CW01496909

# INTO THE REICH

OSPREY
PUBLISHING

# DEDICATION

For Craig Sneed, a true Texan gentleman

# PRIT BUTTAR

# INTO THE REICH

## THE RED ARMY'S ADVANCE
## TO THE ODER IN 1945

OSPREY PUBLISHING
Bloomsbury Publishing Plc
Kemp House, Chawley Park, Cumnor Hill, Oxford OX2 9PH, UK
Bloomsbury Publishing Ireland Limited,
29 Earlsfort Terrace, Dublin 2, D02 AY28, Ireland
1385 Broadway, 5th Floor, New York, NY 10018, USA
E-mail: info@ospreypublishing.com
**www.ospreypublishing.com**

OSPREY is a trademark of Osprey Publishing Ltd

First published in Great Britain in 2025

A catalogue record for this book is available from the British Library

ISBN: HB 9781472866998; PB 9781472867001; eBook 9781472867018; ePDF 9781472866981;
XML 9781472866967

25 26 27 28 29   10 9 8 7 6 5 4 3 2 1

Plate section image credits are given in full in the List of Illustrations (pp. 7–8).
Maps by Prit Buttar
Index by Fionbar Lyons

Typeset by Deanta Global Publishing Services, Chennai, India
Printed and bound in Great Britain by CPI (Group) UK Ltd, Croydon, CR0 4YY

MIX
Paper | Supporting
responsible forestry
FSC® C013604

Osprey Publishing supports the Woodland Trust, the UK's leading woodland conservation charity.

To find out more about our authors and books visit www.ospreypublishing.com. Here you will find
extracts, author interviews, details of forthcoming events and the option to sign up for our newsletter.

For product safety related questions contact productsafety@bloomsbury.com

# CONTENTS

# LIST OF ILLUSTRATIONS

The shattered city of Warsaw had been deliberately destroyed by the Germans as vengeance for the 1944 Warsaw Uprising. (Photo by: Photo12/ Universal Images Group via Getty Images)

Soviet gunners dislodging the Germans during street fighting in Poznań in February 1945. The prolonged resistance of the Poznań garrison complicated supply issues for the Red Army. (Photo by: Sovfoto/ Universal Images Group via Getty Images)

Soviet troops in an anti-tank ambush in Hungary in January 1945. The siege of Budapest had begun in late December and would last for 50 days. (Photo by: Sovfoto/Universal Images Group via Getty Images)

A Soviet armoured division under the command of Lieutenant General Pavel Pavlovich Poluboyarov advancing along the western bank of the River Oder in January 1945. By March the Red Army would hold a wide bridgehead across the river. (Photo by: Sovfoto/Universal Images Group via Getty Images)

Wehrmacht soldiers watching Soviet positions from a village near the Oder in February 1945. Militarily and industrially, the Vistula-Oder offensive was a fatal defeat for Germany. (Photo by Heinrich Hoffmann/ullstein bild via Getty Images)

In a village in Pomerania in February 1945, Waffen-SS soldiers dismount from a truck. Many of the soldiers carry a *Panzerschrek*, a type of anti-tank rocket launcher developed by Nazi Germany. (Sueddeutsche Zeitung Photo / Alamy Stock Photo)

German grenadiers armed with anti-tank projectiles ride on bicycles during a defensive battle in Silesia. After two successful Soviet offensives, the Wehrmacht eventually lost control of the region. (Photo by ullstein bild via Getty Images)

Two German grenadiers stationed on the outskirts of Breslau (the pair are a father and son deployed in the same unit). The success of the Vistula-Oder operation enabled Soviet forces to encircle Breslau, marking the genesis of the USSR's Lower Silesia offensive. (Photo by ullstein bild via Getty Images)

Troops of 1st Ukrainian Front move through a street in former Gleiwitz. The German-occupied Silesian city would be captured by the Red Army in February 1945. (Photo by: Sovfoto/Universal Images Group via Getty Images)

German soldiers fight against Soviet forces in an attempt to maintain military dominance over major Silesian territories. The region would eventually fall into Soviet control. (Sueddeutsche Zeitung Photo / Alamy Stock Photo)

Armed German civilians march together towards the western banks of the Oder in March 1945, ready for defence. In the final months of the war, German civilians were conscripted to serve in a militia known as the *Volkssturm*. (Photo by Mondadori via Getty Images)

Four Soviet sappers crawl along a rubble-strewn street in Breslau whilst dragging containers of explosives. Their comrades operate machine guns from surrounding buildings to provide cover. (Photo by: Rob Welham/Universal History Archive/Universal Images Group via Getty Images)

Breslau central square photographed in ruins during late 1945. In front of the bombarded city hall are piles of recycled materials, ready to be used for the building's eventual reconstruction. (Photo by: Photo12/Universal Images Group via Getty Images)

# LIST OF MAPS

# DRAMATIS PERSONAE

## GERMANY

**Ahlfen, Hans von** – Oberst, commander eponymous *Sperrverband*, later garrison commander Breslau

**Audörsch, Oskar** – Generalmajor, commander 25th Panzer Division

**Baer, Richard** – Sturmbannführer, last commandant of Auschwitz

**Bärmann, Karl** – Oberst, regimental commander 88th Infantry Division

**Benicke, Fritz** – Generalleutnant, senior engineering officer in fortification construction in Silesia

**Bracht, Fritz** – *Gauleiter* Upper Silesia

**Brücker, Otto-Hermann** – Generalleutnant, commander 6th Volksgrenadier Division

**Brux, Albert** – Oberst, commander 17th Panzer Division

**Busse, Theodor** – General, commander Ninth Army

**Decker, Karl** – Generalleutnant, commander XXXIX Panzer Corps

**Dietrich, Josef ('Sepp')** – Oberstgruppenführer, commander Sixth SS-Panzer Army

**Dorow, Otto** – Oberst, regimental commander, 337th Volksgrenadier Division

**Drabich-Waechter, Adolf-Friedrich** – Oberstleutnant, chief of staff XLII Corps

**Edelsheim, Maximilian Reichsfreiherr von** – General, commander XLVIII Panzer Corps

**Eicke, Theodor** – Obergruppenführer, first commandant of Dachau

**Eismann, Hans-Georg** – Oberst, operations officer Army Group Vistula

**Erpenbach, Werner** – Hauptmann, commander *Hetzer* company

**Estor, Fritz** – Oberst, chief of staff Eleventh SS-Panzer Army

**Finger, Arthur** – Generalmajor, commander 291st Infantry Division

**Flacke, Fritz** – Oberstleutnant, deputy commander *Festung Posen*

**Fölkersam, Adrian von** – Sturmbannführer, garrison commander in Inowrocław (Hohensalza)

**Forster, Albert** – *Gauleiter* Danzig-West Prussia
**Frank, Hans** – head of *Generalgouvernement*
**Fries, Walter** – General, commander XLVI Panzer Corps
**Fullriede, Fritz** – Oberst, *Kampfkommandant* Kolberg
**Gareis, Martin** – General, commander XLVI Panzer Corps from 19 January
**Gehlen, Reinhard** – Oberst, head of *Fremde Heere Ost*
**Gille, Herbert** – Obergruppenführer, commander IV SS-Panzer Corps
**Gonell, Ernst** – Generalmajor, commander *Festung Posen*
**Gräser, Fritz-Hubert, General** – commander Fourth Panzer Army
**Greim, Robert Ritter von** – Generaloberst, commander *Luftflotte 6*
**Greiser, Arthur** – *Gauleiter Reichsgau Wartheland*
**Guderian, Heinz** – Generaloberst, chief of German general staff
**Hanke, Karl** – *Gauleiter* Lower Silesia
**Harpe, Josef** – Generaloberst, commander Army Group A
**Hassebroeck, Johannes** – Sturmbannführer, last commandant of Gross-Rosen
**Hax, Heinrich-Georg** – Oberst, later Generalmajor, commander 8th Panzer Division
**Heinrici, Gotthard** – Generaloberst, commander eponymous group/First Panzer Army, later commander Army Group Vistula
**Henrici, Sigfrid** – General, commander XL Panzer Corps
**Heuthaus, Hermann Schulte** – Generalmajor, commander *Brandenburg* Panzergrenadier Division
**Hölz, Johannes** – Oberst, chief of staff Ninth Army
**Hossbach, Friedrich** – General, commander Fourth Army
**Hübner, Rudolf** – Generalleutnant, commander *Infanterie-Division Döberitz*
**Jauer, Georg** – Generalleutnant, commander 20th Panzergrenadier Division, later commander of *Grossdeutschland* Panzer Corps
**Jeckeln, Friedrich** – Obergruppenführer, commander eponymous corps group
**Källner, Hans** – Generalleutnant, commander 19th Panzer Division
**Keitel, Wilhelm** – Generalfeldmarschall, head of *OKW*
**Kinzel, Eberhard** – Generalleutnant, commander 337th Volksgrenadier Division
**Klein, Gerhard** – Oberst, commander Ninth Army *Waffenschule*
**Koch, Erich** – *Gauleiter* East Prussia
**Koch-Erpach, Rudolf** – General, commander *Wehrkreis VIII*
**Krappe, Günther** – Generalleutnant, commander X SS Corps
**Krause, Johannes** – Generalmajor, *Festungskommandant Breslau*
**Krebs, Hans-Georg** – Major, chief of staff 17th Panzer Division
**Kretschmer, Theodor** – Generalmajor, commander 17th Panzer Division
**Krüger, Friedrich-Wilhelm** – Obergruppenführer, commander V SS-Mountain Corps

**Lammerding, Heinz** – Gruppenführer, chief of staff Army Group Vistula

**Liebisch, Hans-Günther** – Major, panzergrenadier battalion commander, 17th Panzer Division

**Liss, Ulrich** – Generalmajor, commander 304th Infantry Division

**Luck, Hans von** – Oberst, commander eponymous battlegroup

**Lüdecke, Otto** – General, commander *Festung Thorn*

**Lüttwitz, Smilo Freiherr von** – General, commander Ninth Army

**Mäder, Hellmuth** – Generalmajor, commander *Führer-Grenadier* Panzergrenadier Division

**Manteuffel, Hasso von** – General, commander Third Panzer Army

**Marcks, Werner** – Generalleutnant, commander 21st Panzer Division

**Mattern, Ernst** – Generalmajor, commander *Festung Posen*

**Metzner, Rudolf** – deputy *Gauleiter* Upper Silesia

**Moll, Otto** – Hauptscharführer, commander eponymous *Sonderkommando*

**Müller, Dietrich von** – Generalleutnant, commander 16th Panzer Division

**Munzel, Oskar** – Generalmajor, commander eponymous corps group

**Natzmer, Oldwig von** – Generalleutnant, chief of staff Army Group Centre

**Nehring, Walther** – General, commander XXIV Panzer Corps

**Niehoff, Hermann** – Generalleutnant, commander 371st Infantry Division, later *Festungskommandant* Breslau

**Pantenius, Hans Jurgen** – Major, later Oberstleutnant, officer in 337th Volksgrenadier Division

**Pohl, Oswald** – head of *SS-Wirtschaftshauptamt*

**Raegener, Adolf** – Generalmajor, *Kampfkommandant* Küstrin

**Rampf, Leonard** – Kreisleiter in Bydgoszcz (Bromberg)

**Raus, Erhard** – Generaloberst, commander Third Panzer Army

**Recknagel, Hermann** – General, commander XLII Corps

**Reinefarth, Heinz** – Gruppenführer, *Kampfkommandant* Küstrin

**Reinhardt, Hans-Georg** – Generaloberst, commander Army Group Centre

**Reischenbeck, Wilhelm** – Obersturmführer, officer involved in Auschwitz death marches

**Remlinger, Heinrich** – Oberstleutnant, garrison commander in Piła (Schneidemühl)

**Rosskopf, Maximilian** – Generalmajor, commander 168th Infantry Division

**Rundstedt, Gerd von** – Generalfeldmarschall, commander Wehrmacht forces in the west

**Sachsenheimer, Max** – Generalmajor, commander 17th Infantry Division

**Saemisch, Siegfried** – Major, commander *Schwere Panzer-Abteilung 424*

**Salisch, Otto von** – Standartenführer, chief of police Bydgoszcz (Bromberg)

**Saucken, Dietrich von** – General, commander *Panzer-Korps Grossdeutschland*
**Schlieper, Franz** – Generalmajor, commander 73rd Infantry Division
**Schmalz, Kurt** – deputy *Gauleiter* Wartheland
**Schmauser, Ernst-Heinrich** – Obergruppenführer, *HSSPF* Upper Silesia
**Schörner, Ferdinand** – Generaloberst, commander Army Group A
**Schulz, Friedrich** – General, commander Seventeenth Army
**Sieler, Ernst** – Generalleutnant, commander 304th Infantry Division
**Speer, Albert** – armaments minister
**Steiner, Felix** – Obergruppenführer, commander Eleventh SS-Panzer Army
**Thamm, Norbert** – Leutnant, officer 97th Jäger Division
**Tippelskirch, Kurt von** – General, former commander Fourth Army, chair of standing court martial in Torgau
**Unrein, Martin** – Gruppenführer, commander III SS-Panzer Corps
**Weber, Friedrich** – Generalleutnant, *Festungskommandant* Warsaw
**Wenck, Walther** – General, deputy chief of German general staff
**Wöhler, Otto** – General, commander Army Group South
**Xylander, Wolf-Dietrich von** – Generalleutnant, chief of staff Army Group A

## SOVIET UNION

**Antonov, Aleksei Innokentovich** – General, acting chief of the General Staff
**Antonov, Viktor Semenovich** – Colonel, commander 301st Rifle Division
**Babadzhanian, Amazasp Khachaturovich** – Colonel, commander XI Guards Tank Corps
**Batov, Pavel Ivanovich** – General, commander Sixty-Fifth Army
**Belov, Pavel Alekseevich** – Lieutenant General, commander Sixty-First Army
**Beria, Lavrentiy Pavlovich** – head of the *NKVD*
**Berzarin, Nikolai Erastovich** – Lieutenant General, commander Fifth Shock Army
**Bogdanov, Semen Ilyich** – Colonel General, commander Second Guards Tank Army
**Bukshtynovich, Mikhail Fomich** – Major General, chief of staff Third Shock Army
**Cherniakhovsky, Ivan Danilovich** – General, commander 3rd Belarusian Front
**Chuikov, Vasily Ivanovich** – Colonel General, commander Eighth Guards Army
**Chuprov, Nil Danilovich** – Colonel, commander X Guards Tank Corps

**Dremov, Ivan Fedorovich** – Major General, commander VIII Guards Mechanised Corps

**Esipenko, Khariton Fyodorovich** – Colonel, chief of staff XXIX Guards Rifle Corps

**Glazunov, Vasily Afanasevich** – Lieutenant General, commander IV Guards Rifle Corps

**Glukhov, Mikhail Ivanovich** – Lieutenant General, commander LXXVI Rifle Corps

**Gluzdovsky, Vladimir Alekseevich** – Lieutenant General, commander Sixth Army

**Gordov, Vasily Nikolaevich** – Colonel General, commander Third Guards Army

**Gusakovsky, Iosif Iraklievich** – Colonel, commander 44th Guards Tank Brigade

**Gusev, Dmitrii Nikolaevich** – Colonel General, commander Twenty-First Army

**Ivanov, Sergei Alekseevich** – Major General, commander VII Guards Tank Corps

**Katukov, Mikhail Efimovich** – Colonel General, commander First Guards Tank Army

**Kolpakchi, Vladimir Iakovlevich** – Colonel General, commander Sixty-Ninth Army

**Konev, Ivan Stepanovich** – Marshal, commander 1st Ukrainian Front

**Koroteev, Konstantin Apollinovich** – Colonel General, commander Fifty-Second Army

**Korovnikov, Ivan Terentyevich** – Lieutenant General, commander Fifty-Ninth Army

**Kosenko, Pyotr Ivanovich** – Lieutenant General, commander of artillery, Fifth Shock Army

**Kozlov, Georgy Kirillovich** – Lieutenant General, commander Nineteenth Army

**Kryukov, Vladimir Viktorovich** – Major General, commander II Guards Cavalry Corps

**Kurochkin, Pavel Alekseevich** – Colonel General, commander Sixtieth Army

**Lelyushenko, Dmitri Danilovich** – Colonel General, commander Fourth Tank Army

**Novikov, Vasily Vasilyevich** – Major General, commander VI Guards Tank Corps

**Orlov, Vasily Fedorovich** – Colonel, commander VI Guards Mechanised Corps

**Oslikovsky, Nikolai Sergeyevich** – Lieutenant General, commander III Guards Cavalry Corps

**Panfilov, Aleksei Pavlovich** – Lieutenant General, commander III Guards Tank Corps

**Perkhorovich, Frantz Iosifovich** – Major General, commander Forty-Seventh Army

**Poluboyarov, Pavel Pavlovich** – Lieutenant General, commander IV Guards Tank Corps

**Pukhov, Nikolai Pavlovich** – Colonel General, commander Thirteenth Army

**Rokossovsky, Konstantin Konstantinovich** – Marshal, commander 2nd Belarusian Front

**Romanovsky, Vladimir Zakharovich** – Lieutenant General, commander Nineteenth Army

**Roslyi, Ivan Pavlovich** – Major General, commander IX Rifle Corps

**Rybalko, Pavel Semenovich** – Colonel General, commander Third Guards Tank Army

**Ryvsh, Vsevolod Ezupovich** – Lieutenant Colonel, commander 16th Guards Mechanised Brigade

**Shemenkov, Afanasy Dmitrievich** – Major General, commander XXIX Guards Rifle Corps

**Shtemenko, Sergei Matveyevich** – Colonel General, head of operations directorate, *Stavka*

**Shugaev, Vasily Minaevich** – Major General, commander 47th Rifle Division

**Simoniak, Nikolai Pavlovich** – Lieutenant General, commander Third Shock Army

**Tsvetayev, Vyacheslav Dmitrievich** – Colonel General, commander Thirty-Third Army

**Vainrub, Matvey Grigorievich** – Major General, commander armoured and mechanised forces, Eighth Guards Army

**Vasilevsky, Aleksandr Mikhailovich** – Marshal, chief of Soviet general staff

**Vesterman, Arkady Grigorevich** – tank crewman, 1st Belarusian Front

**Zhadov, Alexei Semenovich** – Colonel General, commander Fifth Guards Army

**Zhukov, Georgy Konstantinovich** – Marshal, deputy supreme commander, commander 1st Belarusian Front

## OTHERS

**Stanislav Poplavsky** – General, commander First Polish Army (Poland)

# INTRODUCTION: TOWARDS
# A GRIM WINTER

Despite his scarred appearance, Oberst Claus Schenk Graf von Stauffenberg was a striking figure. Tall and slim with dark hair and wearing an immaculate Wehrmacht uniform, he was all the more memorable for the patch that covered his empty left eye socket. The black leather gloves that he wore even in midsummer were another notable feature, hiding the absence of his right hand and half the fingers of his left – wounds that he had sustained in an air attack in North Africa in April 1943. But it was more than his appearance that made him memorable; he had a commanding and confident presence, as Kurt Salterburg, a soldier on guard in the *Wolfsschanze* ('Wolf's Lair'), Hitler's headquarters near the Prussian town of Rastenburg, later recalled. It was not unusual for officers to leave a conference with the Führer before the meeting had ended, and as he passed the saluting Salterburg, Stauffenberg appeared to be self-assured and calm, as he always was. Nor did Stauffenberg have any difficulty bluffing his way past three checkpoints as he departed the *Wolfsschanze*. As the car drove to the nearby airfield, Stauffenberg glanced back one last time. A cloud of smoke rose slowly into the hot summer sky; both Stauffenberg and his adjutant, Oberleutnant Werner von Haeften, were convinced that Hitler was dead.

But for three chance events, they would probably have been correct. The briefcase that contained Stauffenberg's bomb had originally held two explosive devices, but when he attempted to arm the bombs in a small room next to the conference room with his maimed left hand, Stauffenberg was successful only with one bomb – outside, an orderly was impatiently calling to them saying that the conference was about to commence. Haeften removed the other bomb and disposed of it as they drove away from Rastenburg. The briefcase was left under the conference table next to where Hitler would be sitting, but another officer struck his knee against it and moved it, placing it behind a thick wooden table leg. Even then, the single explosive charge would probably have been sufficient to kill Hitler if the conference had been held in its usual location, an underground concrete bunker. But due to the summer heat, it was moved at the last moment to a wooden building, which was less able to contain the blast. Unlike Hitler, both Stauffenberg and Haeften would be dead before the end of the day, executed by a firing squad as the coup attempt against Hitler's regime collapsed. The fallout from the failed plot was to shape the rest of Germany's lost war, with terrible consequences in terms of loss of life.

Whilst the men and women involved in the July Plot of 1944 are generally regarded as heroes, it should be remembered that few, if any, intended to replace the Nazi regime with anything approaching a modern representative democracy. Stauffenberg and others were in favour of retaining much of the territory that Germany had seized from Poland in 1939 and wished to negotiate an end to the conflict only with the Western Allies – they fully intended to continue the war in the east against the Soviet Union. They planned to insist that Germany would not be occupied by any foreign power at the end of the war, and that prosecution of any war criminals would be a matter purely for German courts. Such demands were of course unacceptable to the Allied Powers, and even if Stauffenberg's bomb had succeeded in killing Hitler, there was no guarantee that the coup attempt would have succeeded. In particular, Himmler was absent from the conference, and he would have attempted to use the SS to seize power himself. Given the widespread dismay across both civilian and military populations when news of the coup attempt broke, it is likely that there would have been a period of considerable turmoil and perhaps even civil war following the assassination of Hitler. Such circumstances might have represented Germany's best hope of avoiding the disaster that actually unfolded in the period between the bomb blast in Rastenburg and the end of the war. During those ten months, Germany suffered nearly half its wartime military casualties and more than half its civilian losses.[1] Even if Stauffenberg and his fellow conspirators had failed to win the inevitable power struggle that would have followed Hitler's death, it is likely that the turmoil would have made it almost impossible for the Wehrmacht to continue to hold the armies of the Allied Powers at bay and the war would probably have ended within weeks. As a consequence of the failure of the plot, the conflict would continue until the Third Reich had been ground into dust.

The years of Nazi rule had seen several figures rise to prominence alongside Hitler, though the supremacy of the Führer remained unchallenged throughout. By mid-1944, many of these figures were no longer at the centre of events. Rudolf Hess, at one stage second only to Hermann Göring in status amongst Hitler's followers, was imprisoned in Britain. Göring – still officially the nominated successor to Hitler – had fallen out of favour due to the inability of the Luftwaffe to defend Germany from the increasingly devastating bombing raids of American and British air forces. Others who had played major roles in the early years of Hitler's rule – men like Joachim von Ribbentrop, the foreign minister, and Alfred Rosenberg, the racial theorist of the Nazi Party and head of the *Ostministerium*, one of several bodies that competed for control of the occupied regions of the Soviet Union – had also fallen from favour. As the dust began to settle, both literally and figuratively, from the failed assassination attempt, several individuals tried to manipulate events to increase their already substantial power. Apart from Hitler, they would be the most prominent figures at the top of the Nazi regime during the last months of the war.

*Reichsführer-SS* Heinrich Himmler was already a man with immense sway over Germany. As head of the SS, he controlled the police and security forces of Germany as well as the Waffen-SS, the combat arm of the organisation. In the event of civil unrest across Germany, there were plans for the *Ersatzheer* ('Replacement Army', tasked with preparing drafts of men as replacements for front-line units) to maintain order, which the conspirators had intended to manipulate in order to use the *Ersatzheer* to take control of Germany. Hitler and his close associates therefore decided to place this substantial force under tighter control. In many respects, the July Plot demonstrated a huge failure on the part of Himmler's security apparatus, but Hitler was quick to appoint Himmler as the new commander of the *Ersatzheer*, numbering up to 2 million men; this body added considerably to Himmler's power.

Another major 'winner' in the aftermath of the July Plot was Martin Bormann, Hitler's personal secretary and effectively the man who both controlled access to the Führer and oversaw the functioning of the Nazi Party. After coming to power in 1933, the Party had reorganised local government across Germany, dividing it into regions. Each region or *Gau* was overseen by a *Gauleiter*, answerable to Hitler and reporting to Bormann; the *Gauleiters* in turn controlled their regions through *Kreisleiters*, who were each responsible for a *Kreis* within the *Gau*. Although the July Plot had been largely confined to the ranks of the military, with the addition of a small number of civilian politicians and little or no involvement of the general public, the Nazi Party used the aftermath of the plot to tighten its grip on all aspects of German civilian life. As the Red Army approached German territory in the east, Hitler authorised the creation of the *Volkssturm*, a mobilisation of the civilian male population to form a last line of defence. It might have been expected that this force was placed under the command of the army, but such was the fall from grace of the military that the *Volkssturm* became the responsibility of the *Gauleiters* and therefore of Bormann.

The third person whose influence grew in the weeks after the failure of the July Plot was Joseph Goebbels, the propaganda minister. Unlike Himmler and

Bormann, he played a significant role in derailing the coup attempt, earning him the recognition and gratitude of the Führer. As Hitler unleashed his vengeance on the conspirators, Goebbels increased his propaganda efforts to re-energise the German people in their will to resist and to continue the war. Goebbels now became *Reichsbevollmächtiger für den totalen Kriegseinsatz* ('Reich Plenipotentiary for the Total War Effort'). At the end of the Stalingrad battles in early 1943, Goebbels had announced the adoption of a policy of 'total war', but in reality this was diluted in the following weeks and Goebbels repeatedly lobbied Hitler for a greater emphasis on 'total war'. In order to maximise the number of men available for front-line service, every government agency was to be stripped of 'superfluous' administration personnel and many categories of workers who had previously been exempt from conscription were now to be called up for military service. Those who worked in German factories and mines would be required to work longer hours to increase production and more women were to be employed in factories, and although in many respects Goebbels had to work through agencies controlled by his rivals – for example, his 'rationalisation' of government at local and central level was carried out via the *Gauleiters*, who were under Bormann's jurisdiction – he threw himself into this work with great energy. The impact on the conflict would be too limited to change the ultimate outcome, but by mobilising hundreds of thousands of men, Goebbels certainly helped prolong the fighting. Moreover, he effectively condemned many of those men to death. There would not be sufficient time for them to undergo full training and many were not physically fit for combat operations, especially in the brutal conditions of the Eastern Front.

Despite these changes at the highest levels of the Nazi regime, Germany faced the near certainty of defeat as 1944 drew towards a close. The nations arrayed against it were in no mood to compromise. In such circumstances, the only real purpose in continued resistance was in the hope of achieving a situation in which better terms for peace might be negotiated. Hitler continued to insist that he would only negotiate from a position of strength, and wished to make one last great offensive in the west. If a major setback could be inflicted upon the Western Allies, they would realise that the human cost of storming the defences of Germany was too great, and would abandon their insistence on unconditional surrender. The only other options were that there might be some unexpected circumstances that led to the break-up of the alliance arrayed against Germany, or through the development and deployment of new weapons that could change the course of the war. Otherwise, there was no prospect of a negotiated end to the conflict that was rapidly encroaching on German territory. Hitler had repeatedly emphasised the zero-sum nature of the war with the Soviet Union – in his mind, there was no place for both Bolshevism and Nazism in the world. One would triumph over the other. If Germany could not win the war, it would mean that the German people had failed. In that case, they would deserve the devastation that was widely feared.

Despite the widespread destruction of German cities as a result of air raids and the huge casualties suffered by the Wehrmacht in the summer of 1944 both in the east and in the west, it seems that there remained general confidence in military circles – perhaps more so in the west than in the east – that Germany might still prevail, or at least would be able to ensure a better outcome than that intended by its enemies. A last extraordinary surge in armaments production delivered unprecedented quantities of tanks and guns to replace equipment that had been lost, and sharp checks were inflicted upon the British and Americans at Arnhem and Metz; in the east, several panzer divisions succeeded in mounting a successful counterattack to the east of Warsaw, boosting morale and giving many soldiers and officers hope that German prowess was not yet spent. But to the rear of the combat units straining to hold back the armies of the Allied Powers, life became steadily more difficult for civilians living in Germany's cities and rural areas. Many basic foods were increasingly scarce and most Germans had been touched by the war – either they had lost family members in the conflict, or they knew of others who were bereaved. Marion Dönhoff, who was running the family estate in East Prussia, described a typical moment:

Frau Duttke was … a self-confident but at the same time modest, outstanding woman. She looked after the pigs and was proud that she hadn't missed a day's work for many years. She and her husband had simply worked all their lives so that their children should have something better. Their younger son was killed in France and the older was an NCO – a magnificent, straightforward, reliable chap, that any army in the world would have regarded with pride: he was certain to become an officer one day, and then all the drudgery would be worthwhile.

But this day didn't come; instead, a day came in autumn 1944 when I saw Frau Duttke crossing the estate yard, a bucket in each hand. The handsome woman looked old, absent-minded, a ghost of her former self. 'In God's name, Frau Duttke, what's happened?' She looked at me with dead, staring eyes, put down the buckets – and suddenly threw her arms around my neck, and cried and cried: 'Karl is dead, the news came today. Now everything is at an end. Everything was for nothing – our whole lives.'[2]

It wasn't just the losses of family members in the front line that ground down morale in German towns and cities. The intensity, frequency and reach of air raids increased from the late summer of 1944 as it became possible for American and British aircraft to operate from captured airfields in France. The authorities no longer even tried to suggest that the Luftwaffe could defend the German homeland from such widespread destruction. German propaganda attempted to portray the Western Allies as murderers who sought the complete physical destruction of Germany's cities, but amongst the hundreds of thousands of civilians who lived amidst the rubble of Hamburg, Berlin, and Cologne, the prevailing view was that the Luftwaffe had failed to protect them from attacks.

Berlin had never been particularly sympathetic to the Nazis, and as they moved around their increasingly devastated city, many Berliners resorted to the lugubrious gallows humour that often accompanies such circumstances. A joke circulated in the windowless trains and rubble-strewn streets as Christmas approached in 1944, and people wondered what would constitute an appropriate gift: be practical, they advised each other, buy a coffin. But although there might be grumbling and jokes, any thought of more serious protest ran the risk of arrest, imprisonment, and even execution. There would be no recurrence of the unrest that swept through Germany in 1918. Intelligence reports received by Goebbels highlighted the widespread war-weariness. Many believed that 'peace at any price' was preferable to continuing the war and despite the widespread fear and repression, there were signs of 'outright anger towards the Party, held responsible for the war and its consequences'.[3]

In the early years of the war, there was little attempt by Hitler and others to hide his ambitions for reshaping Europe. The boastful pronouncements about the Thousand Year Reich, the establishment of a huge land empire in the eastern parts of Europe, and the creation of a racially pure continent dominated and controlled by Germany were proclaimed widely. Many might have found this distasteful or even unacceptable, but there was also extensive support, particularly as German armies swept forward in triumph. Even after the failure to defeat the Soviet Union before the end of 1941, German propaganda continued to portray the war as the pursuit of total victory for the Third Reich. It was only after the disaster at Stalingrad in the winter of 1942–43 that the rhetoric began to change, particularly with regard to the war against the Soviet Union. The conflict was now portrayed as a crusade to save Europe from Bolshevism, and the Red Army was seen as a destructive horde that would bring devastation both to Germany and the other states of Europe. The threat from the east was described as 'Jewish Bolshevism' or 'Asiatic Bolshevism', or sometimes as a synthesis of both, and a threat to European civilisation that had to be defeated. This narrative continued into the years after the war as German veterans attempted to portray their military service in the best possible light; Hans Schäufler, a signals officer in 4th Panzer

Division, wrote extensively about his wartime experiences and his view was typical in many respects of soldiers and officers in the Wehrmacht, though few would have dared express such opinions about the leadership of Germany prior to the end of the war:

> Confidence in the military leadership ... from the front line to the highest levels of the Wehrmacht was deeply shaken, given the completely false evaluation of the facts by these leaders. All that remained now was to save innocent victims of the senseless war from the retaliation of the Red Army, driven on by the vengeful Soviet demagogues.[4]

Such an assessment was disingenuous. The 'senseless war' had been started by Germany and the devastation visited upon the Soviet Union was vast. Millions of Soviet citizens were dead, others had been taken from their villages and towns as slave labourers, and it is inconceivable that Schäufler was unaware of the atrocities that had been committed in the occupied territories. He was correct in fearing the retaliation of the Red Army, but the personal experiences of Soviet soldiers – from the scenes they had witnessed, or had described to them in letters from their families – were such that such retaliation was inevitable, with or without the influence of 'Soviet demagogues'.

Just what was likely to happen when the Red Army reached German soil was already clear. In the second half of October 1944, the Soviet 3rd Belarusian Front, commanded by General Ivan Danilovich Cherniakhovsky, penetrated into East Prussia. Determined defensive fighting brought both shoulders of the attack to a halt, but some Soviet units broke through in the central sector and advanced to and beyond the village of Nemmersdorf. When German forces counterattacked and retook the area, they were shocked by what they discovered:

> When we moved through the village, we found no more Soviets. But we were greeted by grisly scenes of the people who had been caught up there, which reminded me of the atrocities suffered by Soviet villagers from their own soldiers, something that I had often seen during our retreats early in 1944. Here there were German women, whose clothing had been torn from their bodies, so that they could be violated and finally mutilated in horrific ways. In one barn we found an old man whose throat had been pierced with a pitchfork, pinning him to the door. All of the feather mattresses in one of the bedrooms had been sliced open and were stained with blood. Two cut-up female corpses were lying amidst the feathers, with two murdered children. The sight was so gruesome that some of our recruits fled in panic.[5]

Whilst any atrocity is terrible, the comments of this soldier about similar scenes in the Soviet Union are striking. If he saw mutilated and violated corpses during the Wehrmacht's long and painful retreat across the western Soviet Union, it was unlikely that these people were victims of the Red Army – after all, he and his comrades were presumably retreating through territory held by German forces, and it seems far more probable that the corpses represented last moments of revenge and brutality from the occupying forces. Moreover, although the Germans recorded about 70 victims in Nemmersdorf and about 95 more in the nearby village of Schulzenwalde, such numbers were tiny compared to the killings carried out by German forces in the Soviet Union.

The Germans attempted to make the most of the events in and around Nemmersdorf both at home and abroad. There was already a sense of fear about the risk of the Red Army attacking civilians. In the years after the war, two mythical versions of the past became widespread. The first was that many, perhaps most, German civilians had no awareness of the crimes committed by Nazi Germany in the occupied regions of Europe, particularly in the east. Similarly, many soldiers and officers who survived to write their memoirs would claim either that they too had no knowledge of such matters, or that all such crimes had been committed by a small minority, largely made up of SS personnel and locally recruited paramilitary formations. Both of these descriptions are untrue. Every part of the German military machine was involved in atrocities in the Soviet Union, Poland, and elsewhere. Regular army formations provided logistic support to the *Einsatzgruppen* that slaughtered hundreds of thousands of Jews and others in the second half of 1941, and all parts of the army became involved in operations to suppress the rapidly growing partisan movement behind the front line. Such operations made little distinction between partisans, their supporters, and innocent civilians who were unfortunate to be in the path of their sweeps. When soldiers returned home on leave, many told their families about what was happening in the east – they may have denied personal involvement, but knowledge of mass killings in the occupied territories was widespread. Inevitably, this contributed to the rising anxiety that Soviet soldiers would inflict similar violence upon German civilians. Joseph Goebbels, the propaganda minister, was swift to realise the potential value of Nemmersdorf. The scale of the killings was deliberately exaggerated and graphic newsreels were shown across Germany.

The impact of these propaganda efforts on the civilian population of Germany was varied, almost in proportion to the threat posed by the Red Army. For towns and cities in East Prussia, Pomerania and Silesia, where there was a major risk of the Red Army arriving in the coming months, the pre-existing fears of rape, murder, and pillage were now reinforced by the terrible images from Nemmersdorf. Further west, the reaction was largely one of indifference. Attempts by Goebbels to portray the Western Allies as little or no better than the Red Army – in particular, propaganda repeatedly described how the arrival of the US Army would unleash a wave of African Americans and Jews into German homes – were treated with disbelief.

Red Cross officials from neutral countries were invited to visit East Prussia in an attempt to elicit sympathy. But even though the suffering of the civilians of the area around Nemmersdorf was shocking and unjustifiable, news of the killings made little or no impact outside Germany and was dwarfed by information released by the advancing Red Army. That summer, Soviet troops had reached and liberated the concentration camp of Majdanek near Lublin. Here, they found plentiful evidence of the industrial scale of German killings and many Soviet units were sent to the camp so that the soldiers could see first-hand how the Germans had behaved. The comments of one soldier in a letter to his family are perhaps typical of the attitude of the men who visited Majdanek or had passed through the devastated towns and cities of the Soviet Union as they advanced towards the west:

> Our soldiers have not dealt with East Prussia any worse than the Germans did with Smolensk. We hate Germany and the Germans deeply. In one house, for example, our boys found a murdered [German] woman and her two children. You can often see civilians lying dead in the street, too. But the Germans deserve the atrocities that they unleashed. You only have to think about Majdanek … It's certainly cruel to have killed these children, but the cold-bloodedness of the Germans at Majdanek was a thousand times worse.[6]

Veteran German soldiers of the long war against the Soviet Union continued to show good discipline and determination to fight, but the replacement drafts that joined them were less willing to continue the struggle. Günter Emanuel Baltuttis was a member of a group of recruits sent to the Eastern Front and described the hostile reception this group received from their new company commander, who warned them that he wouldn't hesitate to court martial any whom he regarded as cowards. During the winter of 1944–45, Baltuttis' company suffered two suicides; two men were executed, one for cowardice and one for self-wounding; and two died as a result of botched attempts at self-wounding. Such incidents were not new, with both the Wehrmacht and the Red Army recording desertions throughout the war – even in the closing days of the conflict, there were cases of Soviet soldiers deserting in attempts to avoid being caught up in the last battles of the war – but Baltuttis noted that all of these casualties, and the small number of desertions, involved the new recruits.[7]

The mood in Germany in the closing weeks of 1944 was therefore varied. Civilian sentiment was grim and largely hopeless, but the grip of the Nazi Party was so great that there was no possibility of any popular unrest bringing down the regime. Within the Party itself, different factions and individuals continued to compete for power and influence, but they were too suspicious of each other ever to combine in any meaningful manner to threaten Hitler's supremacy. The large numbers of men mobilised in the last convulsions of 'total war' and the surge of armaments produced by German industry had allowed at least some of the losses of the year to be made good, but there was no doubt that the war was now far closer to Germany's borders. The past year had seen Germany's last strategic hope – of maintaining a stubborn defence in the east while all available forces were used to crush the anticipated invasion in the west – end in failure. The Western Allies fought their way out of their initial beachhead in Normandy before bursting out across northern France, and although the attempt by British and American forces to seize a crossing over the lower Rhine at Arnhem ended with heavy losses in the autumn of 1944, this was of little comfort to the German forces. The fighting across France cost the Wehrmacht over 290,000 men killed, wounded or taken prisoner and fewer than 150 of the tanks committed to the battles escaped destruction or capture.[8] This represented a catastrophic setback, but was dwarfed by German losses in the east. Commencing in the third week of June, the Red Army launched a rolling programme of major offensives that pushed the front line out of Soviet territory and drove the Germans from huge parts of Eastern Europe. In the process, the Wehrmacht suffered further irreplaceable casualties. Operation *Bagration* and the offensives that followed cost the Germans at least 450,000 further men. The replacement drafts fell some way short of making good this loss, and in any case were no substitute for the veterans who had been killed, wounded or taken prisoner.

Despite this, Hitler's increasingly sporadic broadcasts didn't fall on entirely deaf ears. At the end of 1944, he proclaimed that thousands of *Volkssturm* had been mobilised and the Wehrmacht's divisions had been re-equipped with the newest weapons. To an extent, such statements were true; notwithstanding the devastation visited upon German cities, tank production actually peaked in December 1944 with over 1,800 tanks and assault guns being completed. This was equivalent to six months' production in 1941, but it represented a final surge that consumed the rapidly diminishing resources of raw materials. Stocks of metals required for the production of high-quality steel were practically exhausted, and there were increasingly common reports from the front line that anti-tank rounds often shattered on impact on enemy vehicles rather than penetrating their armour – a reflection of the reduced tungsten content of warheads. Even relatively common resources like brass were growing short, and ammunition manufacturers were forced to use steel to produce cartridges for rifles and machine-guns. These cartridges had different thermal expansion coefficients than their brass predecessors, resulting in frequent jams.

Inevitably, the inexorable tilting of the balance of power against Germany had a major impact upon the nations that had been coerced or persuaded to fight alongside the Wehrmacht, and changes on the Eastern Front in 1944 hastened the disintegration of alliances previously imposed upon the states of Eastern Europe. Romania and Bulgaria took advantage of the Soviet advance to seek a way out of the war. Bulgaria had avoided committing any soldiers to fight alongside the armies of Germany, but the Romanian Army – which had played a significant part in the invasion of Ukraine and had been heavily involved in the mass killing of Jews across the region – switched sides. Henceforth, Romanian troops would fight against Germany. Perhaps even more significant was the loss of access to the Romanian oilfields around Ploiești. Fuel had always been in short supply for the German military, and shortages now became even worse.

In addition to Bulgaria and Romania, there were signs of disaffection and rebellion elsewhere in Eastern Europe. Tens of thousands of Slovaks took part in uprisings against Germany in late August; although the Germans succeeded in restoring control, they lost a further ally, and many of the men who had fought in Slovakian units alongside the Germans now took to the forests and mountains of their homeland to wage a partisan war. Like Romania, Hungary had committed its troops to the war against the Soviet Union but in March 1944 the Germans became aware of the intention of the Hungarian government to seek peace with the Allied Powers. In Operation *Margarethe*, the Wehrmacht moved to seize control of Hungary and a new pro-German government was installed. In October, Miklós Horthy, the Hungarian regent, attempted to secure an armistice with the Soviet Union but was arrested and forced to resign. For the moment, Hungarian Army units remained in the front line on the Eastern Front, but their reliability was open to question.

On the other side of the front line, the Allied Powers arrayed against the Third Reich faced the winter with increasing confidence and expectation. The preceding year had seen major victories against Germany almost everywhere, and the few setbacks were mainly restricted to occasions when Allied forces had overreached themselves and the Germans had been able to mount successful counterattacks. Total victory seemed purely a matter of time, and many – both military figures and politicians – were already looking beyond the end of the conflict to the future shape of Europe. The expectations of Hitler, Goebbels and a few others that the differences between the Soviet Union and the Western Powers were too great to allow the alliance to endure were not without some justification; by the end of 1944, there were distinct signs of strain and it was clear that Stalin, Churchill and Roosevelt had very different opinions on how the world would look after the end of the war. Whilst defeating the Germans remained the obvious priority, these divergences would be increasingly important in the concluding months of the war.

For Stalin and the Soviet Union, the scale of the damage inflicted by the Germans between the summer of 1941 and the end of 1944 was clear to see. With so many Soviet cities and towns in ruins and the numbers of dead at almost incomprehensible levels, the desire for revenge was great, but so too was the need to ensure that there could be no repetition of this invasion. Ever since the fall of the tsars, Russia's new rulers had regarded the territories lost in the west as rightfully belonging to Russia – although the Bolsheviks had agreed peace terms with the Baltic States and had conceded great swathes of territory to Poland, these regions had already been reclaimed by the time war broke out with Germany in 1941. But Stalin's plans were now altogether more ambitious. He intended to ensure that his troops were in control of all of Eastern Europe so that pro-Soviet governments could be installed in the nations bordering the Soviet Union, thus creating a buffer in the path of any future invasion. And mixed with the desire for revenge, the Soviet leadership wanted to seize German industrial machinery as compensation for the damage inflicted upon Soviet cities. In addition to helping Soviet industry to rebuild, this would also deny any future German nation a firm, established industrial base. It was therefore important for the Red Army to push as far west as possible before the conflict came to an end.

For the senior officers of the Red Army, the war had started as a desperate struggle purely to survive in more than one sense. It had been clear from the outset that the Germans were determined to destroy the Soviet Union as an entity and had embarked upon a programme of deliberate killing in order to reduce the population – by killing millions of Soviet urban residents, or allowing them to die through starvation, the Germans calculated that they would be able to seize huge agricultural supplies from the countryside for use elsewhere in Europe. In such circumstances, the Soviet commanders had rapidly realised that defeat was unthinkable. But there had long been another threat to their lives. The purges conducted by Stalin that had ripped through the ranks of the Red Army were recent memories and in the opening months of the war, several senior officers were summarily arrested and executed for failing to hold back the Wehrmacht. With victory over the hated German invaders now in sight, the threat from Stalin's wrath might have diminished a little, but the commanders of the Soviet Union's armies began to position themselves for the post-war era. Of particular importance was the question of which commander would be able to seize the ultimate prize for the assault on Berlin. But it was also clear that Stalin intended the post-war narrative to be dominated by himself; there was always the risk that any senior officer who attracted too much fame and credit might pay a severe price.

It was against this backdrop that the armies of both sides faced each other in late 1944. For the Germans and their few remaining allies, it was essential to keep the Red Army as far from German soil as possible to avoid the terrible revenge that had been seen in and around Nemmersdorf from occurring on a far larger scale. The divisions that had been replenished and re-equipped in the late autumn might have been expected to be deployed to face the Soviet forces, but instead they were to be thrown into one last gamble. Hitler intended to use them in a great offensive in the west with the intention of reaching and capturing Antwerp and inflicting a strategic setback on the Western Allies. This was, in his opinion, a far better path for Germany to pursue than merely defending its frontiers. The consequence was that the German formations facing the Red Army remained dangerously weak.

For the Soviet forces, the end of the war and final victory over the hated Fascists seemed almost within reach. The Red Army had successfully overcome resistance during 1944 in the face of far stronger German defences, though the cost had been high. The battles of 1944 around Leningrad and the Baltic States, the drive from the Dnepr over the Dniester into Romania, and the immense battles of *Bagration* and its accompanying operations had cost the Red Army a staggering 2.1 million casualties, but such was the scale of recaptured territory that hundreds of thousands of men had been immediately conscripted into the ranks as replacements. They clearly lacked the experience of many of their predecessors, but the huge production of armaments and the steady flow of aid from the USA and Britain ensured that sufficient proportions were well armed and supplied. Many – both veterans and new recruits – were strongly motivated to seek revenge on the hated Fascists for their crimes in the occupied regions of the Soviet Union. Few would have been able to imagine the horrors they would find as they advanced across Poland.

Poland, which was to suffer a greater percentage loss of population as a result of the war than any other country, would be the battlefield where this great campaign would be played out. The southern edge was made up of the Tatra Mountains, but most of the terrain was relatively flat, dominated by the great rivers – the Vistula, Warta, Oder, and Neisse. Flowing across the country, these rivers were often flanked by marshy ground and much of the landscape was covered by forests. The winter weather made many of the swamps and rivers passable, at least to infantry, but the few good roads that ran across Poland were vital for both sides.

The last months of the war would see repeated Red Army assaults on the German forces trapped in the Courland peninsula in Latvia, and a major offensive into East Prussia. In the south, Soviet troops would advance to Budapest and would conduct a bloody siege before storming the city and continuing west to and beyond Vienna, but the most important phase of the offensive operations would lie between these sectors, across central Poland. This was the route that led to Berlin, widely seen as the ultimate objective of the Red Army. The bitter experiences of Soviet soldiers in preceding years suggested that the Germans would fight hard, particularly as they were now defending their homeland, but such was the scale of destruction inflicted upon German fighting strength in 1944 that there was little doubt that the end was near. The only question that remained to be answered was just how near this would be, and the scale of losses that would have to be suffered to bring it about.

# CHAPTER 1

# PREPARING FOR ARMAGEDDON: THE WEHRMACHT

The bitter war on the Eastern Front had seen many titanic clashes of arms. Towards the end of 1944, there could be no doubt that the coming campaign – the Soviet drive into and across Poland – would be at least as huge as any battle that had preceded it. Both sides made their preparations; one side with determination and a sense of anticipation of final victory and the other with a grim sense of doom. Almost no officers and soldiers in the Wehrmacht divisions facing the Red Army were aware of the imminent German offensive in the Ardennes upon which Hitler had staked the future of the Third Reich; all they knew was that they were badly outnumbered here in the east.

The first occasion on which the Wehrmacht was forced to make a major withdrawal in the entire war was during the Battle of Moscow in late 1941. The last German attempt to reach the city was carried out by divisions that were exhausted by months of fighting and far from full strength, struggling forward through deep snow and combating terrible weather conditions with inadequate winter clothing. When the Soviet counteroffensive began in early December, the Wehrmacht units were in completely the wrong posture to defend, with their remaining strength still concentrated in their spearheads. The fighting that followed saw the Germans driven back a considerable distance, but as they redeployed into a defensive mode, they rapidly brought the Soviet advance to a halt. For Hitler, the lesson that was learned from this was that resolute, determined defence was the only way of stopping Soviet attacks. Many senior officers had wanted to make more substantial withdrawals, but Hitler insisted – with only partial justification – that his policy of standing fast had prevented disaster. This set the tone of his attitude towards future defensive battles. It was essential for defensive fighting to be conducted as far forward as possible, and every metre of ground had to be held with grim determination. From the Moscow fighting onwards, orders from Hitler and *OKH* (*Oberkommando des Heeres* or 'Army High Command', which had overall control of the Eastern Front) repeatedly used the adjective 'fanatical' to describe the required level of commitment to holding ground. Undoubtedly, the determination of soldiers to hold their positions is an important factor in whether they will prevail, but for Hitler and his associates this 'fanatical' will to win became a substitute for other, more material factors. If German defences failed, Hitler blamed officers and soldiers for lacking the required determination to prevail rather than recognising that his armies were outnumbered and outgunned.

This doctrine of forward defence had several consequences, one of which was to deny the Wehrmacht perhaps its only realistic option for conducting a successful defence. From the First World War onwards, the near inevitability of German defenders using counterattacks to try to restore their front lines became almost proverbial and was deeply ingrained in German military thinking and doctrine. When panzer divisions were first devised in the 1930s, one of their anticipated roles was that they would be used to make powerful counterattacks against major enemy penetrations, operating behind a front line held by infantry divisions, and as the war progressed many German commanders saw the use of mobile forces in such counterattacks as almost the only manner in which they might prevail against the huge numerical superiority of the Soviet Union. Even in late 1944, the tactical expertise of German units remained higher than that of their Soviet opponents, particularly in fluid and rapidly changing circumstances. Creating such circumstances was therefore one of the few ways in which the Germans could expect to succeed, and senior officers repeatedly requested permission to make withdrawals both to free up sufficient reserves and to move from defending static lines to forcing the Red Army to fight in the more confused and unpredictable conditions of mobile warfare and encounter battles where the Germans would have their best chance of success.

But from the Battle of Moscow until the end of the war, Hitler was deeply suspicious of any such withdrawals. He argued that on every occasion that he had granted permission for such a withdrawal, the promised benefits had failed to appear, and he had then been faced with more demands for withdrawals. Whilst this statement was strictly true, it ignored two important points. Firstly, Hitler repeatedly refused permission for withdrawals until it was too late for any benefit to occur, with the formations that senior officers had wanted to withdraw often being forced to fight long defensive battles that greatly reduced their strength before they were finally permitted to pull back. Consequently, the planned counterattacks often failed to achieve their purpose or were impossible to carry out as the overall situation had deteriorated too far.

The second flaw in Hitler's logic was perhaps a more important one. If it was genuinely the case that the Wehrmacht's withdrawals were failing to create the circumstances in which a more successful defence could be fought, it was surely time to face reality and recognise that Germany was outgunned and could not hope to win the war. To continue the conflict in such circumstances was to condemn tens of thousands of men to death in futile battles; these were men who might help Germany rebuild after the war, and without whom their families would be left to struggle alone. But for Hitler, the distorted view of Darwinism that prevailed in so much Nazi thought was being put to the ultimate test in the war against the Soviet Union. If Germany couldn't prevail, the nation deserved defeat and destruction. For the Wehrmacht, there was a strange sense of compartmentalised thinking. Every senior officer – with the exception of a small number of diehard Nazi supporters – knew that final defeat was now inevitable, as did many of the rank and file. But many – particularly in the lower ranks of the military – continued to believe in some last-minute change in Germany's fortunes or in the advent of some new wonderful weapon that would alter the course of the war.

In his book *Vor dem Sturm* ('Before the Storm'), set in the winter of 1812–13, the author Theodor Fontane wrote:

> All couch potatoes constantly demand the 'ultimate sacrifice'; but all trained soldiers, with the experiences of fifty battles on the one hand, knowing the poor levels of organisation and the emotions of simply staggering back, who know what it means and how heroic it is just to perform ordinary tasks, all of them think very calmly about matters of bravery and as a rule have long since stopped seeing everything around them through rose-tinted spectacles.[1]

The contempt felt by soldiers in the front line for those who sit in relative comfort at home and demand ever greater sacrifices is as old as war, and many German soldiers awaiting the next onslaught of the Red Army would have known from their personal experiences that such senseless 'sacrifice' would not change the course of the conflict; yet discipline remained strong, and most men kept such thoughts to themselves. For those who recognised the reality of the catastrophe facing Germany, there was the dark memory of the failed July Plot to kill Hitler and the brutal revenge wreaked upon the conspirators by the Nazis. Most soldiers were genuinely shocked by the revelations about the plot and accepted the official Nazi propaganda that the plotters had been a small clique of self-serving individuals in the upper echelons of the army. But even amongst those who condemned the plot, there were many who could see what lay ahead. Most soldiers on the Eastern Front would fight on grimly to hold back the Red Army from their homeland, and in many cases this was further reinforced by awareness of the crimes that Germany had committed across Europe and particularly in the east. The final retribution of the Allied Powers was seen by many as no different from certain death and defeat on the battlefield.

Alongside Hitler's aversion to timely withdrawals was his unwillingness to recognise the need to prepare proper defensive positions. He repeatedly refused permission for work to be carried out on defences to the rear of the main battle line on the grounds that such work would encourage soldiers to look to these new positions as a place of safety and would thus weaken their willingness to show the required level of 'fanatical' resistance in the front line. During 1942 and 1943, German defences in the northern and central sectors had repeatedly come under heavy attack from the Red Army, and the Soviet forces suffered disproportionate casualties on every occasion as they attempted to batter their way through German defensive lines; what was required, Hitler insisted, was that the new front lines were fortified and defended in the same manner as had been the case in the past so that similar battles could be repeated. But again, this ignored important realities. Firstly, the German defences of 1942 and 1943 had generally been in far more favourable terrain for defensive fighting. Secondly, the Germans had benefited from many months of occupying those lines and had steadily strengthened their positions. Finally, the task of the defenders was supported by significant defensive firepower in the form of artillery and machine-guns to inflict huge losses on Soviet troops struggling forward through the defensive belts.

The German lines across eastern Poland in late 1944 were in terrain that was often far from favourable to the defenders. Although the Germans were arrayed broadly along the middle Vistula, the Red Army had seized several substantial bridgeheads across the river and would be able to concentrate its resources within these bridgeheads so that its soldiers could attack without having to force a river crossing. The German defenders had not been in position for long enough to create the dense defences that had characterised earlier battles on the Eastern Front; nor had they received the material resources needed for such defensive fieldworks.

Even if there had been sufficient concrete and barbed wire to build fortifications, the German divisions on the Eastern Front no longer had the numerical strength to defend the Eastern Front. The huge losses of 1944 could not be replaced. Throughout the war, the frontage that each division was required to defend increased steadily and by late 1944, the divisions on the Eastern Front were holding up to 15 miles (25km) of defences; experience of earlier battles had shown that defending a sector of more than six miles (10km) per division was likely to result in defeat.[2]

The quality of the troops in the front line was also poor. Rolf Hinze, who was a young soldier in the artillery regiment of 19th Panzer Division in the closing years of the war, later described the mixture of raw recruits, including men who had been regarded in the past as medically unsuitable for front-line service, on whom Germany would depend for this last series of battles:

> For a considerable time, greatly overextended frontal widths had been necessary in terms of defensive density because there was a shortage of sufficient numbers of soldiers to occupy the front line securely. Such an over-extended situation required the construction of front line and supporting positions, especially as the Soviets, according to their repeated practice, began each attack with an artillery strike that consumed a great deal of ammunition in a barrage that lasted several hours and could plough up the entire front line, thus crushing any resistance. However, there was a shortage of personnel and construction materials to build positions. Additionally, repeated redeployments of troops lessened attention in construction of fortifications. The great majority of the deployed units were not made up of experienced troops but of new arrivals, some of them territorial reservists, i.e. men from older groups that were not normally subjected to military conscription. This included battalions with stomach problems, eye and ear disorders – scraping the bottom of the barrel! ...
>
> In many cases the divisions were poorly prepared for emergency action, so training courses of all kinds and field exercises were organised to improve the efficient use of weapons and above all to try to produce smooth cooperation between different weapons branches.
>
> However, all efforts of this kind didn't compensate for the lack of combat experience and didn't provide the front-line infantry divisions with shelters and positions that could withstand heavy artillery fire. Added to this was the stretched ammunition situation, which meant that our artillery was unable to detect and engage enemy firing positions. Fuel had to be used extremely sparingly and was managed centrally. This later resulted in the risk that it couldn't be distributed in a timely manner as required by the combat situation, and that the enemy would rapidly seize the storage locations from which fuel was to be distributed.[3]

Another area of constant friction between Hitler and the senior commanders of the Wehrmacht was his policy of declaring positions to be fortresses. In March

1944, as he formulated his strategy for the coming year, Hitler described the establishment of a series of *Fester Plätze* ('fortified locations') that were to be treated in a different manner from other military positions. Senior commanders were to ensure that these fortresses were prepared for all-round defence and provided with suitable garrisons and supplies; when the Red Army advanced, they were to be held at all costs and would act as breakwaters to hinder the Soviet advance, tying up Soviet units and disrupting their further operations by retaining control of key communications nodes. The commandant of each location was to be selected by the relevant army group commander, and withdrawal from the fortress would require the permission of the army group commander – who in turn had to have Hitler's explicit approval.[4] Once the German defences had reorganised, it was expected that powerful counterattacks would be launched to restore contact with the fortress and to return the front line to its previous position.

The 'fortress strategy' explicitly referenced the use of fortresses in previous wars, but failed to acknowledge a fundamental truth. In the First World War, the armies of both sides inherited a series of fortresses that had been constructed in the 19th century and had then been repeatedly modernised at great expense. Despite this expenditure, there were few occasions when fortresses functioned as expected. The fighting around Verdun was perhaps one such case, but the French fortifications served more as part of the front line than in the traditional role of a fortress permitting the enemy to envelop it. On the Eastern Front, the Austro-Hungarian fortress of Przemyśl, in what is now southeast Poland, was encircled twice as the Russian Army advanced towards the west. The first encirclement in the autumn of 1914 lasted less than a month before contact was restored, but there is little to suggest that the Russian units encircling the city would have had a significant effect had they been available to be deployed elsewhere. The siege was renewed after about three weeks and lasted until March 1915 when the exhausted, starving garrison surrendered. Over 125,000 defenders were killed or captured and in addition the failed attempts to advance to relieve the siege cost the Austro-Hungarian forces over half a million further losses.[5] In every respect, the fortress had a greatly negative effect on the ability of the Austro-Hungarian Empire to conduct its war strategy.

The repeated modernisation of fortresses in the 19th century was largely due to the increasing power of artillery, and the capabilities of firepower to crush fortifications continued to improve, augmented by the development of air power. When he drew up his fortress policy, Hitler was undoubtedly influenced by important sieges that had already taken place after the invasion of the Soviet Union in 1941. During 1942, the fortress city of Sevastopol in Crimea – widely regarded as one of the strongest fortresses in the world – was stormed successfully by the German Eleventh Army, though at considerable cost and after a lengthy battle. Stalingrad too had been besieged and although the German Sixth Army was eventually destroyed in the ruins of the city, its prolonged resistance tied down considerable Soviet forces that would have been highly effective had they been available for use elsewhere. Clearly, the fortress policy attempted to harness these two examples, but from the outset the strategy had serious flaws. The prolonged Soviet defence of Sevastopol was possible because the terrain was highly favourable to the defenders, with a series of rugged ridge lines covering the approaches to the city itself; moreover, substantial forces had retreated into the region as the Germans advanced across Crimea. Stalingrad too was defended by a large force, and the resistance of Sixth Army came at a huge cost for the Luftwaffe in its attempts to supply the city. The new fortresses that were designated across the Eastern Front were rarely in locations where the terrain favoured the defenders; nor were they provided with large garrisons in advance. Although orders were issued for the preparation of extensive defences, competition for building materials between fortress commanders and field armies that needed concrete, mines, and barbed wire to strengthen their front lines meant that little was done to turn the locations into proper fortified areas. In many cases, it was also impossible to stockpile sufficient food and ammunition to ensure prolonged resistance.

Perhaps the biggest flaw in the strategy was the expectation that German armoured forces would be able to lift the siege of the fortress before the garrison was forced to surrender. There had been several occasions when German relief forces had reached isolated and encircled units – Demyansk in 1942 and the Cherkassy-Korsun encirclement of 1944 were the largest examples – and it was largely on the basis of these operations that Hitler expected relief operations to be successful in future. But by the spring of 1944, the rescue of the isolated First Panzer Army and the extraction of the garrison of Tarnopol was only possible through the temporary transfer of two SS panzer divisions from the west to the Eastern Front. After the invasion of Normandy by the Western Allies, such transfers were impossible and given the growing strength of the Red Army and the weakening of the Wehrmacht, it was increasingly unlikely that successful relief operations could be mounted in future.

For the officers and soldiers of the Wehrmacht, the fortress policy was deeply unpopular and was associated with a high likelihood of death or capture. Commanders at army and army group level resented the diversion of resources to fortresses that they regarded as indefensible, particularly as it was usually impossible to provide anything approaching the number of men that were required to defend such large locations even by adding units that retreated to the fortresses from the front line. Furthermore, the list of locations that Hitler drew up when he first promulgated his policy might have taken account of the importance of these cities as rail and road hubs, but rarely made any allowances for the local terrain. Most of the fortresses were in areas that weren't particularly suited to defensive operations and true to Hitler's wish for defence to be carried out as far forward as was possible, they were often located immediately behind the front line. Consequently, there would be little opportunity for retreating units to be directed to them, or for further reinforcements to be sent before they were encircled.

As a consequence of all of these flaws, the fortress policy was generally a failure from the summer of 1944 onwards. The fortresses in the central sector – Vitebsk, Orsha, Mogilev, and Bobruisk – were rapidly overwhelmed by the advancing Red Army. Soviet losses in the fighting in these cities were substantial, but no more so than when field positions had been attacked and captured; nor did the fortresses have any significant effect as breakwaters that delayed the Soviet advance. They became the focus of an almost endless series of arguments between army group commanders on the one hand, who were anxious to abandon them before it was too late to save their garrisons, and Hitler on the other hand, with the chief of the general staff reduced to little more than a powerless go-between. Such disputes consumed significant amounts of time and energy when other crises of the front line demanded everyone's attention.

By late 1944, the person holding the post of chief of the general staff at *OKH* was Generaloberst Heinz Guderian, one of the pioneers of armoured warfare in the Wehrmacht. He inherited the post in the summer of 1944; General Kurt Zeitzler, who had been chief of the general staff since immediately before the Stalingrad encirclement, suffered a complete nervous collapse largely because of the relentless stress of dealing with Hitler's failure to accept reality shortly after the Soviet summer offensive commenced in late June. He was replaced temporarily by Generalleutnant Adolf Heusinger, who was wounded in the explosion of Stauffenberg's briefcase bomb in Hitler's conference room on 20 July and consequently was unable to continue in his post.

At this stage of the war, Guderian was a rather different figure from the impatient firebrand that is portrayed in his memoirs of earlier years. The attack through Belgium and northern France in 1940 firmly established his reputation as a hard-driving panzer commander, prepared to argue energetically with superiors who disagreed with him, and his reward for the successful campaign in the west was to be given command of Second Panzer Group, later renamed Second Panzer Army, for the invasion of the Soviet Union. Although his forces made a series of dazzling advances in the central sector, he fell from favour at the end of 1941 when he ordered his formations to retreat in the face of the Soviet counterattack during the Battle of Moscow. Although his decision was undoubtedly correct and probably saved some of his units from disaster, the manner in which he conducted the withdrawal – making little or no attempt to inform his neighbours of his decision – added considerably to the criticism levelled at him and he was dismissed. He remained sidelined until March 1943, when Hitler recalled him and appointed him *Generalinspekteur der Panzertruppen* ('Inspector-General of Armoured Forces'). He was tasked with restoring the fighting power of Germany's panzer divisions, a role in which he worked closely with the armaments minister, Albert Speer, and implemented a series of reforms. Wherever possible, officers in charge of training and organisation were to be men with combat experience; there was no shortage of such officers from panzer divisions who had been rendered unfit for front-line service by their wounds. Tank production was rationalised and panzer divisions reorganised, but his attempts to expand his remit to include the assault gun formations of the army (which remained under artillery leadership) and to gain a veto over the creation of new Luftwaffe and SS armoured formations were blocked by more experienced political operators.

Suffering from raised blood pressure and occasional heart problems, Guderian wrestled with the difficulties of introducing new, often unreliable tanks into service while fending off the demands of Hitler for their immediate deployment. As the Wehrmacht prepared for the Battle of Kursk in the summer of 1943, this resulted in a series of delays in commencing the operation, which had been intended to take place as soon as the spring thaw was over and before the Red Army's tank formations had recovered from their losses of the previous winter, when they had been roundly defeated in the German counteroffensive along the Donets River. But whilst the delays permitted the panzer units to come to terms with their new equipment and for at least some of the teething problems of the Panther tanks to be resolved, it also ensured that the Red Army had ample time to prepare for the German onslaught. And despite Guderian's repeated appeals to Hitler to abandon what he saw as a pointless offensive, much of the good work done by Guderian and Speer was wasted in the battle that followed.

One of the first tasks that Guderian faced when he became chief of the general staff was dealing with the fallout of the failed plot. In 1942, he had been approached by the conspirators but had declined to join them, and it seems that he had advance knowledge of the plot; he had suddenly retired to his country estate on the day of the assassination attempt. Now, he showed considerable energy in implementing the Nazification of the army. In addition to acquiescing to demands for the normal military salute to be replaced by the 'Hitler salute', he arranged for the swift dismissal of suspected plotters from the army so that they could be brought before the *Volksgerichtshof* ('People's Court') rather than face court martial.[6] As a result, those who were found guilty of involvement were condemned to death by hanging, in many cases with piano wire or narrow ropes being used deliberately to prolong their agony, rather than by firing squad as would have been the case if a court martial had reached a similar verdict. Guderian later claimed that he found this task repulsive and had attempted to avoid involvement, but there is little to support this, and no evidence that he raised the formal objections that might have been expected from the chief of the general staff.[7] But to a large extent, he had little room for manoeuvre. Any resistance to the vengeful reaction of Hitler and the Nazi Party could easily have raised suspicions of personal sympathy with the conspirators and their cause. Guderian also showed no hesitation in issuing an order on 29 July demanding that all officers were to join the Nazi Party, and accelerated the promulgation of Hitler's order of late 1943 requiring the appointment of *Nazionalsozialistische Führungsoffiziere* ('National Socialist Leadership Officers', usually abbreviated to *NSFO*); these were selected officers who, in addition to their military duties, were responsible for organising lectures and discussions to increase the commitment of the rank and file to the Nazi Party.

The military duties facing Guderian were severe enough without having to be involved in Hitler's brutal revenge upon those involved in the July Plot. The catastrophic retreat of the German Army Group Centre across Belarus to the Vistula finally came to a halt outside Warsaw, largely through logistic limitations and partly due to an energetic counterattack by IV SS Panzer Corps to the east of the Polish capital. At the same time, the Warsaw Uprising erupted immediately to the rear of the front line and Guderian showed little hesitation in supporting its suppression, which included the slaughter of thousands of civilians. As the long series of Soviet offensives came to a halt, he surveyed what remained of German positions in the east. Army Group North was isolated in northwest Latvia in the Courland peninsula; although it tied down substantial Red Army forces, it nonetheless represented a considerable drain on German resources. Guderian repeatedly suggested its withdrawal so that reinforcements could be released for other sectors, arguing that even if this inevitably resulted in Soviet resources being released too, at least the logistic burden of transporting munitions by sea to Courland would be eliminated; characteristically, Hitler refused to countenance any such plan. Army Group Centre, which had been driven back by the Red Army in Operation *Bagration* and had effectively been destroyed, had been rebuilt with a series of improvised formations and reinforcements sent from other theatres, and was defending a long line along the frontiers of East Prussia to the Vistula; between it and Army Group North was the city of Memel (now the Lithuanian city of Klaipėda) on the Baltic coast, isolated from all other German positions.

The formations to the south of Army Group Centre had undergone various name changes since they formed Army Group South during the invasion of the Soviet Union in 1941. In September 1944, the northern part of what had been Army Group South but had been renamed Army Group North Ukraine earlier in the year was given a new designation of Army Group A, a tacit recognition that it was no longer on Ukrainian soil. To its south had been Army Group South Ukraine; it too was renamed in September, taking up the title of Army Group South after most of the units of Army Group South Ukraine were destroyed or driven back in disarray after the collapse of German positions in Romania. Although all these army groups retained the armies and corps that had been present since the commencement of the war with the Soviet Union, they were shadows of their former selves. Their divisions were far from full strength and the replacement drafts that joined them in the second half of 1944 lacked the training of their predecessors, and perhaps more importantly they had no experience of the realities of fighting on the Eastern Front. It was fortunate that the Red Army needed a lengthy operational pause during the first half of the winter to bring forward supplies and reinforcements; it gave the German divisions a desperately needed opportunity to improve the training of these new conscripts.

The pause also gave Guderian an opportunity to revisit Hitler's fortress policy. A new series of fortresses were designated, but there were fundamental differences with what had happened in early 1944. Most of the new fortresses were further from the front line, in recognition of the ease with which the Red Army had overrun Hitler's original fortresses in the first assaults that broke the German front line during *Bagration*. There would be greater opportunity for defending units to retreat to the fortresses, and the fortress commandants were given greater priority than had been the case in the past in terms of building up stockpiles of supplies and constructing fortifications. Moreover, unlike the cities of the Soviet Union that had formed the first fortresses, the cities of Poland and Germany that now received the designation were larger and hadn't suffered as much destruction. Unlike many Soviet cities, they were largely built of brick and stone, and converting them into fortified positions was a more straightforward task. In most cases, they were also the locations of factories producing munitions and other supplies.

But even if the new fortresses were more likely to hold out in the face of an attack, there remained an important question: what would happen next? On many occasions through 1944, it had proved almost impossible for the Wehrmacht to mount relief operations to rescue the garrisons of isolated fortresses, and if the new fortresses were enveloped, it would be in the context of German units being driven back into Germany itself. In such circumstances, the likelihood of any relief operation was very low. The preparation of these new fortresses can thus be seen to be part of what amounted to a plan for a last line of military resistance. By the time that they were put to the test, there were no longer any strategic options open to Germany to create a situation that would see a favourable end to the war – if such a situation were to arise, it would be the consequence of events beyond German control. All that the Wehrmacht could hope to do was hang on as long as possible.

Even this policy, which in some respects was a successor to Hitler's previous fortress strategy, was only implemented with grudging approval from the Führer – the construction of fortresses to the rear of the main defensive line was seen by him as another example of creating fortifications that might encourage soldiers to withdraw rather than fight in the front line with the required 'fanatical' determination. But by framing the new plans as a continuation of the previous fortress policy, Guderian was able to persuade Hitler that the fortification work should commence. He added a further argument in favour of the new fortifications being further to the rear of the front line than had been the case in the past. The fortresses across the Soviet Union had come under attack almost as soon as Soviet troops broke through the front line, and consequently the Red Army's units were still at full strength, particularly if they were divisions that had been held in reserve to exploit the initial success. By positioning fortresses further back, Guderian hoped that the Red Army formations that attacked them would be rather more depleted.

There was only one fortress that was effectively part of the front line: the shattered city of Warsaw, which had been deliberately destroyed by the Germans as vengeance for the 1944 Warsaw Uprising. Defence of this sector came under the control of General Smilo Freiherr von Lüttwitz and his Ninth Army, and he later wrote about the impracticalities of the Warsaw fortress:

For those of us in [Ninth] Army, the plans for the fortress seemed wholly faulty. We believed, quite rightly, that the strategic value of the fortress would not be a decisive factor in the defence of the Vistula line. All the bridges in Warsaw and the long railway tunnel in the city had been destroyed. If the enemy overran the city, he would face long weeks with substantial construction units to make the place suitable once more for traffic. It would be far easier for the enemy to create road and rail routes across the Vistula by bypassing the city to the north and south, something that we assessed was quite straightforward in view of the existing road and rail network. Crucially, these routes were beyond the reach of the fortress …

Even during the planning phase, it was clear that the available garrison and equipment was in no respect adequate for satisfying the requirements for the changes needed in this front-line fortress …

All of these objections from Ninth Army were submitted in writing to *OKH* in a substantial memorandum and raised in telephone conversations with Army Group [Centre], which endorsed them in every respect. The only result was the appearance of another *OKH* commission in Warsaw. After that, construction of fortifications was ordered to commence in early October 1944.

Up until shortly before the Russian attack [of January 1945], the Warsaw fortress had been expanded by laborious work so that the outer ring of defences, consisting of an anti-tank ditch with barbed wire in its bed, had been completed. The garrison consisted of three regiments of infantry and an artillery battalion equipped with captured guns and about 12 anti-tank guns. Most of the soldiers were old, members of security regiments with little combat experience, i.e. *Landwehr* or disabled former front-line soldiers. For example, one battalion was made up of men from a hospital specialising in ear disorders. Barely any of them had good hearing and almost half had to be treated for suppuration from their ears every day. The regiment commanders had no front-line experience and were all at least 49 years old.[8]

The first 12 months of the First World War had seen extensive fighting between German and Russian armies in this region. The suitability of various defensive lines was well known to both sides, and preparatory work to fortify these lines began in the autumn of 1944. As was so often the case, the front line had solidified where the fighting of earlier campaigns ended and was far from suitable from the German point of view. The Red Army had seized three bridgeheads across the Vistula south of Warsaw, and between them the front line remained along the river. The first bridgehead was around Magnuszew, about 31 miles (50km) south of the centre of the Polish capital, immediately south of where the Pilica River flows into the Vistula. The second bridgehead was a similar distance further south at Puławy, and the largest was around Sandomierz, a further 53 miles (86km) to the south of Puławy; in German accounts, this last bridgehead is often named after the town of Baranów. By pulling back to a front line that continued to face the Magnuszew and Sandomierz bridgeheads but abandoned the Vistula line between them and the line facing the Puławy bridgehead, German staff officers calculated that they would be able to hold a new line that shortened the front by 60 miles (100km).

This line, known as the *Hubertus-Stellung* ('Hubertus Position') would also run through more favourable terrain. A little further west was the *A1-Stellung*, running along the Rawka, Pilica and Nida Rivers; this would involve abandonment of Warsaw and the central Vistula region. In the southern half of Poland, there was a further option to pull back to a line closer to Kraków – this was roughly where the German Army had stopped the Imperial Russian Army in December 1914 and was known as the *A2-Stellung*. Further defensive lines – the *B1-Stellung* and the *B2-Stellung* – ran roughly along and to the west of the Warthe River.

Generalleutnant Fritz Benicke, who was assigned responsibility for preparing these rearward defences, described some of the problems that he faced in addition to the ubiquitous shortages of workers, equipment and materiel:

> As was the case in other provinces, Upper Silesia was governed by the *Gauleiter*, appointed by the [Nazi] Party leadership ... and as *Reichsverteidigungskommissar* had almost unlimited power. In order to adapt the idiosyncratic wilfulness of people who thought entirely in a provincial framework to the operational needs of defending the entire area, but at the same time to ensure their cooperation, which was necessary since the construction of fortifications was largely done by the local population ... there were constant compromises in the planning, management and execution of the immense project: the Wehrmacht leadership determined the overall layout of the lines and their conformity with areas of military command; the *Gauleiters* were responsible for management and deployment of civilian labour and to this end established new staff organisations around senior engineer officers.[9]

The *Gauleiter* of Upper Silesia was Fritz Bracht, a relatively anonymous figure in the Nazi hierarchy. He had served briefly as a rifleman at the end of the First World War and therefore had at least a little military experience, but like all *Gauleiters* he owed his position to his obedience to the Party and his abilities as a political organiser. It was a common feature of Nazi thinking that Darwinian principles could be applied to almost every aspect of life and self-promotion and intense competition was common amongst *Gauleiters*; in this respect, Bracht seems to have been an exception, as an evaluation of his performance in 1939 summarised:

> His basic modesty is impeccable and must be treated as a positive character trait. It has led here and there to disappointment, which, however, was a good [lesson] for him, and as a result he has become harder.[10]

In October 1944, Bracht presided over the creation of Silesia's *Volkssturm* battalions. During the war of 1813 against Napoleonic France, Prussia had raised a large number of *Landsturm* battalions that fought in a variety of roles, serving both as guerrilla forces and regular units. The *Volkssturm* was a reimagining of this concept. In many respects, it was an act of desperation. The Wehrmacht no longer had the manpower to hold back Germany's enemies, and the Nazi Party proposed the creation of a new force of 6 million militia. Orders were issued in September 1944 with an official launch on 18 October, the anniversary of the Battle of Leipzig in 1813 when French forces were effectively forced to retreat from German territory.[11] The *Gauleiters* of German provinces were assigned the task of recruiting and organising these new forces and Bracht addressed a parade of youths, men beyond conventional military service age, and others who had been invalided out of the army:

> My *Volkssturm* soldiers and German men and women. At the same time as we are gathered here and have proclaimed our determination to fight to the end, to fight fanatically with all the means at our disposal, persevering in the face of doubt and temptation, steadfast and alert until our banners are victorious, I have ordered a *Volkssturm* unit led by my deputy to go to the memorial for fallen *Freikorps* warriors at Annaberg [a memorial to the Battle of Leipzig].
>
> There, this unit, as a delegation of the German *Volkssturm* of Upper Silesia, binds us in reverent gratitude with those who remained true to the German people and the Reich in Germany's most shameful hour, who remained undaunted and held to their beliefs, who obeyed only their inner conscience in the struggle for their native German soil, for German honour and liberty, sacrificing their lives for German women and children ... [They were] German men and youths in action to the very last, prepared if necessary to make the ultimate sacrifice when the Fatherland, their homeland, was threatened ...
>
> We know that now we have truly begun to wage total war and that in the shortest possible time we will be a nation in arms in the truest sense of the words and the laurels of victory cannot be snatched from us ...
>
> Now it is too late for our foes. Now it has truly become a total, holy war, one we have been forced to wage.[12]

As soon as the concept of the *Volkssturm* was first raised, there were doubts amongst Wehrmacht officers about the military usefulness of such a measure. Some pointed out that whilst a *levée en masse* might have had some usefulness in earlier eras, it had little place in the midst of a mechanised war. Moreover, as the new *Volkssturm* battalions would explicitly not be part of the army but would be under the control of *Gauleiters*, they would not be covered by the Hague Convention. As a result, it was possible, if not likely, that they would be treated in the same manner that German forces had treated partisans and suspected partisans in the occupied parts of the Soviet Union.[13]

By late 1944, Bracht was suffering from tuberculosis and Benicke had to work with the deputy *Gauleiter*, Rudolf Metzner. Benicke was able to negotiate a working relationship with Metzner but faced another potential area of overlapping responsibilities. Military administration of Germany was carried out via a series of *Wehrkreise* or military districts. These were responsible for matters such as recruitment and basic training of new personnel. Silesia, which faced the threat of Soviet invasion if the Red Army were to break through the defences to the south of Warsaw, came under the control of *Wehrkreis VIII*. Depending on the personalities of the *Wehrkreis* commander and particularly the local *Gauleiter*, this often resulted in further friction. The commander of *Wehrkreis VIII* was General Rudolf Koch-Erpach, an experienced soldier who did all he could to aid Benicke in his work. At least in this region, there was little interference from the office of the *Gauleiter*.

Despite his best efforts, both in terms of military engineering and diplomacy, Benicke soon found himself confronted by the realities of the way that Darwinian competition within the Nazi hierarchy frequently degenerated into jealous squabbles and obstructionism. Part of the defensive line proposed for Silesia would run through the territory of the *Generalgouvernement*, the rump of Polish territory that had not been annexed by Germany. The *Generalgouvernement* was overseen by Hans Frank and even where the plans for defences amounted to no more than the erection of barbed wire entanglements and anti-tank obstacles, Frank refused to permit work parties from Silesia to cross the border into his territory. Both Bracht and Frank made representations to Berlin, and the matter remained a source of friction until the end of German rule in the area.

It was important to establish as much of the new defensive lines as possible before the arrival of winter weather. Benicke suggested to Bracht that *Volkssturm* battalions should be deployed for brief spells in the fortifications to allow them to become accustomed to field conditions, but this proved difficult to organise; many of the personnel of the new battalions were also working in factories and mines in the industrial heartland of Silesia and securing their release was almost impossible. This was a source of considerable frustration for Benicke. Fortifications without troops to hold them were pointless, and past experience had shown that front-line units retreating under pressure from the Red Army were often in too poor condition to take full advantage of such defensive lines. Denied access to the *Volkssturm*, Benicke approached Koch-Erpach and requested the deployment of new recruits in his fortifications. The commander of *Wehrkreis VIII* was sympathetic but turned down the proposal. Such deployment would interfere too much with the basic training of the recruits, which was already detrimentally truncated.

In December Benicke organised a large-scale wargame to simulate the coming Red Army offensive. To the anger of Bracht and Metzner, he assigned low capabilities to *Volkssturm* units in anti-tank warfare – for them, the value of such an exercise was to show everyone (particularly Bormann and therefore Hitler) that the *Gau* was in good shape for whatever might lie ahead. Despite this friction, a few important improvements in the defensive lines were identified and further work was undertaken, but the main issue remained the lack of any standing garrison. As 1944 came to an end, Benicke wrote to Berlin and asked once more for the release of *Volkssturm* battalions. Bormann, the longstanding jealous guardian of the rights and authority of the Nazi Party, refused. The *Volkssturm* were to remain under the direct command of *Gauleiters*, at least until they were committed to combat.

The construction activity to the rear of the front line inevitably resulted in field commanders considering the prudence of moving from their current positions to shorter lines to the rear. Generalleutnant Wolf-Dietrich von Xylander, chief of staff at Army Group A, drew up detailed plans for such a withdrawal under the codename *Schlittenfahrt* ('Sleighride'). The Wehrmacht had good experience of how to conduct such operations; the evacuation of the Demyansk and Rzhev salient had been carried out in earlier years with great success and both operations had resulted in withdrawal to a shorter, more defensible line and the release of substantial reserves. *Schlittenfahrt* would shorten the overall front line by 60 miles (100km) and if the withdrawal was timed carefully, it would be possible for retreating German units to pull out immediately before the Red Army's massive artillery preparation for its next offensive; the bombardment would land on abandoned positions and it would take considerable time for Soviet artillery units to be brought forward and supplied in the new front line. The German forces that were to pull back to the *Hubertus-Stellung* would be in better terrain for defensive warfare; at the same time, the reserves that would be created by the adoption of a shorter front line would be available to deal with the anticipated Soviet assault from the Magnuszew bridgehead.

The planned withdrawal would have consequences for both military and civil authorities, and Xylander recognised this in his plans. Consequently, he proposed that the various parts of Frank's *Generalgouvernement* administration should withdraw to the west in early December and work should commence immediately on the preparations for destruction of bridges, railway lines and embankments, locomotive watering facilities, etc. Such steps would ravage the Polish countryside to the west of the Vistula, but the consequences for the civilian population were irrelevant to Xylander. When he summarised the benefits of his plan, Xylander stressed the positives: it would buy time, as the Red Army would face the laborious task of moving forward over devastated terrain and would have to concentrate its resources in front of the new German lines. Aware of Hitler's favourable attitude towards powerful counterattacks, Xylander stressed the possibility that German reserves released by the withdrawal could be used to inflict a telling blow on Soviet forces advancing from the Magnuszew bridgehead. Such outcomes were unlikely to result in the overall tide of the war turning in favour of Germany, but at the very least it would put off the evil hour when Soviet troops broke into Germany itself. If the war was to be lost, most German commanders quietly accepted that occupation by the Western Allies was preferable to the vengeance of the Red Army.

The forces of Army Group A, which would face the full strength of the coming Soviet offensive, waited with increasing anxiety for a decision to be made about *Schlittenfahrt*. The commander of the army group was Generaloberst Josef Harpe, who had long experience of war on the Eastern Front. He had led 12th Panzer Division, XLI Panzer Corps, Ninth Army and Fourth Panzer Army with considerable skill before taking up command of Army Group North Ukraine shortly before it became Army Group A. But like almost every senior officer who served on the Eastern Front, he had been involved in war crimes. In March 1944, when he was commander of Ninth Army, Harpe oversaw the clearance of large numbers of civilians from the area under the control of his army and issued orders for the creation of a makeshift set of concentration camps near Ozarichi in Belarus. Here, about 40,000 civilians were interned and used as forced labour, with many being executed for minor infringements or because they were too weak to work. There were no buildings for shelter and the internees were forbidden even from lighting fires to warm themselves.[14] Whilst most accounts written by former Wehrmacht officers and soldiers after the war would attempt to place the blame for all such camps upon the SS, there can be no doubt that on this occasion as on many others, the Wehrmacht was fully involved. In addition to Harpe's explicit order for the creation of the camps, the war diary of the logistics section of LVI Corps, part of Ninth Army, stipulated that in the event of the Wehrmacht being forced to retreat from the area, the camp was to be destroyed by artillery fire before the Red Army could reach it.[15] This order was duly carried out when the withdrawal took place.

The most southerly formation of Harpe's army group was what remained of First Panzer Army, now known as *Armeegruppe Heinrici* after it took the Hungarian First Army under its command. The commander of this eponymous force, Generaloberst Gotthard Heinrici, was another experienced Eastern Front officer. He was unpopular with senior Nazi figures. He was a devout Lutheran Christian and refused repeatedly to join the Nazi Party and was frequently insulted and mocked by Göring, who drew attention to the fact that one of his wife Gertrude's parents was Jewish. Heinrici was able to prevent any steps being taken against his family by securing a *Deutschblütigkeitserklärung* ('German Blood Certificate') signed by Hitler that confirmed the Aryan status of both himself and Gertrude. Despite his familial connections with the Jews – or perhaps partly in an attempt to show how they did not affect his commitment to Nazi Germany – Heinrici had little hesitation in embracing the Nazi concept of 'Jewish Bolshevism' as the enemy of the German people. During the Wehrmacht's advance towards Moscow in 1941 he made numerous entries in his diary about the successes of elements of his XLIII Corps against partisans, making little distinction between actual partisans and civilians who were suspected of collaborating with them.[16] But as the war continued, he became increasingly concerned about the crimes being committed by German forces on the Eastern Front and refused to obey orders to lay waste the city of Smolensk when it was abandoned by the Wehrmacht in 1943. He was an astute, skilful field commander with a reputation for successful defensive warfare and was widely respected both by those who served under his command and his contemporary senior officers. He was a slight figure, known for his precise manner of speaking; many of his subordinates privately referred to him with a degree of respect and affection as *Unsere Giftzwerg* ('our poison dwarf').

The 'poison dwarf' would require all his defensive skills in the fighting that lay ahead. His command consisted of the German XI and XVII Corps and XLIX Mountain Corps, together with V Hungarian Corps; between them, they fielded eight German infantry, mountain or Jäger divisions and four Hungarian divisions, together with a weak Hungarian reserve division. It was usual for infantry corps to have independent tank battalions or assault gun battalions attached to them; none was available for any of these units. They would have to deal with Soviet armour with the very limited divisional assets available to them. In October, orders arrived for German troops to disarm the Hungarian reserve division as it was regarded as no longer reliable. Major Hans Jürgen Pantenius was one of the officers ordered to carry out this task, which was made worse by the way they had spent considerable effort improving their cooperation and relationship with the Hungarians during discussions about transferring control of a sector to German troops:

> Without any major fanfare, I travelled to Natolin and explained the situation and my mission to the [Hungarian] commander and asked him for his pistol, not out of any sense of danger to my own person but because I wanted to prevent a suicide attempt. The commander was completely helpless, tears filled his eyes, and he couldn't and didn't want to issue orders; he silently handed me his weapon. The adjutant ... issued the orders I wished, concerning the replacement, disarmament, and internment. Due to previous discussions about replacement and the positional maps that been prepared, the action was carried out comparatively swiftly and without difficulty. Naturally, the Hungarians could see no reason for their disarmament and like their commander were concerned and agitated. This didn't prevent their officers and NCOs from taking care to list what weapons and equipment they handed over.
>
> I never found out who at army, corps or division level actually issued the order for the disarmament of the Hungarian reserve division. Did those in higher commands really think that the division would desert to the Poles? If they had asked the 'front line', in other words our general or our regimental commanders, for our advice beforehand, we would have told them that we never doubted the camaraderie of the Hungarians. But the views of subordinates were not sought. But the very same day came a counter-order. The Hungarian division was to be given back its weapons immediately, the internment was to be stopped, and the division was to prepare for transfer to Hungary the next day. The whole affair was a mess. I was now tasked to make my 'colleagues' who remained in Natolin aware of the new situation and to return their weapons to them with expressions of regret. The Hungarians were delighted with the prospect of returning to their homes in Hungary ... [The division commander] was almost speechless with anger.[17]

To the north of *Armeegruppe Heinrici* was Seventeenth Army, under the command of General Friedrich Schulz. The original Seventeenth Army was effectively destroyed in Crimea in April 1944 and then reformed using survivors of units that had been evacuated by sea from the peninsula. Schulz took command of the army in July 1944. A quiet, efficient officer, he oversaw the rebuilding of his army into a formation that was once more capable of combat,

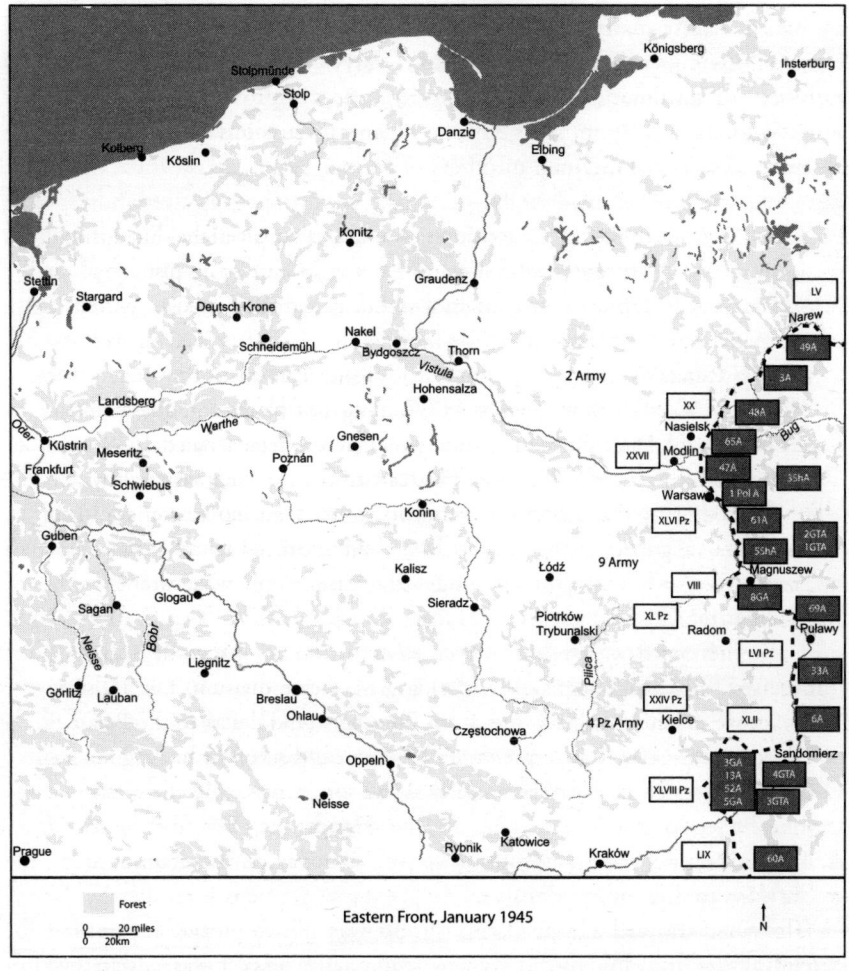

Eastern Front, January 1945

but must have been concerned about the quality of the personnel at his disposal. His army consisted of two corps, XI SS Corps and LIX Corps. These fielded two infantry divisions and three of the new divisions raised since the disasters of the summer of 1944. Two were *Volksgrenadier* divisions, largely made up of the large numbers of men released by Goebbels' 'total war' effort, with their ranks stiffened by handfuls of veterans or the remnants of divisions that had been smashed in combat. The third was termed a *Volkssturm* division. A 'standard' German infantry division consisted of three regiments each with three battalions; by contrast, *Volksgrenadier* divisions had just six battalions in three regiments, with an additional 'fusilier' battalion as division reserve, though in reality many regular infantry divisions had been forced to disband some of their battalions by late 1944. They were equipped with plentiful numbers of automatic weapons and light anti-tank weapons such as the *Panzerfaust*. In addition to their newly mobilised soldiers and a few army veterans, they also contained numbers of former naval and air force men who were released – often grudgingly – to make good the manpower shortages of the army. Perhaps their biggest weakness was the same problem that confronted so many German formations in late 1944: the loss of so many irreplaceable NCOs and junior officers resulted in a significant deterioration in the quality of German military leadership in the field.

Fourth Panzer Army, to the north of Seventeenth Army, covered the front line from the Vistula about 48 miles (77km) east of Kraków to a point close to Radom. General Fritz-Hubert Gräser had inherited command in September 1944, having previously led XLVIII Panzer Corps in its ultimately unsuccessful attempts to destroy the Soviet bridgeheads on the west bank of the Vistula. In earlier years, a panzer army might have had more panzer formations than infantry units, but that was no longer the case. Gräser's former command, XLVIII Panzer Corps, had three infantry divisions; XLII Corps had a further four together with *Sperrverband von Ahlfen*, one of the many eponymous improvised formations that were increasingly commonplace in the Wehrmacht; and a short distance behind the front line was XXIV Panzer Corps, with a battlegroup from 10th Panzergrenadier Division and all of 16th and 17th Panzer Divisions and 20th Panzergrenadier Division. Although this corps was technically part of Fourth Panzer Army, it was under the control of Army Group A. Its positioning was to become a source of repeated disagreements in the weeks prior to the Soviet offensive.

The final army of Harpe's army group was Ninth Army, responsible for defending the front line in the Warsaw region. Almost completely destroyed in the course of Operation *Bagration*, it had been rebuilt around the remnants of the divisions that were shattered in the great Soviet assault and was now led by Lüttwitz. He was a man accustomed to leading from the front – during the course of the war, he was wounded five times – and was in many respects a very traditional Prussian soldier with a strong sense of duty and responsibility for his men. His army consisted of XLVI and LVI Panzer Corps and VIII Corps; they fielded five infantry divisions, three *Volksgrenadier* divisions, and the Warsaw garrison. Like Gräser's army to the south, he had a further formation, XL Panzer Corps with 19th and 25th Panzer Divisions, as his operational reserve, but this corps was under the control of Army Group A.

As well as having operational control of the two panzer corps described above, Harpe also had IV SS-Panzer Corps as an army group asset. It was a powerful formation with two panzer divisions, *SS-Wiking* and *SS-Totenkopf*. Of all his armoured assets, this was perhaps the most important. If committed in a timely and decisive manner, it could be expected at least to blunt a Soviet offensive. In August 1944, the two divisions had taken part in successful counterattacks on Red Army tank forces immediately to the east of Warsaw, and the soldiers of the two divisions were experienced and confident.

The individual formations that manned the front line were weak, made worse by the requirement to hold such long sectors of front line that they had few reserves. It was normal for corps and division commanders to have up to a third of their available manpower ready for counterattacks, but by late 1944 it was almost impossible to have more than a battalion as a local reserve. At army and army group level, there was serious concern about the positioning of XXIV Panzer Corps. Both Harpe and Gräser wanted it to be held further to the rear, but Hitler insisted on its deployment immediately behind the front line. For the field commanders, this made little sense. The local road network was sufficient to ensure its rapid movement from a more rearward position, and by positioning it so far forward it was at great risk of being caught up in the initial Soviet offensive rather than being available for a decisive counterattack. Having completed his proposals for *Schlittenfahrt*, which would release significant forces to function as local reserves and would release XXIV Panzer Corps and permit it to function as a proper operational reserve, Xylander submitted his plans to Guderian at *OKH* at Christmas 1944. As an experienced front-line commander, Guderian could see that *Schlittenfahrt* made good sense – indeed, it was the only possible option that avoided an early catastrophic defeat when the expected Soviet offensive broke. When he consulted Generaloberst Hans-Georg Reinhardt, commander of Army Group Centre and defending the front line in East Prussia, he found that Reinhardt had similar proposals. By abandoning a modest amount of ground, the mismatch between the length of front line and the resources available could be narrowed considerably.

Guderian advised Xylander that he approved of the plan for *Schlittenfahrt*; however, he added that it could only be implemented with Hitler's explicit approval and he doubted that this would be forthcoming. Trying to move matters forward, Oberst Georg Freiherr von Weitershausen – Xylander's operations officer – contacted Frank, the head of the *Generalgouvernement*, to ask him for support. The response was disheartening. Frank wrote back that he felt he no longer had any influence with Hitler and had no confidence that the Führer would listen to representations from him.

Hitler still dreamed of implementing his failed strategy of holding the Red Army at arm's length while he crushed the Western Allies and his final gamble commenced on 16 December. In the Ardennes region, a force of over 400,000 men, backed by about 1,200 tanks and assault guns, launched what would become known as the Battle of the Bulge. Enjoying a substantial numerical superiority and complete surprise at the outset, the German forces broke through the American lines but both shoulders of the offensive encountered heavy resistance. The German forces were forced into an increasingly congested network of small roads, many of them made impassable by the winter weather, and the Americans and British were able to bring more forces to the theatre – crucially, improving weather allowed them to deploy their massively superior air power from about 24 December. The offensive failed with the loss of about half the tanks and assault guns that the Germans had committed, resources that would have been hugely valuable in the face of the coming Soviet offensive.

Hitler had moved to his *Adlerhorst* ('Eagle's Nest') bunker complex in western Germany to be closer to the operations against the Western Allies. As the fighting in the Ardennes offensive turned against Germany, Guderian visited him there on 24 December. He came prepared with the latest intelligence estimates of Red Army strength and capabilities. This assessment was based upon the work of *Fremde Heere Ost* ('Foreign Armies East' or *FHO*) the military intelligence department responsible for the Eastern Front. Its head, Oberst Reinhard Gehlen, had limited assets at his disposal – in particular, the near-collapse of the Luftwaffe deprived him of aerial reconnaissance. Nonetheless, he had prepared a report in November 1944 on the situation along the Vistula. He concluded that 1st Ukrainian Front intended to attack into Upper Silesia through the Kraków region while 1st and 2nd Belarusian Fronts to its north would clear the Vistula line, enveloping Warsaw and then advancing with their main forces on the northern bank of the Vistula. At this stage, he did not anticipate any deep operations towards the Oder River, but rather typically he hedged his bets, concluding:

> One must expect that because of the extended preparation time that has permitted the enemy to replenish his units and because of possible expansion of objectives (Prague, Breslau, Posen, Graudenz, Danzig and last of all the route to Berlin) that the Soviet leaders intend this forthcoming operation to achieve a decisive victory and to destroy the German armies in the east.[18]

Gehlen added that he expected the Soviet offensive to commence in mid-January. Whilst incomplete, this assessment was fairly accurate and his estimates of the strength of Konev's forces in the Sandomierz bridgehead were close to the true figures.

Guderian took this assessment to the meeting with Hitler together with the proposals from Army Groups A and Centre for limited withdrawals. He further suggested that in order to provide more robust resistance to the expected Soviet attack, he proposed the evacuation of Army Group North from Courland and consideration of abandonment of Norway and part of the Balkan region. Unfortunately for Guderian, the reputation of *FHO* had been sinking for some time. As was repeatedly the case with assessments that contradicted his personal wishes, Hitler rejected Gehlen's report with little consideration, ignoring Guderian's attempts to use it as evidence of the growing threat. The Führer insisted that the estimates were incorrect, as the losses suffered by the Red Army during the war had to mean that the Soviet Union was close to the end of its manpower resources. Guderian doggedly insisted that his assessment was accurate, and Hitler lost his temper, telling Guderian that Gehlen should be sent to a lunatic asylum.[19] To make matters worse, Guderian was dismayed to learn that despite the clear failure of the German armies in the Ardennes to achieve success, a further offensive was being planned in the west with an assault on the American forces in Alsace. News arrived that evening to plunge Guderian into even greater gloom: despite so much of the Wehrmacht's strength being committed to stopping the Red Army advancing across Hungary, the Soviet forces had reached and encircled Budapest.

On Christmas Day, Guderian returned to Berlin. While his train travelled through the bombed-out cities of Germany, he learned that Hitler had ordered the transfer of IV SS-Panzer Corps from Harpe's Army Group A to Hungary, where it was to be used to try to lift the siege of Budapest. After the disheartening conversations with Hitler and others the day before, this further weakening of what Guderian regarded as the most critical sector was a further blow. With increasing exasperation and a sense of desperation, he tried once more to secure reinforcements. He spoke to Generalfeldmarschall Gerd von Rundstedt, who was at least nominally in command of German forces in the western theatre, though in practice he was often reduced to little more than passing on Hitler's instructions. Rundstedt and Guderian knew each other well and they agreed on the importance of the threat posed by the Red Army. To Guderian's relief, Rundstedt told him that he had ordered three divisions deployed in northwest

Europe and another in Italy to prepare for transfer to the east. Assured that these transfers could be made without catastrophic weakening of German defences in the west, Guderian returned to the *Adlerhorst* to discuss matters with Hitler again on the last day of December. With great reluctance, Hitler agreed to the transfer of the four divisions, but insisted that they were sent to Hungary. The armies defending Poland were left without any meaningful reinforcements.

Guderian now embarked on a tour of the various headquarters on the Eastern Front. His first stop was at the headquarters of Army Group South, where he had a conversation with General Otto Wöhler, the commander. Wöhler was not a firebrand or argumentative and aggressive figure like some of his better-known contemporaries; rather, he had a reputation for steadiness and calm in every situation. But he couldn't hide his pessimism as he informed his visitor that the attempt by IV SS-Panzer Corps to break the siege ring around Budapest had failed. Guderian then travelled to the headquarters of the panzer corps where he discussed matters with Obergruppenführer Herbert Gille. The balding, bespectacled SS officer was a popular commander with both his contemporaries and subordinates; although there was considerable distrust and animosity between senior officers in the army and the SS, Gille was generally regarded by his army colleagues in a somewhat more favourable light than many other SS commanders. Gille's divisions had a good reputation – he had previously been commander of *SS-Wiking* and had led it to success in several dangerous situations, including two occasions when it was encircled in the first half of 1944. But Guderian now found that Gille had a far more pessimistic attitude. The attempt to reach Budapest had failed with over 3,000 casualties, and Gille responded to Guderian's questions with a resigned shrug. 'We no longer have the material of 1940,' he replied. 'I now need three men where before I could have made do with two, or even one.'[20] It was perhaps characteristic of senior German figures that Gille ascribed his failure entirely to the lower quality of his troops; like all German commanders, he took little or no account of the huge improvements in the fighting abilities of Germany's opponents.

Guderian's next stop was Kraków, where he met Harpe and Xylander and they had further discussions about *Schlittenfahrt*. A further refinement of the plan since the withdrawal of Gille's IV SS-Panzer Corps was to position the four panzer divisions in the army group in two pairs, either side of the expected Soviet offensive. They would then be able to make a pincer attack to strike against the advancing Red Army. The staff of Army Group A also presented Guderian with their assessment of enemy intentions. Substantial

Soviet forces of 1st Ukrainian Front were massed in the Sandomierz bridgehead, and there were further concentrations by 1st Belarusian Front in the two smaller bridgeheads between this and Warsaw. Units were being rotated frequently, permitting Soviet commanders to ensure that all of their troops were familiar with the terrain. As he outlined his proposals for *Schlittenfahrt*, Xylander was honest about his overall expectations, concluding that perhaps the best that could be expected was to halt the Red Army on the *Hubertus-Stellung*:

> If we succeed in intercepting the Russian attack in the *A1-Stellung* or even on the Silesian border in mobile battle, in which we are still superior to the Russians, we will be able to say that we have accomplished our mission. Nothing more can be achieved than that. But the industrial area of Upper Silesia will still be able to continue working, the enemy will be held away from German soil, and time will be gained for the supreme leadership of the Reich to convert the military situation that we have created into political action.[21]

Therein lay the real difficulty. During the summer of 1944 when the German Army Group Centre was being destroyed in Belarus, the Western Allies were simultaneously defeating every German attempt to crush the Normandy beachhead and were slowly pushing towards open country. Generalfeldmarschall Wilhelm Keitel, head of *OKW*, had asked Rundstedt what he suggested should be done. Rundstedt's contemptuous reply was characteristically blunt: 'Make peace, you fools, what else can you do?'[22] But perhaps the only possibility of such a turn of events had disappeared with the collapse of the July Plot. Although Xylander and others could plan for achieving a sufficient stalemate to give an opportunity for negotiations, there was no possibility of either the Allies or Hitler initiating such discussions.

Leaving all such considerations to one side, Guderian assured Harpe and Xylander that he was in full agreement with them about the proposals, but again expressed doubts that Hitler could be persuaded. Harpe's reply was that of a professional man whose advice was being ignored despite the weight of supporting evidence; he told Guderian, 'He should cashier me then. I am only doing my duty.'[23] The staff officers of Army Group A continued their preparations and anticipated that it would be possible for most of the military parts of *Schlittenfahrt* to commence on 10 January, roughly when the great Soviet offensive was expected to begin.

Before returning to Berlin, Guderian spoke to Reinhardt at the headquarters of Army Group Centre by telephone. It was imperative, Reinhardt told him, that

Army Group Centre should be permitted to withdraw to a shorter line. This would necessitate the abandonment of much of East Prussia and the civilian population should commence evacuation immediately. This would require the cooperation of the *Gauleiter* of East Prussia, Erich Koch, and Guderian promised to raise the issue at his next meeting with Hitler. The final conversation was also deeply disheartening. Generaloberst Robert Ritter von Greim, the commander of the Luftwaffe's *Luftflotte 6*, was responsible for air cover on the critical sector of the Eastern Front. He advised Guderian that on paper, he possessed about 300 fighter aircraft, but many were unserviceable due to shortages of fuel and spare parts. By contrast, the Soviet forces were estimated to be supported by over 10,000 planes.[24]

Armed with the results of his swift tour, Guderian returned to the *Adlerhorst* on 9 January. Here, he presented his findings and made one last effort to persuade Hitler that withdrawals to a shorter, more defensible line were essential. Guderian later described the course of the conversation after these transfers had once again been rejected:

> The prevailing mood in *OKW* was a vague hope that our reports of the Russian preparations for a major offensive amounted to no more than a huge bluff. They believed only what they wished to believe and closed their eyes to reality. Ostrich-like politics and strategies! At the end of the discussion, Hitler tried to comfort me by saying, 'The Eastern Front has never before possessed such a strong reserve as now. This is your doing, and I thank you for it.' I replied, 'The Eastern Front is like a house of cards. If the front is broken through at one point, all the rest will collapse.' ...
>
> With Hitler's last words – 'The Eastern Front must help itself and make do with what it's got' – I returned to my headquarters in Zossen in a grim mood.[25]

Guderian might have been severely disappointed by Hitler's refusal to accept the proposals he presented, but he was not surprised. He sent a signal to Army Group A, informing Harpe's headquarters of the outcome. The army group commander was away visiting the army and corps headquarters of the units facing the Sandomierz bridgehead, where he received the latest intelligence reports. There was a steady increase in enemy activity, and there were unmistakeable signs that a new Soviet offensive was coming. Red Army raiding parties were active, attempting to capture German soldiers for interrogation; there had been extensive aerial reconnaissance; numerous front-line units reported increased sounds of vehicle movements at night; and a small number of deserters continued to cross the front line, bringing with them reports that an assault was imminent. When Harpe reached Kraków, Xylander awaited him with the signal from Guderian:

[Xylander said,] 'The Führer has rejected everything – Courland, reinforcements from the west, and *Schlittenfahrt*. The front line stays where it is, and the situation remains the same. The Führer does not believe the Russians will attack.'[26]

In East Prussia, Reinhardt also learned of Hitler's intransigence. To add to his difficulties, he was refused permission for any evacuation of civilians from behind his immediate front line, as such a measure would be seen as defeatist.

Hans Jürgen Hartmann, a young officer facing the northern side of the Sandomierz bridgehead, had endured a dispiriting December. He had been wounded in the summer of 1944 in the southern sector of the Eastern Front and spent six weeks in a hospital in Germany, which proved to be something of a blessing – while he was recovering, his 294th Infantry Division was destroyed when the German Sixth Army was torn apart in August. The remnants were gathered together as a single regiment and sent to the Vistula sector to bolster the weak divisions on the front line. His diary gives a good picture of life in the German front line at this point of the war. On 18 December, Hartmann was enjoying a few days of rest in the rear area when news broke about the great German offensive in the Ardennes, but the celebrations were short-lived. The Red Army units facing the regiment made repeated attempts to capture prisoners for interrogation – such individuals were known to their captors as 'tongues'. When Hartmann returned to his company after his short break, he learned that one of his men had been taken:

During the night of 15–16 December, a man from the company, who had been next to the lane through the minefield, climbed out of the trench, nobody knew why – perhaps to stretch his legs, or perhaps to fetch wood from the ruins for a fire – in any case, he disappeared into the darkness. A few minutes later there was wild gunfire from submachine-guns, the crack of hand grenades, and screams and groans from the ruins. It was over in 30 seconds, a few shadows fleeing amongst the ruins in front of the barbed wire were all that were seen. A few angry bursts of gunfire were fired into the night and then it was still again, as if nothing had happened. But three wounded men groaned amongst the rubble and we found one bloodstained corpse torn to pieces. They were all from the night patrol and had been trying to pass through the lane in the minefield when they ran into the Russian raiding party in the ruins. Just two men from the patrol escaped unhurt.

At dawn, we found a Russian cap and a pair of old gloves, the only traces in the minefield lane and the rubble. The one man who had climbed out of the trench was gone and remained missing. They must have caught him. It was a huge mess …

I finally got back to the company late in the afternoon. But I was exhausted and my knees were like rubber. There was no longer any sense of confidence in victory or recovery, instead I was depressed that I had left the company and had enjoyed a few lovely days in the rear area while here in the front line they were now criticised and treated with suspicion on top of everything else. I sat for a long time in the evening with Oberwachtmeister Lang and the men who had witnessed the drama either directly or from a distance.

Nobody saw the Russian raiding party. The night was pitch black and the Russians probably only settled into the ruins shortly before the tragedy, as two patrols had passed earlier unmolested and hadn't noticed anything suspicious. So how could anyone talk about guilt or failure so off-handedly? The blame lies with the huge gaps in this pitiable front line, there are gaps of up to 800m without a single sentry, just a few weak patrols. What can they do in an emergency? …

For the first time in a long while, I'm really scared again when I go on night patrols. I see ghosts, I hear cracks and quiet calls and I'm startled when a flare hisses up unexpectedly. Now, on the orders of Wissmann [the battalion commander], a few sentries lurk in the rubble at night, but of course that leaves gaps elsewhere. Not a single replacement has come to us and we are short four men, the dead, wounded and the missing man. And the Russians certainly won't come to the same place twice, despite the nice lane through the minefield.

Since last night my nerves are in shreds. Even in the second line I no longer feel safe. Maybe it's partly because Wissmann threatened little Leutnant Zang and Oberwachtmeister Lang with taking the next raiding party – to prove themselves and as punishment![27]

Although there was an eerie calm, Soviet snipers took a steady toll of any soldier unwary enough to raise his head for long from the trenches. In his bleaker moments, Hartmann wondered whether he should simply emulate them to bring his existence to an end and to find peace. Christmas Day saw the appearance of a few parcels of cigarettes and even some alcohol, though consumption was restricted to just a mouthful to avoid drunkenness. Wissmann, the battalion commander, was already held in low esteem by the company due to his criticism of them, and his performance at Christmas did little to improve matters.

He informed Hartmann that he wanted to walk through the company trench at 1500 to wish the men a happy celebration:

> I was ready at 1500 and waited for Wissmann. As it started to get dark shortly after 1600, we had to hurry if we wanted to find the men in their bunkers. But at 1600 I was still waiting, sick to my stomach, waiting for the guy. Finally, I saw him approaching with the doctor across the darkened fields. He was 'unfortunately a little late'. This idiot, he even had to ruin this day for us. But on this occasion he probably preferred the darkness to the light of day.
>
> Of course, the men had been standing outside [their bunkers], they had been looking forward to the little chat that had been announced – but now you could only exchange a few words with them at their guard posts. The Christmas atmosphere at dusk, with candlelight in the bunkers, was ruined. The machine-guns had to be fired in, passwords exchanged. And besides, Wissmann had to go back very soon, there was still a lot to do, you know! Oh yes, we knew. When it was dark he was always busy in his command post.[28]

Hartmann accompanied Wissmann to battalion headquarters and when he returned to his company, he found more bad news waiting for him. Breuer, an older soldier who had been 'combed out' of a rear area unit and had been sent to the trench, had volunteered in place of a younger man to go to collect the evening meal for his platoon; such meals were usually prepared in a central kitchen and then brought forward to the soldiers. A mortar shell suddenly landed on the trench parapet and left him with bad head wounds from shrapnel. Shortly after, news arrived that Breuer had died of his wounds. Hartmann and his men sat in the darkness, reminiscing about previous Christmases and carefully avoiding any discussion of the future. As a company commander, Hartmann was responsible for passing on political lessons that reiterated messages of the past – Bolshevism was the mortal enemy of Germany, and Jews were 'world parasites'. Like many of his fellow officers, he tried to avoid such odious duties as much as possible, even after the increased emphasis on the activity of *NSFO* after the July Plot. For men in a thinly manned front line, mourning the sudden death of an old comrade who had been killed by the terrible timing of a random mortar bomb just as he was climbing out of the trench, any such messages would have felt completely out of place.

By the second week of January, most soldiers in the Wehrmacht knew that the German offensive in the Ardennes had failed. As a consequence, morale sank once more. Diaries and letters from men on all fronts show a mixture of despair at their personal situation and grim determination – particularly on the Eastern Front – to continue fighting. There were undoubtedly soldiers who remained fanatically committed to the Führer, particularly in the ranks of the SS, but the majority of veterans had experienced the realities of fighting against superior enemy forces. For officers like Hartmann, their nerves close to collapse from the constant strain of trying to keep their men alive, the personal bonds of loyalty to old comrades were perhaps the greatest motivation of all.

As threatened, Wissmann ordered a night raid on the Soviet positions to be carried out early in January; the two men he had singled out for blame in the incident of the ambushed patrol were in command. The soldiers in the trench endured a cold New Year's Eve; they were denied any alcohol, but heard loud, boisterous celebrations from battalion headquarters, which did little to raise Wissmann in their esteem. As the day of the planned raid approached, a cable was laid from battalion headquarters to the company position and Hartmann was bombarded constantly with demands for information. He grew increasingly worried that any Soviet soldier lying silently in no-man's land would overhear the constant calls and would guess that something was being planned. Even after the raiding party set off, there were further telephone calls, despite Hartmann requesting that Wissmann avoid drawing attention to the sector by such unnecessary activity. After what seemed like an endless wait for the raiding party to return, there was a sudden burst of firing from the Soviet positions. Hartmann requested an artillery strike to cover the withdrawal of the raiders. Finally, a few men appeared out of the darkness and reported to their company commander. Zang and Lang, the two men ordered to lead the raid, had just entered the Soviet trench when firing began. They were hit by gunfire and caught in grenade explosions – the Red Army unit clearly knew that a raid was coming and the trench was full of soldiers.

As the January days passed, Hartmann and his men waited for what they knew was inevitable, fearing both the Soviet troops in front of them and the military police patrols to their rear. Fortunately for the company, their battalion was rotated out of the front line on 11 January and placed in reserve. On the one hand, it meant that they might not have to face the full force of the Soviet attack, but on the other hand, if such an attack came, they would be required to carry out an immediate counterattack against numerically superior forces. And an attack was coming. Everyone from Guderian to the soldiers in the front line could see this; only Hitler and his immediate entourage believed that the Red Army's preparations were a huge bluff. The thoughts of Rolf Hinze in 19th Panzer Division were probably shared by most soldiers facing the expected offensive:

> The German front line was in an extremely unfavourable position at the beginning of 1945. The front-line soldier had a keen sense of the hopelessness of the situation, and therefore made the most of the days of training and rest while waiting for the inevitable storm.[29]

# CHAPTER 2

# THE RED ARMY: 'FORWARD, FORWARD AT ANY COST!'

Even as the drive across Belarus into eastern Poland and the Vistula was coming to an end in the summer of 1941, the Red Army was planning a further assault towards the west. To date, operations had permitted the Soviet Union to recover territory that it had lost, including the Baltic States and the parts of Finland and Poland that had effectively been seized in 1939 and 1940. Now, there was the prospect of plunging deep into the heartland of the Third Reich and carrying the war to Berlin.

Prior to 1944, there had been considerable friction between Stalin and the Western Allies on two main issues. The first was the repeated demand by Stalin that the invasion of Western Europe had to commence without further delay. Churchill's rejection of such demands in 1943 on the grounds that a premature attempt might result in 120,000 casualties for little or no gain was met with incomprehension: Soviet planners anticipated such losses in almost every operation that they mounted, and the reluctance of the Western Powers to do the same left them with the impression that Churchill and Roosevelt were content to allow the Soviet Union to suffer huge losses while they did nothing. This reinforced a widespread suspicion in Moscow that the delays were deliberate, part of a plan by the west to permit the German and Soviet forces to bleed each other white before mounting an invasion. Finally, the assembled forces of the Western Allies landed on the beaches of Normandy on 6 June 1944. One of the main areas of dispute with the Soviet side was therefore removed.

The other issue was rather more complex. For some considerable time, Roosevelt and Churchill had stipulated that the end of the war should see the restoration of pre-war frontiers, and Stalin had broadly agreed. The problem lay in the wording. For Churchill in particular, the intention had been a restoration of the frontiers of September 1939; but for Stalin, the war had commenced in June 1941, by which date the Soviet Union had seized territory in Finland and Poland and had annexed the Baltic States. The Polish government-in-exile was naturally opposed to Stalin's interpretation, but Churchill had effectively conceded the point at the conference in Tehran in 1943. He attempted to rationalise the concession to Stalin – made without any discussions with the Polish politicians in exile in London – on the grounds that the territory that Poland would lose in the east amounted to little more than swamps and forests, whereas it would in return gain far richer territory from Germany, namely the southern parts of East Prussia, and all of Pomerania and Silesia. In reality, Churchill and the exiled Poles had no choice. The Red Army would be in the region long before the British and Americans could arrive.

Silesia was of great interest to the Allied Powers but particularly to Stalin. By the second half of 1944, the German industrial heartland of the Ruhr was producing only a small proportion of its previous output. The cities of the region were largely reduced to rubble by incessant American and British air raids, and the railway network functioned only due to endless repairs and improvisations. This was particularly disrupting coal transportation, which in turn had an impact on electricity generation. By contrast, the industrial output of Silesia remained high. Capturing this region would deprive Germany of its last major source of new military equipment, thus bringing the end of the war nearer. It was also an opportunity for loot. Stalin intended to seize German industrial equipment and to transport it to the Soviet Union as part of the reparations he was demanding as compensation for the devastation inflicted by the Germans since their invasion of 1941, and the factories of Silesia were an obvious target.

As the senior officers of *Stavka* – the Soviet high command – took stock at the end of the summer of 1944, they considered the options for the future. Army Group North was cut off in Courland, where it had set up a strong defensive line. Soviet post-war accounts repeatedly stressed that destroying the 'Courland bridgehead' was not regarded as important – the Germans were isolated and unable to impose their will upon the Red Army, and their defences were formidable. Consequently, screening off the bridgehead was sufficient. But these accounts contain a substantial amount of rationalisation. Between the creation of the Courland bridgehead and the end of the war, the Red Army launched no fewer than six major assaults on the German lines. The losses suffered during these attacks – estimated to exceed 300,000 killed, wounded or missing – suggest strongly that the fighting was more than just an attempt to pin down the German divisions. Nonetheless, the Courland battles were not going to decide the outcome of the war. The best that the Red Army could achieve was completion of the recapture of Latvia.

To the south of the Courland bridgehead was the main part of the Eastern Front. The ratio of forces facing each other broadly along the northern and eastern frontiers of East Prussia was strongly in favour of the Red Army, but although successes could be anticipated in this sector, overrunning East Prussia would not strike a mortal blow against Germany. The decisive battle, it was agreed, would involve the capture of Berlin, and the road to Berlin was through Poland. Of course, the Germans too were aware of this and the Red Army could expect strong resistance. The distance from the front line near Warsaw to the German capital was about 323 miles (520km), and given the expected heavy fighting, Colonel General Sergei Matveyevich Shtemenko – head of the operations directorate of *Stavka* – and his staff concluded that a single operation to carry the Red Army from the Vistula to Berlin was unrealistic. By the end of October, the thrust to Berlin was therefore already intended to be made up of two phases. But should the German lines disintegrate completely, it might still be possible to end the war in a single drive from the Vistula to the German capital.

Even as fighting died down along the middle Vistula in the last weeks of 1944, Soviet efforts to reach and capture Budapest continued, and as has already been described these had the result of diverting German resources away from the vital Vistula sector. Undoubtedly, the capture of Budapest and a subsequent advance to Vienna would be huge blows against the Third Reich, but the Polish sector and the road to Berlin remained of paramount importance. It is arguable that defending the Hungarian axis was important for Germany, but if the only way of doing this was to weaken the still more important Warsaw-Berlin axis, it is further evidence – if any were needed – that Germany was at the end of its resources. As Soviet planning continued, Shtemenko emphasised the importance of operations both in Hungary and East Prussia. These were significant in themselves, but would also prevent the Germans from shifting reinforcements to Poland. East Prussia was seen as a potentially difficult sector as the terrain was judged to favour prolonged defence; the Masurian Lakes divided the region in two, with armies forced to operate either to the north of the lakes or to their south. Taking account of these defences, *Stavka* concluded that an attack on East Prussia would require the forces of two Fronts in order to overcome the defences and to tie down the German units in the region. The task was assigned to 2nd and 3rd Belarusian Fronts.

The forces that would attack across Poland were commanded by some of the most formidable and accomplished Soviet commanders; like their subordinates, they were confident of success. Even though the Germans could be expected to put up strong resistance as the Red Army entered Germany itself, the victories of the previous year had surely paved the way for one final series of operations.

The southern half of the offensive across the middle Vistula would be conducted by 1st Ukrainian Front, commanded by Marshal Ivan Stepanovich Konev. A bullet-headed, aggressive commander, he had survived numerous setbacks during the war that might have resulted in his demotion or removal from command, but it seems that at an early stage he caught Stalin's eye as a ruthless and capable commander. Consequently, the Soviet leader gave him a degree of leeway, allowing him to learn from his mistakes. His contemporaries generally held him in high regard. Marshal Aleksandr Mikhailovich Vasilevsky, who was chief of the Soviet general staff at this point of the war, later wrote:

> Knowing him by his work at the front I must say that he very much liked being among the troops. Normally, as soon as a decision was taken on an operation he would set off at once for his armies, corps or divisions, wherever his rich experience could be employed preparing the troops for hostilities. As a rule, all remaining business connected with the plan of operation would be done by his headquarters.[1]

Shtemenko had a similar opinion:

> In military circles Konev was known as a firm and resolute commander. Many of us had a friendly envy of his energy and drive. Whatever the circumstances he insisted on seeing the battlefield for himself. He made very careful preparations for every operation and in his efforts to investigate every aspect of it literally made his subordinates sweat.[2]

Konev was aware of the special status that Stalin accorded him and was not slow in taking advantage of it. He frequently telephoned the Soviet leader during operations with suggestions and to share his frustrations, sometimes to the disadvantage of his contemporaries. During the encirclement of much of the German Eighth Army in what became known as the Cherkassy pocket in Ukraine, Konev – at that time commanding 2nd Ukrainian Front – was operating alongside General Nikolai Fedorovich Vatutin, who commanded 1st Ukrainian Front. Inevitably, the operation did not unfold precisely as planned and Konev was not slow to take advantage of this, ensuring that it was Vatutin who was criticised for making errors. After the war, many Soviet setbacks were blamed upon Vatutin's impetuousness, and it is unfortunate that he died as a result of wounds after an attack by Ukrainian nationalist partisans in the first third of 1944; consequently, he had no opportunity to write his memoirs and give his version of events. But if Konev was astute in his political footwork, he backed it up with a sure hand on the battlefield. From the Battle of Kursk onwards, he eliminated his earlier errors, showing greater energy in ensuring that the reports and plans drawn up by his subordinates accurately reflected reality.

The northern part of the great Soviet offensive would be conducted by 1st Belarusian Front. It was now under the command of perhaps the most famous of Soviet officers. Marshal Georgy Konstantinovich Zhukov, a barrel-chested and powerfully built man, first rose to prominence in the defeat of the Japanese forces in Mongolia at the battle of Khalkhin-Gol in August 1939. In the early phases of the war with Germany, he was credited with saving first Leningrad and then Moscow, and became deputy supreme commander of the Soviet armed forces. He had a reputation for being blunt and for speaking his mind, as Shtemenko recalled:

> He was a man with a great gift for generalship, daring and original in his thinking and very firm in the practical execution of his decisions, who would stop at no obstacle in pursuit of the aims for which the war was fought. When he felt himself to be right over some controversial matter, Zhukov would contradict Stalin fairly sharply, which was something that no one else dared do.[3]

Vasilevsky, who was studiously self-effacing in his memoirs and generally very generous in his opinions of his contemporaries, also praised Zhukov:

> The strength of Zhukov's skill as general and his resolve were particularly in evidence during the vital battles between 1943 and 1945 ...
> I always admired his unquenchable energy, the scope and depth of his strategic mind ... Once he had taken a decision, he mustered all efforts to see it put into effect. It seemed that there were no insuperable barriers for him; his powerful will would brush aside anything that stood in his way.[4]

There are some clues in this to a less favourable picture of Zhukov. Vasilevsky praised him for his contribution to the successes of the battles that took place in 1943 and later, ignoring Zhukov's responsibility for the hugely costly failures to destroy the German-held Rzhev salient through 1942. On many occasions, both at Rzhev and in the north around Leningrad, Zhukov was responsible for insisting that operations were executed in rigid accordance with his plans even when the reality on the ground suggested otherwise. This was one of the reasons why the Red Army suffered such appalling casualties in the battles along the

Volkhov River in the north and around Rzhev in the central sector. He was often harshly critical of his subordinates if they failed to carry out his instructions. During the successful breaking of the siege ring around Leningrad in early 1943, he unreasonably criticised Lieutenant General Nikolai Pavlovich Simoniak for not attacking high ground to the south of the main breakout, even though – as the man overseeing the entire operation – Zhukov must have been aware that this high ground lay outside Simoniak's sector and that the terrain was highly unfavourable for an attack in that direction. The two men argued bitterly over the telephone when Zhukov implied that Simoniak's soldiers were cowards and the rifle division commander then refused a direct order from Zhukov to attack the high ground, stipulating that any order had to come via the proper chain of command. No such order subsequently appeared.[5] Marshal Konstantin Konstantinovich Rokossovsky, who was now in command of 2nd Belarusian Front immediately to Zhukov's north, was blunt in his assessment of Zhukov, who was his superior during the Battle of Moscow:

> Insistence on the highest standards is an important and essential trait for any military leader. But it is equally essential for him to combine an iron will with tactfulness, respect for his subordinates, and the ability to rely on their intelligence and initiative. In those grim days our Front commander [i.e. Zhukov] didn't always follow this rule. He could also be unfair in a fit of temper.[6]

Whilst Zhukov's willingness to resort to brutal bullying might have been regarded as a good trait by Stalin, others found it much more unpleasant and difficult. He was also acutely aware of the importance of retaining Stalin's favour. During the summer offensives of 1944, *Stavka* appointed Zhukov to coordinate matters on the southern half of the drive across Belarus while Vasilevsky performed a similar role in the northern half. As the campaign unfolded, Zhukov became increasingly alarmed that Vilnius would fall to the Red Army forces under Vasilevsky's supervision before his own forces reached and captured Baranovichi, and he demanded that General Pavel Ivanovich Batov, commander of Sixty-Fifth Army, should show greater energy. Batov later wrote:

> Together with Radetsky [the political commissar of Sixty-Fifth Army] I made my way from Alekseev's command post, just 3km from the city, to the small village of Velka to my army headquarters. All the army staff had gathered here already under the command of Bobkov [Batov's chief of staff]. For the first time in several days we had an opportunity to do something about our appearance. But we had barely finished shaving and cleaning our boots when several trucks approached

our huts. 'It's Zhukov,' said Radetsky after a quick look through the window. We hurried to the door intending to give the *Stavka* representative an optimistic report. But it turned out differently.

'That's all very well,' grumbled the marshal, 'You're shaving and perfuming yourselves, but Baranovichi still hasn't been taken.'

We urged Zhukov to go into the hut with us. But he still didn't calm down. Never in my long service did I ever encounter such humiliating behaviour. Radetsky's face was frozen. When I finally got a chance to speak and reported that our troops were making good progress, and that the city could be taken at any moment, the marshal started raging again.

'The army commander's report corresponds with the facts,' said Radetsky. But he was ignored. When Radetsky repeated himself, the marshal turned on him too. This undignified scene ended with Zhukov ordering Radetsky to go to Baranovichi and not to return until the city was in our hands. He then kicked aside his chair and left the room, slamming the door behind him.

There was an oppressive silence. 'Don't worry about it,' Radetsky assured me. 'We don't serve Zhukov, we serve the Soviet armed forces. Let's have our evening meal. It's all nonsense. But I'd like to know what got the marshal so agitated.' I didn't really care, but Radetsky continued. 'I think I can see what's going on. Vasilevsky's already outside Vilnius. Zhukov's wrestling with him for attention, to be the first to report a major success to *Stavka*. But I'll have to go. Orders are orders!'

So I was left alone. I didn't have to worry about my troops. The battle was proceeding as planned. Still, I couldn't find any solace. We army commanders were unaccustomed to being treated like this by our superiors. Late that night [7–8 July] Radetsky contacted me. 'Everything's going as planned.'

'Where are you calling from?'

'I'm in Baranovichi. I've driven around the whole city with Alekseev. I'm in Grebennik's command post [15th Rifle Division] in the cemetery. Our troops are about 1.5km further west, advancing successfully.'

A senior officer was hunched over a briefcase in front of the hut where Zhukov was sleeping. I had the marshal awakened and informed him that Baranovichi had been taken.

'Are there any reports from Vilnius?' he asked. 'No? Then I'll sleep a little more.'[7]

In some respects, Zhukov's status at the beginning of 1945 was declining. For much of the war, he was Stalin's personal trouble-shooter and was one of a small number of senior officers who were given wide-ranging powers to coordinate the activities of several Fronts in order to mount large-scale operations, but he was now in command of just one Front, albeit on the most important axis that led to Berlin. With the end of the war now coming into sight, it is likely that Stalin wished to ensure that he personally would receive as much credit as possible for the final victory of the Soviet Union and was therefore moving other figures out of the limelight. But regardless of Stalin's wishes to sideline Zhukov, his name was known to almost everyone in the Soviet Union and his reputation was firmly established. By late 1944, many soldiers of the Red Army were aware of the saying that 'Where there is Zhukov, there is victory'; many would also have known that his presence was usually associated with heavy casualties.

After overseeing the southern half of *Bagration* during the summer of 1944, Zhukov had been sent to the Balkans, where the Red Army took advantage of the increasing weakness of the Wehrmacht to break the German defensive lines in Romania. The result was that Romania rapidly changed sides, leaving the Axis and committing its forces to the war against Germany, and Bulgaria sued for peace. He returned to the central sector of the Eastern Front in September, when the Warsaw Uprising was raging. The Red Army's summer offensive had brought it to a line within artillery range of the Polish capital, but despite repeated pleas from the Poles, the Soviet forces did not march to their aid. The tensions around this episode were obvious at the time: the uprising was being conducted by the *Armia Krajova* or *AK*, which was loyal to the Polish government-in-exile in London, and Stalin had no intention of allowing it to seize control of Warsaw. It suited the Soviet leadership for the Germans and Poles to fight each other while the Red Army stood to one side. After the war, there were repeated assertions by Soviet writers that aid for the uprising was impossible, and it was certainly true that after the victorious march across Belarus, Soviet units were in desperate need of a prolonged operational pause to replenish their ranks and bring forward supplies. There were some attempts to force crossings over the Vistula near Warsaw and there were some supply drops by Soviet aircraft, but not on a scale that was likely to alter the outcome of the uprising. In his memoirs, Zhukov described a conversation involving himself, Stalin, Lavrentiy Beria (head of the *NKVD*), Vyacheslav Molotov (the Soviet foreign minister), and Rokossovsky, commander of 1st Belarusian Front, in which he made the case for pausing offensive operations:

> I unfolded the map and began my report. I could see that Stalin was nervous: he would approach the map, then move away, then come back, peering intently with his sharp gaze first at me, then at the map, then at Rokossovsky ...

'Comrade Zhukov,' Molotov interrupted me, 'you propose to stop the offensive when the defeated enemy is unable to withstand the pressure of our troops. Is your suggestion reasonable?'

'The enemy has already managed to create a defensive line and bring up the necessary reserves,' I objected. 'He is now successfully repulsing the attacks of our troops. This is causing us unjustifiable losses.'

'Zhukov believes that our heads are in the clouds here [in Moscow] and we don't know what's happening at the front line,' quipped Beria with an ironic smile.

'Do you support Zhukov's opinion?' asked Stalin, looking at Rokossovsky.

'Yes, I think it's necessary to give the troops a break and reorganise them after a long period of strain.'

'I think the enemy will use this respite just as effectively as you,' said the supreme commander …

'I believe that [a further attack to the northwest of Warsaw] will give us nothing but casualties,' I reiterated. 'And from an operational point of view, we do not particularly need this sector. The city must be taken by bypassing it from the south, while at the same time inflicting a powerful thrust towards Łódź and Poznań. The Front doesn't have the forces needed at the moment, but they should be concentrated.'[8]

According to Zhukov, Stalin reluctantly accepted the advice of his commanders and ordered Rokossovsky to take command of 2nd Belarusian Front; Zhukov was to replace him as commander of 1st Belarusian Front. He stayed in Moscow for the moment; a short distance beyond the Soviet front line, the *AK* continued its hopeless struggle against the Germans until laying down its arms at the beginning of October 1944. Whilst it is unquestionable that the Red Army was badly in need of a pause in major operations, there was much that it could have done to assist the uprising through the use of artillery or air operations; the lack of such activity at a meaningful scale undermines the Soviet assertions that they did all that they could and it is inconceivable that the Red Army would have been so passive if the uprising had been carried out by pro-Soviet Polish forces.

As planning continued, Shtemenko took stock of German responses to ongoing Soviet pressure in Hungary and to the perceived threat from East Prussia:

Soviet attacks in November–December 1944 caused the enemy, according to our calculations, to concentrate 26 divisions (including seven panzer divisions) in East Prussia and 55 divisions (including nine panzer divisions) near the capital of Hungary. As became known later, Hitler considered at the time that in 1945 the

Soviet Army would deliver its main attack not on the Berlin sector [i.e. from the middle Vistula] but through Hungary and Bohemia, and the main forces of the Wehrmacht were moved accordingly. The German high command was once again compelled to obey our will and left only 49 divisions, including a mere five panzer divisions, on what was for us the main sector of the front.

The fact that the enemy's strategic front had acquired such an odd shape, with strong groupings on each flank and a relatively weak centre with few reserves, made us reconsider ways of attacking on the main line of advance. Would it not be better to give up the idea of a steady advance along the whole front, which would merely push the enemy back? Would it not be better to punch straight through this relatively weak centre, split the German strategic front and without wasting time develop the offensive on Berlin? This course of action would split up the enemy forces and make them easier to deal with, and thus hasten the achievement of the ultimate objective.[9]

On a cold, dark day in late November 1944, Konev and Zhukov travelled to Moscow for a conference with Stalin, where they presented him with their outlines for the forthcoming offensive. Konev described the options available to him – his Front could aim to overrun Silesia, or it could press into Germany in order to secure crossings over the Oder River in preparation for a final assault on Berlin. Conceivably, it could carry out both missions provided reinforcements were received:

I well remember how thoroughly Stalin studied the plans. He examined the Silesian industrial region on the map with particular attention. There was a huge number of commercial concerns and mining operations with considerable equipment in this region and a variety of industrial complexes. All this, taken together, presented significant obstacles for troops engaged in mobile operations during the offensive.

Even on the map, the scale of the Silesian region and its industrial power looked impressive. Stalin emphasised this fact clearly to me, pointed his finger at the map, circled the area and said: 'Gold.'

It was said in such a way that it required no further elaboration.[10]

Whilst there were gold mines in Silesia, Stalin clearly emphasised the value in a more general sense. But Konev's point about the difficulties of manoeuvring in an industrial region were valid. In addition to the numerous industrial and mining complexes that might provide shelter for defending forces, the terrain was increasingly mountainous towards the southern part of Silesia. Konev described how he planned to avoid fighting in the industrial centres because it was important to preserve these for the benefit of Poland, which would inherit the region after the war; he was probably also aware that Stalin intended to appropriate much of the heavy machinery before handing over the factories.

Despite determined German counterattacks in the late summer of 1944, the forces of 1st Ukrainian Front that had secured the large bridgehead over the Vistula at Sandomierz succeeded in holding the area, providing Konev with an excellent starting point for an advance to the west. He intended to make full use of this, aiming to achieve a breakthrough that would be up to 24 miles (40km) wide; this would allow him to commit the maximum number of units for the exploitation phase in the shortest time, whilst also creating a breach that the Germans would not be able to pinch off with counterattacks. From the breakthrough, 1st Ukrainian Front was to advance through Radomsko and Częstochowa, to the northwest of Kraków, and thence towards Breslau (now the Polish city of Wrocław). At the same time, Zhukov's 1st Belarusian Front would break the German defences around Warsaw and head west. The Red Army had identified the main concentrations of the German formations and this operation would permit both the northern and southern flanks of these defences to be turned before they were enveloped and destroyed. At the same time, the armies on the left flank of Konev's Front were to advance into Silesia and attempt to bypass the main potential areas of resistance from the south.

To carry out such a major operation, Konev had considerable resources. The total strength of 1st Ukrainian Front was, according to Konev's memoirs, no less than 1.2 million soldiers, with 3,660 tanks and assault guns, more than 17,000 guns and mortars, and 2,580 aircraft. Even without the additional resources of 1st Belarusian Front, this amounted to far more than the German forces attempting to defend the Vistula line. Konev's troops were divided amongst eight combined arms armies and two tank armies, with an additional four independent tank corps, a cavalry corps, and several independent artillery units.[11]

The two tank armies of Konev's Front, which would be vital in the coming campaign, were led by highly experienced men. Fourth Tank Army was under the command of Colonel General Dmitri Danilovich Lelyushenko, one of the few senior officers to emerge from the Winter War with Finland in 1939–40 with any credit. He was involved in the bloody attempts to reduce the German-held Rzhev salient in 1942 before leading First Guards Army in the encirclement of Stalingrad. He was seriously wounded near Kharkiv in the battles that followed and took command of Fourth Tank Army in March 1944; he then led it with skill and determination during the attack through Lviv to the middle Vistula. As he and his men awaited the new operation, he ensured that training continued at a high intensity, not least because his formations had been brought back to full strength with new recruits. Lelyushenko described two distinct phases of training: first, there was general training and preparation; then, when missions for the forthcoming operation had been assigned to the army, training shifted to focus on the specific problems it would face.

The Germans would of course expect a major attack from the Sandomierz bridgehead and would have organised their defences accordingly, and in order to assist the initial breakthrough phase, Lelyushenko received valuable reinforcements in the shape of two regiments of heavy JS-2 tanks.[12] At the beginning of the war with Germany, Soviet armoured formations had consisted of a mixture of light, medium, and heavy tanks in the same unit, but this proved to be problematic. The vehicles moved at different speeds, with the result that the light tanks often arrived on the battlefield first and found themselves outgunned. The Germans then had sufficient time to organise a defensive line so that they were able to halt the medium tanks, and the arrival of the heavy tanks was too late to make a difference. Moreover, the heavy tanks – mainly KV-1s in the first phases of the war – often damaged roads and particularly bridges, making resupply of the armoured units difficult. The solution was to move the heavy tanks into dedicated breakthrough regiments, so that they could operate in a role in which their slow speed was less critical. The JS-2 had impressive armour and a powerful gun, but it suffered from a low rate of fire and carried limited ammunition. Again, the impact of these factors was minimised by allocating them to breakthrough regiments, which were not expected to join the exploitation forces as they drove forward.

When the Germans brought new tanks into service, they almost always gave crews an opportunity to train with the vehicles before being deployed. By contrast, many Soviet tank crews had to come to terms with their new equipment in the field as they prepared for the offensive. Ashot Apetovich Amanuti was an officer in a regiment that received the new heavy tanks:

> When we first saw our new JS-2 heavy tanks, they made a strong impression on us. We prepared them with particular care. Despite the fact that there were almost no technical facilities for servicing tanks in the field, our teams maintained the tanks carefully. We conducted technical inspections and examined the mechanism of the drive train, and tank commanders took part in meetings to share their experiences in operating different types of tanks.[13]

The other major tank formation of 1st Ukrainian Front, Third Guards Tank Army, was led by Colonel General Pavel Semenovich Rybalko. He was appointed to that post when the army was created as Third Tank Army in 1943 and had an inauspicious start – this was his first proper combat appointment of the war – when his army was badly mauled in the German counteroffensive that restored the front line in March. Despite this, he was noted to have shown great resourcefulness in rapidly changing the axis of advance of his formations. He oversaw the rebuilding of the army and it took part in the Battle of Kursk and the subsequent advance across central Ukraine to and over the Dnepr River.

To date, most Soviet operations had suffered heavy losses, particularly when breaking through the German lines. Konev placed particular importance on swiftly overcoming the German defences so that his two tank armies could be committed to their exploitation roles as intact as possible – in the past, it had often been necessary for the exploitation troops to have to be used to help achieve the initial breakthrough, resulting in a weaker exploitation force than had been planned. The two tank armies were moved into the Sandomierz bridgehead in order to minimise any delays that might occur if they were held further back. With an operational start date initially set for 20 January, there was a strong possibility that the weather might prevent the deployment of air assets, and in keeping with longstanding Soviet practice, artillery would be used to smash the German defences to ensure the breakthrough. This necessitated all of the artillery assets being deployed for the initial assault, with sufficient ammunition for them to achieve their missions:

> We tried to plan the artillery offensive in such a way that with all the massed firepower we could completely suppress the entire tactical defence zone of the enemy and his immediate operational reserves to a depth of up to 18–20km [11–12 miles]. By this time we had gathered accurate intelligence data, the entire enemy defensive line had been repeatedly photographed, and any changes that took place were immediately recorded ...
>
> However, our planning had yet to be conveyed to the front line, down to regimental artillery groups. We didn't shy away from delving into all the details, believing that since the senior artillery commanders had accumulated considerable valuable experience, it was essential that this experience was passed on to divisions and batteries so that it reached, in a sense, the very roots ... To this end, during the preparation of the offensive, senior artillery commanders taught the men in firing positions about specific conditions, specific terrain ...
>
> We saw a well-organised artillery offensive as the embodiment of the power of our armies. We thought that everything we achieved through artillery fire instead of bayonets would be to our great advantage and would save the troops from unnecessary losses.[14]

There could be no question about the weight of firepower that the Red Army could deploy in its initial bombardment, but in the past artillery preparation had often failed to suppress German defences. In the First World War, there were occasions when the wrong type of gun or shell was used, with high explosive being used where shrapnel would be more effective and vice versa. Accurate reconnaissance was therefore essential and Konev gave specific instructions for gunners to avoid the wasteful use of artillery to bombard entire areas in an indiscriminate manner: shelling was to be targeted at specific German positions, with the most effective type of ammunition and weapon being used. During the first years of the war with Germany, Red Army bombardments usually concluded with a short, intense bombardment using *Katyusha* rockets; their distinctive shriek was thought to be a useful means of terrifying defenders who were already shell-shocked by the heavy bombardment. But the imprecision of bombardments and the manner in which the Germans constructed their defences meant that the defenders spent most of the bombardment in hardened shelters where, unless they took a direct hit from a particularly heavy shell, they were generally unscathed. In those circumstances, the distinctive sound of the *Katyusha* wave merely served as a signal that the end of the bombardment and the commencement of the assault were imminent. By the second half of 1944, additional refinements had been added. Although the use of *Katyushas* in the closing phase of the artillery preparation remained widespread practice, it was now often followed by a further intense shelling of the front-line positions to catch any German troops that had emerged from their bunkers in anticipation of the Red Army's attack.

There was a further innovation that had appeared during 1944. During the closing phase of the bombardment, gunners were assigned fire missions that left untouched diagonal lanes through the zone being shelled. In theory, this permitted the assault troops to start moving forward towards the German lines even before the bombardment had ended, with a curtain of shells in front of them hiding their movement from the defenders. But implementing this was difficult. It required considerable precision in terms of accurate fire and timing on the part of the gunners, and there were numerous cases of this tactic resulting in Soviet losses. Secondly, it required infantrymen who were prepared to advance through what must have seemed to them to be a continuous artillery barrage. On several occasions in 1944, assault troops – particularly when units had recently been brought up to strength with fresh drafts – showed considerable unwillingness to take such risks, and just as it was important to ensure that the gunners made full use of the experience of previous bombardments, it was equally vital for the assault troops to be sufficiently prepared so that they would not hold back and thus give the Germans time to take up defensive positions. Experienced veterans and new drafts were therefore often mixed together, and during the weeks of preparation for the offensive there were exercises using live artillery fire in order to acclimatise the new recruits to the thunder and confusion of bombardments.

The Red Army had come a long way in a short time, learning painfully how to fight and win. Many factors had contributed to earlier failures or had resulted in avoidable losses, and Konev's Front took great measures to avoid such problems in the coming offensive. Traffic congestion behind the front line had been a recurring problem, with exploitation troops trying to move forward having to compete with ammunition columns for road space, while a stream of wounded attempted to move in the opposite direction. Konev's engineers repaired or created hundreds of miles of roads, attempting to ensure that each rifle division and tank brigade would have at least two routes available to it. About 30 bridges were constructed across the Vistula, supplemented by three ferries, though the latter were hindered by ice for much of the winter. Just as important as the construction of roads and bridges was ensuring proper traffic control. Western armies had learned this lesson well and had established good procedures with dedicated military police units responsible for entry to and exit from river crossing points, and the direction of traffic flow was strictly controlled; in this respect, the Red Army still had much to learn.

The changes in command at 1st and 2nd Belarusian Fronts became official in mid-November. When Zhukov travelled to his new appointment, he was pleased to learn that the staff had already carried out extensive work for the forthcoming offensive. Despite the immense resources of the Soviet Union, losses in the years of bitter fighting had been so great that it was no longer possible to bring all units up to full strength. Numerically, the tank armies and the other armies that were designated to lead the offensive received priority, with the result that divisions in many of the other armies were barely at 50 per cent of their establishment strength.

On the last day of 1944, Stalin summoned senior figures to his dacha outside Moscow. It was an unusual gathering; to date, there had been no opportunities for Soviet commanders to enjoy the luxury of time for celebrations. After making a short speech just before midnight praising the great efforts of the Soviet people in the war against Germany, Stalin welcomed in the new year and the gathering became more relaxed. Marshal Semyon Mikhailovich Budyonny, an old comrade of Stalin from the days of the Russian Civil War, produced an accordion and entertained the gathering with a mixture of traditional Russian tunes, and in the small hours the party dispersed. As they travelled back to their homes, Shtemenko and the others were aware that this was a very different occasion from when they had marked the turn of the year earlier in the war:

> This really was a peaceful beginning to the new year. A party at the supreme commander's house, a night at home – not a bit like the strict regime that the general staff had maintained all through the war.
>
> But Moscow still retained its wartime appearance. We drove along the dark, deserted streets, past freezing houses with closely curtained windows. Yet even here an occasional timid gleam showed through a chink. The commandant's patrols and anti-aircraft defence guards were no longer quite so strict on such offences.
>
> In short, everything that night reminded us that the war was coming to an end.[15]

Millions of bereaved families across the Soviet Union perhaps felt rather differently about the conflict.

One of the areas where the Red Army improved its performance significantly as the war progressed was in the gathering of intelligence. It was only after the Germans evacuated the Rzhev salient in early 1943 that Soviet commanders realised just how extensive German defences were, and this knowledge led to greater efforts to secure good-quality information about the lines they were going to attack in future operations. Despite this, the strength of German defences continued to surprise the Red Army throughout the rest of 1943 and it was only in the summer of 1944 that assessments of the scale of the task ahead became more realistic. Information was gathered through a number of sources and all of these – aerial reconnaissance, signals intelligence, the capture of prisoners in trench raids for interrogation – improved steadily, but the advance across the German-held parts of the Soviet Union was aided considerably by information from partisan groups operating behind German lines. In addition to reporting the locations of German units, supply dumps etc., the partisans acted in an increasingly coordinated manner, both with other partisan groups and with the Red Army. Immediately before the onset of *Bagration*, partisans across Belarus carried out extensive attacks on road and rail infrastructure to hinder any German reaction to the offensive. Now that the Red Army was entering Poland, it lost this valuable source of help. There were anti-German forces operating behind the German front line, but these were made up of units of the *AK* and there was no love lost between the soldiers of the *AK* and the Red Army even before the tragedy of the Warsaw Uprising. Zhukov's memoirs, like those of other senior Soviet figures, described how the

Polish population of the areas already under Soviet control was largely friendly and cooperative, but there is plentiful evidence that many Poles across eastern Poland were hostile to the Red Army, and that the Red Army's troops behaved with brutality towards the Poles. Zhukov wrote about the steps that were taken to try to avoid such problems in future:

> On the instructions of the Central Committee [of the Communist Party], the army's Party organisations had done a great deal of explanatory work on the behaviour of our troops abroad, where we were marching not as conquerors but as liberators from enemy occupation. In all front-line formations, it was necessary to expand educational work still wider so that from the very beginning of our stay in Poland there would be no ill-considered acts on the part of our soldiers and officers.
>
> We established normal relations with the local authorities and Polish public, and they helped us in any way they could. In turn, our troops shared everything they had with the Poles. Thus from the first steps, from the first meetings, the foundation was laid for the fraternal friendship of the Soviet and Polish peoples, who had endured the burden of the enemy's occupation.[16]

There may well have been such efforts to encourage good behaviour amongst Red Army personnel and there were undoubtedly many occasions when such good behaviour did take place, but there were also many other occasions when Soviet soldiers treated the Poles badly. Looting was a widespread habit, tempered only by the relative poverty of Poland after the years of German occupation, and whilst the scale of rapes was small compared to what was to follow in the eastern parts of Germany, these unquestionably occurred on many occasions. But post-war Soviet orthodoxy required the Red Army to be portrayed as a liberation force that was welcomed by the ordinary people of Eastern Europe. Anything that painted a different picture was ignored or suppressed.

Zhukov's armies would attack from the smaller bridgeheads across the Vistula close to Warsaw. The problems of traffic control across the Vistula were far greater than in the Sandomierz bridgehead to the south and Zhukov paid special attention to rehearsing and controlling troop and logistic movements. One of the formations in the Magnuszew bridgehead was Eighth Guards Army, under the command of the redoubtable Colonel General Vasily Ivanovich Chuikov. With his thick, dark hair and blunt features, Chuikov was a well-known figure all across the Soviet Union; the defence of Stalingrad by his Sixty-Second Army – after which it was renamed Eighth Guards Army – was already part of the growing folklore of the Second World War. Chuikov's memoirs are colourful and engaging, but almost certainly contain an element of 'creative writing'; nonetheless, they remain a valuable source of information. He described the situation in the bridgehead:

> By this time [autumn 1944] there was a continuous saturation of the Magnuszew bridgehead with troops, equipment, weapons, and ammunition. It was like a mainspring, compressed before release. Mobile field hospitals were deployed in the bridgehead, and crossings were built and expanded across the Vistula. A total of 23 divisions and 5,348 artillery pieces were deployed around Magnuszew before the offensive. In the planned breakthrough sector, artillery density reached 282 barrels per kilometre of front line. The breakthrough lane for Eighth Guards Army was restricted to just 7km [four miles].
>
> All of this, of course, required enormous efforts from the logistic units of the army and the Front. They were able to transfer tens of thousands of tons of cargo of the most diverse nature into the bridgehead in good time.
>
> In December, ice began to form on the Vistula. The army's troops, especially our engineering personnel, faced a lot of difficulties. Bridges were threatened not just by ice floes drifting on the surface of the Vistula … When it ran into the pile supports of bridges, the ice formed dams extending deep into the water and this increased the swiftness and pressure of the stream still more. The water often washed away the banks and the riverbed near the pile supports. All our engineering and road troops had to be mobilised to safeguard the bridges. Three companies of demolition personnel and a road construction battalion were assigned to each bridge, and additional emergency teams were created. The commandants of the crossings had motor vehicles and tractors at their disposal, as well as a battery of 120mm mortars for breaking up large ice floes.[17]

In early 1944, Chuikov's troops had faced the Dniester just as winter was coming to an end and had been forced to abandon their planned crossing due to widespread flooding; many of his engineers were therefore experienced with the difficulties of such matters and that expertise was now put to good use. Much of Zhukov's Front remained on the east bank of the Vistula due to the limited size of the two bridgeheads; his total strength was similar to that of Konev's 1st Ukrainian Front, but he was aware that a large portion of his artillery assets would bombard German lines from their positions to the east of the Vistula and would then have to cross the river before being available in the event of the advancing troops encountering resistance. Similarly, the huge quantities of supplies needed to sustain a prolonged advance would have to be brought forward, potentially adding to traffic problems.

As plans were drawn up, Zhukov was unwilling to make firm decisions beyond the initial attack. He anticipated a thrust towards Poznań, about 175 miles (282km) to the west, but further operations would depend on many factors such as the losses suffered during the advance and German reactions. There was also the possibility that if 2nd Belarusian Front, to Zhukov's north, encountered unexpected resistance in its attack to enter and isolate East Prussia, it might become necessary for Zhukov to release forces to assist Rokossovsky – advancing deep into Poland while German forces remained intact and active in East Prussia risked exposing the northern flank of 1st Belarusian Front to counterattacks.

The plans submitted to *Stavka* by Zhukov called for three combined arms armies – Fifth Shock Army, Sixty-First Army, and Chuikov's Eighth Guards Army – to attack from the Magnuszew bridgehead. Fifth Shock Army was commanded by Lieutenant General Nikolai Erastovich Berzarin, who had been arrested by the *NKVD* in 1938 on suspicion of involvement in imagined conspiracies against Stalin. In most cases, such arrests were based upon denunciations by earlier arrestees who offered names to their interrogators in the hope of avoiding further beatings; in Berzarin's case, it seems that the evidence was far more circumstantial and he was soon released. He took command of Twenty-Seventh Army in newly annexed Latvia, fighting in numerous defensive battles through 1941, and at the end of the year he led Thirty-Fourth Army in the Soviet counteroffensive that encircled the German forces around Demyansk. However, the failure of his badly depleted formations to halt the German relief column that ended the Demyansk encirclement resulted in his demotion and for the rest of the year he served as deputy commander of armies in the central sector around the Rzhev salient, where he was seriously wounded in the fighting near Vyazma resulting in several weeks in hospital.[18] With his rank restored, he took command of Thirty-Ninth Army in the fighting around Smolensk and Vitebsk in the winter of 1943–44 before being appointed to lead Fifth Shock Army. After heavy fighting in the Soviet assault across the Dniester into Romania, the army was pulled out of line and spent a month in western Ukraine recovering its strength before being assigned to Zhukov's Front. Berzarin had served under Zhukov's command during the battles around the Rzhev salient and the two men knew each other well; they appear to have had a good working relationship.

Sixty-First Army was also led by an officer who had served under Zhukov, Lieutenant General Pavel Alekseevich Belov. In the last phases of the Soviet counteroffensive outside Moscow in the winter of 1941–42, Belov's I Guards Cavalry Corps was committed in a thrust through the German lines in what became known as the Rzhev-Vyazma Operation. The penetration was rapidly cut off by German counterattacks but Belov's cavalry was able to link up with scattered forces of paratroopers, and with a total of up to 30,000 soldiers and partisans under his control he made a thorough nuisance of himself for several months, sometimes controlling vast swathes of territory. The Red Army made several fruitless attempts to break through to him and eventually the Germans organised a major sweep of the area with 5th Panzer Division and several infantry divisions. Belov's troops had been struggling with shortages of ammunition and food almost since the outset of their operation and had little choice but to attempt a breakout; this was carried out successfully with the bulk of the cavalrymen and paratroopers succeeding in reaching safety.[19]

Belov was almost a caricature of a typical cavalry officer with a prominent moustache more in keeping with fashions of the First World War and earlier, but he was loved by his men for the trouble he took to look after them. He argued with superiors on several occasions about the futility of making pointless attacks that had no chance of success, resulting in frequent clashes with Zhukov. Just before the attack that resulted in his cavalry corps being isolated behind German lines, he sent a signal to Zhukov's headquarters expressing doubts that his divisions – which were understrength from earlier fighting – were strong enough for the mission. Zhukov responded by dispatching Major General Georgy Fedorovich Zakharov, his deputy at the headquarters of Western Front, to Belov's headquarters. Zakharov was a favourite of Zhukov, not least because of his reputation for bullying and brutality, and this visit proved to be typical. Zakharov confronted Belov and his officers with a blunt and uncompromising message:

> The task assigned by the Front is clear to you: you must break through the Varshavskoye highway into the rear of the enemy or die. And let me make it clear: either a brave death on the highway, as heroes behind enemy lines, or a shameful death here. I repeat, this is a task set by Zhukov, the Front, *Stavka*, and Stalin himself. I was sent here to force you to complete the task by any means possible and I swear I will make you complete it, I will drive you into the rear of the German lines even if I have to shoot half your corps to do this. You must break through to the rear of the enemy with the means that you now have. That is why here, in our discussions we can only talk about how to complete the task, not about what is required to complete it.[20]

During the period that Belov and his troops operated behind German lines, Zhukov sent orders that often showed a complete disregard for the reality of the situation and moreover often contradicted himself. At one stage, Zhukov ordered the isolated Soviet forces to attack and capture Vyazma. The assault failed for several reasons. The cavalry and paratroopers lacked heavy weapons and suffered shortages of ammunition for the weaponry that they had, and Zhukov refused permission for Belov to concentrate his forces for the operation, insisting that cavalry units continued to be deployed further west. Belov was then ordered to reinforce these positions to the west, only to receive criticism from Zhukov for moving away from Vyazma. The signal went on to imply that Belov might face severe consequences for his perceived disobedience; the intelligence officer in Belov's headquarters noted that Belov merely shook his head and muttered, 'What a cruel and soulless man.'[21]

Zhukov may have been critical of Belov, but the Germans held the cavalry commander and his men in high regard. Oberst (later General) Günther Blumentritt, who was chief of staff at Fourth Army until the end of January 1942, wrote:

How [Belov] managed to obtain supplies was a mystery to us ... Only Russians and Russian horses can exist on absolutely 'nothing'. Nobody was able to catch him. German forces in the rear areas were too weak and not suited for that type of Indian warfare in the wintry forests ... [The escape of Belov and his men] caused many humorous remarks at the time and the motorised troops that had taken part in the operation became the butt of these jokes. I admired General Belov and I was secretly glad that he had escaped.[22]

The long operation behind German lines – due to the presence of large numbers of paratroopers, the Soviet-held territory earned the nickname of the 'Landing Republic' – was in many respects the phase of Belov's career that gave him the greatest pride. After his successful breakout, he took command of Sixty-First Army and was involved in the recapture of the city of Oryol in the summer of 1943 and the crossing of the Dnepr to the south of Gomel at the end of the year, for which he was awarded Hero of the Soviet Union. His units would now be involved in the drive from the Magnuszew bridgehead.

After the three combined arms armies had broken the German defences, Zhukov intended to introduce First and Second Guards Tank Armies to exploit deep into Poland. Colonel General Mikhail Efimovich Katukov had commanded First Guards Tank Army from early 1943, when it was still titled First Tank Army, and he led it with distinction on the southern flank of the Kursk salient during the summer. His units were involved in the Soviet advance through Lviv to the Vistula and played a major part in seizing the Sandomierz bridgehead before being withdrawn into *Stavka* reserve for rest and replenishment. He held the distinction of having commanded the first Soviet armoured formation – 4th Tank Brigade – to be given the honorific title of 'Guards', and was regarded as a highly capable field commander. In late 1944, Katukov and his staff joined Zhukov for a wargame to assess the likelihood of success in the coming offensive:

[The German defensive lines] could only be broken through with the help of powerful artillery and air strikes. This was well understood both at *Stavka* and at Front headquarters. That was why the breakthrough armies received major artillery reinforcements. Over 220 barrels were planned for every kilometre of front breakthrough – one for every 4–5 metres.

The concentration of tank and rifle units was unusually dense. Rifle divisions, deployed in three echelons, crowded along the front line in sectors of 2.5–3km. There were 35 tanks for every kilometre of the front line. We had not seen such a powerful concentration of troops on such a narrow sector in the entire war. Now the Red Army had a numerical superiority over the enemy in all types of weapons. The troops of 1st Belarusian and 1st Ukrainian Fronts, which faced the Hitlerite Army Group A on the main strategic axis, had superiority of more than five times as many men, almost seven times as many guns and mortars and six times as many tanks and assault guns. It was in this final phase of the war that it was especially clear how much Hitler's intelligence services underestimated the economic power of our country, which managed in a short time to create armed forces on such a scale and of such quality that could not be matched by all of Europe's industries harnessed to Hitler's war machine. We returned from the wargame in high spirits.[23]

Second Guards Tank Army was commanded by Colonel General Semen Ilyich Bogdanov. Like Berzarin, he had been arrested during the purges of the late 1930s and was dismissed from the army in May 1938; a year later, he was sentenced to two years' imprisonment on spurious charges but was released within a short time. After leading tank and mechanised corps with skill in the middle years of the war with Germany, he took command of Second Tank Army in September 1943 when it was pulled out of line and placed in reserve. The army took part in Konev's thrust to the Vistula; during the advance, Bogdanov was wounded and temporarily replaced by his deputy, Major General Aleksei Ivanovich Radzievsky. After reaching the Vistula, Radzievsky was ordered to turn north in order to cut the German lines of communication at and north of Warsaw – if this had been successful, the remnants of the German Army Group Centre, still staggering back after their defeat during *Bagration*, would have been isolated and destroyed completely. Instead, Second Guards Tank Army, as it was now designated, ran into a powerful and skilfully led counterattack that destroyed much of its strength. Bogdanov resumed command in November 1944; like

Katukov, he was generally highly regarded both for his organisational skills and his personal courage.

In addition to these forces, Zhukov had one additional army – First Polish Army, commanded by General Stanislav Poplavsky. There were tens of thousands of Poles in the Soviet Union when the war with Germany commenced in 1941; some had fled, but many were being held as prisoners. Almost immediately, there were requests from the Polish government-in-exile in London for these men to be organised into combat units, but matters were complicated by the fact that Stalin had ordered the execution of thousands of Polish officers at Katyn and other sites. Nevertheless, several Polish formations were raised but they proved to be difficult to integrate into the Red Army's operations and were finally allowed to cross the frontier into Iran, from where they were transferred to British control. The Soviet authorities chose to see this as a positive step with the removal of a large body of men who were regarded as politically unreliable, and immediately commenced work on raising a more pliant force. In August 1943, a Polish infantry division and a tank regiment, together with a fighter aircraft regiment, were combined to form I Polish Corps; although many of its personnel were Poles, others were Soviet citizens who had grown up in the western border regions and who spoke Polish.

In the spring of 1944, the corps was regarded as being ready for battle, but the mass murder at Katyn and elsewhere and the departure of the first wave of Polish recruits via Iran meant that the new units were badly short of officers. Nonetheless, the corps was now redesignated First Polish Army and continued to grow; by the summer, it consisted of four infantry divisions, an anti-aircraft division, an armoured brigade, a cavalry brigade, and five artillery brigades as well as support units. It was subordinated to 1st Belarusian Front and its entry into Polish territory on 20 July during the Soviet advance in the aftermath of *Bagration* was highlighted by Soviet propaganda services. Even as it moved forward, the army continued to grow, and large numbers of men were conscripted from the parts of eastern Poland that were now under Soviet control. After reaching the Vistula, First Polish Army attempted an assault crossing near Warsaw in September 1944. This was portrayed as an attempt to link up with the *AK* fighters still struggling against the Germans in the ruins of the Polish capital, but there was little support from other elements of the Red Army and the Poles were forced back across the river after suffering heavy losses.

Poplavsky took command of the army in December 1944. He was the son of a Polish farm labourer but was born near Mogilev, in the depths of Russia. He became a member of the Red Army in 1923 and like so many others he was dismissed from the armed forces as part of Stalin's purges; he was reinstated a year later. After commanding various units, he briefly took command of the new Second Polish Army in September 1944 before taking command of First Polish Army. In many respects, he was typical of the senior officers of the Polish forces under Soviet control; he might have a link to Poland and was portrayed as being a Pole, but he was a thoroughly Soviet citizen.

Extensive reconnaissance was carried out to determine the strength of German defences and to finalise decisions on the axes of attack. Colonel Viktor Semenovich Antonov was commander of 301st Rifle Division in Fifth Shock Army:

> We received orders [in late November 1944] to conduct a reconnaissance of routes in the direction of Warsaw and Praga [on the east bank of the Vistula, directly opposite Warsaw itself]. [Lieutenant] General [Ivan Pavlovich] Rosly [commander of IX Rifle Corps] warned me that the division was to be constantly ready for an advance.
>
> It was a clear and frosty day. The road ran west across a plain with scattered copses towards the suburb of Praga. Before us was a mass of ruins. From the top of the ruins we could survey the area – open and flat to the south, east and north of Praga, with dark forests in the Vistula valley. Through binoculars, we could see the smoking ruins of Warsaw. On the west bank of the Vistula and on the river ice, there lay corpses in civilian and military clothing. The skeletons of huge buildings loomed bleakly against the sky.
>
> We were shocked by this terrible picture.[24]

Zhukov had intended to use Fifth Shock Army in a direct assault through Warsaw, but based on Antonov's findings, the plan was altered. Such an attack through ruins would give the German defenders a huge advantage. Instead, Fifth Shock Army would bypass Warsaw to the south. This increased congestion in the Magnuszew bridgehead, but that was preferable to the losses that would result from a direct assault on Warsaw.

A feature of all Soviet offensives was the widespread use of deception or *Maskirovka*. It was regarded as an essential aspect of Red Army operations:

> [*Maskirovka* is] a complexity of measures, directed to mislead the enemy regarding the presence and disposition of forces, various military objectives, their condition, combat readiness and operations, and also the plans of the command.[25]

Deception was intended to be carried out at all levels, from large-scale strategic planning to front-line tactical preparations. Bitter experience had taught Soviet commanders that the Germans were adept at using information from a variety of sources to compile an accurate picture of Red Army intentions and steps were taken to avoid this. Wherever possible, radio communication was kept to a minimum, and in particular the earlier practice of mechanised units carrying out radio checks when they reached their deployment areas was discontinued. Discussions were held face-to-face, with paper copies of orders limited to the absolute minimum quantity required. Troops were moved at night wherever possible and their preparation areas were extensively camouflaged; staff officers regularly overflew the areas under their command to check whether camouflage was adequate and sometimes repeated the exercise with unit commanders to show them where they needed to make improvements. Such steps might limit the ability of the Germans to make an accurate assessment of Red Army strength in key areas, but *Maskirovka* also included a significant element of misdirection, to give the Germans the impression that the Soviet effort would fall elsewhere. Radio traffic simulating the location of key armoured formations was widely used; in order to draw German attention to the extreme south of 1st Ukrainian Front, large numbers of fake tanks were constructed. By 21 December, over 300 fake tanks, 250 other vehicles and 600 field guns had been built. They were then moved into position with a degree of camouflage that would persuade the Germans that they were part of a real formation, and to add to this several functioning T-34s were sent to the area to drive around and give the impression of activity. As a result, German maps showed the presence of IV Guards Tank Corps in completely the wrong location.[26]

In many respects, the intended axes of the Soviet operation would have been obvious, with major assaults expected from the bridgeheads across the Vistula, but *Maskirovka* was successful in misleading the Germans as to the strength of the attacks. Although the later figures produced by *FHO* and at a lower level by Army Group A were worrying enough, they underestimated Soviet strength substantially. The German calculations of Red Army rifle strength fell about 40 per cent short of the true total; the underassessment of tank forces was even worse, about 60 per cent short.[27]

The success of *Maskirovka* is striking. When German assessments of the dispositions of the Western Allies are examined for the same period, they seem to be far more accurate, despite the Western Allies having a greater degree of air superiority (and thus preventing aerial reconnaissance) than was the case in the east. Once fighting began in Poland, German situation maps became much more accurate, suggesting that the success of *Maskirovka* was partly – and perhaps mainly – due to good radio discipline. Once the campaign was underway, the need for good communications ensured that there was far more radio traffic for the Germans to intercept.

Many of the young recruits brought into eastern Poland to strengthen the Red Army were relatively poorly trained – like their German counterparts, they were rushed to the front after completing just part of their training – but the Red Army had inherited a practice from the armies of the tsars (and that it passed on to the modern Russian Army). Completion of training of new recruits was regarded as a task of the units receiving the recruits; this was often haphazard, resulting in many recruits being thrown into battle with poor levels of training. Where possible, Zhukov and Konev attempted to gather new drafts together so that they could undergo further training at Front and army level before going to their divisions. Natan Markovich Levin was a 17-year-old in 1945, and decades later he recalled his experiences:

> We were taken to the Sandomierz bridgehead and put in barracks. There, we underwent a 'young soldier' course for a month. Every day there were live-fire exercises and almost every night we went on forced marches or stood guard. The training was difficult and the food was very poor. Every day, 'buyers' from the front line came and took soldiers away. At first, nobody was taken from our team – we had not yet faced enemy fire. Then the 'buyers' came again, we were lined up, and a representative of the unit came up and asked us a few questions. He asked me, 'What did you do before the war?' I said I had finished seven years of school before working as a turner in a factory for two years. 'Come on then,' he said, and took me away. He was the commander of a sapper battalion, by the name of Nosov. He told me, 'You're being assigned to 275th Independent Sapper Battalion, part of 172nd Pavlograd Rifle Division.'[28]

Almost immediately, Levin found himself involved in the final preparations for the great offensive. There were extensive minefields between the two front lines – some laid by the Red Army when it was fending off German attempts to eliminate the bridgehead in the autumn of 1944, and larger minefields laid by the Germans. Much of the elimination of these minefields would be done by artillery fire, but it was essential to ensure that key routes for advancing units were completely mine-free.

> Our POMZ mines had been laid there – it was very difficult to remove them because these mines stood on short poles, disguised in bushes, with a wire running from the mine to a peg. If someone walked past, their foot caught the wire, the pin popped out, and the mine jumped up (it had two charges, one to launch it, and its combat charge), exploded, and scattered shrapnel. It was terrible – everything within several metres was struck by shrapnel. The sapper's task was to

straighten the pin carefully and then remove the peg attaching the wire. I removed several of these mines and worked my way to the barbed wire. The Germans swept the area several times with machine-guns firing tracer rounds. When they fired, I fell flat, lying in the mud and waiting to be hit. But God saved me.[29]

The hard core of veterans in the Soviet formations that awaited the assault had few illusions about what lay ahead. Although they sensed the end of the war was approaching, they knew from bitter experience that there would be plenty of costly fighting before the last shots were fired. Many, like the rifleman Mark Mikhailovich Grinstein, dealt with this with a sense of fatalism:

Nobody in the infantry believed they would survive. If you were in a rifle company, your chances of survival were zero. We were young men, ready to die for the Motherland whenever we had to. We were raised that way. On the front line, our perception of the world changed. We understood that we had already been sentenced to death and we saw each new day as our last. We couldn't escape our fate.

We submitted to it, understanding that we had to – we had to attack, advance under fire, because if we didn't, who would? We needed to do it because the Motherland needed us to do it. Conscience, a sense of duty, the desire for revenge.

These words sound pompous and pretentious, but we sincerely thought that way. And many didn't put it into such words but simply did their duty to the end and died in battle. They removed a dog tag from one dead lad and in the capsule, instead of his address and personal data, there was only a note, a short text with obscenities, but the meaning was clear: 'I'm dying without ever knowing a woman.'[30]

In addition to bringing combat units up to strength where possible, the Red Army had to move huge quantities of supplies into position. When railways were built in the 19th century, the Russian Empire deliberately adopted a wider railway gauge than the rest of Europe; this was partly to hinder the ability of any invading army to use railways to move supplies. Conversely, as they entered Poland, the Soviet forces faced an identical problem and many railway lines across eastern Poland were re-pinned during the autumn of 1944 to permit trains to carry supplies to the Vistula bridgeheads. The requirements were considerable: the daily consumption of food in Zhukov's 1st Belarusian Front alone amounted to 1,500 tons of bread and 220 tons of meat.[31] For the operation to be a success, huge quantities of shells required for the initial bombardment had to be moved forward, together with fuel and ammunition for all weapons to allow several replenishments as the operation unfolded. And once these supplies reached the middle Vistula, they had to be stored either in the bridgeheads or immediately behind them.

The lanes cleared through minefields by Levin and other sappers were used by raiding parties attempting to capture German soldiers for interrogation. Soviet authorities had always regarded anyone exposed to non-Soviet influences with suspicion, even in wartime conditions. Consequently, soldiers who became separated from their comrades on such raids faced a difficult return to Soviet lines. Mikhail Lvovich Shinder, an officer in a reconnaissance platoon, later recalled one such incident:

> Twelve men, Sergeant Major Kulik's squad, went out on reconnaissance. The Germans ambushed them and cut down the group about 50m from their trenches. The group, consisting entirely of experienced reconnaissance troops, made their probe wearing heavy camouflage but someone gave themselves away by speaking, or there was some other misfortune, and nobody returned that night. Two days later, when the general offensive began, Sergeant Major Kulik crawled back with frostbitten toes across the battlefield, strewn with our dead from the attack. He was immediately taken to the counter-intelligence team and they began to interrogate him to find out how he survived and what had happened to his squad. Kulik told them about the ambush and that when the Germans came out to finish off the wounded, he pretended he was dead and they didn't shoot him.
>
> I went to the regiment's 'special officer' [from the *NKVD*] to find out what was happening and he retorted, 'I know all about your platoon, you're a lieutenant and you talk too much.'
>
> I said, 'This isn't about me, I'm asking about Kulik.'
>
> 'What about your Kulik? Everyone was killed, but he apparently survived? We'll deal with him later. You'd better think about your own skin.'
>
> A day later, this officer was killed in an air raid and Kulik was taken somewhere for further investigation. We never found out what eventually happened to him. A new 'special officer' joined the regiment, but from his expression I immediately realised that it was useless to ask him anything about it.[32]

As detailed planning continued, Zhukov and Konev adopted different approaches; to a degree, this was the consequence of their starting positions. With his forces operating out of the smaller bridgeheads, Zhukov opted for attacking with his combined arms armies as his initial assault. These units were to break out of the bridgeheads and secure crossings over the Pilica River on the second day; the tank armies would then be unleashed. This allowed for at least parts of these tank armies to form up on the eastern bank of the Vistula, from where they could enter the limited space of the bridgeheads once the combined arms armies had moved forward. The two tank armies would enter combat on the second and third days of the operation with the intention of reaching the area either side of Kutno – roughly midway between the Vistula and Łódź – within a further three days, an advance of about 92 miles (148km). By contrast, Konev had sufficient space in the Sandomierz bridgehead to allow his armour to line up alongside his combined arms armies. He intended to use his two tank armies as part of the initial hammer blow that would shatter the German lines.

As Guderian journeyed across the shrunken territory under German control in his last attempts to persuade Hitler to see reason, the Red Army completed its preparations. Colonel Amazasp Khachaturovich Babadzhanian was commander of XI Guards Tank Corps, part of Zhukov's Front. He first met Zhukov personally just before the offensive when he and the other senior officers of tank and mechanised corps were summoned to 1st Belarusian Front headquarters. His recollection is perhaps rather more favourable than that of other men who had served under Zhukov:

Everyone knew the marshal's tough temper, and everyone was of course worried. I must say that the stories about Zhukov's temper are not without foundation. But it isn't true that he was unreasonably rude and gave himself freedom to insult the dignity of his subordinates. He admired people who were courageous and organised, energetic and brave. But he was merciless towards cowards and idlers … Personally, I never heard him speak humiliating words about his subordinates, but he was always intransigent about irresponsibility and frivolity …

We were pacing in agitation at the threshold of a small brick house where the commander sat. Finally, a general emerged with a list of special assignments. Everyone froze. He slowly looked at all of us, as if choosing one person, and suddenly pointed at me. 'The marshal wants to see you.'

'Me?' I said involuntarily. Trying to suppress my agitation – I'm not sure I succeeded – from the eyes of everyone else, I went through the door. The marshal sat at the table, surrounded by generals …

Zhukov shook hands and asked me to take a seat. 'How are the tankers doing? Are they prepared for the upcoming battles?'

I reported briefly on the combat readiness of the corps. Zhukov listened without interruption. He then asked a few questions about technical matters and training. I could see he was satisfied and began to relax. This didn't escape the marshal's attention. He looked at me again, suppressing a smile … and suddenly asked: 'There are two types of commanders – some dream of dying in their bed surrounded by relatives and friends, others prefer death on the battlefield. Which are you?' Well, of course I selected the second. Zhukov chuckled and smiled broadly. 'I didn't expect any other answer. But now, to the point. The operation is going to be difficult and apart from us, two other Fronts will be taking part – 1st Ukrainian and 2nd Belarusian. I want you to consider the special tasks facing the tank forces. Armoured formations must cut through the enemy's defences, penetrate rapidly as deep as possible into the enemy's rear to sow panic and spread disorganisation. We must not permit the enemy to cling to their lines and to create new nodes of defence. Press on, only forwards. Don't be afraid of anything: we will keep up with you. You won't be isolated. Is that clear? Forward, forward at any cost!'[33]

# CHAPTER 3

# KONEV'S HAMMER BLOW: 12–13 JANUARY

The intended start date for the offensive across central Poland and the reasons it was altered are surprisingly controversial topics. According to Soviet accounts, 20 January would see the Red Army begin its assault, and preparations in both 1st Ukrainian Front and 1st Belarusian Front were organised so that the last movements would take place immediately before this start date. Complete secrecy was of course impossible, given the huge numbers of troops and equipment squeezed into the three bridgeheads, but *Maskirovka* extended beyond disguising troop concentrations and probable intentions; misleading the Germans on the matter of timing was just as important. It seems that at the last moment, timings changed. Konev wrote in his memoirs:

> It was 9 January, and we had 11 days left before the start of the operation. All the main work had been completed but of course, as always before major undertakings, there was still a great deal to do. On that day, General [Aleksei Innokentovich] Antonov, the acting chief of the general staff, called me on the VHF radio set and said that because of the difficult situation they faced on the western front in the Ardennes region, the Allies had turned to us with a request to expedite the start of our offensive as swiftly as possible. After this appeal, *Stavka* revised the timing of the start of the offensive operation. Instead of attacking on 20 January, 1st Ukrainian Front was to commence operations on 12 January.
>
> Antonov passed on Stalin's decisions. Since the operation had already been approved by *Stavka* and planning was complete, no changes other than the timing were proposed, with no other fundamental issues being considered. I replied to

Antonov in our discussion that the Front would be ready for the offensive by the new start date set by *Stavka*.

I don't want to exaggerate or belittle in hindsight the difficulties that immediately confronted us in connection with the change in the start date. In essence, we were ready for the operation, which is why I had no hesitation in replying to Antonov. But more than eight days, which we lost in an instant, had to be made up for by the most intense work, putting all our efforts into the remaining two and a half days. Enormous organisational work was required from the commanders at all levels to bring preparations to completion.

In recent months we had received reinforcements who had just completed their training before the offensive. A whole programme of exercises had been organised, but now this programme had to be curtailed and reduced at its final stage, which of course was not easy. Many other shortcomings were revealed, but we eliminated them in an exceptionally short time.

In brief, those eight days that were taken from us were in truth highly valuable to us. But this change was made in order to help the Allies, and we in the front line – I speak for my Front, but I believe that the picture was the same everywhere – understood that the change was dictated by considerations on the general strategic level and therefore we just had to accept it. As a Front commander, I personally agreed with the decision taken by *Stavka*.

But one of the reasons that the change in start date didn't please us was because of the weather forecasts. For the last ten days of January, the forecast was more favourable than for the middle of the month. By preparing to launch the offensive on 12 January, we had to take into account that due to bad weather, we would have to suppress the German defences with artillery alone and without air support.[1]

Other Soviet accounts make similar statements, that the change in timing was triggered by requests from the Western Allies – in particular, from Churchill personally in the first week of January – for an earlier start to the Soviet offensive, but this is unlikely to be true. Stubborn resistance by American forces on the shoulders of the German offensive through the Ardennes – along the Elsenborn Ridge to the north and at Bastogne in the south – greatly hindered the German advance, as did the complexity of moving armoured units through the mountainous terrain. The panzer divisions had advanced through this region with great success in 1940, but conditions were very different in late 1944. The earlier advance had been in May, whereas there was now deep snow. The tanks of the German divisions were now more than twice as heavy as those used in 1940, adding to mobility difficulties. Despite being taken by surprise, the Western

Allies responded quickly and the encircled American troops in Bastogne were relieved on 26 December; at the same time, with improving weather permitting British and American air power to intervene with great effect, the tide had turned against the Germans even before the end of 1944.

The Soviet assertions that they brought forward their start date at the request of Churchill are therefore questionable. Firstly, the British forces in Belgium played only a small part in the fighting – out of a total of about 82,500 casualties, British losses were fewer than 1,500, with the US Army bearing the brunt of both the combat and losses. Secondly, relationships at the highest levels were more cordial between Roosevelt and Stalin than between Churchill and Stalin, and it seems likely that any such request would have been more likely to come from the Americans. Thirdly, given that the Germans were effectively defeated by the end of December, a request for Soviet assistance a week later makes no real sense.[2]

This begs the question of why the attack was brought forward, given that this change was certain to cause difficulties for Zhukov and Konev. The answer may lie in the next round of high-level meetings. Roosevelt, Churchill and Stalin had met in Tehran in late 1943 and had agreed the outline of their operations for 1944; their next meeting was scheduled to take place in Yalta, in Crimea, at the beginning of February. It is likely that Stalin intended to ensure that his forces were in possession of the territories immediately to the west of the Soviet frontier so that he would face little resistance from his western counterparts with regard to his plans for Eastern Europe. If the offensive had gone ahead on 20 January, there was the risk that any delay in the Soviet advance might result in Stalin having to meet Roosevelt and Churchill while the outcome of the battle remained uncertain; Churchill, who had made no secret at the Tehran Conference of his unhappiness with Stalin's intentions to impose his will on Eastern Europe after the war, might use any such setback to resurrect old arguments about the restoration of pre-war borders.

But even this explanation is problematic. The timing of the Yalta Conference had been agreed many months in advance, and when *Stavka* set the start date for the Vistula offensive as 20 January, all those involved (including of course Stalin) would have been aware of the proximity of the forthcoming meeting of the 'Big Three'. Another clue, though, lies in weather forecasts. Although Konev asserted that the forecast was more favourable for air operations in the last days of January, there were also predictions that there might be a partial thaw. Frozen ground was essential to permit heavy armoured forces to move across country in the winter, and if the thaw were prolonged, there was the risk of the Vistula River ice breaking up and hindering the movement of supplies and reinforcements.

To confuse matters still further, some documents suggest that Konev was originally to start his offensive on 9 January and the switch to 12 January actually represented a delay rather than bringing the start date forward.[3] Given the scale of preparations and postponements of earlier operations due to delays in getting units into position, a delay rather than bringing forward of the start date seems more realistic. Indeed, bringing the start date forward by so many days would surely have created considerable difficulties in terms of ensuring supplies and troops were all in their designated places. If this is correct, then the official Soviet view that the operation was brought forward to aid the Western Allies may be little more than an attempt to portray the Soviet Union as a magnanimous ally.

The Germans knew that an attack was imminent and monitored the Soviet lines closely. Many commanders hoped to emulate tactics that had evolved over the previous year, with German units pulling back from their forward posts at the last moment before the Soviet preparatory artillery bombardment began – this greatly reduced casualties and ensured that the main defensive line, a little further to the rear, was fully manned. The final Soviet preparations would involve a great deal of unavoidable noise and in order to disguise this, loudspeakers had played loud music every night throughout the Sandomierz bridgehead for several nights. Late on 11 January, a Red Army deserter made the perilous journey across the front lines to the positions of the German 304th Infantry Division. He informed his interrogators that the attack would come the following morning, and this information was passed to higher commands immediately. In many cases in the past, the Germans might have been tempted to use their artillery to conduct spoiling barrages against Soviet concentrations, but such was the imbalance between the resources on either side of the front line that the German artillery planners preferred to keep their guns silent. Any benefit from a spoiling bombardment, they calculated, would be offset by revealing the location of their guns and inviting massive counter-battery fire. In any case, they would need all their precious ammunition to deal with the actual assault.

There is a tendency for armies to adopt a certain approach to operations and then to refine it over time. This has the advantage of evolutionary change and improvement, and implementing operations becomes easier if soldiers and officers are following a familiar pattern. The disadvantage, of course, is that the enemy will also recognise this pattern and will take appropriate countermeasures. For several years, the Red Army had adopted a policy of 'reconnaissance in force', with battalion-sized attacks the day before the main offensive. These served several purposes: they helped clarify the enemy's front-line positions, potentially detecting fortifications that had been missed; they might force the enemy into using concealed artillery, thus revealing its location; and they captured favourable start lines for the main offensive. Opinions on the usefulness of reconnaissance in force were almost proportional to the distance from the front line itself. Senior officers regarded it as a positive measure and felt that it enhanced the offensive greatly; soldiers who had to carry out the mission often saw it as little more than an exercise in suffering pointless casualties. Red Army generals sometimes described how battalions were trained specially for reconnaissance in force, but such training rarely amounted to more than a walk-through of the planned attack and in many cases there was no training at all. Konev was aware that regardless of the merits of reconnaissance in force, the Germans had become so accustomed to it that any benefit was far outweighed by the disadvantages of having to launch the main attack against an enemy who was thoroughly alerted. He therefore came up with a new version.

The timing of the initial Soviet bombardment is reported as commencing at different times in different accounts. Some of this may reflect the fact that German units always operated on Berlin time, whereas some accounts give the timing based upon local time. Regardless, the initial shelling commenced before dawn and lasted less than 30 minutes, far less than the massive bombardments that had fallen upon German positions in previous offensives. Despite this, the fire was heavy and devastated the few buildings that remained relatively intact in the front line. Then, the bombardment suddenly moved on to the German rear zones, and Soviet rifle battalions, which had already been moving forward cautiously through diagonal avenues that had been left free of shellfire, stormed several German front-line positions. Some of these initial probing attacks were made by penal units, which consisted of soldiers charged with a variety of misdemeanours and who had been given a chance to redeem themselves by conspicuous performance; other attacks were made by regular troops, particularly those that were closely supported by tanks and assault guns.

Hartmann and his regiment – who had been rotated out of the trenches the day before – had been sent some distance to the rear, but even from their new location they had no doubt what the thunder meant:

As I was returning from a walk to my bunker before dawn … and had sat down with the usual morning reports, there began some distance from us a huge series of blows, a distant, heavy rumbling and humming – the great Russian offensive! We tumbled out of the door into the darkness and saw in the distance to the southwest and west that the clouds were lit up by innumerable, constant, shimmering lights beyond the horizon, but so far away, so blurry and muted, that we couldn't hear individual explosions or make them out with our eyes. It was the

Russian offensive, the new overture. Nothing happened near us for some distance. We were already lying in the bottom of a gigantic sack, which the Russians apparently wanted to close west of Kielce or at Łódź. So why would they make a big fuss over us?[4]

Hartmann sent messengers to his platoons, ordering the men to prepare for action, but there was no need: everyone knew what the distant thunder meant, and what they should do. Shortly after, he received an order by telephone to prepare to return to the front line. As his company was the only one in the battalion with telephone contact to higher headquarters, he dispatched runners to the other companies. Almost immediately, the phone rang again: they were to stay where they were, ready to move at short notice. The messengers were sent out once again, but the phone rang even as the men left the dugout: the battalion was to set off immediately, as originally ordered. To add to Hartmann's dismay, he was to deploy his company in a sector previously unknown to him with a penal company on either flank. He and his men were led forward by a guide:

> We had long since left the dirt road and were walking across bare fields. Ivan paid close attention to the villages or other locations in the hinterland with heavy calibre weapons. Every few minutes a few heavy loads whistled over our heads, often half a dozen in quick succession. When the rolling noise had passed, all we could hear was the clattering and shuffling of the soldiers and vehicles in the darkness. Barely noticeable hollows and elevations enlivened the landscape during daylight, but in the darkness there were only the milky stars in the moonless sky and the faint glow of distant shots and explosions.
>
> After about half an hour, I asked the guide whether we were close to our destination. He began to stammer and said he had probably led us too far forward and we would have to turn right and then right again and he would then be able to orient himself. When I showed him my map, he couldn't make any sense of it. The front line wasn't marked and the few contour lines in this godforsaken area meant nothing to him. Fifteen minutes later he was completely downcast and at his wits' end.[5]

Hartmann sent out three-man scouting parties in all directions with strict instructions to return after no more than ten minutes. Accompanied by two men, he walked over a small crest and found a small village. He could hear the engines of heavy vehicles perhaps half a mile away, but suddenly shells began to rain down. He returned to his company where the other scouting parties appeared shortly after, and based upon their reports Hartmann made a guess of where he was on his map. He decided to attempt to retrace his steps and his men laboriously pushed their few vehicles until they had been turned around:

> I was now walking with the platoon commanders and the company headquarters group at the head of the column ... when a particularly dense salvo of heavy shells roared right above us and fell far in the hinterland. And then suddenly – I heard only a hellish screech, saw flames, was deafened, and flew through the air and landed heavily, sparks before my eyes. I thought I heard screams and staggered to my feet in the darkness, smelling gunpowder – people were screaming, there were figures on the ground, shouting, moaning, whimpering. 'What happened?'
>
> Finally I saw by the light of the stars overhead, the dark shapes of three men rolling on the ground. Oh God. 'Steinberg!' His skull was cut in half, a mass of blood and scalp. And Iglhaut [a veteran NCO]: 'My stomach, my stomach!'[6]

There were several dead and Hartmann had a thigh wound. He and his men stumbled through the darkness with their wounded, finally reaching battalion headquarters an hour later. After a short rest, they were led forward once more by a different scout and found themselves occupying a large stretch of entrenchments for which they had too few troops. The best that they could do was set up a series of strongpoints and hope that it would be sufficient.

In some sectors, careful preparation of hardened bunkers proved to be highly effective. The initial bombardment on the positions of 304th Infantry Division towards the southern end of the battle zone, for example, resulted in just five men being wounded in one battalion's positions. But this was unusual and in most cases the losses and damage were more extensive. The powerful infantry probes that followed overran much of the forward line of German defences, penetrating in places up to 600m.

Suddenly, the Soviet attacks slackened and the Germans waited to see what would happen next. The brief but intense bombardment and the very aggressive infantry attacks had convinced many that this was the main Soviet assault, but it was actually Konev's new version of reconnaissance in force. Suddenly the Red Army's massed artillery opened fire again. This second bombardment was far heavier and lasted a little more than 90 minutes, devastating German trenches and bunkers. Shelling ranged deep into the rear of the German positions; the headquarters of Fourth Panzer Army, identified by reconnaissance photographs, was badly hit and temporarily put out of action. Having emerged from their hardened shelters after the first Soviet bombardment, many German troops were now caught in their fighting trenches and losses were heavy. In some estimates, up to a quarter of the defenders were killed, wounded, or fled.[7]

Georgy Aleksandrovich Melikov was a rifle platoon commander, waiting to join the attack on the German lines. He watched the artillery preparation in awe:

I can't describe everything that happened. The roar was so loud that my eardrums burst and I started bleeding from my ears. We could barely imagine the hellish conditions over there among the German positions. Huge masses of earth flew into the air, together with all the bits of what had been fortifications, positions, equipment, artillery, and so on. I remember how the continuous flashes from explosions merged into a single all-consuming fire. It seemed as if the very earth was burning, which actually happened, as we later saw. The barrage lasted 90 minutes, and suddenly everything became quiet. After the terrifying roar: a terrifying silence, just as frightening as the noise. A low-level flight of attack aircraft appeared, firing on anything the artillery hadn't destroyed. I asked myself: what could have survived that hell? But it wasn't over – soon the artillery barrage resumed with similar force, this time transferred into the depths of the enemy's defence. I don't remember how long it lasted. Then the 'queen of the battlefield' went forward – infantry, with tanks in support. For the first few kilometres we encountered practically no resistance. In the destroyed trenches lay dead German soldiers with hideous faces, half-covered with earth. Everything that we saw was shocking. Only death, chaos, destruction, fires, smoke – it was impossible to breathe.[8]

From north to south, Konev's first wave of troops consisted of Sixth Army and Third Guards Army facing north, with Thirteenth, Fifty-Second, Fifth Guards, Fifty-Ninth, and Sixtieth Armies facing west. Facing the northern face of the Sandomierz bridgehead on the German side were three infantry divisions of XLII Corps; the German lines continued along the western face with XXIV Panzer Corps and XLVIII Panzer Corps. In some areas, German defenders fought doggedly and held on for many hours, but these were exceptions – in most sectors, attackers like Melikov encountered little resistance. Konev had intended to burst out of the bridgehead with a single massive blow and this was largely accomplished. Despite suffering few losses in the initial bombardment, the German 304th Infantry Division was now in disarray, as Lelyushenko described:

At midday, [Colonel General Nikolai Pavlovich] Pukhov [commander Thirteenth Army] and I learned that the infantry of the first echelon had already captured the enemy's first line and was moving forward. I gave the command for the forward detachments of Fourth Tank Army to follow the infantry.

From the powerful bombardment of our artillery, many Fascist soldiers were maddened and terrified. Soon, captured Fascists appeared at our command post. Many of them were taken prisoner in their trenches in a maddened state, half crazed. It was impossible to get anything intelligible from them at that moment. 'All *kaput*, Hitler *kaput*,' they said, frightened to death. After a time, having recovered his senses, a senior corporal said, 'I have never experienced such horror. It was real hell. There was a continuous howling in the trenches. The wounded screamed for help, but nobody could give it to them. After enduring this horror, I surrendered.' Prisoners of 574th Infantry Regiment of 304th Infantry Division told us, 'With the beginning of the full Russian artillery preparation, we lost control and the soldiers fled. Most of them were killed or wounded.'[9]

Assuming that these were genuine encounters, it is worth remembering that the men who surrendered were more likely to be those who had been overwhelmed, physically or mentally, by the shock of the Red Army's assault, and that their words may not be typical of the rest of the German forces. But German accounts also describe widespread devastation from the intense, second Soviet bombardment and the ferocity of the attack that followed. In many areas, German soldiers were seen fleeing from the battlefield even before the end of the artillery preparation, an almost unprecedented event on the Eastern Front. Hans von Ahlfen, who held the rank of Oberst at the time – he would be promoted to Generalmajor at the end of January – commanded an eponymous group in XLII

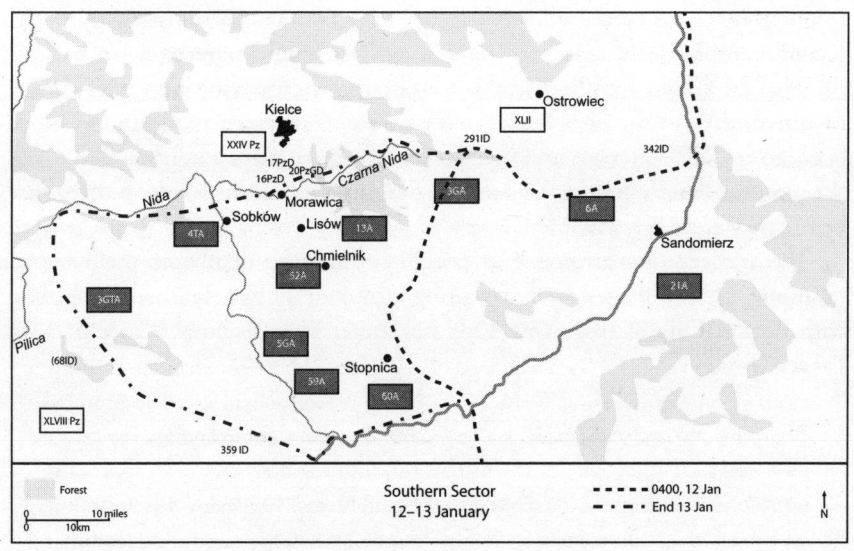

Corps, roughly midway between the northern edge of the Sandomierz bridgehead and the southern tip of the Puławy bridgehead, and his description was based upon reports that passed through his headquarters:

> It wasn't just that the majority of combatants were physically or mentally crushed; the detonations of the drumfire hurled up great clouds of smoke and earth that combined with the enemy's smokescreens to create a bank of cloud up to 10km [six miles] deep over the battlefield and that darkened the sun in the cloudless sky. Observation conditions were no better than those on a moonlit night. When one thinks of our modest forces and the few heavy weapons on such a broad front line – for example, there was only one heavy anti-tank gun per 750m of front – it becomes clear that the enemy, often unobserved by us and therefore not brought under fire, was able from the outset to drive forward and during the first day of the attack to break through the front line.[10]

The description of 'cloudless skies' is at odds with every other account; Konev, for example, noted that snow was falling heavily during and immediately after the bombardment, and this would have added to the German difficulties in seeing what was happening. The initial Soviet bombardment, whilst heavy, was not unusual in comparison to earlier Soviet offensives. What seems to have made a difference was that it was far more precise, with a greater percentage of shells landing on designated targets rather than being squandered in general area bombardments. The innovation introduced by Konev to mount his reconnaissance in force sandwiched between two bombardments, with the second bombardment being the heavier, was also highly effective. Up to two-thirds of the German artillery in the front line was destroyed, either in the initial bombardment or by the Soviet troops surging forward. Communications between artillery observers and their batteries were almost completely destroyed; the gunners rapidly found themselves engaging the Soviet troops in direct fire before they were overwhelmed.

The artillery bombardment extended through the depths of the German positions, and the limited reserves waiting further to the rear watched the shelling with horror. One of these was 40th Panzergrenadier Regiment, part of 17th Panzer Division:

> Between 0300 and 0500 on 12 January, there was a continuous barrage of artillery units firing all calibres in an extent that had hitherto been unknown to us. The horizon was as bright as daylight. Between 0800 and 1000, this fire storm was repeated and ... our impression was of the heavens falling down to the earth.[11]

Leading the assault on the German XLVIII Panzer Corps was Fifth Guards Army, commanded by the capable Colonel General Alexei Semenovich Zhadov. Contrary to Ahlfen's description, Zhadov in his account highlighted the low cloud and snow, which threatened to turn to rain as the day progressed. His army was supported by two tank corps and these entered the battle alongside Zhadov's second echelon as the riflemen moved forward through the German defences. The close cooperation between the tanks and infantrymen was a great improvement on earlier offensive operations, which had often foundered when tanks pressed on into the German positions while the infantry struggled to advance through withering machine-gun and artillery fire. Neverthelesss, although his units reported that they had advanced up to nine miles (15km) on the first day of the offensive, Zhadov was not completely satisfied. Movement had been slower than he had hoped, and he blamed this more on poor ground conditions, worsened by the snow and sleet, than on German resistance.[12]

To an extent, Zhadov's account was unfair on the German defenders. The town of Stopnica in particular had been heavily fortified and it took until early afternoon for Fifth Guards Army to clear the defenders from their positions. Many of 304th Infantry Division's minefields were intact despite heavy shelling and the Soviet tanks and assault guns struggled to keep up with the advancing riflemen. But after the capture of Stopnica, progress rapidly accelerated. German artillery was silenced by counter-battery fire and ammunition shortages as the day progressed, permitting Red Army sappers to clear lanes through the minefields.

Rybalko's Third Guards Tank Army moved forward at about midday to form the southern exploitation group of Konev's 1st Ukrainian Front, but found that only two lanes had been cleared through the German minefields. As they moved forward, the soldiers of 51st Guards Tank Brigade encountered determined resistance and recorded the loss of 15 tanks in close-quarter combat. Attempts to force new paths through the minefields resulted in further losses, but the Soviet units continued to grind forward. Once they had used their single-shot *Panzerfaust* anti-tank weapons, the ability of the German infantry to resist declined rapidly.[13]

A little to the north, the initial Soviet attack by Fifty-Second Army encountered relatively intact positions, held by the German 68th Infantry Division. A regiment of heavyweight JS-2 tanks had been deployed to assist the Soviet breakthrough but many of these were knocked out at close range by German infantrymen armed with *Panzerfausts*. In earlier Soviet operations, such a check might have been followed by stubborn, increasingly costly attacks at the same point, but the Red Army of 1945 had learned a great deal from its earlier mistakes. Colonel General

Konstantin Apollinovich Koroteev, commander of Fifty-Second Army, switched his point of effort to his southern flank, where Zhadov's army had already overrun the German defences, and inserted his armoured support through a gap in the German lines. The Soviet tanks then turned north into the flank of the German defences that were holding up the main attack, only to run into a battalion of *Sturmgeschütz III* assault guns. The German battalion claimed to have destroyed dozens of Red Army tanks by the end of the day, but was nonetheless levered from its positions and forced to withdraw.[14]

Lelyushenko had started moving his tanks forward late in the morning and at 1400 Konev granted him permission to commence the exploitation of the breakthrough. Less than an hour later, Lelyushenko received the welcome news that his leading elements – a Guards mechanised brigade and a Guards tank brigade – had overtaken the rifle units that had made the initial attack and were engaging the German tactical reserves. He immediately moved his command post forward to keep up with the offensive.

The disputes in German circles about where to position their reserves now became increasingly relevant. The closeness of the reserves to the front line – at Hitler's insistence – meant that many of the units and their headquarters had been caught in the initial Soviet bombardment. As a result, even if their losses were lower than those suffered by the infantry in the front line, it would take time for them to restore their signals cables and other equipment. But the rapid advance of Lelyushenko's tanks meant that time was in very short supply. Moreover, the long-standing requirement for Hitler to give his personal approval before panzer units were granted permission to move continued to cause difficulties.

The commander of XXIV Panzer Corps, General Walther Nehring, was a veteran of armoured warfare with a reputation for leading from the front. He had led 18th Panzer Division during the invasion of the Soviet Union in 1941 before being given command of the *Deutsches Afrika-Korps*; Rommel, who has always been associated with this formation, was the overall commander of German forces in North Africa with Nehring as his subordinate. At the end of August 1942, Nehring was badly wounded in an air raid and evacuated, though he returned to take command of forces in Tunisia before the end of the year whilst still recovering from his wounds. He left North Africa before the final German surrender and took command of XXIV Panzer Corps in Ukraine, where he was wounded in August 1943, his fifth serious wound of the war. Intermittently, he took command of Fourth Panzer Army and, still struggling with his wounds and general ill-health, he was now the man who controlled the only significant German forces available to deal with the Red Army's forces that were erupting through the shattered front line.

By the standards of the Wehrmacht in January 1945, XXIV Panzer Corps was a strong formation. The main fighting power was provided by 16th and 17th Panzer Divisions, with the valuable addition of *Schwere Panzer-Abteilung 424* ('Heavy Tank Battalion 424'). Each panzer division was intended to have a panzer regiment of two panzer battalions, two panzergrenadier regiments each with two battalions, an artillery regiment, an anti-tank battalion, and other support services. After suffering heavy losses in Ukraine in 1944, 16th Panzer Division had just half its panzergrenadier strength and its panzer battalions were also below strength. Its sister formation, 17th Panzer Division, had also lost a panzergrenadier regiment but still had three panzergrenadier battalions and a full complement of tanks. The companies of *Schwere Panzer-Abteilung 424* fielded an impressive 52 Tiger tanks, a mixture of the tried and trusted original Tiger and the newer, heavier, and somewhat less reliable King Tiger; the corps was therefore capable of making a potentially decisive intervention.

Aware that permission for movement would probably be slow in arriving. Nehring issued verbal orders as soon as the Soviet bombardment began for his units to begin assembling, but the severity of the shelling was such that even where these orders were passed on, units were still struggling to reach their positions when Lelyushenko's armour appeared from the east:

> At the headquarters of II Battalion, 64th Panzer Regiment [part of 16th Panzer Division] the men were busy loading up large quantities of materiel when suddenly at about 1500 tank shells landed close by. The Russians had arrived. Bitter close-quarter fighting began, one half-track after another was shot up and left ablaze, and the [battalion] commander was wounded. At other locations the Russians surprised the tanks of 16th Panzer Division in their 'boxes' [emplacements for protection against artillery fire]. It was only at 1800 in the evening, about 15 hours after the beginning of the offensive, that the first orders for an operation by the panzer regiment arrived. The Russians had already penetrated 20km [12 miles] into the hinterland and had swept past the division's preparation area.[15]

After the war, Nehring summarised the day's fighting in a few brief words, which highlight the degree to which communications had broken down as a result of 1st Ukrainian Front's massive artillery bombardment. Nehring's account is wrong in several aspects:

> Through the huge gap [in the German front line] the Russian armoured forces immediately surged towards the west, using the German principles of leadership that they had adopted in the course of the war, into the depths of the German

positions and by evening had already outflanked the unprotected right [southern] flank of my corps, which suffered heavy losses in the fighting. The commander of 17th Panzer Division [Oberst Albert Brux] was taken prisoner. *Schwere Panzer-Abteilung 424* was destroyed in its preparation area and its commander, Major von Legat, was killed. All reports were bad. Despite this it was vital to hold our nerve and to take countermeasures.

Despite my repeated suggestions and those of the army commander the corps had been left too close to the immediate front line and it was thus impossible for it to use its operational strength properly as an armoured formation – in mobile operations – but orders arrived to stay in position and hold the key location of Kielce. Apparently, the high command believed that the enemy penetration could still be brought to a halt. We were to do everything in our power to support the wavering front.[16]

As will be seen later, much of what he described took place the following day rather than on 12 January. The account is also mistaken about the commander of the Tiger battalion – Legat had been replaced as battalion commander by Major Siegfried Saemisch. Before the offensive, many of Lelyushenko's tank and anti-tank crews had taken advantage of an opportunity to fire at captured Tiger tanks that had been left crippled on earlier battlefields. They had learned that these behemoths, even the newer and better armoured King Tigers, were not as impregnable as many believed; at medium and close range, their side armour could be penetrated, and like all tanks they could be disabled by damage to their tracks. Accounts of the battle that followed are somewhat confused, both in terms of the day on which it happened and the details of the fighting. According to some accounts written by Soviet officers, the German tanks were busy refuelling and were immobile when Lelyushenko's tanks burst into the preparation area of *Schwere Panzer-Abteilung 424*. These accounts suggest that *Schwere Panzer-Abteilung 424* was rapidly destroyed before it could go into action, but other accounts, including those by Soviet commanders with the leading tank formations, describe a rather different story that seems to be closer to the limited information available from the fragmentary German accounts. It is possible that some of the Tigers were caught refuelling and were rapidly destroyed, but most would make their presence felt the following day.

The city of Kielce, close to the northern part of the Sandomierz bridgehead, was a position that would have to be held if the Germans were to stop the Red Army's breakout, but such considerations were already out of date by the end of 12 January. The Soviet Sixth Army erupted out of the north-facing part of the bridgehead close to Sandomierz, rapidly forcing back the infantry of the German XLII Corps; by doing so, the Soviet units threatened to take Ostrowiec, to the east of Kielce. With the major breakout to the south of Kielce proceeding with more hindrance from the weather than the German defences, the usefulness of Kielce was very limited.

Originally, all of Hartmann's regiment had been intended for use in a counterattack, but during the afternoon of 12 January the men were ordered to set up a new front line. As darkness fell, the infantrymen were told to pull back. When they reached their new positions, the men were pleased to discover that bunkers and trenches had already been prepared there – one of the numerous defensive lines to which Xylander had wanted to withdraw before the onset of the Soviet offensive. The soldiers prepared for action and listened with varying degrees of disbelief to rumours of the exact location of the advancing Red Army.

As the headquarters of Fourth Panzer Army restored its communications links with both higher and subordinate commands, it passed on the orders from *OKH* for Nehring to concentrate his corps at Kielce. The closest formation was 16th Panzer Division and it managed to reach the city relatively intact, but 17th Panzer Division lay further to the south. Brux, the division commander, later recalled the day:

> [The day] began with a heavy artillery barrage preceding the Soviet major offensive. I can remember waiting in vain for orders from the panzer corps. Communication with the panzer corps was interrupted. When communications were restored in the evening, an order came in. I could only tell the chief of staff that this order was perhaps fit to be printed [i.e. it was perhaps still of value] but that an 'order to mount' a few hours earlier would have been more to my liking. Communications were interrupted again. I could still give battle orders to the Tiger battalion under my command, and then about 100 enemy tanks moved through the division command post.[17]

Brux's chief of staff was Major Hans-Georg Krebs. He had been in post since before Brux took command:

> Even before Oberst Brux became the new division commander, 17th Panzer Division had several times demanded of XXIV Panzer Corps to change the rigid concept of this linear form of defence. To counter the imminent Soviet general offensive it was of the utmost importance for the division to be free [to manoeuvre] in order to counter the Soviet attack. Even the supreme commander of the army

group ... was unable to change this operational concept. The possibility of the manoeuvrability of an armoured reserve force no longer existed.

The number of tanks in 17th Panzer Division was 210, a very high number in those days. Due to untrained crews, the losses at the beginning of the battle were more than 25 per cent ...

The only way to breach the encirclement was an attack with all available forces to the north. There they would reach the position of 16th Panzer Division at the River Nida. This goal was achieved. Both divisions [then] tried in a combined attack to reach the city of Kielce. During this operation, the staff of 17th Panzer Division was scattered.[18]

Part of 17th Panzer Division was overwhelmed as it struggled north and the rest of the division fell back to the west, with most of Konev's two tank armies advancing in the gap between these units and the rest of XXIV Panzer Corps to the north. Nehring's command had effectively been cut in two.

Communications between Nehring's corps headquarters and Fourth Panzer Army remained intermittent at best, but were still markedly better than between Fourth Panzer Army and Nehring's southern neighbour, XLVIII Panzer Corps. During the years of fighting across Ukraine and the Don valley, XLVIII Panzer Corps had been one of the most successful German formations, regularly fielding several panzer divisions and taking part in numerous important and effective counterattacks; now, it fielded just three infantry divisions with no armoured support. By the end of 12 January, General Maximilian Reichsfreiherr von Edelsheim, the corps commander, had little or no contact with any of his subordinate units or with Gräser at Fourth Panzer Army's headquarters.

For the Germans, the day was one of disaster and confusion. By contrast, Red Army commanders were increasingly jubilant as reports flowed in. Lelyushenko's leading formations had advanced up to 12 miles (20km) and the breach in the German front line was nearly 24 miles (40km) wide. The weather improved slightly towards the end of the day, allowing reconnaissance flights to monitor German movements; the concentration of XXIV Panzer Corps around Kielce was identified and Lelyushenko moved his units into position to deal with any German attempt to strike south from the city. For Konev, the smooth introduction of his tank armies into the battle was a source of considerable pride.

With regard to the timing of the introduction of tank formations into a breakthrough, there is a considerable volume of military-historical literature. There were different opinions on this matter during the war and I too had my personal opinion. In 1943, 1944 and 1945, the Fronts that I commanded invariably included tank armies or tank and mechanised corps, and based upon my experiences I developed my personal approach to the issue. I believed that under pressure from some tank commanders, *Stavka* often showed unnecessary hesitancy when it came to introducing tank armies into a breakthrough. This was because of the fear – sometimes excessive, I would add – of exposing the tank forces to heavy losses in the fight to overcome the forward positions and main battle line of the enemy's defences. Sometimes, *Stavka* intervened directly and dictated the timing for the introduction of the tanks. Of course, nothing good ever came from this because when they attempted strict control of the timings of inserting the tanks, this often didn't coincide with the specific conditions in the front line. As a rule, schedules imposed from high above had a high risk of failure. In practice, the situation that developed during operations was very variable and when making decisions, it was necessary to take into account local factors that could not be anticipated in advance or seen clearly from afar. There truly is no place for an imposed template.[19]

The Soviet doctrine of introducing tank armies into a breakthrough had undergone several evolutionary steps as the war progressed, in recognition that on many occasions, the process had not produced the expected results. Much of this was due to the organisation of armoured formations. From their inception, panzer divisions had a good mix of tanks, motorised infantry and artillery, and support arms – in particular, vehicle recovery teams and workshops that could restore damaged or disabled vehicles to service quickly. Moreover, the practice of concentrating the best armoured assets in a panzer division into an armoured battlegroup played a major role in increasing their efficacy in attacks and counterattacks. With a history of neglecting support services that had been inherited from the old imperial armies of the tsars, the Red Army constantly adjusted the makeup of its armoured units as the war progressed.

By early 1945, Soviet planners were concentrating on two factors that they regarded as of great importance: the organisation and deployment of tank forces as they moved into the breakthrough; and command and control of tank forces as they exploited the initial successes. The individual tank corps advanced in two or more columns, with each column led by an armoured reconnaissance group. This was followed closely by an advance detachment made up of tanks, motorised artillery, and 'tank rider' infantry, with other units – anti-aircraft and anti-tank battalions, and the bulk of the tank units – following behind. Bitter experience had taught Soviet commanders that the Germans would attempt to counterattack from the flanks and the columns were deliberately configured so that if they did come under flank attack, they would be able to deploy quickly from the line of march to deal with such a threat and either drive it back or bring it to a halt.

The second factor was how the tank army was to function after it had passed through the combined arms armies that had achieved the breakthrough. In battles across the Soviet Union, the Wehrmacht repeatedly engaged Soviet tank forces that had penetrated the front line and destroyed them in detail; in a quick-moving 'encounter battle', German tactical expertise remained superior to that of the Red Army. Soviet analysis of these engagements identified several factors that had contributed to the poor performance of their tank units, particularly addressing how tanks often outran their support. The result was the continuing evolution of the structure of tank armies and of their interaction with other units. The rate of advance of tank forces was deliberately reduced to ensure that units didn't become widely separated and so that slower units, such as artillery and rifle formations, could keep up.

Command and control in a fast-changing battlefield is a complex matter and the Red Army rapidly realised that its pre-war doctrine, with its emphasis on top-down command, was too rigid and inflexible. Even by 1943, it was unusual to have radio communications below battalion level; the expectation was still that companies would be issued with orders and would then be expected to carry them out, and that any feedback from those companies to battalion headquarters was of little value. This explains at least in part why Red Army losses were so heavy – company commanders knew the consequences of failing to carry out their orders, and simply threw their men at German defences even when it became clear that such attacks were futile. By early 1945, radio communications to company and in some cases to platoon level were widespread, improving the ability of commanders at every level to react better to unexpected setbacks and changing circumstances.

All through the night that followed, Red Army supply columns moved forward to replenish the combat formations that had torn apart the German lines; this was another developing area of Red Army doctrine, with far more attention being paid to logistic and support elements. Lelyushenko was ready to deal with any attack by the German armour concentrating in Kielce, and the engineers of Rybalko's Third Guards Tank Army continued to clear wider lanes through the minefields that had channelled the Soviet attacks earlier in the day, and also created crossing points at a number of small rivers and streams that were hindering movement. Konev was confident that his forces would build on their success in the coming days. By contrast, Gräser at the headquarters of Fourth Panzer Army had no clear picture of what was happening. The intermittent reports from Nehring suggested that the concentration of XXIV Panzer Corps at

Kielce was taking place as ordered, but there were gaps in the German positions to the east and south of the city. In an attempt to shore up the line, Gräser ordered 72nd Infantry Division, deployed where the northern part of the Sandomierz bridgehead met the Vistula, to pull back to the west; he intended to send its battlegroups as reinforcements for the infantry divisions of XLVIII Panzer Corps that had experienced the full weight of the Soviet assault, but in order to do so he needed better knowledge of what was happening. At the headquarters of Army Group A, Harpe was also desperate to get a clear picture of what was happening, but it was clear to everyone that the 'house of cards', as Guderian had described the Eastern Front, had either collapsed already or was in the process of disintegration without substantial reinforcements.

Facing the northern side of the Sandomierz bridgehead, Hartmann and his company were fortunate not to come under attack on the first day of the offensive; their lines were too thin to have put up much resistance. In his diary, Hartmann recorded that he felt completely drained, physically and emotionally. His leg wound was increasingly painful and the senseless march before dawn, culminating in the sudden shelling and resultant casualties, had taken its toll. But his diary shows that this was merely the endpoint of a long period of physical and mental attrition. Months of combat, of watching comrades die or be wounded, of having to obey senseless orders, and enduring long, demoralising retreats – all had taken a toll. During the First World War, the British psychologist William Rivers worked with many soldiers suffering from what became known as shell shock. At an early stage of his work, he recognised that of all the factors that kept soldiers motivated to overcome their fears and remain in action, the most important was camaraderie and a sense of loyalty to other soldiers. He also recognised how the resilience of men could be worn down by a series of events, both major and minor, with the result that a final collapse could be triggered by relatively small stresses.[20] Hartmann's increasing indifference to what was happening around him would have been familiar to Rivers, and was replicated in thousands of cases in a Wehrmacht brought to its knees by years of fighting an increasingly hopeless war. Eventually, Hartmann was persuaded to return to the battalion command post to seek medical help; a doctor told him that his wound required hospital treatment and congratulated him – a wound serious enough to remove a soldier from the front line but not to threaten life or limb was known as a *Heimatschuss* ('home shot'). He was evacuated to a field hospital further to the west.[21]

Had Hitler not diverted so many forces to Hungary, reinforcements to deal with the Soviet offensive might have been available. Furthermore, they made little difference to the deteriorating situation in Hungary. The only significant unit that could be dispatched to try to repair the damage inflicted on Fourth Panzer Army was the oddly named *Fallschirm-Panzer-Division Hermann Göring* ('Parachute Panzer Division Hermann Göring'), part of the newly formed *Fallschirm-Panzer-Korps Hermann Göring*. The division, whose name was often abbreviated to *HG*, was organised in a similar manner to Wehrmacht panzer divisions; although some of its panzergrenadiers were former paratroopers, most were simply regular soldiers who had been assigned to the unit – like all 'parachute' formations, it was technically part of the Luftwaffe, but operated under army control. Since the short-lived Red Army penetration into East Prussia in the autumn of 1944, the *HG* Panzer Division had been stationed close to the Prussian town of Gumbinnen, and it was now ordered to move immediately by train to the city of Łódź, renamed Litzmannstadt by the Germans in honour of the First World War general who defeated a Russian army near the city in 1914. The redeployment of the *HG* Panzer Division would take several days, and even though Łódź was over 60 miles (100km) behind the front line, there were already concerns that the front line might have reached this area by the time that the formation had concentrated its resources. Reinhardt's protests that he needed the division as a reserve in East Prussia were overridden.

By dawn on 13 January, Nehring already knew that it was unlikely that he would be able to hold on in Kielce. He ordered his staff to begin preparations for a withdrawal to the northwest while he waited for official permission to make such a move, but he also delayed for another reason. He was aware that General Hermann Recknagel's XLII Corps, immediately to the east of Kielce, was heavily engaged in combat with the Soviet units that were now breaking out of the northern side of the Sandomierz bridgehead. Still struggling to establish reliable communications links, Nehring sent a messenger to Recknagel's headquarters, advising his colleague that he was going to withdraw and that the troops of XLII Corps should try to fight their way through to Kielce as soon as possible.

At the headquarters of Fourth Panzer Army, Gräser continued to work in near-complete ignorance. After a brief discussion with Harpe at Army Group A headquarters, it was decided that XLVIII Panzer Corps should be reassigned to Seventeenth Army, Gräser's southern neighbour. When Harpe contacted Schulz, the commander of Seventeenth Army, to make him aware of the change, he was unable to offer any clear information about the current status of XLVIII Panzer Corps and its subordinate formations; Schulz decided to drive to the area personally to try to make contact with Edelsheim. He reached Kraków in mid-morning without incident, travelling through a worryingly empty landscape; he had expected to encounter the withdrawing rear area elements of the corps, but most of these had already been overrun and destroyed by the Red Army.

A short time later, Edelsheim and his headquarters staff made contact with their new army commander. At the outset of the battle, XLVIII Panzer Corps had three infantry divisions in the front line – from north to south, 168th, 68th and 304th Infantry Divisions. The northern division had largely been destroyed on 12 January and Edelsheim had no contact with it; its survivors were retreating in small groups towards the west and northwest. The other two divisions, in slightly better shape, were falling back towards Silesia. In addition, Edelsheim had been given 359th Infantry Division on the eve of the Soviet attack; originally part of Seventeenth Army to Edelsheim's south, the division was still moving on foot and was ordered to occupy the A1 and A2 lines, but it lacked the mobility to reach far enough north to make any difference to the breach in the German lines. Nevertheless, Schulz ordered the division to push energetically northwards along the line of the Nida River as far as possible.

Warned about the concentration of German armour around Kielce, Lelyushenko's formations crossed the Nida on 13 January and engaged both of Nehring's panzer divisions, together with the surviving Tiger tanks.[22] Heavy fighting continued throughout the day and into the next, but Konev was anxious not to waste time in such a battle and ordered Lelyushenko to avoid being tied down:

> [Bypassing German units] is a characteristic feature of the Vistula-Oder Operation, and indeed the last period of the war. We no longer sought at all costs to create a double – external and internal – front around each such enemy group. We believed, quite correctly, that if we developed the offensive at a sufficiently rapid pace, we had no need to be concerned about the rather substantial enemy forces cut off and still functioning in our rear zones. Sooner or later they would be defeated and destroyed by the second echelon of our armies.[23]

The southern approaches to Kielce were protected by the small Czarna Nida River, just wide enough to make crossing by vehicles problematic. Lelyushenko directed 16th Guards Mechanised Brigade, part of VI Guards Mechanised Corps, to seize crossings over the river at Morawica, just nine miles (15km) south of Kielce, and there was a fierce clash between this Soviet force and elements of 16th Panzer Division that were probing south. The Germans came off worse and as they pulled back, Lieutenant Colonel Vsevolod Ezupovich Rycsh, commander of 16th Guards Mechanised Brigade, took advantage of the confusion to push his leading companies over the Czarna Nida near Morawica. Immediately, these units came under attack from elements of 20th Panzergrenadier Division, which had been directed by Nehring to protect Kielce. The result was that Rycsh was forced to adopt a defensive position, but the retreat of 16th Panzer Division left Lelyushenko with the mistaken impression that the German forces defending Kielce had suffered a major defeat. He therefore ordered X Guards Tank Corps to push on to the west; VI Guards Mechanised Corps was now to slip past the western edge of Kielce.

But the German armoured forces – both in Kielce and those that had been driven away to the west on 12 January – were far from finished. After regrouping overnight, 17th Panzer Division with the surviving Tiger tanks of *Schwere Panzer-Abteilung 424* concentrated their resources and counterattacked northeast into the flank of Lelyushenko's tank army. The first attack came from woodland near the village of Chmielnik towards the northeast and struck the flank of one of Lelyushenko's tank brigades, knocking out several tanks. The Soviet armour hastily withdrew to the village of Lisów where it was reinforced by infantry and anti-tank guns from Thirteenth Army as well as parts of VI Mechanised Corps. The Soviet units rapidly adopted a defensive technique that had proved highly effective in the past year: anti-tank units, infantry and sappers organised a line of anti-tank guns under coordinated command into a *Pakfront* and the German attack was brought to a halt. Reacting swiftly to the German attack, Lelyushenko sent an urgent signal to Colonel Nil Danilovich Chuprov, commander of X Guards Tank Corps. His tanks were now approaching the Nida River near Sobków, but Lelyushenko ordered him to turn around and attack towards the southeast, i.e. into the flank of the German armoured force. During the afternoon and evening, confused fighting continued across the area; clearing skies permitted Soviet aircraft to join the battle. At first, the longer range and accuracy of the German tanks resulted in several Soviet tanks being destroyed, but this advantage was swiftly lost as the battle developed into close-range combat in and around Lisów. At such ranges, the 85mm gun of the improved T-34s that formed the bulk of the Soviet armour was able to engage almost all German tanks with a good chance of success, and additionally the Soviet 13th Heavy Tank Regiment, with several heavyweight JS-2s, also joined the battle. Many of the Tiger tanks had penetrated into Lisów where they found themselves in a trap, and Saemisch, the battalion commander, was killed in the fighting.

To the south, Rybalko's Third Guards Tank Army reached the Nida River early on 13 January and a battalion of dismounted infantry crossed the ice to the west bank. A ford had been identified before the operation began but this proved to be unusable. Red Army sappers attempted to construct a bridge and were dismayed to find that although the river was largely as had been expected, the banks had been flooded resulting in widespread soft ground. Instead of a span of no more than 60m, they had to build a bridge of about 100m in length. Fortunately, the bridging columns accompanying Rybalko's armour were at full strength in terms both of personnel and equipment. The first bridge over the Nida was ready for tanks to cross before the end of 13 January and VI Guards Tank Corps, much of which had struggled across at an alternative fording point, began to probe west. Here, its leading units soon encountered German infantry and assault guns and engaged in inconclusive duels at long range. Rybalko sent an irritated message to Major General Vasily Vasilyevich Novikov, commander of VI Guards Tank Corps:

> You are losing time and control of your forces. I categorically order you to concentrate the main forces on the west bank of the Nida by the morning of 14 January. Organise a concentrated force, don't rush into an attack … if necessary, destroy the enemy instead of bypassing him.[24]

Although the Germans had anticipated that the main Soviet effort would emerge from the three bridgeheads on the west bank of the Vistula, they also had to consider the possibility of a surprise attack across the river itself. In order to cover this possibility and also to hinder any Soviet attack out of the Puławy bridgehead, *Sperrverband von Ahlfen* had laid thousands of 'ice mines', explosive charges placed on and in the river ice, to the south of the Soviet bridgehead. It was Ahlfen's intention to detonate these charges to break up the ice, which would then flow downstream to the north and thus into the rear of the Puławy bridgehead. Unfortunately, he lacked the sappers to make this plan a reality – early on 13 January, Ahlfen was ordered to release his *Heerespionierbrigade 70* as Army Group A struggled to create sufficient reserves to respond to the crisis to the south. Because of this withdrawal, the only two men left in the *Sperrverband* with suitable training were Ahlfen himself and his chief of staff. To make matters worse, the detonators required to trigger the charges had been repeatedly delayed and had still not arrived when Konev began his offensive out of the Sandomierz bridgehead. With his group's front-line strength reduced to three battalions of reservists and a single machine-gun battalion of regular troops, Ahlfen was more dependent than ever on his modest artillery, consisting of a motorised battalion of light howitzers. The news arriving from the south was increasingly alarming – if Soviet forces had advanced as far as reports suggested, they were already up to 60 miles (100km) to the west of the troops still nervously watching the Vistula. The only limited consolation was that at least for the moment, there was no activity in the Puławy and Magnuszew bridgeheads. Nonetheless, the concentration of Soviet forces in these bridgeheads meant that an offensive was surely just a matter of time. After securing the required permission from *OKH*, Harpe ordered 19th and 25th Panzer Divisions to start moving towards the two northern bridgeheads, together with a battlegroup from 10th Panzergrenadier Division.

The German lines facing the western side of the Sandomierz bridgehead had effectively disintegrated. To make matters worse for the Germans, the Soviet Fifty-Ninth Army had yet to make an entry into the fighting and as the rest of 1st Ukrainian Front exploded through the old German front line, Lieutenant General Ivan Terentyevich Korovnikov's army – reinforced by IV Guards Tank Corps – took up positions between Sixtieth Army to the south and Fifth Guards Army to the north. To a large extent, Korovnikov was advancing into open space. The German 304th Infantry Division, which had faced the southern side of Konev's massive assault, was still broadly intact, though it had lost most of its artillery and heavy equipment; between the northern flank of Generalleutnant Ernst Sieler's division and the next intact German unit – the hard-pressed troops of 17th Panzer Division, falling back after the failed attempt to counterattack towards Kielce – there was almost no defensive formation left. As Konev's exploitation developed on 13 January, the gap in the German lines was up to 30 miles (50km) wide.

The two tank armies deployed by Konev faced different tasks. Rybalko was aware that the limited resistance in his path could be suppressed rapidly if his leading elements concentrated their firepower, and by the end of 13 January a large section of the Nida River had been crossed. Although this broadly satisfied the objectives that had been assigned to Third Guards Tank Army for the opening phase of the operation, Rybalko fretted at what he saw as errors. His report to Konev highlighted the shortcomings:

> The leading detachments moved too slowly. The main corps were deployed in an untimely manner, as were the anti-tank units. When the enemy conducted ambushes on small roads and in villages, there was little attempt to bypass these obstacles. This led to the leading elements moving on and the main strength being left waiting to get into action. Another problem was traffic jams at river crossings ... and anti-tank ditches, mined roads, and difficult terrain ... The leading brigades moved to the Nida River quickly but showed little skill in manoeuvre or bypassing any delays they encountered. By contrast, the main forces should have progressed faster.[25]

In the headquarters of Army Group A, Harpe continued to be frustrated by a lack of accurate information. He was unsure of the exact status of Nehring's corps with its precious armoured resources, but at best the two panzer divisions were merely holding the northern shoulder of the Soviet breakthrough. Further to the south, much of Fourth Panzer Army had simply disappeared; remnants were known to be retreating, but the limited reports reaching Harpe indicated that the divisions that had been in the path of 1st Ukrainian Front had been blown to pieces. Seventeenth Army to the south remained intact, but lacked the strength do to anything about the huge hole in the German lines. For the moment, the best that Harpe could hope for was that reinforcements would arrive from other sectors to permit him to bring the Soviet advance to a halt, though even at this early stage it was clear that a great deal of territory would be lost. But matters were about to get far worse. Zhukov's 1st Belarusian Front was about to join the Soviet offensive.

# CHAPTER 4

# ZHUKOV JOINS THE OFFENSIVE: 14–16 JANUARY

Ever since the great Brusilov Offensive of 1916, Russian and Soviet armies had followed a practice of commencing major offensives in a staggered manner. To an extent, this was driven by logistic and command limitations, and allowed attention to be concentrated on each sector in turn over a few days, but there were significant tactical and operational advantages. The most important was that any major assault would result in German reserves being sent to that area in preparation for counterattacks. Starting major offensives simultaneously all along the front line might tie down German forces wherever they were located, but by staggering the start date, there was an increased chance that the Germans would have started transferring troops towards the first sector where fighting had started and would thus have fewer assets available to respond to further offensives elsewhere in the front line.

Covering the southern half of the Magnuszew bridgehead was the German 6th Volksgrenadier Division. The original 6th Infantry Division had been almost completely destroyed during the Soviet advance across Belarus in the summer of 1944 and a new 6th Grenadier Division was then created from the remnants. Barely at the strength of a single infantry battlegroup, it was dispatched to the Vistula in September to try to restore the shattered front line and in October it was renamed 6th Volksgrenadier Division. The quiet weeks that followed were put to good use by Generalleutnant Otto-Hermann Brücker, the division commander, and his staff as they tried to bring the division up to something approaching combat strength; Brücker had commanded several infantry formations and his experience in rebuilding these units was invaluable. In addition to ensuring the training of his officers and men, he took particular care to ensure that his division's field positions were as strong as possible:

> Throughout this period [leading up to 14 January] there was great emphasis on building field positions in the main battle line by the troops themselves and in the rear through the use of construction battalions … Each position was to be dug in according to our fire-plan. The division attached particular importance to three points in planning its main battle line: depth of positions; flank protection; and the construction of strongpoints. The depth of positions for the infantry in the main battle area reached past the battalion command posts to the high ground where the regimental headquarters were placed and then on to the defensive positions around the artillery. Machine-guns were deployed on the flanks of every firing point, in positions that had to be screened from observation and fire from the front, with alternative positions for firing to the front and for close-quarter fighting as well as for action at night or in fog. The heavy machine-guns deployed in echelon past the battalion command posts towards the rear provided the bare bones for the infantry fire-plan. It would have been desirable to support the infantry with 20mm machine-guns, but unfortunately these weren't available.[1]

Large-calibre machine-guns weren't the only items in short supply. As he reviewed his artillery's fire-plans, Brücker had to contend with shortages of ammunition; despite persuading Generalleutnant Hans Källner, commander of 19th Panzer Division, to hand over a large quantity of shells – the panzer division was expected to intervene in 6th Volksgrenadier Division's sector, and Brücker argued that by having the artillery ammunition already in the front line, the panzer division would be able to use the shells when it arrived without having to carry them forward – the artillery regiment of Brücker's division had barely sufficient ammunition, far less than the official requirement that would have sufficed for two or three days' fighting. But perhaps one of the most valuable morale-boosting measures for the Volksgrenadier division came from unusual acts of improvisation:

> The 'Seven White Ravens', a small cabaret troupe made up of members of the division, will always be remembered by our men. Sister Leni Magris, a representative of the *Deutschen Frauenwerk* ['German Women's Association'] was particularly involved with supporting our division. She repeatedly visited our troops in their trenches, always being greeted with great joy, bringing gifts from the homeland. A rest centre was established under her control in Radom for the division, where she provided excellent care and groups of our men spent short periods of rest and relaxation.[2]

As they considered how they would fight the forthcoming battle, Brücker and other senior officers of the division agreed that the dense concentration of Soviet units in the Magnuszew bridgehead formed a perfect target for heavy artillery bombardment – such a firestrike would badly disrupt any Soviet attack. But there was insufficient ammunition or artillery, particularly if shells had to be kept for dealing with advancing Soviet units; instructions from the headquarters of VIII Corps were that artillery should be used with forward observers directing the fire as the Soviet troops moved forward. Brücker regarded this as a mistake on the grounds that the smoke and dust that would be kicked up by the preliminary Soviet artillery preparation would make observed fire almost impossible, and managed to secure permission to use a third of the available ammunition for a spoiling counter-bombardment.

Alerted by Red Army deserters, the Wehrmacht correctly estimated that the Soviet offensive out of the Magnuszew and Puławy bridgeheads would commence on 14 January, and 6th Volksgrenadier Division's artillery opened fire as planned before dawn on the dense positions of the Soviet forces facing it in the Magnuszew bridgehead. Soviet accounts make no mention of this spoiling bombardment, suggesting that it had little impact. By contrast, the artillery preparation planned by 1st Belarusian Front was on a completely different scale. The commander of 6th Volksgrenadier Division later described the bombardment as heavier than any that he or his men had ever experienced. Opposite the German division was Fifth Shock Army's Soviet 301st Rifle Division, commanded by Colonel Viktor Semenovich Antonov. He described the morning of the offensive:

> It was 0630 local time, still dark. And suddenly a mighty glow, flaring up swiftly in the east, illuminated the Vistula valley. The thunder of artillery fire from the east and the explosion of shells on the frozen ground of the enemy's defences merged into a continuous roar. The entire Nazi defence system disappeared in the explosions of howitzer and mortar shells. The artillery preparation had begun ...
>
> The artillery preparation lasted 25 minutes. The signal 'Attack!' was given and the leading battalion from 1052nd Regiment moved forward.[3]

Like Konev, Zhukov had modified earlier Red Army doctrine in terms of artillery preparation. Early on 14 January, the massed guns of 1st Belarusian Front struck the lines of the German LVI Panzer Corps opposite the Puławy bridgehead and VIII Corps facing the Magnuszew bridgehead; these were subordinated to Lüttwitz's Ninth Army. For 25 minutes, an intense bombardment rained down on the German positions. When the shelling ceased, about 22 rifle battalions reinforced by heavy tanks and assault guns moved forward to conduct what was effectively an energetic reconnaissance in force. The necessity for rigid plans that had to be followed regardless of how they were progressing was a thing of the past; Zhukov intended to await the outcome of this initial attack before deciding whether a further artillery bombardment was necessary. If the reconnaissance in force made good progress, he would commit his main assault forces without any further shelling. As had been the case with Konev's offensive, the weather was unfavourable for air operations.

From his division command post, Brücker peered into the thick fog, trying in vain to see what was happening; although shells had landed all around his headquarters, casualties were modest, but most telephone cables had been destroyed and signallers set out to find and repair the breaks. His frustration that so much of his artillery ammunition had been held back so that it could be used in observed fire was obvious to his staff, particularly as foggy conditions had prevailed for several days and the conditions on the day of the attack were therefore predictable. The best that the gunners could do was open fire on pre-designated sectors in the hope that the Red Army would attack as the Germans had anticipated.

When they advanced, the Soviet battalions conducting the reconnaissance in force rapidly overran the first line of German defences, with the reduced visibility greatly hindering the ability of German anti-tank gunners and machine-gunners to use their weapons to maximum effect. With barely a pause, the attackers pressed on to the second line, their accompanying tanks and assault guns rapidly suppressing bunkers and strongpoints. The initial bombardment had been highly effective, leaving the German divisions in considerable disarray and knocking out much of their artillery. As reports began to arrive of these initial Soviet successes, Zhukov decided to commit his main forces without any further artillery preparation.

Zhukov had squeezed two combined arms armies into the Puławy bridgehead – Sixty-Ninth Army in the north and Thirty-Third Army in the south; such were the constraints on space that it was necessary for most of the two tank corps assigned as exploitation forces to wait on the east bank of the Vistula. The larger Magnuszew bridgehead also contained two combined arms armies – Fifth Shock Army in the north and Eighth Guards Army in the south – with First and Second Guards Tank Armies waiting beyond the Vistula for their chance to enter the action. Antonov rapidly committed the first echelon of his 301st Rifle Division to support the successful reconnaissance probes and his troops were soon picking their way forward through dense woodland. It took until midday to clear the German second defensive line fully. The next objective was the Pilica River and Antonov directed an assault engineer battalion, reinforced by assault guns, to

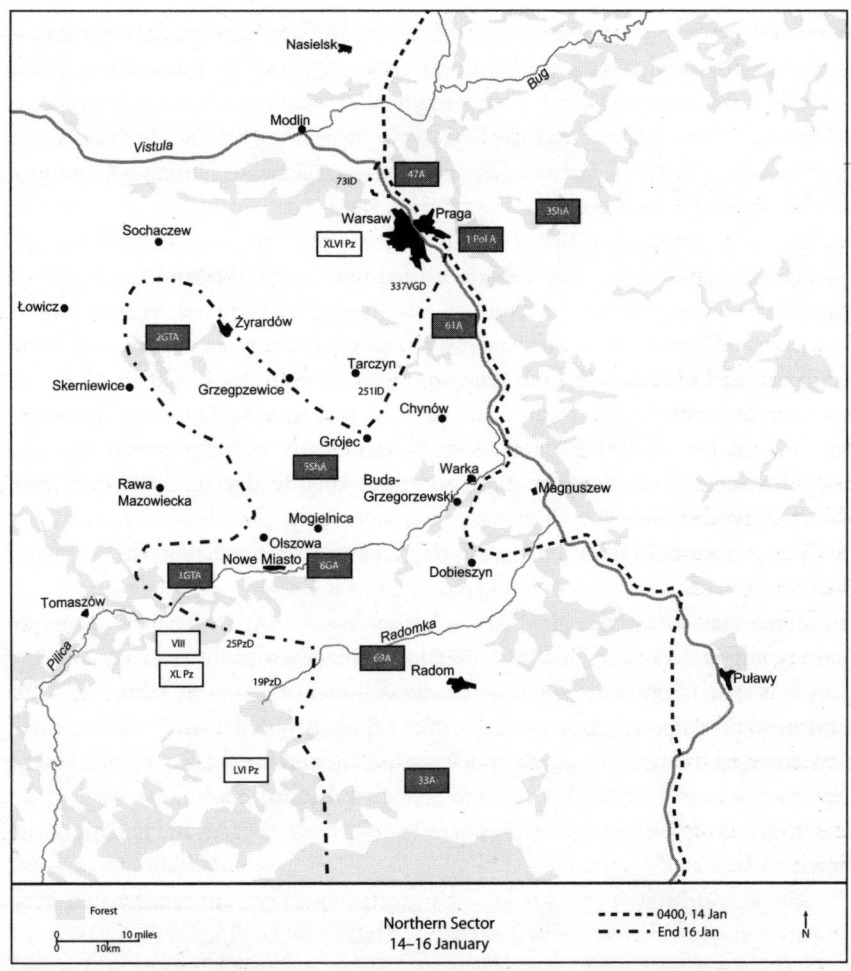

Nasielsk

Modlin

Vistula

73ID

47A

Warsaw  Praga

XLVI Pz  1 Pol A

3ShA

Sochaczew

Łowicz

337VGD

2GTA  Żyrardów

61A

Skerniewice  Grzegpzewice

Tarczyn

251ID

Chynów

Grójec

5ShA  Warka

Rawa  Buda-

Mazowiecka  Grzegorzewski  Magnuszew

Mogielnica

Olszowa

Rawa  Nowe Miasto  8GA

Tomaszów  Dobieszyn

Pilica  Radomka

VIII  25PzD

XL Pz  69A

19PzD  Radom  Puławy

LVI Pz

33A

Bug

1GTA

Forest

10 miles

10km

Northern Sector
14–16 January

━ ━ ━  0400, 14 Jan
━ · ━ ·  End 16 Jan

N

seize crossings. To the south, Chuikov's Eighth Guards Army also made steady
progress through the German lines; having avoided the need for a second
bombardment, Chuikov's artillery commanders were able to allocate substantial
fire support for operations the following day. Late in the morning, as the attacking
rifle formations encountered stiffening resistance, Eighth Guards Army's massed
guns – Chuikov estimated that he had up to 250 barrels per kilometre of front
line – fired a further brief bombardment.[4] But there was a marked contrast to
events further south. Unlike Konev's 1st Ukrainian Front, the assault by Zhukov's
1st Belarusian Front failed to achieve the devastation inflicted by the forces that
erupted out of the Sandomierz bridgehead. To an extent, this reflected different

geography, with Zhukov's armies having to operate from two smaller bridgeheads and facing forested terrain as they moved forward. However, Zhukov had a long record of not taking account of the ground over which his forces were expected to advance. Such failures cost the Red Army huge casualties in 1942 and 1943, particularly around the Rzhev salient and the approaches to Leningrad, and now his formations once more paid a heavy price in blood.

The two panzer divisions that had been alerted and ordered to move into preparatory positions a day before were thrown into counterattacks. Acting under the direct control of Harpe's army group headquarters, 19th Panzer Division had started to concentrate just to the east of the town of Mogielnica and 25th Panzer Division had formed up around Radom. A combined attack by the two divisions was of course the best option and they were directed to deal with the Magnuszew bridgehead first; if the Soviet attack here could be halted, the divisions would then be sent south to the Puławy bridgehead. Källner's 19th Panzer Division moved to Dobieszyn, its deployment hindered by the thick fog with several columns losing their way. The terrain of low hills and dense woodland was far from ideal for armoured operations, and the persistent fog eliminated the substantial advantage that the German tanks enjoyed with their better accuracy at long range. Still struggling to re-establish contact with his regiments, Brücker was told that 19th Panzer Division would commence its counterattack at 1130 and used his intermittent communications to alert his infantrymen; but when the designated time arrived, the attack was postponed for two hours because the division was still struggling to move into position. Only one of its two panzergrenadier regiments had reached the forming up area before the Soviet offensive began.

This second start time was also abandoned and it was only later that 19th Panzer Division finally probed forward. Almost immediately, it ran into the leading elements of Eighth Guards Army, moving forward from the Magnuszew bridgehead. Briefly, there was a potentially dangerous moment for the Soviet forces, with German armour appearing on the flank of Chuikov's army, but the anti-tank units that Chuikov had already deployed to protect his attacking formations stopped 19th Panzer Division's battlegroup. Due to the delays, the original German plan for a major counterattack was reduced to a far less ambitious operation, aiming just to buy some time for the infantry divisions in the front line to move their artillery further to the rear. The incident gets no more than a passing mention in Chuikov's account and barely disrupted his forward movement. For the hard-pressed soldiers of 6th Volksgrenadier Division, the delays proved costly. By midday, one of the division's regiments was effectively surrounded.

In keeping with the doctrine described by Konev, Chuikov's forces pressed on, leaving the isolated Volksgrenadiers to their second echelon. A German artillery officer who had moved forward in a vain attempt to direct artillery fire from his guns was killed when the isolated regimental headquarters was hit by shellfire, and the regiment commander died shortly afterwards as he tried to shoot at a passing Red Army tank with a *Panzerfaust*.

The reports of 19th Panzer Division describe a course of events completely at odds with Soviet accounts, with the division's panzer regiment and a panzergrenadier regiment combining in a powerful and effective counterattack that knocked out over 50 Soviet tanks and forced the rest to withdraw.[5] For this attack, the commander of the panzergrenadier regiment was awarded the Knight's Cross, but regardless of the true timing and nature of the battle, any German success was short-lived and 19th Panzer Division was forced to pull back late on 14 January. Communications between Brücker's 6th Volksgrenadier Division headquarters, subordinate units, neighbouring formations, and higher commands remained intermittent at best, but all the reports that arrived were bad. A second regimental commander was killed as the day progressed, and there was almost no contact with individual battalions. During the afternoon, Soviet riflemen and tanks penetrated into the division's artillery positions and were engaged in direct fire. It was an uneven fight and the gunners were soon killed, taken prisoner or driven off. By the evening, the artillery regiment had been reduced to just eight guns.[6] This is in complete contrast to the account of the fighting described in the history of 19th Panzer Division, which suggests that it was possible for the infantry division to withdraw its artillery as a result of the limited counterattack of 14 January.[7]

On the northern flank of 19th Panzer Division, 25th Panzer Division fared a little better, pushing back the first units it encountered. These were the leading elements of Fifth Shock Army and confused fighting continued throughout the afternoon of 14 January with substantial losses on both sides, but the Soviet forces were in a better position to absorb such casualties. The German counterattack had a significant impact on Antonov, whose division was leading the advance of Fifth Shock Army:

> The enemy suddenly appeared in front of our combat units as if emerging from the ground. Either he approached us under cover of the forest or he mounted a rapid counterattack. And our forward units met the enemy face to face …
>
> The German command clearly wasn't prepared to accept the loss of its second line along the railway line and threw its reserves into a counterattack on a broad front. The dark forest began to roar with the sounds of combat. The German

counterattack against Colonel Radaev's regiment ran into Major Hayrapetyan's battalion. The battalion opened fire and engaged them in hand-to-hand combat. Fighting raged for an hour. Supported by the regiment's artillery group, the battalion defeated the enemy infantry and advanced forward rapidly …

Fierce fighting continued in the forest for two hours but the Germans were defeated. Major Ishak Gumerov's regiment went forward to the Pilica River. Radaev's regiment turned to face north and reached the edge of the forest east of Marynka. Dense lines of German infantry supported by tanks counterattacked from Buda-Grzegorzewski. The enemy's heavy artillery began to fire from the area to the northwest of Warka. I reported the situation to [Major] General [Ivan Pavlovich] Roslyi [Antonov's corps commander] and asked for suppressive fire against the Warka area. The request was passed to the army commander, who decided to respond with the entire army's artillery group.

The army artillery commander, Lieutenant General Pyotr Ivanovich Kosenko, personally took control of 10th Artillery Brigade. About ten minutes later, shells flew over us with a loud hiss towards the enemy's artillery positions. The bombardment of my leading regiment lessened steadily.

During the afternoon, the enemy continued to counterattack fiercely with large numbers of tanks. Major Sotnikov's artillery engaged the tanks …12 tanks and assault guns were knocked out.[8]

Despite this intense fighting, Fifth Shock Army continued to move forward, reaching and crossing the frozen Pilica River during the evening. Antonov was most of the way over the river when a German shell landed nearby, smashing the ice. He was briefly stunned by a chunk of ice that struck his head and fell into the river; one of his officers hauled him up the far bank. Temporarily, Antonov's chief of staff, Colonel Mikhail Ivanovich Safonov, took command of the division.

The steady disintegration of 6th Volksgrenadier Division was typical of the fate of the German infantry formations facing the Soviet offensive. As the short winter day drew to a close, it had ceased to function as a coherent fighting unit. Most of its artillery was gone and Brücker had command of just one of his three regiments; the remnants of the other two had been subordinated to the panzer divisions. When a signal arrived from Oberstleutnant Müller, the regiment commander, that he was being forced to adopt all-round defence, Brücker ordered him to withdraw; he had already seen his other two regiments isolated and almost completely destroyed while they waited in vain for the panzer divisions to counterattack. Fortunately for the Germans, further help was at hand.

The German Pz.III tank was effectively obsolete by the end of 1942 but production of the tried and tested chassis continued throughout the war; instead of being built as a tank, it was used as an assault gun with a long-barrelled 75mm gun in a fixed mount. Although this had limited lateral traverse, it was a potent tank-killer and, organised into brigades, these *Sturmgeschütz* formations provided invaluable support for the Wehrmacht. One such formation was *Heeres-Sturmgeschütz-Lehr-Brigade 920* ('Army 920th Training Assault Gun Brigade') under the command of Major Wolfgang Kapp and deployed as part of 19th Panzer Division. As his brigade moved forward, Kapp encountered a small group of Soviet tanks, destroying or driving them off, and was then ordered to move forward to establish contact with Müller's isolated regiment. Early in the evening, the assault guns reached Müller's headquarters. Müller wasted no time, breaking out to the south with the aid of the assault guns.[9]

The only significant German reserves available to Ninth Army were now tied down, and even if they had brought the Red Army formations immediately in front of them to a halt, they were unable to intervene against other formations. The only hope for such modest reserves to make a decisive difference had been if they could achieve quick successes, and that possibility was lost. By the end of the day, 1st Belarusian Front was moving forward at a satisfactory rate, though the German lines were still just about intact. But Zhukov's tank armies had yet to enter the battle, and the ability of the Germans to resist such powerful formations was very limited.

Generally, the Soviet units were fighting well, but with the end of the war clearly not far in the future, some men inevitably began to think about how they might increase their chances of surviving to see peace. This sometimes resulted in unusual incidents. Arkady Grigorevich Vesterman, a tank crewman, described an episode involving a crew from his formation:

> One crew came back from the battlefield on foot, all without any injuries, and the commander of the T-34 reported that a shell hit the side of the tank, the vehicle was set ablaze, and somehow they miraculously survived unscathed. But the tank was in an area held by us and when the brigade's repair crews approached the burned tank, they found no hole left by any shell. And the ammunition should have detonated after such a hit, but this hadn't happened. The repairmen were suspicious and reported their findings to *SMERSH* and a senior 'special officer' immediately rolled up his sleeves and began to pressure the crew hard. One of the tankers broke ranks and 'betrayed' the crew, admitting that they all decided together that they didn't want to die and by agreement threw an anti-tank grenade into their tank. The crew was shot after court martial in front of the entire brigade.[10]

Meanwhile, in the south, Konev continued to urge his units forward on 14 January. The German 17th Panzer Division remained concentrated in woodland between the town of Chmielnik and the Nida River, but lacked the strength to continue its attempts to break through to the rest of XXIV Panzer Corps. There were continuing clashes between Lisów and Chmielnik, with the scattered units of both sides now intermingled; this made intervention by air power and artillery almost impossible. With his division now effectively fighting as individual battalions and companies, Brux had little control over the battle. During the afternoon of 14 January, his command post was overrun and he was taken prisoner. The Soviet forces also suffered losses of senior personnel; the commander of a tank brigade was badly wounded and died a few days later.[11]

The small Soviet bridgehead over the Czarna Nida to the south of Kielce had been expanded overnight, but for the moment the Soviet forces here lacked the strength to drive off 20th Panzergrenadier Division. Lelyushenko was already moving his formations away towards the west, and Konev directed Third Guards Army to attack and destroy the German forces around Kielce.

Confident that they would not encounter any strong German formations, the Soviet tank forces rapidly reorganised into an 'exploitation deployment' with a forward reinforced tank brigade leading each tank corps; in addition to their tanks, these brigades had motorised infantry, mounted mainly on trucks but in a few cases in US-supplied half-tracks, with combat engineers, anti-tank guns, mortars, and *Katyusha* rocket-launchers. These brigades in turn sent forward smaller reconnaissance detachments. If German units were encountered, the brigade commander had to make a choice between overwhelming the enemy or bypassing him, depending on his strength. It is a measure of the growing skill of the Red Army's officers that they were able to show such initiative, something that would have been almost unknown in operations up to (and in many cases during) 1944. Whilst the Kielce fighting may have tied down some of Lelyushenko's units, Rybalko had no such constraints. During 14 January, Third Guards Tank Army secured a bridge over the Nida River at Motkowice; leaving a small force to hold the crossings until Fifty-Second Army arrived, Rybalko motored onwards. By the end of the day, his leading units had reached Nagłowice, 40 miles (64km) from the original front line.

The Germans were in no position to do anything to hinder the armies of 1st Ukrainian Front. Too many divisions had disintegrated on 12 and 13 January, and after the heavy fighting around the approaches to Kielce the two panzer divisions of Nehring's corps were short of ammunition and fuel. The lines of the German XLII Corps, on the Vistula to the north of the Sandomierz bridgehead

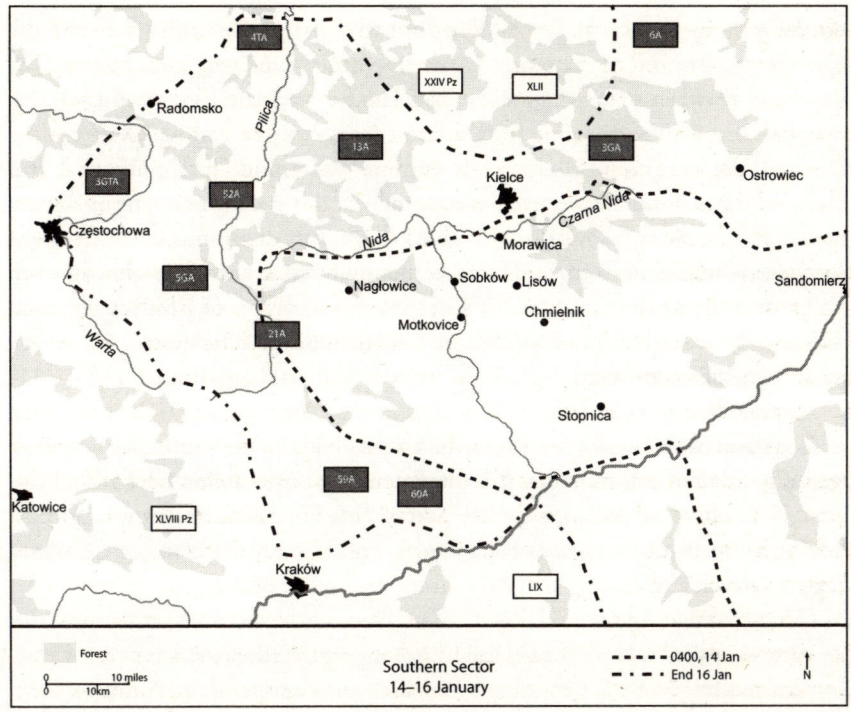

Southern Sector
14–16 January

– – – – 0400, 14 Jan
–·–·– End 16 Jan

Forest

0        10 miles
0      10km

N

and to the south of the Puławy bridgehead, remained largely quiet, though the troops could hear the sounds of artillery fire and fighting on either side and there were some local penetrations. Despite worrying reports slowly arriving from either flank, Recknagel's orders remained unchanged – he was to continue holding the Vistula bank. Past experience had taught all German commanders that permission for a withdrawal often arrived too late, and Recknagel issued verbal orders to his divisions to start moving all 'non-essential' troops back from the river.

From the headquarters of Army Group A, Harpe sent a signal to *OKH*. The Soviet forces that had effectively smashed Fourth Panzer Army were unstoppable with the units available. There was a high likelihood of a threat developing towards Upper Silesia and its industrial resources; without substantial reinforcements, it would be impossible to prevent the last major intact industrial region of Germany from being overrun. It must have been very clear to Harpe that reinforcements on the scale required were not going to be provided. The situation was already disastrous for Fourth Panzer Army and was rapidly deteriorating for Ninth Army to its north. So far, the front line around the two northern bridgeheads was just holding, but the German defenders were rapidly approaching the end of their strength. Harpe ordered the surviving remnants of the forces that faced the Magnuszew and Puławy bridgeheads to pull back to a new line that ran northwards from a point just north of Radom. Whether the battered, depleted units could reach the line was doubtful. The fog that had persisted throughout the day had dispersed a little and as his division headquarters moved to its new location, Brücker could see flickers of gunfire in the darkness to the east where isolated remnants of his units continued to fight. His 6th Volksgrenadier Division was reduced to just the survivors of Müller's regiment – about 200 men – and the handful of guns that escaped the destruction of the division's artillery regiment.

Zhukov had held back his tank armies in the expectation that the combined arms armies would break the German defences, and both tank army commanders restlessly awaited the moment that they would go into action. Babadzhanian, whose XI Guards Tank Corps formed part of First Guards Tank Army, was in the headquarters of XXIX Guards Rifle Corps, one of the formations of Chuikov's Eighth Guards Army:

After the combined arms armies had broken through the enemy's tactical defence zone to a depth of 15–20km [up to 12 miles], our First Guards Tank Army was tasked with exiting the Magnuszew bridgehead, entering the breakthrough on the the second morning, and then rapidly developing the offensive towards Nowe Miasto, Rawa Mazowiecka, Skierniewice, Łovicz, Kutno, and by the end of the fifth day of the operation we were to capture the Kutno-Lechnitsa area and continue the advance towards Koło and Poznań. Throughout the day [14 January], thousands of tanks, assault guns, and armoured personnel carriers crossed seven bridges over the Vistula to the roar of the powerful artillery fire. The steel armada, ready to go into battle, was just waiting for the command.

At the command post of XXIX Guards Rifle Corps ... there was animation and the bustle of work; communications officers scurried about, radio and telephone operators shouted into microphones. The staff of [Major] General Afanasy Dmitrievich] Shemenkov [the rifle corps commander] glanced at us repeatedly in expectation. Finally, Shemenkov lost patience and asked, 'When, my tanker friends, are you going to start hostilities? Or will you only be picking up loot for my infantry?'

I understood his impatience, but he had to understand that we didn't make our own orders. 'Someone should pick up the loot,' I replied to him ... I felt uneasy with the enforced wait. The advance detachment ... crossed to the west bank of the Vistula on the night of 14–15 January.[12]

In an attempt to break the last German resistance, Chuikov had organised a fresh artillery bombardment for the morning of 15 January, taking advantage of the ammunition that had not been used the previous day. Despite intensive shelling, the German lines continued to hold up Eighth Guards Army for several hours, slowly falling back to the railway line running from Radom to Warka. Chuikov was aware that Zhukov and the two tank army commanders were increasingly impatient and that while his army was still moving forward, it was now several hours behind schedule:

At noon, our troops attacked the enemy-held railway embankment. How much would air strikes have helped us at this moment, but the planes were still unable to take off from their airfields due to fog.

After speaking to the commanders of Fifth Shock and Sixty-Ninth Armies … and reporting my situation and decisions to the Front commander, I went forward to IV Guards Rifle Corps with [Major] General [Alexei Mikhailovich] Pronin, a member of my military council, and a group of other officers. We drove in the fog along roads clogged with vehicles, making our way with difficulty to the village of Ignacuvka where Lieutenant General [Vasily Afanasevich] Glazunov's command post was located. He reported that 47th Rifle Division had made the best progress. The division commander was [Major General] Vasily Minaevich Shugaev, a strong-willed, enterprising general with admirable courage. He had fought all through Ukraine and usually led from the front. Shugaev was in his command post near the railway at the very centre of events.

I decided to visit him. Along the way, Glazunov showed me 12 completely serviceable German six-barrelled rocket launchers captured in the village. They stood in a fighting position facing east. There were piles of shells nearby. The enemy hadn't fired a single shot from these weapons. They simply didn't have time. Our attack mixed up the Nazis so much that they abandoned everything without even having time to destroy the launchers.

From Shugaev's command post we watched the attack of the division as its battle formations climbed a ridge north of the village of Olszowa. Satisfied with the successful development of the attack we went north … Here we met the commander of the armoured and mechanised forces of my army, [Major] General [Matvey Grigorievich] Vainrub. He had assembled a tank group and together with the commanders of rifle units from XXIX Corps, led the battle for the railroad, ensuring cooperation between the tanks and infantry.

The enemy resisted stubbornly, taking advantage of the station buildings and adjacent forest. The fire from his anti-tank guns and machine-guns blocked our advance. Behind Vainrub's rifle regiments and tanks stood the columns of First

Guards Tank Army. They were the vanguard of Katukov's units, waiting for the breakthrough to be cleared. We had to drive the enemy from the railway line and then the tank army, breaking into operational space, would split the enemy's front. We prepared a fresh artillery strike to be followed by an assault by infantry and tanks – this would tip the balance in our favour. But the sun was already setting and there was only about an hour of daylight left.[13]

Babadzhanian was finally unleashed in mid-afternoon. The leading detachment of his XI Guards Tank Corps was 44th Guards Tank Brigade, under the command of the redoubtable Colonel Iosif Iraklievich Gusakovsky. From the moment that he took command of a tank brigade during the Battle of Kursk when his predecessor was killed, he led with great flair and distinction, and his brigade – now reinforced with assault guns, mortars, anti-aircraft guns and combat engineers – surged past Chuikov's riflemen and pressed on, exchanging fire with German strongpoints. The rest of the corps followed swiftly. Such advances had often ended in disaster in the past; German infantry formations would allow Soviet armour to move through their line and would then reform, preventing infantry from joining the tanks. Without the tanks, the Soviet riflemen were then crushed with artillery and machine-gun fire while they tried desperately to follow the armour, and the unaccompanied tanks were easy prey for anti-tank units. But now, the German forces lacked the strength needed for such tactics. The infantry formations were too weak to restore their positions after the Red Army tanks had rampaged past, and what few anti-tank weapons were available were all committed to the front line. Moreover, the Soviet rifle regiments were accompanied by tanks and assault guns that belonged to their division and were under strict orders not to press on into the depths of the German positions on their own.

The entry of XI Guards Tank Corps into the battle was not without difficulties; the northern flank in particular struggled in the face of German resistance and terrain issues, but Babadzhanian was quick to exploit the success of Gusakovsky's brigade on his southern flank. He showed a level of tactical adaptability that hitherto had been a hallmark of German operations and left a reinforced battalion of motorised infantry to defend against German units to the north of his corps; he switched the rest of the corps to follow Gusakovsky's advance. The first tanks reached the Pilica River as darkness fell. A small bridgehead was swiftly established and Gusakovsky's combat engineers reported that they thought they had found a ford. Immediately, Gusakovsky ordered his armoured vehicles to cross. But either the engineers were mistaken, or the vehicles deviated from the ford – a few tanks succeeded in crossing, but six T-34s and two assault guns had to be abandoned in the icy water.[14] The tank crews faced a further frustrating wait while bridging engineers worked through the night, erecting a pontoon bridge.

Chuikov's Eighth Guards Army and First Guards Tank Army were attacking towards the southwest in the corridor of land between the Pilica and Radomka Rivers; to their north, Fifth Shock Army and Second Guards Tank Army pushed west and northwest. Throughout 15 January, 19th Panzer Division and Kapp's assault gun brigade continued to put up tough resistance with the support of the remaining elements of 6th Volksgrenadier Division, but there was no real contact with 25th Panzer Division, which was meant to be operating close to the Pilica River. During the afternoon, the Red Army took advantage of this breach in the German lines. First Guards Tank Army moved into the gap, rapidly making the position of the German forces still holding the line to the north of Radom untenable. Fortunately for the survivors of 6th Volksgrenadier Division, 19th Panzer Division had sufficient motorised transport capacity to take the surviving infantrymen with it as it pulled back to the southwest over the Radomka River.

Throughout the first half of 15 January, Antonov's 301st Rifle Division had its hands full dealing with repeated German counterattacks from Generalmajor Oskar Audörsch's 25th Panzer Division:

> The situation on the battlefield was getting worse. A new wave of German tanks and infantry appeared from Grzegorzewice and advanced towards our 1052nd Rifle Regiment. Black lines of soldiers moved towards 1050th Rifle Regiment ... It was a particularly strong counterattack. The Germans advanced through our artillery barrage and broke into the division's positions. Close-quarter fighting began ...
>
> Another line of Fascists broke through the artillery barrage and climbed the steep slope to our ridge. I ordered the division reserves into battle. Colonel Safonov [Antonov's chief of staff] gave a signal. A series of red flares soared over Lechanica. My deputy, Colonel Vasily Emelyanovich Shevtsov, led the division reserve forward. Colonel Kazantsev commanded his assault gun battalion to attack the enemy.
>
> Dense lines of riflemen from the division reserve and machine-gunners rolled over the crest of the ridge on a frontage of about 2km next to our command post. The roaring engines of the assault guns added to the general thunder of shellfire. The blow by the division's reserves was so strong that not only did the enemy fall back, but positively fled before our eyes.
>
> However, this didn't stop the enemy. Soon, more columns emerged from the forest and deployed in line. [The division's artillery commanders] transferred the fire of their artillery regiment from one attacking wave of Fascists to another.

By midday we had repulsed five counterattacks. Gunfire thundered ceaselessly. In the morning, the landscape had been covered with pure white snow, but now everything had turned black. The earth was scarred by the explosions of artillery shells. There were corpses of soldiers everywhere. Tanks burned brightly.[15]

Bogdanov's Second Guards Tank Army began crossing the Pilica at midday, together with elements of II Guards Cavalry Corps. Isaak Izrailevich Uritskiy, a tank crewman, was one of those waiting to move forward:

Ahead of us, a penal company led the attack in black pea jackets and opened the way for us, their corpses lying everywhere on the battlefield. We entered the breakthrough, our tanks moving like an avalanche, a mixture of T-34s and JS-2s. We formed a line to make the attack. In front of us was a stream and low-lying ground that was covered by water. There was a steep hillock on the other side and we thought there might be 'Faustniks' [i.e. German troops with *Panzerfausts*] on the crest. We crossed the stream but couldn't climb the hill. Just as we reached the ridge, our tank stopped and skidded backwards. The rest of the brigade broke through the defences and moved on. They threw some rations to us and told us to wait for recovery. A tractor came up with a crane, but it couldn't pull us out. Another tractor arrived, but they could barely move us. It was now dark. We had to remove two engine covers, then remove the crank case, drain the water from the cylinders, and then reassemble everything. We managed this with difficulty overnight and then set off to catch up with everyone else.[16]

By now, the German counterattacks had come to an end and the German defences were in no shape to resist the appearance of fresh forces. A mixed group of tanks and cavalry, accompanied by riflemen from Antonov's division, rapidly seized the villages from which 25th Panzer Division had made its repeated attacks. The Soviet armour then motored on through the evening towards the northwest, aiming to cut the roads and railways running west from Warsaw.

The attacks by 25th Panzer Division were accompanied by other German attempts to counterattack. The line of the Vistula immediately south of Warsaw was held by 337th Volksgrenadier Division. The division commander, Generalleutnant Eberhard Kinzel, had been head of *Fremde Heere Ost* before the German invasion of the Soviet Union in 1941 and had overseen the collection of information that led to a catastrophic underestimate of Red Army strength. Although he had held several staff roles including chief of staff of Army Group North, this was his first significant front-line command. General Walter Fries, commander of XLVI Panzer Corps, ordered Kinzel to organise a battlegroup for use against the Magnuszew bridgehead as soon as Zhukov's attack began; the group consisted of two of the division's Volksgrenadier regiments, the personnel and trainees of Ninth Army's *Armeewaffenschule* ('Army Weaponry School', a training establishment to allow new recruits to learn how to use a variety of support weapons), and perhaps a further company of troops, and concentrated at the southern edge of the division's sector at Chynów.

As Bogdanov's tank army began to cross the Pilica, the battlegroup from 337th Volksgrenadier Division came under increasingly heavy artillery fire. Although the group was known as *Kampfgruppe Kinzel*, the senior officer in Chynów was Oberst Gerhard Klein and he ordered an immediate attack against the Soviet bridgehead over the Pilica. Pantenius, who had earlier been involved in the attempt to disarm Hungarian troops, was on the west flank of the counterattack with his regiment:

> The preparation area of I Battalion was very close to the firing position of a 210mm mortar battery, but this had already left the area when we arrived; we couldn't expect its support. The enemy had spotted the preparation area and laid down such a heavy artillery bombardment that any major movement was impossible. The regiment staff, which was close behind I Battalion, was unable to take command, at least for the moment; communications were cut. Although the leading elements of the rifle companies managed to gain a little ground, the attack was soon brought to a standstill by fire from the massed Russian artillery and heavy weapons. The amount of terrain gained was small. Orientation in the fairly featureless terrain was made even more difficult by the dense haze created by shell impacts all around. Although the enemy didn't attack towards us any further, the battlegroup's intention to throw the enemy back across the Pilica was hardly begun before all attacking groups had to stop.[17]

Given that there was no longer any real prospect of preventing the Soviet forces on the northern side of the Magnuszew bridgehead from breaking through the German lines, Fries contacted Lüttwitz, commander of Ninth Army. He pointed out that if his XLVI Panzer Corps stayed in and around Warsaw, it faced certain destruction – the only sensible option was an immediate withdrawal to the A2 line to the west of the city. Moreover, it would only be possible to hold Warsaw for any significant period if most of XLVI Panzer Corps retreated into the city, which would effectively leave no German forces in the path of 1st Belarusian Front's advance towards the west. Lüttwitz agreed and passed on the request to Harpe at the headquarters of Army Group A, who in turn had to try to get permission from

Guderian at *OKH*, but the chief of the general staff was absent from his headquarters. Instead, the head of the Operations Department, Oberst Bogislav von Bonin, promised to locate Guderian as quickly as possible. In the meantime, Warsaw had to be held. Harpe knew that even once Guderian was informed, he would have to secure Hitler's permission for the abandonment of Warsaw. Even in the best possible circumstances, such an arrangement was cumbersome and likely to be overtaken by the rapidly changing events on the ground.

Whilst unwelcome, such delays were now so commonplace that they came as no surprise. Soviet forces were converging from north and south around Warsaw and it was vital for Fries' XLVI Panzer Corps for the road and rail links to the west to be kept open in the hope that permission for a withdrawal would arrive before it was too late. Accordingly, Fries ordered the creation of a new battlegroup under the command of Oberst Otto Dorow, commander of one of 337th Volksgrenadier Division's regiments. Using all available means of transport, Dorow's regiment was rushed to Żyrardów, about 26 miles (42km) from the centre of Warsaw, with orders to carry out a limited attack towards the south – this would effectively be into the flank of the Soviet armour threatening the lines of communication from the south. At the same time, 337th Volksgrenadier Division's sappers, reinforced by corps-level units, would continue to hold the old front line. Pantenius was to take up a position midway between his current position and *Kampfgruppe Dorow*:

As ordered, I Battalion disengaged during the afternoon after fighting in which neither side made any headway and left the bicycle-mounted II Battalion to act as the rear guard … I Battalion and regimental units marched … to Tarczyn, 15km [nine miles] north of Grójec on the main road to Warsaw with orders to halt the enemy's thrust towards this vital road junction. Most of *Kampfgruppe Kinzel* and the remnants of 251st Infantry Division subsequently moved towards Jeziorna. The line of march to Tarczyn was about 30km [18 miles]. Without II Battalion, the regiment reached Tarczyn at about 2200. In order to familiarise myself with the situation at our new location I drove ahead in a Volkswagen with a radio team, checking a wide area around Grójec and Tarczyn, reaching the latter as darkness fell.

An amazing surprise awaited me in Tarczyn. I was greeted cheerfully by the commander of a heavy artillery battalion of 210mm mortars from whom I learned that not only this heavy battalion but also another artillery battalion, an anti-aircraft battalion, and two heavy anti-tank companies with 88mm guns were there without any infantry cover and most importantly without any further instructions as they had no contact with corps headquarters of 251st Infantry Division. We quickly agreed that as the senior staff officer, I would temporarily take command of this considerable force and that I would immediately deploy the approaching I Battalion on the high ground south of Tarczyn and would try to establish contact with my division. With such artillery and anti-tank firepower, we could repulse any attack along the road to Tarczyn.

The biggest handicap of this force was the almost complete lack of fuel and the four motorised artillery units were practically immobile. We had no contact with the enemy. The resistance of the sappers at Grójec had made the Russians cautious. With the arrival of I Battalion and our mortar company, we were able to provide a degree of infantry protection. But the men were completely exhausted from their earlier fighting and the strenuous march; apart from sentries and scouting parties, everyone was ordered to get some sleep. No enemy attack was expected until 16 January.[18]

The German lines facing the Puławy bridgehead had also collapsed during the day and the Soviet Sixty-Ninth and Thirty-Third Armies were now rapidly approaching Radom from the east. The exploitation forces in this bridgehead consisted of VII Guards Cavalry Corps and IX and XI Tank Corps. The cavalry corps had been held back due to the limited space available in the bridgehead and spent most of 15 January crossing the Vistula, but the two tank corps went into action at about midday. They rapidly found gaps in the German lines and by nightfall XI Tank Corps had reached and bypassed the northern outskirts of Radom. IX Tank Corps was similarly operating in open space to the south of the city. There was still a narrow gap between the Soviet forces breaking out of Zhukov's two bridgeheads, and two German divisions – 45th Volksgrenadier Division and 17th Infantry Division – began a desperate race to try to escape encirclement. Generalmajor Max Sachsenheimer, at 35 the second youngest general in the German armed forces, gathered together what remained of his 17th Infantry Division and conducted a determined fighting withdrawal, clashing repeatedly with Soviet units that had bypassed the Germans. By the time it reached Radom, Sachsenheimer's division was reduced to barely 1,000 men and had abandoned all its artillery and heavy equipment; 45th Volksgrenadier Division broke up and was almost completely destroyed on 15 and 16 January.

In the south, the tank armies that had burst out of the Sandomierz bridgehead continued to motor onwards. Lelyushenko had turned his XXV Tank Corps to bypass Kielce to the west, while X Guards Tank Corps and VI Guards Mechanised Corps moved into open space to the northwest. Supported by the tanks of XXV Tank Corps, the riflemen of Thirteenth Army and Third Guards Army moved into Kielce during 15 January. There was heavy fighting on the eastern and southern approaches to the city throughout the morning, with much of the urban area falling to the Red Army by midday. Nehring had been ordered by Gräser to hold the line of the Czarna Nida to the south of Kielce, but although much of 20th Panzergrenadier Division remained on the river, this was clearly an untenable position. Nevertheless, the commander of XXIV Panzer Corps wanted to hold on for as long as possible to give the neighbouring XLII Corps time to pull back. However, even as the orders from Gräser arrived, most of Nehring's troops were being driven out of Kielce. There were effectively no major German formations left between Nehring and the German Seventeenth Army to the south, and the only resistance encountered by Konev's forces came from the battered survivors of the divisions of Fourth Panzer Army that had disintegrated on the first day of the offensive. Rybalko's Third Guards Tank Army was hindered more by difficulty in finding suitable crossing points over streams and rivers than by German resistance.

As they entered Kielce, the Soviet troops found a devastated city. When the Wehrmacht invaded Poland in 1939, the city had a population of about 80,000 people, of whom 35 per cent were Jews. After months of persecution, the Jews of the city and the surrounding area were confined in a ghetto in April 1941; as was the case with most ghettos, it was organised as a large ghetto and a neighbouring small ghetto – the two could be sealed off separately, allowing the Germans to take measures against the small ghetto's population and then to redistribute the Jews between the two sites.[19] At its peak, the ghetto was home to about 27,000 people, and the overcrowding led to outbreaks of disease that killed thousands. In the summer of 1942 the ghetto was 'liquidated', with those unable to work being executed on the spot or put aboard trains to Treblinka, where they were killed. Only 2,000 survived the liquidation and sporadic killings continued until the arrival of the Red Army. Accompanied by a modest number of Polish partisans – most of the Polish partisans operating in the region were part of the *AK* and therefore hostile to the Red Army – the Soviet forces found that nearly half the pre-war population – including most of the Jews – was gone. Inevitably, Soviet-era accounts portray the local Polish population as welcoming the Red Army with enthusiasm. The reality was that for most Poles, the arrival of Soviet forces was seen as the replacement of one occupying army by another, but some Red Army soldiers were shocked by the open antisemitism of many Poles. Semen Ruvimovich Tsvang was a tank crewman who later recalled one such encounter:

In some places, the Poles may have greeted the Red Army with joy, but I remember a more wary or even hostile attitude towards us. I often had to listen to reproaches from the Poles – 'Why did you come here? We have our own army!' We walked through a village and an old man showered us with curses. One of the soldiers couldn't restrain himself and struck the old man with his rifle butt, shouting 'Shut up, you dog!'

Once, we entered a Polish hut and a woman treated us to crushed potatoes with curdled milk. She said in a hateful voice, 'The Jews are to blame for everything! They sold Poland!' How is it possible, I thought, to suffer for five years under the German yoke and to blame the Jews for everything? One of the other tankers, listening to this Polish woman, asked me, 'Aren't you going to give her a slap?' At times I was afraid my temper would snap and I would shoot someone for saying the word 'kike'.[20]

Nehring was able to extract most of the troops that had gathered under his command as he abandoned Kielce, but due to a mixture of fuel shortages and breakdowns, he was forced to abandon dozens of vehicles. The Red Army claimed to have captured over 200 tanks when the city fell, but many of these would have been knocked-out vehicles previously recovered from the battlefield and taken to repair workshops. Konev was anxious not to give the Germans any opportunity to reorganise and ordered Colonel General Vasily Nikolaevich Gordov, commander of Third Guards Army, to seize the area to the north of Kielce – this would trap the retreating elements of XLII Corps before they could withdraw from their positions along the Vistula. The terrain here was heavily forested and the Soviet units struggled to establish a coherent front line; to complicate matters further, Recknagel had ordered his two main formations, 291st and 72nd Infantry Divisions, to abandon the Vistula line and fight their way west and there were fierce clashes to the north of Kielce throughout the afternoon.

By the end of 15 January, the outcome of the battle along the Vistula was not in doubt. The only matter to be decided was the scale of the German defeat, and Zhukov and Konev were energetically urging their forces onwards to ensure that this was as large as possible. To the north of Warsaw, the Soviet Forty-Seventh Army began to move forward against the German 73rd Infantry Division on the morning of 16 January. The first probes across the river took place the preceding day but the bulk of Major General Frantz Iosifovich Perkhorovich's army waited until the following morning to take advantage of the crossings that had been secured over the frozen Vistula. The German 73rd Infantry Division had built substantial defensive positions along the riverbank and Perkhorovich was reluctant to waste his troops in costly attacks, preferring instead to move forward in a more deliberate and careful manner.

The original 73rd Infantry Division was destroyed in Sevastopol in 1944 and the new division was formed in mid-June and sent to the front line three months later. By mid-morning, the Red Army had broken the division into several fragments. Bridging engineers swiftly established a crossing over the Vistula and during the afternoon Soviet armour began to move forward, reaching and overrunning most of 73rd Infantry Division's artillery positions.[21] Most of the Soviet rifle units had only moved about a mile beyond the Vistula, but this placed Forty-Seventh Army in a position to threaten an advance towards the southwest, cutting off Warsaw. At the same time, the First Polish Army, facing Warsaw across the Vistula, began bombardments of German positions and small formations crossed the Vistula immediately north of the Polish capital. To the south of the Poles, between their lines and those of Fifth Shock Army, Sixty-First Army also moved forward and threatened Warsaw from the south.

Throughout the morning of 16 January, Zhukov's two tank armies exploited their successes of the preceding day to the full. The heavy fighting of 15 January had exhausted the resources of 25th Panzer Division and it could do little to intervene. Bogdanov's Second Guards Tank Army dispatched two tank corps towards the northwest and by dusk the leading formations were about two miles to the southeast of the important road junction of Sochaczew, threatening the lines of communication between Warsaw and the west. Other elements of Second Guards Tank Army were approaching the town from the south, having reached and cut the road running south from Sochaczew to Skierniewice. With the exhausted remnants of the German armour now falling back towards the southwest, Fifth Shock Army had a far easier day; Antonov congratulated his officers and men on their determination of 15 January and organised marching columns to move forward in the wake of Bogdanov's tanks. The advance was swift, with Antonov's riflemen covering about 18 miles (30km) during the day; compared to the hard battles of 15 January, the relative calm must have felt almost unreal.

Meanwhile, the German plan to position *Kampfgruppe Dorow* for a counterattack against the southern threat to the line of retreat from Warsaw was rapidly falling apart. XLVI Panzer Corps was unable to supply sufficient fuel and the few units that were able to move found that Soviet units were already blocking their path. During the morning of 16 January, a group of about 35 Soviet tanks approached the position established by Pantenius around Tarczyn but drove off without attacking; Pantenius and the artillery officers watched helplessly, knowing that the crippling fuel shortage meant that most of the precious guns would have to be abandoned if the force was ordered to withdraw. Shortly after, the anticipated orders arrived: Pantenius' regiment was to move to support *Kampfgruppe Dorow*. He withdrew from Tarczyn during the afternoon, leaving a small rearguard in the hope that fuel might miraculously appear and permit the withdrawal of the artillery battalions. An hour after his troops left Tarczyn, Soviet tanks entered the town and pushed on to the north. The German artillerymen destroyed their guns and retreated. A few of the heavy mortars were towed away by the trucks from Pantenius' regiment for which fuel was available. Even without proper contact with higher commands, Pantenius and his colleagues knew that the complete encirclement of XLVI Panzer Corps – a panzer corps only in name, without a single tank at its disposal – was imminent. Still waiting for permission to abandon Warsaw and pull out to the west, Fries ordered the scattered elements of 337th Volksgrenadier Division to march to Sochaczew to secure the vital line of retreat.

Fries now travelled to Warsaw where he met Generalleutnant Friedrich Weber, the commandant of the fortress garrison. The two men agreed to make quiet preparations for the speedy abandonment of the city, but their scope was limited. Few trucks were available, and fuelling them also posed considerable problems. Meanwhile, Guderian returned to *OKH* where Bonin informed him of the request from Army Group A to abandon Warsaw. It seems that this was discussed in the most general terms and concentrated mainly on the precise line that XLVI Panzer Corps would then attempt to defend – this was based on the assumption that Warsaw had already been abandoned or overrun by the Red Army. With only intermittent radio contact with Weber and the 'fortress' garrison, Guderian approved the abandonment of Warsaw and set off for Hitler's bunker for the evening situation report.[22]

To the south of Second Guards Tank Army, Katukov's First Guards Tank Army faced difficulties in crossing the Pilica River. Towards the end of 16 January, 19th Guards Mechanised Brigade approached the small town of Nowe Miasto on the river and a vital bridge that was still intact; the Germans were awaiting the arrival of their armour that was falling back to the river line. A small detachment of T-34s and assault guns, accompanied by motorised riflemen, edged up to the river late on 16 January and arrived almost at the same moment as a retreating column of German tanks and trucks. In the gathering darkness, the Soviet vehicles joined the German column and crossed the bridge without incident. The accompanying riflemen infiltrated across the river ice and suddenly a firefight developed. To the dismay of the lieutenant leading the Soviet tanks, explosive charges on the bridge were detonated. Nevertheless, Nowe Miasto was captured and it was possible for Katukov's formations to commence crossing via a ford immediately south of the town. Amongst the loot secured in the town was a vehicle from the headquarters of the German Ninth Army; the maps and documents in it were rapidly passed on to Zhukov's 1st Belarusian Front headquarters.[23]

Konev's tank armies were also continuing their advance. Followed by Fifty-Second Army, Rybalko's Third Guards Tank Army approached the city of Radomsko during the afternoon of 16 January. Remnants of the German 68th and 168th Infantry Divisions had pulled back to Radomsko where they were reinforced by a construction battalion and a small group of soldiers from the *Russische Befreiungsarmee* ('Russian Liberation Army'). These men were demonised by Soviet writers during and after the war as traitors; they were former Red Army soldiers who had been captured by the Germans and had been organised under the command of General Andrei Andreyevich Vlasov, the former commander of Second Shock Army who was captured when his army was encircled and destroyed near Leningrad in 1942. Some of the Russian 'volunteers' in this new force were strongly motivated to fight against the Soviet government for a variety of reasons, but most chose to serve in Vlasov's units because conditions in prisoner-of-war camps were so bad. Many volunteered in the hope of being able to defect back to the Soviet side. Known to the Soviets as 'Vlasovites', they could expect no mercy if they were captured. Those who did succeed in crossing the front line in the hope of rejoining the Soviet forces were immediately arrested and treated with great suspicion; most ended up in prison camps or were executed. The first formation from Third Guards Tank Army to reach Radomsko was VI Guards Tank Corps, and its 53rd Guards Tank Brigade, reinforced by a field artillery regiment and an assault gun regiment, stormed into the city after a brief artillery bombardment. Streetfighting continued throughout the evening, but the last German units were destroyed or driven off by midnight. A little to the south, the larger town of Częstochowa also came under attack from Katukov's leading units. VII Guards Tank Corps dispatched a tank brigade, a motorised rifle brigade, a regiment of assault guns, and artillery towards the town; the force crossed the Warta River to the northeast of Częstochowa shortly after dusk on 16 January and then entered the northern part of the town. Here, the attack came to a halt in the face of determined resistance and rather than risk losing troops in a night battle, Major General Sergei Alekseevich Ivanov, commander of VII Guards Tank Corps, ordered his units to move up to the town from the east and south so that a major attack could be made the following morning.

From the headquarters of Army Group A, Harpe finally issued orders for the abandonment of Warsaw during the evening of 16 January. The garrison received detailed instructions at about 2230; it was to organise itself into three regiments reinforced with artillery and anti-tank weapons and march along the main highway running west from Warsaw to Łódź. Most of the 37 anti-tank guns that belonged to the garrison – largely guns seized from French and Soviet units in earlier years – couldn't be removed due to lack of vehicles and were destroyed. But even as the last preparations were made – Weber was anxious to begin the withdrawal under cover of darkness – a fresh order arrived just before midnight signed by Oberst Johannes Hölz, chief of staff of Ninth Army:

Führer order! [Previous] radio message superseded. Fortress is to be held.[24]

It seems that Guderian had been acting on the assumption that Warsaw had already been lost; when he learned that the city was still in German hands, he had no choice but to make Hitler aware of this. The result was another of Hitler's frequent outbursts of temper against the unreliable Wehrmacht officers who failed to show the required level of fanatical resistance. The new order caused consternation in Warsaw, but given that so much equipment, including the majority of the garrison's anti-tank guns, had already been destroyed, even a short-term defence of Warsaw was impossible. Weber concluded that this new order was impossible to obey and continued with his planned withdrawal.

Near Kielce, Nehring and the surviving elements of his XXIV Panzer Corps were isolated to the south of the city. In accordance with Konev's orders for first echelon units to exploit into the depths of the enemy positions and to leave isolated German formations to be destroyed by the second echelon, the Soviet units that had smashed the German defences in the area were moving off to the northwest. Kielce was now occupied by the relatively weak Soviet CII Rifle Corps; its two rifle divisions had started the offensive at about two-thirds of their establishment strength and had suffered further losses in the assault on Kielce. After being driven from the ruins of the city, Nehring had moved to the forests to the south between Kielce and the Czarna Nida, where he made contact with the remnants of 17th Panzer Division and 20th Panzergrenadier Division; infiltrating their way forward from the south, the elements of 17th Panzer Division and *Schwere Panzer-Abteilung 424* reached the river and crossed at a ford, leaving behind them most of their vehicles. Reconnaissance patrols sent out by Nehring reported that significant numbers of Soviet troops had moved out of Kielce to block the road between the city and the river and, concluding that it was likely that only weak forces were left in Kielce itself, Nehring decided to make a surprise attack on the city. Led by the remaining tanks and assault guns, the German force caught the Soviet defenders by surprise and rapidly retook Kielce. Reacting rapidly to this alarming setback, the Soviet units counterattacked, but Nehring had no intention of holding Kielce. His men now withdrew to the northwest and set up a position for all-round defence. The Soviet rifle divisions that had recaptured Kielce had already suffered heavy losses in earlier fighting around the city and were in no state to pursue in strength; they were limited to a few probes to locate the German positions.

The first phase of the great Soviet offensive was now over, with the armies of 1st Ukrainian Front and 1st Belarusian Front streaming westward through the gaping holes that had been created in the German front line. Despite some concerns about delays, the assault had unfolded well from the Soviet point of view. Given its clumsy and hugely costly operations of earlier years, the Red Army had performed well. A staff officer in the Wehrmacht later gave a decidedly German interpretation of the development of the Red Army:

> In summary, it can be said that the Russian conduct of attacks was largely based upon the German offensive doctrine of 1941–1942. The teacher of old was unable to counter it successfully, since Hitler's orders made established German defensive tactics impossible and in fact rendered them worthless ... Hitler placed severe operational and tactical restraints upon German commanders, allowing the Russians to operate as we had in 1941–1942, and forced us to operate in a manner that was contrary to our regulations.[25]

This was a recurring theme in German accounts after the war: if it hadn't been for Hitler's interference, many veterans argued, they would have been able to mount a far more effective defence of the Reich against the Red Army. There is undoubtedly much truth in this argument, and Hitler's rigid imposition of orders robbed field commanders of any flexibility. German defensive doctrine was based on the ability to mount swift counterattacks at both tactical and operational levels, often by making temporary withdrawals, and there simply wasn't enough time for approval to be secured from a distant headquarters if such operations were to be mounted effectively. Moreover, the deployment of XXIV Panzer Corps so close to the front line on Hitler's insistence further handicapped the Germans, as its entry into the battle was unquestionably hindered by being caught up in the initial Soviet bombardment. But simply blaming Hitler for the defeats suffered by the Wehrmacht ignores two important points. Firstly, few Wehrmacht figures had questioned the wisdom of prosecuting campaigns of conquest earlier in the war, which had led to the current situation. Secondly, the Germans failed to recognise how the Red Army had evolved during the war. The operational and tactical leadership of the Red Army of 1945 might have been very similar to that of the Wehrmacht in earlier years, but the same could be said of the armies of the Western Allies. It wasn't necessarily that the enemies of Germany were copying German doctrine; rather, the Germans had realised some of the realities of warfare in the mechanised age sooner than Germany's enemies. It was only a matter of time before the Soviet Union, Britain, and the USA caught up with such thinking. Moreover, the huge industrial resources of the enemies of Germany permitted them a level of motorisation that the Wehrmacht never achieved.

# CHAPTER 5

# WARSAW – KRAKÓW – ŁÓDŹ: 17–19 JANUARY

During the great encirclements at Stalingrad in late 1942 and Korsun in early 1944, the Red Army struggled with the issue of how to conduct an envelopment. By trapping many German formations in the ruins of Stalingrad – the number of Germans caught in the encirclement came as a surprise to the Red Army – a huge hole was torn in the German front line, but exploitation of this gap proved to be difficult because so many Soviet units had to take up positions around Stalingrad itself. Moreover, the first attempts to overwhelm the trapped Sixth Army were strongly repulsed and although the Germans were unable to extract the encircled units, they performed an important 'negative role' by tying down significant Soviet resources while the Wehrmacht rebuilt its front line further to the west.

When large parts of the German Eighth Army were encircled at Korsun in 1944, the problems encountered at Stalingrad were taken into account and the tank forces that led the two pincers of the encirclement operation were ordered to turn outwards to drive back the German units outside the encirclement. This too proved to be problematic, with the units directed to hold the perimeter around the trapped German units being too weak to prevent the Germans from creating a firm defensive position. This made it impossible for the 'besieging' Soviet units to overwhelm the pocket and ultimately most of those encircled were able to escape.

The solution that was adopted during *Bagration* in the summer of 1944 and then further developed in the months that followed was to concentrate on continuing the attack into the depths of the German positions. As Konev described, the intention was to leave any isolated German units to be destroyed by second echelon units; in any case, if the front line could be pushed far enough to the west, it would be impossible for any bypassed German forces to make such a long journey to link up with any new front line.

From the German perspective, the threatened and actual encirclements at Stalingrad and Korsun – and later along the Vistula and elsewhere – highlighted two problems. Firstly, Hitler's military mindset was increasingly obdurate and his earlier unwillingness to consider any tactical withdrawals became a rigid and inflexible policy. Perhaps drawing on his experiences of fighting on the Western Front in the First World War, he had a curious attitude to the strength of defensive positions. On the one hand, he had learned that properly entrenched troops could withstand heavy bombardments and attacks despite the numerical superiority of the attacking force. But on the other hand, he repeatedly lauded the abilities of German mechanised formations to overcome defences with their superior mobility, yet failed to recognise that other armies could also use mechanised forces with great effect against static, fortified positions. The result was that German forces were repeatedly left defending exposed positions that practically invited encirclement. When grudging permission was given for a withdrawal to a shorter, safer line, it was often too late for the orders to be executed without heavy losses. Hitler would then use these failed withdrawals as justification for forbidding retreats on other occasions, not recognising that the problem had been his tardiness in granting permission.

The second problem for the Germans had dogged their campaigns throughout the war. Every new German offensive – Poland in 1939, Belgium and France in 1940, and the Soviet Union in 1941 – was preceded by a period of careful stockpiling of fuel. The only major source of oil extraction available to Germany was in Romania and after this was lost in late 1944, the German forces were almost completely dependent upon synthetic fuel production and a small quantity from Hungary. The volume required for military use was so great that it was impossible in the best conceivable circumstances to manufacture sufficient synthetic fuel; in any case, the relentless bombing of German cities by American and British bombers reduced production far below planned levels. Consequently, even when permission was granted for withdrawals, the threatened units were too immobile for a quick retreat. Indeed, Hitler's refusal to permit a breakout from Stalingrad by Sixth Army was justified on the grounds that the encircled German units lacked the fuel to reach safety.

Both of these problems, and the issues created by the modified Soviet tactics, left Nehring and his XXIV Panzer Corps facing great difficulties. The Germans had been isolated near Kielce and had surprised the Soviet forces by briefly retaking the city but they were cut off, with limited supplies of fuel, ammunition, and food. Even local counterattacks regarded as essential for the survival of the group had to be conducted with great care to avoid excessive consumption of fuel and ammunition. Moreover, Nehring and his men had little idea of where the nearest German forces were and therefore the distance that they would have to cover to reach safety.

Nehring wasn't the only German commander having to deal with the possibility of being cut off. As darkness fell on 16 January, it was clear that the fall of Warsaw was imminent, with the two Soviet pincers close to closing. The only sensible option for XLVI Panzer Corps in and around Warsaw was an immediate withdrawal to the west in order to avoid destruction – even if the current Red Army policy didn't result in a proper encirclement, the German units would only be able to escape at the cost of abandoning their heavy equipment and their wounded unless they retreated rapidly. Accordingly, orders were issued late on 16 January by Ninth Army and XLVI Panzer Corps for all units to take up a new line roughly midway between Warsaw and Łódź. This effectively represented that last opportunity for an orderly withdrawal; the shortages of fuel in individual units and the difficulty in distributing the limited supplies available meant that even now, this retreat would necessitate the loss of a considerable quantity of equipment.

The confusing series of orders issued to XLVI Panzer Corps – dictated from above by Hitler, leaving both Army Group A and Ninth Army with no option other than to pass them on without alteration – stipulated that Ninth Army was permitted to establish a new defensive line, but it was to run from the city of Piotrków Trybunalski (renamed Petrikau by the Germans), 80 miles (128km) southwest of Warsaw, to the Polish capital. Lüttwitz, the army commander, replied to Harpe shortly after midnight during the night of 16–17 January. The defensive line that he had been ordered to hold was unachievable as substantial Soviet armoured forces had already passed it. Warsaw had been abandoned, and XLVI Panzer Corps was attempting to concentrate sufficient forces to recapture the town of Sochaczew, 32 miles (51km) west of Warsaw – this was essential if any of the German forces in and around Warsaw were to escape. In an attempt to ensure the success of this attack, Lüttwitz contacted Fries, the corps commander, asking him to take personal control of the attempt. He decided to visit the headquarters of XLVI Panzer Corps personally, but was detained by an increasingly common development: the appearance of a senior Nazi Party official.

When Germany annexed large areas of Polish territory in 1939, the western parts of Poland became *Reichsgau Wartheland*. Arthur Greiser, who had grown up in what was then the German city of Hohensalza (now the Polish Inowrocław) and was fluent in Polish, joined the Nazi Party in 1929 and rose rapidly through its ranks in the city of Danzig (now Gdańsk) where he clashed repeatedly with his rival in the Party, Albert Forster. After the defeat of Poland, he took up his new post as *Gauleiter* of Wartheland and was diligent in pursuing a policy of 'Germanisation': Jews, who formed about 8 per cent of the population, were first moved to ghettos and then transferred to the Kulmhof extermination camp near Chełmno; up to half a million Poles were deported to the *Generalgouvernement*; Poles with serious illnesses such as tuberculosis were to be given 'special treatment', which in this context meant their murder; the remaining Poles were treated as inferiors and subject to harsh restrictions; and up to 350,000 ethnic Germans, mainly people who had returned to the Reich from eastern Poland and Romania, were settled in the region.[1]

As the war approached the region, Greiser – like the other *Gauleiters* – took on responsibility for the *Volkssturm*. In keeping with the orders imposed by the Nazi Party, he refused to permit plans to be drawn up for civilian evacuations in the event of further Soviet advances – any such suggestions were condemned as 'defeatist'. Now, in the middle of a battle that might leave the Red Army free to advance into Wartheland almost unopposed, Greiser turned up at Harpe's headquarters and proceeded to lecture him on the importance of rigid defence.[2] Greiser's history of military service amounted to a spell in the German Navy in the First World War, a short period as a fighter pilot (he was shot down and seriously wounded in Belgium at the very beginning of his aerial career), and two years in a non-combatant role in the ranks of the *Freikorps*, the German 'volunteers' who remained in uniform at the end of the First World War and fought against a number of opponents inside and outside Germany. He was in no position to give Lüttwitz or any other military officer advice on how to conduct a modern battle; nonetheless, he now delayed the commander of Ninth Army for a considerable time with repeated demands for the shattered and poorly supplied Wehrmacht units to show greater 'fanatical' commitment to defending Germany. The degree to which individuals believed that fanaticism was in some way adequate to correct the material imbalance on the battlefield was usually in inverse proportion to personal experience of the front line.

One of the key locations on the road and rail lines running west from the Polish capital was the town of Skierniewice, 40 miles (64km) from Warsaw, and Antonov and his 301st Rifle Division reached and crossed the frozen Rawka River to the northeast of the town during the night of 16–17 January. From their foothold on the west bank, Antonov and his headquarters staff could hear fighting in Skierniewice and succeeded in making contact with Colonel Pashkov, commander of 220th Tank Brigade. Pashkov was delighted with the unexpected appearance of Antonov's riflemen; his unit was struggling to penetrate into the town without infantry support. At first light on 17 January, Antonov attacked

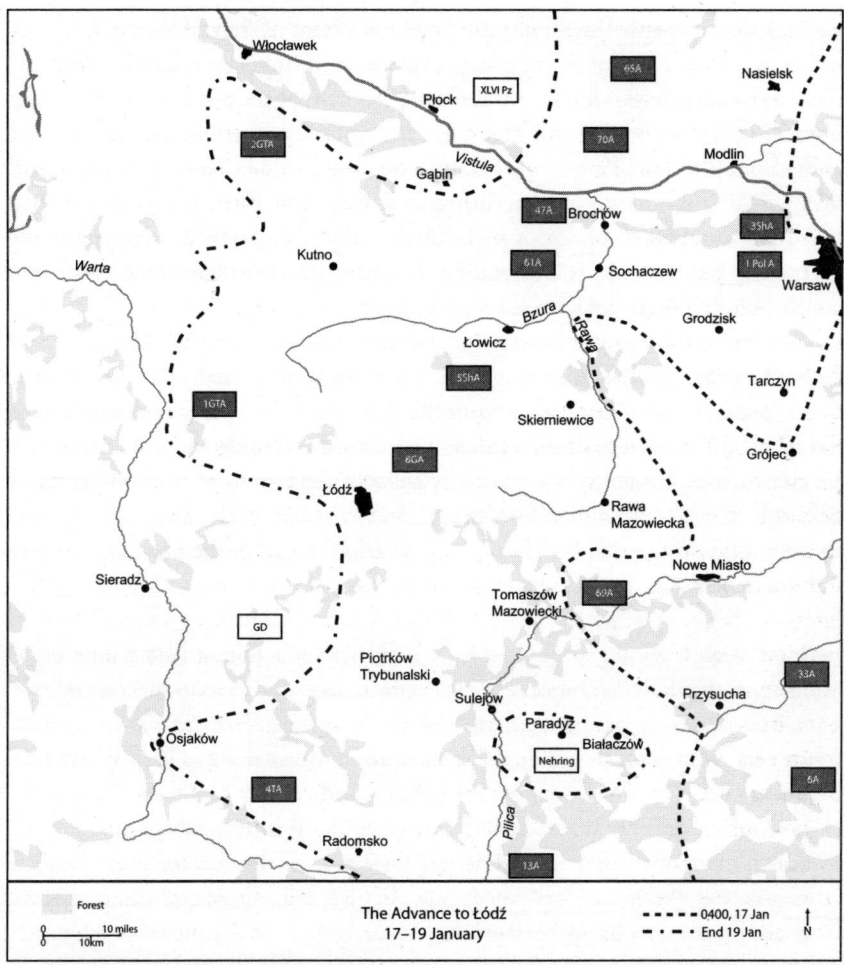

The Advance to Łódź
17–19 January

– – – – 0400, 17 Jan
– · – · – End 19 Jan

Forest

0   10 miles
0   10km

N

from the north while Pashkov sent his tanks in a sweep around the southern part of Skierniewice; by midday, the town was in Soviet hands.[3] A little to the south, the town of Rawa Mazowiecka was attacked by Gusakovsky and his 44th Guards Tank Brigade. When he encountered determined resistance, he swiftly manoeuvred his brigade past the northern edge of the town.[4]

Pantenius and his 690th Volksgrenadier Regiment were ordered to move to Chylice, near Tarczyn. After the forced marches of the past day through deep snow, Pantenius knew that his men needed rest. He halted in a small copse, but almost immediately a Polish farmer appeared and informed him that Soviet tanks were a little to the southwest. It was the only information that Pantenius had on the location of enemy forces; nor did he know where the rest of his division was, as he was unable to establish radio contact with any other units. While he considered what to do, four German assault guns appeared, survivors of a group from 251st Infantry Division that had been driven back from the Magnuszew bridgehead. The assault gun commander willingly joined Pantenius' regiment. Meanwhile, a scouting patrol returned and informed Pantenius that they had spotted a motorised column a little to the north, crossing the path that the Volksgrenadier regiment was intending to follow; Pantenius hurried forward and rapidly identified the vehicles as being a Soviet force.

The Soviet column was headed for the small town of Grodzisk and Pantenius dispatched the four assault guns, with a company of infantry riding on their hulls, to attack the Soviet group from the rear. While he considered whether he should abandon his remaining vehicles and attempt to infiltrate to the west with his men on foot, Pantenius was joined by another German force – the *Waffenschule* of Ninth Army, commanded by Oberst Klein. The two columns now combined and marched on towards the north, but towards the end of the day they ran into a group of Red Army tanks. Pantenius described the fight that followed:

I was in my Volkswagen with the last battalion when we heard loud sounds of fighting, the shots and impacts of tank rounds, and soon a group of T-34s that had been tracking us appeared. The tanks were probably from a tank battalion that had been called in to help the reconnaissance group that had been attacked in Grodzisk … The men scattered immediately and the vehicles also attempted to head off in different directions. At that time, the Russian tanks had no gun stabilisation and as they fired while they were moving they hit remarkably few targets, but the impact on morale was decisive and our march temporarily degenerated into wild flight; there was no cover and the few bushes and trees barely blocked line of sight. The anti-tank teams with their 'stovepipes' [*Panzerschrek* anti-tank weapons, similar to bazookas] tried here and there to return fire but had little success. Attempts to gather together the scattering riflemen and make it clear that running away meant certain death, whereas staying here and dodging the tanks at the last moment at least offered a chance of survival, were only partially successful. Although my Volkswagen was a big target, were hit. Peper, my driver, turned left and right so skilfully … that the tank that was targeting us didn't get a clear chance. Then, completely unexpectedly, a company of *Hetzer* light assault guns appeared like guardian angels and immediately engaged the T-34s in battle. They were so fast, skilful and manoeuvrable that the enemy tanks were unable to oppose them. The *Hetzers* scored far more hits than the Russians, some T-34s were shot up and the rest

turned around and disappeared. That was the fortune of war at that moment …
The regiment's losses were not severe, but were painful enough, as two officers,
including my orderly officer, Leutnant Son, were killed along with about 12
NCOs and men, and one officer was missing.[5]

Like the *Sturmgeschütz* assault gun, the *Hetzer* was another highly effective use of
an obsolete tank chassis. Originally, it had formed the basis of the Czech-built
Pz.38 light tank, which was effectively outdated by the time that the Wehrmacht
entered the Soviet Union in 1941 but continued in service with several panzer
divisions. Instead of building more such tanks, a 75mm long-barrelled gun was
mounted on the chassis with limited traverse. Although the armour of the *Hetzer*
was modest and no more than 60mm thick at its strongest point, it benefited
from a considerable slope that helped deflect incoming rounds. Weighing only
16 tons and having a height of just a little over two metres, the *Hetzer* was a
highly manoeuvrable and nimble tank killer. With the *Hetzer* company added as
a rearguard, the German column continued its march towards the north along
the frozen roads, encountering other German groups struggling west from
Warsaw from time to time. The confused fighting of the day is typical of the
clashes that took place all along the front, a direct consequence of the Red Army
doctrine of avoiding the use of large numbers of men to establish firm
encirclements.

Meanwhile, Harpe, Lüttwitz and Fries continued to try to make sense of the
confused situation. The attempt to recapture Sochaczew rapidly ground to a halt
during the morning of 17 January; Fries reported to Lüttwitz that he was
outnumbered and in any case much of XLVI Panzer Corps' forces that had been
designated for the attack were still struggling to reach the area. Besides, there
were reports of Soviet tanks now operating far to the west of the line designated
by Harpe and Lüttwitz. The reply from the headquarters of Ninth Army was
uncompromising. Sochaczew had to be recaptured by nightfall if the German
units to the west of Warsaw were to escape. Once the city had been taken, Fries
was to try to establish a new line south to Skerniewice; even if Soviet tanks were
already further to the west, at least this would prevent the Red Army's rifle units
from joining the armour. Even as the order was sent, Lüttwitz and his staff were
packing up their equipment and moving from the city of Łowicz, about ten miles
(16km) to the west of the Sochaczew-Skierniewice line, to a northern suburb of
Łódź. The move came just in time. Just 15 minutes after the Germans left Łowicz,
a group of about 50 T-34s burst into the city.

As was increasingly common as the war progressed, Hitler responded to
setbacks on the battlefield by making changes in senior appointments. Harpe was

told that he was being dismissed as commander of Army Group A and replaced by one of the diminishing number of men in whom Hitler had confidence: Generaloberst Ferdinand Schörner. The physically intimidating Schörner – a tall, heavily built man – was a veteran of the First World War, having been awarded Germany's highest honour, the *Pour le Mérite*, in battles on the Italian Front. He commanded 6th Mountain Division and later XL Corps before taking control of Seventeenth Army and Army Group South Ukraine. During this latter spell, he gained a reputation for imposing rigid discipline with regular arrests and executions of soldiers who were suspected of leaving the front line without permission; he was then assigned to command of Army Group North, before replacing Harpe.

Schörner's fanatical faith in Hitler and his often brutal attitude towards any signs of weakness or disobedience earned him Hitler's approval, but the distaste and contempt of many of his contemporaries. Guderian opposed his appointment as the new commander of Army Group A, but was overruled by the Führer. Ordinary soldiers under his various commands had mixed views. On the one hand, many detested his rigid imposition of discipline, with men often being treated as 'guilty unless proved innocent'; but on the other hand, he earned the approval of many front-line personnel by his ruthless combing out of rear area formations in order to transfer personnel to combat units. Like every army in history, the soldiers who marched and fought in the Wehrmacht had a low opinion of men they regarded as individuals who enjoyed comfortable lives in the rear areas, and Schörner clearly shared this view.

While Hitler replaced commanders with men he regarded as more likely to show and enforce the required level of 'fanaticism', German columns like that of Pantenius' regiment and the *Armeewaffenschule* continued to try to reach safety. The main road running west from Warsaw via Blonie to Sochaczew was choked with traffic and Pantenius led his men to the north. Fortunately, the group had a good map and were able to find a series of small roads and tracks that allowed them to turn west; other units were left sitting helplessly, waiting for traffic to move forward while casting anxious eyes skyward and to the east. Behind them, the soldiers of First Polish Army, accompanied by units from the Soviet Second Guards Army and Third Shock Army, began to move into Warsaw. Some of the Polish soldiers were from Warsaw and had left the city before the arrival of the Germans in 1939; others had visited the Polish capital before the war. They found a completely changed landscape.

After Poland was occupied by German and Soviet troops in 1939, resistance to foreign occupation continued with varying degrees of organisation and coordination. To bring more order to the fight against the Germans and

Soviets, General Władysław Sikorski, the Polish prime minister in exile in London, issued orders in November 1939 for the creation of the *Związek Walki Zbrojnej* ('Union for Armed Struggle' or *ZWZ*). This functioned in two groups, one in the Soviet zone and one in the German zone, but after the *NKVD* captured General Michal Tokorzewski-Karaszewicz, commander of the *ZWZ* in the east, there was a need to reorganise once more. Despite this attempt to create a unified structure, there were numerous resistance groups operating relatively independently of each other and sometimes even clashing; there were particularly difficult relationships between Polish and Jewish groups in eastern Poland and the Vilnius region of Lithuania.[6] In February 1942, the *ZWZ* was reorganised into the *Armia Krajowa* ('Home Army' or *AK*) under the overall control of the London-based government-in-exile. Many of its units were built around the surviving elements of the Polish Army and as the front line approached Polish territory in 1944, plans were drawn up for a series of risings in the cities of eastern Poland. These uprisings, under the overall codename of *Burza* ('Storm'), were intended to seize control of cities immediately before the arrival of the Red Army; there was little expectation that the pro-London *AK* would then be able to retain possession of the cities, but it would at least allow the Polish leadership to claim that the Red Army hadn't liberated the cities.

Stalin had no intention of permitting armed groups that were loyal to the government-in-exile to seize control of Polish cities, if only temporarily, and the Soviet military repeatedly refused to cooperate with the *AK*. In most cases, the attempted seizure of cities was defeated by the Germans before the Soviet forces arrived, and thereafter the Red Army rapidly disarmed any *AK* units it encountered and often arrested and imprisoned their leaders. *Burza* came to a dramatic climax in August 1944 when an attempt was made by the *AK* to seize control of Warsaw.[7] Unlike the earlier risings in the cities of the east, this was intended to be a permanent seizure of control; Warsaw was within flying range for the air forces of the Western Allies and there were expectations that in addition to providing logistic and military support, the British would permit the immediate transfer of Polish-manned RAF squadrons and Polish paratroopers to Warsaw.

When the Warsaw Uprising started, the Red Army was approaching Warsaw from the east in the aftermath of *Bagration*. At the same time, a tank corps from a Soviet group that had reached the Vistula at Sandomierz moved north along the east bank of the river and threatened to capture the Warsaw suburb of Praga. Such a move would effectively sever the last lines of communication for the German Army Group Centre, retreating in disarray from Belarus. But Polish expectations that the imminent arrival of the Red Army would at least divert German strength from Warsaw and at best would lead to Soviet forces breaking the German grip on the entire region proved to be incorrect. The Soviet armies that had smashed the Germans in Belarus were badly depleted and operating at the end of long lines of communication; the Germans had brought significant reserves to the region and were about to launch a powerful counterattack to the east of Warsaw against the tank forces attempting to advance north from Sandomierz; and in any case, it suited Stalin for the Germans to crush the Warsaw Uprising before he took control of the Polish capital.

The bitter struggle for Warsaw raged from August until the beginning of October when the last elements of the *AK* surrendered to the Germans or slipped away into the surrounding countryside. For many Germans, the uprising was as much an opportunity as it was a threat. As early as the summer of 1939, before the Second World War began, Hitler showed interest in a proposal that suggested that the existing city was to be largely destroyed and its population eliminated. In its place, a new German provincial city was to be built on the west bank of the Vistula, with a slave colony on the east bank. As the uprising began in August 1944, Himmler spoke to Hitler in Berlin:

> My Führer, the timing is unfortunate, but from a historical perspective what the Poles are doing is a blessing. After five or six weeks we will leave the area. But by then Warsaw, the capital, the head, the centre of intelligence of this former state of 17 million Polish people will be extinguished, these people who have blocked our way to the east for seven hundred years and have stood in our way ever since the Battle of Tannenberg [a reference to the defeat of the Teutonic Knights in 1410 rather than the battle of 1914]. After this, the Polish problem will no longer be a great historical problem for the children who come after us, nor indeed will it be for us.[8]

From the outset, German conduct of operations against the *AK* was brutal, even by the standards of the Eastern Front. Both SS and Wehrmacht units showed no hesitation in using civilians as 'human shields' and executing prisoners; the *AK* also shot many German soldiers who surrendered to them. Killing of civilians by German forces rapidly escalated and one of the worst examples was the execution of about 35,000 men, women and children by SS troops under the command of Gruppenführer Heinz Reinefarth in the western parts of Warsaw on 5 August – Reinefarth even recorded that he would have killed more if ammunition had been available in larger quantities.[9] With little meaningful support from the Red Army and only modest amounts of supplies being delivered by the air forces of the Western Powers, the *AK* was ground down and negotiated a surrender at the beginning of October. The Germans agreed to treat the fighters of the *AK* as prisoners of war. Himmler immediately issued instructions to senior SS figures:

> The city must disappear from the face of the earth and serve only as a transport station for the Wehrmacht. No stone can remain standing. Every building must be razed to its foundation.[10]

About 16,000 *AK* fighters died during the Warsaw Uprising. Civilian deaths were far higher, and up to 200,000 were killed – some were caught in the crossfire, but most were deliberately massacred by the Germans. Estimates of German casualties vary considerably, from a lower figure of 2,000 dead and 9,000 wounded to a higher figure of 10,000 killed and 17,000 wounded.[11] Despite the assurances given to the *AK* at the time of the surrender, the civilian population of Warsaw was largely expelled from the ruined city and sent to a special transit camp in the southeast part of Warsaw. Orders were issued for the creation of this camp as early as mid-August under the jurisdiction of the *SS-Wirtschafts-und Verwaltungshauptamt* ('SS Main Economic and Administrative Office' or *SS-WVHA*). The scale of what was intended was clear from the outset. A week after the SS started organising the camp, the *SS-WVHA* requested the supply of 400,000 uniforms – the infamous 'striped pyjamas' seen in so many photographs of concentration camp survivors. Towards the end of August, Himmler issued fresh instructions:

> Many able-bodied men and women will be used for work in concentration camps, and as such only women with small children will be accepted as local Polish labourers.[12]

The significance of this wording was that Poles regarded as 'able-bodied' would be dispatched elsewhere for use as forced labour. Despite the final surrender agreement at the end of the uprising, which promised that civilians would not be deported and mistreated, Himmler's instructions were followed to the letter. Up to half a million Poles passed through the camp, starting in late August. Of these, 90,000 were dispatched to labour camps across the Reich, 60,000 were sent to concentration camps, and the rest were dispersed across the *Generalgouvernement*.[13] Most of the civilians who were sick or suffering from wounds incurred during the uprising were simply executed. Eulalia Matusiak was aged just 12 when she arrived at Auschwitz from the transit camp in September 1944:

> We were driven to the barracks. It was already night when I entered Block 16 of the *FKL* [*Frauenkonzentrationslager* or 'Women's Camp'] ... I entered the barracks. It was completely dark there, I didn't know how to get about and then behind us came a scream to go in faster. There was no room in there and finally someone inside asked, 'And who are you?'
>
> [I replied] 'They call me Lilka,' it was my nickname.
>
> 'Well then, come here.' Someone gave me a hand and I climbed onto the topmost bunk. The women there were saying to each other, 'Look, it's a kid! Where are you from?' and I said, 'I'm from Warsaw.' And they continued, 'What's going on in Warsaw?' I said, 'An uprising.' 'Uprising in Warsaw?' Then I had to explain over and over again about the uprising.
>
> They were delighted with the news. Finally I fell asleep. I think they gave me a piece of bread. When I awoke in the morning, the piece of bread was gone. Who that was, who were these women, Polish women, I have no idea. Then our life in the barracks started. There were about 500 children there.[14]

About 12,000 Warsaw civilians were sent to Auschwitz; several were women in advanced pregnancy, who gave birth in the concentration camp. Thousands perished in the winter that followed, but an even worse ordeal lay ahead for the survivors, as is described later. Prior to the war, Warsaw had a population of about 1.3 million people, of whom 300,000 were Jews. Up to 70,000 civilians were killed or wounded in the fighting of 1939, which left about one-eighth of the city in ruins. The fighting of the autumn of 1944 destroyed much of the city and as soon as the remaining civilians had been dispatched to the transit camp, the Germans commenced a programme of deliberate destruction. Special squads of *Brandkommandos* ('arson squads') and *Sprengkommandos* ('demolition squads') commenced the systematic levelling of Warsaw, concentrating particularly on buildings of historical importance. Even at this stage of the war, with the final outcome beyond doubt, Hitler and Himmler still clung to their dream of creating a German settlement on the ruins, with perhaps a large artificial lake that would drown the old city centre.[15]

When Soviet and Polish troops cautiously entered the deserted ruins of Warsaw on 17 January, they found that over 85 per cent of the city had been levelled. About 40 per cent of this destruction had taken place since the suppression of the Warsaw Uprising. Georgy Gavrilovich Semenov was a staff officer in the headquarters of Third Shock Army, which was moving forward as part of 1st Belarusian Front's reserves, and monitored the progress of Soviet and Polish troops as they secured the ruined city:

> Having learned [of the capture of Warsaw] from Front headquarters via the VHF set, [Major] General [Mikhail Fomich] Bukshtynovich [chief of staff of Third Shock Army] ordered me to go with a small group of officers to Warsaw; it was necessary to assess the state of the roads for the next movements of the army's troops. We drove in two vehicles along the highway where units of Forty-Seventh Army had recently advanced. At the end of the day, after running the risk of setting off German mines, we made our way with great difficulty to the northern part of Warsaw.
>
> The city was quiet. The scale of destruction was astonishing. All buildings were reduced to ruins. Piles of broken bricks littered the streets. The few surviving residents emerged from the basements. With tears of joy in their eyes, they hugged and kissed us, warmly greeting every Soviet and Polish soldier.[16]

A little over 100,000 people had remained in Warsaw, hiding in basements and moving from one area to another as the German destruction squads methodically destroyed the city. How enthusiastically they welcomed the Soviet soldiers is open to question; some would have remembered the joint victory parade held by the Red Army and the Wehrmacht through the streets of Warsaw in late 1939.

Generalleutnant Friedrich Weber, the commandant of Warsaw, and his 'fortress' garrison had left the city before dawn on 17 January. They succeeded in linking up with the rearguard of 337th Volksgrenadier Division to the west of Warsaw. When he learned of the abandonment of Warsaw, Hitler had another outburst of rage. Despite Guderian's protests, he ordered Bonin, the head of the Operations Department of *OKH*, and two of his subordinates to be arrested at gunpoint for permitting the abandonment of Warsaw. The three officers were detained at gunpoint and handed over to Ernst Kaltenbrunner, the head of the *Reichssicherheitshauptamt* ('Reich Main Security Office'). Bonin's two subordinates were released after questioning after a few weeks, but Bonin was less fortunate. He was sent to the concentration camp at Flossenbürg in Bavaria and later to Dachau. As the end of the war approached, Bonin was held with several senior prisoners – a mixture of former officers and the family members of some of those involved in the July Plot – in Niederdorf, in northern Italy. Fearing that he and the other prisoners would be executed before the war ended, Bonin tried to contact Generaloberst Heinrich von Vietinghoff, commander of Army Group C in northern Italy and a personal acquaintance. On 30 April, Vietinghoff's chief of staff sent a group of soldiers to the town where the prisoners were being held. With American troops expected at any moment, the SS guards fled and the prisoners were moved to a nearby hotel until they were taken into US custody.[17]

To the south of the ruins of Warsaw, Chuikov's Eighth Guards Army was advancing swiftly, crossing the Pilica in the wake of Katukov's First Guards Tank Army. Chuikov met Katukov near the Pilica and the two men discussed progress to date. German resistance had largely disintegrated and even in the areas where some Soviet forces seemed to be moving forward slowly – Sixty-Ninth and Thirty-Third Armies were lagging behind the main advance – there was little concern. The Germans were in no shape to take advantage of any discontinuity in the Soviet front line. The German 19th Panzer Division and 45th Volksgrenadier Division were on Chuikov's southern flank but were hurrying west towards Tomaszów Mazowiecki, where the newly arrived *HG* Panzer Division was still detraining. The remnants of 6th Volksgrenadier Division had placed themselves under the command of 19th Panzer Division; from time to time, the retreating units clashed with small groups of Soviet tanks. The German line of retreat was strewn with broken and abandoned equipment and corpses.

Between Zhukov's armies in the north and Konev's armies in the south, the divisions of the German XXIV Panzer Corps and XLII Corps were cut off from German lines. Nehring discussed options with Generalleutnants Dietrich von Müller and Georg Jauer, commanders of 16th Panzer Division and 20th Panzergrenadier Division respectively. For the moment, the pressure from Soviet units seemed to have slackened, and the three men correctly concluded that this was because the bulk of Soviet forces were pressing on to the west and northwest. From what little information they had, it was clear that the best option for escape was to try to head northwest – travelling directly west would require the use of inferior roads and they suspected that the Soviet armies that had burst out of the Sandomierz bridgehead would be operating in this region. However, before they could attempt their escape, there was the question of the infantry divisions of XLII Corps to the east. In many respects, the chances of a successful breakout were highest if the operation was attempted at the earliest possible moment, but the three officers agreed to do all they could to hold open a line of retreat for Recknagel's corps. Nonetheless, it was important to start a withdrawal and the bulk of 16th and 17th Panzer Divisions were ordered to commence a march towards the northwest after dusk on 17 January. They were to be followed by 20th Panzergrenadier Division and 342nd Infantry Division, with 168th Infantry Division forming the rearguard – Generalmajor Maximilian Rosskopf, the division commander, was under orders to withdraw as slowly as he could without losing contact with the rest of the column.

Meanwhile, with the front line to north and south disintegrating, Recknagel had taken matters into his own hands and pulled back from the Vistula. Ahlfen, the commander of the small blocking unit at the northern end of XLII Corps' positions, had received orders by radio late on 16 January to move with all possible speed to the small town of Iłża, to the south of Radom:

> *Sperrverband Ahlfen* is to march with all speed back to the Hubertus Line via the road junction of Iłża, which must be defended. This most important task is to shield the northern flank of the corps, which is marching west. God protect you![18]

It was the last signal that Ahlfen received from Recknagel. Fortunately for Ahlfen, his group was joined by the armoured pioneer battalion of 16th Panzer Division; these combat engineers were used as battlegroups throughout the war, particularly in the latter stages, and their experience in armoured warfare proved crucial. Ahlfen's relatively weak infantry came under heavy attack in Iłża and was wavering when the pioneer battalion arrived and restored the situation, its half-tracks taking the Soviet units by surprise. A nearby mortar battalion also intervened and caught a Red Army column hurrying forward in the open; in the lull that followed, Ahlfen was able to break contact and continue his retreat. His men pulled back to the west, keeping as much as possible to roads that ran through forested areas. Other units regularly joined the group, and Ahlfen ordered all equipment and vehicles not strictly essential for combat to be abandoned. With no radio contact with higher formations, his command laboured west, followed by the Soviet Sixth Army. Meanwhile, Nehring received a radio message from Recknagel: the commander of XLII Corps had reached the lines of 168th Infantry Division, which was the last unit of Nehring's main group, and had taken command of the rearguard.[19]

Lelyushenko's Fourth Tank Army was some considerable distance further west. His leading units were across the Pilica and captured Sulejów, near Piotrków Trybunalski, early on 17 January. By the end of the day, Fourth Tank Army was within striking range of Piotrków Trybunalski. To the south, Third Guards Tank Army had taken Radomsko and probed north to close the gap with Lelyushenko's troops and there were limited advances further towards the west, but Rybalko used the day mainly to bring up fuel and ammunition, giving his units a chance to regroup. On his southern flank, Fifth Guards Army faced Częstochowa, and Zhadov ordered two of his rifle corps to attack the city. Supported by formations of Third Guards Tank Army, XXXII Guards Rifle Corps turned the northern flank of the German defences; to the irritation of the Soviet troops, the Luftwaffe made a rare appearance and bombed several Red Army columns approaching the city. Nevertheless, Częstochowa was largely in Soviet hands by the end of 17 January. It was a moment of considerable pride for Zhadov – the capture of Częstochowa had been set as his objective to be achieved by 23 January, and his men had taken the city four days ahead of schedule.[20]

To the south of Konev's 1st Ukrainian Front was the city of Kraków. German troops had approached the city on 6 September 1939, less than a week after crossing the frontier into Poland, and rapidly took control of the area; the Wehrmacht units were swiftly followed by two SS *Einsatzgruppen* (roughly translated as 'task forces') that immediately began to arrest and execute anyone thought to be a real or potential threat to German rule. Jews, of course, were a priority target. In early November 1939, Hans Frank established his administration in Kraków, making it the capital of the *Generalgouvernement*. Unlike other Polish cities, it was not intended for depopulation and demolition; on rather spurious grounds, Frank claimed that the city had German origins and was therefore worth preserving. Nevertheless, massacres of Jews and Polish intellectuals continued and a Jewish ghetto was created in March 1941 under the control of Otto Wächter; it became home to about 15,000 Jews, living in an area that had accommodated just 3,000 people before the war. A little over a year after the creation of the ghetto, the Germans began its systematic depopulation with thousands being taken either to labour camps or to Auschwitz and Bełzec where they were killed. It formally ceased to exist in March 1943; nearly all of the Jews were dead. As the Red Army approached the city, led by IV Guards Tank Corps, the defenders – mainly 344th Infantry Division under the command of Generalmajor Georg Kossmala – prepared the hopeless task of trying to hold back Konev's assault. But other German units were also arriving – 712th Infantry Division transferred from the Netherlands; 75th Infantry Division and 97th Jäger Division sent north from Hungary; and 269th Infantry Division from Alsace. If a little time could be bought, there was a possibility that a new defensive line could be established. Just how durable this new line would be was open to question.

Hans Frank, who had been the Governor-General of the non-annexed parts of Poland, would later claim at his trial in Nuremburg that he made no fewer than 14 attempts to submit his resignation to Hitler, but was turned down on every occasion. There is no evidence to support this assertion; by contrast, his implementation of Nazi occupation policies was extensively documented. At the end of 1941, he addressed a meeting of senior occupation officials in Kraków:

> What should we do with the Jews? Do you think they will be settled in Ostland [the former Baltic States], in villages? We were told in Berlin, 'Why all this bother? We can do nothing with them either in Ostland or in the *Reichskommissariat* [the

new administrative regions of occupied Soviet territory across Ukraine and Belarus]. So liquidate them yourselves.' Gentlemen, I must ask you to rid yourselves of all feelings of pity. We must annihilate the Jews wherever we find them and wherever it is possible.[21]

Frank showed a similarly callous attitude towards non-Jewish Poles. In January 1944, after his train was derailed in an unsuccessful assassination attempt and in retaliation, he approved the execution of about 100 Poles held in Montelupich Prison in Kraków. Now, with the fall of Kraków imminent, Frank and many other senior Nazi figures took the opportunity to flee.

In his memoirs, Konev wrote about visiting the headquarters of Fifty-Ninth Army on 19 January, as Korovnikov was preparing to attack Kraków, but other accounts give earlier dates for the fighting around the city. The daily situation maps of the Red Army suggest that much of Fifty-Ninth Army was within a few miles of the city by the end of 17 January; Fourth Guards Tank Corps was operating in front of Korovnikov's army and had already dispatched a tank brigade to cut the main road running west from Kraków. Holding the city was impossible and Kossmala ordered his 344th Infantry Division to commence a withdrawal. Regardless of the value of the city, there was better defensive terrain to the south. No time was wasted in the commonplace practice of preparing demolitions of major buildings, power stations and water pumping facilities, but Frank and the administration of the *Generalgouvernement* ordered the use of precious transport resources to evacuate many of the city's art treasures.

The German forces reeling back from Warsaw were in a completely different state. Pantenius' mixed column reached the Bzura River at Brochów, where it found a pontoon bridge and crossed to the west bank; the soldiers then set up defensive perimeters on either bank to protect the bridge and keep open a line of retreat for other German units that continued to appear from time to time. After the chaos of the preceding couple of days, there was now at least the first signs of a more organised German position. Patrols were sent north and south and reported that the line of the Bzura to the north to and beyond the Vistula was held by 73rd Infantry Division, and other elements of 337th Volksgrenadier Division were appearing along the river to the south of Brochów. Trying to bring some order to his scattered formations, Fries travelled to the river line and ordered one of the first battalions to arrive there to attack south towards Sochaczew to re-open the main line of retreat; the attack failed after making no significant progress. Fries tried again later in the day after gathering reinforcements and on this occasion the attack managed to penetrate into the western parts of Sochaczew.

Even if these attacks succeeded, the new German line now occupied by Fries' corps was merely holding back the combined arms armies of Zhukov's 1st Belarusian Front – both of Zhukov's tank armies were already across the Bzura and advancing westwards and heavy Soviet attacks to the north threatened to turn the flank of 73rd Infantry Division. With Soviet tanks operating freely behind his line, Fries concluded that it was impossible to continue holding the Bzura and ordered 73rd Infantry Division to concentrate its forces north of the Vistula. The rest of XLVI Panzer Corps was to fall back towards Płock and Gąbin.

To the south of the positions held by 337th Volksgrenadier Division along the Bzura, the Red Army moved against the city of Łowicz during the morning of 18 January. Much of Antonov's 301st Rifle Division had become strung out over the preceding days and it now formed up properly for a formal assault. The German entrenchments around Łowicz were fairly extensive, but the garrison lacked the numbers to hold them and within hours the city was in Soviet hands. Further south, Chuikov's Eighth Guards Army was approaching Łódź, mopping up small German garrisons in its path that had been bypassed by the fast-moving tank armies. VIII Guards Mechanised Corps, the leading formation of First Guards Tank Army, penetrated into the northern part of Łódź but moved on to the west, aiming to secure crossings over the next water obstacle. The Warta River, running northwards about 34 miles (55km) west of Łódź before turning to the west, was a formidable obstacle and Babadzhanian approached it towards the end of 18 January with orders to establish a bridgehead across the river. Lacking bridging equipment, Babadzhanian asked permission to avoid a time-consuming and potentially costly battle to seize a crossing; he suggested instead that he should follow the north bank of the Warta after it turned to the west, thus approaching the city of Poznań. The suggestion was rejected, and he reluctantly prepared to strike over the river as ordered.[22]

The city of Łódź was the scene of heavy fighting in the first winter of the First World War, when the Russian Second Army – rebuilt after being largely destroyed at the Battle of Tannenberg – marched through the area. The Germans mounted a powerful counterattack from the north under the leadership of General Karl Litzmann, striking to the northwest of Łódź with the intention of isolating the Russian Second Army in the city, but a further Russian attack left Litzmann's force isolated. Undaunted, Litzmann led his men to safety, turning a threatening situation into a surprising victory and taking with him the prisoners he had captured.[23] After the area was occupied by the Wehrmacht in 1939, the Germans imposed the name of Litzmannstadt; street names were also changed – Piotrkowska, one of the main thoroughfares in the city centre, became Adolf-Hitler-Strasse. This was part of the overall German plan for the city. Unlike

Warsaw and other major urban centres further to the east, Łódź was to be part of the new *Reichsgau* of Wartheland and was therefore part of Germany. Litzmannstadt would be the capital of one of three *Regierungsbezirke* or administrative districts. Consequently, the city was not one of those listed for eventual destruction.

Historically, the city had been under Prussian control in the past before becoming part of the Russian Empire. Large numbers of Germans moved to the region during the 19th century and although many of them left after the re-establishment of an independent Poland at the end of the First World War, there were still about 54,000 Germans living there when the Germans invaded in 1939, roughly 8 per cent of the urban population of 672,000. As was the case elsewhere, Polish intellectuals and other potential leaders of anti-German resistance were systematically rounded up; some were sent to concentration camps, but many were executed in the nearby forests and about 10,000 ethnic Poles were simply expelled to the *Generalgouvernement* to make way for German settlement.[24] Just over a third of the pre-war population of Łódź was Jewish and although many were fortunate enough to escape before the arrival of the Wehrmacht, most came under German control either within the city itself or as the advancing German forces overtook refugee columns and forced them to turn back. After the initial waves of killings and expulsions, the remaining Jews were confined to the newly established ghetto, and as the surrounding rural region was 'cleansed' of Jews, the population of the overcrowded ghetto steadily increased, reaching about 148,000 in May 1941.[25] Trains began to transport groups of Jews to the Chełmno death camp about 117 miles (188km) north of Łódź in 1942 and Himmler ordered the closure of the ghetto in the summer of 1943. The intention was to move the remaining Jews to a new work camp that would be created near Lublin, but the deteriorating military situation on the Eastern Front made this impossible. Instead, Oswald Pohl, head of the *SS-WVHA*, ordered an inspection of the ghetto. Accompanied by Adolf Eichmann, whose self-proclaimed status as an expert on Jewish matters had led to his rise in the management of mass deportations of Jews, Pohl's subordinate Max Horn drew up a report criticising the local authorities for their management of the ghetto. Too many Jews were working in areas not directly related to the war effort; there were large numbers of non-productive children; many of the factories where the Jews worked were too far from the ghetto, resulting in time being wasted while they were marched to and fro; and the only solution was to convert the ghetto into a concentration camp.[26]

This proposal was an unwelcome development for Greiser, the *Gauleiter*; he saw it as direct interference with his personal authority. Far from being decided purely on economic grounds, the continued existence of the ghetto became a matter of personal prestige and influence. In February 1944, Greiser took advantage of a visit by Himmler to secure agreement that the ghetto (which was under the jurisdiction of Greiser, who benefited from any profit from its work activities) would not be turned into a concentration camp (which would have been under SS control, with Pohl's *SS-WVHA* profiting from its work). However, the population was to be reduced significantly, a task that would be carried out by a *Sonderkommando* ('Special Detachment') under the command of Hauptsturmführer Hans Bothmann, commandant of the Chełmno death camp.

The camp at Chełmno was established by Sturmbannführer Hermann Lange in October 1941 after he had conducted experiments in the killing of Jews and Polish prisoners using gas vans – large vans that had their exhausts diverted to their cargo compartments. These vans proved to be inefficient, and Lange selected the village recently renamed by the Germans as Kulmhof as the location for a new camp. At first, the camp was used to kill up to 50 people at a time in gas vans; when the secretary of the local Polish council, Stanisław Kaszyński, attempted to raise awareness of what was happening, he was arrested, interrogated, and then executed along with his wife. Bothmann inherited command of the camp and oversaw modifications to the process of murdering Jews – additives that made the exhaust fumes more poisonous were introduced and a special machine to help grind down the bones of victims was procured.

By the summer of 1943, Bothmann's death camp was winding down operations, having eliminated most of the 'surplus' Jewish population of Wartheland. In early 1944 there were still about 80,000 people living in the ghetto in Łódź and killings at Chełmno resumed in the summer. As much of the previous infrastructure had been dismantled, Bothmann set up a new group of wooden barracks and crematoria and once again most of the killings were done using gas vans. When the camp was finally closed at the end of 1944, the remaining Jews – groups of up to 80 Jews at a time were retained as workers to empty the vans of the dead victims, and these groups were periodically killed and replaced – were either executed or sent to Auschwitz. As part of the widespread *Sonderaktion 1005* ('Special Action 1005'), strenuous efforts were made to remove all traces of the crimes committed at Chełmno and elsewhere, with mass graves being exhumed and the remains burned. The total number of victims is estimated at being between 152,000 and 340,000. Accurate figures are impossible to determine because so many documents were destroyed to hide the activities of the SS, but the true figure is probably closer to the high estimate. Bothmann was assigned to other duties, including a spell in the 7th SS Mountain Division *Prinz Eugen*. He became a British prisoner of war, and hanged himself before his involvement in mass murder in Poland had been recognised.

When Bothmann ceased his killings in Chełmno, there were still about 68,000 Jews in the ghetto in Łódź. Himmler had now reissued instructions for the ghetto's liquidation, but the Warsaw Uprising led to delays in implementing his orders. Even at this stage of the war, when most Jews knew of the death camps, the Germans continued to take steps to avoid possible unrest and resistance by implying that those being taken from the ghetto were going to be employed elsewhere. On 2 August 1944, a proclamation appeared in the ghetto:

> On the instructions of the mayor of Litzmannstadt, the ghetto will be evacuated. The workshop crews will go as units, together with their families ...
>
> Luggage is not to exceed 20kg per person ... The families of the evacuees will go with the same transport so that no family will be separated.[27]

A few days later, Hans Biebow, the head of the German administration of the ghetto, made further assurances to Jews who were going to be removed from the camp:

> Siemens, AG Union, Schukert, every place where munitions are made, need workers. In Czenstochau, where workers are employed in munitions plants, they're very satisfied, and the Gestapo is also very satisfied with their work. After all, you want to live and eat, and you will have that ... I assure you that we'll make every effort to continue doing our best and – by transferring the ghetto [population] – save your lives.[28]

In the last months of 1944, trains left Łódź regularly carrying thousands of Jews, mainly to Auschwitz. The ghetto was steadily reduced in size, but despite repeated searches by the SS, 877 Jews – including three children – remained there; some were in hiding, but most were part of labour gangs being used to clear equipment from the ghetto's workshops. Numerous detention camps were created in and near Łódź in the years of occupation in addition to the ghetto; perhaps the cruellest was the *Polen-Jugendverwahrlager* ('Polish Youth Custody Camp'), set up at the end of December 1942 next to the Jewish ghetto. Children from all over Poland were brought to the camp and assessed for potential Germanisation. Those selected were sent to adoptive parents in Germany to be raised as Germans. Although most were aged between eight and 14, the youngest children were only two years old. Many of the children were forced to work in workshops that formed part of the ghetto.

As they approached Łódź, the Red Army units of 1st Belarusian Front crossed a significant line: they were now on Reich territory, part of Germany rather than areas occupied by the Germans. Consequently, the area had a far higher density of German civilians, albeit made up largely of newcomers to the region. Evacuation of some families from Łódź – mainly those of army and SS officers – started in late 1944, but as was the case throughout the eastern territories of the Reich, Hitler refused to consider mass evacuation as the Red Army advanced. The Führer insisted that the proximity of German women and children would bolster the will of the army to resist the approaching Soviet forces. As 18 January drew to a close, those forces were at the very gates of the city. In preceding days, thousands of German civilians had massed around the railway station in the hope of finding a means of escape, and hundreds more ventured out onto the frozen roads running west. Soviet aircraft attacked these columns from time to time and the chaotic situation greatly hindered the arrival and deployment of German reinforcements.

Hitler had ordered the troops of the *Panzer-Korps-Grossdeutschland* to move to the sector when the Soviet offensive began from its positions in East Prussia. Almost as the first trains departed for Łódź, Rokossovsky's 2nd Belarusian Front and Cherniakhovsky's 3rd Belarusian Front commenced their offensives against East Prussia; the result was that for several critical days, *Grossdeutschland* was unable to intervene either at its original location or at its intended point of redeployment. Guderian protested about its move to Łódź on the grounds that this would leave the forces defending East Prussia fatally weakened, but Hitler's decision and Guderian's arguments merely highlight the bankruptcy of resources that faced the German military. Bolstering one sector required weakening another, and the strength of Germany's enemies was now so great that there were no 'quiet' sectors from which troops could be drawn.

Like the British Army, the Wehrmacht had a tradition – albeit comparatively short-lived – of regional recruitment, with most of the rank and file of regiments and divisions being drawn from a specific military district or *Wehrkreis*. An exception was the *Grossdeutschland* Infantry Regiment, created in the summer of 1939 from a ceremonial guard regiment based in Berlin and composed of recruits from all over Germany. The regiment was rapidly motorised and then expanded steadily; in March 1942 it was an infantry division and a little over a year later had expanded to a panzergrenadier division. Like SS panzer and panzergrenadier divisions, it was significantly stronger than its Wehrmacht equivalents with an integral assault gun battalion and panzer battalion even when it was still an infantry division.

During the disastrous German defeat in Belarus in the summer of 1944, several corps were disbanded because their subordinate formations had ceased to exist. The remnants of XIII Corps – some of the staff and rear area elements – were used to create a new *Panzerkorps Grossdeutschland* in September 1944. It was fortunate to have as its commander General Dietrich von Saucken, a highly experienced officer who had led 4th Panzer Division with distinction in earlier fighting. In many respects, he was the epitome of the Prussian officer; photographs show him almost always immaculately dressed, usually with a monocle in place. His stern, austere expression was familiar to his men; he spent a great deal of time visiting front-line units and was highly regarded for the lengths he took to ensure the well-being of his men. But given the great limitations on resources available to the Wehrmacht by this stage of the war, assembly of the corps and its support elements proved to be a protracted affair and was still incomplete in January 1945.

In terms of combat elements, the new corps was intended to have the original *Grossdeutschland* Panzergrenadier Division and the *Jäger-Division Brandenburg*. Originally, the various elements of *Brandenburg* were used in similar roles to those of British commandos and SAS units, but as part of the creation of the new *Grossdeutschland* corps the disparate regiments were to be gathered and deployed as a new panzergrenadier division. Its commander was Generalmajor Hermann Schulte Heuthaus and he spent the last weeks of 1944 overseeing the transformation of his various regiments from units that had been used primarily in anti-partisan warfare in Yugoslavia into panzergrenadiers. Like other panzergrenadier divisions, *Brandenburg* was intended to have a panzer battalion, but although it was formed in Germany and equipped with Panther tanks, it was immediately deployed in Hungary and would never join its parent division.[29]

When orders were received for Saucken to move his corps to Łódź in January 1945, the *Grossdeutschland* Panzergrenadier Division was already heavily committed in fighting in East Prussia, where Rokossovsky's 2nd Belarusian Front was threatening to break through the German lines. As a result, the division was detached from the corps and left in place; the corps-level units together with *Brandenburg* were to deploy at Łódź to stop the threatening advance of Zhukov's two tank armies. In addition, Saucken was given control of the *HG* Panzer Division. Even if they had been at full strength, these two divisions would have been unlikely to be able to deal with the weight of Soviet armour that was pouring west. The first trains left East Prussia late on 14 January and as they rolled through the frozen landscape, the soldiers stared out of the carriage windows at columns of German refugees struggling to escape the advancing Red Army. In earlier years, it had been German troops who swept past such columns of civilians, pushing them aside or often opening fire on them; now it was the turn of German civilians to be caught up in a terrifying battlefield.

The first units of Saucken's *Grossdeutschland* corps reached Piotrków Trybunalski, about 25 miles (40km) south of Łódź, late on 16 January and detrained with the sounds of fighting clearly audible to the east. It was the first time that *Brandenburg* was being used in combat as a coherent division and Heuthaus' men got off to a bad start. A battalion deployed to the southeast of Piotrków Trybunalski came under sudden attack by Soviet armour from Fourth Tank Army before dawn on 17 January and was scattered. With little clear information about the precise location of Red Army units (and indeed of Wehrmacht formations retreating from the east), the rest of *Brandenburg* was ordered to detrain further north, and then to concentrate in forested countryside to the east of Piotrków Trybunalski. Almost immediately, there were clashes with probing Soviet units and the Germans – still far from full strength – fell back towards Łódź. Other parts of *Brandenburg* were still detraining here when there were sounds of fighting in the northern suburbs. There were confused clashes between *Brandenburg* units and the Soviet VIII Guards Mechanised Corps, but the railway line running to Łódź from the north had been cut. There was no possibility of the rest of the German division reaching Łódź. A regiment deployed around the town of Kutno, 32 miles (52km) north of Łódź, where it almost immediately came under attack. Two of its battalions were scattered and effectively destroyed in the days that followed.

Saucken arrived in Łódź on 18 January and set up a command post on the city outskirts. His corps had been subordinated to Ninth Army and Lüttwitz ordered him to carry out a counterattack towards the southeast as soon as he had sufficient strength. Shortly after he arrived, he learned that Nehring's corps was still in existence and attempting to march northwest towards Łódź; he decided that a counterattack as ordered was doomed to failure, particularly given that there were reports of Soviet armour approaching the line of the Warta River to the west of Łódź. He issued orders for his units to concentrate in the southern parts of Łódź, from where they would secure crossings over the Warta at Sieradz to the west of Łódź and would attempt to hold a position there in the hope that Nehring would be able to reach them.[30]

A measure of the success of the Red Army to date can be seen by a review of the German forces in Poland. When the Soviet offensive began, the German line from north to south was made up of XLVI Panzer Corps, VIII Corps, XL Panzer Corps, LVI Panzer Corps, XLII Corps, XXIV Panzer Corps, and XLVIII Panzer Corps. By the end of 18 January, many of these had effectively ceased to exist as coherent, united formations. After abandoning Warsaw, XLVI Panzer Corps was struggling to establish a new defensive line to the west. VIII Corps had disintegrated southeast of the Pilica River. XL Panzer Corps' remnants were struggling back towards Łódź, and the surviving elements of LVI Panzer Corps, XLII Corps, and XXIV Panzer Corps were somewhere in the rear of the advancing Soviet units. XLVIII Panzer Corps had borne the brunt of Konev's surge out of the Sandomierz bridgehead and had also effectively ceased to exist.

Far behind the Soviet tanks streaming towards the west, Nehring and his fellow senior officers attempted to make sense of their predicament on 18 January. They still had little clear idea of where friendly and hostile forces were, and fuel shortages were becoming an increasingly severe constraint. Finally, Nehring received a radio signal from Saucken's temporary headquarters in Łódź and decided that this was the direction in which there was the greatest chance of escape. The German column continued its slow trek, attempting whenever possible to avoid moving during daylight. Roads through woodland offered some protection from air attack, but increased the risk of clashes with Polish partisans; some of the Germans took to shooting at any Polish civilians they encountered.[31]

Despite their perilous situation, the officers and men in what became known as 'Nehring's wandering cauldron' remained confident that they would reach safety. Jauer, commander of 20th Panzergrenadier Division, later wrote:

> The strange thing was that despite all the hardships and worries, we never had the feeling that we would meet our end in the pocket. This was not least because everyone had trust in each other and everyone gave their best efforts.[32]

During 18 January, more survivors of Recknagel's XLII Corps began to link up with Nehring's troops. One such group, largely the remnants of 342nd Infantry Division, reached the column near Białaczów; it had a battery of 12 howitzers, but limited fuel to move them. The first objective was now to reach and cross the Pilica River. A reconnaissance group reported that the road through the village of Paradyż to the west was clear, but there were clashes with Soviet troops to the north at Przysucha. Nehring therefore decided to turn west in order to avoid contact with this Soviet force.

The units that had been encountered in Pryzsucha were part of the Soviet Thirty-Third Army, the southern wing of Zhukov's 1st Belarusian Front. It was the good fortune of the Germans in the wandering cauldron that by chance, they found themselves precisely on the junction of 1st Belarusian Front to the north and 1st Ukrainian Front to the south. With both Soviet fronts intent on continuing their advance towards the west, there was a limited opportunity for

Nehring to slip away before the Red Army could establish a continuous front line. Time was of the essence, but Nehring wanted to hold open the line of retreat for other units further to the east. He concluded that a determined thrust to reach the Pilica would have to take place no later than 19 January.

Ahead of Nehring's forces, the Soviet tank armies continued their advance. Lelyushenko's Fourth Tank Army crossed the Pilica in strength during 18 January and seized Piotrków Trybunalski. To the south, Rybalko's Third Guards Tank Army was advancing through almost open space with no major German units in its path. Fresh orders arrived from 1st Ukrainian Front as the day progressed: Rybalko was to cross the frontier into Germany at Miedźno on 19 January. There were concerns that the fortifications prepared by the Germans along the Reich frontier would give retreating Wehrmacht units a chance to catch their breath, and it was important to seize them before any German resistance could harden.

At the southern end of the great Soviet offensive, Konev's troops were about to enter Kraków. After the war, Konev's account of the attack on 18 January was part of a widely accepted narrative:

I went to the observation post of Fifty-Ninth Army to see [Lieutenant] General Korovnikov. The advancing army troops, deployed from the second echelon, were lined up to strike directly at Kraków from the north and northwest. From the observation post we had a clear view of the city.

After assessing the situation on the ground with the army commander, we decided to send IV Guards Tank Corps, attached to this army ... to bypass Kraków from the west in combination with the advance of Sixtieth Army, which at that time was approaching the southeast and southern outskirts of Kraków, a manoeuvre that threatened the Kraków garrison with encirclement.

The troops of Fifty-Ninth Army itself were already preparing for the assault. They were tasked with breaking into the city from the north and northwest and capturing the bridges across the Vistula, depriving the enemy of the opportunity to strengthen their defences in the city itself. It was very important for me to achieve swift action by all the troops participating in the attack on Kraków. Only our speed could save Kraków from destruction. And we wanted it intact. The Front command rejected artillery and air strikes on the city. But nevertheless, we subjected the fortified approaches to the city, on which the enemy defence relied, to heavy artillery fire that morning ...

The attack was successful. The Nazis opened fire on our troops with rifles, machine-guns, artillery, and at times tanks, but despite the constant noise, it was clear that the fire was slackening and that in essence the enemy's resistance was broken. The threat of encirclement ended any determined attempt to cling tenaciously to the city … The enemy had only one road left – southwards to the mountains. And he began to leave quickly.

On this occasion, we didn't set ourselves the task of cutting off the last escape route of the Nazis. If we had done so, we would then have had to spend a long time digging them out and this would undoubtedly have destroyed the city. No matter how tempting it was to create an encirclement, we turned this down even though it was within our capabilities …

During the evening, smashing the enemy's rearguards, Korovnikov's troops moved through the entire city with units of IV Guards Tank Corps entering from the northwest, and parts of Sixtieth Army from the east and southeast inflicted heavy losses on the enemy as he left Kraków. Thanks to the skilful actions of the troops of Korovnikov, [Colonel General Pavel Alekseevich] Kurochkin [commander of Sixtieth Army] and [Lieutenant General Pavel Pavlovich] Poluboyarov [commander of IV Guards Tank Corps], the oldest and most beautiful city in Poland was taken safe and sound …

The Nazis had laid more than enough demolition charges in the city – under all the main buildings and structures – but they didn't have time to trigger them. Immediately, our sappers began their tireless work.[33]

This version of events – that it was the swift action of Konev's armies that drove the Germans from Kraków before they could destroy the city – was repeated many times in the years after the war. As late as 1987, just two years before the end of Communist rule in Poland, a new statue of Konev was erected in Kraków. But whilst it is true that the threat of encirclement triggered the German retreat from the city, there is little evidence to support Konev's assertion that the Germans were planning widespread demolitions. Most of the explosives that they had planted were small anti-personnel mines and the only systematic destruction was at the headquarters of the Gestapo and police. In other cities in Eastern Europe, both in Poland and further east in the Soviet Union, the Germans carried out a ruthless scorched earth policy as they withdrew. There was clearly little effort to repeat this in Kraków, perhaps through a lack of time or resources. But it suited the Soviet Union to portray Konev as a great liberator who took particular care to prevent the destruction of the city; this may have been a conscious attempt to counter the criticism levelled at the Red Army for its failure to intervene during the Warsaw Uprising.

On 19 January, Soviet troops in the north moved into Łódź in strength. Even if he had been inclined to defend the city, Saucken lacked the troops for such a battle and his *Grossdeutschland* Corps completed its withdrawal to the area around Sieradz. Chuikov's Eighth Guards Army, temporarily out of contact with Zhukov's Front headquarters, had spent much of 18 January paused to the east of Łódź, giving the troops a much-needed opportunity to rest and reorganise. Chuikov drew up orders for his troops to sweep through the northern and western parts of Łódź to avoid heavy fighting in the city centre, but suddenly received a signal from 1st Belarusian Front: his army was ordered to take up the positions it had already occupied by the end of 19 January. Chuikov decided that the signal was out of date and proceeded with his plan to overrun the city and his troops moved forward shortly after dawn. They encountered little serious resistance, though Vainrub, in command of Eighth Guards Army's tanks and mechanised forces, was seriously wounded during a brief German artillery bombardment. As was the case with Kraków, Łódź was captured without heavy urban fighting. Chuikov drove into the city during the afternoon:

> We drove through the streets. The Fascists had remade everything here in their own manner. The main square, formerly called Liberty Place, had been renamed Germany Square. With such changes, the Nazis wanted to emphasise that Poland would never be free, that Germany would rule here and the Poles would be powerless slaves. On street corners, there were signs with German street names. All store signs were in German. There were signs on the doors of cafés and restaurants: 'Only for Germans. Poles are not allowed to enter.'[34]

Chuikov continued with a description of the rapturous welcome his soldiers received from the Poles, but this account is undoubtedly exaggerated. Most Poles would have welcomed liberation from German rule and some may have been enthusiastic about the arrival of the Red Army, but this latter group was probably a minority.

The two tank armies of Zhukov's Front were further to the west. Babadzhanian's tanks encountered elements of the German *Brandenburg* Division, scattering them with ease. To his relief, he was permitted to move most of his forces to approach Poznań directly rather than attempting an assault across the Warta and by the end of the day his leading elements were approaching the city. For many years, the city had been under Prussian or German control and was known as Posen; it was returned to Poland at the end of the First World War. As a result, about half of the remaining German population left. In 1939, the city once more came under German control. About 100,000 Polish inhabitants were forcibly expelled to the east and there were mass executions of Jews and others, mainly in a camp that was established at Fort VII, part of the 19th-century fortifications.

It would have come as no surprise to any of the German forces in the area when Hitler declared Posen a fortress, to be held to the last man. The designated commandant was the corpulent Generalmajor Ernst Mattern, a former police officer with little field experience; he had commanded a number of training units or newly raised units that were building up to full strength, but rarely in combat. Most of the soldiers available to him were poorly armed *Volkssturm*, but their ranks were stiffened by the presence of the personnel of several training establishments in the city. Despite the determination of the officer cadets in his garrison to defend Posen, Mattern had no such illusions. He issued the necessary orders for preparations, but it was clear to his staff that he felt that the task was hopeless.[35]

Meanwhile, early on 19 January, the leading elements of Nehring's group attempted to seize the next objective in their line of retreat, the small village of Paradyż. After an initial success, the Germans were brought to a standstill by the arrival of Soviet reinforcements and it wasn't until the surviving tanks of Nehring's corps appeared – at first, they were mistaken for Soviet tanks and nearly came under fire – that the village was taken. Shortly after, Nehring led his men to the Pilica to the east of Piotrków Trybunalski. The Germans found an intact wooden bridge, permitting infantrymen to cross to the west bank. The sappers with the column began the arduous task of finding and strengthening a ford where the German tanks would be able to cross. Several half-tracks and an artillery tractor broke through the ice of the river and were swept away; eventually, two tanks were sacrificed to create the piers of an improvised bridge. In the meantime, large numbers of soldiers began to mass on the east bank, looking nervously at the sky, but the weather had deteriorated and few Soviet aircraft appeared.

At about the same time, Lelyushenko's tanks reached and captured Osjaków on the Warta, about 46 miles (74km) to the west of Nehring's men. With his units now approaching and reaching the Warta on a broad front, Lelyushenko ordered a brief halt. Many battalions were dangerously low on fuel and ammunition, and a short pause was needed. Further south, Rybalko's tanks began to encounter increasing German resistance, as did the combined arms armies operating in the wake of the two tank armies. The southern flank of the great Soviet advance was now facing an increasing number of newly arrived formations, and the rapid penetration into the Silesian industrial heartland that Stalin had expected was looking more complex. It was time to consider whether the headlong drive towards the west would have to be modified.

All across the frozen landscape, people were on the move. Soviet tanks had made spectacular advances and in many sectors were still pushing on to the west; Soviet infantry marched along frozen roads in their wake, accompanied by columns of trucks carrying food, fuel and ammunition. Bypassed German groups were everywhere, sometimes laying down their weapons in exhaustion when they encountered Soviet troops and sometimes fighting fiercely. Civilians – mainly Germans, but also some Poles – tried desperately to make their way to whatever constituted safety. But there were also others on the move in one of the most tragic and deadly episodes of German atrocities in the occupied lands of the east.

# CHAPTER 6

# ROADS OF SUFFERING
# AND DEATH

In the years that followed the end of the Second World War, German accounts of the closing months of the conflict on the Eastern Front began to appear. Some were personal memoirs of both soldiers and civilians caught up in the chaos; others were historical accounts of the campaigns. But although many of these German accounts drew attention to the plight of German refugees as they struggled to escape before the arrival of the Red Army, few made any mention of another mass movement that was taking place at the same time.

The German concentration camp system started to develop as soon as the Nazis came to power. The first camps were used to incarcerate political opponents of the regime, and Theodor Eicke, the commandant of Dachau, instigated a regime of harsh, strictly enforced rules that imposed a climate of terror. As word of these conditions spread across Germany, the effect was seen by many within the regime to be beneficial and Eicke's policies soon became the normal modus operandi for all camps; from the outset, Jewish prisoners were treated with particular brutality.[1] With the creation of Sachsenhausen in 1936 and its subcamp Neuengamme two years later, a new policy began to develop, with the use of camp inmates as forced labourers. Both of these camps were used for making bricks and roof tiles, but productivity was far lower than in ordinary places of work – there was inadequate investment in equipment and the mistreatment of prisoners left many too weak to work effectively. Nevertheless, Himmler – whose SS had control of the camps – was keen to develop the economic potential of the people in the camps and he appointed Oswald Pohl to run the *SS-Wirtschaftshauptamt*.

A longstanding and fanatical member of the Nazi Party, Pohl was also an efficient administrator and organiser and there was considerable friction between his aims and those of Eicke, who wished to use the camp system to crush any dissent and saw the value of his regime as a means of identifying and selecting men who would rise to high rank within the SS.[2] But the demands of the German economy meant that Pohl's star was in the ascendant. In 1938, the *Deutsche Erd- und Steinwerke* ('German Earth and Stone Works') was created under Pohl's control; it would grow into one of the largest users of concentration camp labour. There was a further development in 1939, when Himmler was appointed *Reichskommissar für die Festigung Deutschen Volkstums* ('Reich Commissar for the Strengthening of Germandom'). He was to oversee the creation of new German settlements across the territories of Eastern Europe as they came under German control, and from the outset it was Himmler's intention to use the concentration camp population as the workforce for this project. New camps would be created as required, and the planned scale of German population engineering was so great that there were no concerns about the consequences of high death rates in the camps.[3]

Following the outbreak of war, German industry began to suffer from widespread manpower shortages. Many workers had been mobilised into the armed services, and although numerous technicians were later released there remained major problems. In late 1941, there were suggestions that the large numbers of prisoners of war captured in the Soviet Union might be put to use, but the death rate in prison camps was shockingly high – over 3 million Soviet soldiers were captured in the first months of the war with the Soviet Union, but two-thirds of them were dead by February 1942 through a mixture of malnutrition, disease, and deliberate murder. Workers were recruited, usually with little choice, across Poland and the occupied parts of the Soviet Union, but there continued to be serious shortages. A different solution was required.

The first phase of the Nazi attempt to exterminate the Jewish population of Europe gathered pace shortly after the German invasion of the Soviet Union. Each German army group was accompanied by one or more *Einsatzgruppen*, and working with other units – security and police battalions, and local paramilitaries – these SS units carried out what became known as the 'Holocaust by bullets'. From the Baltic States to Ukraine, there were mass shootings of Jews, Roma, the disabled, suspected and actual Communists, and anyone else who was regarded as unwanted. Those killed were buried in mass graves, usually at the site of the shooting; in many cases, they were shot in pits, a layer of soil was sprinkled on them, and the next group of victims was then brought forward and executed while standing or lying on those already killed. The expectation was that the war against the Soviet Union would be over in a few short weeks and thereafter the

Jews of Germany and Western Europe would be transported to the east where they would be worked to death, building roads and railways across the newly conquered territories. But given the demands of German industry for workers, Pohl was now given control of the concentration camp population as a source of workers. This was distinct from Himmler's original intention to use these men and women as workers in the construction of the new towns, railways and roads that would spread across the eastern territories. The intention now was to create work camps that were specifically intended to aid the German war industry. This also marked a shift in the plans to implement the destruction of the Jews of Europe. The overall objective – the complete extermination of all Jews – remained unaltered; but economic constraints would have to be taken into account, necessitating many Jews being kept alive until the war was over.

Pohl steadily replaced the harsh disciplinarians that Eicke had left in commanding roles in the concentration camps with men of his own. In the autumn of 1942, he met Speer to provide more labour from the camps for the armaments industry. The result was a proliferation of subcamps around the main concentration camps, with each subcamp providing labour for one or more industrial concerns. But the increasing use of camp labour for the war industry meant that the terrible conditions in the camps – where malnutrition was widespread, medical care was almost non-existent, and arbitrary punishments and even killings remained an everyday event – had to be improved. In October 1942, a group of prisoners was transferred from Dachau and Ravensbrück to Auschwitz, where they were to be used in the Buna subcamp, the location of a chemical factory run by I.G. Farben. The camp administration was unimpressed:

> The 499 prisoners transferred from Dachau are in very bad physical condition and none of them is suitable for work in the Buna plant. Barely a third of them can be employed in other work and these only after a two-week recovery time. Fifty of the arrivals could be employed in their profession; 162 have no profession; and 267 of the transferees are farm workers. The 186 workers transferred from Ravensbrück were in better physical condition than those from Dachau.[4]

Pohl issued instructions to all camp commandants and their medical staff, telling them that the death rate – in 1942, he estimated, it was at about 10 per cent per month – was unacceptable.[5] The camp population increased greatly in the following months; some of this was due to better conditions in the camps, but most was due to larger numbers of people being incarcerated. The transfer of prisoners from one camp to another had another effect: the original populations of each camp became steadily diluted and more heterogeneous. Originally, the camps that were intended as depots of slave labour were mainly for prisoners of ethnic backgrounds that did not necessarily result in their inclusion in German genocidal plans, but by the last months of the war, these 'racially acceptable' prisoners were greatly outnumbered in work camps by Jews, Poles, other Slavs, and Communists from Italy, France and elsewhere. Indeed, by the summer of 1944, Jews formed more than 50 per cent of the overall concentration camp population.

As the end of the war approached, the death rate in work camps began to increase again; but by the beginning of 1945, Pohl estimated that about 29 per cent of the concentration camp population – about 207,000 out of 714,000 prisoners – was working directly or indirectly for the German armaments industry.[6] This created considerable tensions between those who were trying to keep Germany's war production running and those who were still focused on the extermination of Jews and other undesirable populations on ideological grounds. In mid-1944, Himmler wrote to Pohl to advise him that Hitler had approved the transfer of 200,000 Hungarian Jews to the Reich as labourers. However, he added that this was to have no bearing on the fates of the families of the workers selected.[7] Those who were not suitable as labourers were to be killed.

As the war dragged on far beyond the original expectations of Hitler and his inner circle, there was growing concern about the mass graves of those killed in the Holocaust by bullets and the consequences if they were ever uncovered at a future date; even if Germany was eventually victorious, it was possible that future generations would not understand the necessity of the mass killings and would condemn those who had carried them out. At a more practical level, the mass graves at Chełmno and elsewhere were causing problems with foul vapours and liquids oozing from the ground, and there were worries about groundwater becoming contaminated.[8] In early 1942, Reinhard Heydrich, the senior SS figure who oversaw much of the mass murder committed by the Nazis, ordered the implementation of a new plan known as *Sonderaktion 1005* ('Special Action 1005'). This involved the disinterment of the victims of recent killings and the incineration of their corpses. Implementation of *Sonderaktion 1005* was delayed when Heydrich was assassinated in June 1942 but not long after, experiments were conducted by Standartenführer Paul Blobel, who had directed the slaughter of thousands of Jews at Bila Tserkva and Babi Yar in Ukraine. His first experiments at the extermination camp at Chełmno using incendiary bombs to set fire to mass graves were unsuccessful and after several setbacks he determined the most effective way to proceed. After being exhumed by forced labour parties from concentration camps, the corpses were placed on a grid of railway tracks in layers with firewood between each layer and were then set ablaze. Periodically, the labour parties were shot and added to the pyres.

In mid-June 1944, with Germany facing multiple threats on all fronts, Himmler issued fresh instructions to the concentration camp commandants. The document stated that in the event of a major alert, the police chief in each region – the *HSSPF* – would temporarily assume authority over concentration camps and the staff in each camp would be subordinated to him.[9] The precise nature of what constituted a major alert was not specified. After the war, several concentration camp officers and other senior SS figures described how they interpreted this as an instruction that devolved decision-making about the fate of camp prisoners to the *HSSPF*, particularly about whether they should be evacuated, left to be liberated by the enemy, or killed out of hand. In the *Generalgouvernement*, Walter Bierkamp, head of the security police in the district of Radom, made his own interpretation:

> The liberation of prisoners or Jews by the enemy, be it the Western Powers or the Red Army, must be avoided under all circumstances, nor may they fall into their hands alive.[10]

Himmler's new directive was based upon recent events. In early 1944, evacuation of the concentration camp at Majdanek, immediately east of the Polish city of Lublin, was ordered. Prisoners began to leave at the beginning of April for concentration camps elsewhere, mainly in overcrowded cattle railcars with few if any sanitary arrangements. Despite this, most reached their destinations, but the last evacuation from the camp and nearby factories took place just a day before the Red Army reached the camp. About 1,200 prisoners were marched to Kraśnik, about 26 miles (42km) to the southwest, where they were to board trains that would take them to Auschwitz. What followed was a precursor of events that would unfold across German-occupied regions in the last months of the war. The guards forced the prisoners to march at a pace that was barely possible for the fittest amongst them; those who faltered were shot. Barely half of the prisoners survived to reach Auschwitz.[11]

When the Red Army reached Majdanek, the soldiers were confronted with horrifying evidence of the mass killings that had taken place. Despite being hardened by their personal experiences and the horrors they had already witnessed, the Red Army troops saw scenes that haunted them for the rest of their lives:

> The most striking thing was the heaps of shoes ... Whole warehouses. A man who guided us was a servant or maybe a security guard. He showed us the ovens. There was a recess next to them and a German used to stand there with a club. When prisoners could no longer work [throwing corpses into the ovens for cremation],

he hit them on the head as they passed him. They were then thrown into the ovens. He showed us the barrels in which ashes had been collected for scattering on the fields.[12]

Some of the furnaces were still warm and the ashes from human corpses were everywhere. There were three heaps of ashes in the yard, about 1.5m high. We went looking for rags to clean our vehicles' guns. We found a warehouse where it looked like victims had been undressed. What struck me was this: the clothes and shoes were all so clean, smoothed out and folded, children's shoes separated from women's shoes, everything laid out tidily. And there were lengths of women's hair bundled together. It was terrible. How could anyone do something like that?[13]

The Soviet government rapidly made the discoveries at Majdanek and also at the dismantled extermination camp of Bełzec widely known and photographs appeared in newspapers and newsreels all over the world.

After the Soviet capture of Majdanek, the SS urgently considered the risk of further camps falling into Soviet hands. There were evacuations in several areas, and the ordeal of the prisoners varied. Generally, camps in the eastern parts of German-held territory tended to have higher Jewish populations, and these always suffered the highest death rates. In some cases, there were deliberate attempts to kill Jews in work camps if evacuation was likely to be difficult. One such example took place in Vilnius, where the city was already almost encircled by the Red Army. Jewish workers in a vehicle repair workshop complex attempted to hide at the last moment; SS personnel searched the buildings and managed to find perhaps half of the 600 Jews in hiding, killing most of them immediately.[14] When a labour camp being used for the dismantling of the former Warsaw Ghetto was cleared in the summer of 1944, those who were unfit for evacuation were executed. The rest spent three days marching without food or water, and anyone who attempted to ask local people for either was shot. When they reached Żychlin, 57 miles (93km) west of Warsaw, they were crammed into railcars – again without food or water – and taken to Dachau. Most didn't survive the journey.[15]

In eastern France, the Germans had established a concentration camp with several subcamps at Natzweiler-Struthof, about 24 miles (39km) to the west of Strasbourg. As American and French forces approached the area, evacuation from the camp commenced. Conditions in the camp were better than in many camps to the east and the prisoners – mainly from France, Norway, Belgium, and the Netherlands – were in comparatively good health. Evacuation was also generally conducted in a more organised manner; it commenced in September 1944, but several of the subcamps continued to function. These were essential for local factories working for the German armaments industry, and the collective population of these camps was over 13,000. There were even inward transfers of additional prisoners from camps like Dachau.[16] Most of those who were evacuated from the main camp survived to reach their destinations, but conditions there were often far worse than in Natzweiler-Struthof itself. A large group was sent to the village of Huttendorf; they had been given no food or water during their march and their condition deteriorated rapidly. When he became aware of their condition, the local mayor visited the compound where they were being kept, despite attempts by the officer in charge of the guards to stop him, and then organised food and water supplies for them – even the commander of the local *Volkssturm* helped by providing personnel.[17] But such acts were unusual. Most civilians were too scared to offer help, or chose not to do so.

On 21 December 1944, several weeks before the great Soviet offensive in the east commenced, Bracht – the *Gauleiter* of Upper Silesia, in whose territory Auschwitz and most of its satellite camps lay – ordered arrangements to be made for the evacuation of all prisoners of war, forced labourers, and concentration camp inmates from his province. They were to be taken further west where it was expected they could continue to contribute to Germany's armaments industries. Despite this, several weeks passed with almost no steps being taken. As Konev's 1st Ukrainian Front began to move closer to Katowice and Auschwitz, Ernst-Heinrich Schmauser, the *HSSPF* for Upper Silesia, telephoned Berlin and spoke to Pohl to ask for instructions. He was told that no healthy prisoners were to be left in the camps.[18]

Prisoners finally began to leave the subcamps of Auschwitz on 18 January. About 2,200 were taken directly to other camps in Germany, and the population of the main camp was reduced to 8,000, with another 500 in Birkenau; these were all people who were categorised as too weak to be marched away. Terrified that the SS would kill them, many of the sick and disabled tried desperately to join the columns being marched away. It is likely that given their weakened status, they didn't survive the ordeal that followed. A prisoner described the chaotic scenes of the last moments of the concentration camp:

> One morning there was suddenly unusual noise, and the SS roused the dying women, who were sleeping, worn out from their labours, with unprecedented sadism. Within minutes, we were standing ready in lines of five; each of us was given a loaf of bread, which the starving women ate immediately ... We wrapped our feet in newspapers before shoving them into our heavy wooden clogs so that we would be warmer on the road, which was covered in a thick, slippery layer of snow. None of us knew what lay ahead.[19]

By contrast, prisoners in other blocks had been told the evening before that they would be leaving and there had been a more orderly assembly of columns and distribution of food, further evidence that despite Bracht's orders for plans to be drawn up in advance, little or no such preparations had been made in a systematic manner. Several of the emptied huts in Auschwitz were set ablaze and the sounds of explosions as the SS destroyed camp equipment added to the terror of those who lay in their bunks, too weak to join the marches. By 25 January, the remaining SS and SD staff had destroyed much of the documentation in the camps; immediately before they left Birkenau, the SD officers separated 300 Jews from other prisoners who were still present and executed them.[20]

In the last months of a war that had unleashed industrialised cruelty and murder across Europe, the determination of some Germans to kill the last Jews in their custody seems almost incomprehensible. Their dream of a racially pure Europe was in ruins and the enemy was quite literally at the gates; yet many still managed to find time for further killing. To an extent, this seems to have been the culmination of the tension that had prevailed ever since the end of 1941, between those who were determined to implement the genocidal policies of the Third Reich and those who wished at least to postpone such activities and to use prisoners for labour. Either policy was now pointless given the imminent final defeat of Germany; yet the killings continued, some of it driven by a desire to ensure that the hated Jews didn't survive to see the downfall of Nazi Germany. Such killing took place both in the camps and during the marches that followed the evacuations. Obersturmführer Wilhelm Reischenbeck left Auschwitz with a column of 3,900 prisoners on 19 January. The destination was Loslau (now the Polish Wodzisław Slaski), about 33 miles (53km) to the west. The prisoners had little or no protection from the winter weather. During the march, temperatures regularly fell to -15°C and the roads were covered in deep snow. Reischenbeck claimed that Sturmbannführer Richard Baer, the last commandant of Auschwitz, had ordered that any stragglers should be executed; whilst this is possible, Baer had shown little interest in organising the evacuations and had already fled, and it is more likely that each column commander made up his own mind about such matters. As exhausted prisoners dropped by the roadside, the guards killed them with a single shot. There was no opportunity to bury them in the frozen ground, with the rumble of the artillery of the Red Army clearly audible.

One of the columns that left Auschwitz on 18 January consisted of about 3,000 prisoners, almost all of them Jews from Hungary, France, and Poland. On 20 January, they reached Gleiwitz (now the Polish Gliwice), a journey of 32 miles (52km), and boarded trains for a further journey of 11 miles (18km). About 290 died either in the short train journey from Gleiwitz or were shot shortly after.

After combining with other prisoners from Auschwitz subcamps, the column made its way on foot to the concentration camp at Gross-Rosen (now the Polish Rogożnica). In total, about 1,000 died or were killed during the week that it took the prisoners to travel from Auschwitz to the new camp.[21]

Conditions in Gross-Rosen were amongst the worst in the entire concentration camp system, and now deteriorated further with the arrival of additional prisoners from Auschwitz. Wooden barracks that had been intended to hold perhaps 100 prisoners had at least 400 occupants; although ten extra barracks were constructed, there were over a thousand prisoners in each building in extreme cases.[22] Food supplies that had been inadequate for the existing population were now distributed – usually haphazardly – to even more prisoners, many of whom were only able to lie down outside the huts on the frozen mud. Some of the new arrivals later described their experiences:

As soon as we entered, we were left to our own devices without guards, like a flock of sheep without a shepherd, but there were SS men standing around. In the camp there were no barracks, no bunks, nothing except for earth and mountains and around the area were scattered thousands of corpses, thousands of skeletons. Suddenly the order was given … to pick up the corpses and arrange them in lines … Two men picked up each corpse, a man at each end, and threw the corpses … It grew dark and we continued to throw them one after the other automatically. Our strength ran out and we sank down where we were standing in order to rest a little. We crowded together in order to keep warm and fell asleep …

The entire camp stank of burned flesh and the smoke rose and rose. We were concentrated in huts without anything, only walls, no beds, nothing. We were jammed in one on top of the other, there was no room to sit, everyone had to stand.[23]

The Red Army was drawing ever closer. Petr Markovich Katsevman was a pilot flying ground attack missions in support of 1st Ukrainian Front as it moved into Silesia:

Our mission … was to bomb enemy troops unloading at a railway station. According to aerial reconnaissance, many trains had accumulated at the station. But nobody told us, the pilots, that there were trains at this railway station from the Auschwitz camp. And who in the regiment headquarters could have known this? … When we broke through the clouds at an altitude of over 2,200m [7,200ft] we saw the station with trains standing on the tracks, and in the distance – rows of warehouses. We had no idea that these were barracks for Auschwitz prisoners. Bombing from such a high altitude was ineffective and our commanders of course knew this. Usually, bombing was done in a dive from a height of 600m or lower – we didn't have bombsights and only the nose of the aircraft and the crosshairs on the windshield served as a sight. But we were ordered to bomb from a high altitude largely to spread panic. We carried out this task … [After the liberation of Auschwitz] the surviving prisoners said that many of the German guards and other Fascist personnel, after seeing our Ilyushins over the camp, got into their cars and drove off in a panic without having time to kill the last prisoners in the camp and eliminate evidence of their crimes. If this really happened, then for me this mission is the most important of my career. If, even indirectly, the concentration camp prisoners were saved by our attack, I can be proud of this mission to the end of my life.[24]

There was growing chaos behind the German front line. With Soviet units rapidly moving forward, some columns of prisoners marched for days along the snowy roads only to be turned back and forced to retrace their steps. Although some prisoners had been given food before they set off, almost no further rations were issued and for the badly malnourished prisoners, exhaustion and exposure took a huge toll. One survivor compared their ordeal to that of another march through bitterly cold conditions:

> Anyone who has seen the film about the 1812 Russian-French war, and the scenes of the retreat of the French from Moscow, the snow-covered soldiers, the soldiers with ice crystals on their lips, on their moustaches, soldiers without head coverings and with a layer of snow, and soldiers retreating with torn boots and toes protruding from the torn leather, soldiers who collapsed out of weakness, starvation – it was nothing compared to the hell of the death march.[25]

Some of the civilians who lived along the routes of what became known as the death marches tried to help, throwing food to the prisoners; this usually resulted in anger on the part of the guards. On occasion, prisoners who slipped away from the columns were given shelter. Constantly fearing that they were about to be overtaken by Soviet troops, the guards often resorted to brutal measures to keep their columns moving. One group of prisoners from Auschwitz and its satellite camps reached a work camp at Blechhammer, roughly midway between Katowice and Oppeln, before being taken onwards to Gross-Rosen. About 100 who were assessed as too weak to continue were left in the camp and a doctor amongst their number tried to organise care, looting the abandoned SS barracks. A small group of prisoners decided to leave the camp rather than await the arrival of the Red

Army; they were the fortunate ones. On 26 January, a company of SS arrived and searched the camp, executing any prisoners they found. The bodies were piled together and set ablaze. Fewer than a dozen prisoners survived to tell the tale.[26]

Intelligence officers in Sixtieth Army had briefed Kurochkin, the army commander, about the existence of the concentration camps in his path and on 25 January he issued orders for the leading units to form special advance detachments of tanks with infantry riders. On 27 January, two days before the German Seventeenth Army was given belated permission to withdraw from Katowice, Soviet troops reached Auschwitz. The troops of Sixtieth Army had been threatening to turn the eastern flank of the German positions around Katowice and a soldier from 100th Rifle Division, part of XXVIII Rifle Corps, was the first Soviet soldier to reach the camp shortly after dawn.[27] Leontiy Veniaminovich Brandt was a scout with one of the leading units, who was interviewed about his experiences over half a century later:

> There are things that are impossible to forget. So many years have passed, but before my eyes there is still an image: our reconnaissance group was entering the Auschwitz camp. Barracks, long rows of barracks. And the prisoners in striped rags, waving their arms, shouting to us in different languages. Exhausted, completely exhausted – they apparently couldn't leave the camp when others left and the guards, hearing the thunder of our guns, hastily fled. And they met us, clinging to the barbed wire, laughing and crying. It was a terrible scene. But the worst thing lay ahead: the crematoria, which were still warm, and mountains of women's hair – of different colours and different lengths. Piles of shoes, including children's shoes.
>
> Everything had been done in an orderly fashion. The belongings of the dead were kept in numbered paper bags – perhaps prepared for shipment back to Germany. And hair and human skin was used for 'economic' purposes. Skin with tattoos was highly valued – we learned that handbags were made from it. And next to this horror were well-kept houses where the guards lived, with flowers in the front gardens. Sports grounds, a swimming pool – all that was needed for a good rest after hard work.[28]

Aleksander Leonidovich Limin was a 19-year-old rifleman who found himself in one of Kurochkin's advance detachments:

> It was snowing, it was bitterly cold and we had stopped in some kind of orchard to have a meal. And some of our tanks rolled up, about 12 or 14 of them. They stopped and a short, stocky major got out of the tank and said that they had

received an order that a concentration camp was located 30km [18 miles] away and they needed help to liberate it. 'I can't do it alone, I don't have any infantry riders for my tanks … Give me some riflemen.'

… We drove forward for about 90 minutes and came to this place, Auschwitz. There was a guard post – some kind of wooden house and a barrier. There was a German at the post with straw in his boots to keep his feet warm. Our tank drove straight up to the barrier and crushed it. He shouted, '*Du bist verrückt! Was machst du?*' ['You're crazy! What are you doing?'] I shouted back, '*Jetzt aufhängen!*' [literally 'hang it up now', but intended to mean, 'We'll hang you now']. And we did so.

Then we began to try to restore order in the camp. There was someone else in a watchtower, but he was also dealt with. Then another rifle unit arrived from 1st Ukrainian Front and we looked at what had been going on there. My God, the horror.[29]

At the same time, hundreds of thousands of German civilians took to the frozen roads. The atrocities committed by the Red Army in and around Nemmersdorf had been widely publicised and most Germans had little expectation of good treatment from Soviet soldiers who were almost universally feared. As they struggled along the roads of the collapsing Reich, German civilians came across scenes that could only add to their sense of horror. One boy aged 13 was fortunate to be put aboard a train that left Poznań before the siege ring closed:

Along the road we saw German soldiers who had been hung. There were signs around their necks saying: 'I was a coward and I tried to run away.'[30]

On occasion, columns of refugees were overtaken by the advancing Soviet forces. Horst Wegner was a 16-year-old in one such column:

The Russian tanks caught up with us just before we reached Kolberg. The infantry sitting on top of the tanks started to shoot wildly all over the place. My father got shot right through his thigh. We were near a farmer's house, and sneaked into the barn to catch our breath and rest a little … The Russians found us and pulled us out of the barn. They were Mongolians. They had huge scars and pockmarks on their faces. And they were draped with jewellery – they wore watches up to the elbows. They came in and pulled out everyone wearing anything military – a military coat, for example. They were taken behind the barn, shoved against a wall, and shot. They weren't even all Germans; some of them were foreigners. They even shot the private who had bandaged my father's leg.[31]

Many Soviet soldiers gathered as many wristwatches as they could – some had never seen such items before, and had no idea that if they stopped, they could simply be rewound. Without question, many Red Army soldiers sought to exact revenge upon German soldiers for the events they had witnessed earlier in the war – the deaths of comrades, evidence of German atrocities, etc. – but the preparation of the Red Army for the final phase of the war also played a major part. Military newspapers urged the soldiers to show no mercy; there was encouragement to kill any German soldiers without any distinction of whether they had surrendered or were still fighting; and as is the case in almost every war, the urge to violence rapidly spilled over into looting and rape. Many Germans later described the first wave of Soviet soldiers as tough but disciplined, and said that these men often warned them that the men following behind were less disciplined; but just as almost every German unit, army or SS, was involved in atrocities on the Eastern Front, so too were most Red Army units.

It must have been clear to everyone by late 1944 that the war was going to reach German territory. In such circumstances, prudence dictated that plans should be drawn up for possible civilian evacuations; the Germans had sufficient experience of modern warfare to know the impact of fighting on civilians. But although some orders were issued for plans to be drawn up, this was on a haphazard basis and there was little or no attempt to assess the plans to see if they were adequate. Crucially, there was almost no consideration given to the likelihood that the main roads and rail links would be in demand for military use. Plans should therefore have included extensive discussions with railway officials about the numbers of trains that might be available, and any road movements should have been planned for side roads rather than the main highways. Indeed, some military commands attempted to make these very points, but they were largely ignored.

In July 1944, there was a meeting in Katowice involving Wilhelm Stuckart, Reich Minister of the Interior, and officials in Silesia. It was stressed that a proper timetable was essential to give people sufficient time to prepare for evacuation. Once evacuation routes had been agreed, there should be provision for rest, medical care, and supplies at key locations; and plans should be drawn up in advance about which records were to be destroyed before areas were overrun by the Red Army. Despite agreeing to these measures, there is no evidence that Stuckart issued any instructions to turn them into reality in a consistent and organised manner. Instead, decisions were left to *Gauleiters* and their subordinates and were largely under the control of the *Nationalsozialistische Volkswohlfahrt* ('National Socialist People's Welfare' or *NSV*), an organisation that was originally a charity affiliated to the Nazi Party but rapidly became an integral part of the Party. Given how Hitler, Himmler, Bormann and other senior Nazi figures decried any precautionary steps towards evacuation as defeatism, it was inevitable that few officials were prepared to risk attracting the wrath of Berlin by making detailed plans.

In some cases, local Nazi Party officials organised evacuations that took place with varying degrees of order and success. In many other cases, the officials used their authority to guarantee the evacuation of their families and then fled, leaving the population to manage as best it could. In Silesia, the officials who had met with Stuckart drew up some preliminary plans but were unable to start implementation without the approval of Bracht and Hanke, the *Gauleiters*. In mid-January, as details began to filter back to Silesia about the disaster unfolding along the Vistula front, Herbert Mehlhorn, district president in Oppeln, made personal contact with Wehrmacht officers in Poland and was given a stark picture of what was happening. He later described the situation that unfolded in Silesia:

> Although I, with the help of district administrators and their gendarmerie departments, managed to get a clear picture of the situation that was often superior in detail to the official Wehrmacht reports, local Party officials often believed that on the basis of misguided assessments of the military forces they could contradict the evacuation plans I had made based upon the real situation. In some cases, hasty evacuations took place, particularly in Oppeln, where my evacuation order, which I obtained after a telephone conversation with Bracht, was then delayed by twelve hours due to counterproposals by the *Gauleiter's* administration, resulting in completely avoidable haste in the evacuation with all the resultant disadvantages.[32]

A good example of the refusal of local officials to accept reality unfolded around Namslau (now the Polish Namysłów) in Lower Silesia. Despite columns of refugees arriving in the area from further to the east, the local Party chief calmly announced on 19 January that the military situation gave no cause for concern. One of the local regional administrators was a former soldier and energetically intervened. That night, five trains were organised to move about 7,500 civilians to the west; he contacted authorities at the destinations for the trains, asking them to organise accommodation in schools and churches. He ordered the rural population to evacuate by road, informing Hanke's office that he had taken these steps on his own authority; he later estimated that he managed to evacuate over 90 per cent of his district over 24 hours.[33]

Whilst Party officials often abandoned their posts and rarely made adequate provisions for the welfare of those who were fleeing the advancing Red Army, church organisations went to great lengths to care for the frozen, terrified civilians. Pastors oversaw the use of churches, schools and other buildings to house refugees and attempted to make arrangements for their onward journeys to the west; they also often chose to stay with those who either refused to leave their homes or were too old or ill to attempt evacuation. Many died attempting to protect women from Soviet troops bent on rape and murder.

When civilian columns were overtaken by Soviet columns, there were further atrocities. Many of the refugees then wearily retraced their footsteps to their homes, often finding that they had been looted and wrecked. There was a great deal of deliberate destruction carried out by men of the Red Army; in many cases, they were stunned by the relative wealth and luxury they found in German homes compared to what they had left at home, and this enraged them still further – it seemed incomprehensible to them that the Germans, who clearly lived far better lives than people in the Soviet Union, had chosen to inflict such suffering on people in conquered territories.

As they tried to reach some sort of safety, the columns of civilian refugees sometimes crossed paths with the prisoners from concentration camps who were on forced marches. A prisoner from Stutthof remarked:

> As we walk along, I will never forget this, hundreds of Germans are fleeing like us. They look the same, these heroes. They are fleeing, on horse-drawn carts, on foot, the heroes are fleeing like us, and they look so pathetic, just like us.[34]

There was inevitable congestion on the roads. Harry Haffner, the prosecutor-general in Upper Silesia, described the situation in his province in late January:

> The previously determined evacuation routes had to be partly abandoned because the roads were either too congested or within the range of enemy action. The traffic jams on the roads resulted from the fact that around 1.5 million of the people living in the endangered areas were now on the move, some in columns on foot. For days on end, huge convoys of vehicles slowly moved down the few roads leading west or southwest. In addition to that, there were the retreating columns of the Wehrmacht and police. Finally, the prisoners of the Auschwitz concentration camp were also sent out on these roads – apparently 50,000 men and women, along with thousands of British and Russian prisoners of war. I have been told that of 3,000 men in one particular POW column only 1,000 reached their

destination. Bearing in mind the total disorder on the roads, made even worse by enemy air attacks, I do not find this hard to believe. Words simply cannot describe the horrific scenes. The countless human corpses, dead horses and upturned vehicles were scattered along the roads.[35]

In such circumstances, priority was given to military traffic; civilian refugees and prisoners of war were next in line. The starving, emaciated concentration camp prisoners, with utterly inadequate clothing for the winter conditions, had the lowest priority and were often forced to wait for several days at a time while other columns shuffled past. This resulted in ever rising death rates from exposure and starvation. In some cases, steps were taken to hide the presence of concentration camp prisoners from German civilians:

> Those who stopped, everyone who fell on the road, was shot, no difference whether it was a man or a woman … We left [the concentration camp] after the women … and along the route we saw many dead bodies of women on the ground. We marched at night and had to rest during the day, so that the people should not see us being led through, and in the evening when it was dark we marched on again.[36]

By 21 January, an estimated 600,000 German civilians were on the move across Silesia; huge numbers were also fleeing from what is now western Poland, and from East Prussia. Amongst them were deserters from the front line, who had thrown away their weapons and uniforms. In some cases, refugees tried to protect these men; in many instances, they handed them over to military police without hesitation. Those who were arrested were usually executed within a day, left hanging on makeshift gibbets by the roadside with placards around their necks proclaiming that they were cowards who had failed to protect the German people. Soldiers weren't the only ones to try to hide amongst the refugees; senior Nazi Party officials also attempted to flee, wanting to hide their identity both from the pursuing Soviet troops and from the refugees themselves, who were generally bitterly angry at the chaos and the failure of the Party to organise timely evacuations.

Many in Breslau and the other cities of Silesia thought that their best option was to head for the railway stations – surely, the Party and the railway authorities would have organised sufficient transport. The station and surrounding lanes became littered with abandoned bags as helpless refugees crowded into the buildings and onto platforms. Mothers became separated from their children, dozens of whom were trampled to death when the few trains appeared and crowds surged forward, desperate to secure places. Inevitably, railway stations were frequently bombed, adding to the chaos and casualties.

One of the columns that left Breslau heading west and southwest was headed for the town of Kanth (now the Polish town of Kąty Wrocławskie), in what became known to the survivors as the *Känther Todesmarsch* ('Kanth death march'). The bitterly cold weather immediately took a toll on the weakest in the column. Small children and babies froze to death; some were buried in the park on the southern side of Breslau, where over 50 graves accumulated in just the first days of the evacuation.[37] Other small corpses were left in roadside ditches, along with some of the baggage that the refugees had taken with them. When a group of *Volkssturm* followed the path of the column, they found 400 corpses of varying ages littering the road.[38] About 60,000 civilians left Breslau, mostly in columns on foot. It is estimated that nearly a third perished in the days and weeks that followed.[39]

The first destinations of the refugee columns were merely interim halts; the intention was to move them onward. But Silesia had experienced a boom in its population because it was largely out of range of the bombers of the Western Allies that were causing such devastation to other German cities, and there was now a growing sense of danger as refugees reached places that had been hit repeatedly by air raids. Increasing numbers of refugees from all eastern parts of the Reich began to gather in Dresden, one of the few cities in Germany that had escaped serious bombing apart from at the railway yards. This would have tragic consequences when Dresden came under heavy attack in mid-February. By then, up to 200,000 refugees had reached the city. It is estimated that up to 25,000 people, many of them the survivors of harrowing journeys across the frozen landscape, were killed in the great air raids.[40] As refugees gathered in the Baltic ports, Admiral Karl Dönitz, head of the Kriegsmarine, implemented a plan that had been drawn up hastily by Konteradmiral Conrad Engelhardt, the head of sea transport in the German military. Engelhardt had compiled lists of ships that might be used in an evacuation. Several large ocean liners were docked in the ports where they had been used as accommodation for trainee U-boat personnel and the intention was that the evacuation, codenamed *Hannibal*, was officially to transfer these trainees to ports further west where they could continue their training. However, a supplementary order to carry as many civilian refugees and wounded soldiers as possible during the journeys to the west was in reality the true purpose of *Hannibal*. Such evacuation was urgently needed. The ports in the Danzig region were now crammed with over 100,000 refugees, with similar numbers in ports further to the east. Because many of the ships that were to be used had been tied up in ports for much of the war, considerable work had to be done to make the vessels seaworthy. Fuel shortages would also play a major part in limiting operations.

Commencing on 20 January, *Hannibal* ran until the end of the war – several ships completed their last evacuation voyages after the unconditional surrender of Germany. Three of the five greatest losses of life at sea in history occurred during the operation, but it was nevertheless a great success. Under hostile skies and over a sea patrolled by Soviet submarines, Engelhardt's ships evacuated over 2 million German soldiers and civilians. In many cases, people were brought to safety and then evacuated again to ports further west as the Red Army continued its inexorable advance. In the context of the utter collapse of Germany, it was an extraordinary achievement.

# CHAPTER 7

# DRACONIAN PUNISHMENT, FANATICAL DEFENCE

When Germany was created as a state in 1871, Helmuth von Moltke was chief of the general staff of the Prussian Army; he then became chief of the general staff of the new German Army. He was largely the military architect of the wars against Denmark, Austria and France that created the German Empire, and he wrote extensively about his military theories. In one of his works, he codified the principles that had made the Prussian war machine so effective:

> Diverse are the situations under which an officer has to act on the basis of his own view of the situation. It would be wrong if he had to wait for orders at a time when no orders can be given. But productive are his actions when he acts within the framework of his senior commander's intent.[1]

He went on to add that subordinate commanders had to have a clear understanding of the overall intentions of their superiors, and that these intentions had to be laid out in a manner that gained the support and approval of subordinates. This would then permit those subordinates to improvise in crises, achieving the objectives of their superiors without slavishly following plans that might be unworkable. This delegated decision-making became known as *Auftragstaktik* or mission-based tactics, and was one of the major reasons for the success of Prussian and German armies – indeed, the victories of the early years of the Second World War were due as much to this flexibility of command as they were due to the creation of panzer divisions. But the relationship between Hitler and many of his generals was never an easy one. Hitler believed – correctly – that many of the senior officers of the Wehrmacht,

197

drawn from the Prussian *Junker* class of landowners, regarded the Nazis in general and Hitler in particular with contempt and disdain. While Germany was victorious, these tensions were of limited importance, but after the setback outside Moscow in December 1941, the lack of trust on both sides became a more problematic issue.

Increasingly, Hitler attempted to impose his will on Wehrmacht officers he regarded as insufficiently committed to the National Socialist vision of Germany and the world. While Stalin gradually learned to trust his senior commanders and gave them greater leeway in their decision-making, Hitler moved in precisely the opposite direction. The result was a steady erosion of the principles articulated by Moltke and that were deeply embedded in the German military system, particularly amongst its highly trained and carefully selected staff officers.

On 21 January 1945, Hitler went a step further and issued a new set of general orders to all officers of division command and higher. In many respects, it merely reiterated what was already established practice, but was effectively the final act of removing any ability for decision-making by professional soldiers who had been trained from their earliest military experiences to be prepared to think and act without waiting for instructions. Henceforth, the experienced senior commanders of the Wehrmacht would have to abide by the strict whims of a man who had risen to the rank of corporal in the First World War:

> The supreme commanders [army and army group], commanding generals [corps] and divisional commanders are personally responsible to me, in that:
>
> Every decision concerning an operational movement;
>
> Every intended attack by a divisional unit, which does not fall within the scope of the general instructions of the highest leadership;
>
> Every attack on quiet fronts … ;
>
> Every intended withdrawal or retreating movement;
>
> Every intended surrender of a position, a local strongpoint or fortress;
>
> – must be reported in sufficient time to allow me to intervene in the decision-making process, and to allow any countermanding order to reach the most forward troops in time.
>
> The supreme commanders, commanding generals and divisional commanders, the chiefs of staff, and every individual staff officer … are responsible to me in that every report made directly or through official channels to me contains the unvarnished truth. I shall in the future inflict draconian punishment on any attempt at obfuscation, whether it occurs intentionally, by negligence, or through carelessness.[2]

This was a direct response to the events that surrounded the abandonment of Warsaw. The order was absurd on so many levels. For all such decisions to be sent to Berlin was an impossible undertaking given the scale of the war, particularly for headquarters units that were involved in desperate battles for survival and had far more pressing demands on their energy. Any information that was sent to Hitler would be meaningless without full context, and this either necessitated further time-consuming work by the units submitting reports or relied on Hitler being fully aware of operational and even tactical nuances at a local level. Even if all division, corps, army and army group commanders had been able to send the required information to Hitler, to do so 'in sufficient time' to allow Hitler to oversee the decision was impossible given the pace at which battles unfolded, and it was clearly impossible for any one individual, however capable he might be, to absorb all the required information to make sensible decisions every day, covering the battlefields of the Eastern Front, Italy, and the west. The final part – threatening punishment for misleading information – was an attempt to eliminate the tendency of officers to present information in a selective manner so that Hitler would have no choice but to grant their requests.

This was not the only change. In an attempt to reorganise Wehrmacht forces on the Eastern Front to take account of the drastically altered circumstances, Hitler made a series of changes to the command arrangements of what remained of the field formations. From the beginning of *Barbarossa*, Sixteenth and Eighteenth Armies – now trapped in the Courland pocket – had been the main strength of Army Group North. They were now designated Army Group Courland. Army Group Centre, which had been fighting a desperate battle in East Prussia, now became Army Group North; and the remnants of Schörner's Army Group A became Army Group Centre. There was a substantial gap between these latter two army groups, stretching from the scattered battlegroups in the path of Lelyushenko's tanks in the south to the threatened fortresses of Schneidemühl, Bydgoszcz, and Toruń, and a new army group was created to fill this. It would inherit the remnants of Ninth Army from the newly named Army Group Centre and Second Army from the new Army Group North in addition to the various fortress formations that had been improvised to defend against the Soviet advance. Oberst Hans-Georg Eismann had served in a variety of staff roles in the war on the Eastern Front and had just been nominated to become an instructor in a training establishment, having spent the autumn of 1944 as chief of the liaison staff with the Hungarian Army, but before he could take up his new post he received fresh instructions. The head of the training establishment informed him that he was to depart for the east, where he would become Ia – the head of operations

– for a new Army Group Vistula. He also learned the name of the man who would command this new army group.

If it was to function with any efficacy, it was vital for the new army group to be led by an experienced and capable officer. Guderian and Hitler had discussed the matter at length and Guderian suggested that the post be given to Generalfeldmarschall Maximilian von Weichs. After commanding XIII Corps in Poland in 1939, Weichs led Second Army into France in 1940 and into the Soviet Union in 1941; in 1942, he became commander of Army Group B in Ukraine, but fell from favour during the German setbacks in and around Stalingrad. In August 1943 he took command of Army Group F in Greece and the Balkans and conducted a competent and orderly withdrawal from the region in late 1944, contrary to Hitler's orders; Weichs managed to justify the withdrawal by claiming that significant Soviet forces were threatening to isolate and destroy his units. Perhaps because of this, Hitler rejected Guderian's suggestion that Weichs be sent to take command of Army Group Vistula, telling the chief of the general staff that Weichs was too old and tired for the role. At first, Generaloberst Alfred Jodl, chief of staff at *OKW*, was supportive of Guderian, but when he saw that Hitler was opposed, he changed his opinion, stressing that Weichs' strong religious views were not compatible with the degree of fanaticism that the current situation required. When Hitler announced his decision, Guderian was unable to hide his dismay. The man who would be responsible for coordinating and welding together the ragtag of improvised battlegroups, *Volkssturm*, a few reinforcements, and the remnants of retreating units into an army group tasked with defending West Prussia and Pomerania would be Heinrich Himmler.

Born in 1900, Himmler was too young to serve in the First World War; he was a trainee recruit when the conflict came to an end. He joined the Nazi Party in 1923 and was a close associate of Ernst Röhm, the founder of the SA. Two years later, he joined the SS. By 1929, he had risen to become *Reichsführer-SS* and presided over the rapid increase in the size and responsibilities of the organisation; the appointment of senior figures who were involved in the Holocaust and other atrocities, such as Reinhard Heydrich and Theodor Eicke, was overseen by Himmler. He also created the Waffen-SS, which ultimately fielded nearly 40 divisions (though many of these were raised late in the war and were small and barely reached regimental strength).

Himmler was an unimpressive figure – a slight man of medium height with rimless spectacles, a precisely trimmed moustache, and a receding chin. He was often paternalistic towards his subordinates and protected his favourites in even the most egregious cases; by contrast, he insisted upon 'decency' and strict morality amongst others. Despite his considerable administrative skills and almost unfettered power within the Third Reich, Himmler had no military field experience or formal military training whatever. In 1944, he was briefly appointed as *Befehlshaber Oberrhein* ('Commander Upper Rhine') in the west, but it was a post that involved him in making few if any serious decisions, with most of the work being done by the staff of Generalfeldmarschall Gerd von Rundstedt, the overall German commander in the west. Nonetheless, Himmler made a poor impression on the professional Wehrmacht officers during this brief spell. Such views weren't restricted to the Wehrmacht. Senior SS officers also had a low opinion of Himmler's military abilities. Oberstgruppenführer Paul Hausser, one of the most capable commanders to serve in the ranks of the Waffen-SS, wrote:

> Himmler had no authority as a military leader … he was also unaware that he lacked military experience and knowledge … it was a tragedy – no, a crime – to entrust this army group to Himmler in this most desperate situation.[3]

To make matters worse, Himmler – who had been troubled by intestinal complaints for most of his life – insisted on following a strict diet and regime of regular rest that made it impossible for him to work more than five hours a day and remained in his luxurious personal train, refusing to visit any field units to discover the reality of the situation.

Eismann, the new operations officer for the army group, made a dispiriting journey to his new post:

> The journey via Frankfurt-an-der-Oder and Küstrin revealed to me the full extent of the confusion and suffering of the homeland that had hitherto been completely unknown to me and about which I had had no suspicions during my posts abroad. Endless processions of refugees from the east choked every highway. Amongst them were Wehrmacht vehicles and even troops. It was often unclear which direction the refugee columns were trying to move. There was a general impression of disorder. The state of the people and animals in these columns was utterly deplorable.[4]

When he reached Schneidemühl (now the Polish Piła), he found that nobody seemed to be aware of the existence of a new army group. Finally, an acquaintance in the headquarters of the city garrison directed him to Deutsch-Krone (now the Polish Wałcz), a little to the northwest of Schneidemühl. Here, he found Himmler's personal train, *Steiermark*. He was taken to Himmler's office in the train, and Himmler gave him a 'somewhat erratic' briefing and outlined the yawning gap that Army Group Vistula was tasked to repair:

> I then asked, 'What will we use to close this breach and then hold the new front line?' The entire campaign in the east had been fought with no reserves, or at least no strategic reserves and usually without tactical reserves either ... Up to this point, Himmler had been speaking while sweeping his pointer energetically around the map. The core of his rather rambling briefing, however, had been that he would bring the Russians to a halt with Army Group Vistula and would then crush them and throw them back. This was quite a declaration. Any great field commander should of course strive for the highest objectives with self-belief ... But a degree of sound judgement regarding the relevant military circumstances must accompany this. Here, I had the involuntary impression that I was talking about colours with a blind man ...
>
> It was clear to me that the great breach created by the penetration would persist and that the army group's mission would be impossible unless the high command provided fresh formations as quickly as possible. Therefore I asked Himmler what additional forces would be provided, and when they would arrive.
>
> Instead of an answer, I now received a rather loud and rude lecture from my new commander about my typical 'general staff attitude' that climaxed with an accusation that staff officers only had misgivings, were too academically trained, couldn't improvise, had defeatist attitudes, and so on. He, Himmler, would end any such misgivings by attacking with ruthless determination. That was the only way that such difficult problems could be overcome.[5]

Eismann was also informed that the chief of staff of the new army group would not arrive for several days and he would have to take this role too in the interim. The chief of staff would be Gruppenführer Heinz Lammerding, a personal favourite of Himmler who had commanded the panzer division *SS-Das Reich* through much of 1944. Since its creation by Himmler, the Waffen-SS had struggled to find sufficient numbers of experienced and suitably trained senior officers for its formations, and men like Paul Hausser had been brought into its ranks to improve matters, but many in senior posts owed their positions to Himmler's patronage and were poorly equipped for such responsibilities. Lammerding had little or no formal military schooling and had risen through the ranks of the SS to his current post where many – including fellow SS officers – regarded him as being out of his depth as a division commander.[6] But whatever shortfalls he might have had in tactical and operational expertise, he sought to impress Himmler with his ruthless determination and fanaticism. His division was responsible for a series of brutal atrocities as it moved through France in the summer of 1944, culminating in the notorious massacre of at least 654 French civilians in the village of Oradour-sur-Glane, a reprisal for the killing of an officer of *SS-Das Reich*. When his division reached the Normandy battlefields, Lammerding was wounded and although he subsequently returned to command his division for a brief spell, he was soon replaced. Shortly after, Himmler selected him as his chief of staff in Army Group Vistula.

When he finally reached Army Group Vistula, Lammerding made a poor impression on Eismann:

> With him, there was always the impression of insecurity. That was compounded by the fact that he was a cautious man who was inclined to compromise. In his new post, he avoided taking personal responsibility … At first he didn't involve himself in the business of commanding the army group and took a laissez-faire attitude. He was reluctant to express his views on the operational situation to Himmler.[7]

The role of a chief of staff in a German formation included the need to challenge the decisions of the commanding officer, thus providing a swift 'sense check' on any decisions. Reluctance to speak truth to power was, therefore, a major handicap. Army Group Vistula, which was responsible for defending the main axis of advance by which the Red Army would threaten Berlin, was commanded by a man with no experience of military command, aided by a chief of staff with no staff officer training and little inclination to challenge his boss.

It was commonplace for senior Nazi figures to try to accumulate power by holding multiple posts, often far beyond the ability of even the most capable person to oversee so many different concerns. When he became commander of Army Group Vistula, Himmler was still the head of the SS; in addition, he was also Interior Minister, the head of Germany's police, commander of the *Ersatzheer*, and held several other posts. His subordinates for all of these concerns had their personal offices aboard *Steiermark* and there was almost no space for the personnel who would be needed to run Army Group Vistula:

> For communications there was a telephone system, one teletype and one radio set. The so-called staff of the army group was directed politely to set itself up in this situation that had been organised for completely different functions. Even for a limited time in an emergency, it was impossible to command an army group from a single room the size of half a railway car in which civilian secretaries and ministry clerks worked at every conceivable task, sitting at the corner of a table that belonged to someone else, with a telephone that had to be shared with ten other people.[8]

This begs the question: why was Himmler appointed to such a post? The top leadership of Germany had increasingly retreated into an unreal world of fantasy and Himmler managed to hold mutually incompatible views about the course of the war. Outwardly, he remained completely committed to Hitler and competed to seek the approval of the Führer; but in private conversations with several figures, he was actively seeking a way of negotiating an end to the conflict with the Western Powers. Other senior figures – it seems that Martin Bormann, Hitler's personal secretary, was particularly active in this – saw an opportunity to manoeuvre Himmler into a post where he was certain to fail, thus weakening his standing. The fact that this failure would have catastrophic consequences for the Wehrmacht and for Germany as a whole was simply ignored.

As Eismann struggled to create a functioning headquarters, Himmler told him that he intended to take control of Second and Ninth Armies without delay. Eismann protested that this was impossible; even with the help of the signals section of *OKH*, there was only limited secure communications with Second Army and effectively no secure communications with Ninth Army. It would take at least four days to create sufficient links for even the most rudimentary control to be exercised, but Himmler remained adamant and informed *OKH* early on 18 January that he had assumed command of the two armies. Eismann laboured on with increasing despair:

> [Himmler] was simply not capable of a strategic evaluation of the big picture. He just stared as if spellbound at the huge breach that he had to close. He looked at the Russian advance towards Poznań as a unique opportunity to attack the flank of the Russian armies from a line running from Schneidemühl to Bydgoszcz and thus to destroy them. He constantly used words like 'aggressively' and 'thrust into the flank'. It never seemed to occur to him that the Russians might be planning a flank attack against the hard-pressed Second Army. One look at the map that was always spread before him should have made that obvious.
>
> For him, 'attack' seemed the only option …
>
> Himmler wanted to direct the battle himself. He issued orders indiscriminately to individual battalions until it was possible for us to put a halt to this. I particularly remember that he seemed to not know how to measure distances on a map and constantly confused the scales of the standard general staff maps; he sent a battalion out from Schneidemühl completely on its own with the simple mission of attacking the enemy and then holding him until the flank attack could take place … The battalion commander, an elderly reservist, was completely nonplussed. He didn't dare raise objections against the army group commander. The battalion would end up in open countryside 30km [18 miles] south of

Schneidemühl without any communications or contact on its flanks because Himmler had no comprehension that a 10cm distance on the map represented 30km on the ground. No more was ever heard of that battalion.[9]

Guderian later wrote that he had argued strongly against the appointment of Lammerding as well as Himmler, but was overruled by Hitler. He also described a meeting that he had on 25 January with Joachim von Ribbentrop, the German foreign minister, the day after Himmler was given command of Army Group Vistula. In this meeting, Guderian tentatively suggested to Ribbentrop that the two men should approach Hitler together to secure permission to seek a ceasefire with at least some of Germany's enemies. Given the nature of the conflict with the Soviet Union, this could only be possible in the west. Guderian gave an account of the discussion:

Ribbentrop: I can't do it. I am a loyal follower of the Führer. I know for a fact that he does not wish to open any diplomatic negotiations with the enemy and I therefore cannot address him in the manner which you propose.

Guderian: How would you feel if in three or four weeks' time the Russians were to be at the gates of Berlin?

Ribbentrop: Good heavens, do you believe that that is even possible?

Guderian: It is not only possible, but – due to our actual leadership – certain.[10]

Guderian suggested to Ribbentrop that they should keep this conversation confidential, but the foreign minister wrote a report in which he described a discussion with 'an exceptionally high-ranking officer at present in active service in the most responsible position'. That evening, at the regular conference, Hitler bitterly denounced Guderian for having the meeting with Ribbentrop. There was little point in denying the conversation and Guderian resolutely repeated his suggestion for seeking a ceasefire in the west. Hitler rejected it out of hand.

Gradually, new formations were appearing on the maps of Army Group Vistula. V SS-Mountain Corps had existed since the summer of 1943, operating in the Balkans, and its headquarters staff now moved to take command of the front line to the west of Poznań. Its commander, Obergruppenführer Friedrich-Wilhelm Krüger, had served in the First World War and subsequently had been an active member of the Nazi Party, SA, and SS. After the conquest of Poland, he became *HSSPF* first in Łodz and then the *Generalgouvernement*; in this role, he supervised the mass murder of Polish intelligentsia and imposed brutal reprisals for any attacks on Germans; he also oversaw the forcible seizure of tens of thousands of Polish children, who were sent to special foster homes for

'Germanisation'.[11] When he led the SS division *Prinz Eugen* in the Balkans, his experiences in Poland were replicated by brutal atrocities against civilians suspected of aiding anti-German partisans. Whilst he may have carried out such duties with a level of fanaticism that raised his standing in Himmler's eyes, it seems that he was aware of the criminal nature of what he was doing. In early 1944, he wrote in a letter to a friend:

> In my four-year fight in the *Generalgouvernement*, I have lost honour and damaged my reputation.[12]

He now found himself in command of a corps headquarters that controlled almost no field units. Apart from a few battalions of *Volkssturm*, Krüger had just a single assault gun battalion.

On the northern flank of V SS-Mountain Corps was the newly created X SS Corps. It was formed around the staff of XIV SS Corps, which had itself been created in November 1944 and took part in the inconclusive Operation *Nordwind* against American troops to the north of Strasbourg. Its commander, Obergruppenführer Erich von dem Bach-Zelewski, is today best known for his role in the brutal suppression of the Warsaw Uprising in the autumn of 1944. He had served in the First World War with the distinction of being possibly the youngest volunteer in the German Army (he was aged just 15). He remained in the army after the end of the First World War before resigning in 1924 and becoming a member of a series of right-wing, often violently antisemitic organisations; he blamed his resignation from the army on his three sisters, all of whom had married Jewish men. He was a prominent member of the SS when the Second World War broke out and played a leading role in the forced expulsion of Poles from parts of Silesia; shortly after the invasion of the Soviet Union he became *HSSPF* in Belarus, where he energetically conducted campaigns of extermination of the Jewish population. It seems that he coped with the 'stresses' of this work by resorting to opiate abuse, which required a spell of hospitalisation in early 1942.[13] After discharge from hospital, he was considered as a replacement for Reinhard Heydrich, the *Reichsprotektor in Böhmen und Mähren* ('Reich Protector of Bohemia and Moravia'), who was assassinated in the summer of 1942, but his anti-partisan operations in Belarus had caught Himmler's imagination and he oversaw the adoption of similar tactics across the entire Eastern Front. The result was the widespread slaughter of civilians – estimates suggest that nearly a quarter of a million were killed in sweeps across large parts of the countryside.[14] Like V SS-Mountain Corps, the new X SS Corps controlled no field formations of any significant value.

A little further north was Obergruppenführer Karl Maria Demelhuber's XVI SS Corps, extending the front line as far as the Vistula. He fought in the ranks of the *Freikorps* after the First World War and was a police officer in Bavaria for many years. He took part in anti-Jewish activities in Poland after 1939 and was then given combat roles, commanding a motorised brigade of SS infantry and then the *SS-Nord* Division in 1941–42. His new corps consisted almost entirely of a single formation, 15th *SS-Waffen-Grenadier* or 1st Latvian Division.

Originally raised from Latvian volunteers and police battalions, the division was first known as a volunteer legion; it suffered heavy losses in the withdrawal from Leningrad and across Latvia in 1944 before being evacuated by sea to the Danzig area in September 1944 for replenishment. Although it was officially made up of Latvian volunteers, many young men were effectively conscripted and had no choice about serving in its ranks. One veteran later recalled the journey from Riga to Danzig:

> There were a lot of youngsters from Latvia called up on that boat, very few of them in uniform. The Germans were catching people in the street and sending them to Danzig. There were lots of people drunk, and suicides too: people jumping over the side of the ship.[15]

Most of the new recruits brought in to replenish the division were aged 18 or 19, and had undergone little or no training prior to leaving their homeland. They were housed in villages in Pomerania together with Latvians who had already been transported to Germany as forced labourers and were now being incorporated into the division. Its establishment was similar to that of a regular German infantry division, but just like those infantry divisions it was far from full strength, with about 10,000 Latvians being assembled in Pomerania. The most pressing problem was to find sufficient weapons for them and as it wasn't possible to arm them all, about 1,500 were organised into three construction battalions. Oberführer Adolf Ax, who would take command of the division a few days later, inspected a regiment of the division on 22 January and came away unimpressed. Nearly all the men had no combat experience – many had not even fired live ammunition. There were few heavy weapons and no artillery. Although morale and motivation seemed to be good, it was doubtful that this would survive the first battle with the Red Army as the lack of weaponry and training would put the men at a huge disadvantage.

While Army Group Vistula was going through its troubled birth process, a completely different campaign was being pursued: Hitler's wrath at the abandonment of Warsaw continued to seek victims. On 19 January, Walter Fries, whose XLVI Panzer Corps had been defending the Warsaw sector, was dismissed from his post. His replacement was General Martin Gareis, an experienced infantry commander whose 98th Infantry Division had served on the central sector of the Eastern Front for much of the war; thereafter, he became commander of 264th Infantry Division in the Balkan region.

Fries returned to Berlin where he was told that he had been placed in 'Führer Reserve'. After languishing in limbo for several weeks, he was brought before a court martial in Torgau to answer charges that he had authorised the withdrawal of XLVI Panzer Corps contrary to Hitler's orders for Warsaw and the neighbouring region to be held. Lüttwitz, commander of Ninth Army, and Weber, the designated commandant of the Warsaw 'fortress', were also dismissed and arrested. The new commander of Ninth Army was the bespectacled General Theodor Busse. He was an experienced staff officer who had enjoyed a long and cordial working relationship with Erich von Manstein on the Eastern Front; although his performance in his staff roles was highly regarded, he often resorted to passing on orders from Hitler that he knew were unworkable with no attempt to mitigate or modify them. He was therefore one of the few Wehrmacht officers still regarded by Hitler as reliable.

Lüttwitz was questioned briefly and then released, but summoned once more in early February and interrogated at length about why he had disobeyed a direct order from Schörner not to retreat. During a break in the interrogation, Lüttwitz asked General Hans-Karl von Scheele, one of the other officers present – the two men had served alongside each other in the winter fighting outside Moscow in 1941–42 – why he had been summoned to Torgau for further interrogations. Speaking in private, Scheele informed him that Keitel had ordered the arrest and interrogation and had told Scheele that the heads of senior officers would have to roll because of the failure to hold Warsaw. Keitel was regarded with contempt by many of his contemporaries for his blind and rigid obedience to Hitler and it is highly likely that either he had been ordered specifically by the Führer to take such action or was acting on his own initiative, either seeking to secure Hitler's praise or attempting to atone in some way for the role of the army in the July Plot.

Realising that his life might be at risk, Lüttwitz demanded that Oberst Johannes Hölz, the chief of staff of Ninth Army, should be brought to give evidence; he also pointed out that to date, his replies to questions had been based upon his personal recollections but he now insisted on having the war diary of Ninth Army in order to refresh his memory. A week later, proceedings resumed. With the war diary available to him, Lüttwitz was able to demonstrate that his earlier answers had been correct, and that Fries and Weber had acted in accordance with orders from Ninth Army. In the circumstances, it was a brave stance: he was effectively taking full responsibility for the abandonment of Warsaw.

The senior prosecuting officer in the court martial was General Kurt von Tippelskirch, who had commanded units on the Eastern Front until he was injured in an air crash in the summer of 1944 when he was head of Fourth Army. He travelled overnight from Torgau to Berlin to report on proceedings to Keitel, who ordered him to seek the death penalty for all three accused officers. Such instructions would have horrified Tippelskirch, who had personal experience of being given impossible orders from Hitler, but the documents relating to the court martial are incomplete and it is therefore not clear whether he made any protest. In any event, the court partially acquitted Lüttwitz. Aided by General Maximilian Fretter-Pico – who had commanded German forces in southern Ukraine and Romania and like all senior German officers had repeatedly been given impossible orders with inadequate resources – Fries was able to persuade the three presiding officers that although he had failed to obey Hitler's orders, given the circumstances in which he was operating – lacking heavy weapons and tanks, with few supplies, and with his men almost exhausted – it would have been impossible to continue to hold Warsaw and the designated defence line without the complete destruction of XLVI Panzer Corps. Moreover, the war diary of Ninth Army showed that he had acted in accordance with Lüttwitz's instructions and he too was acquitted.

In earlier trials, senior army officers had been acquitted only to be arrested almost immediately by the *Sicherheitsdienst* ('Security Service' or *SD*, effectively the intelligence arm of the SS). On this occasion, the presiding officer of the court martial quietly made a car available to Lüttwitz and Fries so that they were able to slip away from Torgau unnoticed. Both became prisoners of the Western Powers at the end of the war. Lüttwitz later joined the West German Bundeswehr, rising to become one of its senior commanders; he died in 1975. Fries died in 1982 in a small town in Hesse, close to where he had been born.

Weber, the former commandant of the Warsaw garrison, was less fortunate. When the fortress policy was first instigated, Hitler specified that their commandants were directly answerable to him, and this prevented Lüttwitz's evidence from protecting him. Moreover, in October 1944, when he was commander of 131st Infantry Division, Weber's unit was involved in a chaotic withdrawal in the face of a Soviet attack and he was criticised for not showing sufficiently forceful leadership and was replaced as division commander. His case was not helped by a statement from Guderian, which informed the court martial that even a short period of resistance around Warsaw would have delayed the Soviet advance significantly. There is little to support such an assertion, particularly given that the Red Army was deliberately not allowing trapped German units to hold up its advance and was leaving them to be destroyed by second echelon formations. Despite his assertions that the garrison had been completely inadequate for the task assigned to it and that the order countermanding his withdrawal from Warsaw arrived two hours after his men had commenced the destruction of their equipment, he was found guilty of disobeying Hitler's orders. Fortunately, Keitel's urging for the death penalty was ignored and Weber was sentenced to three years' imprisonment; this was immediately altered to probation and he was released from captivity. He didn't receive any further appointments and like the other two officers he was held by the Western Powers until 1947. He died in 1974.[16]

At a time when the enemies of Germany had crossed the frontiers to the east and west, when most of Germany's cities had been reduced to ruins, when every drop of fuel had to be treated as a precious resource – when the inevitability of total defeat could no longer be avoided – it seems extraordinary that so much energy was spent on pursuing these officers for their alleged disobedience. Nor were they the only targets of the wrath of the Führer. In East Prussia, the German Fourth Army found itself cut off from the rest of Germany when Rokossovsky's 2nd Belarusian Front advanced to Elbing (now the Polish city of Elbląg) and the Baltic coast. General Friedrich Hossbach, the highly experienced commander of Fourth Army, gathered his rapidly dwindling resources and attempted to counterattack towards the west, aiming to cut the corridor that Rokossovsky had created to the coast. It was his intention to abandon much if not all of East Prussia, and he made his preparations and started his counterattack without the knowledge or approval of *OKH* and Hitler. Reinhardt, commander of Army Group Centre, was aware of the plans and had made repeated pleas to Berlin for permission to conduct a fighting withdrawal from East Prussia but as was so often the case, Hitler responded to a request that he didn't want to face with silence. At first, the attack made good progress but then lost momentum – several of the divisions that Hossbach had intended to use as his second echelon to sustain the offensive had to be deployed in the east and north to prevent the complete collapse of German positions in East Prussia. Just as Fourth Army's counterattack slackened, Erich Koch, the odious *Gauleiter* of East Prussia, apparently made a crucial intervention. He had a personal bunker in the small town of Neutief, on the shore of the saltwater lagoon known as the Frische Nehrung, and he had retreated there as Soviet troops invaded East Prussia. According to some accounts, he now sent a telegram to Hitler:

> Fourth Army is fleeing towards the Reich. It is cravenly trying to escape to the west. I am continuing to defend East Prussia with the *Volkssturm*![17]

More recently, the existence of this telegram has been disputed. Koch denied ever sending such a message and no copy has survived. Indeed, most accounts that describe the telegram rely on the reminiscences of Generalmajor Erich Dethleffsen, who was Hossbach's chief of staff at the time. Dethleffsen later wrote that he heard about the telegram but hadn't actually seen it.[18] Nonetheless, whether as a result of a message from Koch or due to suspicions that Hossbach was about to withdraw entirely from East Prussia without permission, Hitler dismissed the commander of Fourth Army. Reinhardt had already been dismissed a few days earlier. Hossbach returned to Germany and underwent medical treatment for an ear infection, but in early April – the last Soviet offensive to take Berlin was imminent, and the Western Allies were pressing into Germany in the west – a group of Gestapo and SS officers appeared at the hospital in Göttingen to arrest Hossbach. There was a brief firefight, with Hossbach opening fire on the Gestapo and SS from the balcony of his room with a pistol, before the arresting party departed hastily as US troops approached.[19]

Nor were such measures restricted to senior officers. On all front lines, soldiers who had been executed for alleged cowardice were hanged from lamp posts, trees, and buildings, usually wearing placards around their neck proclaiming their crimes. Some may have fled the front line only to be arrested by the widespread military police patrols that then took them to face a summary court martial, but others were innocent of any crimes. In some cases, men who had been sent back to obtain supplies or to collect vehicles from repair workshops, but whose instructions had been given verbally rather than in writing, were rounded up and executed. Such activity was particularly commonplace under Schörner's command, and after the war he would face prosecution for ordering such executions. Nor did Schörner restrict his behaviour to his subordinates. Oberst Thilo von Trotha had been chief of staff in the headquarters of First Panzer Army through the winter and was dismissed in February 1945. He made little secret of his anger at his removal and particularly the behaviour of senior

Nazi Party figures when he returned to Berlin, and he then received a letter from Schörner, an old acquaintance:

> I received a hint yesterday, most confidentially of course, that your attitude to the Party and its representatives is occasionally somewhat reserved. One could have the impression that you don't place sufficient value in certain things such as the National Socialist leadership of the army … I trust you have understood me. Either we succeed in having fanatical supporters and unconditional loyalists of the Führer at the very top, or things will go wrong again.[20]

There were increasing numbers of soldiers behind the front line on all fronts. In many cases, they were genuine stragglers who had been separated from their units, but some were simply attempting to stay alive until what they saw as the inevitable end of the war. The existing military police measures against such individuals were enhanced by a new decree from Hitler on 15 February. Each area threatened by the armies of the Allied Powers was to establish a *Standgericht* ('summary court martial') chaired by a judge, a senior member of the Nazi Party, and an officer of the Wehrmacht, SS, or police. These were to be appointed by *Gauleiters* and were empowered to deal with any infringements that might endanger military morale. They could reach only three verdicts: exoneration; transfer to a formal court; or the death penalty. This was followed a few weeks later by the establishment of the *Fliegendes Standgericht* ('flying court martial'), which roamed across all areas still under German control, executing anyone with little judicial process and no right of appeal. The views of ordinary soldiers to these events were complex. Many were bitterly angry at the behaviour of the military police, who were not taking part in front-line fighting but spent their time pursuing and executing their victims; others had more nuanced views, deploring those who fled from the front and left their comrades in peril.

The involvement of so many senior officers in these vindictive attempts to prosecute men like Lüttwitz, Fries, Weber, and Hossbach is also striking. Guderian was adamant that Weber should not have abandoned Warsaw, yet in December 1941 he had withdrawn his divisions from their exposed salient to the south of Moscow despite explicit orders from Hitler to hold his positions, an act that cost him his post. Tippelskirch had commanded Fourth Army during *Bagration* in the summer of 1944 and had seen his divisions destroyed or badly mauled due to Hitler's refusal to countenance a timely withdrawal – these losses contributed directly to the weakness of the German positions along the Vistula. At least in his case, the court martial in which he was a senior officer acquitted Lüttwitz and Fries, but nonetheless convicted Weber. Almost 80 years later, from an era in which information is far more freely available than in Nazi Germany, it is difficult to understand the mindset of such figures, caught up in the catastrophic collapse of their nation but still continuing to obey the unforgiving edicts of the man who had brought so much destruction upon Germany and its neighbours. Many were mindful that their families were effectively being held hostage by the regime and might suffer repercussions if they were seen to be anything other than utterly loyal; others claimed later that they were bound by their oath of loyalty. But any such oath ignored other realities. They were ultimately responsible for the lives of their men, and were servants of the German nation, not just of the Führer. One of the bitter legacies of the failed July Plot was that even if senior officers had wanted to take steps to stop the senseless killing, the level of suspicion and scrutiny was so great that any coordinated action was impossible. Instead, they found themselves trapped in the disaster that was unfolding around them.

# CHAPTER 8

# POZNAŃ AND THE NORTHERN SECTOR

On the battlefield, Soviet troops continued their relentless advance. The German formations that staggered back from the Vistula front were too weak to do more than put up token resistance, and many of the units rushed to the region found themselves fighting isolated and often hopeless battles, struggling to obey orders that were out of date even before they were issued. The near-complete disintegration of Fourth Panzer Army left the Germans fighting a series of disconnected battles and gave the Red Army an opportunity to pursue objectives on diverging axes with little need to worry about potential countermeasures by the Wehrmacht. To make matters worse for the Germans, the westward rout of the formations from the Vistula front meant that there was now a yawning gap in the north to the German forces fighting in East Prussia. Consequently, the events of the campaign became focused on a distinct series of theatres. In northern Poland, Zhukov's combined arms armies consolidated their hold on Łódź and prepared to push on to the west; the two tank armies were already moving closer to their next objective, the city of Poznań and the Warta River. In the central sector, on the seam between 1st Belarusian Front to the north and 1st Ukrainian Front to the south, Nehring and his surviving troops continued their attempts to march to the west while Saucken's *Grossdeutschland* panzer corps struggled to hold open an escape route. To the south, Konev was facing the prospect of sustaining an advance on diverging axes with Lelyushenko's Fourth Tank Army pushing west and northwest while the rest of his armies began to face the challenge of advancing southwest into Silesia. These military developments are described in turn below.

While Hitler relentlessly pursued those who had failed to show sufficient fanaticism and devotion to the cause, the Red Army moved to destroy the German forces holding the 'fortress' of Poznań. Extensive fortifications had been built around the city in the 19th century when it was part of Prussia and although these were largely obsolete, they nonetheless provided a degree of protection for defending forces and there had been extensive work to improve them, with the clearance of buildings and trees to provide better fields of fire for defensive weapons. Chuikov later wrote:

> Reconnaissance by the leading tank crews suggested that it would not be easy to take Poznań. But wasn't this what had been ordered in the Front's directive? The liberation of Poznań was developing into a complex military task. Further reconnaissance and interrogation of prisoners showed that all the forts and the central area of Poznań were prepared for defence. In terms of military science, Poznań could be considered a classic fortress, built according to the general schemes of Vauban, the famous architect of fortifications. There were forts around the centre, with the main defensive centre being the citadel. Both the forts and the citadel had substantial underground structures that could accommodate a very large garrison.
>
> To what extent these old structures were being used by the Nazis, we didn't know at the time, and we had no information on the manner in which the fortress had been strengthened. However, it was obvious that it would be impossible to take such a fortress in a day.[1]

As the man who had overseen the defence of Stalingrad in 1942 against the German Sixth Army, Chuikov had every reason to be cautious. He knew that numbers and even firepower counted for little in urban warfare; even if the German garrison of Poznań was modest in strength, it could still inflict heavy losses on an attacking force and lead to major delays in the offensive. After ordering energetic reconnaissance to be carried out in order to assess the likely strength of German defences early on 20 January, he spoke to the commanders of his neighbouring formations. Berzarin, whose Fifth Shock Army was to the north, told him that there were indications that the Germans were preparing to defend the city of Schneidemühl. Chuikov then drove to the headquarters of First Guards Tank Army for discussions with Katukov. The two men agreed that if possible, they would simply bypass Poznań. Even if the Germans had a substantial garrison in the city, it was likely that it would lack the mobility to be able to strike against the supply lines of the units that continued the Soviet advance to and over the Warta River.

That evening, *Gauleiter* Greiser addressed his staff in Poznań. One of his audience later described him as looking pale and exhausted. The man who in the middle of a battle had lectured senior Wehrmacht officers on the need for fanatical resistance was expected to issue a rallying call for the determined defence of the 'fortress', but his words were rather different:

> Gentlemen, the Russians will be in Posen within one or at the most two days. Here I lay down my life's work, uncompleted. My connection with this land could be no stronger, and my son rests in its earth. Tonight I leave Posen. An order from the Führer has summoned me to Berlin to fulfil a task under the direction of the Reichsführer-SS [Himmler], and my deputy will take over the direction of the Warthegau.[2]

Like other senior Nazi officials, Greiser had been a determined competitor in the pseudo-Darwinian world of Nazi Germany. He made no attempt to hide his utter contempt and disdain for Poles and others he regarded as lesser humans and clashed repeatedly with those he saw as his rivals, such as Albert Forster, the *Gauleiter* in Danzig-West Prussia. He was particularly proud of his 'Germanisation' of Łódź – he oversaw the repression of the Catholic Church across Wartheland and was open about his involvement in the Holocaust. It was perhaps fitting that the competitive rivalry that was such a prominent feature of the Nazi Party proved to be his downfall. With the Red Army still some distance from Poznań, Greiser had contacted Hitler and Bormann and secured permission to leave, but when he reached the city of Frankfurt an der Oder he discovered that Himmler denied authorising any such move. Goebbels was quick to condemn him as a coward and a traitor and demanded that he be punished by being sent to fight in a *Volkssturm* battalion, but Hitler was unwilling to take such a step, perhaps embarrassed that he had been conned into ordering Greiser's recall.[3] He was permitted to travel to the Alps for a rest cure. On 17 May, Greiser was captured by American troops and subsequently handed over to the Polish government; he was found guilty of mass murder, mass deportation, the use of forced labour, and numerous other crimes. Despite pleas from Pope Pius XII, he was hanged on 21 July 1946 in Poznań.[4]

Greiser's deputy in Poznań, Kurt Schmalz, was already effectively head of the *Volkssturm* in Wartheland. His term as *Gauleiter* of the province would have been brief in any event, but he chose to flee before Poznań was completely isolated. He disappeared in the increasing chaos of Germany's collapse and became a British prisoner of war before being released in 1947 – his captors were unaware of his past record. In 1950, court proceedings against him for his activities in Wartheland commenced in the German state of Braunschweig, but he went on the run and

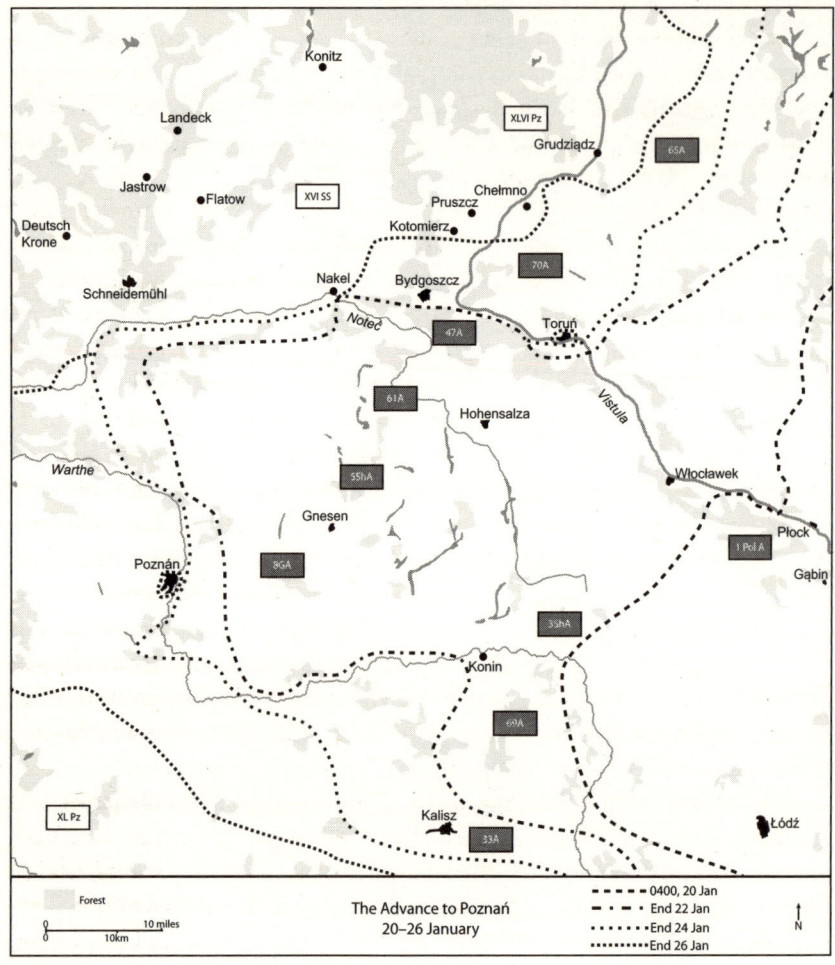

The Advance to Poznań
20–26 January

Forest

0       10 miles
0    10km

- - - - 0400, 20 Jan
- · - · End 22 Jan
········· End 24 Jan
·········· End 26 Jan

N

successfully evaded arrest. He died in 1964, one of a large number of senior Nazis who never faced trial for their actions.[5]

On 21 January, the leading formations of Second Guards Tank Army continued their rapid advance towards the northwest, with the Vistula River on their northern flank and the Noteć River to the south. Like the cities of Poznań and Łódź, this was an area where there had been extensive settlement with ethnic Germans from the Baltic region and the Soviet Union – before 1941, the Germans had secured an agreement with Moscow for these civilians to be permitted to leave Soviet territory as part of a programme that became known in Germany as *Heim ins Reich* ('Home in the [German] Reich'). Inevitably, large numbers of Poles had been expelled or – in the case of Jews – killed in areas that were now incorporated into Germany. The Polish city of Bydgoszcz had been the scene of particularly troubled events. As German troops approached in September 1939, there was violence between Polish civilians and soldiers and ethnic Germans in the city, who formed about 10 per cent of the population of 117,000 people. After German troops secured the area on 6 September, Hitler ordered an enquiry into the killings of German civilians. This reported that between 3,500 and 5,800 people had died, at least partly when they were caught in the crossfire between the two armies. The number also included ethnic Germans who had been killed in the general area rather than specifically within Bydgoszcz.[6] The report, which became known as the *Weissbuch* ('White Book'), was passed to Hitler, who reacted with anger to its contents. He demanded that the number of dead had to be increased tenfold; the result was that German propaganda proclaimed that 58,000 Germans had been slaughtered by the Poles, and this was used as justification by Forster, *Gauleiter* of Danzig-West Prussia (under whose jurisdiction the city fell) for widespread repression. Now known by its German name of Bromberg, the city had already seen the murderous activity of several SS units including *Einsatzgruppe IV* and *Einsatzkommando 16*; just three weeks after the Germans took control of the area, local Polish officials were summoned to a meeting with their new German masters and were taken to nearby woodland where they were summarily executed.[7] Over the following months, a total of over 10,000 citizens of Bydgoszcz were killed, a mixture of Poles and Jews.

The first Soviet troops to approach the city were from IX Guards Tank Corps and the local Nazi Party *Kreisleiter*, Leonard Rampf, waited in vain for instructions from above. As the first panicky reports of Red Army columns probing towards the city began to circulate, he had a brief meeting with Standartenführer Otto von Salisch, the police chief in the city, and the two men concluded that waiting for definitive instructions from higher authorities would result in disaster. Rampf took matters into his own hands by ordering the civilian population – by 1945, the majority were Germans, most Poles having been expelled in the preceding years – to leave immediately. When reports of the evacuation reached Berlin, the response was almost immediate. A proclamation was issued a few days later:

> Administrative authorities, in particular district administrators, mayors, and regional heads of administration are to continue performing their duties in the territories threatened by the enemy to the last moment and are then to join the troops in combat. Reports should highlight men who display particularly brave conduct. Immediate action should be taken against those who fall short. They must be removed from office and replaced by suitable personnel.

In a teleprinter message, the Reichsführer-SS [Himmler] has ordered amongst other matters:

'The heads of all military and civilian administrations must be aware that abandoning their posts without orders will result in the death penalty.'

Accordingly, the Reichsführer issued the following punishments in his order of 30 January:

1. The former Standartenführer von Salisch, head of police in Bromberg, is demoted by me for cowardice and neglect of his duties and is to be shot immediately.

2. The former regional head of administration in Bromberg, [Walther] Kühn, and the former mayor of Bromberg, [Walter] Ernst, are stripped of their decorations and honours for cowardice and neglect of duty and demoted. They are to serve as probationary soldiers in a penal battalion after witnessing the execution of Salisch.

The former *Kreisleiter* of Bromberg, Rampf, who has been expelled from the Party and demoted on the orders of the Party Chancellery, is likewise ordered to a penal battalion, where like Kühn and Ernst he will be assigned to arduous and dangerous duties.[8]

Salisch was shot as ordered. Rampf and Ernst were killed in combat in March 1945; Kühn survived and later became a politician in West Germany. But the order to commence the evacuation of Bydgoszcz resulted in many civilians leaving the city by road and rail before the advancing Soviet forces cut all lines of communication.

The city of Bydgoszcz had the usual mixture of *Volkssturm* and training units as its garrison, but a panzergrenadier battalion from 4th Panzer Division was also present. Until January, 4th Panzer Division was one of three panzer divisions trapped in the Courland pocket, but it was transferred by sea to Danzig as part of a trickle of reinforcements that Hitler grudgingly permitted to be extracted from the 'Courland bridgehead'. Oberstleutnant von Arnim, the commander of the cavalry school in Bydgoszcz, had been appointed garrison commander and he tried in vain to obtain clear instructions. Matters were further complicated by command arrangements – the panzergrenadier battalion, easily the most powerful force in the city, was not under Arnim's command. When the panzergrenadier battalion commander informed him that Generalleutnant Clemens Betzel, commander of 4th Panzer Division, had ordered the battalion to move north to link up with the rest of the division, Arnim ordered the rest of his garrison to prepare to march north with them rather than conduct a pointless defence of the city.

Meanwhile, the leading elements of First Guards Tank Army were probing the German defences around Poznań. They had a moment of considerable good fortune when a reconnaissance group encountered a small body of German troops and rapidly overwhelmed them, killing several and taking the rest prisoners. Amongst those captured was Oberstleutnant Fritz Flacke, the deputy commander of *Festung Posen*. Katukov later wrote that Flacke was very forthcoming with information about the city's defences:

> Flacke drew us a detailed plan of the Poznań fortress with all its forts, reinforced concrete positions, and other fortifications. The all-round defence of Poznań consisted of three lines. The first passed along the city outskirts, the second along Polna Street to Sołacz, and the third – most central – line included the old city and the citadel. On the city outskirts, all buildings had been adapted for defence: loopholes were punched in walls, windows were sandbagged, and basements were connected by tunnels. According to Flacke, the fortress garrison numbered 20,000 men. Subsequently we learned that 65,000 Nazis were in the fortress.
>
> 'Poznań,' Flacke readily told us, 'is the main defence point on the Warta line.' To the west there was a further line – along the Obra River and even further back a powerful fortified area known as Meseritz [now the Polish town of Międzyrecz]. The area between the Warta and Oder Rivers was full of defensive structures forming a fortified quadrangle.[9]

Just how readily Flacke volunteered this information is by no means clear; in any event, the garrison was far smaller than Katukov suggests in his memoirs. A training establishment for junior officers yielded 325 instructors and about 1,300 recruits; a heavy anti-aircraft battalion in the city had 32 88mm guns; there was a police regiment made up of three weak battalions; there were four *Volkssturm* battalions; and there was a single weak battalion of Latvians. Perhaps somewhat more powerful was what was termed the *Festungs-Reserve* ('fortress reserve') of an SS panzergrenadier battalion, an assault gun battalion with 32 Sturmgeschütz III and IV (including 15 vehicles that had been intended for onward transport to East Prussia but were now assigned to the battalion); and a tank platoon of a single Tiger, a Pz.IV and two Panther tanks. In total, the garrison numbered about 25,000 men.[10] Military personnel from neighbouring towns eventually boosted this figure by an additional 5,000.

Whilst Flacke was being interrogated, Babadzhanian's XI Guards Tank Corps had reached the Warta River to the north of Poznań and was preparing to cross:

> My 44th Brigade failed to capture the bridge over the river – while retreating, the enemy managed to blow it up. I decided to bypass the city and move into the rear of the German positions. But how to transport the main forces of the corps across

the river? The bridging battalion had fallen far behind and was awaiting delivery of fuel. It was the same old story. There was no alternative: we would have to use improvised means of transporting the motorised infantry of 27th Brigade, the machine-gun battalions of 40th and 45th Tank Brigades, and some of the artillery to the other side.[11]

It proved impossible to get the bulk of XI Guards Tank Corps across the river and Babadzhanian's intention to bypass Poznań quickly was frustrated. Other elements of First Guards Tank Army were moving closer to the city further south but they too were unable to achieve a quick success. The capture of Poznań would have to await the arrival of the combined arms armies that were still moving forward some distance to the east.

At the highest levels of the German leadership, decision-making continued to be obstructed by Hitler's refusal to face reality. Albert Speer, Germany's armaments minister, described a meeting where Guderian – who had earlier been holding discussions with Hiroshi Oshima, the Japanese ambassador in Berlin – lost his temper at Hitler's intransigence:

> We took our positions on the window side [of the huge map table]; Hitler sat facing us.
>
> The German armies in Courland were hopelessly cut off. Guderian tried to convince Hitler that this position should be abandoned and the armies transported across the Baltic Sea. Hitler disagreed, as he always did when asked to authorise a retreat. Guderian did not give in, Hitler insisted, the tone sharpened, and finally Guderian opposed Hitler with an openness unprecedented in this circle. Probably fired by the effects of the drinks he had had with Oshima, he threw aside all inhibitions. With flashing eyes and the hairs of his moustache literally standing on end, he stood facing Hitler across the marble table. Hitler too had risen to his feet.
>
> 'It's simply our duty to save these people, and we still have time to remove them!' Guderian cried out in a challenging voice.
>
> Infuriated, Hitler retorted: 'You are going to fight on there. We cannot afford to give up these areas!'
>
> Guderian held firm. 'But it's useless to sacrifice men in this senseless way,' he shouted. 'It's high time! We must evacuate these soldiers at once!'
>
> What no one had thought possible now happened. Hitler appeared visibly intimidated by this assault. Strictly speaking, he really could not tolerate this insubordination, which was more a matter of Guderian's tone than his argument … Hitler stuck to his decision.[12]

On 22 January, when the leading elements of Bogdanov's Second Guards Tank Army probed the German lines near Bydgoszcz, they crossed a line that had been drawn up prior to the commencement of the great offensive – the so-called Bydgoszcz-Poznań line. There was a great deal of satisfaction at every level of command. The original plans had called for the tank armies to reach the line in the first week of February; the advance had proceeded at least ten days faster than expected. There was little time for the tank crews to celebrate as they continued their thrust and the forces to their rear – Forty-Seventh Army to the south of the Vistula and Seventieth Army on the north bank – moved closer to the city known to the Germans as Thorn and to the Poles as Toruń. In the 19th century, it had been one of the numerous locations along the Vistula where the Prussian Army had constructed substantial fortifications. After the end of the Franco-Prussian War in 1871, the new German state faced an increasing threat that France and Russia would ally against Germany and attack from east and west at the same time, and the purpose of these fortresses along the Vistula was to create a barrier at which the Russians could be held until the French could be defeated in the west. It was inevitable that Hitler would declare it a fortress. About 22 miles (35km) to the southwest of Toruń, the town of Hohensalza – now the Polish Inowrocław – was another location that was to be held at all costs. The garrison commander was Sturmbannführer Adrian von Fölkersam, the commander of a small SS 'special forces' unit. By early 22 January, the town was completely encircled and under constant bombardment and Fölkersam contacted his commander – the renowned Obersturmbannführer Otto Skorzeny, who had conducted several daring missions during the war. Skorzeny realised the futility of trying to hold the shattered town and gave permission to Fölkersam to attempt a breakout. It was the penultimate communication with the small garrison; a signal was received shortly after, informing Skorzeny that Fölkersam had been badly wounded by a bullet that struck his head. Fighting died down during the morning as Soviet troops took control. The fate of Fölkersam is not known. He may have died in the fighting for the town, but there are suggestions that he became a Soviet prisoner of war; these records lose track of him in about 1949.[13]

The small garrison of Hohensalza was believed to have been annihilated, but remarkably, a small number of soldiers escaped. Two months after the battle, a group of two officers and 13 men reached German lines, which at that time were about 204 miles (340km) to the west. They were the last survivors of Fölkersam's special forces unit and they reported that the garrison, reduced from its original strength of 800 men to 200, had broken out of the town in two groups, with the unconscious Fölkersam in the last remaining half-track. The vehicle and one of the groups disappeared in the confused fighting and the other group became increasingly fragmented. No prisoners from this battle returned to Germany after the war, and these 15 men can be assumed to be the only survivors.[14]

Katukov continued his attempts to bypass Poznań. Babadzhanian's bridgehead across the Warta River to the north of the city was of little value without an intact bridge, and VIII Guards Mechanised Corps attempted to penetrate the eastern suburbs of Poznań. It was repulsed and Zhukov intervened, sending orders for the Soviet tank units to avoid being drawn into urban combat. Instead, Major General Ivan Fedorovich Dremov, commander of VIII Guards Mechanised Corps, was to bypass the southern outskirts. In 1944, the Soviet Fifth Guards Tank Army had suffered heavy losses in its advance through Minsk, Vilnius and Kaunas, resulting in its commander being dismissed; Zhukov was determined to avoid a repetition and wanted to retain his armoured forces as intact as possible so that the advance could be continued. The combined arms armies, which would have the task of seizing Poznań, were still several days' march to the east, and they too received orders: they were to accelerate their advance. For army commanders who were struggling with the difficulties of moving sufficient supplies to their combat units to sustain mobility, such instructions were largely unnecessary. They were already doing the best that they could. Meanwhile, the German authorities in Poznań – no longer hampered by the presence of Greiser and other senior Nazis – completed the generally orderly evacuation of German civilians from the city; over the preceding two days, trains had left for Danzig in the north and for other destinations to the west, and many had set out on foot along the icy roads from the city. Almost all the 90,000 Germans had left, together with perhaps a third of the 140,000 Poles who still lived in the city.

The continued German presence in Poznań began to have an impact on Red Army operations to the north, where Second Guards Tank Army faced little significant resistance but were left with a long southern flank. On 23 January, Bogdanov's leading units were penetrating into the southern edge of Bydgoszcz and were closing with Toruń; at the same time, XII Guards Tank Corps was now close to the city of Schneidemühl. This too had been declared a fortress, though for the moment only a limited number of *Volkssturm* had been made available. Just on the outskirts was an important factory, the *Albatros-Werke*, where components for Me-262 jet aircraft were manufactured. The garrison commander, Oberstleutnant Heinrich Remlinger, had arrived in the city on 21 January. He was an experienced front-line officer, having served with 6th Panzer Division in the attempt to break through to the encircled German Sixth Army in Stalingrad in late 1942; he had caught the eye of Himmler, who regarded him as a determined and ruthless officer and therefore far superior to the 'defeatist' generals who had

The shattered city of Warsaw had been deliberately destroyed by the Germans as vengeance for the 1944 Warsaw Uprising. (Getty Images)

Soviet gunners dislodging the Germans during street fighting in Poznań in February 1945. The prolonged resistance of the Poznań garrison complicated supply issues for the Red Army. (Getty Images)

Soviet troops in an anti-tank ambush in Hungary in January 1945. The siege of Budapest had begun in late December and would last for 50 days. (Getty Images)

A Soviet armoured division under the command of Lieutenant General Pavel Pavlovich Poluboyarov advancing along the western bank of the River Oder in January 1945. By March the Red Army would hold a wide bridgehead across the river. (Getty Images)

Wehrmacht soldiers watching Soviet positions from a village near the Oder in February 1945. Militarily and industrially, the Vistula-Oder offensive was a fatal defeat for Germany. (Getty Images)

In a village in Pomerania in February 1945, Waffen-SS soldiers dismount from a truck. Many of the soldiers carry a *Panzerschrek*, a type of anti-tank rocket launcher developed by Nazi Germany. (Alamy)

German grenadiers armed with anti-tank projectiles ride on bicycles during a defensive battle in Silesia. After two successful Soviet offensives, the Wehrmacht eventually lost control of the region. (Getty Images)

Two German grenadiers stationed on the outskirts of Breslau (the pair are a father and son deployed in the same unit). The success of the Vistula-Oder operation enabled Soviet forces to encircle Breslau, marking the genesis of the USSR's Lower Silesia offensive. (Getty Images)

Troops of 1st Ukrainian Front move through a street in former Gleiwitz. The German-occupied Silesian city would be captured by the Red Army in February 1945. (Getty Images)

German soldiers fight against Soviet forces in an attempt to maintain military dominance over major Silesian territories. The region would eventually fall into Soviet control. (Alamy)

Armed German civilians march together towards the western banks of the Oder in March 1945, ready for defence. In the final months of the war, German civilians were conscripted to serve in the *Volkssturm*. (Getty Images)

Four Soviet sappers crawl along a rubble-strewn street in Breslau whilst dragging containers of explosives. Their comrades operate machine guns from surrounding buildings to provide cover. (Getty Images)

Breslau central square photographed in ruins during late 1945. In front of the bombarded city hall are piles of recycled materials, ready to be used for the building's eventual reconstruction. (Getty Images)

failed to hold back the Soviet onslaught. Although Guderian had named the city as one of his potential fortresses before the Soviet advance began, little work had been done to construct any field fortifications and few heavy weapons had been made available. The commander of X SS Corps, Bach-Zelewski, could see no point in holding the town, but Himmler insisted that the fortress had to be defended. As was so often the case, Nazi Party officials had obstructed every attempt to evacuate the civilian population in a timely manner and the first of its 45,000 inhabitants were finally permitted to leave on 24 January; again, in a typical development, there were too few trains provided and large columns of civilians left on foot in temperatures of -25°C.

Remlinger's garrison consisted of about 12,000 men at most, a large proportion of them poorly armed *Volkssturm*. But even if the German force in Schneidemühl was modest and unlikely to make much of an impression on the Soviet armies that were approaching, the southern flank of Second Guards Tank Army looked increasingly exposed, particularly as Katukov's formations were still struggling to cross the Warta River and to bypass Poznań. There were no signs of German units deploying to the north of Poznań to take advantage of this, but there was a potential threat from that direction and Bogdanov ordered I Mechanised Corps to turn south. It was to advance to the line of the Warta River, which turned to the west to the north of Poznań; this had the advantage both of protecting Bogdanov's southern flank and also threatening to envelop German forces in Poznań.

The Red Army made its first probes towards Schneidemühl at about the same time that the civilian population began to leave, but progress was limited by several factors. The weather was terrible, but indiscipline was now a major problem for the Red Army, with Berzarin having to admit that anything up to a third of his army was involved in drunken looting. It wasn't until 31 January that Fifth Shock Army was able to complete the encirclement of the city.

While Himmler's army group slowly formed, the situation continued to deteriorate for the Wehrmacht. The Soviet Seventieth Army was now close to Toruń and General Otto Lüdecke was designated as the fortress commander. Amongst the troops at his disposal were the remnants of the Warsaw garrison, though of course they had lost their heavy weapons when they retreated from the Polish capital; he also had the personnel of a junior officer training establishment and the depleted 31st Volksgrenadier Division, another formation that had been transferred out of the Courland pocket. The defences around Toruń would have required about five divisions for proper defence; Lüdecke had less than half the men he would require and few of the heavy weapons. To make matters worse, he estimated that these heavy weapons had sufficient ammunition for just three days of heavy combat. Most of the German population of the city had already left, joining the civilians streaming away from Bydgoszcz, and the half-abandoned city was now home to about 12,000 Polish civilians who awaited the arrival of the Red Army with a mixture of hope and fear.

On 24 January, the Soviet Seventieth Army commenced its first attacks on the perimeter around Toruń. These attacks were beaten off, but Lüdecke was under no illusions. His weak force might be able to repulse some probes by what were largely reconnaissance units, but once the bulk of the Soviet forces arrived he would be outgunned and lacked the manpower to defend all the key locations around the city – there would be plenty of gaps in the line for the Red Army to exploit.

There was no news on reinforcements for the isolated garrisons attempting to hold the 'fortresses' in the path of the Red Army, but Himmler began to issue orders to the fortress commanders. In Bydgoszcz, Arnim was told that he was not permitted to retreat; the city was to be held. Uncompromising instructions were sent by Army Group Vistula to all fortress commanders, demanding that they compensate for numerical and material shortfalls by commensurately greater fanatical determination.

Katukov was increasingly frustrated by the failure of his leading units to secure proper bridgeheads across the Warta and Zhukov was urging him to push west so that the southern flank of Second Guards Tank Army could be protected. Concluding that the current attempts to force the river line had failed largely because insufficient forces had been concentrated for the attempt, he ordered both Babadzhanian and Dremov to use 24 January to bring forward sufficient forces to conduct proper assaults. They were then to bypass the northern and southern outskirts of Poznań respectively and link up to the west of the city. The chances of success looked much better to the south of Poznań than to the north, and Babadzhanian was accordingly told to loan one of his tank brigades to Dremov. Eighth Guards Army and Sixty-Ninth Army continued to labour forward, but both army commanders informed Zhukov that they would still be at least 20 miles (33km) from Poznań by the end of the day; realistically, a formal attack to reduce the 'fortress' couldn't commence until 26 January.

After regrouping and bringing forward vital bridging equipment, Babadzhanian and Dremov launched their new attacks early on 25 January, rapidly securing proper crossings. As Katukov had anticipated, the southern bridgehead proved to be the best point for crossing the Warta and Soviet units started to stream across the frozen river almost unopposed. Dremov's VIII Guards Mechanised Corps made swift progress past Poznań, overrunning a series of airfields as it advanced, and late on 25 January the corps commander met Babadzhanian and offered to take him on a plane ride. When reports of the day's advance reached Katukov, he was startled by the number of aircraft that Dremov claimed to have captured:

> When they told me the number – 700 – I was dubious; we had never captured so many aircraft. 'Are Dremov's men exaggerating?' I doubtfully asked [Lieutenant General Mikhail Alekseevich] Shalin [Katukov's chief of staff]. 'You know, sometimes people exaggerate. Let's reduce the number to maybe 500.'
>
> As I expected, the staggering number of captured aircraft made a corresponding impression in Moscow. *Stavka* sent a special commission to check this unusual claim, and it later confirmed the original figure: there were indeed over 700 captured aircraft.[15]

It seems an astonishing number of aircraft to be captured at any stage of the war, let alone in the dying phases of the Third Reich when the Luftwaffe was a shadow of its former strength. There was a Luftwaffe base to the southeast of Poznań near the village of Krzesiny where FW-190 fighters were assembled, but this was on the east bank of the Warta and was therefore already in Soviet hands. There was a far larger airbase to the northwest near the village of Ławica where several Luftwaffe training units and repair teams were stationed at various stages during the war. It was used extensively by units that used cargo gliders and it is possible that a number of partially assembled gliders may have contributed to the number of aircraft that Dremov claimed to have captured.[16] The Luftwaffe struggled with shortages of replacement parts throughout the war; to an extent, this reflected poor decision-making when contracts with aviation companies were drawn up and matters worsened as the war progressed and factories were bombed. Cannibalisation of damaged planes took place from the early stages of the conflict and increased as the war progressed, resulting in large numbers of irreparable wrecks accumulating at locations like Poznań. There could therefore have been several hundred airframes at the airbase that was captured by Dremov's troops, but only a very small proportion of these would have been airworthy, and even these would have been of little use given the crippling fuel shortages that prevailed. Study of the war diary of First Guards Tank Army suggests that the figure of 700 aircraft was indeed a major exaggeration. The recorded number of planes destroyed or captured both intact and damaged by the various formations of the army between 15 and 26 January comes to just 265.[17]

On the same day, Chuikov's Eighth Guards Army's first units began to probe into the eastern edge of Poznań; the attacks were beaten off around the ring of forts that formed the main defences of the city. Chuikov asked in vain for support from Sixty-Ninth Army, which was meant to be on his southern flank; at first, he was astonished when the headquarters of 1st Belarusian Front informed him that Sixty-Ninth Army reported that its units were already fighting in the city, but this was soon corrected. The leading elements were still two days' march to the east.[18]

Having crossed the Warta and after completing the construction of a large bridge to the south of Poznań, First Guards Tank Army was finally able to push on to the west. The last remaining road links between the garrison and the outside world were cut and Babadzhanian was given orders to drive on with all speed, and by the evening his leading units were at least 15 miles (25km) to the west of the city. At the same time, Dremov's VIII Guards Mechanised Corps began to attack towards the southwest towards the next objective, a chain of lakes that ran along the old German-Polish frontier of 1939. That evening, Zhukov spoke to Stalin by telephone and gave an understandably upbeat assessment:

> After listening to my report, he asked what we intended to do next.
>
> 'The enemy is demoralised and is no longer able to offer serious resistance,' I answered. 'We have decided to continue the offensive with the goal of the Front's troops reaching the Oder. The main direction of the offensive is towards Küstrin, where we will try to seize a bridgehead. The right wing of the Front is deployed on northern and northwest axes against the East Pomeranian group [of German forces], which does not yet pose a serious or immediate danger.'
>
> 'Once you are on the Oder, you will have a gap from the flank of 2nd Belarusian Front [Rokossovsky's units, fighting in East Prussia] of more than 150km,' said Stalin. 'This cannot be permitted. We must wait until 2nd Belarusian Front completes its operation in East Prussia and regroups its forces across the Vistula.'
>
> 'How long will this take?'
>
> 'About ten days. Please note,' added Stalin, '1st Ukrainian Front will now not be able to advance further and provide you with support on the left [to the south], as it will be busy for some time liquidating the enemy in the Oppeln-Katowice area.'[19]

A bridgehead at Küstrin – now the Polish Kostrzyn – would place Zhukov's forces just 50 miles (81km) to the east of Berlin itself, and this new objective was just 75 miles (121km) from the leading units of First Guards Tank Army. But Stalin's warnings were correct; it would not be possible for the Fronts on either flank to keep pace and prevent German counterattacks. Stalin promised to think further on the matter.

Early on 26 January, the panzergrenadier battalion in Bydgoszcz moved out at first light, heading north to try to link up with the rest of 4th Panzer Division.

The city had been fully encircled the previous afternoon but the units of Major General Vladimir Viktorovich Kryukov's II Guards Cavalry Corps moved swiftly on to the northwest, leaving the first formations of Forty-Seventh Army to take up the task of eliminating Bydgoszcz. The German escape attempt coincided with a narrow space of time between the departure of the cavalry and the arrival of LXXVII Rifle Corps. The weather was also favourable for a breakout, with intermittent snow and patches of fog; led by the panzergrenadier battalion, the rest of the garrison also slipped away, with a group of infantry reinforced by a company of combat engineers forming the rearguard. But when Arnim's column reached Kotomierz, about 12 miles (19km) north of Bydgoszcz, it ran into a substantial Soviet force. It took most of the day for Arnim to secure the village but Soviet forces to the north of the village were clearly too strong for the breakout to continue on its intended path. Instead, Arnim ordered his men to move first east, and then north towards Pruszcz. Fortunately for the Bydgoszcz garrison, elements of 4th Panzer Division were moving towards Pruszcz from the north and took it on 27 January; towards dusk, the troops from Bydgoszcz began to arrive in three columns. About three quarters of the garrison had made it to safety.[20]

Not far away, the German garrison in Toruń was also isolated. During 25 January, it received welcome reinforcements in the shape of about 7,000 men of Generalmajor Franz Schlieper's 73rd Infantry Division, which had been defending a small triangle of land to the east of the confluence of the Vistula and the Narew Rivers, immediately to the north of Warsaw, before the Soviet offensive began. In its long retreat, the division had lost most of its artillery, but nonetheless it added greatly to the strength of the garrison. As soon as he reached Toruń, Schlieper met Lüdecke, the fortress commander, and suggested that there was little to be gained from attempting to hold the city. Lüdecke agreed, but the repercussions of the retreat from Warsaw were still being felt and for the moment the garrison commander decided to hold firm.

Around Poznań, more elements of Eighth Guards Army were arriving and during the morning of 26 January Chuikov was able to organise a more forceful assault. Attacking from the southwest, two rifle divisions took the Germans by surprise and overran Forts IX and IXa, creating a breach in the main defensive perimeter. If sufficient troops had been available to exploit this success, it might have developed into a swift advance into the urban area, but the rapid deployment of the fortress reserve, led by Obersturmbannführer Wilhelm Lenzer, brought the Soviet attack to a halt. But Chuikov was struggling to balance the demands being placed upon his army. On the one hand, he had been ordered to capture Poznań as quickly as possible to open up supply routes from the Vistula to the forces that were pressing on towards the Oder; on the other hand, Zhukov was also urging him to send rifle units forward to support Katukov's tanks as they moved towards the old German-Polish frontier. There were indications that the German forces were digging in along this frontier along what was known to the Red Army as the Meseritz Fortified Area, taking advantage of defensive structures dating from the 1930s, and Zhukov wanted to overrun them as quickly as possible before defences could harden.

At this stage, Chuikov noted the impact of a change of vocabulary in the instructions he received from 1st Belarusian Front:

> It was during these days that the word 'Berlin' appeared for the first time in operational documents, as an integral part of the overall objective. The order of the Front Commander dated 27 January emphasised: 'If we secure the west bank of the Oder River, then the operation to capture Berlin will be absolutely guaranteed.' Zhukov was known in the army as a strictly realistic man who was not carried away by groundless dreams. The word 'Berlin' in his order sounded to us like a new mission. You can imagine how excited we were when we read this order in those days. Having marched through great open spaces across thousands of kilometres, overcoming fire, cold, water barriers and fortresses, we were now faced with the final goal of the war. The orders required each army to allocate one rifle corps reinforced with tanks, assault guns, and mortars, and dispatch them immediately to reinforce the tank units that were already approaching the Oder. We understood that if the enemy managed to take up defensive positions on the approaches to the Oder before our troops crossed the Meseritz Fortified Area, then we would have to expend a lot of energy there. It was all about timing.[21]

Chuikov had led his men – first as Sixty-Second Army, then renamed Eighth Guards Army – all the way from the ruins of Stalingrad. Despite the huge losses suffered by his units as they battled their way across Ukraine, there would have been several veterans who had been involved in the bitter defence of the city on the Volga. When the German Sixth Army surrendered in early 1943, a group of exhausted, starving German soldiers found themselves confronted by a Red Army officer who raged at them. Indicating the sea of shattered rubble that stretched away in all directions, he shouted, 'That's how Berlin is going to look!'[22] The effect of seeing the name of the German capital in the orders arriving from above for forthcoming operations must have been electrifying. An end to their long war was finally in sight.

The Latvian 15th SS Division had taken up positions around Flatow (now the Polish Złotów) after clashing with the Red Army to the east of the town.

On 31 January the Red Army attacked again and together with some German units, the Latvians were swiftly surrounded. What few anti-tank weapons had been issued to the Latvians had already been lost, and when the small garrison broke out it suffered heavy casualties. When the survivors reached Jastrow (now the Polish Jastrowie) to the west, they were once more encircled. A group of Latvians attempted to clear the road running north and a mixture of Latvian, Dutch and German troops managed to pull back along this route to Flederborn (now the Polish Podgaje) under constant attack by the Polish First Army. In barely a week of combat, the Latvian division had been reduced to tattered remnants, as one of its soldiers later described:

> Each hour brought more victims and the roads and courtyards filled up with corpses that no one wanted to collect. There wasn't anywhere to bury them anyway. The ground was frozen and you couldn't walk around because that created more victims. Low clouds, a light mist and the warm, windless weather made the air stink sweetly of spilled blood.[23]

Ax, the division commander, was deeply unpopular with the Latvians; they regarded him as incompetent and willing to sacrifice the lives of his Latvian soldiers to save Germans. On 3 February, he led an attempt by the division to withdraw further north to Landeck (now the Polish Lędyczek). Oddly, he elected to make the attempt at dawn, thus depriving the soldiers of the cover of darkness. As they pulled out of Flederborn (halfway between Jastrow and Landeck) the SS – either the Latvians or soldiers from a Dutch SS division – slaughtered 32 Polish prisoners who had been captured in the preceding days. As the Latvians fought their way towards Landeck, about 400 fell into the hands of either Soviet or Polish troops; they were killed over the following days. The shattered remnants of the Latvian division pulled back in stages to the Baltic coast, having been effectively destroyed as a combat formation.

The battle for Poznań would continue into February. Chuikov sent an ultimatum to the garrison on 28 January, calling on the Germans to lay down their arms and surrender; the message was ignored. Two of the defensive forts were effectively cut off on 27 January and the local commander, Major Helmut Reichardt, ordered his men to make preparations to fight their way through to the northwest. This resulted in furious arguments – Oberleutnant Robert Fütterer, one of the company commanders, protested that they had seen an order from the fortress commander instructing them to make their way to the central defensive position, but Reichardt insisted on the attempt to leave the city. Had he marched towards the central area, he would have been able to link up easily with Lenzer's fortress reserve, but late on 29 January the 1,500 men under his command set off into the unknown. At first, they made rapid progress, but the column gradually split up. After several days, Reichardt reached the Warta near the village of Drezdenko, about 52 miles (84km) to the northwest of Poznań, and found an intact bridge; he led the 500 men accompanying him across the river, but the group was overwhelmed shortly after. Fütterer had better luck. He led about 200 men towards the west, finally reaching German lines at the village of Dölitz (now known as Dolice), about 30 miles (48km) to the southeast of Stettin on 2 March after an exhausting march. Another group managed to slip through to the north from Poznań; about a third of Reichardt's command managed to escape.[24]

On 28 January, Himmler ordered Mattern to be replaced as fortress commander on the grounds that he lacked sufficient field experience for the task, a decision that was indirectly critical of Hitler's appointment of Mattern in the first place. Himmler was also influenced by reports that Mattern had not been as active as he might have been in preparing Poznań for a siege and had allowed various stockpiles around the outskirts to fall into Soviet hands rather than attempting to move them to the central part of the city. The replacement was Generalmajor Ernst Gonell. He immediately imposed harsh discipline on his command, ordering the execution of soldiers who had left the front line without permission or had attempted to surrender.

In bitter fighting, two rifle corps from Chuikov's Eighth Guards Army and a rifle corps from the neighbouring Sixty-Ninth Army – which reached the outskirts of Poznań on 28 January – ground their way into the city. By 12 February, only the central citadel was still in German hands. Throughout the fighting, Gonell had urged his men to fight on in the expectation that a relief attempt would be made to rescue his men. It seems astonishing that at a time when the Wehrmacht was clearly unable to hold back the Red Army, it was possible for men like Gonell to believe that German forces would be able to attack and carry out such a rescue operation, but eventually even he could see that his men were on their own. Fighting intensified around the central citadel in the following week and late on 22 February, Gonell informed his remaining officers that they were free to act as they wished. He shot himself, and command of the remnants of the garrison passed back to Mattern. Led by Lenzer's battlegroup, a number of German soldiers attempted to break out towards German lines, but the group rapidly disintegrated and few if any reached safety. Lenzer and many others were taken prisoner; the SS officer died in captivity in 1949.

Before he killed himself, Gonell had already sent a message to Chuikov to commence surrender negotiations. There are varying estimates of the number of survivors who surrendered with Mattern, from a low figure of 3,000 to a higher figure of 12,000.[25] Many SS soldiers were executed immediately by their captors. The prisoners were marched away through the ruins, with Soviet soldiers repeatedly attacking them to seize watches and other items; as they left the city, there were incidents of attacks by Polish groups. It is impossible to say how many died before reaching prison camps, or before they were finally released back to Germany.

Major General Dmitrii Evstigneevich Bakanov, commander of 74th Guards Rifle Division, contacted Chuikov to inform his army commander that he had taken Mattern into custody. Chuikov summoned Mattern to his headquarters:

> About 15 minutes later, Generalmajor Mattern entered the room where we were sitting, puffing like a locomotive and barely squeezing through the door. Having caught his breath, he gave me a note from Gonell, the fortress commandant, asking the Soviet command to provide assistance to the wounded. 'Where is Gonell himself?' I asked.
>
> 'He shot himself.'
>
> When I asked Mattern how he was feeling, he shrugged. 'What do I care? I'm not a member of the Nazi Party. I don't want to shed blood in vain, given that resistance is useless.'[26]

Mattern survived to return to Germany several years after the war; he died in 1962.

The casualties suffered in the battle for Poznań are difficult to determine with any accuracy. The total strength of the German garrison at the outset of the siege is disputed, as is the number of prisoners taken at its end. A conservative estimate would be that the Germans lost at least 20,000 men killed or taken prisoner. Red Army losses amounted to between 4,500 and 6,000 dead with an unknown number of wounded. Many of Hitler's fortresses had little impact on the course of the war, but the prolonged resistance of the Poznań garrison complicated supply issues for the Red Army, ultimately delaying operations further to the west. Whether this was worth the loss of so many men at this stage of the war is open to question. Any operation in time of war should serve to help deliver a greater operational or strategic objective, and in the context of a war that was clearly lost, the only greater objective that was achieved by the fighting in Poznań was the prolongation of the conflict with, arguably, an increase in the overall loss of life but no change to the final outcome. It was no longer possible to justify the sacrifice of so many men in places like Poznań in the name of buying sufficient time to rebuild the front line – the Wehrmacht and Germany as a whole were so exhausted that any such front line was sure to collapse as quickly as the Vistula front had disintegrated in January. Perhaps the only useful purpose to which the time bought by the battle of Poznań would have been put was to try to seek a ceasefire, but this was unachievable while Hitler and the Nazis remained in power.

Even the suggestion that Poznań bought time to rebuild defences further west is questionable. An operational slowdown was certain to happen in any case, given the length of the Red Army's supply lines, and the men who died or surrendered in the fighting on the Warta River might have been more usefully employed further west. The city itself was badly damaged in the fighting. Most of the city centre was reduced to ruins and an unknown number of Polish civilians were killed; at least 2,000 Poles died in the battles for the central citadel, having been conscripted and thrown into the fighting.

Further to the northeast, the futility of holding Toruń was increasingly clear. One of the Latvian construction battalions – given the disparaging nickname of *Tornas Grāvrači* ('gravediggers of Toruń') by their comrades – was in the city and was working on trenches on the outskirts when it encountered a column of Soviet tanks. The battalion scattered, with some attempting to surrender while others fled, pursued by the tanks. The surviving officers of the headquarters group waited until the sounds of firing died down and then sent a small reconnaissance patrol back to discover what had happened. A veteran of the Latvian division later described the scene:

> Upon arriving on the main road, an unimaginably terrible view was revealed. They were all dead. Some who had fallen on the road had been flattened by tanks. Others lay on the side of the road, but most of them were in a ditch, where they had tried to escape – to hide from the bullets …
>
> Nothing was spared. The first company had … tried to stay in the school. They had not complied with the Russian order to come out, so the tanks fired two cannon-rounds at the school, which exploded inside and destroyed everything.
>
> Many died or were injured in the rubble. The survivors came out. They were lined up and shot.[27]

The Soviet forces operating on the right bank of the Vistula limited themselves to screening the German garrison and pressed on to the northwest, and it became clear that Toruń was tying down far fewer Soviet soldiers than the number of Germans in the garrison. Guderian raised the matter with Hitler with no expectation of securing permission for Toruń to be abandoned, but to his surprise Hitler agreed on 29 January for Lüdecke to commence a breakout. Unfortunately for the garrison, a bridge over the Vistula at Fordon, immediately to the north of

Bydgoszcz, had been destroyed by the Germans on 27 January and the Toruń garrison now faced a long and difficult march to the next likely crossing points, either at Chełmno or near Grudziądz (renamed Graudenz after the German occupation began in 1939).

Lüdecke led his men out of Toruń early on 31 January in three columns, encountering little resistance on the first day of their march. There were clashes with Soviet troops between Chełmża and the Vistula River on 1 February, but two days later most of the garrison reached the Vistula to the south of Chełmno. Schlieper led his 73rd Infantry Division across the frozen river and managed to make his way north to link up with German forces a short distance away, but a rise in temperature made the ice of the river much weaker for the rest of the garrison, particularly for a few vehicles that were carrying wounded men. Moreover, the Soviet Seventieth Army was now making belated attempts to intercept the garrison and shelling of the river broke up much of the ice. Despite this, troops continued to cross the river and followed in the footsteps of Schlieper's men towards the north. About 15,000 men were left trapped to the east of the Vistula, where they came under increasingly heavy attack. The battle continued until 9 February when the surviving 11,000 surrendered. It is estimated that about 2,000 died from their wounds and exposure in the days that followed. About half of the Toruń garrison of 32,000 escaped. The impact of holding the fortress on the overall situation was negligible.[28] Lüdecke, the fortress commander, was one of those who escaped; he surrendered to the Western Allies at the end of the war.

Isolated in Schneidemühl, Remlinger continued his hopeless defence of the city. About a thousand wounded men had been flown out of the city by transport planes bringing in supplies but the airfield was lost on 12 February and Remlinger decided to break out. The garrison made its escape attempt in the early hours of 13 February, leaving Schneidemühl in three columns; they were at least 30 miles (50km) from the nearest German forces. All three columns broke up as they were spotted and came under attack, and small groups of men wandered across the countryside for several days, sometimes combining with soldiers who had escaped from Poznań. Eventually, a few managed to reach German lines. Army Group Vistula recorded that about 120 men reached safety. Remlinger and other senior officers of the garrison were taken prisoner and Remlinger died in captivity in 1951. There were about 15,000 civilians left in the city when the Red Army took possession, and they had to endure rape, looting and arbitrary killings at the hands of the Soviet soldiers.

# CHAPTER 9

# THE WANDERING CAULDRON: KONEV TURNS SOUTH, 20–31 JANUARY

Far behind the advancing Soviet armies, Nehring and his men continued their cautious attempt to escape. In 1944, the German First Panzer Army had been cut off around the city of Kamyanets-Podilski and succeeded in fighting its way back towards the west, attacking the Soviet units in its path while a relief column marched to its aid. For Nehring, the challenge was completely different. He lacked the firepower and fuel to conduct an aggressive breakout; instead, he had to try to conceal his movements from the Red Army and hope that, despite everything, German forces further to the west would be able to reach out a helping hand.

The prospects of a successful escape improved greatly during the night of 19–20 January when the retreating Germans came across an intact fuel dump and were able to fill the tanks of their remaining vehicles. Having crossed the Pilica River, the columns faced a dangerous phase of their escape; the terrain beyond the river crossing was relatively open and there was less chance of the troops being able to avoid detection. After waiting for the short daylight hours to pass, the Germans set off as darkness fell. A few German transport aircraft appeared and dropped fuel and ammunition by parachute; some of the supplies were recovered but most were lost, either falling close to Soviet units or in areas where they were impossible to recover. Fortunately for Nehring's command, thick fog began to develop, shielding the column from observation and also grounding most of the Soviet aircraft operating in the area. There was a further glimmer of good news. At last, Nehring was able to obtain some accurate information about the overall situation late on 20 January when he managed to have a brief radio conversation with *OKH*. Guderian informed him that the *Grossdeutschland* Corps was continuing to hold its positions near Łódź. Nehring reached woodland immediately north of Piotrków Trybunalski before dawn on 21 January; although the overnight fog had persisted, he ordered a halt to give his men a chance to rest, and for stragglers to catch up.

The column had a lucky escape. The best roads in the area were a little further to the north, running from Łódź towards the west, and some of Nehring's staff officers urged him to try to reach these routes. But based upon his assessment that the advancing Soviet forces would regard the capture of Łódź as a priority and would therefore have substantial forces in the area, Nehring chose to head west along smaller roads. Had he tried to escape by marching closer to Łódź, his group would have encountered Sixty-Ninth Army and would almost certainly have been tied down and destroyed.

Nehring wasn't the only recipient of supplies delivered by air. The *HG* Panzer Division received rather more generous quantities of fuel and ammunition – many army officers grumbled that the Luftwaffe was favouring the division because its personnel belonged to the Luftwaffe. Together with the survivors of the scattered elements of the *Brandenburg* Division, the *HG* Panzer Division was now dug in to the northeast of Sieradz on the Warta River, about 33 miles (53km) from Łódź. Elements of 25th Panzer Division had managed to retreat and take up positions along the Warta a little to the north with 19th Panzer Division's survivors in Zduńska Wola to the east, but Soviet units from IX and XI Tank Corps, supported by VII Guards Cavalry Corps, were probing the entire defensive line and further to the north, other elements of the two tank armies of Zhukov's 1st Belarusian Front were already operating far beyond the flank of the fragile German positions around and north of Sieradz. During 20 January, the Soviet IX Tank Corps and VII Guards Cavalry Corps gathered sufficient strength for a deliberate assault on the German lines. Exhausted after their fighting near Warsaw, 19th and 25th Panzer Divisions could do little more than carry out delaying actions.

Parts of *Brandenburg* were holding a small bridgehead on the east bank of the Warta, almost due west of Łódź, and the Soviet XI Tank Corps made a major attack on this position at the same time as the other Soviet forces were pressing back 19th and 25th Panzer Divisions. Despite their reputation as members of an elite unit, many of the troops from *Brandenburg* fell back in disarray while others continued to cling to their increasingly compressed bridgehead. To the horror of some German officers, there were increasing signs of disintegration, with several

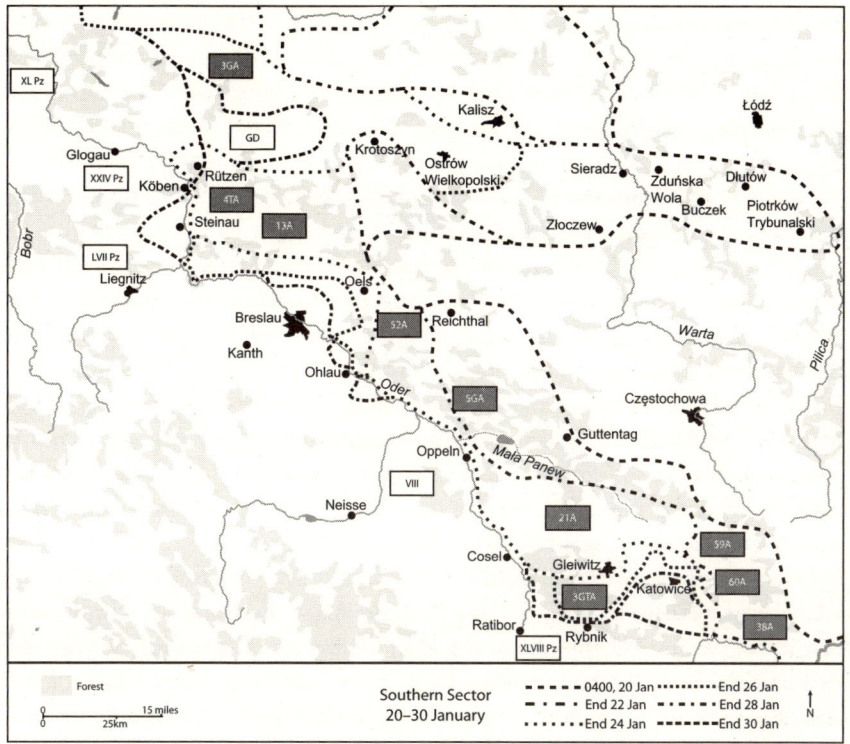

Southern Sector
20–30 January

- - - - 0400, 20 Jan
- · - · End 22 Jan
· · · · · End 24 Jan
· · · · · · · End 26 Jan
· · — · · End 28 Jan
═══════ End 30 Jan

Forest

0    15 miles
0    25km

N

companies conducting unauthorised withdrawals to the west bank of the river. Towards the end of 20 January, the bridgehead was abandoned and the surviving German units pulled back towards the west. They were dismayed to learn that their destination, Konin, was already in Soviet hands and they faced a long detour to the south of the city.

The position held by the *HG* Panzer Division in Sieradz was thus being badly outflanked to the north not only by the leading Soviet tank armies but also by the combined arms armies following in their wake. To make matters worse, the southern flank of Saucken's *Grossdeutschland* Corps was also being bypassed. Fourth Guards Tank Army moved swiftly through the town of Wieluń on 20 January, meeting almost no resistance, and a little to the north the Soviet X Guards Tank Corps encountered a hastily improvised force of *Volkssturm* with a few regular troops from a training camp in the small town of Złoczew. For a few hours, the Germans were able to hold the town, showing surprising resilience for such a poorly armed and trained unit, but once sufficient Soviet units had arrived they rapidly drove the *Volkssturm* away to the east.

While the *Grossdeutschland* Corps continued to try to hold onto its positions, Nehring edged ever closer. After receiving a further small quantity of fuel from an airdrop, 16th Panzer Division led the march towards the west past the southern edge of Łódź. Near the village of Dłutow, 14 miles (22km) south of Łódź, heavy fighting broke out as elements of a Soviet tank brigade attempted to intercept the German column from the north. Both sides suffered losses before the Germans were able to break contact and continue their march, confirming Nehring's suspicion that continuing towards the northwest would have ended in disaster. The cautiously advancing vanguard of the column encountered road signs that bore the insignia of Saucken's corps, an encouraging development, and late on 21 January the head of the column reached Buczek, 11 miles (17km) further to the west. Here, the Germans encountered a reconnaissance company from Saucken's forces. It was the first physical contact between Nehring's men and outside elements and Nehring was finally able to get clear information on what lay ahead. He was informed that the *Grossdeutschland* Corps was attempting to hold positions either side of Sieradz, another 20 miles (32km) to the west, with a small bridgehead over the Warta River. Shortly before midnight, 16th Panzer Division was able to secure a crossing over the smaller Grabia River a little to the east of the Warta and the rest of the exhausted column struggled through the darkness to reach the vital bridge. Behind the leading elements, the column stretched back at least 30 miles (50km), with Recknagel, the commander of XLII Corps, continuing to command the rearguard.

The leading units of Nehring's 'wandering cauldron' might be close to the Warta, but a further 74 miles (119km) to the east, groups of German soldiers from a variety of divisions – 6th, 17th, 45th and 214th Infantry Divisions and 10th Panzergrenadier Division – that hadn't been able to reach Nehring's group were fighting their last battles. The Soviet Sixth Army had been assigned the 'second echelon' task of eliminating such groups. Almost out of ammunition and without any contact with other German forces, these remnants were broken into ever smaller groups and by the end of 21 January had effectively ceased to exist. Some German accounts later described how individual soldiers managed to make their way back to the west over the following weeks, but it is almost impossible to confirm such tales; in any event, the divisions involved were so badly scattered that any escapees might well have been from elements that had been able to accompany Nehring's group towards the west.

Another small group that was attempting to make its way to the west was made up largely of soldiers from 291st Infantry Division, some distance to the south of Nehring's wandering cauldron. Originally, Generalmajor Arthur Finger's division had been deployed in positions on the northern face of the Sandomierz bridgehead and was driven back in heavy fighting; Finger was aware that Nehring's units were to his northwest but he was separated from them by the Opatówka River, and he judged that the ice of the river was too weak to support the weight of his division's heavy weapons. At first, the German division waited for an imminent attack that would overwhelm it, but as the Soviet flood moved west, it became clear that there was perhaps an opportunity for escape. On 17 January, Finger ordered his men to make the attempt. The column was led by a small group of *Hetzer* tank destroyers and while it had been waiting for the breakout, the division had succeeded in collecting sufficient trucks – and just as importantly, fuel – to transport nearly all the men. Early on 18 January, the Hetzers reached Melonek, about 24 miles (39km) to the southeast of Kielce, and captured the village almost without a fight. The rest of the division followed in two columns.

After making contact with the reconnaissance company from the *Grossdeutschland* panzer corps, Nehring had to deal with increasing pressure from the north while continuing his attempt to escape to the west. There was heavy fighting in Piotrków Trybunalski, where Generalmajor Ulrich Liss, commander of 304th Infantry Division, gathered men from different formations to prevent the Red Army from breaking up the retreating German column. Liss was wounded during the day and became a prisoner of war; he would remain in captivity until 1955. Recknagel took personal command of the German troops in the town as the rest of Nehring's command continued its march to the Warta. The first men crossed to the west bank during the morning of 22 January, but their relief at linking up with other German forces was tempered by the growing realisation that Saucken's *Grossdeutschland* Corps around Sieradz had no effective contact with any other German units. Indeed, there were reports that Soviet armour had reached the town of Krotoszyn, a further 56 miles (90km) to the west. Nonetheless, by crossing the Warta the head of the column was now in a location where German transport aircraft could land rather than attempt to drop supplies from the air. The planes discharged a precious cargo of fuel and ammunition and then flew back to the west with the worst of the wounded from 16th Panzer Division.[1]

The Soviet tanks that had reached Krotoszyn were the northern flank of Lelyushenko's Fourth Tank Army, held back more by lengthening supply lines than German resistance. After a discussion with Lelyushenko, Konev ordered Thirteenth Army to hurry forward as quickly as possible to support the tank army. Pukhov, the army commander, did his best, while deploying troops along his northern flank to attack Nehring's retreating columns. The Red Army's policy of advancing deep into the German positions and leaving any isolated German forces to be destroyed later had permitted Nehring's men to survive, but time was running out with growing pressure from both north and south. On 23 January, the Soviet Thirty-Third Army attacked Piotrków Trybunalski in strength and Recknagel's men were barely able to hold their positions. The Red Army wasn't the only enemy that they faced; during the afternoon, Polish partisans opened fire on Recknagel's headquarters and he was fatally wounded. Command of the Germans fighting in and around Piotrków Trybunalski passed to Oberst Karl Bärmann, an officer from 88th Infantry Division – the commander of his division, Oberst Carl Anders, was still some distance to the east with the stragglers of Nehring's group. Bärmann continued to cling to the ruins of Piotrków Trybunalski while he waited for the last stragglers to march west.

Throughout 24 and 25 January, heavy fighting continued in Piotrków Trybunalski. Bärmann was killed in the battles and command passed to Oberstleutnant Adolf-Friedrich Drabich-Waechter, who had been Recknagel's chief of staff. A little to the south, the last of the wandering cauldron plodded on towards the west and the Warta crossings where their tenuous escape route was still held open. The pressure on the northern flank of the *Grossdeutschland* Corps was unrelenting. Nehring and Saucken had hoped to withdraw through the city of Ostrów Wielkopolski but Soviet units from Thirty-Third Army had already seized the area, forcing the Germans to angle further to the south. A small group of men from *Brandenburg* had been isolated to the north of Ostrów Wielkopolski and managed to fight their way past the northern edge of the city.[2]

The retreating German units were now close to the old German-Polish frontier, beyond which lay the Oder. Although they continued to come under attack from the north, Nehring and Saucken were also aware that the Soviet Fourth Tank Army, on the northern flank of Konev's 1st Belarusian Front, had continued its advance and was now effectively in their path. Lelyushenko's army was led by 17th Guards Mechanised Brigade, which reached the Oder on 23 January at the town of Köben (now the Polish Chobiena); nearby, it captured a train carrying military supplies including a number of new tanks.[3] Over the next few days, Lelyushenko's men crossed the Oder, where the river ice had melted, and rapidly expanded their bridgehead. A ferry was improvised using prefabricated bridge sections, but the crossing didn't go smoothly. Lelyushenko and Colonel Vasily Fedorovich Orlov, commander of VI Guards Mechanised Corps, had already crossed to the bridgehead and watched the transfer of further troops:

A T-34 was being transported on a ferry towed by a motorboat. In the middle of the river, the boat's engine stalled and the ferry drifted downstream. Not without a degree of anxiety, Orlov and I waited to see what would happen and what the tank crew would do in such a dangerous and unforeseen situation. They turned the turret towards the enemy and the crew opened rapid fire with the gun at pillboxes past which the ferry was sailing. While the Nazis scrambled to respond, the battleship tank drifted out of their field of fire.

'Well done!' exclaimed Orlov. 'I'll nominate them for an award!' I shared his opinion. About 30 minutes later the crew managed to land on the eastern bank of the river. Unharmed, the tank rejoined our forces.[4]

Operating at the end of long supply lines and with their supporting combined arms armies still several days' march to the east, the formations of Lelyushenko's tank army were far from full strength. In addition to the losses suffered in combat, particularly in the opening phase of the battle against the relatively strong divisions of XXIV Panzer Corps, the tank brigades had left a stream of broken down or stranded vehicles in their wake. The ability of integral engineering and workshop teams to recover these – and to repair battle damage to other vehicles – was far greater than had been the case earlier in the war, but the sheer scale of the advance meant that it was impossible for the recovery crews to be everywhere at once. They had to compete with combat formations and supply columns for road space, and this congestion hindered the forward movement of bridging units. The tank armies had been given additional bridging resources at the outset of the operation but many of these had already deployed their prefabricated bridge components. Until further supplies arrived, there was little they could do to help the Soviet units secure more than modest bridgeheads across the Oder.

Throughout 26 January, Nehring's and Saucken's troops continued to head west under heavy pressure. From the north, XVI Rifle Corps from Thirty-Third Army attacked repeatedly, and from the south there were constant thrusts by Third Guards Army's CXX Rifle Corps. At the same time, Finger's 291st Infantry Division, some distance to the south, also came under increasing pressure. At first, Finger attempted to find a way past the Soviet troops in his path, but rapidly it became clear that this was impossible. Ammunition for the heavy weapons was soon spent and Finger was killed on 27 January, but the surviving infantrymen fought on for another two days until the last remnants were overrun.

On the same day that 291st Infantry Division was destroyed, the bitter defence of Piotrków Trybunalski came to an end. Drabich-Waechter was killed in the fighting together with perhaps 15,000 German soldiers, but their stand had bought time for the rest of the German forces to move west. The first elements of the combined remnants of the *Grossdeutschland* Corps and Nehring's units reached and crossed the Oder at Glogau (now the Polish Głogów); Saucken had given priority to the exhausted soldiers of Nehring's command to cross first. It was a remarkable achievement. Almost since the onset of the Soviet offensive on 12 January, Nehring and his units had been isolated, but they had escaped through a combination of circumstances. The deliberate policy of the Red Army to leave bypassed German units to be destroyed by second echelon formations undoubtedly played a considerable part, and it was unquestionably the correct policy to follow. Almost all the artillery, tanks and other heavy equipment of Nehring's divisions was lost during the retreat – although thousands of German soldiers escaped, their combat efficacy was vastly diminished. If the Red Army had deliberately tried to encircle and crush XXIV Panzer Corps in or near Kielce, this would have resulted in heavy losses and would have delayed the westward exploitation of the initial breakthrough. Nehring and Saucken also benefited from being on the seam between two Soviet Fronts, and the sheer determination of the men to escape was also an important factor, as was the skilful leadership of their commanders. Finally, the weather contributed considerably to the German escape; the frequent snow, fog and heavily overcast skies limited the ability of Soviet aviation to monitor and interfere with the German march.

It would be wrong to assume that German discipline was flawless during the retreat. Writing after the war, Hans-Günther Liebisch, who was a major in 17th Panzer Division and commanded one of its panzergrenadier battalions, described an incident that showed both the strains placed upon discipline by the retreat and the sense of personal loyalty and unit cohesion that was essential for survival:

> Something occurred which immediately portrayed the peculiar situation in which all soldiers were at that time. A confused soldier reported to General Nehring that soldiers from my battalion had snitched fuel from trucks of the corps staff. The general immediately relieved me of my command, although I had nothing to do with the whole matter.
>
> Before dusk, we were ordered to form up, but General Nehring had not expected the ensuing reaction of my Bavarian soldiers. Nobody would move. After about two hours of waiting, the chief of staff suddenly appeared and told me something like 'Forget it' [i.e. Liebisch's dismissal was reversed].
>
> We then formed up into squads and the general with the rest of his staff was close behind us. Never again would this incident be mentioned.[5]

When it crossed the Oder, Liebisch's battalion was at only one-third of its original strength; it was still the largest relatively intact element of 17th Panzer Division to escape.

In 401 BC, the Persian Cyrus the Younger raised an army of 10,000 Greek mercenaries and led them into Persia to try to seize the throne. The army won a victory near Babylon, but Cyrus was killed and the Greeks were left in a precarious situation. In the weeks that followed, the men conducted an extraordinary march across Mesopotamia and Asia Minor, finally reaching the Black Sea coast near the modern Turkish city of Trabzon; here, they were able to contact Greek ships and arrange transport back to Greece. The story of the march was immortalised by the Greek writer, soldier and philosopher Xenophon in his *Anabasis* and Guderian and others likened the march of Nehring's men to this ancient episode. In the dark days of 1945, the escape of the German group was a small crumb of comfort for a nation and its armed forces as they faced annihilation. Inevitably, Soviet accounts took a different viewpoint and highlighted the losses of men and equipment suffered by the retreating column, but the march of Nehring and his men, staying together, evading Soviet troops when possible, and fighting with determination when necessary, remains an almost forgotten but nonetheless outstanding example of the principles that had served the Wehrmacht so well: discipline; highly trained officers and NCOs; and an ability to improvise in the face of uncertainty and adversity.

Even as they crossed the Oder, the soldiers knew that there was little prospect of a period of rest to recover from their ordeal; the German lines were threadbare at best, and every man who was available would be needed for immediate deployment. In particular, Guderian was anxious about the bridgehead that Lelyushenko had established over the Oder near Steinau (now the Polish Ścinawa) and wanted the *HG* and *Brandenburg* Divisions to attack here as soon as possible. The remaining units of 19th Panzer Division – effectively reduced to just a modest battlegroup – would cover the northern flank of this planned attack. Accordingly, Saucken received orders for his corps not to proceed west towards the crossings at Glogau, but to angle south to attack the Soviet units that were still to the east of the Oder.

Lelyushenko had ordered his men to secure bridgeheads across the Oder to both the north and south of Steinau. The northern bridgehead was around the town of Köben. At the same time, 62nd Guards Tank Brigade launched a surprise attack on Steinau itself on 25 January. This thrust took the poorly equipped garrison by surprise and the vital bridge over the Oder was swiftly captured by the Soviet force, but the Germans rapidly rallied. In the tight streets of the town, the Soviet tanks were at a disadvantage without supporting infantry and the commander of the tank battalion that had seized the bridge was badly wounded. Many of his tanks were knocked out and the Germans managed to regain control of the western end of the bridge; they promptly triggered demolition charges and destroyed the crossing. The remaining Soviet tanks trapped in Steinau were hunted down and destroyed.

The Soviet forces on either side of Steinau enjoyed greater success, and despite repeated German attacks they were able to expand both bridgeheads. On 29 January, Saucken's counterattack from the north began. The battlegroups of the *HG* Panzer Division and *Brandenburg* had concentrated immediately east of the Oder and made a limited advance towards the south, but the attack was effectively brought to a halt in Rützen (now the Polish Ryczeń). To add insult to injury, the Soviet defenders – the leading units of Third Guards Army – used the old walls of the castle in the town to good effect; before the war, this had been the property of the family of the operations officer of the *Grossdeutschland* Panzer Corps.[6] Lelyushenko had directed VI Guards Mechanised Corps to defend this northern shoulder of his tank army and the Germans realised that they were outnumbered by the forces they were attacking. Finally, Saucken called off the attack and ordered a withdrawal to the west where a bridging detachment had constructed a bridge over the Oder. Drifting ice in the river damaged one of the trestles of the bridge, leading to growing traffic congestion on the east bank, but the Germans were able to cross to the safety of the west bank during the night of 31 January–1 February.

The failure of the counterattack led to sharp exchanges between Saucken and higher commands. Harpe, who was aware of the disparity of strength between the two German divisions and the Soviet units in their path, sided with Saucken, but Schörner strongly criticised the leadership of the *Grossdeutschland* Corps. Saucken had a reputation for not accepting what he regarded as undeserved criticism and acerbically pointed out that his units had been effectively isolated for many days before being ordered south to launch a counterattack without receiving adequate supplies or any reinforcements. Regardless of the German arguments, Lelyushenko's bridgeheads across the Oder had managed to coalesce and the units that had crossed the river were able to seize control of Steinau. Any future German counterattacks would have to be made west of the Oder.

While the escape of the troops commanded by Nehring and Saucken was taking place, there were major developments on the southern flank of the great Soviet offensive across Poland. After taking Kraków to the south, 1st Ukrainian Front now faced growing German resistance. From the outset, Stalin had made clear to the commander of 1st Ukrainian Front that overrunning Upper Silesia and its industrial centres was a high priority and Konev was increasingly concerned that the Germans would be able to conduct a stubborn, slow retreat through the region; in such circumstances, his troops would have to endure heavy fighting:

> We were faced with three tasks, which ultimately combined into one: to defeat the enemy's Silesian group without major losses on our part; to do this as quickly as possible; and to preserve the industrial resources of Silesia intact.

A decision was made to carry out a deep bypass of the Silesian industrial region with tank formations and then, in cooperation with combined arms armies advancing on Silesia from the north, east and south, force the Nazis – under threat of encirclement – to withdraw to open ground, and to defeat them there.

To this end, Rybalko's Third Guards Tank Army received orders from the Front command on 20 January to change the direction of its offensive. Previously, Rybalko's troops were aimed at Breslau, but due to the situation in Upper Silesia it was necessary to turn his army sharply to the south. For Rybalko, this order was not only unexpected, but also very difficult: turning an entire tank army, already aimed in a different direction and on the move, is a challenging task.[7]

Whilst it was a difficult undertaking, Rybalko had performed similar manoeuvres before. He swiftly issued fresh orders to his leading formations. VI Guards Tank Corps was ordered to reach the Oder River near Oppeln (now the Polish Opole), while VII Guards Tank Corps aimed for the river a little further to the south. On his left flank would be IX Mechanised Corps, with the intention of eventually turning towards the east to outflank the German line defending Upper Silesia. Konev also modified the orders to his combined arms armies. All three armies on his southern flank – from north to south, Twenty-First, Fifty-Ninth and Sixtieth Armies – were to attack towards the southwest.

As Third Guards Tank Army turned south, Koroteev's Fifty-Second Army continued to advance west towards the city of Breslau (now the Polish Wrocław). The city had a long history of being home to a mixed population of Germans, Poles, and Jews, with the Germans usually forming a substantial majority, and it became a Prussian possession in the 18th century. Many Poles left at the end of the First World War and widespread poverty and unemployment resulted in fierce clashes between Communists and Nazis in the early 1930s. By the outbreak of the Second World War, Breslau was a firmly established centre of support for the Nazis and there was considerable violence against the Jewish population, the fourth largest Jewish urban community in Germany. During the war, there were numerous subcamps of the main concentration camp at Gross-Rosen (now the Polish Rogoźnica), with factories producing goods for various war-related industries. The city lies on the Oder River, which divides into several channels as it enters the city from the east; some urban areas – Bischofswalde and Zimpel – are between the main channel of the river and smaller channels to the northeast, while others – Rosenthal and Karlowitz – are entirely east of the waterways. The Ohle River – now known as the Oława – enters the city in the southeast part and joins the main channel of the Oder immediately to the east of the city centre. With so many waterways running through the urban area, there were dozens of bridges for rail, road and foot traffic. The population grew steadily as it was perceived to be out of range of the bombers of the Western Allies, but as early as August 1944, Hitler nominated Breslau as a future fortress. *Gauleiter* Karl Hanke, in charge of Lower Silesia, was declared the interim commander of the fortress with responsibility for preparing defences around the city.

The *Gauleiters* of Nazi Germany were a heterogeneous group. Some, like Koch in East Prussia, had started their political careers leaning towards socialism, while others emerged from the multiple right-wing groups that proliferated in Germany in the 1920s. Hanke was a Silesian by birth and was 15 years old when the First World War came to an end; he served a year in the post-war army before becoming a miller. When he was in Berlin working as a teacher for apprentice millers, he joined the Nazi Party and demonstrated an enthusiasm for agitation and political organisation that rapidly drew the attention of senior figures. During this period of his life he became close friends with Albert Speer, who was an architect at the time, and Joseph Goebbels, who was *Gauleiter* in Berlin. Goebbels took Hanke under his wing, but the close relationship between the two men had serious consequences. On the one hand, it provided Hanke with opportunities for rapid political progress and promotion within the Party; on the other hand, as a family friend of the Goebbels, Hanke became acquainted with Goebbels' wife Magda. The extramarital affairs of Goebbels were common knowledge; and perhaps from a starting point of deploring these activities, Hanke drew closer to Magda and in 1938 tried to persuade her to leave her husband and to marry him, producing evidence of dozens of women with whom Goebbels had had liaisons. When he became aware of this, Hitler intervened. He told Goebbels that a divorce was out of the question and insisted that his propaganda minister repair the rift in his marriage. Goebbels duly did so, at least for outward appearances, but the affairs continued. Hanke continued to hope for a change of situation, but by the outbreak of the Second World War his relationship with Magda was over. Unlike many *Gauleiters*, Hanke found himself in the army, joining 3rd Panzer Division and then being assigned to 7th Panzer Division, where he distinguished himself in fending off a French counterattack in the 1940 campaign. The division commander, Erwin Rommel, recommended Hanke for the Knight's Cross, but withdrew his recommendation when Hanke boasted about his Party rank placing him above Rommel.

In 1941, Silesia was a single *Reichsgau* under the control of Josef Wagner, but the *Gauleiter* was falling out of favour, particularly with Martin Bormann and Heinrich Himmler, whose scheming against Wagner was aided by the active cooperation of Wagner's deputy, Fritz Bracht. After a tireless campaign by

Bormann, Hitler reluctantly agreed to divide Silesia into Upper and Lower Silesia with Bracht becoming *Gauleiter* in Upper Silesia; the post of *Gauleiter* in Lower Silesia was given to Hanke. Wagner, whose Catholicism brought him into conflict with many in the Nazi Party, was first sent to Westphalia-South as *Gauleiter*, then dismissed and eventually expelled from the Party and incarcerated in a concentration camp, where he would be hanged by the Gestapo in the closing days of the war.[8] In the meantime, Hanke took up his new post with enthusiasm, moving against those he regarded as the enemies of Nazi Germany. Top of the list, inevitably, were the Jews of Breslau, the capital of Lower Silesia; all had been expelled by mid-1943. When he visited Auschwitz, Hanke was shocked by the events he witnessed, but continued his ruthless pursuit of enemies of the Reich. Over 1,000 were executed on his orders in and around Breslau.

Hanke was not a personally charismatic or popular figure. Many Silesians regarded him – like many Nazi figures – as someone who had an over-inflated opinion of his own abilities and importance, and in view of his clear enthusiasm for public executions, there was much wordplay with the similarity between his name and *Henker*, the German word for hangman.[9] Even as the Red Army drew closer to Breslau, Hanke continued to impose ruthless justice on those he judged to have transgressed. The deputy mayor of Breslau, Wolfgang Spielhausen, tried to use his Party influence first to evacuate his family from the city and then to secure a post for himself in Berlin. He failed to achieve the latter and was promptly arrested on Hanke's orders. After being driven around the city on the back of an open truck, he was shot by a firing squad of *Volkssturm*, but was still alive; one of Hanke's officials then executed him by firing several shots into his head.[10] Further harsh measures followed. Three other senior Nazi figures were sentenced to death in the days that followed, as were many ordinary citizens. Even military personnel were not safe. An intelligence officer, Major Hans Meyer, was accused of defeatism on account of comments he made to a mixed group of *Volkssturm* and Wehrmacht soldiers and was brought before a court martial at Hanke's instigation. Despite the attempts by several senior Wehrmacht officers to intervene on behalf of Meyer, he was found guilty and shot.

As he prepared his city for its role as one of Hitler's fortresses, Hanke also had to address the urgent need to evacuate civilians while it was still possible. Plans had been drawn up for a major evacuation using the railway, but this was largely theoretical and dependent on about 100 trains being available every day – there was little discussion with railway officials about how much capacity could be provided. This was an era in which railways played a critical part in the movement of war materiel, particularly in the eastern parts of Europe where roads were inferior to those further west; moreover, the fuel shortages in Nazi

Germany meant that even when trucks and other road transport were available, keeping them running was highly problematic. Despite heavy bombing of railway yards, the *Reichsbahn* continued to function, though of course at reduced capacity, but the requirements placed upon it were impossible. In addition to moving troops, ammunition and food, the trains were also increasingly in demand for evacuations across the eastern parts of the Reich and precious railway capacity was also needed to move large numbers of prisoners from prisoner-of-war camps and concentration camps. Generalmajor Johannes Krause had been appointed to oversee military aspects of the fortress and he repeatedly urged Hanke to evacuate the city during the winter before the Soviet offensive began; Hanke rejected his suggestions each time.

Late on 18 January, Breslau suffered an air raid that left fuel storage tanks on the banks of the Oder ablaze. That night, after becoming aware of the approach of Soviet tanks near Reichthal (now the Polish Rychtal), *Gauleiter* Hanke authorised the evacuation of civilians from Breslau, but even at this stage this was limited. Most of the population were shocked by a sudden announcement on the public address loudspeakers that were in place around the city shortly after the end of the air raid:

> The civilian population must evacuate every district of Breslau east of the Oder immediately. The Oder bridges in the city are being prepared for demolition by engineers. Every person in the eastern part of the city must leave their home immediately and proceed on foot to the western side of the city where every measure has been taken to prepare for their arrival.[11]

As people began to cross the bridges, they found that few steps, if any, had been taken by the authorities. Within hours, tens of thousands of civilians were gathering helplessly in the frozen streets and squares as more snow fell. The evacuation also resulted in the separation of many families; men had been summoned for duty in the *Volkssturm*, and teenage boys were ordered to join groups of Hitler Youth who were being armed and prepared for the coming battle. Some Party officials were deeply worried by the lack of provision for the evacuees and demanded firm action, but others were still in the grip of the fantasy world that dominated the Party: the new weapons that Hitler had promised would soon turn the tide in favour of Germany, and in any case the reports of Soviet tanks approaching the city were exaggerations. Hitler had assured the nation that the Red Army was at the end of its strength.

A lucky few – those with wealth and connections – had already left for the west, but the people from the eastern suburbs now joined the increasingly anxious population in the western and central parts of the city. Hanke made a brief broadcast, attempting to assure people that the evacuation had been purely precautionary and that if any further evacuations were required, they would be organised in a timely manner. He had a poor reputation as a public speaker, and it is unlikely that this announcement did anything to allay the fears of Breslauers.

The local *Volkssturm*, under the control of Hanke, soon had a baptism of fire. One group was transported to an area east of Breslau on 19 January where the men were ordered to complete the construction of a series of positions known as the Berthold Line; thereafter, the 600 men of the battalion were to hold a frontage of about six miles (10km). Even as they deployed, the first Soviet tanks appeared – three T-34s, which ran into a different *Volkssturm* battalion near Reichthal. This battalion had also been labouring on defensive positions and was almost weaponless. The several dozen *Volkssturm* battalions that had been raised across Silesia should have had about 650 rifles and between 30 and 40 machine-guns each but in practice, there were rifles of various nationalities with no more than 15 rounds of ammunition per gun to arm just one-third of their soldiers and like most *Volkssturm*, the men in Reichthal had no uniforms.[12] They were instead wearing civilian clothes and coats with an armband inscribed with the words *Volkssturm – Wehrmacht*. The Soviet tanks left the village littered with dead Germans, including most of the *Volkssturm*.

On 20 January, there was a further announcement in Breslau. Civilians were to leave the city on foot and were ordered to proceed to Opperau, on the southwest edge of Breslau, or to Kanth (now the Polish Kąty Wrocławskie), a further ten miles (16km) to the southwest. No transport was available and the citizens wrapped themselves in as many layers as they could before venturing out. The temperature was -20ºC and there was deep snow, which muffled the sounds of crying children and adults shouting to try to find lost family members. Some gathered in railway stations and watched helplessly as the few trains that were running passed without stopping; most were already heavily laden with refugees. It is estimated that the number of refugees struggling along the snow-covered roads of Silesia exceeded half a million people.[13]

On 21 January, further information appeared from Hanke, either on billboards or in the newspapers. The city was formally declared a fortress and the proclamation assured everyone that all possible measures were being taken to safeguard the evacuees. All the men who had been ordered to remain in Breslau were to fight to defend the city. The announcement made no mention of how long they would have to resist. The defenders were the usual mixture of retreating Wehrmacht units and local *Volkssturm*. As was often the case, there were also some training units that were pressed into use; one such was *Jäger-Ersatz- und*

*Ausbildungsbataillon 83* ('83rd Jäger Replacement and Training Battalion'), which was normally responsible for preparing new drafts for 28th Jäger Division. Hastily mobilised for combat, the battalion's soldiers had only rifles and light machine-guns – no mortars or heavy weapons, and critically little by way of signals equipment. Its personnel were a mixture of veterans from 28th Jäger Division and recruits who had perhaps two months' training behind them. There was feverish activity as the city was prepared for battle. Trees were chopped down and, with trams and other vehicles and toppled monuments, were used to create roadblocks and barricades. Even gravestones were used, and barbed wire was festooned across open ground. Despite the shortage of rifles and machine-guns, the Germans had one weapon in abundance: the single-shot *Panzerfaust*, the precursor of modern light anti-tank weapons and rocket-propelled grenades, which could penetrate the armour of any tank. It was a short-range weapon and the approved manner of using it was to prepare deep foxholes and to allow Soviet tanks to approach as close as possible before engaging them. The sprinkling of veterans in the garrison watched the preparations with a mixture of despair and contempt. One commented:

> Russian tank crews will need just fifteen minutes to get past these barriers. Fourteen minutes to stop their belly laughs, and one minute to push the junk aside.[14]

The numerous bridges in the city – there were 64 over the various waterways – were prepared for demolition. To the east, the occasional sounds of artillery fire and explosions began to grow louder.

Even as these preparations were taking place, there was increasingly heavy fighting along the improvised defensive line to the east of Breslau. Suffering heavy losses, particularly amongst its veteran officers and NCOs, 83rd Training Battalion was forced to pull back towards the west where it was relieved to run into the first elements of 269th Infantry Division, just arriving from the Rhine front, but there was no respite; after the briefest pause to reorder its depleted ranks, the battalion was sent forward to attack Soviet units that were probing down the main road running from Łódź in the north to Breslau. At first, it seemed as if the Red Army units had pulled back, but they were merely regrouping. The small town of Oels (now the Polish Oleśnica) was fiercely contested until 24 January. At one stage, when German troops managed to regain control of parts of the town before being driven back, they found the corpses of several civilians. One elderly resident searched the rubble for his wife. He found her corpse in a cellar; she had been raped before being killed.[15] Wherever the retreating Germans moved through areas where Soviet troops had been operating, they reported similar scenes.

Outflanked to north and south, first the training battalion and then all of 269th Infantry Division were forced to conduct a hasty retreat from Oels to the edge of Breslau. Their losses were heavy, but the delay that they imposed on the Red Army's advance permitted many of the defensive fortifications to be completed and for more of the civilian population to leave. An attempt by the Red Army to seize crossings over the Oder to the southeast of Breslau failed when German aircraft intervened; the Soviet forces were operating so far forward that their previous air cover was now limited until airfields could be made operational in the newly seized areas, and Stuka dive-bombers made repeated attacks as the Soviet engineers made futile attempts to erect a bridge.

The consequences of Konev's change of direction with Rybalko's Third Guards Tank Army turning south were increasingly apparent on 21 January. Zhadov, commander of Fifth Guards Army, now had Rybalko's formations crossing his line of march and met the tank army commander to try to sort out road use. With increasing reports of widespread traffic congestion and heated arguments between field commanders, the two men agreed that the leading formations of Third Guards Tank Army would have priority to march south; thereafter, Fifth Guards Army's leading units would march west towards the Oder, and the rear area formations of both armies would then take turns to move through the area. It was a compromise intended to ensure that the leading combat units weren't delayed, but the consequence was considerable logistic disruption for both armies. A force made up of elements of the two armies seized the small town of Guttentag (now the Polish Dobrodzień), to the east of Oppeln, threatening the roads running between Oppeln and Katowice. The German lines immediately to the east were now steadily solidifying along the line of the Mała Panew River, but there was a gap between these formations – under the command of the reconstituted XLVIII Panzer Corps – and Oppeln. If Rybalko could move his tanks through this gap quickly, there was every likelihood of the precious industrial regions of Upper Silesia being isolated and captured. Moreover, the concentration of German units around Katowice created a further opportunity. By outflanking these units from the west, the Red Army could inflict a further major defeat on the Wehrmacht. The leading Soviet tank units reached the river late on 21 January but found that the bridge they had been aiming to capture had already been destroyed.

Stalin wasn't alone in stressing the importance of the industrial resources of Upper Silesia. Albert Speer, the German armaments minister, had made clear to Hitler that with the Ruhr region effectively no longer functioning as an industrial centre, the Silesian factories constituted the only means by which Germany could continue the war. On 21 January, he visited Schörner's headquarters in Oppeln. The two men could hardly have had greater physical dissimilarities: Speer was a relatively slight figure in civilian clothes, and the physically intimidating Schörner was in full uniform. But their areas of expertise and responsibility were so far separated that each had to respect the opinions of the other. Speer stressed the critical importance of Upper Silesia: the region had 104 coal mines, which produced 95 million tons of coal per year; there were 15 steelworks producing about 2.4 million tons of steel; and the factories in Katowice were the main centre of production for the famous 88mm guns used with such effect against aircraft and tanks by German forces.[16] In his memoirs, Speer repeatedly stated that by this stage of the war, he was convinced that defeat was inevitable and that he used every opportunity to try to dissuade other senior figures from implementing Hitler's orders to carry out a scorched earth policy, and he managed to secure agreement from Schörner that only materiel that could be put to immediate use by the Red Army would be destroyed; bridges and railways, however, would have to be destroyed in order to try to limit the mobility of the Red Army.

Despite his personal high standing with Hitler and his clear devotion to the Nazi desire for fanatical resistance, Schörner had no doubts about the reality of the situation facing his troops:

> He informed me [his army group] existed in name only. Their tanks and heavy weapons had been destroyed or captured in the course of a lost battle. No one knew how far the Russians were from Oppeln. In any case, the headquarters officers were leaving.[17]

Schörner's comments weren't entirely accurate, as his army group was now receiving reinforcements from the south, but it was certainly true that the few units that had staggered back in the face of Konev's tremendous assault were barely functioning. That evening, Speer sent a teleprinter message to Hitler suggesting that given the almost complete lack of impact of Luftwaffe units against the Western Allies, perhaps those aircraft might serve a more useful purpose on the Eastern Front where the Soviet forces were operating at the end of increasingly long and potentially vulnerable supply lines. Hitler ignored the suggestion. The following morning, Speer attempted to drive to Katowice but his car collided with a large army truck and he was forced to return to Berlin. He later described how he had attempted to show Hitler photographs he had taken of Silesia, with long columns of German refugees struggling through the snow in attempts to reach safety; this too was ignored by the Führer.

Rybalko's tank units completed their difficult transition across the line of march of Fifth Guards Army during 22 January and began to close in on Oppeln from the north. In theory, this sector of the German line was defended by VIII Corps, but its total strength was perhaps less than a full division, made up of the remnants of several divisions and hastily mobilised rear area units in improvised battlegroups. General Walter Hartmann, commander of VIII Corps, had little hope that his men could do much more than delay the Red Army's drive towards the south and he warned Schulz, commander of Seventeenth Army, that even when the various reinforcements he had been promised actually arrived, he would still be hugely outgunned. The German line north of Katowice looked strong in principle, but it was also now coming under intense pressure as the Soviet Twenty-First Army began to press down from the north. Third Guards Tank Army's tank corps attacked either side of Oppeln and achieved a substantial penetration to the south, where there were only a few improvised groups of German defenders. The leading regiment of 100th Jäger Division arrived towards the end of the day and managed to halt the Soviet drive, but the Soviet I Guards Cavalry Corps was also attacking a little further to the southeast, forcing the rest of 100th Jäger Division to take up defensive positions around the town of Cosel (now the Polish Koźle).

It was clearly impossible for the Germans to hold Oppeln, particularly as it lay some distance to the east of the Oder. After a skilful series of rearguard actions, the local garrison – directed personally by Hartmann, whose VIII Corps was defending this sector – abandoned the city on 24 January. At the same time, there was a dangerous development to the east of Katowice, where Fifty-Ninth Army broke through the German line at the seam between 75th Infantry Division to the north and what remained of 10th Panzergrenadier Division to the south. The result was that 75th Infantry Division now faced being encircled to the east of Katowice; its destruction would open the way for a swift Soviet advance into the city.

The city of Katowice was part of the region that the victorious Entente Powers considered handing to Poland at the end of the First World War. There was a plebiscite in the region with inconclusive results; the rural population voted by a small majority in favour of union with Poland, but the urban population was strongly in favour of remaining part of Germany. There were three uprisings in and around the city between 1919 and 1921, resulting in Katowice becoming part of Poland, but it once more became part of Germany after 1939. The Jewish population of the city, numbering between 8,000 and 9,000, was swiftly expelled and sent either to concentration camps or to the *Generalgouvernement* and many Poles were also driven out. Street names were changed, the use of Polish was forbidden (even when celebrating mass in church), and when anti-German resistance groups began to increase their activity a guillotine was set up in the city prison; at least 700 Poles were executed in public including several priests.[18] The city was the capital of the *Gau* of Upper Silesia, but Fritz Bracht, the *Gauleiter* who had demanded great deeds from the *Volkssturm*, had already departed and was now in Oppeln with Schörner. Shortly after arriving in Oppeln, Bracht suffered a severe heart attack and was sent to hospital in Neisse. His deputy Metzner now became *Gauleiter* of a rapidly shrinking *Gau*, but matters were further complicated by many of the administrative duties of the *Gau* and the title of *Reichsverteidigungskommissar* ('Reich Defence Commissar') being given to Fritz Reckmann.

The German 20th Panzer Division had been badly degraded in fighting in 1944. First, it was caught up in the huge disaster that overtook Army Group Centre during the summer; then, it was rushed to the southern sector of the Eastern Front in a vain attempt to prevent Soviet forces from breaking into Romania. In August, the remnants of the division were pulled out of line and sent to East Prussia for reconstitution and replenishment. Given the general pressures upon the Wehrmacht by this stage of the war, it was inevitable that this proved to be a difficult process and parts of the division were swiftly diverted to deal with the constant crises that were erupting along the Eastern Front. Nonetheless, Generalleutnant Werner Marcks' division was at almost full strength when it was sent to Hungary on 5 January 1945. On 19 January Marcks was ordered to pull his units out of line: they were being sent to reinforce the shattered XLVI Panzer Corps in Katowice. The intention was for the division to deploy on the eastern flank of the corps in Sosnowiec, immediately to the east of Katowice, but the southward drive of Third Guards Tank Army reached and overran the western suburbs of Katowice on 25 January. Much of the division was now directed to this sector where it found itself in combat against VI Guards Tank Corps. Part of 20th Panzer Division's artillery was supporting 100th Jäger Division further west against the Soviet VII Guards Tank Corps and other Soviet units exploited the gap between the two German divisions, advancing to the edge of Rybnik (23 miles or 37km to the southwest of Katowice). The exposed German 75th Infantry Division withdrew hastily from the salient in which it had been threatened to the east of Katowice, but the German position in the city was becoming increasingly precarious, with the Soviet Fifty-Ninth and Sixtieth Armies attacking from the east. Edelsheim, commander of XLVIII Panzer Corps, had already experienced the problems arising from having to hold an indefensible position and had seen his divisions scattered and destroyed in mid-January. He could now see his corps being encircled and crushed in Katowice and discussed the matter with Schulz, the commander of Seventeenth Army. Schulz agreed about the dangers faced by XLVIII Panzer Corps and submitted a proposal to Schörner for a withdrawal to a shorter line that would run closer to Rybnik. This would necessitate the abandonment of Katowice, but it would save XLVIII Panzer Corps and would still protect the coal mining region to the south. Schörner in turn had to submit these proposals to Guderian at *OKH*, who would take them to Hitler at the next briefing. It was a cumbersome way of making decisions in a fast-moving campaign.

While Schulz waited for a response from Schörner at the headquarters of Army Group Centre, the situation continued to deteriorate. The battlegroups of 20th Panzer Division managed to hold back the Soviet forces attacking to the southwest of Katowice on 26 January, but Third Guards Tank Army was still gathering its strength. For Rybalko, it was a frustrating day. Although his formations reported that the gap between the German defences around Katowice and Cosel was still largely undefended, several bridges had been destroyed and there were constant delays due to mines that had not been cleared. The units that had been ordered to seize Rybnik were struggling to bring forward sufficient ammunition and fuel to brush aside the weak German garrison. Konev was also having to consider the best way to proceed. Attacking Katowice risked a drawn-out battle in an urban setting:

I could clearly see how much it would cost us to destroy the enemy who was being surrounded in the Silesian industrial basin. However, it wasn't easy to turn our backs on it. I won't hide that I faced a dilemma. The situation was further complicated by the fact that a few days before when I gave the order to try to encircle the region at the beginning of the operation, when we had yet to approach the Silesian region, we did not have time to assess properly what losses and destruction would result from prolonged fighting in this area. As I drove to Rybalko's headquarters, the thought was growing in my mind that we must take the Silesian industrial region in one piece, which meant that we must release the Nazis from this trap and finish them off later in open ground. But this situation was the highest form of operational art. How could we turn our backs on it? It wasn't easy for me, a military professional, brought up in the spirit of striving to encircle the enemy when possible by cutting his lines of communication and not allowing him to escape, to smash him – suddenly, instead of this, I might have to proceed contrary to the established doctrine and firmly established principles …

I tried calmly to assess the pros and cons.

On the one hand, we could surround the Nazis in the Silesian industrial basin. We estimated there were about 100,000 enemy troops there. Half of them would be destroyed in battle and half would be taken prisoner. This, it seemed, was the sum total of the advantage.

But what about the disadvantages? Having closed an encirclement as a result of the operation, we would be forced to lay waste to this entire area, causing enormous damage to the largest industrial centre that was to become the property of the new Poland. In addition, our troops would suffer heavy losses, because they would have to storm factory after factory, mine after mine, building after building. Even with an advantage of firepower, in such battles for cities where we would have to clear the area house by house, we would pay a heavy price in life. And we had already suffered enough human losses in four years of war. The prospect of a victorious end to the war was not far off. And wherever possible, I really wanted to save lives, to achieve victory with them still alive.[19]

This section of his memoirs is problematic in several respects. Firstly, the plans for the January offensive stipulated that encirclements were to be avoided; they were increasingly seen as a diversion of forces that would be better used to deepen the breakthrough, leaving any bypassed German units to be mopped up by rear area elements. Even when this policy failed to destroy the troops themselves, the crippling fuel shortages facing the Wehrmacht ensured that most of the heavy equipment of the bypassed units had to be abandoned, greatly reducing their combat power unless they could be re-equipped. Secondly, given the emphasis that Stalin had placed on seizing Upper Silesia in order to secure its industrial assets, it is surely inconceivable that it was only in the last week of January that Konev started to think about the practicalities of how this was to be accomplished in the most efficient manner possible. Thirdly, although this region was to be passed to Poland after the war, Stalin intended to seize considerable amounts of factory equipment from all occupied parts of Germany for use in the Soviet Union – whilst comments about ensuring that factories, mines, etc. were handed over to Poland intact might have fit the political narrative after the war, it is highly unlikely that it played a major part in Soviet thinking during the conflict itself. And finally, Konev's apparent desire to minimise casualties in his forces would have been driven more by the need to ensure that his armies had sufficient strength for further operations rather than any concern for the survival of his men. Like Zhukov, he had shown little anxiety about huge casualties in the past other than purely in the sense that such losses disrupted military operations.

The German Fourth Panzer Army had nominal control of the units facing the Red Army along the Vistula from Glogau in the north, through the bridgeheads secured by Lelyushenko, past the fortress of Breslau, and down to the southern flank of VIII Corps to the west of Katowice. The line from here onwards fell under the control of Seventeenth Army. The likelihood of Schulz's formations defending Upper Silesia successfully had always been dubious. In a straight line, the frontage they would have to hold came to over 70 miles (120km), and the density of cities, towns, and industrial facilities meant that a single full-strength division would have been able to hold less than a tenth of this. If Schulz had controlled a dozen divisions, he might have had sufficient to man a continuous defensive line – with adequate reserves held behind it – to blunt and even turn back the Red Army. Instead, despite the reinforcements that he had received his total strength fell far short of this, not least because most of those reinforcements were far from their establishment strength. On his left flank, in and immediately to the west of Katowice, XLVIII Panzer Corps had the remnants of 68th and 304th Infantry Divisions, badly depleted after their retreat across central Poland; the first was reduced to less than a single regiment in strength and the second was even weaker, amounting to little more than a reinforced battalion. The corps had received 75th Infantry Division from First Panzer Army to the south and had also been promised two additional divisions – 97th Jäger Division from First Panzer Army and 712th Infantry Division from the Netherlands – but barely half of these divisions had arrived. Much would depend on 8th and 20th Panzer Divisions, but the latter was already tied down in defensive fighting and the bulk of XLVIII Panzer Corps was fighting Soviet forces to the west, north and east of Katowice. The B-1 and B-2 defensive lines that had been constructed at such effort by Benicke prior to the Soviet offensive were already largely overrun; Benicke had been refused permission to deploy the *Volkssturm* in these positions so that the soldiers could familiarise themselves, and when they were hastily sent forward the command and control of these poorly equipped and almost untrained units proved to be non-existent. Technically, they remained under the control of the Nazi Party, but in practice they were simply left to their own devices. Retreating Wehrmacht units hastily commandeered them and threw many of the *Volkssturm* into gaps in their own ranks, where they melted away when they faced their first Soviet attacks.

On 26 January, Schulz sent a further message to Schörner demanding permission to pull back from Katowice. His report summarised the unequal struggle his men were facing:

> Today, the continuation of the enemy's offensive operation resulted in extraordinary strain, especially in the area around the industrial centres [i.e. in Katowice]. Seventeenth Army is engaged in very heavy defensive fighting against an enemy who is attacking with four armies, 33 rifle divisions, five tank corps, a cavalry corps, and an independent tank brigade, and the southern flank [further

to the southeast] was pushed back. There were several deep penetrations in the front line around the industrial area and there was also a tactical breakthrough to the southeast of Katowice. Attacking from southeast of Gleiwitz, 20th Panzer Division drew on itself the majority of the enemy tank units approaching from the northwest and inflicted considerable losses on them. However, its own attack could not achieve the broad objectives that had been set. Between Gleiwitz and the Oder, other elements of the Enemy's Third Guards Tank Army moved south and reached the Rybnik-Ratibor road with armoured spearheads. Several improvised battlegroups have been deployed against them.[20]

On the other side of the front line, Konev issued a series of orders in his attempt to avoid a drawn-out battle in and around Katowice. It is striking that the senior officers in both the Red Army and the Wehrmacht were anxious to avoid such fighting, but Konev had the advantage that Stalin gave him permission to act on his own initiative – as the war progressed, Hitler imposed ever greater micromanagement on his senior commanders, whereas Stalin increasingly relaxed his top-down control, especially with commanders like Konev, Zhukov and Rokossovsky who had repeatedly proved their worth. Konev drove to the headquarters of Twenty-First Army to the northwest of Katowice, having already sent written instructions to Fifty-Ninth and Sixtieth Armies to the northeast and east of the city to keep up their pressure. When 1st Ukrainian Front turned south to attack Upper Silesia, the orders issued to Colonel General Dmitrii Nikolaevich Gusev's Twenty-First Army were to screen the northwest and western sides of Katowice and thus protect the flank of Third Guards Tank Army; Konev now ordered Gusev to apply direct pressure to the city. In combination with the two armies attacking from the northeast and east, this would squeeze the Germans and force them to evacuate to the south.

Konev then drove on to Rybalko's headquarters, where he informed his subordinate that having completed one radical change of direction with Third Guards Tank Army, he would now have to repeat the process. Fortunately for Konev, one of Rybalko's three corps was still moving forward to join the other two corps in the front line; this corps was now directed immediately to strike towards Ratibor while the other two corps stopped their advance and regrouped.

It was increasingly clear to Schörner that Hitler, faced by a decision that he wished to avoid, had resorted once again to procrastination. On 27 January, with the situation growing ever more urgent, the army group commander decided to act on his own authority and informed the Führer that he was granting Schulz and Edelsheim permission to pull back from Katowice. When he spoke to Hitler by telephone to explain his decision, there was a general expectation of another of the increasingly frequent outbursts of anger from Berlin; instead, a weary-sounding Hitler replied, 'Yes, Schörner, if you wish, you're already showing good leadership.'[21]

Many officers feared that permission to abandon Katowice had been granted too late. Extracting the troops in Katowice was difficult, given the increased Soviet pressure on all sides; it took until 29 January for all the units to pull back. The fighting resulted in substantial casualties and the loss of much of the heavy equipment of the defenders and due to these losses, it looked highly unlikely that the new line to the south of Katowice could be held for long. Konev claimed that his troops captured Katowice and its industrial resources largely intact, but in reality there was substantial damage to much of the city. Although most of the German population had left the city, there were thousands of Poles. Soviet writers after the war wrote about the liberation of Katowice and other Polish cities, describing in glowing words how the Red Army was greeted by crowds of cheering Poles. The reality was usually very different. There was considerable indiscipline amongst the Soviet units that moved into Katowice, adding to the Polish resentment of the new occupiers.

# CHAPTER 10

# 1ST BELARUSIAN FRONT: THE ADVANCE TO THE LOWER ODER

On 26 January, just as Chuikov was gathering his strength for his first full attack on Poznań, Zhukov discussed the overall situation with Stalin. The Germans were utterly demoralised and broken, he reported, and provided the so-called Meseritz Position, along the old German-Polish frontier, could be overrun quickly, he anticipated little difficulty in pushing on to the lower Oder. Once there, he would be able to establish bridgeheads and could then advance directly on Berlin. There would be a need for one or more logistic pauses, but he considered these to be of the order of just a day or two. Whilst he welcomed this positive assessment, Stalin had concerns about the threat that might result to the flanks of 1st Belarusian Front, particularly from German forces in Pomerania. He wanted Zhukov to consider waiting until Rokossovsky's 2nd Belarusian Front, which had completed the isolation of East Prussia by reaching the Baltic coast to the east of the Vistula estuary, regrouped and deployed its forces to advance alongside Zhukov's formations, but Zhukov urged Stalin to allow him to continue. The potential threat from the north was minimal, he insisted, and even if any such threat emerged there would be plenty of time to regroup to deal with it. The most important consideration was to penetrate the Meseritz Position quickly and to deny the Wehrmacht any opportunity to reorganise.[1]

On the same day, the leading reconnaissance elements of First Guards Tank Army reached and penetrated the Meseritz Position. Interrogation of the first prisoners to be captured suggested that the German units were still forming up in the defensive positions, strengthening Zhukov's case for speed. He ordered Katukov to assault the German positions and overrun them without delay, which caused some alarm in the headquarters of First Guards Tank Army:

There was no example in military history of a powerful fortified area being broken through by a tank army. Typically, fortifications of this kind were destroyed by heavy artillery fire and air strikes, and only then did sappers and rifle formations complete the destruction of pillboxes and bunkers.

The Front command had set us a difficult task! Under other conditions, the order might have seemed impossible to fulfil, but now the offensive momentum of the troops was so high that any difficult task seemed within the grasp of the tank crews. Of course, the matter was complicated by the fact that with such a rapid rate of advance, the rear echelon was always lagging behind with our fuel supplies. But even here they found a solution. [Colonel Pavel Grigorevich] Dyner [head of tank repair and supplies in First Guards Tank Army] suggested the use of captured alcohol for wheeled vehicles, and the rear area units managed to supply sufficient diesel for us.[2]

Katukov exaggerates the scale of the Meseritz Position. Work had started on the construction of a defensive line in this area in 1934; in many respects, the plans were for the creation of defences similar to those in the west, forming the *Westwall* or 'Siegfried Line'. A series of obstacles using local waterways was planned, with movable bridges and barriers that could be used to block movement rapidly. A total of 160 different fortifications were planned, but only 60 had been built when work effectively stopped in 1939. Thereafter, much of the equipment that had been installed – telephone systems and weapons, for example – was removed and transferred first to the *Westwall*, and later to the Atlantic Wall. Once American and British bombers began to hit Berlin regularly, many art treasures were moved from the German capital to the bunkers of the Meseritz Position.

The construction of fortifications resumed in late 1944 and a series of barbed wire entanglements and protected firing points for machine-guns provided fighting positions for about 25 battalions of infantry or *Volkssturm*. The fortifications were therefore far from the formidable obstacle that Katukov described; nonetheless, his tank army lacked sufficient infantry for prolonged fighting. Zhukov's assessment was broadly correct, and if the forward momentum of 1st Belarusian Front was to be sustained, the tank army would have to sweep through the German lines before they could be established properly.

In the makeshift headquarters of Army Group Vistula, the maps continued to show a deteriorating situation. Second Army was suffering heavy casualties trying to hold back Rokossovsky's forces to the east and was in no position to spare any units that might reinforce the lines further west. Eismann, who was still functioning as operations officer whilst bringing Lammerding, the chief of staff, up to speed, urged Himmler to make Hitler see sense – it was only by abandoning Courland and perhaps East Prussia that sufficient troops could be released to restore the front line. Even then, Eismann held no hope of actually stopping the Red Army for long. His main consideration was to extract as many German soldiers as possible from encirclement in the east so that, when the inevitable end of the war came, they would be able to surrender to the Western Allies rather than to the Soviet Union. After listening to the presentation, Himmler agreed to raise the matter with Hitler and headed for Berlin on 26 January:

> We held few hopes. When he returned late in the evening, we immediately saw that something new was up, apparently even, something positive. My scepticism was, however, already so great that I could not believe that Hitler had made a decisive decision in our favour.
>
> That was correct. There was, however, something entirely new, as Himmler put it an 'extremely great thing'. At last the time had arrived when the army group would deal the Russians a shattering blow. The Führer had, indeed, rejected all of our proposals, but – and now Himmler told this to myself and the chief of staff with almost childlike zeal: a great panzer army was immediately to be concentrated in the area east of Stettin. The army group would attack the rear of the Russian armoured forces assembled in the area north of Küstrin, destroy them and then – up to this point the matter still sounded entirely reasonable, but now it became risky – the further objective would be either the destruction of the enemy in the area south of the Warthe River or a turn to the east against the rear of the enemy facing the south flank of Second Army – thus, march directly towards Bromberg and Thorn.[3]

This account was written many years later and contains an error: at the time of the conference that Himmler attended, the Red Army had not yet reached the Küstrin area. But orders were issued on 26 January for the activation of the headquarters of a new Eleventh Army in Pomerania, which would form the core of this counteroffensive. The original Eleventh Army had conquered Crimea in 1942 before its units were sent north in anticipation of a renewed assault on Leningrad, and the new headquarters was created using personnel from *Oberkommando Oberrhein* ('Upper Rhine High Command'). In addition, the headquarters of Third Panzer Army was to be transferred from East Prussia to Pomerania – the few remaining units under the command of Third Panzer Army would be left in East Prussia. Even as these arrangements were being put in place, Himmler intervened and insisted that the new army should be a formation of the Waffen-SS and should be named Eleventh SS-Panzer Army. Its commander would be Obergruppenführer Felix Steiner.

After serving in the German Army in the First World War, Steiner fought in the ranks of the *Freikorps* in the chaotic months after the end of the conflict before joining the regular army in 1921. He left the army in 1933 and became an active member of first the Nazi Party, then the SA, and finally the SS. During the invasion of Poland, he led the motorised infantry regiment *SS-Deutschland*. He caught the eye of Himmler, who appointed him to oversee the creation of the new division *SS-Wiking*, which he commanded during the invasion of the Soviet Union. He then took command of the new III SS-Panzer Corps in the retreat from Leningrad to Estonia and subsequently in northern Estonia. Unlike many senior SS officers, he was a skilful and experienced officer with a deserved reputation for expertise in setting up modern training programmes; he was therefore a valuable addition to Himmler's army group.

News of the creation of this new army reached the Soviet leadership through a number of channels and the confusion around German orders played an important part in Soviet reactions. At first, there was little understanding that Eleventh Army, Third Panzer Army, and Eleventh SS-Panzer Army were actually the same formation. There was at least a possibility that the Germans were concentrating three different armies in Pomerania; whilst one army would be a threat that could be contained, three armies constituted a substantial danger. Although senior figures in the Red Army were aware that Germany was close to the end of its resources, there were constant fears that even at this last moment, the Germans might come to an accommodation with the Western Allies, releasing substantial forces for deployment in the east. Consequently, Soviet plans evolved to deal with a substantial force attacking out of Pomerania.

These new plans were part of the continuing pattern of thoughts and beliefs circulating in the utterly surreal world of Hitler's inner circle. Throughout history, there have been episodes in which rulers retreated into a fantasy world as their realms collapsed around them. For example, even as protesters were thronging the streets of Petrograd in early 1917 and the previously loyal Cossack regiments were refusing to use brutal force against them, Tsar Nicholas II continued to insist that the military could restore order. When Mikhail Vladimirovich Rodzianko, chairman of the Russian Duma, sent him an urgent message describing the worsening state of anarchy in the capital, Nicholas told Vladimir Frederiks, the Minister of the Imperial Household.

> Again, this fat Rodzianko has written to me lots of nonsense, to which I shall not even deign to reply.[4]

Within days, Nicholas was under arrest and centuries of rule by the tsars had come to an end. In a similar manner, Hitler and those around him continued to dismiss reports of the growing disasters on all fronts. The Red Army had to be near the end of its strength, he insisted. It was inconceivable that the Soviet Union could produce troops in sufficient numbers to continue the war. The alliance against Germany was made up of nations with mutually incompatible beliefs and systems, and just as the anti-Prussian alliance had disintegrated at a key moment in the Seven Years' War – the so-called 'miracle of the House of Brandenburg' – Hitler and Goebbels repeatedly predicted that there would be a similar turn of events in coming weeks. The new weapons – jet aircraft, new tanks, and rockets and missiles – would give the German armed forces superiority on the battlefield, and Germany would be saved. All that was required was for the nation to weather the current storm. In the meantime, some – particularly Bormann and Himmler – continued to plot and scheme, attempting to increase their personal power and authority in the rapidly shrinking Reich.

It had become customary for Hitler to make a speech to the nation on 30 January, the anniversary of his accession to power, and he duly delivered his address by radio, stressing the threat to the world from Bolshevism and portraying Germany as a bulwark that protected the rest of civilisation from this menace:

In the years before our assumption of power the bourgeois world was incapable of opposing [Bolshevism] effectively on a small scale, just as it is incapable of doing so today on a large scale. Even after the collapse of 1918 this bourgeois world failed to realise that an old world was vanishing and a new one being born and that there is no use in supporting and thus artificially maintaining what has been found to be decayed and rotten, but that something healthy must be substituted for it. A social structure that had become obsolete had cracked and every attempt to maintain it was bound to fail ...

We were granted only six years of peace after 30 January 1933. During these six years tremendous feats were achieved, and even greater ones were planned, so many and such huge ones that they caused envy among our democratic, impotent neighbours ...

The horrid fate that is now taking shape in the east and that exterminates hundreds of thousands in the villages and marketplaces, in the countryside and in the cities, will be warded off in the end and mastered by us, with the utmost exertion and despite all setbacks and hard trials ...

The fight against this Jewish Asiatic Bolshevism had been raging long before National Socialism came to power. The only reason why it had not already overrun Europe during the years 1919–1920 was that it was then itself too weak and too poorly armed ...

In this fateful battle there is therefore for us but one command: he who fights honourably can thus save his own life and the lives of his loved ones. But he who, because of cowardice or lack of character, turns his back on the nation shall inexorably die an ignominious death …

I now appeal to the entire German people and, above all, to my old fellow-fighters and to all the soldiers to gird themselves with a yet greater, harder spirit of resistance, until we can again – as we did before – put on the graves of the dead of this enormous struggle a wreath inscribed with the words: 'And yet you were victorious'.

Therefore I expect every German to do his duty to the last and that he be willing to take upon himself every sacrifice he will be asked to make; I expect every able-bodied German to fight with complete disregard for his personal safety; I expect the sick and the weak or those otherwise unavailable for military duty to work with their last strength; I expect city dwellers to forge the weapons for this struggle; I expect the farmer to supply the bread for the soldiers and workers for this struggle by imposing restrictions upon himself; I expect all women and girls to continue supporting this struggle with utmost fanaticism.

In this appeal I particularly address myself to German youth … No people can do more than that everyone who can fight, fights, and everyone who can work, works, and that they all sacrifice in common, filled with but one thought: to safeguard freedom and national honour and thus the future of life.

However grave the crisis may be at the moment, it will, despite everything, finally be mastered by our unalterable will, by our readiness for sacrifice, and by our abilities. We shall overcome this calamity too, and this fight too will not be won by Asia but by Europe; and at its head will be the nation that has represented Europe against the East for 1,500 years and shall represent it for all times: the Greater German Reich, the German nation.[5]

Soldiers across the shrinking Reich listened to the speech on their radio sets. Some were struck by the complete absence of any mention of new, wonderful weapon systems. Many could see the emptiness of Hitler's speech, but few were prepared to speak out loud, limiting themselves to wry smiles. Almost inevitably, the Führer's words had their greatest impact on the youngest listeners. Hans Dalbkeyermeyer was aged 15 and together with his fellow Hitler Youth group he had been sent to Küstrin to assist in preparing the city for defence. Here, he and his friend Manni Roeder were attached to a group of older soldiers:

We both listened reverently, convinced we must give everything asked of us by the Führer and Fatherland. As the only youngsters amongst so many soldiers we sat silently just like the others after the speech, but our thoughts flowed down different channels. I still believed in final victory, which for me had never been in question.[6]

On the same day, Speer submitted a lengthy memorandum to Hitler. He described in detail the consequence of the loss of the Upper Silesian industrial region, describing how production of tanks, guns, and even ammunition would now decline sharply. He concluded that no amount of fanaticism or courage would be sufficient to compensate for the ever-growing material imbalance between Germany and its foes. On 1 February, he and Karl Saur, a senior subordinate in the armaments ministry, were summoned to the Führer's presence. Speer feared the worst – at the very least, an angry outburst, and at worst, arrest for defeatism – but instead there was a calm discussion about the difficulties faced by German industry. It was only at the end of the meeting that Hitler revealed his anger:

> [Hitler said,] 'You are perfectly entitled to let me know your estimate of the armaments situation, but I forbid you to convey such information to anyone else. You are also not permitted to give anyone else a copy of this memorandum. But as for your last paragraph,' – at this point his voice became cool and cutting – 'you cannot write that sort of thing to me. You might have spared yourself the trouble of such conclusions. You are to leave to me the conclusions I draw from the armaments situation.'[7]

Speer had already sent copies of the memorandum to six separate departments of the general staff; he asked for them to be returned, aware that many would have read the contents and had probably come to similar conclusions already. But such was the fear generated by Hitler that Speer continued to find his attempts to impose reality upon the situation were repeatedly blocked. Saur had a habit of undermining Speer's pessimistic reports by telling Hitler what he wanted to hear, and in the days that followed he did so again despite assuring Speer that he would support the armaments minister – instead, he suddenly produced drawings of a new four-engined jet bomber that might be able to reach North America, and Hitler launched into a fanciful discussion about the impact of German air raids on New York. The reality that even in normal circumstances, it would take many years to progress from drawings to operational aircraft, and that Germany was rapidly running out of factories that could manufacture planes – which would then have had no fuel available – was ignored.

Meanwhile, Katukov's forces began their attempts to penetrate the Meseritz defences. The first strong attacks took place on 28 January in a bitterly cold blizzard. Friedrich Helmigk, a 44-year-old who managed a substantial family estate near Pinnow, northeast of Berlin and immediately west of the Oder, was with a *Volkssturm* battalion that had been sent to man the defensive positions near Meseritz. His company was holding a position with six turreted bunkers by a blocked sunken road and came under attack from a group of Katukov's tanks:

> The first tank now appeared from the sunken road, followed by a second and a third. They came to a halt before the obstacle. I had my hunting binoculars and my rifle with a telescopic sight, which had been accurately calibrated. The turret hatch of the leading tank opened and several Russians climbed out. A portly officer with a stick walked to the barrier with two others and took a close look ... They behaved as if it were peacetime. I spoke briefly to my sergeant-major and put the crosshairs on the officer, aiming at his centre of mass, and fired. The range was just 150m, and he folded up like a penknife. The Russians scattered in all directions at the sound of my shot and our machine-gun blazed away at them. We had already agreed that a shot would be the signal for the six turrets to open fire and at the same time our mortar struck the Russians with a sequence of maybe a dozen bombs. Lightning-fast, the sergeant-major and I dashed to our bunker. We had only just got inside when five or six 152mm rounds blocked the doorway with rubble. The machine-gun fell silent, wrecked by the shelling. One of our men was lightly wounded. We didn't know what casualties, if any, the Russians had suffered.[8]

In some areas, the Soviet forces were repulsed; Helmigk's company was comparatively well-armed by *Volkssturm* standards, but most units had plentiful supplies of *Panzerfausts* and these were often used with good effect. But in other sectors, the Red Army was more successful. Babadzhanian's units, led as usual by Gusakovsky's 44th Guards Tank Brigade, were in the forefront of the attack:

> Luckily, Gusakovsky's unit came across a movable gate in the reinforced concrete walls of the Meseritz Position. At the same time, other weaknesses had been noticed in the seemingly impregnable defences. The structures in the front line weren't fully manned by the enemy, but were held as strongpoints, and this made it possible to penetrate the defensive system between the pillboxes. Many of these were held by random groups of enemy officers and soldiers who had retreated to the area and didn't know the full defensive system or how to deploy the anti-tank obstacles. Some of these in the depths of the defences were completely unmanned.
>
> Having passed through the gate, Gusakovsky's brigade took advantage of the absence of an enemy response and rushed west without notifying the main forces of the corps ... and the enemy, spotting the hole in the defences, immediately sealed it. When 45th Brigade arrived, it was met by a storm of fire. Attempts to break through with the main forces of the corps ended in failure.

Reconnaissance probes were sent north and south. They reported that south of Hochwalde, the forward edge of the defence line was not occupied by enemy troops and the reconnaissance group managed to pass through the pillbox line and establish contact with Gusakovsky's brigade as well as units of Dremov's mechanised corps, which it turned out had also taken advantage of these movable gates and penetrated into the depth of the position.

Over the following half-day, our corps rapidly regrouped in the area north of the town of Schwiebus [now the Polish Świebozdin] and without encountering much resistance, moved to the rear of the Meseritz Line. Sensing they were surrounded, many garrisons of the 'Eastern Wall' began to surrender to the combined arms armies following us.[9]

The combined arms armies that Babadzhanian mentions – elements of Sixty-Ninth and Thirty-Third Armies – were in the process of mopping up the numerous small groups of German troops still trying to retreat from the Vistula towards the west. The main German forces attempting to stop the Red Army consisted of V SS-Mountain Corps, which at this stage lacked any significant field formations; the best that it could do was provide limited artillery bombardment of Soviet units. One of its few assets was an improvised battlegroup made up of two battalions of trainee SS officers and replacement drafts, commanded by Brigadeführer Werner Ballauff. This was thrown into the confused battle immediately and Ballauff drove forward towards the front line with little idea of the location of friendly or hostile forces. Near Zielenzig (now the Polish Sulęcin), he almost literally collided with tanks from Gusakovsky's tank brigade. Hastily, Ballauff abandoned his car and escaped through nearby woodland; amongst the documents in his car was a detailed map of the Meseritz Line.[10] It was taken immediately to Gusakovsky, who passed it on to Babadzhanian.

While First Guards Tank Army was picking its way through the Meseritz Line, Army Group Vistula developed plans for the great counteroffensive that Himmler confidently predicted would destroy the Soviet armour and would hurl the Red Army back deep into Poland. Eismann was overwhelmed with work, and his first priority was to discover what forces were going to be made available:

Himmler had made such imprecise statements regarding this most important question that during the night [of 26–27 January] I sought immediate clarification of these matters from the Operations Department of *OKH* … Bitter experience had taught us much about the promises of Hitler and *OKH* … The chief of staff, Lammerding, took only a relatively small part in the preparation of such an important operation. At least initially he left all the work, especially the clarification of all questions that were obscure, to the operations officer. Since the rest of the war, however, was still going on, the operations officer would have very much appreciated some support from him.[11]

Eismann learned that the new Eleventh SS-Panzer Army would receive forces that, at least on paper, were formidable. These included 10th *SS-Frundsberg* Panzer Division, 4th *SS-Polizei* Panzergrenadier Division, 18th Panzer Division, *Führer-Begleit* and *Führer-Grenadier* Divisions, a new *Panzer Division Holstein*, and two additional SS divisions (*SS-Nordland* and *SS-Nederland*). Over the next days, the promise of troops grew with several assault gun brigades expected to be transferred to the region. Eismann calculated that if all of these units were at full strength, Eleventh SS-Panzer Army would be a formidable force with up to 1,500 armoured vehicles, but the chances of these units having anything near their establishment strength was small. Indeed, *Panzer Division Holstein* only commenced its formation at the end of January in Denmark and consisted of just a single weak battalion of Pz.IVs, two panzergrenadier regiments (also far from full strength) and a single artillery battalion – this amounted to less than half the usual tank strength and a third of the artillery strength of a conventional panzer division, meaning that *Holstein* was little more than a battlegroup.

When he investigated further, Eismann's doubts about the likely strength of the units being sent to Eleventh SS-Panzer Army were confirmed. *SS-Polizei* had been badly mauled in 1944 and was currently undergoing replenishment, and several other units – particularly *SS-Frundsberg* and the *Führer-Begleit* and *Führer-Grenadier* Divisions – had been involved in heavy fighting in recent weeks and were far from full strength. Moreover, it was doubtful that sufficient railway capacity could be provided for them to be sent to Pomerania quickly. The information that was available was of doubtful accuracy and Eismann concluded that he would simply have to wait until the units arrived before he was able to make a sensible assessment of their strength.

The operation was given the codename *Husarenritt* ('Hussar's Ride'), an optimistic title that recalled the days of light cavalry exploiting battlefield victories in the 18th and 19th centuries and sweeping across the land in pursuit of a defeated enemy. The challenges facing Eismann and Steiner's new staff – his chief of staff, Oberst Fritz Estor, had previously held a series of senior posts, most recently as operations officer of Eighth Army – were considerable, not least because conventional principles of military thinking dictated that an operation could only be devised after considering the strength of both friendly and enemy forces. And accurate information on both was missing. Initially at least, Himmler insisted that the operation start as soon as possible, adding further strain.

Throughout this period, Katukov's First Guards Tank Army, now supported by the first elements of Thirty-Third and Sixty-Ninth Armies, was completing its penetration of the Meseritz Line. There was heavy fighting in Schwiebus, where VIII Guards Mechanised Corps found itself struggling to overcome the German defences, but despite running short of fuel a reconnaissance detachment managed to advance past the northern flank of the German units on 30 January, struggling forward through alternating snow and icy rain showers. The detachment was led by Colonel Alexei Mikhailovich Sobolev, Katukov's chief of intelligence, who had a copy of the map that had been captured a day before:

About 35km [21 miles] north of Schwiebus, the lead detachment reached a canal. On the other side, through the morning gloom, the tiled peaked roofs of a village were visible. The windows were closed by shutters. Sobolev got out of the tank and compared the scene with the fortified areas marked up on the map. In this area the enemy had reinforced concrete firing points and pillboxes, and deep anti-tank ditches.

Having crept up to the canal, the sappers found a bridge which, with the help of some ingenious counterweights, had been drawn back to the far bank. Only a reinforced concrete slab remained upright, but if this could be pulled towards us, it would create a crossing.

The opposite bank was silent. Was it a trap? Or were there really no troops here? The soldiers brought up a tank, threw a cable to the west bank, and succeeded in looping it over the slab. The tank reversed and the slab fell across the canal. Three trucks were the first to cross. Then a tank crossed and its weight drove the far end of the slab into the ground.

As the enemy didn't appear on the far bank, the tankers grew bolder and gathered near the canal in preparation for an advance. But at that moment, a man with a long grey overcoat that dragged in the snow ran out of the last house of the village, which seemed to be deserted. He stopped at the bank of the canal and shouted something in German, waving his arms. 'He wants to lower the bridge,' someone amongst the tankers suggested. Soon the German turned a winch recessed into the mechanism and the bridge was laid across the canal. Rumbling loudly, the tanks crossed it, and then the wheeled vehicles.

From a conversation with their unexpected assistant, the men learned that just yesterday evening there were two companies of grenadiers in the village but during the night, hearing the roar of our approaching T-34s, the enemy soldiers abandoned their positions. Thus, the detachment managed to cross the canal without firing a single shot.[12]

The small Soviet force drove forward through the snow, reaching the village of Lugau during the afternoon. As they were preparing to attack the village, white flags appeared. To their surprise, the advancing Red Army soldiers found themselves surrounded by a crowd of men shouting in French and English: a column of prisoners of war that had been marched east to this area had been abandoned by its guards in Lugau.

The fighting in Schwiebus continued to delay the advance of First Guards Tank Army, but further north the leading units of Second Guards Tank Army enjoyed greater freedom of movement. Bogdanov's first formations, IX Guards Tank Corps and I Mechanised Corps, swept past the northern edge of Landsberg an der Warthe (now the Polish Gorzów Wielkopolski) on 30 January into open space. They were closely supported by the leading elements of Fifth Shock Army, whose troops crossed the battlefield of Zorndorf where Russian and Prussian forces had clashed in 1758, a battle that saw both sides lose nearly a third of their men in an inconclusive struggle. On this occasion, the silence was broken not by the sounds of desperate battle but the roar of engines and the tramp of marching men.

Part of the German defence force was made up of the so-called *Woldenberg* Infantry Division, which was tasked with defending Landsberg-an-der-Warthe. Its commander, Generalmajor Gerhard Kegler, found that his new command consisted of barely sufficient soldiers to form a battlegroup. One of its officers was Leutnant Rudolf Schröter:

> I had about 400 recruits at my disposal, some of whom had yet to be inducted properly, mainly youngsters who had just completed their pre-military Hitler Youth training and were at the beginning of their next phase. Sergeants and other NCOs were completely absent, so their roles were filled by recruits with some military knowledge and who seemed to be the most suitable …
>
> During the afternoon of 30 January the Russians attacked and took Lorenzdorf. The Hungarians withdrew without notifying us, their northern neighbours, without orders or even a brief message, but the fire of our heavy weapons into the enemy's flank stopped his advance. We forced him to withdraw and abandon Lorenzdorf with our reserves supported by a King Tiger, during which a captured recruit from my company was released.
>
> I had no idea what my superior formation was or who commanded it. Since being given my orders in the barracks I had not received any further instructions and had no communications whatsoever with any staff. No officer or messenger came looking for me. I only knew that the Russians were attacking and that, since the departure of the Hungarian reservists, I had an

open and unprotected gap of nearly 3km to the Warthe through which the Russians could renew their attack …

As it was suspected that the town commandant of Landsberg had fled in panic and that Soviet infantry could slip into the city by outflanking us, I decided after discussion with my northern neighbour and the SS sergeant-major [who commanded three King Tigers] to withdraw to save lives and retain our combat capability. The untrained recruits would also not be involved in possible urban fighting. This withdrawal was effected during the night through deep snow and along woodland tracks without enemy interference.[13]

Kegler, the division commander, was also inclined to avoid pointless slaughter of his poorly equipped and barely trained men. When he arrived near Landsberg to take command of his new unit, he was downcast – but not surprised – that the reality of the division was far from what he had been told to expect:

I found the division's command post east of Friedeberg [now the Polish Strzelce Krajeńskie, about 15 miles or 25km northeast of Landsberg]. It had no signals unit and there were no communications with superior commands … The 'division' had no anti-tank weapons, no ammunition or food supply arrangements … [or] a divisional medical officer. The artillery consisted of two horse-drawn batteries. The 'division' was not a 'strong battlegroup', nor were the troops fit for battle.[14]

Describing his troops as a 'pitiful bunch of people in uniforms', he ordered the division to retreat towards Küstrin and managed to get through to the headquarters of Ninth Army by using a local telephone. He spoke to Busse, the army commander, informing him of his decision. Characteristically, Busse retreated into the mindset of simply imposing orders from above that he must have known were unworkable – he demanded that Kegler reverse his decision and return to Landsberg. Kegler stuck to his decision. When he learned of this, a furious Himmler ordered Kegler to be arrested and executed and Kegler was detained as soon as he arrived in Küstrin. From there he was summoned to the standing court martial in Torgau and charged with dereliction of duty, but it proved almost impossible for the prosecutors to proceed as most of those they wished to interview were by then trapped within Küstrin. But Himmler continued to demand Kegler's execution and he was found guilty of abandoning Landsberg without orders. The presiding judge secured Himmler's permission for Kegler's death sentence to be postponed until the end of the war; in the meantime, he was sent to serve as a private soldier in another improvised unit, *Division Doberitz*. He was badly wounded in April 1945 but survived the war.

With Soviet troops now moving through Landsberg, the lower Oder lay just a short distance to the west and Colonel Khariton Fyodorovich Esipenko, the chief of staff of XXIX Guards Rifle Corps, decided to continue forward with a small group. On 31 January, the Soviet group reached the frozen Oder. On the far bank, they could see the town of Kienitz, with smoke rising from chimneys and people moving freely through the streets:

At 0800 on 31 January, Majors Platonov and Cherednik led their battalions across the Oder on foot across thin ice and captured a small bridgehead in the Kienitz area. The rifle units immediately began to prepare defences. Tanks and most of the self-propelled artillery couldn't cross to the west bank; the ice was too weak. Instead, they took up positions on the right bank in readiness to provide fire support for the advanced detachments ... At this point, the main forces of Fifth Shock Army were still 30–40km [18–24 miles] from the bridgehead.

The rapid advance of Soviet troops to the Oder was so surprising to the Fascist command that they didn't even have enough time to suspend railway movements. Without firing a single shot, our soldiers captured a military train that arrived from Berlin at the station in Kienitz, complete with six anti-aircraft guns and 13 officers and 63 cadets from the anti-aircraft artillery school. The appearance of Soviet troops also threw the German civilian population into confusion. After all, Berlin Radio had just broadcast a message that 'the valiant troops of the Führer, successfully conducting an organised battle, are pulling back to previously prepared positions on the Bzura River'. And here, just 68km [41 miles] from Berlin, there were Soviet tanks and artillery, and Russian voices could be heard ...

The station chief turned to Colonel Esipenko: 'Will you permit me to dispatch the train to Berlin?'

With exaggerated politeness and a serious demeanour, Khariton Fyodorovich replied, 'I'm sorry, Station Manager, but it's impossible. Passenger traffic to Berlin will be interrupted for a short time – well, at least until the end of the war. Please take your passengers to the basements and bomb shelters.'[15]

It was a momentous scene: Soviet troops were standing unopposed within a day's march of the German capital. As they probed the surrounding area, Esipenko's men came across a prisoner compound a little to the north where they liberated several Soviet soldiers; they were immediately incorporated into the ranks of the rifle battalions. For the soldiers of Fifth Shock Army, there was considerable pride that after an advance of 340 miles (570km) in just 17 days, they had crossed the Oder before the units of either of Zhukov's tank armies.

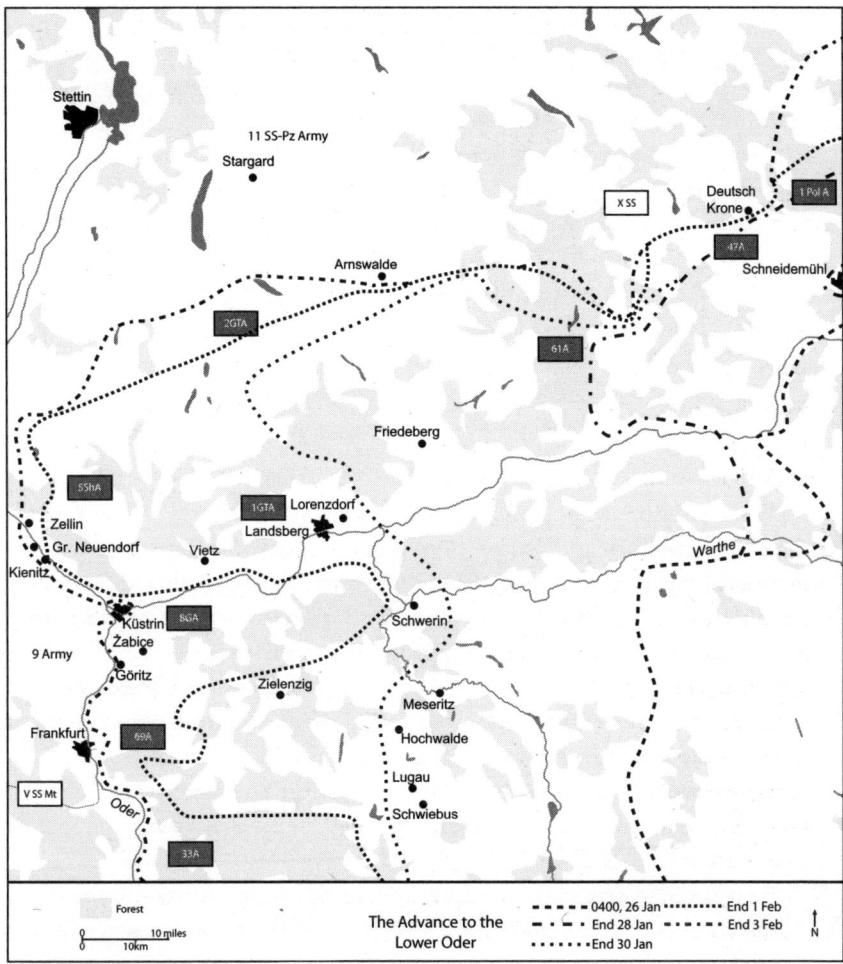

The Advance to the
Lower Oder

Forest

0   10 miles
0   10km

- - - - 0400, 26 Jan
- - · - · End 28 Jan
· · · · · End 30 Jan
· · · · · · · · End 1 Feb
- · - · - · End 3 Feb

N

As January drew to a close, Zhukov took stock of the situation. The successes achieved during the month were hugely impressive, but logistic problems and the long northern flank facing Pomerania were increasingly important considerations. Zhukov issued a fresh set of orders to his armies:

> The enemy in front of 1st Belarusian Front does not yet have any large counterattack groupings. The enemy doesn't have a continuous defensive front. He is now covering certain areas and in others is trying to remedy matters with active operations.

We have preliminary intelligence that the enemy has moved four panzer divisions and up to six infantry divisions from the west and is transferring these units to the east. At the same time, the enemy continues to draw units from the Baltic region and from East Prussia.

It is likely that in the next seven days, the enemy will concentrate troops from these areas on the Schwedt-Stargard-Neustettin line to cover Pomerania, prevent us from reaching Stettin, and block our access to the Pomeranian coast ...

The tasks of the units of the Front are to consolidate the success already achieved in the next six days with active operations, bring up everything that is lagging behind the advance, replenish supplies to a level of two full fuel loads and two full ammunition loads, and then progress to capture Berlin with a swift attack on 15–16 February.[16]

The order continued with instructions for Fifth Shock Army, Eighth Guards Army, and Sixty-Ninth and Thirty-Third Armies to seize bridgeheads across the Oder. At the same time, the Polish First Army, and Forty-Seventh and Sixty-First Armies, backed by Second Guards Tank Army and II Guards Cavalry Corps, were to secure the northern flank by penetrating to the Oder estuary. Rear area units were ordered to ensure that tanks and other vehicles were recovered speedily and returned to their units to bring them as close to establishment strength as possible. It was an ambitious task, particularly as several German 'fortresses' – particularly Poznań – continued to hold out, and the the roads were in a poor state as a consequence both of the military traffic and alternating episodes of freeze and thaw.

There was now a scramble by both sides to respond to the developments on the battlefield. As panicky reports reached Berlin of the Soviet presence on the west bank of the lower Oder, reconnaissance planes were dispatched and confirmed the presence of Soviet troops, with more columns sighted to the east and approaching rapidly. Berzarin, commander of Fifth Shock Army, ordered XXVI Guards Rifle Corps to move forward as quickly as possible to reinforce the bridgehead while Esipenko organised his small force to defend Kienitz. The first German attacks came on 1 February with several air strikes, reducing much of the town to rubble. The first German ground troops appeared later in the day and mounted increasingly powerful attacks; although under growing pressure, the two Soviet rifle battalions, together with the prisoners of war they had rescued, held onto their positions with considerable fire support from the east bank. Soviet accounts described no fewer than 12 German assaults on the bridgehead, but given the almost complete absence of German units in the area, it is likely that the number of real attacks was significantly lower and that many – perhaps most – were little more than reconnaissance probes. In particular, the nine tank attacks described by Lieutenant General Fedor Efimovich Bokov, a senior member of Fifth Shock Army's military council, are unlikely to have taken place as described.[17]

For Zhukov's 1st Belarusian Front, reinforcing this small bridgehead posed major challenges. The leading elements of Fifth Shock Army now had exposed flanks both to the north and the south. Much of Eighth Guards Army was still fighting in Poznań, and the formations that Chuikov had been able to send forward were now heavily engaged with the German garrison of Schwerin. Second Guards Tank Army was badly weakened by its long advance and its units were desperately short of ammunition, fuel and food; until vehicle recovery teams could salvage stranded and damaged vehicles, its leading units were far from effective strength. Moreover, the weather took a turn for the worse. Fierce winds had been driving snow almost horizontally across the landscape and the roads were rapidly blocked by huge drifts; now, as February began, the temperature rose and much of this snow melted, creating muddy morasses everywhere.

In order to secure the southern flank of Fifth Shock Army's salient to the Oder, Berzarin sent XXXII Rifle Corps into the rear of the German forces holding Schwerin; the leading units encountered little resistance and were ordered to turn west with the intention of reaching the Oder to the south of the small bridgehead at Kienitz. The main difficulties the Soviet soldiers experienced were caused by the sudden thaw and by columns of German refugees struggling to reach the questionable safety of the Oder, but the soldiers of 416th Rifle Division pushed forward as fast as they could towards their objective.

Küstrin lies at the confluence of the Warthe and Oder Rivers, predominantly to the northeast of where the rivers join. Astride one of the main routes to Berlin from the east, it was always regarded as a militarily useful location as evidenced by the major fortress that was first built in the 13th century and substantially enlarged 300 years later. Modifications to the course of the Warthe improved the defensibility of the central part of the city during the 19th century, and its importance as a crossing point was perhaps further increased by the advent of the railway age. By the Second World War, there were five large and three small rail and road bridges across the Oder.

The first refugees from German regions to the east began to arrive in Küstrin on 20 January. These were the lucky ones who had been able to leave while scheduled train services were still running; they were largely the families of middle and lower ranking officials (the families of senior Nazi Party members would have travelled by car). Over the days that followed, the fully loaded trains were gradually replaced by increasingly overcrowded trains, often with unheated freight cars pressed into service. Most of the passengers were unloaded in Küstrin where they awaited onward transportation.

On 24 January, as civilians began to accumulate in and around the railway station, the local *Volkssturm* was mobilised and the following day, Hitler declared that the city was to be yet another fortress and designated Generalmajor Adolf Raegener as its commandant. He had last commanded a field unit in February 1941; having lost a leg due to a serious wound early in the war, he was then assigned to numerous training posts. Before the First World War, there had been substantial defensive positions immediately to the east of Küstrin, but these were dismantled at the end of the conflict as part of the Versailles Treaty. Like other fortress commanders, Raegener found himself with few reliable troops, but his long experience of running training establishments proved to be highly useful. His garrison consisted of a wide mixture of men: there were Luftwaffe anti-aircraft crews; a battalion of Hungarian soldiers; the now usual mix of *Volkssturm* and Hitler Youth; and even a battalion from the *Turkistanische Legion*, former Red Army soldiers who had been captured earlier in the war and had volunteered with varying degrees of willingness to fight for the Germans. Trust in these men was limited – the Germans regarded them as racially inferior to Aryan Germans, but were willing to use them in France, Yugoslavia and Italy, avoiding the risk of exposing them to the Red Army. Now, a battalion found itself facing the Red Army's assault on Küstrin.

Raegener's first task was to improve the defences of the city, an undertaking that was greatly hindered by the frozen ground. To provide the fixed defences with some much-needed anti-tank firepower, a shipment of turrets intended for Panther tanks was sent to Küstrin, together with prefabricated wooden frames to support them; there was a surplus of such turrets and there was little prospect of them being built into new tanks, and in any case the crippling fuel shortages of the Reich would have rendered such tanks almost useless. Hans Kirschhof, a corporal who had been selected for officer training, was part of the unit that was with the turrets with the intention of being deployed further east along the lower Vistula:

> Our company consisted of three platoons each with four turrets, and each turret had a five-man crew. Our train stopped at Vietz as our ultimate destinations were no longer reachable having already fallen to the Russians and we were sent to Frankfurt, Küstrin and Stettin, a company of 12 turrets to each place.

The Panther turrets were to be fitted to earthen bunkers with wooden frames and linings previously fabricated by the Todt Organisation, but the earthen bunkers had to be built first.

One of our turrets slipped off its sledge during the move and was so badly damaged that it was no longer usable. The remaining 11 were sent to their allotted positions around Küstrin but before they could be installed, eight fell into the hands of the Russians. Only three turrets became serviceable …

Following the loss of so many Panther turrets even before going into action, we were later given two 37mm anti-tank guns and a captured Russian 45mm anti-tank gun.[18]

The first Soviet units reached Küstrin late on 1 February. Their leading unit was supported by perhaps ten or 12 US-built Sherman tanks from 219th Tank Brigade, which swept through Drewitz, immediately north of the town, and then rushed into Küstrin itself in an attempt to seize the bridges over the Warthe and Oder before the Germans could react. As had been the case during their advance to the Oder, they were hindered more by the streets of the city being choked with refugee traffic than German resistance, but they still took Raegener's garrison by surprise and reached the centre of the town. Now, they found themselves in a difficult situation: tanks operating in urban settings without adequate infantry support are highly vulnerable and the small groups of tank riders clinging to the rear decks of the Shermans were too few in number to provide proper protection. A platoon of panzergrenadiers was one of the German units that responded to this sudden attack:

A tank with infantry sitting on it raced past us at extraordinary speed on the street leading into the town. Nobody could have stopped it. Even our sergeant was struck speechless. It wasn't long before other tanks, again carrying infantry, raced past in the same direction. This occurred twice more. We were shocked that they disregarded us entirely.

During one of the breaks, our sergeant shouted, 'There are more coming. I'm going to take a *Panzerfaust* and try to knock one out.' With my comrades I had taken up a firing position behind the rubble of a stone wall …

It wasn't long before another tank carrying infantry followed and stopped near us. The Russians jumped off and went towards the foxholes of our neighbouring platoon on the far side of the street. Their sergeant opened fire and shot one of the attackers. We were terrified when we saw the sergeant fall in a burst of machine-gun fire and our ten comrades being shot down.

When the tank was about to move off, there was an explosion that blew off a track. Our sergeant had been true to his word. However, he was unlucky as he had been standing in a doorway and the back-blast from the *Panzerfaust* had rebounded off the doorposts behind him and burned his back. The Russians dismounted again and fled towards the town, but a machine-gunner cut them down ...

When we tried to cross the road to reach the dead on the other side, we couldn't believe our eyes when the tank turret turned and a shot was fired from the gun. The shell went through the wall behind which I was standing with my comrade from Guben. Our corporal jumped on the tank, pulled out a hand grenade, and threw it into the turret. After the explosion, all was quiet.[19]

The first units of 25th Panzergrenadier Division were just arriving in Küstrin and were detraining at the railway station in the Neustadt, the eastern part of the city that lay to the northeast of the Warthe. The startled German soldiers suddenly found themselves under fire from the small group of Shermans, but the panzergrenadiers and other tank-hunting teams armed with the lethal *Panzerfausts* rapidly went into action and hunted down most of the Shermans. Four managed to retreat to the north and 25th Panzergrenadier Division was pulled back to the west over the Oder, where it could be held in readiness to deal with Soviet penetrations on a broader battlefield. More Soviet tanks and assault guns approached Küstrin from the northeast late on 2 February, cautiously probing the German defences around the edge of the Neustadt, but although several locations in the city came under artillery fire, it was clear to the Soviet commanders that they would have to wait until further units arrived before they could make a formal assault.

Antonov's 301st Rifle Division was part of the forces of Fifth Shock Army that were moving up to the Oder along the stretch of river downstream of Küstrin. A little to the north of Kienitz, another small bridgehead had been secured by a Soviet reconnaissance group but then abandoned when it came under pressure. The Soviet advance left the leading units vulnerable to air attack; although Soviet aviation vastly outnumbered the Luftwaffe and air units could relocate to captured airfields as 1st Belarusian Front advanced westwards, supplying those units was part of the huge logistic challenge that all Soviet forces faced. Antonov, who had been wounded early in 1942, now became the victim of a sudden intervention by German aircraft:

At noon on 2 February, the corps commander summoned me urgently by telephone to go to his observation post in the village of Zellin [now the Polish Czelin] and to prepare my regiments for crossing the Oder immediately to the west of the village. All my staff gathered and I gave them their orders. With my adjutant Vasily Konozobko, I drove from Klossow to Zellin in a jeep.

En route, we were involved in an unpleasant incident. Before we had driven far, a Messerschmitt turned and dived on us. The car stopped instantly and we dived into a ditch, and a burst of machine-gun fire ripped up the tarmac. We jumped back into the car and rushed off again, but Hitler's pilot didn't want to leave us alone. He flew towards us from the rear and fired again with his guns. The Fascist attacked us five times, and on each occasion we plunged into the mud in the ditch.

Then we reached the outskirts of Zellin. There was a sharp whistling sound and a mighty explosion. I don't remember what happened next. Later, officers who were in the courtyard of the corps headquarters told me how a Messerschmitt flew over from the direction of the Oder and dropped a bomb. The bomb exploded near our car. My adjutant, Captain Konozobko, and my driver, Fyodor Panov, were killed by shrapnel. I was thrown from the car onto the pavement. The car was set ablaze.

I awoke in the dugout of [Major] General [Ivan Pavolovich] Rosly [commander of IX Rifle Corps]. Lieutenant Ustimenko, the doctor, was bent over me. General Rosly and [Major] General [Aleksandr Mikhailovich] Kushchev [chief of staff, Fifth Shock Army] entered. I tried to sit up but Kushchev waved to me to lie down. 'You scared us, don't get up yet.' He turned to the doctor. 'How is his head?'

'It's a deep wound, but the skull hasn't been broken,' she answered.

'When you've been treated, we'll get down to business.'

I was there for perhaps half an hour. Then I got up and sought out Rosly and Kushchev. My head was still swimming and my legs felt weak. 'Well,' said the chief of staff of the army, 'as you're here, you are given this mission,' and told me about the situation of 248th Rifle Division, which had lost its bridgehead on the west bank of the Oder. 'Your division is a veteran unit. You're ordered to reinforce the bridgehead.'

The task was very clear. We left the dugout and headed for the observation point. At that moment, a Messerschmitt suddenly appeared from beyond the forest and dropped a bomb. It landed on a house near the dugout. The roof of the house and its walls collapsed, but the dugout withstood the blast. All the cars in the yard were damaged by shrapnel.[20]

Still feeling groggy from his wound, Antonov moved his men into position closer to the river. In many cases, accounts written by men on either side often exaggerated the difficulties their troops faced to make their successes look all the more impressive, but the re-establishment of the lost bridgehead in the face of resistance was without question a challenging task:

> The right [east] bank of the Oder was higher than the left bank. Below was the icy white sheet of the Oder. A kilometre from us, we could see a curling black strip – it was where the melted snow exposed a black embankment on the west bank. The villages of Neu-Bornim and Ortwig were visible in the distance. The Germans were digging on the embankment, installing their machine-guns. Half-tracks stood near Gross-Neuendorf and fired at the east bank. German fighters screeched overhead, chasing every vehicle, even individual men. The main burden of restoring the lost bridgehead fell on my 301st Rifle Division. At the same time, a regiment each from 230th and 248th Rifle Divisions would enter the battle ... To cross the Oder, I assigned 1050th and 1052nd Rifle Regiments to the first echelon. All artillery battalions were deployed with the rifle regiments for close support. The divisional artillery group was created from howitzer batteries and a separate self-propelled artillery division ...
>
> The Nazis had already become thoroughly familiar with our tactics of conducting river crossings. To surprise them, we decided to carry out the Oder crossing and attack the west bank without any artillery preparation, without noise, and even without the traditional battle-cry of 'Urrah!'
>
> Preparations continued at full speed. The regiments moved from their concentration areas and, under the cover of the forest to the west and northwest of Berwald, almost fully regrouped during the day. They formed up about 10km [six miles] from the Oder shore.
>
> It grew dark. All field gun batteries with the rifle regiments rolled their guns to the shore for direct fire at the firing points on the embankment. The rifle battalions approached the shore in complete silence. The signal was given and the crossing began. Riflemen, submachine-gunners, and machine-gun crews quietly descended from the steep bank onto the river shore without firing a single shot. Batteries of 45mm guns accompanied the infantrymen.
>
> We listened intently. Suddenly, a rocket soared into the sky from the other bank and exploded, and a series of glowing flares hung over the river. The white ice sheet became clearly visible, and on it the moving dark lines of our regiments.
>
> At the same moment, enemy machine-guns opened fire from the embankment and a fiery stream of white tracers pierced the darkness of the night. Our guns fired back at the enemy machine-guns. Barkov's regimental battery destroyed two machine-guns and an enemy field gun in one salvo. The shots of our guns smashed into the enemy embankment and crushed his firing points.

The rifle companies rushed across the ice at a rapid pace. Now for the embankment! Here, they could no longer restrain themselves from roaring 'Urrah!' A great wave rolled over the embankment and a battle began in the darkness on the west bank of the Oder.[21]

Before dawn on 3 February, Antonov and his staff crossed the Oder into the newly re-established bridgehead. Temperatures had risen above freezing and the ground turned to a sea of mud. Ammunition was running out, as similar conditions on the east bank of the river made it almost impossible to bring supplies forward to the river. Antonov later described eight fierce counterattacks by German tanks and infantry that were repulsed. Towards the end of 3 February, another German counterattack overran part of the defensive line. Further heavy fighting continued over the following days, but the bridgehead survived.

Some of the German counterattacks were made by a battlegroup from 25th Panzergrenadier Division; it was supported by a number of units assembled in haste from the usual mix of rear area units, replacement drafts, and stragglers. These had been given the collective title *Infanterie-Division Döberitz*, under the command of Generalleutnant Rudolf Hübner, but the total amounted to far less than even the weak infantry divisions that had manned the Vistula line in early January. After several days of futile counterattacks, it was barely able to field a single weak battlegroup.

At the same time, the leading elements of Chuikov's Eighth Guards Army – much of it was still fighting in Poznań – reached the Oder to the south of Küstrin, accompanied by some tanks from First Guards Tank Army. Chuikov immediately ordered his leading IV Guards Rifle Corps to seize a bridgehead and to close up with Küstrin from the south:

The crossing area needed protection from air attack. At my request, the Front commander assigned me 16th Anti-Aircraft Artillery Division … It was supposed to arrive at the crossings by dawn [of 2 February]. But the gunners were delayed by more than a day by fuel shortages.

At 1000 on 2 February, I was in the observation post of the commander of IV Guards Rifle Corps, Lieutenant General [Vasily Afanasevich] Glazunov, in the ruins of a fort near the village of Żabice, to the south of Küstrin. The corps troops had already deployed on the embankment between Küstrin and Göritz [now the Polish Górzyca], preparing for the crossing. Through the stereoscope I looked over the Oder … The ice was so fragile that even infantry, let alone any equipment, couldn't venture out on it without risk. We didn't have any proper bridging or transport equipment. Yet, under cover of artillery fire, the guardsmen began to move towards the west bank. They carried with them poles, boards, and bundles of brushwood. As they moved, they built decks and in some places they managed to transport light anti-tank guns. These were rolled by hand across the ice, with their wheels on improvised skis.

Unfortunately, the crossing attempt didn't last long. German Focke-Wulf fighters appeared above our Guardsmen. In groups of up to nine planes, they flew over the crossing at low altitude, dropping bombs and firing their machine-guns. How we needed the anti-aircraft gunners of General Seredin's division! But they weren't there, nor were our fighter aircraft – they were relocating to new airfields closer to the Oder, but they too lacked fuel. Companies of anti-tank rifles and machine-guns entered the fight. It wasn't possible to see how many hits they scored but two Focke-Wulfs caught fire before my eyes and crashed in territory that we had already seized. A pilot who was captured by our soldiers told us that German aviation had been ordered to disrupt the crossing of the Oder.

And it must be admitted that they succeeded. We had to pause until dark. We resumed our attempt at night, but the crossing became even more difficult: the already fragile ice had been broken in many places by their bombs.

Although only a few units crossed to the left bank, they managed to capture some small bridgeheads.[22]

Over the next few days, Chuikov's small bridgeheads coalesced into a slightly more secure, larger bridgehead. When they moved into a small town, they came across an old prison where up to 1,000 prisoners had been held. Just a few days before the Red Army arrived, a group of Gestapo personnel – part of *Sonderkommando Moll* – arrived in the town and over about four hours executed over 800 prisoners. A handful of survivors, former soldiers of the Red Army who had been prisoners of war, informed their liberators of the massacre.[23]

The anti-aircraft division arrived on 3 February and immediately went into action, shooting down three aircraft in the first Luftwaffe attack of the day. This forced the Luftwaffe to switch from squadron-sized attacks to sending just two or three planes to attack the Soviet bridgeheads at low level, and it was now possible for larger numbers of soldiers to cross. However, the bridging columns attached to Eighth Guards Army were still struggling forward, a long way further east. Without those bridges, it was impossible to transfer any tanks or heavy equipment to the west bank, with the result that the exposed bridgehead remained under heavy pressure. Slowly, German ground units began to make their presence felt against the bridgehead, and the Soviet forces suffered additional losses from encounters with German stragglers still trying to retreat to the Oder from further east. One of Chuikov's division commanders, Major General Leonid Ivanovich Vagin, was caught up in an encounter with one such group and badly wounded.

With fighting progressing around the perimeter of Küstrin and on the Oder both to north and south, Himmler decided that Raegener was not suitably imbued with Nazi fanaticism for the role of commander of the Küstrin garrison. He was to be replaced by an officer from the SS: Gruppenführer Heinz Reinefarth. At the beginning of the war, he served as a non-commissioned officer in Poland and France before he was rapidly promoted through the ranks of the SS, taking up several senior roles in the police forces, and in September 1944 he commanded an eponymous battlegroup that was involved in the suppression of the Warsaw Uprising. His battlegroup included some of the most unsavoury units in the SS, including a brigade led by the notorious Oskar Dirlewanger, and the battlegroup was heavily involved in the killings of tens of thousands of civilians – at one state, Reinefarth complained that had he been given more ammunition, he could have killed far more people. For his role in the brutal suppression of the uprising, he was awarded the Oak Leaves to the Knight's Cross, and then became a corps commander in the west. He was now sent to Küstrin to replace Raegener. The former garrison commander was put in charge of a newly raised division that temporarily bore his name.

After issuing his ambitious order to prepare for an assault towards Berlin in mid-February, Zhukov reassessed the situation at the beginning of the month. His rifle divisions were reduced to an average of just 5,000 men, less than half their establishment strength, and the tank brigades of the two tank armies averaged about 40 vehicles each. The logistics specialists of 1st Ukrainian Front informed him that it was completely impossible to deliver sufficient fuel, ammunition and food to fulfil Zhukov's orders in preparation for a drive on Berlin, even at their current strength. If those units were restored to something approaching their establishment, the logistic problems would increase even further. The consequence was that Stalin and Zhukov agreed to bring a formal end to what became known as the Vistula-Oder Operation on 2 February. There would now be a pause in the westward assaults while the German forces were cleared from Pomerania. Once Rokossovsky's 2nd Belarusian Front was able to secure the lower Oder to the north of Zhukov's armies, and once there had been sufficient time to replenish the depleted units and provide them with adequate supplies, a new offensive to end the war would be unleashed.

Writing after the war, men like Babadzhanian agreed that a significant pause was essential:

> Even after crossing the Oder, units of Eighth Guards Army needed to spend a lot of effort and time – about two weeks – to expand their bridgehead on the west bank

to a size that would allow 1st Ukrainian Front to concentrate the required number of troops there to begin a powerful attack on Berlin. And even after our troops secured bridgeheads on the west bank of the Oder, the enemy continued to hold a fortified bridgehead centred on the city of Küstrin. A significant number of enemy troops, although surrounded, continued to hold important locations like Schneidemühl, Poznan, and Breslau, tying down our forces ... The lines of communication of our troops were now stretched over 500km [300 miles] and more, the railways were not functioning, the railway bridges over the Vistula had not yet been restored, supplies were exhausted, and military equipment and weapons needed repair and replacement. A direct attack on Berlin was out of the question.[24]

But others disagreed with such assessments. Writing after the war in a Soviet historical journal, Chuikov speculated that, whilst risky, a continuation of the attack towards Berlin was still possible:

As for the risk, in war you often have to take chances. But in this case the risk was justified. Our troops had already covered over 500km in the Vistula-Oder Operation and only a further 60–80km remained from the Oder to Berlin ...

If we objectively assess the strength of the grouping of Nazi forces in Pomerania, we can see that any threat to our strike forces on the Berlin axis could well have been contained by the troops of 2nd Belarusian Front.[25]

He acknowledged the supply difficulties, but in a separate article written at about the same time, he concluded:

If *Stavka* and the Front headquarters had organised supplies properly and had managed to deliver the required amount of ammunition, fuel and food to the Oder on time, if aviation assets had time to relocate to the Oder airfields, and the bridging units could ensure the crossing of troops over the Oder, then our four armies – Fifth Shock, Eighth Guards, and First and Second Tank – could have developed a further attack on Berlin in February, advanced another 80–100km [50–60 miles], and completed the gigantic operation by capturing the German capital.[26]

The first word of this section – 'if' – carries a great deal of weight. It is highly likely that there were errors made in bringing forward supplies; in an operation of this scale, it would be extraordinary if that wasn't the case. But the main problems were as described above. The sheer length of supply lines; the lack of adequate bridging capacity across the Vistula, which had formed a large part of the front line until mid-January; the destruction of bridges, railway embankments, and other installations by the retreating Germans; and the weather conditions – all made it impossible for the most skilful staff officers to ensure that supplies were moved forward in sufficient quantities. It had taken many weeks to build up the stockpiles that were expended in the last two weeks of January, and despite Zhukov's initial enthusiasm of a few days before, a logistic pause was badly needed. It was also highly likely that the Germans would commit whatever troops they could to defend Berlin, and in such circumstances an attack with weakened units that were far from their establishment strength, even if they had been adequately supplied, would have been a hugely risky undertaking. Finally, Chuikov's comments about the threat from German forces in Pomerania being contained by 2nd Belarusian Front contain large amounts of hindsight. At the time, Soviet intelligence was trying to get to grips with the multitude of armies that were appearing in German orders with little awareness that this was at least partly due to Third Panzer Army being renamed first as Eleventh Army, and then as Eleventh SS-Panzer Army.

Chuikov also described a meeting that took place at the Headquarters of Sixty-Ninth Army that was attended by Zhukov, Chuikov, Berzarin (Fifth Shock Army), Colonel General Vladimir Iakovlevich Kolpakchi (Sixty-Ninth Army), Katukov (First Guards Tank Army), and Bogdanov (Second Guards Tank Army) on 4 February. Stalin took part by telephone and ordered Zhukov to stop plans for an immediate resumption of an advance towards Berlin and to concentrate instead on destroying German forces in Pomerania. Zhukov denied that this meeting took place and wrote that he was at the headquarters of Sixty-First Army at the time on the right wing of his Front; moreover, the timing of the cessation of the Vistula-Oder offensive on 2 February means that it would not have been necessary two days later for Stalin to order operations towards Berlin to be stopped.[27] Chuikov's and Zhukov's accounts are clearly not compatible, and the other officers who were apparently present at this meeting made no mention of it in their memoirs; Chuikov suggested that this was because of the cult of Stalin's infallibility that prevailed after the war, but the timing of events suggests that, at the very least, Chuikov is mistaken in the date of this meeting.

As the combined arms armies of Zhukov's Front steadily caught up with the tank armies, they added their efforts to secure crossings over the Oder. Colonel General Vyacheslav Dmitrievich Tsvetayev's Thirty-Third Army reached the river to the south of Frankfurt-an-der-Oder, driving before it the wreckage of the German 463rd Division; this had been created out of a number of training units and having had no opportunity to organise properly, it disintegrated in a series of clashes to the east of the Oder. Its remnants were pulled back to Frankfurt and absorbed into the newly formed *Raegener* Division. It was too weak to stop Thirty-Third Army seizing a bridgehead across the river to the south of Frankfurt on 4 February, and another bridgehead developed to the north of the city a day later.

During this period, planning for the German counterstroke with Eleventh SS-Panzer Army continued. The first outline described a concentration of all available armour around the town of Stargard, to the east of Stettin (now the Polish Szczecin); from there, the force would strike towards the southwest, into the flank and rear of the Soviet units that were now pressing up against Küstrin and the Oder. Provided the forces made available sufficed, it was planned to create three armoured groups; the central group would be the main strike force, with the other two – particularly the eastern group – responsible for flank security. The eventual objective was Küstrin; if this was achieved, the result would be the destruction of large parts of Second Guards Tank Army and Fifth Shock Army.

When the proposal was brought before Hitler, the Führer immediately interfered. The eastern armoured group was ordered to strike towards Landsberg. Even Himmler could see that this was stretching the available resources beyond their capabilities, and the commander of Army Group Vistula asked for an additional two infantry divisions – without these, too much armour would be tied down in flank protection, and it would be impossible to contain any Soviet units that were isolated by the attack, but of course no such resources were available.

The next consideration was one of timing. Eismann and his operations staff concluded that it would take at least until mid-February to prepare for the operation. It was now clear that over half of the panzer formations assigned to the new panzer army were barely at half-strength in terms of armoured vehicles. This led to heated exchanges and growing awareness amongst the professional soldiers that the operation was highly unlikely to succeed:

> In this irritating give-and-take it became ever clearer to me that this entire operation was doomed to failure. The forces were, of themselves, inadequate and the delayed onset of the operation deprived it of any chance of success. Finally, the commitment of the last mobile troops of the German Army in this operation was not in any way justified by the anticipated local success with major losses.
>
> I expressed these views both to the Chief of the General Staff [Guderian] and to Himmler. But what could one do against the almighty order from Hitler? ... The time required to prepare the armoured forces was thoroughly discussed with the commander of Eleventh SS-Panzer Army as well as with the commanders of the panzer corps and with most of the division commanders. All shared the same opinion that the attack could not begin before the arrival of the last of the armour.

Most of these men, however, were convinced that the entire attack would be a failure. Such was the state of things when Guderian, as ordered by Hitler, set the day of the attack as 15 February.[28]

This decision ignored a simple reality: it would be impossible for sufficient fuel to be delivered to Army Group Vistula in time for it to be distributed to the divisions that were to take part in the operation. After discussions with higher authorities, Oberst Hans-Georg von Rücker, the senior quartermaster of the army group, concluded that in the best possible circumstances there would be fuel for no more than three or four days of operations. Thereafter, continuation of the attack would depend entirely on the ability of higher commands to provide more fuel. Given the recent experiences in the German offensive in the Ardennes region, when large German concentrations of armour were repeatedly hampered by delays in moving fuel and ammunition to them, Rücker's report left Eismann and his fellow staff officers with a deep sense of pessimism. So much faith was being placed in this offensive, yet it seemed doomed to failure.

# CHAPTER 11

# 1st UKRAINIAN FRONT: THE CONQUEST OF SILESIA

The columns of tanks, trucks, and marching men heading southwest from Katowice were a forlorn contrast to the triumphant advance of the Wehrmacht through the same region in 1939. The confidence of the past was gone; in its place was a mixture of resignation, exhaustion both physical and mental, and fear. The Red Army was close behind. The beleaguered troops of XLVIII Panzer Corps escaped certain destruction, albeit at the cost of having to abandon much of their heavy equipment; but Germany lost control of vital industrial assets, without which it would be impossible for the war to be continued for more than a few weeks. Stalin's designation of Upper Silesia as 'gold' had been correct.

Leutnant Norbert Thamm was an infantry officer who had been badly wounded with a chest wound the previous year. He was on his way back to his 97th Jäger Division when he was directed to Ratibor (now the Polish Raciborz), where units were being cobbled together using convalescents and stragglers. Shortly after his arrival, he drove north where he was put in command of a group of *Volkssturm* to defend the line of the Oder River. The small group of elderly men were in civilian clothes and had just one antiquated machine-gun; closer inspection showed that it was inoperable. Fortunately for Thamm and the *Volkssturm*, no Soviet attacks took place, but events took an increasingly surreal turn. First, a Luftwaffe Leutnant appeared on a motorcycle and told Thamm that a battalion made up of Luftwaffe personnel was meant to be taking over the defences along the river; it was the first that Thamm had heard of this, and he replied that he was unaware of the location of any such Luftwaffe battalion. The *Volkssturm* were then ordered to set up a vehicle checkpoint to catch stragglers and to confiscate any weapons. In bitterly cold conditions, Thamm's men searched the few vehicles that reached their checkpoint, seizing a few *Panzerfausts* and boxes of ammunition, and then a column of cars and trucks appeared out of the darkness. At first, it seemed as if the vehicles wouldn't stop; when they did, the occupant of the first car objected loudly to being halted. Thamm doggedly insisted on checking the documents of everyone in the convoy, and the man, wearing the uniform of a senior naval officer, reluctantly emerged from the car. He informed Thamm that the other vehicles contained most of the Nazi Party leadership of the Katowice area. A search of the trucks in the column revealed that they contained large quantities of fine furniture and artwork; only in the last truck were there some machine-guns, pistols and ammunition. These were seized, and the Nazi officials were permitted to continue with their furniture. Meanwhile, German civilians continued to trudge through the frozen snow of the Silesian roads without any provision being made for their well-being.[1]

For the moment, the battered German units had a small period of time to catch their breath. Like Zhukov's armies to the north, the formations of 1st Ukrainian Front were operating on long supply lines that stretched across a devastated and frozen landscape. The shattered ranks of the German Ninth Army, facing the northern wing of Konev's Front and the southern wing of Zhukov's Front, were made up of the remnants of the divisions and improvised battlegroups that had been overwhelmed in the Red Army's offensive, and staff officers worked tirelessly to reorganise and reorder the survivors. Within a few days, they were able to report that the army had 22 battalions in varying degrees of combat readiness at its disposal. Given that a full-strength infantry division should have had either seven or nine battalions, this amounted to only a modest force for an entire army, but it is a measure of the disaster that befell the Wehrmacht in Poland during January that fielding this many battalions was seen as a considerable triumph.

On the southern flank of Ninth Army was XL Panzer Corps, commanded by General Sigfrid Henrici. A comparison with most of the men who were assigned to command the various SS corps of Himmler's army group shows the gulf in experience between regular officers and those in the SS who owed their status to patronage and Party service. Henrici joined the German Army as a cadet in 1907 and served in the First World War, winning several medals and playing a major role in developing the air forces of Germany. He left the post-war army in 1920 and served as a senior police officer until returning to military service in 1935. He was artillery commander for XVI Corps for several years before taking command of 16th Motorised Infantry Division in early 1941, leading this unit first in the fighting in the Balkans and then in the invasion of the Soviet Union. In 1942, his division was employed to fill the huge gap between the southern flank of the German units in Stalingrad and those marching into the Caucasus region; the men of his reconnaissance battalion had the distinction of becoming the most easterly German forces of the war when they carried out a wide sweep that took them close to Astrakhan, on the shores of the Caspian Sea. He took command of XL Panzer Corps shortly after. He was seriously wounded near Zaporozhye in October 1943 but returned to his corps 11 months later. A bald, bespectacled figure, he was regularly in the front line, embodying the old Prussian principles of duty and ensuring that everything possible was done for the well-being of his men.

As his corps retreated past Łódź towards the west, Henrici was told by Busse, the new commander of Ninth Army, that he was to take under his control all the units in his area and immediately to the north. At the time, he was still trying to salvage the remnants of his 19th and 25th Panzer Divisions. He spoke to Hölz, chief of staff at Ninth Army headquarters, by radio to ask how far north he was expected to extend his line: what was his northern boundary? The reply cannot have been unexpected. Hölz was unable to give him any clear indication of the situation or who his northern neighbour was.

It is a measure of the weakness of XL Panzer Corps that a group of eight half-tracks became the core of an improvised 'fire brigade' that was dispatched to react quickly to news of Soviet penetrations. Repeatedly in action, the small group – commanded by Hauptmann Oskar Lieske – succeeded in driving off several Red Army groups, and when the corps reached and crossed the Oder, Lieske was ordered to eliminate a Soviet bridgehead near Neusalz (now the Polish Nowa Sól). This was successfully achieved, but a new bridgehead was then identified a little to the north, where the Oder curves from its northward path to flow towards the west. With artillery support from a single 100mm howitzer and two captured field guns and supported by a weak battalion of *Volkssturm*, Lieske pressed home the attack. Surprise was on his side and his men penetrated to the bridge that the Soviet troops had captured over the river; a group of combat engineers was able to carry out a hasty demolition before Lieske's men were driven back.[2]

The Soviet bridgehead remained in place and a second attempt was organised to eliminate it. Henrici organised a search of factories in the small town of Freystadt (now the Polish Kożuchów), where several armaments firms had been operating, and as a result it was possible to arm a handful of vehicles with 20mm guns. There was also a small stockpile of rocket fuel that had been intended for V-2 missiles. Combat engineers took possession of this and created explosive charges that were placed on Goliaths, small remote-controlled tracked vehicles that were intended for single-use demolition work. Despite widespread service, the Goliath was not regarded as a significant success; it was easily disabled by small-arms fire and was relatively slow. But on this occasion, the Goliaths proved to be highly effective. Despite the previous attack on the bridgehead, the Soviet troops were once more taken by surprise and the bridgehead was eliminated. Three T-34s were captured and immediately pressed into use.[3]

The ability of the Red Army to seize bridgeheads with improvised crossings and then to expand them rapidly was a recurring feature of the war and the Germans had learned from bitter experience the need to eliminate these bridgeheads as quickly as possible. Attention now turned to the Soviet bridgehead that had coalesced around Steinau. The attack would be made by Saucken's *Grossdeutschland* Panzer Corps; despite its losses in the fighting to the east of the Oder River, it remained the strongest German formation in the area. Saucken had little clear idea of the strength of the units facing him and ordered the armoured reconnaissance battalion of the *Brandenburg* Division to lead the advance. The initial cautious probes of the battalion ran into Soviet troops in the village of Pilgramsdorf (now the Polish Polkowice) and drove them off, but there was no clear picture of the precise location of the rest of the Soviet forces further to the south. Saucken might have preferred to wait until he had more information, but any delay was likely to be of greater benefit to the Red Army than to the Wehrmacht. On 2 February, a mixed force of panzergrenadiers and assault guns began to move east from Pilgramsdorf.

The attack was carried out across relatively open ground with large patches of marshland towards a low ridge, where the Soviet defenders were waiting. In costly fighting, the Germans managed to cover about half the distance between Pilgramsdorf and the Oder, an advance of about nine miles (15km); Heuthaus, the commander of the *Brandenburg* Division, was often in the front line and at one point had to be rescued by an armoured car. On the second day of the attack there was almost no progress, and on 4 February the Red Army began to drive the Germans back. On the southern flank of Saucken's attack, LVII Panzer Corps – the headquarters of which had just moved to the area from the Balkans – was also attacking towards the Oder. The main effort was made by 408th Division, a formation improvised from a variety of training units and commanded by Generalleutnant Heinrich Wosch. One of its battalions was commanded by a reservist Hauptmann who had volunteered to return to service despite his age.

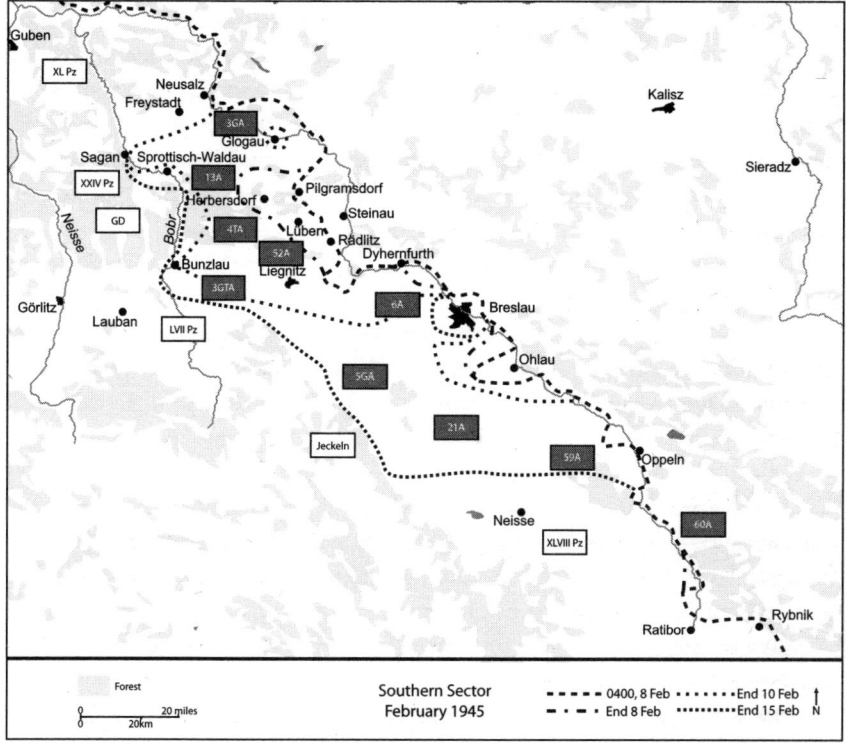

His battalion was typical of the units being cobbled together for the last battles of the war, and he described its state when he joined it:

> They were mostly men on leave who had been gathered together. They were well clad in winter uniforms and equipped with assault rifles and carbines. They had Czech machine-guns, but unfortunately no heavy weapons at all. They made a good general impression and were mostly Silesians; I could expect them to defend their homeland with courage. The quality of the lower leaders varied considerably. In addition to old infantrymen, we had NCOs who had never smelled the gunsmoke of battle. But I didn't know that at the time. I just had to try to get to know the men and have a few words with them … [Later] I was able to secure German MG-34s in place of the Czech machine-guns and to get six light mortars. A light anti-tank platoon [armed with *Panzerfausts*] and an anti-aircraft platoon with a triple mount together with a field kitchen were added later … The battalion needed a few days to get everything organised and above all to establish relationships and trust between the leaders and their troops. But we soon received orders for deployment.[4]

The battalion went into action in an attack on Saucken's southern flank. Advancing across relatively open ground, the unit performed perhaps better than expected and despite substantial casualties it succeeded in taking the village of Rädlitz (now the Polish Redlice). Attempts to advance further resulted in rapidly rising casualties and almost no progress, without adequate heavy weapons and particularly artillery support. The reservist officer, who had recently been ill, felt overwhelmed by the situation:

> Our 3rd Company, which was pretty much the weakest, was badly hit. Leutnant Fink was badly wounded. Leutnant Suchy took over command. In order to get a personal view of the overall situation, I drove to regimental headquarters. A raid against the farm in front of us during the night failed. There weren't enough suitable leaders. The weight of my responsibilities rested heavily on me. I was getting almost no sleep. I had barely left hospital when the damp, the cold, and the food from the field kitchen dragged me down once more. For several days I had had a fever. Things couldn't go on like this. On 7 February I started to write a letter to regimental headquarters that I refused to be answerable for further bloodshed. Leutnant Jung, the adjutant, said I couldn't send it as I would be brought before a court martial. Instead, I sent an oral report. Major Herzog appeared that evening. He was quite sympathetic and concerned. He agreed with calling off the attack. I was to receive 15 soldiers and ten NCOs as replacements. During the evening, four medium mortars were delivered, and three more *Panzerschrecks* during the night.[5]

Before dawn the following morning – 8 February – there was intense artillery fire on the positions around Rädlitz. The massive use of Soviet artillery was an ominous development, indicating that sufficient guns and more importantly ammunition had caught up with the leading Soviet formations. The shelling was followed by an attack with infantry supported by two tanks, but the rising temperature had softened the ground and the Germans were able to bring the slowly advancing Soviet troops to a halt. One of the T-34s was hit and set ablaze with a *Panzerfaust* and the other withdrew to the cover of nearby trees:

> Leutnant Jung, the adjutant, was badly wounded by a shot through his chest. I was hit in the left heel by shrapnel. A cow was torn to bloody fragments by a mortar bomb. I could see soldiers falling back, probably from Rädlitz. The village had been bravely defended so far … I continued to fire, almost alone, from a

skylight. Then my assault rifle jammed and I grabbed a carbine. More tanks appeared from the direction of Rädlitz. Further resistance here was pointless. I ordered a withdrawal to the artillery battery position near Gugelwitz [a short distance to the southwest].[6]

Communications were badly disrupted, with the officers of 408th Division only intermittently in contact with the headquarters of LVII Panzer Corps; they often had to resort to using the partly destroyed local telephone network, which was also being used by the advancing Red Army units, resulting in frequent wild shouting in two different languages at the same time. General Friedrich Kirchner, commander of the corps, had long experience of fighting on the Eastern Front. He commanded 1st Panzer Division in the early stages of the German invasion of the Soviet Union, and then led LVII Panzer Corps for most of the rest of the war. Under heavy pressure from Schörner who repeatedly visited his headquarters, Kirchner ordered 408th Division to continue its attack despite the protests of Wosch that he had little contact with his units and was unable to coordinate or supply them. Over the following days, losses mounted without any benefit and before long the division was in full retreat.

Saucken too repeatedly advised Gräser at the headquarters of Fourth Panzer Army that he lacked the strength to carry out the elimination of the bridgehead, but – again, under pressure from Schörner – Gräser insisted that the attempts continue. After further heavy losses, a crisis developed on 10 February when a large part of the *Brandenburg* Division, together with elements of the *HG* Panzer Division and 20th Panzer Division, were almost completely cut off by the Red Army around Herbersdorf (now the Polish Soblin). Orders for Heuthaus – who was in the encirclement – to retreat to the original start line around Pilgramsdorf arrived too late.

At great personal risk, Saucken drove to the encirclement, managing to slip past the encircling Soviet units. At first, the German units trapped in Herbersdorf had become disorganised and there had been a degree of panic, but order was swiftly restored. Led by a small number of tanks and assault guns, the group pulled back first to Parchau (now the Polish Parchów), immediately to the northwest, where there was a brief battle with a Soviet unit, and then onwards to the northwest. Before dawn on 12 February, the column reached Sprottisch-Waldau (now the Polish Szprotawka), where it made contact with outside forces. The counterattack had failed, and large numbers of vehicles had to be abandoned during the retreat. Manpower losses were also significant. If the *Grossdeutschland* Panzer Corps had been regarded as a powerful force at the beginning of February, this was no longer the case.

Throughout the fighting in Poland, Saucken had led his units with skill and determination. The *Brandenburg* Division had been forced to deploy near Łódź before it had the chance to gather its strength, but had still fought well; risking the complete destruction of his corps, Saucken had then held open the line of retreat for Nehring's troops. The two counterattacks he was then ordered to make – one to the east of the Oder in the last days of January, and then the second to the west of the river in the first week of February – were doomed to failure from the outset and the lack of success was in no respect due to any failing on the part of Saucken. Indeed, his energy had been vital in extracting his troops from the attack to the east of the Oder, when he ordered a bridge to be thrown over the river so that he could pull back to the west, and he personally took command of the encircled units a few days later to the west of the river and led them to safety. Despite this creditable performance, he was now summoned to the headquarters of Army Group Centre: he was being replaced as commander of the *Grossdeutschland* Panzer Corps.

Saucken travelled to see Schörner via Gräser's headquarters. The commander of Fourth Panzer Army was clearly embarrassed by this turn of events. He personally thanked Saucken for his actions in saving the encircled units from probable destruction, and assured him that he had no idea why he was being replaced. When he reached the headquarters of Army Group Centre, Saucken was kept waiting for several hours. He then had a private interview with Schörner; the officers in the adjacent room could hear raised, angry voices, but were unable to determine what was being said. When he emerged, Saucken was tight-lipped and pale with fury.[7]

The dismissal of Saucken appears to have been triggered by Schörner. The exact reasons are not recorded, but it seems likely that Schörner needed a scapegoat for the two failed attacks on either side of the Oder. It was irrelevant that neither stood any real prospect of success; to retain his good standing in Hitler's eyes and to show the required level of ruthless determination, Schörner had to blame the setbacks on a subordinate, and Saucken was the undeserving victim. It was not the end of his military career. On 13 March, he was summoned to Hitler's presence and told that he was being sent to Danzig. Here, he was to take command of the German units that had been compressed against the Baltic coast, a group that later became known as *Armeeoberkommando Ostpreussen* ('Army High Command East Prussia'). As he gave Saucken this assignment, Hitler added that the new army commander was to take his orders from Albert Forster, the *Gauleiter* of Danzig and West Prussia. For those who knew this precise, austere East Prussian, his reaction was in many ways predictable. Saucken had previously shown little reluctance to speak his mind; in the summer of 1944, a junior officer in 4th Panzer Division – which had been under Saucken's command earlier in the war – witnessed an incident involving Saucken and Generalfeldmarschall Walter Model, at that time the commander of Army Group Centre and another of Hitler's favourites:

> Next to my Pz.IV, Generalfeldmarschall Model had gathered a whole row of generals. His discontent at the delays in troop movements was being vented in berating the generals. When it was the turn of our former division commander, General von Saucken let his monocle fall from his eye and said in the quiet tone that was so well known to us, 'You will not speak to me like that, Herr Feldmarschall.' Then he walked away. We grinned mightily.[8]

When he was summoned by Hitler in March 1945, Saucken pointedly gave the Führer a normal military salute in place of the Nazi salute that was now enforced; he also – probably deliberately – omitted that required greeting of 'Heil Hitler!' In response to the instructions that he was to be subordinated to *Gauleiter* Forster, he stared back at the Führer and then replied, 'I have no intention of placing myself under the orders of a *Gauleiter*.' The other senior officers present braced themselves for an outburst from the Führer; but after a moment of silence, Hitler looked away and muttered, 'Very well, Saucken, keep the command yourself.' Saucken turned and left without any further salute or the slightest hint of a bow.[9]

Saucken was to remain in command of the small German enclave around the Vistula estuary until the end of the war. As the final surrender became imminent, Dönitz – who had replaced the dead Hitler as German head of state – sent a plane to evacuate Saucken; in a characteristic gesture, he had the plane loaded with wounded men instead and sent back to the west. Saucken's last act as a commander was to negotiate successfully with the opposing Soviet forces for his men to take their last vehicles with them after they surrendered, which permitted them to carry wounded comrades and supplies of food for at least part of their long march into captivity. He remained a prisoner in the Soviet Union, often mistreated badly, until 1955. He died in 1980.

Saucken's dismissal as commander of the *Grossdeutschland* Panzer Corps was greeted with general dismay amongst the rank and file of his formations; he had been a highly popular and deeply respected figure. But the bitter pill was sweetened a little when the corps learned that Saucken's replacement was Generalleutnant Georg Jauer. He had extensive experience of commanding mechanised formations, having led 20th Motorised Infantry Division – later renamed 20th Panzergrenadier Division – and 25th Panzer Division. He had also served as commander of the artillery regiment of the *Grossdeutschland* Division in early 1942, so he was personally known to many of the senior officers of the corps.

The battles around Steinau and the failed German counterattacks on either side of the Oder were a disappointment for the Germans but they also left Konev feeling deeply dissatisfied, particularly with the escape of Nehring's and Saucken's forces to the Oder and then their subsequent counterattacks. He had expected better of his armies. He described how he had ordered Lelyushenko to turn towards the northwest in order to try to link up with Gordov's Third Guards Army and thus effectively encircle the German armoured formations fighting along the Oder:

> Together, these two armies were supposed to encircle and destroy the enemy group being compressed from the north by 1st Belarusian Front in order to prevent it from crossing the Oder.
>
> I remember my bitterness when the troops of Third Guards Army and Fourth Tank Army failed to complete this task. The Nazis manoeuvred around the north of our intended attack. Our troops still managed to encircle and then destroy about 15,000 enemy soldiers, but the rest – albeit suffering heavy losses – crossed to the west bank of the Oder. So if on the left wing [around Kraków and Katowice] everything unfolded as planned, then the same cannot be said about operations on the right wing.[10]

This account is almost certainly misleading. Konev's memoirs do not give the date of his meeting with Lelyushenko where orders were allegedly given for the tank army to cooperate with Third Guards Army in order to destroy the units of the 'wandering cauldron', but given the context of the narrative it implies that this was during or immediately after the establishment and consolidation of the Red Army bridgehead around Steinau. By that time, Nehring's troops had already crossed the Oder and Saucken was either leading his corps back to the bridge he had ordered to be established over the river, or had already crossed to the west bank. It is likely that regardless of the Red Army's plans to avoid time- and energy-consuming encirclements to destroy German forces, the escape of so many German troops caused consternation and embarrassment, and when he wrote his memoirs in the late 1960s, this was Konev's attempt to pass any blame to his subordinates. Notably, there is no mention of any such instructions in the account left by Lelyushenko, but the tank army commander did describe the difficulties faced by Third Guards Army to his north:

> When the troops of Third Guards Army rushed up to the Oder [at the end of January], some units were badly strung out. Taking advantage of this, the

enemy struck its flank and penetrated to the headquarters of LXXVI Rifle Corps, commanded by Lieutenant General [Mikhail Ivanovich] Glukhov. The corps commander and his advance detachment managed to retreat to join one of his divisions, but six staff officers didn't have time to leave the building where they were stationed and were forced to take refuge in the basement. When the enemy captured the town, he used the same building where Glukhov's headquarters had previously been located as his headquarters, as it was one of the least damaged.

Consequently, there were Nazis on the first floor, and a group of officers from Glukhov's LXXVI Rifle Corps in the basement. The Nazis went into the basement to scavenge for food, but they didn't see our officers because they were hiding in the dark depths of the basement.

The next day, Glukhov regrouped his forces and supported by our 93rd Tank Brigade, 22nd Self-Propelled Artillery Brigade and 49th Mechanised Brigade, reoccupied the town. When our troops entered the headquarters building, some of the Fascist officers hadn't had time to escape and rushed to hide in the basement. Realising what was happening, our comrades in the basement shouted out, '*Hände hoch!*' ['Hands up!'] Twelve Fascists were captured without a shot being fired.[11]

Regardless of Konev's dissatisfaction about the escape of the German XXIV Panzer Corps and the *Grossdeutschland* Panzer Corps, there was considerable pride at the pace at which the advance had unfolded. Looking at his original operational orders, Konev could see that his Front was at least eight days ahead of schedule as the 'Vistula-Oder Operation' formally came to an end in early February:

According to our calculations, in 23 days of fighting 1st Ukrainian Front defeated 21 infantry divisions, five panzer divisions, 27 independent infantry brigades, nine artillery and mortar brigades, and a very large number of different special units and individual battalions. During the operation, 43,000 prisoners were taken and we estimated that more than 150,000 enemy officers and men were killed or wounded. Among the captured materiel were more than 5,000 guns and mortars, more than 300 tanks, more than 200 aircraft, and a very large number of other weapons and military equipment …

If we take the operation as a whole and compare the losses we suffered with the successes achieved, then we can confidently conclude that we achieved victory with less bloodshed than in some other earlier operations. This was a consequence both of our increased technical capabilities and of our maturing military skill.[12]

The German units that had withdrawn in haste from Katowice were now reorganising and taking up defensive positions to the south of the city. They had been further reinforced by the arrival of 8th Panzer Division, which had been fighting in Hungary. Oberst Heinrich-Georg Hax had just been appointed to lead the division and first joined his new command as it began to arrive in Silesia; he was a highly experienced officer with extensive service in infantry and panzer units as well as in staff roles. After receiving a briefing from Xylander, chief of staff of Army Group A, in the main headquarters in Neisse (now the Polish Nysa), he flew to Ratibor where his division was detraining with orders to hold a bridgehead to the east of the Oder. There was little prospect of 8th Panzer Division being granted the luxury of waiting until all its units had arrived; instead, they were dispatched across the Oder piecemeal and strung out along an extended front line of about 21 miles (35km). For a formation that was intended to deliver concentrated blows either in attack or counterattack and that lacked the infantry strength for prolonged or extended defensive duties, it was a singularly inappropriate mode of deployment.[13]

As the rear area units of 8th Panzer Division arrived in Ratibor, they took on the duty of organising the town's defences and also took the *Volkssturm* and Hitler Youth under their wing; no provision had been made to feed or supply the mixture of old men and teenagers. To the right of 8th Panzer Division was 1st Ski-Jäger Division, which had been formed the previous year. It had been fighting in the Slovakian mountains during the winter and like all German units was far from its establishment strength, but at least it was equipped for warfare in winter conditions. Supported by assault guns that belonged to the division and by some of 8th Panzer Division's tanks, the soldiers of the Ski-Jäger regiments swiftly recaptured parts of Rybnik that had been occupied by the Red Army; but attempts to push north ran into growing Soviet resistance. Nevertheless, it seemed as if the threat of a Soviet exploitation of the fall of Katowice had been averted, though in truth this owed more to Konev's logistic difficulties as much as it did to the arrival of German reinforcements.

Despite all the German setbacks over the preceding days and weeks, the front line was beginning to stabilise. Hax was able to issue a cautious report that the general panic and despair that had prevailed when he arrived was being replaced by calm confidence, and that all his men were determined to fight to the utmost of their abilities. Whilst this may have been true in many cases, there can be little doubt that – privately at least – there was a great sense of imminent doom. The Red Army was now on German soil, and it was only a matter of time before it gathered its strength and surged forward once again. Nonetheless, Hax wrote to his wife:

> What else can we do? We must, and want to hold out, and even if things are damned hard sometimes and the troops are completely at the end of their strength, we will still fight on![14]

In addition to the logistic pause that was badly needed by the Red Army, there was another reason for a reduction in the pace of Soviet operations. Stalin's presence and attention was required elsewhere. Given that he had taken upon himself the role hitherto served by officers like Zhukov and Vasilevsky to coordinate numerous Fronts in a single major operation, it was inevitable that his absence from Moscow and therefore from *Stavka* would have an impact. On 2 February, Churchill and Roosevelt met aboard the heavy cruiser USS *Quincy* in Malta as a prelude to the next great conference of all the main leaders of the Allied Powers.[15] The British were concerned about the future of Poland and wished to secure greater American support for the Polish government-in-exile in London to have a leading role after the war. The Americans were more interested in ensuring the success of their plans to create what became the United Nations, and were prepared to make concessions to Stalin to achieve this. The two western leaders travelled on by air to Yalta in Crimea, arriving there on 3 February. The city had a reputation as a great resort, having become very fashionable amongst Russian aristocracy in the 19th century, but the palaces and fine houses were badly damaged by the fighting in Crimea, particularly when the Germans were driven out in 1944. Already feeling gloomy after his preliminary conversation with Roosevelt, Churchill dubbed the city 'the Riviera of Hades'.[16]

Stalin arrived in Yalta by train the following day, 4 February; the Soviet leader had a longstanding aversion to flying. He met Churchill and Roosevelt separately, showing considerable skill in presenting information to them in different ways. To Churchill, he emphasised the great victories of the Red Army; to Roosevelt, he highlighted the operational difficulties that his armies faced. When the conference started with all parties present, there were considerable differences of opinion. The Soviet delegation stressed the possibility of the Wehrmacht transferring troops from west to east and listed several units that had already been moved. When General George Marshall, the US Army's chief of staff, made a presentation about preparations for crossing the Rhine and highlighted the difficulties caused by German rocket attacks against Antwerp that were disrupting the build-up of supplies, Stalin was dismissive. Such attacks were too inaccurate to have much impact, he insisted, implying that the Western Allies were dragging their heels.

The conference continued until the end of 6 February. Stalin agreed to increase pressure upon German forces along the Baltic coast to eliminate once and for all the use of the Baltic Sea as an area for U-boat training, but both sides were mistrustful of the estimates provided by the other side about the German units they faced; perhaps understandably, the Soviet side and the reasonably combined Anglo-American side each hoped to persuade the other to increase its efforts to tie down as many German divisions as possible. The division of Germany into occupation zones had largely been agreed before the meeting in Yalta, but the details, such as the transfer of Polish territory in the east to the Soviet Union and compensatory transfer of territory from Germany to Poland, were finalised. It is worth noting that despite waging a war in the name of democracy, the Americans and British were quite prepared to agree to such territorial reshaping without any attempt to consult the wishes of Poles, Germans and others who actually lived in those regions. But despite securing agreement for the future United Nations, the Western Allies came away acutely aware that the conference had been a major success for the Soviet Union, and with good reason. Stalin, too, had no doubts on that matter. He later joked to his close confidants:

> Churchill, Roosevelt and Stalin went hunting. They finally killed their bear. Churchill said, 'I'll take the bearskin, let Roosevelt and Stalin divide the meat.' Roosevelt said, 'No, I'll take the skin. Let Churchill and Stalin divide the meat.' Stalin remained silent so Churchill and Roosevelt asked him, 'Mister Stalin, what do you say?' Stalin simply replied, 'The bear belongs to me – after all, I killed it.'[17]

One of the consequences of the Yalta Conference was an agreement by the Western Allies to increase their efforts to prevent the transfer of German reinforcements and supplies from the west to the east. This led to the increased bombing of ports and the main axes of railway traffic; the raids on Swinemunde and Dresden, which resulted in so many civilian deaths, were the outcome.

On the ground, *Stavka* reviewed the current disposition of the Soviet armies that had surged across Poland into German territory. There were concerns about both flanks, and Konev was ordered to clear Lower Silesia to eliminate any threat from the south. The intention was to advance beyond the Oder broadly to the line of the Neisse River; to do so, 1st Ukrainian Front's armies would either have to capture or isolate Breslau. Konev and his staff had started work on planning this further advance in the last week of January with the original intention of driving on without any pause. This was only possible if the Fronts on either flank

– 4th Ukrainian Front to the south and 1st Belarusian Front to the north – attacked at the same time, protecting the flanks of Konev's armies and preventing the Germans from shuffling troops from one sector to another. But it was now clear that Zhukov would be pausing his westward advance while he brought up reinforcements and supplies and also cleared the German units overhanging his northern flank in Pomerania. To the south, 4th Ukrainian Front had initially been moving swiftly into and through Czechoslovakia, but its advance had almost ground to a halt in the face of growing resistance and difficult terrain. Finally, the German units that faced 1st Ukrainian Front were now in good defensive positions and had received sufficient supplies to restore at least part of their former strength, whereas Konev's formations were still depleted by their advance and in need of replenishment.

Konev's staff estimated that the German units facing them amounted to about 118 infantry divisions, a ski division, four panzer divisions, and two panzergrenadier divisions. In addition, there were numerous battlegroups and the garrison of Breslau. Although there was recognition that the average numerical strength of the German divisions was low, probably below half strength for most, there were signs that further reinforcements were still being directed to the area. Konev now regrouped his forces with the intention of mounting two major attacks either side of Breslau. The northern group would consist of both tank armies supported by Third Guards Army and Thirteenth, Fifty-Second and Sixth Armies; the southern group would be far weaker, with Fifth Guards Army and Twenty-First Army, reinforced by two tank corps. Finally, a third group of Fifty-Ninth and Sixtieth Armies would protect the southern flank of the advance. It would take several days to prepare for the new operation while supplies were brought forward and troops redeployed – in particular, Third Guards Tank Army was being shifted a considerable distance to the north.

German units were also being redeployed. After being involved in almost constant fighting since the start of the Soviet offensive, the German 371st Infantry Division was badly depleted with most of its battalions reporting combat strength of less than a normal infantry company, and was now inserted into the front line near Ratibor to release 8th Panzer Division so that it could be held ready behind the line to deal with the inevitable resumption of Soviet attacks. As they pulled back towards an assembly area to the southwest of Breslau, the various battlegroups and rear area units of Hax's division took with them as many refugees as they could squeeze into their vehicles. A supply officer later wrote:

> The misery of the refugees, who were only able to take a small amount of
> their belongings with them after they had left their houses and farms in great

haste, demanded strong nerves on the part of soldiers ... Whenever we were able to take back evacuated territory, we saw with horror how the Soviet soldiers, incited by their leadership, had lived in the conquered parts of Silesia. The worst were the rapes, mostly committed under the influence of alcohol.[18]

The behaviour of Soviet troops in the occupied parts of Germany was unquestionably marred by terrible acts of violence and indiscipline. German accounts written by veterans after the war denied any personal involvement in atrocities committed by the Wehrmacht, passing the blame to others; Soviet accounts simply ignored the entire issue of misconduct in occupied areas for several decades. Interviews with veterans give a varied picture. Iosif Bentsionovich Galitsky had fought against the Germans as a partisan in the occupied parts of the western Soviet Union and had witnessed first-hand many of the atrocities committed by the Wehrmacht. He was then incorporated into the ranks of the Red Army as it moved through the region in 1944. Long after the war, he was still reluctant to talk in detail about how Soviet soldiers behaved towards German civilians:

> I have no desire to answer such questions in detail. But in general terms:
>
> In any captured city, for the first three days we could do whatever we wanted, and then, by order of higher authorities, there began a 'merciless fight against looters and rapists' in the first echelon rifle and tank units. But personally, I had the impression that things went according to unspoken rules, according to tradition like in the old days – 'the first three days belong to the victors' – shoot, kill whoever you want, rape, rob, and the commanders turned a blind eye to everything.
>
> And then, God forbid that you should ever lay a finger on a German – you faced being sent to a military tribunal. Discipline in our battalion was a serious matter and the soldiers knew that if the battalion commander ordered us to 'hold back', there should be no more irregular incidents.[19]

Since medieval times, there had been a widespread recognition across Europe that if a city resisted an enemy army, that army could sack the city for three days after its fall, and this could be avoided if the city surrendered without resistance. There were countless episodes when conquering armies simply ignored this and proceeded to loot, rape and murder regardless of whether the city had opened its gates or had resisted. There was certainly no 'rule of war' that recognised this. Arkady Vesterman, the tank crewman who described the incident involving a tank crew trying to claim that their vehicle had been hit by a German shell before they abandoned it, was also relatively honest about events in Germany and Poland:

> I'm not particularly eager to talk about it. You see, you should tell only the truth about the war or say nothing at all. But in Germany, everything happened and there were many dark moments there. I understand the veterans who find it difficult to decide whether it's worth talking openly about it.
>
> At first, German women were raped with impunity at every turn, although both German and Polish women later willingly agreed to be intimate with our soldiers and officers.
>
> Violence was mainly carried out by the infantry. They took revenge on the Germans in different ways. During the war, people became brutalised and savage, and some rifle units resembled undisciplined hordes.
>
> Once, we were in a house on German territory, frying chicken and goose, and the German woman who lived there, aged about 35, told us: 'The Russians came here, all in dirty ragged uniforms, and demanded, "Do you have a watch? Fine, now get on the bed!" Then others came in, shouting "*Uri! Uri!*"' ['Watches! Watches!'] In short, she was raped four times during the first night.
>
> We had a sergeant who was often sent on reconnaissance, he wore five wristwatches on each arm, and he told us how, together with a drinking buddy, he raped two German women, a mother and a daughter, forcing her husband at gunpoint to play the piano during the rapes.[20]

In some cases, soldiers took steps to protect civilians, but these were far outnumbered by the occasions when they either looked the other way or actively took part in atrocities. Dmitry Filippovich Osinovsky was an artilleryman involved in the advance, and inevitably he entered areas after rifle and tank units had already moved through:

> The scars left by our offensive probably were fewer than those of the German offensive against the Soviet Union, but were still impressive. I remember that after we crossed a river that formed the frontier with German territory, we were greeted by a [Soviet] poster: 'This is damned Germany!' And we often came across the corpses of old people, women, and children.
>
> I saw a murdered old woman who had a 1.5m wooden stake inserted into her genitals. Robbery and violence were commonplace … German civilians fled in fear of the advancing Red Army, and those who didn't flee were subject to looting. Taking a watch was considered particularly valuable at that time …

One night I received an assignment: I was to take two other soldiers and go to a farm, a separate building, to guard a German family there – a woman and her children, since she had complained to our commander that she had been raped every night. We arrived at the house and set ourselves up. During the night we detained 12 soldiers who wanted to rape her. When dawn broke, she asked to be taken to another village, where her relatives lived. We walked there with her, about 7km …

In our regiment there was one senior lieutenant who, at every opportunity, raped German women at gunpoint. He told us … that he saw a girl of about 15, took out his pistol and said: 'Come!' Her mother grabbed her, screaming '*Nein, nein!*' but he raped her immediately, in front of her mother. The girl's mother held her head in her hands and wept. One day … when we had already taken up our positions, he suddenly disappeared for several hours. When he returned, I asked him where he had been. It turned out that three days before, he had raped a woman and then discovered he had contracted gonorrhoea. He found a bicycle, went back to her house, and shot her. We were shocked when he said this – it wasn't her fault that someone had infected her. But he replied, 'She won't infect anyone else now.'[21]

Some accounts written later by German civilians described how the hardened veterans of Soviet first echelon formations might have taken wristwatches and jewellery, but often refrained from violence towards civilians; they frequently warned German civilians that the soldiers following in their wake were likely to be less restrained. But even amongst the units that led the Red Army's advance into Germany, there were many who didn't hesitate to rape and murder. In some cases, this was driven by a desire to exact revenge for the suffering of their families, or after what they had seen in liberated towns across the Soviet Union and in locations like Majdanek and Auschwitz. The comment by Osinovsky contrasting the trail of devastation left by Soviet forces across Eastern Europe with the atrocities committed by German troops is interesting. It should be remembered that whilst the Soviet authorities had deliberately stoked the desire for revenge amongst Soviet soldiers, this was largely an attempt to counter war fatigue and there were attempts to stress the difference between fighting with implacable determination and venting rage upon civilians. Nevertheless, the resulting fear amongst Germans was unquestionably a useful development from the point of view of Stalin and others. At Yalta, Churchill had worried that the reassignment of large amounts of German territory to Poland might result in difficulties; the consequence, he told Stalin, might be that 'the Polish goose dies of

German indigestion.'[22] Stalin reassured him that huge numbers of German civilians were already on the move, and the ethnic issues that had played a major part in the origins of the Second World War would not be permitted to recur. There was implicit acceptance by Churchill and Roosevelt that this would result in the forcible removal of all Germans from territory that was being given to Poland.

A lack of discipline played a very large part in the violence inflicted upon the German population by the Red Army; by contrast, the violence of German soldiers towards the civilian population of the Soviet Union was deliberate. The mass killings of Jews; the taking and killing of hostages; the horrific death rate amongst captured Soviet troops in the first months of the war; the indiscriminate slaughter of civilians in so-called anti-partisan sweeps; the forcible deportation of hundreds of thousands of civilians who were used as labourers in the Reich; and the deliberate, calculated use of hunger as a means of reducing the Slav population of the western parts of the Soviet Union to make way for German settlers at the end of the war – these were all policies initiated mainly from the highest levels. Rape, a weapon as old as warfare itself, was widespread in all phases of the Second World War, but was particularly prominent during the Red Army's advance into Eastern Europe and especially on German territory. But again, there was a contrast with more organised German behaviour. Whilst German soldiers unquestionably took part in rapes both in the Soviet Union and elsewhere, the Wehrmacht also organised a network of brothels across the occupied zones, with separate brothels for officers. The women who worked in these brothels did so through little choice. Nor should it be forgotten that other armies were also involved in crimes such as rape. There were hundreds of incidents reported in Normandy and elsewhere. The US Army recorded a total of 208 rapes and murders committed by American personnel in the channel region, almost certainly a considerable underestimate of the true number.[23] A total of 180 soldiers were charged with rape and 29 were executed. Of these, the great majority both of those charged and those executed were African Americans; in many cases, the evidence against them was circumstantial at best.[24] Once American and British forces crossed into German territory, the number of rapes increased, and the number of arrests fell. There seems to have been greater tolerance in both armies about the rape of German women than there had been of French women.

However, when comparing the atrocities committed by the various armies involved in the Second World War, it is essential to remember that crimes cannot be justified by previous crimes. On the few occasions that Soviet-era accounts acknowledged the rapes, murders and looting that occurred as the Red Army advanced into Poland and Germany, this was always portrayed as the inevitable revenge of soldiers who had seen shocking evidence of earlier German crimes. In many respects, the portrayal of crimes in Germany by the Red Army written by Germans after the war was even more misleading. Whilst the suffering of helpless civilians was highlighted, there was almost complete silence about the crimes committed by German forces in Poland and the Soviet Union; if they were mentioned, they were blamed on a small minority. And whilst many of the atrocities committed by Soviet soldiers were driven by a desire for revenge, others were the result of far more basic urges:

> We were young, strong. We hadn't been with a woman for four years, and there just weren't enough German girls. So ten men raped one German girl. They even attacked 12-year-olds. If they cried, we would hit them, stuff a rag in their mouths. We felt ashamed in front of them.[25]

Although civilians in both Poland and Germany were often treated badly, the Soviet soldiers showed particular rage towards the Germans, not least when they saw how rich the Germans were compared to ordinary Soviet citizens – why had such a wealthy country invaded its relatively poor neighbour and inflicted so much harm? Attitudes toward the Poles varied. Anatoly Ivanovich Bogachkin, an artilleryman, described the cautious welcome given by some Poles:

> When we moved through this country and came to a town or a village, the people living there seemed to be afraid of us and hid in the forests. I remember walking through a village where we went into a Polish house. Generally speaking, many of their houses were made of straw and timber. They had entire villages with thatched roofs. As we entered, we saw an elderly man was sitting in the house, at a table that had been set. 'Who is this for?' we asked him. He replied, 'My wife prepared this. She said it is for the first Russians who come here.' 'Where is your wife?' we asked him. 'Everyone ran into the forest and is hiding there.' And there was a lot of food prepared for us. We were warned as soon as we entered Poland that food might be poisoned and we needed to be careful. So I forced this Pole to try everything on the table. If he had shown the slightest hesitation, because he knew which bits of food were poisoned, we would have killed him. But everything was fine. There were poisoning incidents in other units. Fortunately, this didn't happen in our regiment. Generally, the Poles treated us very well.[26]

Indiscipline amongst Soviet units led to more than mistreatment of civilians. Misuse of alcohol was widespread amongst Red Army units, and searching for alcohol was a common activity. Aleksandr Vasilevich Vyatkin, a Soviet airman, described what happened when his bomber regiment came across a substantial supply:

> It was near a town called Guttentag. Our regiment was located in the farm of a wealthy German and as there was a pause in the fighting, a bathhouse was set up for our guys, but it was in a building housing a small distillery. Men went there in groups for baths, carrying all manner of pots. Our 1st Squadron went first and disappeared. Then it was time for the 2nd Squadron and they too vanished. Only when the men of the 3rd Squadron also failed to return did our officers become alarmed. The officers went to the bathhouse, and found everyone drunk and singing. There was a lot of alcohol that had been left in storage tanks and they had laid into it. And just about anyone who could find a container had carried some away. Of course, the senior commanders put a stop to it, but the regiment was completely incapable of action.
>
> The division headquarters staff sent orders for a combat mission but the regiment didn't even respond. This went on for two days and nobody in higher commands knew what was happening. The division commander sent his communications officer with a group of soldiers to the regiment to investigate, but they too disappeared. It later turned out that the regiment had detained them and kept them captive so that they couldn't report what had happened. It was only on the third day that order was restored to the regiment. They tried to hush it up, but the commander of Second Air Army refused to accept this and the division was deprived of its Guards title. After that our 887th Regiment became known as *Bimborsky* – '*Bimbor*' is the Polish word for moonshine. For a month or two they were refused the right to apply for any sorts of awards, though the guys were assigned to the most dangerous missions rather than the operations they had flown before.[27]

An artillery officer, Aleksey Grigorevich Burimovich, described an incident that involved a far more hazardous consumption of loot:

> My battery got hold of alcohol from somewhere and when they showed me the bottles, my hair stood on end: it was methyl alcohol, with a label that said '*Methanol. Vorsicht. Gift.*' ['Methanol. Danger. Poison.'] The alarm was raised across the batteries and the regiment commander was informed of the incident. All the other batteries were warned about it. At first, none of the battery personnel

admitted they had drunk any methyl alcohol. But a group of Muscovites had drunk it – Alekhine was celebrating his birthday with Evseev and Sheikhon. Aware of the possible consequences, the soldiers just stayed silent and waited to see what would happen. For most, nothing happened – they drank a lot of water and ended up with headaches. After a few days, the methanol made itself felt and some were poisoned. Others were poisoned by canned food deliberately left behind by the Germans. And everyone was drinking the alcohol that was issued to front line soldiers. There were steps taken to deal with poisoning – gastric lavage for example, or drinking milk – fortunately, there were plenty of abandoned cows around. Still, three men couldn't be saved. All of them had suffered from malaria in the past. As regiment commander, I was punished with ten days' house arrest. I accepted this willingly, it could have been far worse. The whole incident left an unpleasant memory for the rest of my life. For a long time, I couldn't face alcohol without a shudder.[28]

Indiscipline also played a part in the treatment of captured Germans. Again, there were many occasions when behaviour was shaped by what the men had experienced, both personally and through their families and acquaintances. There was widespread recognition that ordinary German Army soldiers wore the eagle-and-swastika badge on their chest, whereas SS personnel wore it on their arm, and soldiers wearing SS uniforms were less likely to survive capture. This resulted in many attempting to switch uniforms. The use of black uniforms also resulted in captured soldiers being singled out for mistreatment and execution, often in error. When the panzer arm was created in the 1930s, it adopted the black uniform and death's head emblems of the old hussar regiments of the Prussian Army. Unfortunately, the SS also chose to emulate the old Prussian hussars, and as a result many Wehrmacht tank crews were killed by their Soviet captors in the mistaken belief that they were members of the SS. On some occasions, the decision of whether to shoot a prisoner or take him to the rear was made on the spur of the moment. Mark Mikhailovich Grinstein, a rifleman, later recalled:

We didn't take many prisoners, they didn't either. We hated the Germans fiercely. One captured German sticks in my memory. During the winter offensive we were attacking and a T-34 was ahead of us, and they hit it with a *Panzerfaust*. They caught a German *Faustnik*, a very young guy, and he started yelling, '*Nicht schiessen!* ['Don't shoot!'] He begged to be left alive, but the soldiers shot him on the spot.

There's another nuance here. If a company was attacking and fighting forward, which soldier who had been condemned to being in the front line would go to the rear with prisoners without orders from the battalion commander? The 'special officers' [*NKVD* personnel] would immediately seize such a soldier by the scruff of the neck, call him all sorts of names, and accuse him of trying to escape the battle.[29]

Samuil Iosifovich Rozenberg, another rifleman, was clear in his recollections:

If we came across SS men, they weren't taken prisoner. As for the rest – we acted according to circumstances. We took a lot of German prisoners in 1945. That winter, we were involved in a serious battle near Oppeln. There was a small town there, Bytom, in which we surrounded a German group. We moved out from the railway station along the main street and began to comb through the buildings. We walked down both sides of the street, keeping close to the buildings. And then we were ambushed from above, from the windows on upper floors and from below, from the basements. They fired at us and threw grenades. We retreated to the station with losses, but the guys noticed that the people firing at us were in civilian clothes, not in Wehrmacht uniforms.

In the evening, reinforcements arrived and as darkness fell we began to move forward again. We were told that many of the encircled Germans had changed into civilian clothes and that all military men dressed in civilian clothes should be checked carefully. Groups of up to four soldiers were assigned to each house and slowly, building by building, we checked each one. And then it began again, with them shooting at us from basements. Sometimes, when a soldier entered the bedroom of a house and stood gaping in surprise at the German furniture and other goods, a hidden German would shoot him in the back, from the closet.

We stopped again, our officers assessed the situation, and once more we entered the buildings. We went into a house and immediately we fired a burst from our submachine-guns into any closet, or threw grenades into the basement. And in one basement, all the people were in civilian clothes and we couldn't figure out who was who. In short, everyone who was of military age was shot and killed on the spot.

We finished clearing our area and were approaching the town square where our men were assembling. Our chief of staff, an eastern Ukrainian, was standing there and a civilian, a Pole, was brought up to him and addressed him in Polish, 'Sir, Officer, I am a Pole, not a German, don't kill me. I have a good girl for you.' And the officer replied to him, 'Well, bring your woman, we'll see.' The Pole returned a minute later with the woman. The chief of staff looked at them, took a pistol from his holster, and killed the couple with two shots to their heads, saying, 'They're definitely Germans!'[30]

Many of the Germans who were captured wearing civilian clothing were members of the *Volkssturm*, and there hadn't been sufficient time for them to be issued with military uniforms. Even when they were recognised as *Volkssturm*, they were often shot out of hand; the Soviet soldiers remembered that the Germans had refused to treat partisans in the Soviet Union as regular combatants, and they now treated the *Volkssturm* in the same manner.

Despite the widespread hatred of the SS, the treatment of prisoners owed a great deal to the attitudes of the soldiers who happened to capture them. Boleslav Filippovoch Agaltsov, a tank driver, was in a platoon that was tasked with intercepting a German train suspected of carrying military personnel and their families. Their captors were taken to a village:

The men from our advanced detachment gathered near the prisoners. There were six SS men led by an officer. The officer was young, a handsome guy, but trembling. The rest stood like oak trees, strong and healthy guys in black uniforms, only one was in some kind of greenish uniform, a small guy. For some reason I liked him. The battalion commander arrived on a motorcycle and began to interrogate them – we had already reported that we had completed our task and in the meantime the infantry brought us a gift of a whole bowl of watches from those they had captured. They were distributed fairly, like all spoils of war. The battalion commander, Major Belov, was precise and quick in his decision-making and after a brief interrogation, he ordered that the SS men were to be shot. They were not to be taken prisoner. The little guy was fidgeting. They were taken aside and shot near my tank, a bullet in the stomach. This was called execution of thieves, just as the SS did when they captured our Guards. I didn't take part in this, I stepped aside and made myself busy. When I returned, I heard wheezing – the Germans were in a heap near the tank, some were still alive though unconscious. I gave everyone a precise shot in the head to put them out of their misery. And when I had finished, the soldier in the green coat crawled out from under the tank, saw me, and started babbling something, saying '*Meine Kinder, Kinder.*' ['My children.'] And so on. I even remember his name – Richard Leichtling. I saw him and thought, what can I do with him? I couldn't let him go, but I didn't want to shoot him – I generally despised such things and thought it unworthy of a soldier. But of course, I raised my gun. He saw what I was doing, but noticed an accordion tied to the tank by the handrail on the turret, and pointed at it and began to say, '*Ich bin Musiker!*' He started singing something in German, it sounded like a poem. I liked it and told him, 'Here, take the accordion!' He reached for it and started playing wonderfully. And there was great demand for music in the battalion – I could barely sing a note. I decided he could play for us. I told him to take off his hat and to put it in his pocket and to remove his soldier's belt – he would look like a Soviet soldier, because many of our crewmen wore bits of German uniform …

The German stayed with us for a while until something else happened. Although we were tankers, we took turns on guard duty at night. Our orders required us to follow regulations, but we did it carelessly. We slept on the street on straw and hay, threw some rags on top and slept in a heap next to the tanks, and this German slept with us. For a couple of hours, someone would stand guard, then he would come over to the heap and poke the first person he came to with his foot, and he would replace him, taking his submachine-gun and spare magazine. And accidentally, the guard woke the German, didn't realise in the dark, gave him the gun, and Richard was proud that he had been entrusted with guard duty and stood guard all night. At dawn, as luck would have it, Major Belov came around to check our lines. He rode out with an orderly on a motorcycle and when he approached the yard where we had been sleeping, the German heard the motorcycle's engine and was scared. We had told him, 'Avoid Major Belov, he'll kill you.' So he jumped off the road and hid behind the gate and when the officers drove up, they saw a man in German uniform with a machine-gun. The motorcycle swerved suddenly into the ditch and they drew their weapons. Richard recognised the battalion commander, because such checks took place quite often, and ran up to our heap shouting 'Belov! Belov!' and kicking the sleeping men. The first man to wake up saw a German running around with a machine-gun shouting loudly and screamed in fear. I woke up when he stepped on my face. Everyone got up, the German calmed down and threw down his gun, shouting 'I surrender! I surrender!'

Belov came into the yard, lined us up, and said, 'What's going on? Have you degenerated to the point where you don't even remove German insignia from uniforms?' He had concluded that it was one of our soldiers in a captured uniform. He moved down the line, checking everyone, and when he reached the German he asked, 'Where did this scarecrow come from? What's your last name?' He muttered something unintelligible and Belov asked us, 'Is he a Pole or something?' Someone answered timidly, 'German, Comrade Major.' Belov was furious. 'How did this happen?' We explained that when he ordered the SS to be shot, we didn't kill him. He wanted to know who had made the decision and they named me. He raged at me and an article appeared in our front-line newspaper, citing me as an example of a person who decides to make friends with the enemy in wartime. We told him that he helped us, cooked *Kasha* and other stuff, he travelled with us but didn't shoot at anyone – the only question was how he had got a gun. We explained how it had happened by accident.

Belov said angrily, 'Do what you want with him.' We found a broomstick to which we attached a card and wrote on it, 'Richard Leichtling is going to the collection point for prisoners of war and asks for your assistance.' And we slapped some sort of seal on it. He put it over his shoulder like a soldier carrying a rifle, and we told him what to say to everyone – '*Ich bin Sozialdemokrat. Hitler ist kaput!*' ['I am a social democrat. Hitler is finished!'] We later learned that he reached the rear, repeating these words like some kind of prayer. There was a lot of laughter, because a lot of our soldiers were easy-going people, they saw a scarecrow walking with this placard and clutched their bellies laughing when he introduced himself as a social democrat![31]

Richard Leichtling was undoubtedly very fortunate. Vesterman's recollections suggest that there was little mercy on many occasions:

We couldn't exactly put captured Germans in our tanks. Our rage towards the Germans was wild, and as a result our attitude towards prisoners was also wild and extremely cruel. I will say honestly – the infantry may have captured Germans, but we, the tankers, usually left nobody alive.

In one place in Germany, we captured a large group of Germans and we were ordered to continue the advance. We asked Boyko, the brigade commander, what we should do with the prisoners, and he ordered, 'Shoot them on the spot!' We began to divide the prisoners into groups for each crew, about 30 each. When the Germans realised they were going to be executed, they began to run but they were all cut down with machine-gun fire.

The Germans from regular Wehrmacht units often resisted fiercely in 1945, fighting us to the last bullet with the fury of men knowing they were doomed and we simply went mad with anger when we lost comrades in battles so close to the end of the war. And after we liberated the Majdanek camp and saw evidence of the German atrocities there, we no longer spared anyone. If we caught *Faustniks*, we killed them on the spot, but once our tank riders caught a German boy with a *Panzerfaust*. He was only 14 years old. They just punched him in the face and let him go. He was just a kid, his face covered in snot and tears.[32]

Although he had committed his tank armies at an early stage of the initial breakout from the Sandomierz bridgehead, Konev had only released them after his combined arms armies had penetrated the German defences. For the new operation to reach the Neisse River, he ordered his tank armies to support the initial attack – the losses suffered by the rifle divisions during the fighting of January might leave them too weak to overcome the German defences.

In truth, the balance of power was hugely in favour of the Red Army; despite its losses, 1st Ukrainian Front fielded a little under a million troops, nearly 1,300 tanks and assault guns, and over 2,000 aircraft. German resources were far smaller, with barely half as many men and fewer than 300 tanks. As the formations of Konev's armies moved into position, the weather continued to be capricious, with snow flurries followed by warmer spells that turned the ground into a quagmire. Nonetheless, all preparations were complete by the end of 7 February.

On the German side, there had been frantic work to try to create defensive positions. The garrison of Breslau now numbered 25,000 men with plentiful supplies of *Panzerfausts*, but little ammunition for their 50 field guns and 120 anti-aircraft guns. Ammunition shortages weren't the only problem. Hauptmann Siegfried Knappe, an artillery officer, had been sent to Breslau as the garrison's operations officer and worked tirelessly to bring order to the defences, but he received little help from Krause, the fortress commander, who had been forced to take to his bed at the end of January with pneumonia. When Schörner visited the city and demanded to see him, Krause declined to leave his bedroom until Schörner threatened to have him shot. When the two men met an hour later, Schörner was far more conciliatory. He told Krause that it was impossible for him to continue as commandant if he was so ill. He was to be replaced by Hans von Ahlfen, who had commanded a mixed force on the Vistula immediately north of the Sandomierz bridgehead at the start of the Soviet offensive.

One of the few regular German units defending the flanks of Breslau was Sachsenheimer's 17th Infantry Division. On 4 February, Sachsenheimer was summoned to the headquarters of Fourth Panzer Army and was given a special mission. Immediately to the northeast of Dyhernfurth (now the Polish Brzeg Dolny), on the right bank of the Oder to the northwest of Breslau, there was a secret factory that had been producing the nerve agent Tabun. Although chemical weapons had not been used during the war, the Germans maintained considerable stockpiles and these had not been destroyed before the factory was abandoned. A special team – consisting of two scientists, several soldiers trained in chemical warfare, and about 80 former workers from the factory – had been organised, and Sachsenheimer was ordered to launch a surprise attack across the Oder to reoccupy the factory long enough for this team to destroy the Tabun stockpile. Simply bombing the plant might be disastrous if the nerve agent were released.

At the time, Soviet troops were still moving into the area and there was the smallest of windows of opportunity for a swift raid to carry out the mission. Instructions from Schörner's headquarters suggested that a small force of paratroopers should be dropped around Dyhernfurth, but Sachsenheimer felt that this would merely attract the attention of Soviet forces in the area. When he went to the Oder to reconnoitre the situation, Sachsenheimer had a fortunate escape; his group came under fire from the Soviet-held bank and the officers either side of him were wounded. Despite this, he identified a railway bridge as a crossing point and an embankment that led towards the factory. He also noted that the Soviet riflemen in Dyhernfurth were busy celebrating their successes with alcohol they had found in the town.

The raid was carried out late on 5 February. After crossing the railway bridge, the German troops silently overcame two machine-gun positions and advanced swiftly to the factory. The specialists were brought forward just an hour after the operation commenced and set to work. Pumps and other equipment in the factory were still intact and using these, the team pumped the contents of the two Tabun storage tanks into the Oder River, adding chemicals to neutralise the nerve agent. Sachsenheimer then pulled back to his small bridgehead, continuing to hold it through 6 February before evacuating his men back over the railway bridge.[33]

The German lines either side of Breslau were the remit of the newly improvised *Korpsgruppe Jeckeln*. Obergruppenführer Friedrich Jeckeln was its commander, a man whose personal record shows both the lack of military experience of senior SS figures and how their involvement in German atrocities was seen as grounds for their promotion. He had been a police officer before the war and was involved in several murders of opponents of Hitler in the 1930s. Rising steadily through the ranks of the SS, he became *HSSPF* for Ukraine after the German invasion of the Soviet Union and was responsible for the mass killings of Jews in the opening months of the conflict. During this time, he was praised for perfecting a technique known as *Sardinenpackung*, in which Jews would be forced to strip and lie close together in mass graves, where they would be shot. A thin layer of sand or soil would be sprinkled over the victims, many of whom were still breathing, and more Jews would be forced to lie on top of them. He then moved to the Baltic region where he took part in the mass killing of Jews from the Riga ghetto in preparation for the arrival of Jews from Germany. In his desire to demonstrate his zeal, he overstepped his instructions by ordering the execution of a trainload of German Jews who arrived before it was possible to accommodate them in ghettos or camps, for which he was reprimanded. He was then extensively involved in anti-partisan operations, and now found himself overseeing the deployment of several units to defend the front line despite having no real military field experience.

On the morning of 8 February, there was a bombardment of the German lines that lasted for nearly an hour. Despite the period of preparation, ammunition wasn't available in the quantities that the artillery planners might have wished. Nor had there been the same opportunity as at the beginning of the year to carry out careful reconnaissance of German positions and to identify all the strongpoints that would need to be destroyed. As the shelling died away, Konev's armies moved forward. There was bitter fighting all along the front. The Germans had known that a resumption of Soviet attacks was imminent and had spent the preceding week strengthening their fortifications as best they could. The terrain was hilly with widespread forests, favouring defensive fighting; this was particularly the case in the south, where Konev had his weakest group. The attacks by Fifty-Ninth and Sixtieth Armies made almost no impact on the German lines and after two days of rising losses with almost nothing to show for them, it was clear to the Soviet commanders that further attacks were futile. Konev ordered the two armies to switch to a defensive posture, though they were to remain alert for any signs of German withdrawals and were to apply pressure if the Wehrmacht attempted to transfer any units or to pull back its front line.

On either side of Breslau, the attacks enjoyed greater success, not least because of their considerable numerical advantage. Konev estimated that the group to the north of Breslau had an advantage of 2.3:1 for infantry, 6.6:1 for artillery, and 5.7:1 for tanks and assault guns; the group to the south of the city also outnumbered the Germans, with ratios of 1.7:1, 3.3:1 and 4:1 respectively.[34] Combat engineers were deployed in the icy water of the Oder with demolition charges to break up large ice floes that threatened to disrupt crossings. The mixture of exhausted veterans, determined young recruits, and untrained *Volkssturm* fought with varying determination but could do little to hold back the onslaught. Soviet aircraft made repeated attacks on German defences, but despite their overwhelming numerical advantage the recent thaw meant that the improvised airfields behind the front line were often inoperative, and there were few hardened runways available. Nevertheless, by the end of the first day, Lelyushenko's leading units had reached the town of Lüben (now the Polish Lubin), 11 miles (18km) to the west of the Oder. The first probes into the town suggested that the Germans had established strong defences in and around the built-up area and Lelyushenko decided that he would attempt to bypass the town and push on towards the Bobr River, a further 26 miles (42km) to the west.

Towards the end of 9 February, the leading Soviet units reached Liegnitz (now the Polish Legnica); several trains had gathered in the station and left hastily without waiting to take on board any passengers. In 1241, there had been a major battle close to the city when the army of the Polish Duke Henrik II Pobożny was crushed by a Mongol force. Drawing on the memory of that earlier battle, Nazi Party officials urged the *Volkssturm* to hold back this new horde advancing into Europe from the east; reinforced by a few handfuls of regular soldiers, they opened fire on the advancing Soviet troops. Pukhov, the commander of Thirteenth Army, decided to try to take the city with a swift attack. His units were fed into the fighting as they arrived and the battle continued through the night. Casualties were heavy on both sides and a huge fire raged through the urban area, destroying many of the buildings. It took until mid-morning on 10 February for the surviving Germans to be driven off. On the same day, Lelyushenko's southern flank, having slipped past Lüben, captured Bunzlau (now the Polish Bolesławiec) and reached the Bobr River. Further north, VI Guards Mechanised Corps reached Sagan (now the Polish Żagań) and crossed the Bobr. Lelyushenko immediately directed his X Guards Tank Corps to take advantage of this to maintain momentum towards the west.

Breslau was now almost surrounded and a last-minute panic broke out as many of the civilians who were still in the city attempted to leave. Some managed to board the last train from Breslau before dawn on 9 February; they were taken to Schweidnitz (now the Polish Świdnica). Soviet units were already operating some distance further to the west, but they had escaped before the ring finally closed around Breslau. In the city, final preparations for the inevitable siege were under way. Large blocks of buildings around the southern edge of the urban area were demolished to create rubble for barricades, and a group of sappers was given the grim task of killing the animals in the city zoo – there were fears that if they escaped their cages as a result of bombing, they would be a threat to the defenders.[35]

The Soviet troops attempting to encircle Breslau from the north were opposed by Sachsenheimer's 17th Infantry Division. At first, the Germans were able to put up a resolute defence, but Soviet units slowly outflanked them by advancing first west and then south and southeast. Soon, Sachsenheimer could see groups of Red Army tanks moving into his rear area and he was forced to conduct a hasty retreat late on 10 February. For the next two days, 17th Infantry Division was able to hold its new positions, but it continued to be outflanked and on 13 February Sachsenhauser was ordered to pull back towards Breslau itself. The city was surrounded.

The German Seventeenth Army had already taken steps to break the Soviet ring around the city. Fourth Panzer Army made available 19th Panzer Division, which had been recuperating after its involvement in the first Soviet offensive, and 8th and 20th Panzer Divisions were brought up from the south. On 12 February, the force moved forward with 8th Panzer Division in the centre, 20th Panzer Division to the south, and 19th Panzer Division to the north. Despite difficult terrain and the presence of large numbers of Soviet tanks, the German force made steady progress. On the northern flank, 19th Panzer Division managed to establish tenuous contact with the besieged forces before being driven back. In the centre, 8th Panzer Division moved to within nine miles (15km) of Breslau and reached a famous landmark of earlier conflicts. The commander of a panzer company later wrote:

> During one of those days we passed the grave of the Prussian 'Marschall Vorwärts ["Marshal Forwards"]' Marshal Blücher, from the days of the liberation war. The nearby village had for a few years been known as Blüchers-Ruh. The grave was in a small park next to which stood the warden's house. The sarcophagus in the grave vault had been broken open and the body, which had been wearing a uniform, lay next to it. Most of the uniform was missing. Some of the medals and buttons from the clothing were still scattered around. The epaulettes had been cut off. What was particularly horrifying was the discovery that some fingers, which had apparently been wearing rings, had been torn or chopped off. In one corner the Asiatics had left their calling cards, and in the other there were empty vodka bottles and the bloody remnants of slaughtered chickens.[36]

The description of Soviet soldiers as 'Mongols' and 'Asiatics' reflects the German propaganda of the era, which attempted to conflate Bolshevism, Jews, 'Asiatics', and Slavs into some sort of vast threat to Europe. Although the three German panzer divisions had made encouraging progress, they were in danger of being outflanked to the north, where Soviet armour reached and captured the town of Jauer (now the Polish Jawor). The attack was abandoned and the three divisions returned to their start line. Breslau was definitively encircled, but the German Seventeenth Army was ordered to ensure that it held a line as close to the southwest of Breslau as possible, from which a future relief effort could be launched.

To the north of Seventeenth Army, Fourth Panzer Army had to face the reality that it was unable to stop the new Soviet offensive and would be forced back to and beyond the line of the Neisse River. This would result in a catastrophic lengthening of the German front line; even if this line held, it would be wafer-thin and would surely collapse in the face of further attacks. There was no possibility of help being sent from other armies and Gräser, the commander of Fourth Panzer Army, sent a detailed assessment to Schörner. The commander of Army Group Centre might have been a devoted supporter of Hitler, but he was also a highly experienced officer and could see the clear reality of the situation. He was also aware of how Hitler had dismissed such concerns in the past. Schörner therefore decided to send Xylander, his chief of staff, to Berlin with the report to add weight to its contents. Xylander left Silesia and flew north. His plane had to stop to refuel at an airfield in Struppen, near Dresden; unfortunately, this coincided with the devastating air raids on the German city. His aircraft crashed while landing and he was killed. His replacement would be Generalleutnant Oldwig von Natzmer, but it would take several days for him to take up his new post. The planned meeting in which Xylander was to have presented Hitler with the details of the grave situation facing Army Group Centre never took place.

Although Konev's armies were making good progress, they were not enjoying the runaway success that they had experienced in January. Rybalko's tank army had an establishment strength of about 940 tanks and assault guns, but was reduced to about 530 operational vehicles by the end of January.[37] The army was further weakened by the diversion of IX Mechanised Corps to guard the southern flank of Rybalko's advance; when it attempted to move forward to join the tank spearheads, the corps was delayed crossing the Oder by flood waters that washed away several pontoon bridges. The rising temperatures that had released the floodwaters turned the landscape to mud, making movement across country almost impossible even for tracked vehicles. The attack by the German panzer divisions forced a further diversion of Soviet resources, but the grinding advance continued. The Germans were levered out of their positions repeatedly and forced west, albeit at great cost, though Konev fretted about the delays. He was critical of Thirteenth Army, which he felt had not kept up with Lelyushenko's Fourth Tank Army, and the latter was operating sufficiently far in advance of the combined arms armies following it that communications were increasingly difficult. Nonetheless, with Third Guards Army on the northern flank approaching the town of Guben, the advance continued. Lelyushenko established bridgeheads across the Neisse at several points, opening the day for further advances, and Rybalko's leading units approached Lauban (now the Polish Luban).

On 21 February, fresh orders arrived at the headquarters of Army Group Centre from *OKH*. Although they bore the signature of Guderian as chief of the general staff, the tone was entirely consistent with Hitler's thinking. Schörner's army group was to prevent any Soviet advance over a line running from Schwedt in the north to Görlitz – roughly along the current German-Polish border – whilst also defending parts of Pomerania and West Prussia in the north and Lower Silesia in the south. The order added that this would 'create the conditions for transition to an offensive'.[38] Reinforcements would be made available from the north. Writing after the war, Natzmer described how these orders were received with weary smiles and shrugs. For the men who were managing the last armies of the Reich, talk of future offensives was absurd. Their capability had been reduced to a level far below operational thinking; the best they could do was extract minimal tactical reserves from one sector and use them to shore up another, in the clear knowledge that all they were doing was delaying the inevitable.[39]

# CHAPTER 12

# *SONNENWENDE* AND POMERANIA

On either side of the front line that now ran from the lower Vistula across Pomerania to the Oder, there was energetic activity to prepare for the next phase of the war. Zhukov and Rokossovsky were planning to drive north and reach the Baltic coast, eliminating what Soviet accounts later described as the 'Baltic balcony' or 'Pomeranian shelf'; and Himmler continued his plans for a counterattack that would isolate and destroy the Soviet units that had approached the Oder. The date for the German offensive – now renamed *Sonnenwende* ('Solstice') – was set for 15 February. The division, corps and army commanders were almost unanimous in their view that it would not be possible for all the promised armour to assemble in the few days that remained for preparation, but Guderian was adamant that the date could not be changed. Hitler was of a similar opinion – for the moment, at least.

The forces that would be available were far smaller than Steiner, commander of Eleventh SS-Panzer Army, had been promised, but even supplying these divisions posed huge challenges. In particular, fuel remained in desperately short supply. Many of the divisions that were assembling in northwest Pomerania had been transferred from the west, where they had been involved in the winter offensive through the Ardennes, and few had recovered from the losses they had suffered. The Ardennes offensive – known in the west as the Battle of the Bulge – had little likelihood of success in the best possible circumstances, but it too had been handicapped by constant fuel shortages. Indeed, some divisions had anticipated that they would need to capture fuel supplies as they advanced if they were to sustain forward momentum. Those same divisions now faced an operation where once more, they would have limited fuel.

For officers like Eismann, Himmler's chief of operations, there was little doubt that *Sonnenwende* was doomed to failure, and the sense of gloomy anticipation worsened as the ground softened. The assault groups would be forced to use a limited number of roads for their advance, making the task of the Soviet defenders far easier. With a stream of pessimistic reports arriving hourly – and crucially, many of these came from senior SS officers like Steiner – even Himmler was beginning to doubt the likelihood of success. Once again, he contacted *OKH* to request a postponement in the operation until sufficient troops, fuel and ammunition could be gathered. The response from Berlin was blunt. As he often did on such occasions, Hitler had retreated into a mindset that was often described by his inner circle as 'adamant' and refused to countenance any change in plans. Even Guderian seemed to be infected by this, accusing Army Group Vistula of lacking sufficient energy and determination to push forward their plans at the required rate. He had a fiery exchange with Eismann:

> Generaloberst Guderian himself urged daily and accused Army Group Vistula of being sluggish and hesitant. He asserted that it wanted to sabotage the entire operation upon which the fate of the Eastern Front depended. This developed into an ongoing clash with *OKH* which gradually took an extremely bitter form. During a radio conversation with Generaloberst Guderian I had to repeatedly express serious reservations regarding the time set for the attack and the, as yet, incomplete preparations. That drew a reprimand that made the microphone vibrate. It ended with Generalboerst Guderian telling me that he would hold me personally responsible for carrying out all orders and for having the army group ready on the appointed date set for the attack. If the army group continued to work so slowly he would yank me out of the general staff. During the chief of the general staff's tirade all I could get in was an occasional '*Jawohl*'. At the end I informed him that I was merely the First General Staff Officer [the 'Ia', i.e. operations officer] of the army group. Responsibility rested with the commander in chief [i.e. Himmler]. He again shouted at me that he would hold me responsible for everything. I was the First General Staff Officer of this army group and had to influence my commander in chief and chief of staff in whatever way he and *OKH* considered proper.[1]

After the war, Guderian added to his already extensive writing and as his works were translated into English, his version of events was largely accepted without question; it is only comparatively recently that there has been a proper critical analysis that suggests he somewhat embellished his reputation as the great pioneer of panzer warfare at the expense of others who were less able or willing to promote their own roles.[2] Nevertheless, he was an experienced and highly regarded panzer commander, and his attitude in connection with the planned counteroffensive is worth considering in detail. Whilst Guderian had extensive personal front-line experience, he had not commanded troops in the field since being dismissed by Hitler outside Moscow in late 1941. In the intervening years, the nature of the war had changed a great deal. When he left the headquarters of his Second Panzer Army to the south of the Soviet capital, the heaviest tank in his command was the Pz.IV, which weighed about 25 tons. Now, the divisions still fielded large numbers of Pz.IVs, but they also had Panthers that weighed 45 tons and the even heavier Tigers. Originally weighing about 54 tons, the Tiger had developed into the King Tiger with a weight of nearly 69 tons. The Tigers and Panthers had far wider tracks than the older Pz.IV, giving them a lower ground pressure per square metre, but the sheer mass of the tanks meant that however well this weight was distributed, they were still likely to sink into soft ground or to destroy bridges. Their fuel consumption was also far higher than that of their lighter predecessors, and German fuel supplies were far smaller than had been the case in the heady days of Guderian's advance towards Moscow. Prior to becoming chief of the general staff, Guderian had served as *Generalinspekteur der Panzertruppen* ('Inspector-General of Panzer Troops') and therefore had a good level of knowledge about these newer tanks, but this was no substitute for battlefield experience. Although he had a past history of headstrong reluctance to obey orders with which he disagreed, this was all in the context of the first two years of the Second World War when German armies were triumphant and he had intermediate levels of command between him and Hitler. His dismissal in the wake of the failure to reach Moscow was the first occasion that he (or for that matter most German commanders) had been in post when the Wehrmacht suffered a major setback, and subsequently he watched from some distance as senior commanders clashed with Hitler over increasingly unrealistic orders and were consequently dismissed. It was one thing to be insubordinate when German armies were winning great victories and when the chain of command shielded him from Hitler, but he was now in a very different position. There was no buffer between him and the Führer. Moreover, the mood in Hitler's inner circle was very different. The failed July Plot and the resultant widespread belief in Nazi circles that senior officers had failed to win the war largely through their lack of ideological commitment left Guderian with little room for manoeuvre.

Guderian has a formidable reputation as the man who pioneered the use of panzer divisions and after the war, he wrote detailed memoirs that described how he had engaged in passionate arguments with Hitler in often-futile attempts to prevent or mitigate the Führer's disastrous interventions in military affairs.

His innovative and energetic role in the development of German armoured forces is unquestionable; one of his most valuable contributions was early recognition of the value of all tanks being equipped with radios, permitting groups of tanks to coordinate their actions on a rapidly changing battlefield. Nor is there any question about his often-fiery relationship with Hitler, but to a large extent his reputation was established on the basis of his memoirs that appeared at a time when other accounts of events were not available. The last phase of Guderian's military service casts a shadow over his reputation. He was head of the *Ehrenhof* or 'Honour Court', which was responsible for discharging suspected conspirators from the army so that they could face harsh interrogation by the Gestapo and could be brought before the *Volksgerichsthof* or 'People's Court' rather than face court martial. He also oversaw the complete Nazification of the army, with the adoption of the Hitler Salute and issued orders that all officers were to join the Nazi Party; it should be added, though, that this order was poorly enforced.

When he was appointed as chief of the general staff at *OKH*, Guderian was explicitly forbidden from submitting his resignation and had to deal with the ongoing political games that continued to play out as the Reich steadily collapsed. Senior Nazi figures were keen to exploit the failed July Plot to sideline the Wehrmacht leadership, replacing it with strongly pro-Nazi figures and often preferring relatively inexperienced SS officers to the professionally trained soldiers from the ranks of the long-established German staff officers. Even within the Wehrmacht, jockeying for power was widespread. Guderian's *OKH* was responsible for the Eastern Front; the other fronts came under the jurisdiction of *OKW*, where Jodl and Keitel held sway. They were determined to undermine Guderian at every turn, and in many respects he was equally determined to try to increase his authority at their expense. This somewhat arbitrary division of fronts created absurdities. As the armies on the southern flank of the Eastern Front retreated into Romania, Hungary and the Balkan region, they remained under the control of Guderian's *OKH*, but their rear area services were answerable to *OKW*, which had been responsible for this area for several years.

This was the context in which Guderian had first proposed the operation that was now known as *Sonnenwende*. In many respects, it was classical German doctrine – to wait for the enemy's offensive to become over-extended, and then to deliver a powerful counteroffensive to inflict maximum damage. But whilst the overall thinking might have been correct, Germany simply lacked the resources for such an operation to be mounted with the required speed.

Even these resources were being squandered without any real discussion with Guderian. The original plan was for a pincer operation to destroy the Soviet armour in the Oder-Warthe region, but in late January Hitler informed Guderian that Sixth SS-Panzer Army, which consisted of the bulk of the veteran SS divisions that had been heavily involved in the failed Ardennes offensive, was being sent to Hungary rather than to the lower Oder. Despite Guderian's protests, the Führer insisted that the SS divisions were to be used to break through to relieve the besieged garrison in Budapest. Once this had been achieved, the SS divisions might be released for use elsewhere. In the event, the relief attempt failed with heavy losses, not least because the selected terrain was utterly unsuitable for the deployment of so much heavy armour; had they been sent to take part in *Sonnenwende*, they might well have struggled with ground conditions, but the odds of success would have been substantially greater.

Throughout the preparations for *Sonnenwende*, Guderian was rightly concerned that the opportunity to destroy the isolated Soviet armour on the lower Oder was constrained by time: the longer it took for the operation to be prepared, the higher the likelihood that the Soviet combined arms armies would arrive and reinforce the Soviet positions. This, added to the longstanding and mutual distrust between him and senior SS figures – particularly Himmler – lay behind his increasingly ill-tempered demands that Army Group Vistula should adhere to the timetable that Guderian had set. In these circumstances, it was relatively easy for him to assume that the delays in preparation for *Sonnenwende* were due to the inexperience and incompetence of the SS officers who surrounded Himmler. It should also be remembered that his cardiac and circulatory problems were worsening. The twice-daily conferences with Hitler took place 45 minutes' drive from Guderian's headquarters in Zossen, resulting in a total of three hours being lost purely for travel; the conferences themselves lasted between two and three hours. With perhaps eight or nine hours of every day lost in this manner, time still had to be found to deal with the gargantuan tasks of running *OKH*. Guderian's constant struggles with Hitler, having to endure long digressions in which the Führer would launch into irrelevant monologues about his future dreams or would try to impress the professional soldiers by his personal knowledge of the minutiae of various weapons systems, took a devastating toll. He was greatly aided by his able deputy chief of the general staff, General Walther Wenck, who had repeatedly impressed his superiors throughout the war. He had been one of the energetic officers who salvaged the disastrous situation faced by the Wehrmacht in the winter of 1942–43 outside Stalingrad, and had then held a series of staff roles on the Eastern Front.

It was against this background that Guderian made increasingly unrealistic demands of Eismann, who after all was every bit the professional Wehrmacht staff officer that Guderian preferred to the dilettantes of the SS. There was another factor at play here. The German general staff drew its traditions and ethos from the general staff of the old Prussian Army of the 19th century. Highly trained staff officers had been created at that time because there was recognition that the traditional methods of command, with senior officers owing their posts more to their aristocratic rank than their military experience or skills, were often unsuited for leadership on increasingly complex battlefields. The assignment of chiefs of staff to these aristocratic commanders was a means by which a degree of professionalism could be brought into decision-making. Moreover, staff officers were explicitly expected to be able to challenge their commanders and to influence their decision-making; they had the right to raise objections through chiefs of staff at higher levels if they thought this was appropriate. Guderian therefore expected Eismann to show a similar ability to influence Himmler, even though he wasn't the chief of staff. For the operations officer of the army group to challenge the man who was head of the SS and who had already made clear his disdain of the objections raised by professional soldiers around him was of course utterly unrealistic, but Guderian's frustrations with the problems that he faced are perhaps understandable.

But the question of logistics was of paramount importance. Traditional German military doctrine was that logistic concerns should not dictate operational decisions – it was the responsibility of logistics officers to make their commanders' operational wishes possible. Even after the war, senior German officers who cooperated with western military figures and historians repeatedly stressed this point, an utterly unrealistic concept in the era of armies that needed such huge quantities of fuel, ammunition and food to be able to function. Deeply imbued with this traditional doctrine, even visionaries like Guderian often failed to recognise the constraints imposed by Germany's steadily worsening supply problems. Indeed, the memoirs of Guderian, Manstein and others frequently stress Hitler's interference as the cause of their problems, but almost never look at whether German operations should have taken greater cognisance of logistic realities. The planning of *Sonnenwende* – or at least the top-down insistence on unrealistic timetables – was greatly influenced by such flawed thinking.[3]

After finishing his difficult and angry conversation with Guderian, Eismann felt obliged to make Himmler aware of the exchange. Predictably, the commander of Army Group Vistula interpreted this as an attack on his authority and contacted Guderian personally, insisting that he had no right to interfere in the internal planning decisions of the army group. With tempers fraying everywhere, a conference was organised in Hitler's headquarters on 13 February, just two days before the planned start date of the offensive. In addition to the Führer and his usual entourage, Guderian, Wenck, Himmler, and Oberstgruppenführer Sepp Dietrich, commander of Sixth SS-Panzer Army, were all present, but the main account of the discussions was written by Guderian; like all of his memoirs, it should be treated with a degree of caution.

Himmler demanded more time for preparation before launching the new operation, but Guderian's description concentrated on his personal exchanges with Hitler:

> Guderian: We cannot wait until the last barrel of gasoline and the last shell has been delivered. By then, the Russians will be too strong.
>
> Hitler: I beg your pardon, are you accusing me of wanting to delay?
>
> Guderian: I don't blame you at all, but there is no point in waiting for the last supplies to be delivered and thus delaying the designated start date for the attack.
>
> Hitler: I just said I don't want you to accuse me of wanting to wait.
>
> Guderian: And I just told you that I don't wish to blame you, but nor do I want any delay.
>
> Hitler: I forbid you to accuse me of wanting a delay.
>
> Guderian: General Wenck must be assigned to the Reichsführer's staff, otherwise there is no guarantee that the attack will succeed.
>
> Hitler: The Reichsführer is man enough to lead the attack on his own.
>
> Guderian: The Reichsführer does not have the experience or the appropriate staff to conduct the attack independently. General Wenck's presence is therefore essential.
>
> Hitler: I forbid you to say that the Reichsführer is not up to the task.
>
> Guderian: I must insist that General Wenck is assigned to the army group staff to ensure the operations are conducted properly.[4]

The argument continued over the head of Himmler, who was present throughout, for two hours. Then, Hitler backed down and informed the Reichsführer that Wenck would be joining his staff. To date, Hitler had been strongly committed to the offensive starting on 15 February, but perhaps as a result of private conversations with Himmler he now changed his mind and suggested that a brief delay might be required.

Guderian then described an exchange with Keitel as the conference ended:

> I went into the anteroom and sat down at a small table. Keitel then walked up: 'How can you speak up against the Führer like that? Don't you see how much it angers him? What will happen if it makes him unwell?'
>
> I remained calm in front of Keitel: 'A statesman must tolerate contradiction and the truth, otherwise he doesn't deserve the title.' Other men from Hitler's

entourage joined Keitel and once again I had a difficult time until agitated minds had calmed down. Then, I issued the necessary instructions via telephone to my staff. There was no time to lose. One never knew whether the authorisation that we had fought for would be revoked at the next moment.[5]

As already described, the staff of Third Panzer Army, transferred from East Prussia by sea, were to form the core of the new Eleventh SS-Panzer Army. Generaloberst Erhard Raus, the commander of Third Panzer Army, was another highly experienced panzer commander who led 6th Panzer Division during its desperate attempt to reach the Stalingrad perimeter in the winter of 1942–43 before rising first to corps command and then at various stages leading Fourth, First, and finally Third Panzer Armies. His memoirs written after the war are of questionable accuracy in terms of detail – the chronology of the fighting outside Stalingrad, for example, is contradicted by the war diaries of divisions and armies that were involved – but his writing is consistently vivid and probably gives a fairly accurate picture of the personalities with whom he interacted during the Second World War. He met Himmler in Prenzlau late on 13 February:

> [Himmler said] 'The Führer expects decisive results for the outcome of the war from this attack. Originally I had planned to place you, an experienced panzer commander, in charge of this mission. Unfortunately, it was not possible to obtain your release from East Prussia in time. My suggestion of postponing the attack so that the assembly of forces could be completed, and that you and your staff might still be integrated prior to the attack, was rejected by the Führer. Give me your honest opinion as to the course of action and the chances of success in this offensive.'
>
> I replied, 'A comparison of the strength of both sides (our one reinforced panzer army as opposed to the three Russian tank armies and three to four infantry armies) is sufficient to conclude that the attack can lead only to failure. By achieving better coordination of our own units and selecting a shorter route for the attack by your panzer divisions, perhaps some ground may be gained at one point or another, but then they will come to a standstill. Under no circumstances, however, can a decisive success be expected.'[6]

The Soviet forces facing the Germans had two, not three tank armies, but even after correcting Raus' overestimate, his assessment was accurate. He went on to suggest to Himmler that it would be better to hold the panzer formations in reserve and to await the next Soviet offensive before launching sharp counterattacks. Raus went on in his memoirs to describe how he continued his discussion with Himmler in private, and told the *Reichsführer-SS* that the 'supreme command' – a general cipher for Hitler – had repeatedly made serious errors in strategic and operational thinking, and that Germany now faced almost certain defeat if not complete destruction:

> Having finished, I remained silent as we looked at each other for several minutes without uttering a word. Himmler then moved closer to me, bent over, and spoke slowly in a subdued voice, enunciating every word: 'I agree with you.' He then fell silent again.
>
> Astounded by this reply, I drew a long breath and asked, 'Then why have you not informed the Führer?'
>
> After a brief pause, Himmler said, 'I expected that question.' After a second pause, he continued: 'I have already told the Führer all these things.'
>
> 'And what did the Führer say?'
>
> Pointing his finger, Himmler replied after a short time in a raised voice, 'The Führer replied most violently, "You are a defeatist, too!" and in a fit of rage showed me the door.'[7]

We have only Raus' account of this conversation, and the Himmler that he portrays feels like a different person from the army group commander who constantly left Eismann in a state of exasperation, but like many senior Germans, Himmler could hold completely contradictory opinions. Otto Carius, who commanded a company of Tiger tanks in the battles outside Leningrad and later in the Baltic region, was wounded in the late summer of 1944 and was presented with the Oak Leaves to the Knight's Cross by Himmler while he was convalescing in Germany. After a celebratory lunch, he had a private conversation with Himmler; his description of this discussion suggests a frank exchange of views broadly similar to the conversation recorded by Raus. Carius recalled that the two men talked about a wide range of subjects: the survivability of armour in the face of modern anti-tank weapons such as the *Panzerfaust*; the effect of air attacks on German cities; the detrimental effect of bombastic speeches by senior figures when most Germans could see for themselves how desperate the situation was; and the unhelpful rivalry and friction between the Waffen-SS and the regular army.[8] Carius wrote that Himmler remained very confident that the war would be brought to a successful conclusion, but many years after the war he said that Himmler had asked him about this. When Carius replied that he thought the war was now unwinnable, Himmler allegedly paused thoughtfully and then replied, 'That is most interesting.'[9]

The conversation that Himmler had with Carius was several weeks after the July Plot, and there are intriguing clues that Himmler was at least partially aware of the planned assassination attempt. Normally, he might have been expected to be at the conference where Stauffenberg attempted to kill Hitler, but he did not attend. It is possible that he simply kept his knowledge to himself and waited to see if the plot would succeed; with the formidable apparatus of the SS at his disposal, he would then have been in a position to assume power. The consequence was that he faced criticism for appearing not to know that such a widespread plot existed, but he still managed to turn events to his advantage, assuming still greater powers after the plot failed. Within days, his personnel had arrested over 5,000 alleged plotters and anti-government conspirators, suggesting that he had a substantial amount of information about resistance activity.

By early 1945, Himmler was already attempting negotiations to try to persuade the Western Powers to make a separate peace with Germany. Ernst Kaltenbrunner, head of the *RSHA*, was in theory subordinate to Himmler but was perfectly prepared to undermine his boss in order to raise his personal standing with Hitler and passed information to the Führer about Himmler's contacts with Swiss diplomats. Hitler furiously declared that anyone attempting to exchange Jews with foreign powers for any purpose would be shot and Himmler hastily cancelled his plans, but later, using his personal masseur Felix Kersten as an intermediary, he made contact with Count Folke Bernadotte, head of the Swedish Red Cross, with the intention of trading concentration camp prisoners for material support and diplomatic access.[10] Himmler seems to have thought that, whereas Roosevelt and Churchill had ruled out any possibility of negotiating with Hitler, they would be willing to see him as a suitable partner in future; given the role he had played in the war, it is almost inconceivable that any of the Allies might have been willing to negotiate with him. Any insight he had, therefore, can be regarded as limited.

In the absence of Sixth SS-Panzer Army, the original pincer attack against Zhukov's tank armies was now reduced to a strike from the north. The original plan for three attack groups remained in place. To the west, closest to the Oder, was XXXIX Panzer Corps commanded by Generalleutnant Karl Decker, a highly experienced panzer commander, with four divisions: the new *Panzer Division Holstein*; 10th *SS-Panzer Division Frundsberg*; 4th *SS-Polizei Panzergrenadier Division*; and 28th *SS-Freiwilligen Grenadier Division Wallonien*. The central group was formed from Gruppenführer Martin Unrein's III SS-Panzer Corps, with five divisions: 11th *SS-Panzergrenadier Division Nordland*, reinforced by a small group of Tiger tanks; 23rd *SS-Panzergrenadier Division*

*Nederland; Führer-Begleit Panzergrenadier Division;* and two infantry divisions. Finally, the eastern group was made up of the eponymous *Korpsgruppe Munzel* under the command of Generalmajor Oskar Munzel. This was the weakest group, with three divisions: the *Führer-Grenadier Panzergrenadier Division;* 163rd Infantry Division, which was still in the process of being transferred to Pomerania from Norway; and 281st Infantry Division.[11] Given the battered state of Germany's armed forces, it was a remarkable concentration of force, even if none of the divisions involved were at full strength.

Meanwhile, the Red Army had been regrouping in preparation for an offensive operation of its own, aiming to eliminate the German forces in Pomerania. Zhukov's 1st Belarusian Front originally intended for Forty-Seventh and Sixty-First Armies to attack towards Stettin while First Polish Army shielded their flank, but Zhukov had pulled both of his tank armies out of the units massing along the Oder and ordered them to concentrate between Sixty-First Army in the west and First Polish Army in the east, to strike north and northwest. These would later be reinforced by Third Shock Army. Further to the east, Rokossovsky's 2nd Belarusian Front had brought considerable forces across the Vistula with the intention of overrunning eastern Pomerania and West Prussia. From west to east, he had Seventieth Army, Forty-Ninth Army, Sixty-Fifth Army, and Second Shock Army. Like their German opponents, all these formations were far from full strength, but once they were in line, the numerical advantage lay with the Red Army.

After the bruising conference in Berlin, Wenck travelled to Prenzlau, where Himmler's personal train *Steiermark* was currently based. He attempted to have a discussion with Himmler about the final arrangements for the coming attack, but was rebuffed: the commander of Army Group Vistula was having his dinner and insisted that the briefing would have to wait until he had finished his meal. Wenck replied that he had no intention of waiting and was departing for the front line, where he felt he belonged. This angered the *Reichsführer-SS*: was Wenck accusing him of cowardice? Wenck responded that such judgements were not for him to make, and that he had the authority to proceed as he wished. It was hardly the sort of close personal relationship that was essential for a successful military operation.[12]

When he reached Unrein's headquarters, Wenck learned that only a limited offensive was possible on the planned start date. Nevertheless, the attack was launched by *SS-Nordland* and took the Soviet Sixty-First Army by surprise. Belov, the army commander, had ordered his units to be alert for a German counterattack, but the units in the front line had been rotated several times and such orders were passed on with varying degrees of efficiency. In the preceding days, Sixty-First

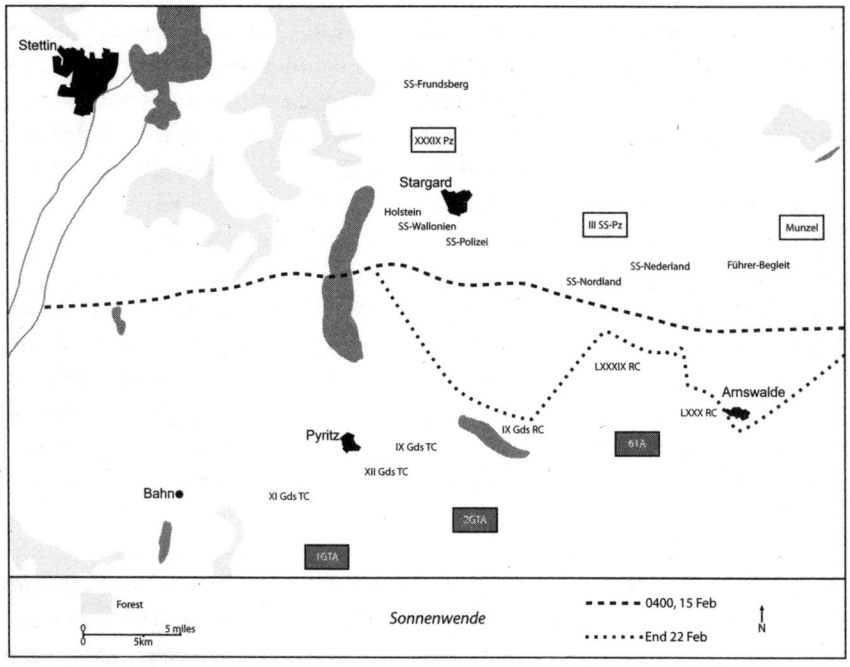

Stettin

SS-Frundsberg

XXXIX Pz

Stargard

Holstein
SS-Wallonien
SS-Polizei

III SS-Pz

Munzel

SS-Nederland    Führer-Begleit

SS-Nordland

LXXXIX RC

Arnswalde

LXXX RC

IX Gds RC

Pyritz

IX Gds TC

61A

XII Gds TC

Bahn

XI Gds TC

2GTA

1GTA

Forest

5 miles

5km

Sonnenwende

– – – – 0400, 15 Feb

· · · · · · End 22 Feb

N

Army had surrounded the small town of Arnswalde (now the Polish Choszczno) and many units were busy roaming through the newly captured German towns and villages, intent on loot and rape. The SS division, led by its small group of Tiger tanks, succeeded in breaking through to the town and linking up with the garrison. *Sonnenwende* was off to an encouraging start.

On 16 February, the bulk of the forces of Steiner's Eleventh SS-Panzer Army went into action. The central thrust by III SS-Panzer Corps widened the narrow corridor that had been created to Arnswalde and the Soviet units were driven back in some disarray for seven miles (12km). But neither of the flanking attacks enjoyed the same success. XXXIX Panzer Corps was intending to reach the Plönersee, a large lake about 13 miles (21km) to the west of Arnswalde, but ran into the units of Second Guards Tank Army that were assembling for an attack of their own. Alerted by the German thrust to Arnswalde the previous day, Bogdanov had told his units to prepare for a possible German attack and there were heavy losses on both sides. Some German units managed to force their way forward to Pyritz (now the Polish Pyrzyce) to the west of the Plönersee but were in danger of being isolated. On the eastern flank, *Korpsgruppe Munzel* managed only a modest advance of perhaps two or three miles.

With fuel and ammunition still very limited, the Germans needed to make greater gains if the operation was to be a success. Wenck was summoned back to Berlin to brief Hitler and Guderian. Wenck and his driver had been awake almost continuously since the morning of 15 February and they arrived at Hitler's headquarters before dawn on 17 February. After a lengthy presentation to the Führer, Wenck drove to Zossen where Guderian was waiting anxiously. Another briefing followed, and the weary general and his even more weary driver, accompanied by Wenck's aide Major Karl Seidel, set off for the headquarters of Army Group Vistula. They had been on the road about an hour when the driver, Hermann Dorn, told Wenck that he was struggling to stay awake and that he couldn't continue. The two men changed places, with Wenck chewing a cigarette in the hope that the bitter taste of tobacco would keep him awake. But shortly after, as they passed Altlandsberg, a short distance to the northeast of Berlin, Wenck too was overcome by exhaustion and fell asleep at the wheel. The car crashed into a motorway bridge.

Both Seidel and Dorn were thrown from the car, which began to burn. Despite being seriously injured, Dorn forced open the door of the car and extracted the unconscious Wenck. The personal weapons of the three men were in the car and as the ammunition began to explode in the flames, Dorn and Seidel rubbed down Wenck's smouldering greatcoat with snow to prevent it igniting. Shortly after, they were able to flag down another vehicle and they were taken to hospital. Wenck was the most seriously injured, with several fractured ribs, a head wound, and concussion.[13]

It was the end of Wenck's assignment to Army Group Vistula. For Guderian, it was a particularly heavy blow: he had been preparing Wenck to take his place at *OKH* in the event of the war lasting long enough for this to become necessary. After treatment in a Berlin hospital, Wenck was sent to Bavaria to convalesce; he would hold one more post before the end of the war and would play an important role in the last battles of the Reich. In his place, General Hans Krebs was appointed both as deputy chief of the general staff and as liaison officer with Army Group Vistula to continue overseeing *Sonnenwende*.

This latter role was largely redundant by the time that Krebs became aware of it. The offensive was running into increasing difficulties and on the day that Wenck was injured the German forces made little or no progress. Zhukov had Third Shock Army in reserve and deployed it in full to confront the German attacks. Late on 17 February, the Soviet forces were ready to launch counterattacks. The commander of Third Shock Army was Lieutenant General Nikolai Pavlovich Simoniak, a highly experienced officer who had played a leading role in breaking the German siege ring around Leningrad.

By nightfall, the leading German units had been forced back by increasingly energetic attacks.

Whatever small possibility of success had ever existed for *Sonnenwende* was now gone. On 18 February, Himmler ordered its abandonment; too many of the remaining powerful divisions of the Wehrmacht and Waffen-SS were tied up in an offensive that was now going backwards. Steiner had doubted the possibility of victory from the outset, and he was now ordered to move west with his headquarters. The staff of Third Panzer Army were to take control of the sector immediately to the east of the Oder. The current commander was still Raus, but Hitler had a low opinion of his abilities because of the pessimistic – though completely accurate – assessments that he had sent to higher commands in the weeks before the Soviet offensive overran much of East Prussia.

Raus described in his memoirs that he was dismayed to find that many of the SS divisions that had just seen action during *Sonnenwende* were already boarding trains for other destinations, depriving him of the means to conduct effective counterattacks against any thrusts by the Red Army into Pomerania. He blamed Steiner for having an 'inadequate defensive scheme', but the reality was that Steiner had been brought in specifically to mount an offensive operation and this had then been abandoned, with Steiner being ordered elsewhere before he had the opportunity to put any defensive plans in place.[14] Raus still had ten divisions under his command, but all were badly weakened and some were new improvised formations created in the preceding weeks. Between them, they fielded just 70 tanks. Raus ordered the construction of anti-tank obstacles to block the areas of clear ground between the numerous forests and lakes of the region, hoping that these might delay the imminent Soviet attack long enough for his weak forces to be able to respond.

While Zhukov completed his preparations for his thrust into Pomerania and recaptured the ground that had been lost to the Germans during *Sonnenwende* – all the German gains had been reversed by 23 February – Rokossovsky drove north into West Prussia, along the west bank of the Vistula. Whilst still refusing to permit the evacuation of the German armies cut off in Courland, Hitler allowed the transfer of individual divisions, like the veteran 4th Panzer Division that had already been brought south by sea to try to halt the advance of 2nd Belarusian Front. The original intention was for the division to leave all its tanks in Courland and to be re-equipped on arrival in West Prussia; although a number of Pz.IVs were available, these proved to have no batteries for their radio sets and eventually the Panther tanks the division had handed over to other units in Courland were shipped out to Danzig. In the

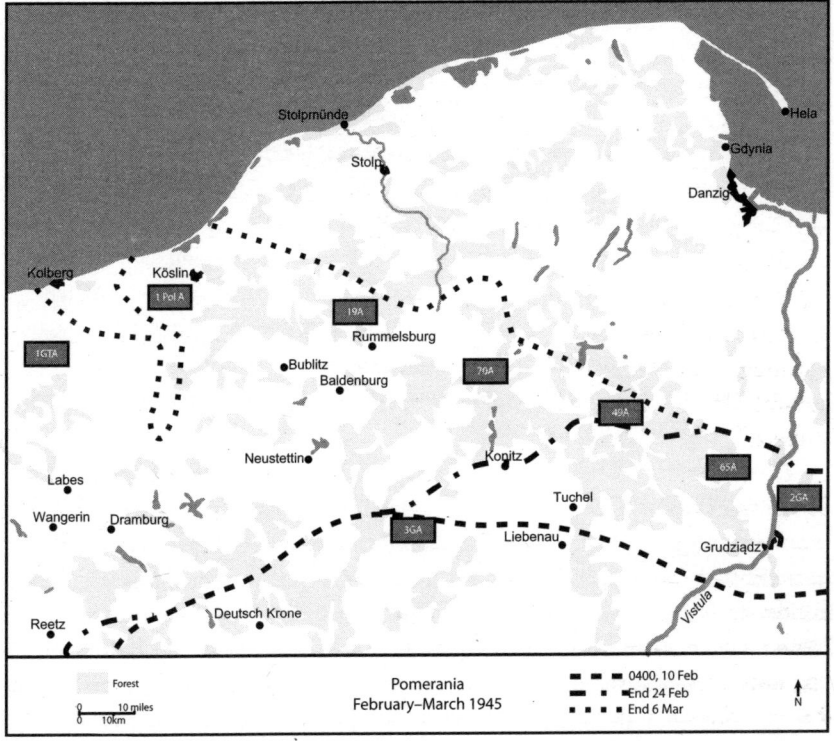

Pomerania
February–March 1945

meantime, the division did what it could. Its first battle took place near the town of Tuchel (now the Polish Tuchola):

We moved through Tuchel, heading south. A road-sign told us we had reached Liebenau. Tired, fought-out soldiers from a Luftwaffe unit occupied trenches in the streets. They waved to us, aware that without our attack they would be prisoners of war of the Russians.

We drove under a railway bridge. Immediately, we saw the red tracer of a Russian anti-tank round coming our way. Our 6th Company deployed by platoons in hull-down positions. Only the vehicle commanders could see over the cover. The platoon commander ordered that we were to fire only on his command. Soon, the first three Russian tanks appeared at the railway bridge. A KV-2, unmistakable with its massive turret, was leading. We opened fire suddenly at 50m range. The three Russians were soon ablaze. The crews bailed out. The following tanks turned rapidly but were caught by flank fire from another platoon. In panic, they disappeared back into the village. We received orders to push into

341

the village and to capture it. A Tiger was assigned to us and soon arrived. I have no idea where it came from. But now it was with us, it was staying with us.

First, we attempted a frontal attack but this failed when we came under fire from all sides. So we drove around the village and attacked from a flank. The Tiger served us well, shooting up the Russian tanks at 2,000m range with its 88mm gun. But when we pressed into the village, we failed once more when the enemy concentrated the fire of all his weapons on us. So we pulled back again and tried once more, this time from the south. Meanwhile, it was growing dark. The flat white surface proved to be treacherous. Suddenly, the ground beneath my tank gave way. We had broken through the ice over a stream. Water poured through the engine compartment. We nearly tilted over and only luck and cunning allowed us to work our way free. But our Tiger – our pride and joy – was hopelessly stuck because of its huge weight.

Our hearts bled when we were ordered to return to our starting positions and to blow up the Tiger.[15]

Like Zhukov's armies, the formations of 2nd Belarusian Front were far from full strength. They had driven across East Prussia to reach the Baltic coast near Elbing, and had then fought a fierce series of actions to prevent the German divisions trapped in East Prussia from breaking out towards the west. Rokossovsky was therefore glad to receive reinforcements in the shape of Nineteenth Army, which had been brought south from Finland, and III Guards Tank Corps. However, these would take a few days to assemble and in the meantime the advance was continued by the tired units in the field. After battering their way through Tuchel, the Soviet forces reached Konitz (now the Polish Chojnice) where once more they clashed with elements of 4th Panzer Division; the advantage lay heavily with the Soviet forces until the German 7th Panzer Division arrived:

Our battlegroup took up positions around the large town square, with our Pz.IV near the red cemetery wall and its turret turned to the rear, and after a short while we were hit. The shell hit the rear, in the engine compartment, which immediately started to burn. We therefore bailed out apart from the driver, who couldn't exit from his hatch because unfortunately the turret locker was overhead. Thankfully, the fire soon went out.

The tank commander, Unteroffizier Schiessl, wanted to rescue our driver from this awkward situation, but every time we climbed onto our tank to get in and turn the turret, the tank took another hit from the Russian gun; this happened three or four times. We didn't know if it was an anti-tank gun or a tank that was firing at us. As Schiessl was determined to help our trapped driver, Obergefreiter Kleinhempel, he sent me to the tank of the commander, Major Brandes, who was about 40m away, to ask for help with covering fire. The commander was positioned facing away from the enemy and like us, had turned his turret to the rear.

For some time, Major Brandes considered whether he could leave his position with his Panther. His tank was in partial cover behind a roadblock, which had been set up at the entrance to another road that he was covering. In order to take cover from the enemy, I stood near the front of his tank and waited.

Finally ... Major Brandes stood up in the turret and nodded to me. He ordered his driver to back up to us. He probably wanted to drive past on the side of the roadblock. His turret remained turned to the rear. The Panther had barely come any distance when the Russians swiftly opened fire on it, but too high, and thus struck Major Brandes' head from his shoulders. Brandes' body fell into the turret.[16]

The normal practice for German tank crews was to turn their vehicles to face the most likely direction of enemy attack in order to take advantage of their strongest armour, and the manner in which these tanks were operating – with their turrets turned to the rear – suggests that either the battle was so confused that the most likely direction of attack was difficult to anticipate, or that they were prepared to move out at speed at short notice. In any case, the episode highlights another factor that was working against the Germans. Brandes had recently been awarded the Knight's Cross and was a highly regarded veteran in 4th Panzer Division. The loss of such experienced and skilful officers played a major role in weakening the ability of the Germans to continue fighting at the same high levels of skill that they had demonstrated repeatedly in the past. Soviet gunners were now far better at identifying German command vehicles – conspicuous because of the greater number of radio antennae – and gave their destruction a high priority.

The presence of 4th and 7th Panzer Divisions, even though they were far from full strength, was sufficient to slow Rokossovsky's advance to a slow grind. It took several more days for the Soviet reinforcements to deploy, and Lieutenant General Georgy Kirillovich Kozlov's Nineteenth Army was finally ready for action by the third week of February. After discussions with Vasilevsky, Rokossovsky deployed his fresh troops on the western wing of his Front so that they would be better able to cooperate with Zhukov's offensive. As had consistently been the case for both sides, logistic difficulties continued to play a major part in preparations:

Our supply lines were badly extended, with the Front's rear echelons stretching back nearly 300km [180 miles]. Most of the Front's depots were located even beyond this area. Communication with them was hampered by the difference in the gauge of Russian and German tracks. Then there was the Vistula and scores of smaller rivers. The Nazis had demolished all bridges, and cargoes had to be shipped over temporary crossings. The break-up of the ice and the rising spring flood waters made it difficult to restore and build bridges. The spring thaw made roads already churned up by shells and bombs impassable ...

In spite of the tremendous difficulties they faced, the rear services had ensured the Front received continuous supplies of everything needed. Their personnel were inexhaustibly inventive. They laid a pipeline to accelerate fuel deliveries across the Vistula.[17]

This was an important difference between the two sides. Whereas the Germans faced difficulties both locating sufficient supplies and then moving them to the front line, the Red Army was comparatively lavishly supplied; its problems related to delivering those resources to the combat units. The pause while Kozlov moved his divisions into place was in some ways a relief, as it allowed ammunition and fuel to be brought forward in sufficient quantities to create sufficient stockpiles for the assault units to be able to operate for longer once the attack was renewed.

Aware that the Red Army was massing its resources for a fresh offensive, the Wehrmacht launched a series of spoiling attacks on 22 February along the Pomeranian front line. However, although Raus wrote that the Germans had spotted the build-up of Soviet units on Rokossovsky's western flank, the deployment of Kozlov's entire army had not been detected and this sector remained relatively quiet. The greatest German pressure was against Sixty-Fifth Army, commanded by the redoubtable Batov, and the Germans briefly succeeded in driving back the Soviet units and Batov's neighbour, Forty-Ninth Army, was temporarily forced out of Osowo. Despite this, the preparations for the resumption of the Soviet offensive continued almost unchecked. On 24 February, after a 40-minute artillery barrage, Kozlov's Nineteenth Army attacked and rapidly overran the German defences in its path. But Zhukov's Front was still completing its preparations and as Kozlov advanced, his western flank became increasingly exposed. Rokossovsky had hoped to hold III Guards Cavalry Corps in reserve until a later date, but was forced to deploy it to shield this flank.

The first day of the offensive, 24 February, saw the Soviet units push up to 12 miles (20km) to the north, though Rokossovsky felt that the advance might have been faster if the attacking troops had been closely supported by tanks. On 25 February, Lieutenant General Aleksei Pavlovich Panfilov's III Guards Tank Corps was deployed to accelerate the advance and by the afternoon it had moved beyond the multiple layers of German positions into open country. Although trenches and other positions had been constructed, the Wehrmacht lacked the men and guns to man them properly, and the description that Raus gave of his dispositions was similar to that of all the formations of Army Group Vistula:

> Division front lines averaged between 26 and 30km [15–18 miles] in length. For every kilometre of front, we deployed one artillery piece, one heavy machine-gun, two light machine-guns, and 40 men. We deployed one anti-tank gun for every 2.5km, one tank for every 4km, and each battalion was stretched across roughly 6km.[18]

Whilst these figures are averages and the armour and heavy equipment would have been concentrated in small packets, the numbers are in stark contrast to those that Rokossovsky described; according to him, Red Army reconnaissance and intelligence had estimated the German strength facing his Front as amounting to 230,000 troops with 700 tanks and assault guns and over 3,000 artillery and anti-tank guns.[19] Given the speed with which the German defences collapsed, it is likely that Raus' figures were more accurate, though the concentration of German forces closer to the lower Vistula, where 4th and 7th Panzer Divisions continued to hold back the Red Army, undoubtedly left the rest of the German line in a weak state.

The entry of III Guards Tank Corps into the battle resulted in a rapid advance. At dawn on 26 February, Panfilov's leading units swept into the town of Baldenburg (now the Polish Biały Bór), about 34 miles (55km) from 2nd Belarusian Front's start line and halfway to the Baltic coast. But just as the initial advance of the rifle divisions of Nineteenth Army had been hindered by a lack of armoured support, Panfilov's tanks now found themselves struggling without infantry support. Rokossovsky had little doubt where the blame lay:

> The swift and resolute action of the tankmen led by General Panfilov, a fine commander, paved the way for Nineteenth Army's rapid advance. Unfortunately, however, the army didn't exploit the opportunity, and in two days advanced only 25km [15 miles]. The fighting to force the enemy out of strongpoints left behind by the tanks consumed much time and energy. This doubtlessly told on the rate of advance, but it was not the only reason, and poor leadership was also to blame. Time and again the army commander, Kozlov, lost contact with his formations and was slow in taking essential decisions. Two days' fighting revealed that he was incapable of handling such a large formation as an army, to say nothing of the attached reinforcing units. In the complex and extremely

fluid situation of the offensive he was at a loss and incapable of influencing the course of events.

This compelled the Front military council, with the sanction of the supreme commander [Stalin], to replace the army commander with [Lieutenant] General [Vladimir Zakharovich] Romanovsky, a seasoned, experienced general with good all-round abilities.[20]

Kozlov had commanded his Nineteenth Army since May 1943, and there had been little reason to doubt his abilities to date. His replacement, Romanovsky, had led armies during the bitter and costly fighting to break the siege ring around Leningrad; he might have lacked the flair of other senior officers, but he was a capable organiser and was in many respect the ideal man to take command of an army that was hindered as much by logistic hurdles as by enemy action.

Poor weather had made it impossible for the full weight of Soviet aviation to be deployed for the first day of Nineteenth Army's assault, but bombers and ground attack aircraft made their presence felt in the following days. With the German lines broken by Nineteenth Army and III Guards Tank Corps, it was possible for Seventieth Army to the east to start advancing, though the gains were more modest. Elsewhere, the energetic German counterattacks close to the Vistula had been halted, but the Soviet armies were unable to recover lost ground. From the point of view of the Red Army in general and Rokossovsky in particular, this was not unwelcome: if substantial German assets were still fighting on the direct approaches to Danzig in the east, then the advance of the left wing of Rokossovsky's 2nd Belarusian Front would be able to trap them if it could continue to the Baltic coast. However, the advance of that flank of the Front was creating problems. Zhukov's armies had not yet attacked, and despite the presence of III Guards Cavalry Corps there were several sharp counterattacks by the German forces in the area, particularly as Rokossovsky's units moved closer to Neustettin (now the Polish Szczecinek). With III Guards Tank Corps pushing north a little to the west of the city, this area was now actually behind the flank of the advancing units, and Rokossovsky later wrote about his concerns that the lack of any movement by Zhukov's armies further to the west was working in favour of the Germans:

The city, to the west of our Front's boundary line, was swarming with enemy forces which might launch an attack against our exposed flank at any moment. I reported this to *Stavka*. A little later I was called to the telephone by the supreme commander. I reported the situation on our Front in general, and on the left wing in particular.

'You mean Zhukov is up to something?' Stalin said.

I said that I did not think he was up to anything, but the fact remained that his troops were not advancing, thereby creating a danger to my exposed flank. I had no forces with which to protect it as my reserves were used up. Therefore I requested that either the Front should be reinforced or 1st Belarusian Front instructed to assume the offensive as quickly as possible.[21]

The implication in Rokossovsky's memoir is that it was largely through his pressure that 1st Belarusian Front's armies finally joined the offensive into Pomerania, but Zhukov had been redeploying his units for several days and was also dealing with *Sonnenwende*. Moreover, given that Rokossovsky had emphasised the problems caused by his long supply lines, the same was even more the case with the armies of 1st Belarusian Front – operating further to the west, their supply lines were even longer. Naturally, Zhukov makes no mention in his recollections of being put under any pressure by *Stavka* to hasten preparations. The relationship between Zhukov and Rokossovsky wasn't particularly warm, and the rivalry between the two men was steadily growing as the end of the war approached. In the summer of 1944, Rokossovsky had led 1st Belarusian Front with considerable skill across Belarus and to the outskirts of Warsaw, and when he was transferred to take command of 2nd Belarusian Front in the last months of the year, he clearly saw it as a demotion:

Stalin ... told me that I was being appointed commander of 2nd Belarusian Front. This was so unexpected that I blurted without thinking, 'What have I done to be transferred from the main to a secondary sector?'

Stalin said that I was wrong, and that the sector was a part of the general western sector on which three Fronts – 2nd Belarusian, 1st Belarusian and 1st Ukrainian – were to operate. The success of this decisive operation depended on the closest coordination of these Fronts, which was why *Stavka* was giving special attention to its choice of commanders.[22]

The only account of this conversation is in Rokossovsky's memoirs, and although he continued by saying that he told Stalin he regarded Zhukov as 'the very man for the job' of replacing him as commander of 1st Belarusian Front, he clearly resented the change. It was clear that 1st Belarusian Front would be on the most important (and therefore most prestigious) axis of the offensive across Poland and the eastern parts of Germany, and the argument that it was important to select the right candidates as commanders of the three Fronts participating in the offensive is of course correct. As deputy supreme commander, Zhukov was given priority over Rokossovsky.

While Zhukov completed his preparations, Rokossovsky ordered Lieutenant General Nikolai Sergeyevich Oslikovsky to use his III Guards Cavalry Corps, reinforced by elements of Nineteenth Army, to eliminate the German presence around Neustettin. On 27 February, Oslikovsky made good use of substantial artillery and aerial support to pin down the defenders of Neustettin while he swept around either flank of the German position. By the end of the day, the city was in Soviet hands. Rokossovsky added wryly that Oslikovsky reported making contact with elements of II Guards Cavalry Corps, the right flank formation of Zhukov's 1st Belarusian Front, immediately to the west of Neustettin – a clear result, he concluded, of his conversation with Stalin.

The Soviet Nineteenth Army was now making better progress, but it was still some distance behind the units of III Guards Tank Corps and Rokossovsky ordered Panfilov to halt near Bublitz (now the Polish Bobolice) while the rifle divisions caught up. But other units were still not pushing forward as fast as Rokossovsky had hoped. Seventieth Army was moving north to the east of Nineteenth Army, but its leading unit – VIII Mechanised Corps – failed to show the energy that the Front commander demanded. It was an unfair criticism; the units of the corps were all far from full strength, and had been in almost continuous movement since mid-January.

The Germans were shuffling their meagre resources to try to counter Rokossovsky's thrust. Although Oslikovsky's III Guards Cavalry Corps was doing an effective job protecting the western flank of Rokossovsky's main thrust, the relatively slow advance of Seventieth Army left the eastern flank also exposed. Weiss, commander of Second Army, ordered the headquarters of VII Panzer Corps, commanded by General Mortimer von Kessel, to take control of *SS-Polizei* and 7th Panzer Division; these were to concentrate around the town of Rummelsburg (now the Polish Miastko), from where they would be able to attack against the potentially open flank of the Soviet Nineteenth Army. Rokossovsky described this force as having 'several dozen tanks and thousands of infantry' – in reality, both divisions had barely half their infantry strength and 7th Panzer Division fielded just 30 tanks and assault guns. The fact that Romanovsky was able to repel this attack with the three divisions of his XL Rifle Corps – although the corps had not been involved in heavy fighting in 1945, it was far from full strength – suggests that the German attack was a weak affair. Indeed, only part of 7th Panzer Division was present, with much of its armour and artillery deployed in small packets to try to reinforce the overall front line.

Even as the fighting around Rummelsburg died down, a threat appeared on the other flank of Nineteenth Army. Rokossovsky described how the Germans massed 15th and 32nd Infantry Divisions with tank support for this attack, but this is incorrect; at the time, 15th Infantry Division was fighting far to the south in the Tatra Mountains and 32nd Infantry Division was in the process of being transferred by sea from Courland to Danzig, with barely a battlegroup being available for action. As was the case with the alleged serious attack from the east at Rummelsburg, this German attack from the west was defeated by a modest force of just one rifle division. Moreover, whilst Rokossovsky might have fretted about his western flank being potentially exposed, his advance had also exposed the eastern flank of Raus' Third Panzer Army. Raus had no choice but to move units to the east, aware that it was only a matter of time before his entire front line came under attack.

On the last day of February, Zhukov's Front completed its preparations for the offensive. To make the best use of his hard-pressed logistic resources, he committed just three armies to the main assault, but they were his most powerful: First and Second Tank Armies, and Third Shock Army. In the case of the latter, the Soviet planners resorted to a tried and tested technique. The Red Army had a unique formation, the *Ukreplyonny Rayon* or 'fortified district' with about 4,500 men. Although it was, numerically, less than half the strength of a rifle division, it was extensively equipped with machine-guns and artillery, and the wartime version was a development of formations that had first appeared in the Russian Civil War. To an extent, they were a response to the necessities of the time: manpower was needed in units that would carry out offensive operations, and Soviet industrial output was at high enough levels to compensate these relatively less mobile formations with a great deal of defensive firepower. An additional 'fortified district' was assigned to Third Shock Army in preparation for the offensive, allowing it to concentrate its offensive units on a tighter front line – although the army covered a front line of 22 miles (36km), it would be attacking on a frontage of just ten miles (16km).[23] By contrast, German infantry divisions, with perhaps fewer than 10,000 combatants, were routinely required to defend over 15 miles of front line. Whereas Raus reported that he had an average of just one tank for every 4km of front line, Katukov's First Guards Tank Army could concentrate 70 tanks per kilometre. To increase the strength of the initial attack, Zhukov assigned a tank corps and three assault gun regiments to support the already formidable forces of Third Shock Army.

Immediately before 1st Belarusian Front attacked, Katukov was summoned to a meeting with Zhukov. He found the Front commander in a rich but unheated German mansion:

> Georgy Konstantinovich was alone. He shivered slightly, straightening his slipping greatcoat with a shrug of his shoulder. It was easy to see that the marshal was in a

bad mood. From my conversation with him, I realised he was worried about whether the tank armies would be able to carry out the instructions from *Stavka* in the required time. 'There's slush everywhere, and almost no roads running north. There's only one with a hard surface. How will such a mass of troops move through here? Only four days are assigned for the entire operation. The Baltic coast is 100km [60 miles] away. That means you have to cover 25km every day. Can you handle it?'

'Don't worry, Comrade Marshal, the army will complete its task on time.'

Zhukov looked at me gloomily. 'You won't let me down?'

'Of course not. During the advance from the Vistula to the Oder, we covered larger distances.'[24]

Given Zhukov's competitive desire to advance faster than his rivals during *Bagration*, it is likely that the successes being achieved by Rokossovsky to the east were playing on his mind.

When the attack began on 1 March, Third Shock Army struggled to penetrate the German defences – the limited number of roads running north had permitted Raus' divisions to concentrate their meagre forces where they would most be needed. The original intention had been to commit First Guards Tank Army into the battle after Third Shock Army had broken the German line, but as had often been the case during the war it was necessary for the tanks to be thrown into action in order to assist the penetration. The German defenders – mainly from 5th Jäger Division – had fought doggedly all morning to hold back the Soviet units and now they gave way around the town of Reetz (now the Polish Recz).

Raus had already dispatched his only army-level reserve – the *Holstein* Panzer Division – to his eastern flank, and he had no reinforcements to send to deal with the Soviet breakthrough. The Soviet attack on 5th Jäger Division was on the western flank of X SS Corps and as the German division pulled back, a gap opened between this corps and III SS-Panzer Corps to the west. As darkness fell on the first day, Katukov committed his entire tank army into the breach. His leading units were soon advancing almost unopposed and swiftly covered the first 15 miles of their march to the sea. Babadzhanian's corps was once more in the lead, heading for Labes (now the Polish Łobez) during the night. Here, the Soviet armour would find itself astride good roads running northeast and northwest. Further exploitation would be far easier. At the same time, Second Guards Tank Army brushed aside the remaining units of III SS-Panzer Corps and drove forward towards Stettin.

The situation for Himmler's Army Group Vistula was already very bad; Rokossovsky's spearheads were within striking distance of the Baltic coast, and the rapid advance of 1st Ukrainian Front was swiftly dismembering Third Panzer

Army to the west. But since the failure of *Sonnenwende*, Himmler had taken to his bed, telling his subordinates that he was suffering from influenza. Despite his high standing in the Nazi hierarchy, he was now being blamed for the failed counteroffensive, with others continuing to seek advancement at his expense. Even if he had been more active in his headquarters – and just as importantly, even if he had been an experienced and skilled senior commander – there would have been little that he could do to prevent the slide from a bad situation to a disastrous one. Throughout 2 March, 1st Ukrainian Front's units advanced with greater hindrance from the mud than from German resistance. Although *SS-Nordland* made several counterattacks during the day from the northwest, these were repulsed with little difficulty. Between this division and the fragmented remnants of 5th Jäger Division, *SS-Nederland* fought bravely but was hopelessly outnumbered; and in any case, much of the armour of Zhukov's two tank armies had already bypassed the SS divisions and was pushing north into almost empty space. By the end of 2 March, Babadzhanian's leading units had reached and captured Labes. They had covered more than half the distance to the coast.

There was little respite elsewhere. Having used their brief pause to bring forward supplies, the armoured units of III Guards Tank Corps, leading Rokossovsky's advance a little to the east, moved forward again and rapidly approached the town of Köslin (now the Polish Koszalin), a little over four miles (7km) from the Baltic coast. If this advance continued, and if Katukov's tank army further west could not be stopped, the German X SS Corps would be cut off and isolated; moreover, all of Weiss' Second Army would be trapped in a large pocket around the city of Danzig and the Vistula estuary. The divisions that had launched the futile *Sonnenwende* counteroffensive might have been effective at this moment, but instead they had left much of their equipment destroyed or abandoned near Arnswalde. In any case, they had already been dispersed to deal with the multiple crises facing Germany.

As was frequently the case, Hitler resorted to the same measures that he had adopted in the past when facing a lack of resources to deal with Soviet attacks. Raus was informed that the city of Kolberg was declared a fortress. The city had no defenders and was choked with refugee traffic, as Raus later recalled:

> The small city was overcrowded with wounded, the railway station filled with hospital trains. Columns of refugee carts blocked the roads, and Russian tanks were only 40km [24 miles] distant. Precisely at that moment the newly appointed fortress commander, Oberst Fritz Fullriede, who was entirely unfamiliar with the situation, was flown in by a Fieseler *Storch*. He was not acquainted with the duties of a fortress commander and had to be briefed in

detail. The 'fortress' was absolutely defenceless. Hitler's attention was called to this fact, but he nonetheless insisted that Kolberg be held as a fortress under all circumstances. In his reply to my protests, Hitler assured me that the Spandau depot would receive instructions immediately to dispatch 12 new anti-tank guns to Kolberg by rail. This was at a time when the single-track railway line to Kolberg was completely blocked and Soviet tanks were expected to appear in the proximity of the city within a few hours.[25]

Fullriede was an experienced soldier, with a distinguished record of field commands in the Soviet Union, North Africa and in the west. It was in this latter theatre that he was involved in an action that was a major blemish on his reputation. After Dutch resistance fighters attacked a staff car late on 30 September 1944, Fullriede was ordered to destroy the Dutch village of Putten. His troops set 84 homes alight – the village had about 2,000 homes, and Fullriede deliberately did the minimum damage he could without contravening his orders entirely and did not execute all male civilians as was commonly the practice in such reprisals. He also refused to deport the men, but SS units deported 588 men and youths to Germany as forced labourers. Fewer than 50 would return to their homes. Fullriede's superiors issued a sharp reprimand and his assignment to a suicidal command like Kolberg was perhaps the ultimate consequence.[26]

Once they had been levered out of their defensive positions, the German units collapsed rapidly. On 4 March, three bottles of liquid arrived at Rokossovsky's headquarters, a gift from the soldiers of Panfilov's III Guards Tank Corps: it was water from the Baltic Sea. The German Second Army was cut off in a pocket around Danzig. The Soviet armour turned east immediately, driving along the coast, while a rifle corps defended the corridor running to the sea from any attack from the west. Such attacks were few and feeble, as X SS Corps was fighting for its life. Babadzhanian's tanks swept past Wangerin (now the Polish Węgorzyno) on 3 March and advanced a further 18 miles (30km) before nightfall, but Katukov was concerned about the potential risk to XI Guards Tank Corps, operating some distance ahead of other Soviet units. Wangerin was captured by Third Shock Army the following day, easing Katukov's concerns, but in any case he had little to fear. The German units in his path were in disarray and falling back on diverging axes. On the same day that Panfilov reached the Baltic coast further to the east, Katukov also received a gift of seawater from one of Babadzhanian's brigades. In addition to the encirclement of the German Second Army, the Soviet advance had isolated X SS Corps. Generalleutnant Günther Krappe, the corps commander, rapidly lost contact with his broken formations and found himself close to his family estate near Dramburg (now the Polish

Drawsko Pomorskie). He was wounded as Soviet troops stormed the estate and taken prisoner. The disparate battlegroups made up of shattered Wehrmacht units and hastily improvised rear area formations that made up his corps were either destroyed or – in a few cases – succeeded in fighting their way through to the west.

Other Soviet units reached the Baltic coast to the east of Kolberg, isolating Fullriede and his small garrison. Despite Hitler's promises to Raus, none of the anti-tank guns from the Spandau arsenal reached the city before it was isolated. Nevertheless, Fullriede did what he could, organising his meagre resources in the hope that it would be possible for German ships to evacuate the thousands of civilians and wounded soldiers who had gathered in Kolberg. Meanwhile, the Soviet forces were regrouping. In order to crush the encircled Second Army as quickly as possible, Katukov's First Guards Tank Army was transferred to 2nd Belarusian Front. Rokossovsky later wrote that Zhukov handed over the army with some reluctance, reminding the commander of 2nd Belarusian Front that this was merely a temporary arrangement and that he expected First Guards Tank Army to be handed back in the same condition.[27] As the tanks refuelled and moved east, the Polish First Army took up positions around Kolberg. To the west, Second Guards Tank Army swept on towards Stettin, reaching the Oder on either side of the city. As had been the case elsewhere, Hitler insisted that the city was held as a 'bridgehead' for future offensive operations. In less than three weeks, Rokossovsky and Zhukov had eliminated the remote possibility of a threat to their northern flank from the German forces in Pomerania.

Zhukov left the reduction of Kolberg to the Polish First Army. After extensive artillery and aerial bombardment, the Poles attacked on 12 March and for two days they battered the defences, suffering heavy losses for minimal gains. After a day of regrouping, the Poles attacked again and forced the German defenders back to the port. A naval evacuation of civilians and wounded soldiers had been underway since 11 March under the direction of Fregattenkapitän Hans Kolbe, who had already conducted a successful evacuation of the port of Stolpmünde, and an astonishing 70,000 people were safely transported to the west in five days.[28] Late on 17 March, the German destroyer *Z 43* and the torpedo boat *T 33* – although classified as a 'torpedo boat', this was a vessel about the size of a small destroyer – left the port with the last of the garrison. Fullriede departed under fire from Soviet guns in a motorboat; Kolbe was amongst the last to leave in another small boat. Kolberg had endured a long siege by French forces in the Napoleonic Wars and Fullriede's defence of the city was regarded as a great triumph by Goebbels. But even though the Poles had suffered heavy losses in the fighting, their overall casualties were similar to those of the German garrison and the fighting had little effect on the outcome of the campaign.

The German defeat in Pomerania resulted in further command rearrangements. Weiss, who had warned that his Second Army faced encirclement and likely destruction, was dismissed for his defeatist attitude; his replacement would be Saucken, recalled from his period of leave after being dismissed by Schörner. Raus had also warned of the danger to his left flank and the imminent encirclement of X SS Corps and he was summoned to see Himmler. He found the commander of Army Group Vistula in a hospital to the northeast of Berlin, apparently recovering from an episode of angina brought on by his recent influenza. Raus later wrote an account of a conversation he had with the *Reichsführer-SS*, but it must be remembered that only he and Himmler were present and there is therefore no corroboration of what was said. Raus blamed the disintegration of his Third Panzer Army on the lack of reserves and on Himmler; during the fighting, he complained that Himmler had either been completely silent or had issued impossible instructions, such as ordering Raus to attack from the Stettin area with a single panzer division towards the east in order to re-establish contact with Second Army, despite the powerful formations of two Soviet Fronts being in the path of any such attack. Himmler apparently replied that he had passed Raus' requests to higher commands but Hitler had refused any suggestions of a timely withdrawal.[29]

Raus was then ordered to report personally to Hitler in Berlin. He reached the German capital on 8 March and gave Hitler a detailed description of events. Himmler had warned him that the Führer would ask for details of how the troops had performed – whilst such information might have been of interest, it was surely irrelevant given the disaster engulfing Germany. At the end of the conference, Raus was told that he was being dismissed. His replacement as commander of Third Panzer Army – its depleted ranks now defended the line of the lower Vistula – would be General Hasso von Manteuffel, a man with a long history of distinguished service in panzer formations.

Himmler's days as a field commander were also coming to an end. After the failure of *Sonnenwende*, he seemed to lose interest in leading Army Group Vistula. For days at a time, he declared himself too unwell to take part in the daily situation reports. After the Soviet advance across Pomerania to the Baltic coast broke the army group in two, the reports from the headquarters of Second Army, hemmed in around Danzig, became increasingly recriminatory. Himmler spoke to Weiss, offering him platitudes and little else. At no time did either Himmler or his chief of staff, Lammerding, attempt to fly to the isolated army to hold discussions face-to-face. Indeed, Himmler's disparaging reports to Hitler about the negative views expressed in Weiss' reports probably contributed to Weiss' dismissal. The toxic atmosphere in the headquarters of Army Group Vistula was worsened by the presence of Gruppenführer Hermann Fegelein, whom Himmler had appointed as his adjutant. Even by the standards of the overpromoted denizens of the upper echelons of the SS, he was a singularly ungifted and talentless individual. In 1940, he faced prosecution for unlawful sexual intercourse with a Polish woman and of procuring her an abortion, but any attempts to investigate the matter were resolutely blocked by Himmler. He commanded cavalry units involved in 'anti-partisan warfare' on the Eastern Front; his operations were largely exercises in mass murder of any civilians who lay in the path of his sweeps. In 1944, Fegelein married the sister of Eva Braun, Hitler's mistress, but continued to have numerous affairs. In his role as Himmler's personal adjutant, he rapidly earned the enmity of professional officers like Eismann, the operations officer of the army group:

He was ... the most lying and evil intriguer whom I ever experienced during this war. He had his filthy fingers into everything. His unashamed arrogant conduct toward older, experienced men was unparalleled. Even toward Himmler, with whom he was familiar, he employed a tone in private which was, at the very least, remarkable.

In the course of time both Lammerding and I discovered that Fegelein calumniated Himmler in the worst possible way with Hitler. He often passed on the most dishonest reports regarding the situation of the army group that were none of his business ...

As Fegelein's trouble-making worsened steadily I persuaded Lammerding to tell Himmler the plain truth about his friend. After several protests, Himmler agreed that Fegelein was out of line. He was unwilling, however, to recall him, even though Fegelein's behaviour was causing him real harm.[30]

Guderian travelled to see Himmler in the third week of March and informed Himmler that he was being replaced as commander of Army Group Vistula. His replacement would be Generaloberst Gotthard Heinrici, who had commanded First Panzer Army in its dogged retreat across southern Poland.

The fantasies in Hitler's bunker took on an increasingly surreal aspect. Guderian described a typical moment:

One night, in the midst of these desperate moments, Dr [Robert] Ley [head of the *Reichsarbeitsfront* or 'Reich Labour Front'] made a new proposal to Hitler. He offered to form a *Freikorps* from Nazi Party political officials who were becoming redundant in the west: 'At least 40,000 fanatical fighters can certainly be raised, *mein Führer*. These men can hold the Upper Rhine and the Black Forest region. Please allow this select *Freikorps* to bear your proud name and to call itself the *Freikorps Adolf Hitler*. The chief of the general staff must deliver 80,000 assault rifles immediately!' Less convinced than Dr Ley of the value of the new formation, I asked him first to tell me the actual number of combatants he had assembled, and then I would see about arming them. I didn't hear from him again.[31]

While fighting raged across Pomerania, the ordeal of the German soldiers and civilians in Küstrin continued. After the Red Army established its bridgeheads across the Oder on either side of the city, their forces then edged closer to each other in an attempt to isolate Küstrin and in early February were only about two miles apart, despite constant air attacks. When comparing the Eastern Front with what was happening in the west, it is striking how often the Luftwaffe was still able to mount attacks against the Red Army despite the huge numerical superiority enjoyed by the Soviet air units. Much of this was due to doctrinal differences between the USAAF and RAF on the one hand and Soviet aviation on the other, but other aspects were due to differences in the performance of aircraft. By 1945, fighter planes flown by the Western Allies had operational ranges that were three or four times greater than those of Soviet aircraft; consequently, they were less dependent on ground forces capturing airfields during advances.

Emil Stürtz, *Gauleiter* of Brandenburg, telephoned Reinefarth on 4 February to give permission for an evacuation of civilians, but Reinefarth chose not to take any action. Meanwhile, the Soviet units that had crossed the Oder gathered their strength in preparation for an attack to link up and thus isolate Küstrin, and on 5 February the railway line running from the city to Berlin was cut. It was now too late for any of the remaining civilians in the city to be evacuated easily. Only the most tenuous connection remained between Küstrin and the rest of Germany.

Within Küstrin itself, Reinefarth imposed discipline in a manner that would not have surprised anyone familiar with his activities in Warsaw. There were dozens of forced labourers from the Baltic region, Poland and the Soviet Union in the city. Fourteen were summarily executed for plundering.[32] Reinefarth divided Küstrin into two defensive zones, separated by the Warthe, and appointed an officer of the *Feldgendarmerie* as commander of the Neustadt zone on the right bank of the river. It was not a good choice; Oberst Franz Walter had no front-line experience and whilst he was prepared to impose iron discipline on his troops – who formed about two-thirds of the city garrison – he showed little tactical awareness in his dispositions. By contrast, the commander of the Altstadt zone on the other side of the Warthe, Major Otto Wegner, was a veteran of both wars with extensive combat experience and several medals for his achievements. For the moment, neither zone came under heavy attack. An attack by 21st Panzer Division from the west managed to open a small corridor, but it was constantly swept by artillery fire and could only be used for major movements during the night; much of the corridor ran across country, and with the warmer weather turning the fields to mud, movement was largely limited to tracked vehicles or people on foot. Having established this corridor, 21st Panzer Division was withdrawn and replaced by 25th Panzergrenadier Division.

In mid-February, sufficient supplies had reached the besieging forces for Soviet gunners to increase their activity. The road bridge across the Warthe was badly damaged, limiting movement across the river, and there was also increased Soviet air activity. The experiences of a sapper in the Altstadt were probably typical of many of the garrison:

We used planks to prop up our position, which kept collapsing in the sandy soil. During this work a shell burst near me and buried me for a short while. However, my comrades quickly pulled me out again. Our losses meanwhile were so high that the number of soldiers was halved within a week by death or wounding …

Sometimes we had to parade briefly for a headcount. These were clearly measures to raise our morale, for we were somewhat depressed. From our positions on the Warthe bridges we could see how the Neustadt was being systematically destroyed by artillery fire. There were fires everywhere. The biggest blaze came when the railway sleeper depot caught fire, giving the dying town a ghostly light.

We had become used to dead comrades, but it was different when women or children were hit. I had to experience a shell splinter hitting a baby in its mother's arms. I was also strongly moved when a soldier was hanged from an A-frame for plundering. His girlfriend was shot in front of the Catholic church.

Our provisions were becoming more meagre. There was hardly any warm food for us any more and a loaf now had to be shared between eight of us. The last meat I remember was strips of raw, albeit briefly smoked horsemeat … That was why we sometimes searched the cellars of abandoned houses for food; but always in great fear of being punished for looting.[33]

Late on 19 February, the first civilian evacuation via the narrow corridor to the west was carried out; Reinefarth issued strict instructions for all those who gathered for evacuation to be carefully checked to prevent any of his garrison taking the opportunity to try to escape. Only two vehicles were available, and it took several hours for those who had gathered to make their way to safety.

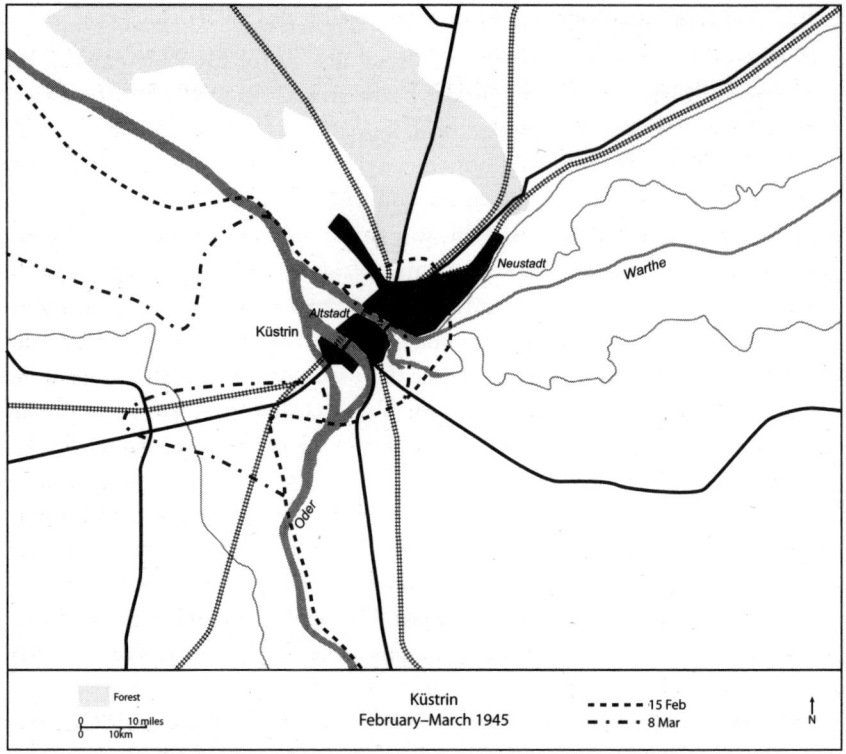

Küstrin
February–March 1945

Forest

0      10 miles
0    10km

- - - - 15 Feb
- · - · 8 Mar

N

There were further evacuations over the following nights, but the waxing moon and clear nights made the endeavour increasingly risky. Nevertheless, all but perhaps a thousand civilians were able to leave.

In the last week of February, the besieging forces were reinforced by troops who had completed the capture of Poznań. The weight of artillery fire increased and on 6 March Soviet forces attacked the Neustadt and again the following morning. Despite their superiority in numbers and firepower, they made little progress; as had been the case in so many urban battles during the war, even modest numbers of defenders could put up determined resistance. With the attacking forces suffering heavy losses, treatment of defenders who fell into Soviet hands was often brutal, as one German soldier near the badly damaged road bridge across the Warthe described:

> Four or five members of my company were captured by the Russians … on the east bank of the Warthe. One of them, whose mother tongue was Polish, was able to understand the Soviet soldiers. They argued as to who should take the prisoners

back and then, as nobody wanted to, they switched their submachine-guns to single shots and shot them one after the other. Only the witness was able to save himself as, thanks to his knowledge of the language, he realised early enough what was going to happen. Knowing the area well ... he threw himself desperately into the water and swam across.[34]

In heavy fighting, the Red Army slowly reduced the German positions in the Neustadt. Late on 11 March, groups of defenders attempted to escape towards the west. Some managed to reach the Altstadt and others experienced a hazardous journey over several days before they reached and crossed the Oder, linking up with other German forces outside the siege perimeter; many such groups were rapidly wiped out by the Red Army. Fighting continued in the ruins of the Neustadt for several days more, even as Soviet forces began to gather for an assault on the Altstadt. By now, Reinefarth had less than half his original defence force left; most of his artillery had been lost, and there was almost no ammunition left for the remaining heavy weapons. To add insult to injury, the Germans realised that many of the shells with which the Red Army was hammering the remaining defenders were of German origin: Chuikov's Eighth Guards Army had amassed hundreds of captured German guns and tens of thousands of captured shells, and was putting them to good use.

When Heinrici reached the headquarters of his new command on 22 March, Himmler subjected him to a rambling lecture about the overall situation and described what he had personally achieved in glowing terms. During the conversation, news arrived that the Red Army had renewed its attacks and had closed the narrow corridor to Küstrin; Himmler simply passed the telephone to Heinrici, telling him that he was now in command of the army group. As Heinrici investigated further, he learned that the Soviet attack had – at great cost – battered its way through the German line and that a counterattack by 25th Panzergrenadier Division and the *Müncheberg* Panzer Division was underway. But the following day, the Red Army started to push the two German divisions towards the west.

Both the Red Army and the Wehrmacht now gathered their strength – the former for a definitive attack to overrun Küstrin, the latter to make one last despairing counterattack to break open the siege ring. The German operation, under the aegis of Ninth Army, was intended to assist the remnants of the garrison in a breakout; by contrast, *OKH* insisted that the fortress had to be held. Moreover, *OKH* ordered that the attack should be combined with an assault out of the beleaguered Frankfurt-an-der-Oder to the south with the intention of isolating and destroying the Soviet Eighth Army. By travelling to Berlin, Heinrici was able to persuade Hitler not to transfer 25th Panzergrenadier Division to

Frankfurt for this operation. The relief attempt was under the control of the tireless Decker's XXXIX Panzer Corps, whose headquarters had moved to the region. On 27 March, the Germans attacked; at first, they made good progress, but were then driven back with heavy losses – the axis of attack had been anticipated by Chuikov and the Soviet anti-tank defences had spent the intervening days preparing for the battle. Küstrin remained isolated.

Hitler's already difficult relationship with Guderian broke down completely. As news arrived in Berlin of the failure of the attack towards Küstrin, a furious Hitler blamed it on Busse at the headquarters of Ninth Army. There had been too little artillery preparation, he lectured Guderian. When the chief of the general staff pointed out that ammunition for prolonged artillery preparation was simply not available, Hitler raged at him that he should have ensured that sufficient ammunition had been delivered in good time. Guderian responded by showing that all the shells available had been sent to Ninth Army, whereupon Hitler retorted that if artillery preparation wasn't to blame, then the attacking troops were responsible for the failure. Guderian's assertion that the heavy losses suffered by the attacking formations demonstrated that they had not lacked determination was rejected.

The following day – 28 March – Guderian was summoned back to Hitler's bunker together with Busse. Overnight, Guderian had submitted a detailed report refuting Hitler's arguments about poor artillery preparation, but the Führer now returned to the issue, raging at Busse for not conducting a longer preparatory bombardment. Guderian interrupted angrily, and Hitler ordered the room cleared, leaving just three men – Guderian, the Führer, and Keitel. According to Guderian, Hitler then told him that he was to depart on six weeks' sick leave immediately after the conference. When the other officers returned, the briefing resumed, though there were no further accusations thrown at Busse or Guderian.[35]

It was the end of Guderian's military career. He surrendered to American troops on 10 May and although Soviet officials wished to have him charged with war crimes, there was no appetite for this amongst the Americans and the British.[36] He joined a group of other senior Wehrmacht figures headed by Franz Halder, who had been one of Guderian's precursors as chief of the general staff; the group worked for the US Army Historical Division and produced numerous documents and publications about the war from the German perspective. Guderian denied any personal involvement in war crimes. He specifically stated that the infamous 'Commissar Order' – which required all suspected Soviet commissars to be singled out and executed out of hand if there were the slightest suspicion that they were encouraging non-cooperation – was not passed to his panzer group in 1941. This is a straightforward falsehood. The order was distributed to all army and panzer group commanders and they were required to pass it on to their subordinates. The conduct of operations against partisans in German rear areas – in which large numbers of civilians, particularly Jews, were murdered – was no different in areas controlled by his forces than any other sector of the front. As chief of the general staff from mid-1944, he was heavily involved in the suppression of the Warsaw Uprising and took no steps to restrain the murderous activities of men like Reinefarth. After the war, he tried to justify the manner in which Germany had fought, claiming that Germany had been fighting for its very existence and had been defending Europe against the spectre of Bolshevism; he was one of many prominent former Wehrmacht commanders who attempted to place the blame for all war crimes on the SS and rear area formations, distancing themselves and regular Wehrmacht formations from any such deeds. He died in 1954.

Guderian had hoped that his replacement as chief of the general staff would be the very capable Wenck, but he was still recovering from his injuries sustained in his road crash. Instead, the role was given to General Hans Krebs, who was also recovering from recent wounds. Krebs inherited an unenviable situation, with the war being lost on all fronts. In the west, the Americans and British had crossed the Rhine in strength. On 7 March, American troops had captured a damaged but intact bridge over the river at Remagen, but it seems that this surprised the Western Allies as much as the Germans and the exploitation of this windfall was uncertain at first.[37] Further crossings – including a major airborne operation – followed. German resistance to the Western Allies had generally been strong after the Wehrmacht recovered from its disastrous defeat in France in 1944, but was now far more patchy. In some sectors, German troops still put up fierce resistance, but in others they had clearly reached the point where junior commanders and soldiers could see that further fighting was pointless. The number of men surrendering rose rapidly and Hitler's angry response was to consider breaking with the Geneva and Hague Conventions – he believed that if he did so, the Americans and British would stop treating prisoners so leniently and this might harden the will of soldiers to continue fighting. It took the combined arguments of most of his close entourage to dissuade him. But as Guderian departed for his period of sick leave, the front line in the west was disintegrating. The remaining industrial production from the Ruhr region ceased as American and British forces swept forward. The Ruhr region would be encircled in early April; the breakout from the Rhine by the Western Allies and the elimination of the Ruhr pocket would account for over 320,000 German troops for the loss of just 10,000 American and British casualties.

In Küstrin, there had already been tentative discussions about a breakout. Soviet attacks continued even as Decker's divisions made their futile attempt to break through the siege ring. The island in the middle of the Oder was abandoned by the defenders, leaving just the Altstadt in German hands. A fresh order arrived for Reinefarth stating that the fortress was to be held to the bitter end, but he chose to ignore it. He told his subordinates that they could conduct a breakout on their personal initiative in the hope that by doing so, he wouldn't personally be blamed for the abandonment of the city. On 29 March, most of the Altstadt was in Soviet hands and that evening, the remnants of the garrison attempted to attack towards the west. The breakout took the Soviet troops in their path by surprise, but the escape attempt rapidly degenerated into chaos. At one point, unaware of the breakout, German artillery to the west started shelling the area, adding to German losses. Nevertheless, Ninth Army reported the following morning that about 1,000 men had reached their lines.

Immediately, orders were issued for the arrest of Reinefarth and other senior officers of the garrison. Characteristically, Busse, the commander of Ninth Army, simply passed on the instructions to his subordinates. Leutnant Victor Hadamczik, who was serving with 20th Panzergrenadier Division, was summoned by Oberst Georg Scholze, the division commander:

> Oberst Scholze ordered me to take two vehicles and two or three men to look for the Küstrin garrison men fleeing through our lines and take them to certain collecting points. He came up close and said: 'Should the commandant of the fortress, an SS officer, be among them, bring him to the division command post.'
>
> During the course of the morning a vehicle carrying an SS-General approached and I informed him of my task. He told me: 'You surely have enough to do,' and had me show him on the map where the command post was. When I reported back to the command post late that afternoon, I was asked about the SS-General. He had not reported there and Scholze threatened me with court-martial for not fulfilling his orders.[38]

The battles around Küstrin cost the Germans about 20,000 dead, wounded and taken prisoner; the Red Army lost a similar number killed and wounded. The outcome was that the Soviet units now held a wide bridgehead across the Oder. Although the bridges had been destroyed, they were either repaired or replaced by new crossings within a couple of weeks. The Germans attempted to portray the fighting as having been essential to disrupt the Soviet plans for a swift advance on Berlin, but in reality, any such rapid thrust had already been abandoned before the siege began. Reinefarth was detained and arrested and sentenced to death for abandoning the fortress. However, the sentence was not carried out. At the end of the war, he surrendered to the British. The Polish government demanded his extradition in connection with his conduct during the suppression of the Warsaw Uprising, but the Western Powers refused; they intended to use him as a witness at the upcoming Nuremburg Tribunals. He was briefly investigated by the Western Powers for war crimes but there was no appetite to proceed and he was released. He became a successful politician in West Germany and then worked as a lawyer, despite repeated demands from Warsaw for his extradition. He died in 1979 without ever facing charges for his crimes, including the massacres of civilians in Warsaw during which he wrote that had his troops had more ammunition, they would have been able to kill even more people.

# CHAPTER 13

# LAUBAN

In the last days of February, Konev's attempts to overrun the last parts of Silesia continued to be frustrated. The slow progress of his armies was due to a multitude of factors: the terrain was favourable for defensive warfare; the ground that had been frozen hard during the triumphant drive across southern Poland into Upper Silesia was now increasingly muddy and difficult for all vehicles, even those with tracks, to traverse; the Soviet units were far from full strength and the long supply lines meant that it was almost impossible to stockpile sufficient ammunition and fuel for sustained high-tempo operations; and in the centre of the region covered by 1st Ukrainian Front, the fortress of Breslau was an increasing drag on the attempts to advance.

Many of these factors were of course beyond Konev's control, but he decided to try to deal with those that he could address. The main one was Breslau. The previous policy of bypassing isolated German formations and leaving them for second echelon formations to mop up was impractical; the second echelon was now badly depleted with much of its strength transferred to the first echelon in an attempt to keep the strike forces as strong as possible, and Konev decided that as a minimum, Breslau had to be encircled tightly – the larger the area under German control, the greater the level of interference with the advance of his armies. Accordingly, orders were sent to Third Guards Tank Army. Once again, Rybalko was ordered to carry out a sudden change of axis for his tank units. He was to divert some of his armour to drive towards Breslau from the west. At best, this might result in a sudden collapse of the defences; as a minimum, it would drive the Germans into a smaller pocket.

The command and control of Konev's armies in this phase of the war was not as precise as the Front commander wished. In some sectors of 1st Ukrainian Front – for example, with Gordov's Third Guards Army around Glogau – the army commanders were able to balance the need to drive the Germans back towards the west whilst isolating bypassed German units. In others, this proved far more problematic. Rybalko's tank army in particular was suffering from the consequences of multiple changes of direction of advance, resulting in delays and the consumption of time and fuel. Whilst some formations of the tank army were turning east to push back the Breslau garrison into a tighter perimeter, the rest of the army fought its way towards the city of Lauban, frequently clashing with German forces. Taking full advantage of the cover provided by woodland and numerous small villages, German infantry successfully engaged the Soviet armour at close range with their lethal *Panzerfausts*. Rybalko made good use of his excellent working relationship with Konev to point out that he needed to concentrate his resources better; the Front commander agreed, and Sixth Army was left with sole responsibility for the Breslau encirclement.

Perhaps trying to make up for this lost time, Rybalko was now ordered by Konev to reach the city of Görlitz on the Neisse River. To achieve this, he decided to try to push forward as rapidly as he could, intending to cross the river either side of Görlitz. First, he had to cross the Bobr River; VI Guards Tank Corps would then move to seize a bridgehead over the Neisse to the north of Görlitz, while VII Guards Tank Corps turned first to the southwest to capture Lauban and then proceeded east to reach the Neisse to the south of Görlitz.[1] His third major formation – IX Mechanised Corps – was still regrouping after its diversion towards Breslau, and he hoped to be able to feed it into the battle once it caught up. His tank brigades were now far from full strength and the combined arms armies were still lagging some distance behind, but the Germans were also surely all but finished. One last effort before the spring weather softened the ground would leave his forces poised to burst into the German heartland after they had been replenished.

The consequence of the increasing dislocation amongst Soviet forces was that the Wehrmacht was given invaluable opportunities. Many German units that were caught up in the Red Army's advance in January were utterly torn apart, either being destroyed completely or reduced to such a weakened state that they were of little military value; there was now a greater chance for these units to withdraw relatively intact. And as the advancing Soviet armoured formations became isolated from the combined arms armies struggling forward in their wake, there was a possibility of mounting effective counterattacks – provided, of course, that sufficient units could be assembled in a timely manner and given sufficient fuel and ammunition for such counterattacks. At the end of the winter of 1942–43, Manstein had conducted a series of such counterattacks across eastern Ukraine with striking success; even with weakened panzer divisions at his

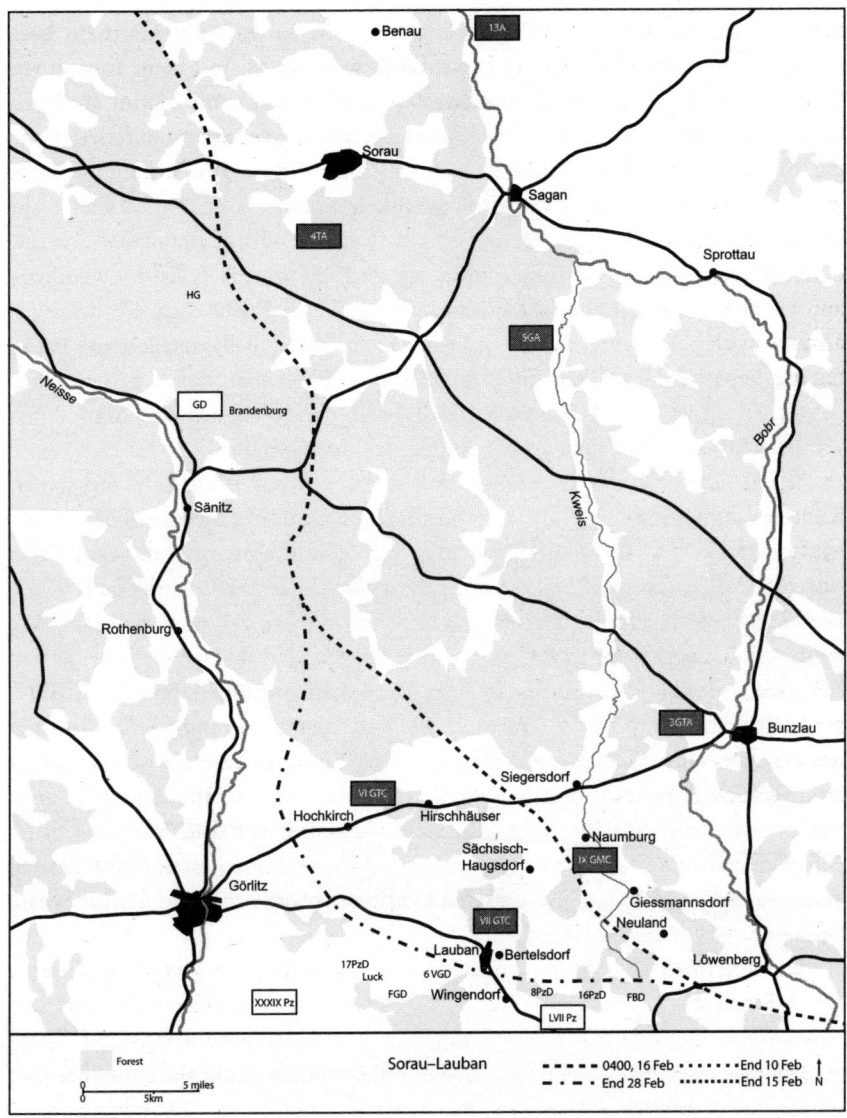

Benau

13A

Sorau

Sagan

4TA

Sprottau

HG

5GA

Neisse

GD
Brandenburg

Kweis

Bobr

Sänitz

Rothenburg

3GTA

Bunzlau

Siegersdorf

VI GTC

Hochkirch          Hirschhäuser

Naumburg

Sächsisch-
Haugsdorf

IX GMC

VII GTC

Giessmannsdorf

Görlitz

Neuland

Lauban   Bertelsdorf

Löwenberg

17PzD
Luck        6 VGD

XXXIX Pz        FGD   Wingendorf        8PzD    16PzD   FBD

LVII Pz

| Forest | | Sorau–Lauban | – – – – – 0400, 16 Feb | • • • • • • End 10 Feb |
| --- | --- | --- | --- | --- |
| 0        5 miles | | | – • – • – End 28 Feb | • • • • • • • End 15 Feb   N |
| 0    5km | | | | |

disposal, he was able to inflict a major defeat on Soviet tank formations, and it subsequently took several months for those units to recover their strength. Would such an opportunity arise once more?

After the failed counterattacks on either bank of the Oder River, the *Grossdeutschland* Panzer Corps found itself in the thick of the fighting against

Lelyushenko's Fourth Tank Army. Between Glogau and Lüben, there were repeated encounters between the two sides, and on one occasion it took the timely intervention of four Stuka dive-bombers, armed with 37mm anti-tank cannon, to beat back a Soviet spearhead that was threatening to cut the German line of retreat towards the northwest. Nevertheless, there were too many Soviet units moving forward and the Germans were levered back from the Oder to the Bobr, both inflicting and suffering losses. The line of the Bobr proved to be indefensible and Lelyushenko's units crossed at several points where they succeeded in capturing intact bridges. Colonel Nil Danilovich Chuprov's X Guards Tank Corps surged west and reached the town of Sorau (now the Polish Żary); Lelyushenko claimed the destruction of a German panzer division, but the remnants of 20th Panzergrenadier Division were able to withdraw intact towards the west.[2] The tank army commander also described how his men seized an aircraft factory in the town where they found 200 partially assembled planes, but this claim seems unlikely. He specifically described how there were many Messerschmitt Bf-109Fs in the factory, but production of this variant had ceased by the summer of 1942; moreover, whilst there were numerous factories producing Messerschmitt aircraft – in Regensburg, Leipzig, and Vienna during 1945 – there were none in this part of Silesia. If such a stockpile of aircraft was captured, it is likely they were damaged planes being stripped down for parts.

The two divisions of the *Grossdeutschland* Panzer Corps pulled back towards the west past the southern edge of Sorau. They found themselves separated by a group of Soviet tanks and immediately launched a counterattack with the *HG* Panzer Division striking from the north while the *Brandenburg* Division deployed its assault guns to the south. The Soviet armour was 62nd Guards Tank Brigade, which had just liberated a prisoner-of-war compound near Sorau, freeing several thousand French and Soviet prisoners. One of the officers in the brigade described the battle with the two German divisions, which took place on 16 February:

> During the morning, the enemy launched fierce attacks from three directions simultaneously: from the east, west, and south. The infantry and tank attacks were supported by massive artillery and mortar fire, and air strikes. The battle for the eastern outskirts [of Sorau] was particularly intense, where two regiments of enemy infantry and 30 tanks were active. In a fierce battle that lasted many hours, my battalion and its supporting artillery battery held their positions. The enemy suffered great damage: ten tanks were left ablaze and more than 150 soldiers were killed. We lost three guns, and numerous killed and wounded in the brigade staff.[3]

It is highly unlikely that any German attacks in this phase of the war enjoyed 'massive artillery and mortar' support, and although the Luftwaffe intervened occasionally, its impact was usually modest. By contrast to this description of the fighting, some German accounts claimed the complete destruction of the Soviet tank corps; the reality was that both sides suffered substantial casualties, but the German divisions were able to continue their withdrawal towards the west, having perhaps inflicted a stinging blow against 62nd Guards Tank Brigade.[4]

The armies on either flank of Lelyushenko's tank army – Thirteenth Army to the north and Fifth Guards Army to the south – were now catching up, allowing Lelyushenko to operate on a narrower frontage. His forces spent a valuable day regrouping and bringing forward ammunition, and the *Grossdeutschland* Panzer Corps took full advantage of this respite to reorder its battered ranks. The southern flank of the corps was on the Neisse River at Sänitz (now the Polish Sanice), and from here the front line ran first towards the northeast before turning north, enclosing a substantial bridgehead on the east of the river.

Lelyushenko barely mentions the battles that followed in his memoirs, merely commenting that the conquest of Lower Silesia was completed by 20 February, but other accounts differ. Vasily Ivanovich Zaitsev, the battalion commander who described the fierce fighting near Sorau, became involved in a bitter struggle for Benau, a short distance to the north of Sorau. He was told that the German *SS-Polizei-Brigade Wirth*, consisting of two weak regiments, had advanced into the gap between the Soviet tank army and Thirteenth Army in the north and had isolated the headquarters of XI Rifle Corps. After clashing with a small group of German tanks to the west of Benau, he was able to make contact with the surrounded Soviet riflemen and was then joined by a group of five JS-2 tanks, adding them to his 11 T-34s. On 19 February, he attempted to clear the Germans from Benau:

> Progress towards the centre of Benau was slowed by stubborn enemy resistance. As we approached a stone house, which together with its outbuildings had been transformed into a miniature fortress, the Nazis opened a heavy fire when we demanded they surrender. Savich [the commander of the JS-2s] had to break open the entrance with his gun in order to take the small fortress. Knocking out the Germans in this manner from each subsequent house, we moved towards the town centre ...
>
> At dawn on 19 February, enemy infantry in battalion strength attacked my group. Our massed fire didn't stop the enemy. Despite losses, a dense wave of enemy soldiers rolled towards us. The outcome was decided by two 37mm anti-aircraft guns.[5]

At the same time that Zaitsev was driving the Germans from Benau, the rest of Fourth Tank Army attempted to break into the German bridgehead on the east bank of the Neisse. The first attack on 18 February made little or no progress and was resumed the following day. In the two days that followed, there was further heavy fighting throughout the sector, with the Germans slowly being driven back to their bridges over the Neisse. Despite constant pressure, it proved possible for the rear area units of the *Grossdeutschland* Panzer Corps to cross safely to the west bank while the Soviet attacks were held at arm's length; finally, after beating off Lelyushenko's formations, the survivors of 20th Panzergrenadier Division, the *HG* Panzer Division, *Brandenburg* Panzergrenadier Division, and the disparate improvised groups of police units and *Volkssturm* were also able to pull back over the river, destroying the bridges behind them.

The successful fighting withdrawal of the *Grossdeutschland* Panzer Corps was largely possible because Lelyushenko was unable to concentrate sufficient strength to pin down the German formations while moving other units into position to overwhelm them. Inevitably, the Germans took great solace from their successful withdrawal, but the reality was that although the pause that followed permitted both sides to replenish their units, the improvement in fighting strength of the German formations was modest; by contrast, Fourth Tank Army would be brought back to full strength before the end of March. The Soviet commander had a great deal to give him a sense of real achievement: since the second week of January, his formations had covered a huge distance in less than seven weeks – 275 miles (443km) in a straight line, and far more along the snow-choked roads of southern Poland and Silesia. Dozens of tanks were still awaiting recovery having been abandoned through breakdowns, fuel shortages, and battle damage – these would soon be back in service. It is therefore entirely understandable that the irritating sense of frustration at the last phase of the great advance led to just the briefest mention in Lelyushenko's personal account; naturally, he preferred to focus his attention on the days of great success. By contrast, the Germans could take great satisfaction from their ability to extract their units more or less intact and to form a new defensive line along the Neisse River, but they could do nothing to hide the reality that they had been smashed in battle and driven back a huge distance.

Further south meanwhile, the German units falling back across the Bobr River to Lauban were struggling to catch their breath. Two battlegroups, roughly at regimental strength, succeeded in escaping from Liegnitz as Soviet forces stormed the city, and then faced a difficult march to the Bobr. Late on 15 February, the exhausted soldiers reached the river close to the town of Löwenberg and crossed to the west bank, where they made contact with elements of 17th Panzer Division. There was no time for rest and the infantrymen were ordered to take up defensive positions to the west of Lauban. They were fortunate; the Soviet 57th Guards Tank Brigade and 23rd Guards Motorised Rifle Brigade reached and swept through Löwenberg shortly after and crossed the Bobr to the south of the town. Without a pause, they continued along the highway from Löwenburg towards the west, encountering little resistance until they reached the village of Wingendorf, just a short distance from Lauban. Here, they ran into the German soldiers who had pulled back from Liegnitz and a battalion made up of *Feldjäger* (military police) and there was a brief but fierce battle. Both sides took losses before the Soviet troops pulled back.[6]

After its tribulations in the retreat from the Vistula, 6th Volksgrenadier Division had withdrawn over the Warthe River at Sieradz and was then transferred swiftly further west, reaching Glogau on 22 January. Here, it had a moment to pause and regroup. Many of its personnel were dead or missing. Some had surrendered to the Red Army, and other missing soldiers had been co-opted into the ranks of other German formations – there was a substantial group with 19th Panzer Division, who would serve with that unit until the final surrender. In a similar manner, Generalleutnant Brücker took the opportunity to round up stragglers from other units retreating to Glogau and used them to try to bring his ranks back to fighting strength. The pause didn't last for more than a few days, and 6th Volksgrenadier Division's headquarters was soon ordered to move to Sagan, where they were told they would receive replacement drafts; understandably, most of the division's remaining officers were doubtful that any meaningful reinforcements would appear. A battalion from the division remained in Glogau, holding a bridgehead over the river, until the advancing Soviet forces forced the evacuation of the town.

In Sagan, Brücker was able to assess the remaining strength of his division. Most of the infantry were gathered within the ranks of 58th Grenadier Regiment, with sufficient men to form barely a battalion. Several hundred men of the division's 6th Artillery Regiment were present, but without any guns. Other elements such as the signals battalion and logistic services were also far below strength and had lost all their equipment. Brücker's doubts about the appearance of replacement drafts proved to be correct; instead, he was told that he was to send staff officers further to the rear to organise the disparate bands of *Volkssturm* into units that could serve in the division. The gunners were reorganised into an infantry battalion, but there was a general raising of spirits when news arrived that the division was to receive two anti-tank units. At the time, the anti-tank battalions of many infantry divisions had been armed with the highly effective *Hetzer* tank-hunter, but hopes that the reinforcements would be armed with these or similar weapons proved to be unfounded. Instead, the two 'tank hunter units' consisted of men from different units that had disintegrated in preceding weeks, armed with personal weapons and *Panzerfausts*. Brücker and his officers distributed them amongst the *Volkssturm* to provide them with a degree of stiffening.[7]

Whilst the *Panzerfaust* was a poor substitute for a motorised long-range weapon, it was nonetheless highly effective. The early versions had an effective range of just 30m, but the later models fired a larger projectile up to 100m.[8] They were thus of maximum value in urban and forested areas where German defenders could engage enemy armour at close range, and it is estimated that up to 70 per cent of Soviet tank losses in German towns and cities during 1945 were caused by *Panzerfausts*; this reflected both the efficacy of the *Panzerfaust* and the reduced numbers of conventional anti-tank guns being deployed by the Wehrmacht. The less well-known *Panzerschreck*, roughly equivalent to a western bazooka, had a slightly longer range, but was available in smaller quantities; it too was a highly effective tank-killer, able to penetrate the armour of any tank deployed against the Wehrmacht.

The efficacy of the *Panzerfaust* was widely known in Soviet tank units by 1945. Isai Borisovich Stratievsky, an infantry officer, recalled after the war that the tank crews feared German troops armed with these lethal weapons and were constantly asking for infantry support whenever they entered areas where close-range ambushes were likely – over 8 million *Panzerfausts* had been produced and cost just 25 Reichsmarks each. Close cooperation between armour and infantry was needed to overcome *Faustniks*:

> The Germans were lying down in a ditch near the highway. On the other side of the road to our left, they had a machine-gun which swept the road with flanking fire and didn't allow us to move forward to knock them out. Two men tried to run across the highway and were cut down immediately by the machine-gun. Then the platoon commander, Erokhin, said to me, 'I'll try,' and he managed to run a few metres before he was killed. I reported the situation via the field telephone and three tanks came to our aid. A tanker climbed out of one. 'Who's senior here?' 'I am, Lieutenant Stratievsky.' 'Climb onto the tank and if you spot a *Faustnik*, hit the armour with your rifle butt and we'll stop.'
>
> We moved along the side of the road and along the highway there were wooden structures. There was a *Faustnik* in one and we spotted him. There was a special lever on the *Panzerfaust* that you moved to set the range but this German was struggling with it and the tankers cleared him away with their guns and

machine-guns. We crossed the highway and the tanks drove straight along the ditch in which the Germans were hiding. They took revenge for everyone at that moment, for Erokhin and the other fallen soldiers.[9]

The hollow charge of the *Panzerfaust* and *Panzerschreck* could burn through up to 200mm of armour if it struck at the right angle, and even incomplete penetration could be lethal – the charge often resulted in metal fragments or 'spall' being blasted from the inside of the armour, and these would then fly around the confined space of the tank with deadly effect, and the concussion from the explosion was also highly disabling. Increasingly, any Germans captured with *Panzerfausts* were killed out of hand by Soviet soldiers.

Additional reinforcements for 6th Volksgrenadier Division came in the form of Luftwaffe personnel from a nearby airfield; as the division retreated, it encountered several hundred ground crew and promptly organised them into infantry platoons. As the Soviet units approached Bunzlau, Brücker ordered an immediate counterattack with his division reserves and the Soviet units were temporarily driven back a short distance. To the southeast of Bunzlau, a small village was defended by the soldiers of an improvised battalion from 6th Volksgrenadier Division, commanded by Hauptmann Wilhelm Buhl. There were fierce clashes with losses on both sides, but for the moment the Germans managed to hold their positions. Nonetheless, the report from Buhl to division headquarters was hardly encouraging: he reported that his command had been reduced to just 30 riflemen. When he was asked what had happened to the rest, particularly the Luftwaffe personnel who had been incorporated into his battalion, he replied that most of them had disappeared during the night.[10]

In Bunzlau, Brücker encountered a police battalion on 10 February and added it into his division. Like the Luftwaffe personnel, the police officers disappeared the next morning without any warning. But finally, some proper reinforcements arrived in the shape of a company of *Hetzers* accompanied by a few half-tracks. Another battalion of infantry, commanded by Hauptmann Werner Erpenbach, was absent and was assumed to have been lost, but it suddenly appeared having made a long journey from Glogau. Brücker's division remained far from full strength – in particular, it still had no artillery – but it was in significantly better shape than it had been just a day or two before.

Despite the widespread confusion, the retreating German units succeeded in destroying most of the bridges over the Bobr. However, there were still sufficient intact crossings for Rybalko's tanks to continue their advance. Although the main road bridge in Bunzlau was destroyed when 6th Volksgrenadier Division retreated over the river through the town on 11 February, an intact railway bridge was captured just to the north of the town. The leading Soviet tanks rumbled over to the west bank, but from here the railway line that crossed the Bobr at this bridge ran through hilly countryside and it took two days for the Soviet troops to reach Siegersdorf, roughly midway between Bunzlau and Lauban. Erpenbach and his battalion headquarters staff were briefly surrounded by the advancing Soviet units but were rescued by the Volksgrenadier division's *Hetzers*. Two of the precious vehicles were lost in the fighting.

Another bridge to the south of Bunzlau fell into the hands of a Red Army group that pushed on to Naumburg. The village was garrisoned by another mix of improvised units reinforced by the tireless Erpenbach, who was badly wounded in the fighting. Some of the German defenders were distinctly unconventional: about a dozen boys aged 14 volunteered to fight the Soviet units. At first, they were used as guides for 6th Volksgrenadier Division's reconnaissance units, but many were then armed with *Panzerfausts* and sent into action against the constantly probing Soviet armour.[11] The Kweis River runs north through this area, and although it is a modest stream, it nonetheless provided the Germans with a useful series of positions on which to anchor their line. Some Soviet tank units succeeded in crossing, but the few fords they discovered were rapidly rendered too muddy for other units to follow.

By the end of 16 February, the remnants of German 17th Panzer Division – in reality, barely enough to form a single medium-strength battlegroup – had arrived, giving Brücker some much-needed support. Early on 17 February, a counterattack gained some ground against the Red Army. Nevertheless, with the other Soviet armour at Siegersdorf now probing south, it was impossible to hold Naumburg and the German positions here were abandoned late on 17 February. The pursuing Soviet tanks moved within shelling range of Lauban; at this stage, Brücker was able to report that his division fielded five weak rifle battalions, though they had little by way of heavy weapons. The left flank of the division near Siegersdorf continued to be held by the *Hetzer* company.

There was now a brief pause while both sides attempted to strengthen their units in the area. Brücker's division, strung out in a north-facing line, was almost exhausted and any meaningful Soviet attack would probably have broken its ranks, but the Soviet units also needed to regroup. On 18 February, 17th Panzer Division mounted a limited counterattack, driving back a dangerous group of Soviet units that had been threatening the western flank of the German position. But to date, the Germans had been sparring with just part of Rybalko's Third Guards Tank Army. The other units were now concentrating in the area, greatly tipping the numerical balance of power in favour of the Soviet forces. However, on a battlefield with dense patches of woodland, rolling hills, and numerous villages – with Lauban itself just to the south – numerical superiority was not as effective as it would have been on more open terrain. The Germans fell back on their traditional military doctrine, as an officer of 6th Volksgrenadier Division described:

> The one tactic that seemed to offer us chances of success in our difficult situation was to exploit every opportunity to attack and counterattack. Every occasion that the enemy was exposed had to be exploited immediately. The enemy's methodical, slow movements proved most useful. We could risk a great deal that would not have been possible if dealing with an enemy composed of German troops.[12]

There were several factors at play here. The German doctrine of swift counterattacks was almost proverbial, with opponents of German armies having long and often bitter experience of the speed with which such attacks could be mounted. The hesitancy and lack of determination to push forward in strength by Rybalko's army was due to several factors. Firstly, its formations were far from full strength and were constantly in danger of exhausting their limited fuel and ammunition. A report from one of the leading corps of the army made this clear:

> [The corps] has not had replenishment with new equipment and replacement parts for tanks and self-propelled artillery, or time for rest and recovery. Its motorised resources and soldiers have greatly reduced combat effectiveness. Daily battles have severely eroded the strength of motorised infantry units and the crews of fighting vehicles. Large quantities of technical material and replacement parts are required to restore units to combat-ready condition. Preparation for each offensive phase requires a minimum of two to three days of preparation, which has not taken place during this period. As a result, the efficiency of the offensive has been greatly reduced. The ground gained by the troops has been insignificant, and often they haven't been able to advance.[13]

Secondly, many formations were still strung out far to the east due to the frequent direction changes imposed by Konev and were still making their way forward over badly degraded roads, with further delays at the choke points of river crossings. Thirdly, it seems likely that there was a degree of war-weariness creeping in. The Soviet units had taken part in a hugely successful sweep across Poland in an offensive that seemed to have torn apart the Wehrmacht; more than half the remaining distance to the German capital had been covered. Surely the end of the war was close – and in such circumstances, it was understandable that the thoughts of so many soldiers turned to the question of their personal survival. Many Red Army veterans later described how they had simply assumed that they personally were unlikely to survive as they fought their way west across the devastated landscape of the Soviet Union, but there was now the prospect of an end to the fighting. In such circumstances, the earlier fatalism was increasingly replaced by hope of living to see an end to the war.

The Red Army reached Lauban on 17 February from the north and northeast, bringing the vital east-west railway line under artillery fire. It was a modest town of fewer than 20,000 residents, many of whom had already left for the hoped-for safety of places further west. The commandant of the small garrison was a reservist, Major Max Tschuschke, who had been in charge of a training battalion stationed in the town. Most of his men had already been sent to the front line and he was left with just a handful of *Volkssturm* and stragglers. Nonetheless, he showed commendable energy in mounting a fierce defence. For several days, there was heavy street fighting; the *Volkssturm* defended their homes bravely, but at a high cost. A small number of German tanks and assault guns joined the defenders, but after accounting for several enemy tanks they were soon knocked out. Another group of reinforcements consisted of two battalions of men who had previously been excused military service on medical grounds. These soldiers had stomach or ear disorders, and they were grouped together in the hope that sufficient medical support could be provided for their similar ailments for them to be able to fight. Although the 'stomach battalion' fought well, the ailments of the soldiers resulted in them rapidly becoming completely exhausted, necessitating their withdrawal. The 'ear battalion' proved more resilient; it fought in Lauban with some distinction, and then remained part of 6th Volksgrenadier Division until the end of the war.

Further reinforcements for the Germans arrived in the shape of a panzer battalion from 8th Panzer Division. Major Walther von Lossow, commander of the division's panzer regiment, later recalled what must have seemed an almost surreal march to the new battlefield:

> In relatively warm weather, nature was stirring everywhere in the early spring. The beautiful Silesian landscape with its low mountains was bedecked with fresh greenery and leaves on the willows. There were no shots, no sounds of battle to be heard. Everything was peaceful. One couldn't have guessed that just a few hundred metres further to our left, the enemy was wreaking havoc in a small hamlet of just a few houses.[14]

The last two *Hetzers* of 6th Volksgrenadier Division were lost at the end of February due to mechanical breakdowns, thus depriving the division of its last motorised anti-tank resources. Just in time, an anti-aircraft regiment arrived from the west, allowing Brücker's division to fight off attempts by Soviet armour to try to bypass Lauban to the west. Nevertheless, by the beginning of March most of Lauban was in the hands of the Red Army. To date, German reinforcements had arrived in a trickle, barely sufficient to enable combat units to remain in action, but finally more substantial help appeared. Even as 6th Volksgrenadier Division was slowly being driven back towards Lauban, plans were afoot for a large German counterattack. Nehring, whose XXIV Panzer Corps had escaped destruction in January by undertaking its epic march across central Poland to link up with the *Grossdeutschland* Panzer Corps, received fresh instructions on 27 February, as Nehring later recalled:

> Orders arrived for a new mission: an attack to liberate Lauban in order to restore the railway line running across Silesia. To that end, *Panzergruppe Nehring* was created, adding XXXIX and LVII Panzer Corps as well as a few infantry divisions.[15]

Oberst Hans von Luck was commander of an eponymous battlegroup, largely created from parts of 21st Panzer Division. He and his men had been involved in heavy fighting in the west since D-Day before being transferred to the east. Here, they experienced a shocking introduction to the harsh regime imposed by Schörner in Army Group Centre. Several vehicles were in a workshop undergoing repairs and Luck sent one of his senior NCOs and a few drivers to collect them. A few days later, one of the drivers returned to the battlegroup:

> In tears, hardly able to control his voice, he said, 'We were sitting together in the evening, after we had made sure that the last vehicle would be finished during the night, in a little inn, eating our day's ration and talking about the future, our homes and all the other things that soldiers talk about. Suddenly the door was pushed open and in rushed a staff officer with some military policemen. "I am Chief Judge Advocate under the direct orders of Generalfeldmarschall Schörner. Why are you sitting about here while up at the front brave soldiers are risking their lives?"
>
> 'My platoon leader replied, "I was ordered by my regimental commander, Oberst von Luck, to bring some armoured vehicles that are being repaired here up to the front as quickly as possible. Work will be going on through the night. We'll be able to go back to the front tomorrow morning."
>
> 'The judge advocate [said] "Where is your movement order?"

'[The NCO's] answer: "I had it from the commander by word of mouth."

'The judge advocate [replied]: "We know about that, that's what they all say when they want to dodge things. In the name of the Führer and by the authority of the commander in chief of Army Group Centre, Generalfeldmarschall Schörner, I sentence you to death by shooting on account of proven desertion."'[16]

The NCO was then shot by the military police accompanying the judge advocate and the rest of Luck's men were forced to dig a grave. Luck angrily demanded the name of the judge advocate, but Generalleutnant Werner Marcks, commander of 21st Panzer Division, refused to take any action.

At about this time, Schörner felt it necessary to send a signal to all army and corps commanders:

I now have a sufficiently clear picture of the attitudes and condition of all troops and staff, in addition to an overview derived from my frequent changes of command.

I note that on this part of the Eastern Front in particular there are some magnificent troops who fight under capable and courageous leaders and face every situation not only with bravery but with a revolutionary determination that has always characterised great times. This marks the kind of achievements that we require, especially in the sixth year of the war.

On the other hand, some formations have declined so dramatically that I have never seen such changes in similar circumstances, and they are more characteristic of the Romanian armed forces than our National Socialist army, which is fighting on German soil in the life-or-death struggle of our great people ...

Almost four years of an Asian war have given the front-line soldiers a different outlook, as once the fighters had before Verdun and on the Somme. These years have hardened them and fanaticised them in the fight against the Bolsheviks. Prisoners are no longer taken on the Neisse these days. The political soldier has developed during the eastern campaign, as had already emerged in the west [in the First World War] and founded the National Socialist front ...

However, this revolutionary movement appears to have passed some people by without leaving a trace. I do not see the required adjustment to the blood-soaked earnestness of the existential struggle that we are engaged in today. There is still a degree of indifference to political and military events amongst the staff that gives the impression of being leftovers of a bygone era. The search for comfortable quarters where one can play landowner, for good food and other comforts, for the opportunities to have sexual relations with foreign whores, a constant celebration of so-called birthdays, contrasted with the exigencies of the front line, are like a slap in the face for front-line soldiers. This must stop immediately ....

    I will no longer tolerate any euphemisms. I am clearly calling for fanaticism, nothing else.[17]

After the loss of his NCO, Luck learned that he and his battlegroup were to form part of the planned attack at Lauban. He later wrote that the plans described this as merely the first phase of a larger operation. After successfully recovering Lauban, reopening the vital railway line and destroying a large part of the Soviet armour that had pushed west, the offensive would be continued to lift the siege of Breslau. The besieged city lay 75 miles (141km) to the east; the experienced officers whose units were being sent to the region knew that whilst retaking Lauban seemed within the limits of what could be achieved, a thrust to reach Breslau – attacking through the various armies of Konev's 1st Ukrainian Front – was utterly utopian.

    The precise genesis of the counterattack at Lauban is unclear. The expression 'Success has many fathers: failure is an orphan' has been attributed to figures as varied as George Washington, Generalfeldmarschall Paul von Hindenburg, and John F. Kennedy, but originates from Tacitus' biography of his father-in-law Agricola: 'It is the singularly unfair peculiarity of war that the credit of success is claimed by all, while a disaster is attributed to one alone.'[18] Given the almost legendary status that the Battle of Lauban assumed after the war, it is surprising that no senior German commanders attempted to claim sole credit for its origins. By contrast, there is clear information about the roles of Guderian and Himmler in the creation and development of *Sonnenwende*. Given the scale of troop movements that took place, it is likely that the plan was drawn up by staff officers at Army Group Centre. Natzmer had become chief of staff after the death of Xylander, and arguably hadn't been in post for long enough to have a sufficiently detailed view of the situation to come up with a plan for a major counterattack. His operations officer, Oberst Georg Freiherr von Weitershausen, had been with the headquarters since the last week of January, and would certainly have at least been involved. The operation would be conducted under the aegis of Seventeenth Army and Schulz, the army commander, was described in one account as being responsible for drawing up the plans together with his chief of staff Generalmajor Joachim Schwatlo-Gesterding and operations officer Oberst Kurt Tarbuk. In any event, it would be the headquarters of Seventeenth Army that had operational control of what became known as Operation *Gämse* ('Chamois'). However, Schulz was wounded in a Soviet air attack at the end of February and control of *Gämse* passed to Nehring.

Regardless of its origins, *Gämse* attempted to take advantage of the relative isolation of the Soviet armoured forces that had penetrated into Lauban and were in the area immediately to the north and east of the town. Here too there is a degree of confusion. Accurate knowledge of the location and identity of the Soviet units was essential for the success of any counterattack, and many of the officers of 6th Volksgrenadier Division, which had been heavily engaged in the battles around Lauban, believed that they were facing the Soviet Sixth Tank Army. They grimly joked about the coincidence of numbers – their weak 6th Volksgrenadier Division was facing the Sixth Tank Army.[19] In reality, Sixth Tank Army – renamed Sixth Guards Tank Army in September 1944 – was operating further south in the Soviet advance towards Vienna. Other German accounts, by contrast, correctly identify the Soviet units around Lauban as belonging to Third Guards Tank Army. But it was clear that until the combined arms armies of 1st Ukrainian Front caught up, there was a brief window of opportunity for a counterattack that might catch the Soviet armour in a disadvantageous position. The plan was for a strike to the north either side of Lauban; the two German pincers would then meet on or beyond the main east-west highway to Bunzlau, *Reichstrasse 115*.

The two panzer corps that were being assigned to Nehring's command had both been involved in recent failed German attacks, as had many of their divisions; Decker's XXXIX Panzer Corps was part of the force that attacked in Pomerania as part of *Sonnenwende*, and Kirchner's LVII Panzer Corps had fought alongside Saucken's *Grossdeutschland* Panzer Corps in the attempt to eliminate Lelyushenko's bridgehead across the Oder River at Steinau. Between them, these corps would control several divisions. To the southeast of Lauban, LVII Panzer Corps took up positions facing north. From east to west, it fielded *Führer-Begleit* Panzergrenadier Division; 16th Panzer Division; and 8th Panzer Division. In addition, it controlled what remained of 408th Division, which had fought as part of Kirchner's corps in the failed attacks on the Oder, and the independent 103rd Panzer Brigade. The combined armour of these divisions was substantial, with over 300 tanks and assault guns. To the southwest and west of Lauban was XXXIX Panzer Corps, with Brücker's 6th Volksgrenadier Division forming its front line. Behind this, Decker had, from east to west, *Führer-Grenadier* Panzergrenadier Division; *Kampfgruppe von Luck*; and 17th Panzer Division. The total armoured strength of the corps came to about 100 tanks and assault guns.

The planning and execution of *Sonnenwende* was severely hampered by supply problems, but there appears to have been little difficulty in gathering sufficient ammunition and fuel for *Gämse*. The divisions arrived and deployed within days of the plan apparently being drawn up, and Brücker was only informed about the counterattack on the eve of the assault. The dates of the various battles that unfolded around Lauban are inconsistent, with variation between different accounts. Too many division diaries have been lost for a definitive, accurate timetable to be established, and the description below is based upon a general amalgamation of the various accounts.

Late on 1 March, as German tanks began to move forward, there was still some confusion about the precise positions and identities of the Soviet units in their path. Only VII Guards Tank Corps had been definitively identified in and immediately to the north of Lauban, and the positions of other Soviet units to the northwest and north of the town were not known with any clarity. Accordingly, 17th Panzer Division was ordered to carry out a reconnaissance probe to the north, past the left flank of 6th Volksgrenadier Division. After moving forward barely two miles, the division – now commanded by Generalmajor Theodor Kretschmer, who had inherited the division from Brux when the latter was wounded and taken prisoner in January – reached *Reichsstrasse 115*. Near the village of Hohkirch, a column of Soviet armour was strung out along the highway, presumably waiting for dawn on 2 March before driving west.

The Soviet tanks were from VI Guards Tank Corps' leading unit, 51st Guards Tank Brigade; the rest of the corps was on the same highway further to the east. After a brief radio conversation with Decker at the headquarters of XXXIX Panzer Corps, Kretschmer was ordered to move to the west and to block the highway. At the same time, *Kampfgruppe von Luck* and *Führer-Grenadier* Panzergrenadier Division were ordered to attack the Soviet column. As a murky dawn broke on 2 March, the German assault struck the Soviet armoured column, which was taken completely by surprise. The Germans claimed to have destroyed over 60 tanks and assault guns for modest losses.

As this battle was raging, German units moved to recapture Lauban; an essential part of *Gämse* was the reopening of the railway line running through the town. This task was delegated to 103rd Panzer Brigade supported by a few infantry battalions, including elements of 6th Volksgrenadier Division. The assault took the Soviet units in Lauban – a brigade of VII Guards Tank Corps – by surprise, but the initial rapid advance resulted in increasingly heavy fighting. Nonetheless, the town was back in German hands by the end of 2 March, though most of it had been reduced to rubble and ashes. Wilhelm Hubner, who had grown up in Lauban, was aged just 17 and was a member of a *Volkssturm* battalion that was involved in the battle:

> The fighting was almost face-to-face. There was fighting for house after house. In all, 48 Russian tanks were destroyed – that's a lot for a small town. And you can

imagine the destruction of houses and the like – and of people. Amongst other things I was a messenger, moving around even at night and through fog. Because I knew the ground, things were relatively easy for me, thank God. Directly beyond [the town] was a small area of woodland, where we played as children – it was the ideal place for children to play. We played at war and in the evening we talked about how things might be if there were weapons lying around everywhere. And in 1945 that became a cruel reality. It was a terrible battlefield. We messengers were billeted in the cellar of the Pestalozzi School with the commander and his staff ... I had to find good routes and I had to know where the front line was at that moment and where streetfighting was because from one hour to the next nobody knew for sure who was in which specific block – our side or the enemy – and I, just a little chap, stood there at the map table ...

You can't survive such situations without luck. Even though I knew the ground, it wouldn't have helped me at night if a shell had landed next to me. And I was lucky: bursts of machine-gun fire from disabled tanks flashed past a metre above my head and struck a fence – that was fortunate. Then four or five rounds from a Stalin Organ landed in the school playground. I was lying there in the middle of these bursting fireworks – not a scratch ... I was one of the smallest, and perhaps that was the reason the bullets passed over me. There were veterans who had taken part in every campaign who stopped me being over-eager and said 'Bubi' ['Lad'] – that's what they called me then – 'Bubi, stay back, we can't do much here. We're just trying to make sure the remaining women and children who are trying to get out can do so safely.'

At the end of the fighting, before I went back to the Hitler Youth, I received the Iron Cross from the commander in the courtyard of the Pestalozzi School.[20]

The divisions of Kirchner's LVII Panzer Corps, to the southeast of Lauban, also commenced their offensive on 2 March. Most of 8th Panzer Division had now assembled and struck north and northwest, seeking to move around the outskirts of Lauban. Remarkably, sufficient artillery ammunition had arrived for the division's artillery regiment to mount a brief but intense bombardment of the Soviet lines before Hax's division moved forward in two groups. As was the case elsewhere, the Soviet units seem to have been taken completely by surprise. Many Soviet tanks and assault guns were shot up before their crews could climb into them and others were destroyed at close range by the panzergrenadiers who accompanied the German attack. A little to the east was 16th Panzer Division, which had been recovering from its losses in January. Unsurprisingly, the division was still far from its establishment strength both in terms of manpower and vehicles, and many of its elements were still en route to the Lauban area.

Effectively reduced to a single battlegroup, this division also achieved near-complete surprise when it attacked during the afternoon of 2 March. In its path was the Soviet 54th Tank Brigade, and it was rapidly overrun.

On the eastern flank of Kirchner's corps and therefore the eastern flank of the entire attack was the *Führer-Begleit* Panzergrenadier Division. The small village of Neuland was rapidly captured, but fighting grew heavier as the Germans moved north into forested countryside. Repeated clashes with small groups of Soviet anti-tank guns slowed the pace of the advance and as the day progressed, it became clear that substantial Soviet forces were in position beyond the eastern flank of the German advance. With losses rising steadily from this flanking fire, Generalmajor Otto-Ernst Remer, commander of the German division, concluded that further attacks would be at too great a price. He ordered his men to regroup and prepare to resume their attacks the following day.

Meanwhile, the Soviet units were recovering from their surprise. Major General Vasily Vasilyevich Novikov, whose VI Guards Tank Corps was fighting to the northwest of Lauban, rapidly deployed his anti-tank guns in a series of *Pakfronts* in woodland to the south of *Reichsstrasse 115*. These were backed by the firepower of his three assault gun regiments. At the same time, he extracted the remnants of the tank brigade that had been badly mauled by the German attack and moved the rest of his corps into better positions. On 3 March, when the *Führer-Grenadier* Panzergrenadier Division attempted to resume its attacks towards the north, the *Pakfronts* rapidly destroyed several German assault guns and the advance was halted. The German division's commander, Generalmajor Hellmuth Mäder – who was awaiting the arrival of his replacement but remained in command of the division for the moment – spoke to higher commands, pointing out that continuing the attack as originally planned towards the north, with the intention of linking up with LVII Panzer Corps near Hirschhäuser and Siegersdorf, would result in increasing losses and was unlikely to succeed. Instead, he proposed turning east so that a link-up could be achieved more quickly. The disadvantage of this was that the original plan had envisaged the complete encirclement and subsequent destruction of all the Soviet armour that had crossed the Bobr and advanced towards Lauban, and a smaller encirclement would eliminate only a smaller proportion.

Perhaps due to Schulz, the commander of Seventeenth Army, being wounded immediately before the German attack began, there was a degree of confusion about decision-making. Decker, commander of XXXIX Panzer Corps, referred the decision to Nehring, who had overall control of the operation. Schörner had meanwhile travelled to the command post of the *Führer-Grenadier* Panzergrenadier Division but refused to give orders to change the operation, rightly pointing out that Nehring was in control and had a better overall view than he did. But Nehring passed the decision back to Decker on the grounds that as he was closer to the action, he should discuss the matter with Kirchner at LVII Panzer Corps and then use his judgement.

In many respects, Nehring was correct to delegate the decision to Decker; this was consistent with the German concept of *Auftragstaktik* with its emphasis on delegated decision-making. But this change of direction had consequences that were far greater than the mission that had been given to Decker. If he turned east instead of pushing on to the original objective, Kirchner's LVII Panzer Corps would also have to alter its plans, and therefore the person in command of both corps, i.e. Nehring, should have been responsible for the decision. Rather than telling Decker to discuss the matter with Kirchner, Nehring should have contacted LVII Panzer Corps and then informed both corps commanders of his decision. There is almost no mention of this incident in Nehring's biography or his personal account of the battle.[21] But regardless of whether Nehring was correct to defer the decision to his corps commanders, the almost inevitable decision was made after a further discussion between Decker and Kirchner. There was no point in trying to pursue the original objective with its high risk of casualties and delay, during which the Soviet units might withdraw to the north. Instead, Mäder's *Führer-Grenadier* Panzergrenadier Division was to turn east immediately while 17th Panzer Division effectively screened off the Soviet VI Guards Tank Corps.

Already, the claimed kills recorded by the German formations were impressive. The attack by Decker's units to the west of Lauban had allegedly accounted for at least 65 tanks and assault guns, and the eastern attack group added claims of many more. On 3 March, the *Führer-Begleit* Panzergrenadier Division changed the axis of its advance in accordance with the new plan. Remer ordered his left (western) battlegroup to attack towards Giessmannsdorf, while the right flank took up a screening role to prevent further Soviet attacks from the east. The division's armoured battlegroup reached the village in the late morning, and in its report later in the day it claimed to have found a group of unmanned T-34s parked amongst the houses. Giessmannsdorf was swiftly overrun.

Rybalko's army was trying to catch up with events. It was difficult for his headquarters to get a clear picture of what was happening; although Novikov's VI Guards Tank Corps seemed to have recovered from its mauling on the first day of the attack and was holding firm to the northwest of Lauban, the town itself was now back in German hands and communications with VII Guards Tank Corps in and north of Lauban had broken down. There had been hopes that the rifle divisions of Fifty-Second Army would be arriving to reinforce Third Guards Tank Army, but these were now not expected to reach Bunzlau until 4 March.

Even as these rifle units were arriving, the Germans continued their attacks. After regrouping, the *Führer-Grenadier* Panzergrenadier Division – to the northwest of Lauban – turned east, leaving 17th Panzer Division to guard against any attempt by the Soviet units along *Reichsstrasse 115* to intervene. To date, two of Rybalko's three corps had been engaged – VI Guards Tank Corps on *Reichsstrasse 115* and VII Guards Tank Corps in and around Lauban. Now, the eastward thrust by the *Führer-Grenadier* Panzergrenadier Division ran into part of IX Mechanised Corps. Again, the reports from the German battlegroup claimed an improbable number of Soviet assault guns had been destroyed. Regardless of how many were actually shot up, Decker's corps – forming the western pincer of the German assault – was now close to the village of Sächsisch-Haugsdorf, astride the road running south to Lauban.

At the same time, Kirchner's corps continued to advance from the east, albeit at a slow tempo. The terrain to the north of Lauban was forested, with few roads running towards the northwest. The leading battlegroup of the *Führer-Begleit* Panzergrenadier Division also encountered parts of IX Guards Mechanised Corps and by the end of the day was barely two miles from the German forces attacking from the west. But the Soviet units that had harassed the exposed eastern flank of the German division were now increasing their pressure and there was heavy fighting all along the protective German line running from Neuland in the southeast to Giessmannsdorf. Although the Soviet attacks were beaten off, the Germans suffered substantial casualties and much of the *Führer-Begleit* Panzergrenadier Division was effectively tied down. It would not be possible to reinforce the attack to link up with Decker's XXXIX Panzer Corps. Closer to Lauban, the units of 8th Panzer Division and 16th Panzer Division moved north towards Sächsisch-Haugsdorf. They were supported by the soldiers of 6th Volksgrenadier Division, one of whose artillery officers demonstrated both the lethality of the *Panzerfaust* and the iron nerves needed to use it at close range. One of his comrades wrote in a letter:

Today, Oberleutnant Bergmann left to go on leave. A few days earlier he had shot up a tank that had reached his B position – at a range of 5m. Two Russian T-34s approached his B position during the afternoon and halted near his barn. With the personnel of his B position and four *Panzerfausts* Oberleutnant Bergmann crept forward in the cover of walls, hedges and houses towards the first T-34. He fired the first *Panzerfaust* at the running gear, rendering it immobile. The second *Panzerfaust* penetrated the turret and the third struck the centre of the tank, whereupon it was blown into the air. Then Bergmann wanted to fire the fourth *Panzerfaust* at the second tank, but it wouldn't work. A misfire! Then, with loud cheers, Bergmann and his group rushed towards the tank, and it engaged reverse gear, firing all the time.[22]

By dawn on 5 March, communications between Rybalko's headquarters and VII Guards Tank Corps to the north of Lauban were reduced to intermittent radio contact; the situation with IX Mechanised Corps a little to the north was only slightly better. German artillery fire was sweeping the few roads to the north of the Soviet armour and heavy fighting continued in and around Sächsisch-Haugsdorf. During the afternoon, the various German attacks – the *Führer-Grenadier* and *Führer-Begleit* Panzergrenadier Divisions from the west and east respectively, and 8th and 16th Panzer Divisions from the south – took possession of the burning ruins, though not without suffering losses. Junior Lieutenant Stepan Mikhailovich Zaborev, a tank commander, had been in the thick of the fighting since the third week of February and had been credited with numerous kills, including the destruction of a Panther tank using a captured *Panzerfaust*. During the battles to the north of Lauban, his tank was destroyed together with its crew, though he was recorded as having shot up another two Panther tanks before he was killed.[23] Most of VII Guards Tank Corps was now definitively surrounded, with IX Mechanised Corps badly disrupted a little to the north. Rybalko sent liaison officers forward on foot to try to establish contact with his units; they issued orders for the survivors to break out to the north that evening. At the same time, VI Guards Tank Corps was ordered to make local attacks to try to tie down the German units to the northeast.

Fighting continued through the night and into 6 March. The Germans would later claim to have destroyed all of VII Guards Tank Corps, but many of its personnel escaped, even if they had to abandon their vehicles. Ivanov, the commander of the corps, was reported by the Germans – on the basis of radio intercepts – to have been killed, but he was amongst those who made their way to the north on foot. He had spent four months in hospital in 1944 after being wounded, and he would be wounded again before the end of the war, a month after his escape from Lauban.

Combat gradually died down across the entire sector. Although there had been talk of pushing on to Breslau – some of the fantasists in Hitler's entourage even dreamed of continuing the advance beyond Breslau into central Poland, linking up with triumphant German forces thrusting down from the north – there was little prospect even of reaching the Bobr, and had Nehring's group attempted to continue northwards they would have encountered the same terrain difficulties that had held up Rybalko's formations as they tried to advance south and west. As they pulled out, the badly depleted brigades and corps of Third Guards Tank Army handed over the sector to the rifle divisions of Fifty-Second Army and were moved to the rear. Here, they would be replenished and brought back to full strength in preparation for the final attacks into Germany. To a large extent, Konev's objective – to capture Lower Silesia – had been achieved. But the German counterattack at Lauban demonstrated beyond doubt that despite the approaching end of the war, and even in the face of the devastating losses suffered by the Wehrmacht in its retreat from the Vistula, the Germans were still capable of concentrating sufficient forces for powerful counterattacks against isolated and overstretched Soviet units.

The Battle of Lauban would become known as 'the last panzer victory' in German accounts of the war. As the Cold War developed in the 1950s and 1960s and translations of the German memoirs and descriptions of the fighting on the Eastern Front began to appear, these formed the basis for the prevailing English-language narrative and the numbers of tanks destroyed by Wehrmacht units were largely unquestioned. In the case of Lauban, matters were not helped by the manner in which Soviet accounts largely ignored the battle. Konev's account in his memoirs is very brief and is a clear attempt to place the blame for the setback at Lauban on the shoulders of Rybalko. His description suggests that despite suffering losses, it was the Red Army that emerged triumphant:

[Rybalko] decided to carry out a bold double envelopment of the entire enemy group around Görlitz with the two corps remaining at his disposal. It must be said that this decision was not one of Pavel Semyonovich's best. The fact is that even before this, VI Guards Tank Corps had already fought several intense battles on this axis without success. Now it was faced with essentially repeating the same task, but it had to attempt it with fewer forces, in a weakened state, and – of course – with even less reason to expect success.

The commander ordered the other corps, VII Guards Tank Corps, to cross the Kweis River and capture the city of Lauban. Fortunately, Rybalko soon realised his mistake and began to regroup his forces. However, by this time the situation in the area had changed dramatically for the worse. The advancing units of VII Guards Tank Corps were forced to engage in battles with approaching enemy armoured reserves in a series of encounter battles. And the remaining units of this corps, having encountered strong resistance along the river, had difficulty in crossing the Kweis.

Over the following days, the Germans transferred 8th Panzer Division, 408th Division, and 10th Panzergrenadier Division to this area, reaching the rear and flank of VII Guards Tank Corps and parts of VI Guards Tank Corps, and began to bypass Rybalko's army from the east. In short, the situation became very tense. Only with joint attacks from all three corps, with the support of troops from Koroteev's Fifty-Second Army, did Pavel Semyonovich finally manage to defeat the enemy group that had broken through northeast of Lauban and throw it back to the south.

During those days, finding myself in the forward command post of General Koroteev, I had the opportunity to assess personally the complexity of the situation that arose in Rybalko's sector. Everyone, including me, knew that many brigades of Third Guards Tank Army had only 15–20 tanks each. And yet the army commander came out of this unenviable situation with honour. We must give him his due: despite at first being somewhat overconfident, overestimating his own strength and underestimating the enemy, he later showed both sober judgement and enviable composure, and this ultimately allowed him to thwart the rather threatening plans of the Germans …

On the day when the Fascist German units began to penetrate into the rear of Third Guards Tank Army, Stalin called me and expressed concern: 'What is happening there with Third Guards Tank Army? Where are its units located?'

I replied that Rybalko's army was fighting particularly intense battles in the Lauban area, but I thought that nothing special was happening to it. 'The army is fighting in a difficult situation, but that's a common thing for tank troops.'

I took Stalin's call at the command post of Fifty-Second Army, not far from Lauban. I assured the supreme commander that if the situation became more difficult, we were on the spot and could take all necessary measures.[24]

As with so many accounts written after the war, this is a misleading version of events. It was on the orders of 1st Ukrainian Front – i.e. Konev – that Rybalko attempted to reach Görlitz and the isolation of his tank corps in Lauban owed more to the delayed arrival of IX Mechanised Corps than the intention to force the Neisse either side of Görlitz. The delay in the advance of IX Mechanised Corps was due to Konev ordering its diversion to compress the Breslau perimeter. It is also noteworthy that Konev's headquarters had informed Third Guards Tank Army on 1 March that it was to be pulled out of the front line for replenishment as soon as Fifty-Second Army could take up its positions. The clear implication in this is that no further advances were expected or required – in other words, the order for the drive onwards to Görlitz and the Neisse was no longer in effect. If Rybalko's army ended up in a precarious situation, this was more due to Konev redirecting one of its corps to seal off the Breslau encirclement than any failure on Rybalko's part.

Konev declared the Lower Silesian Operation to have ended a few days before the end of February, but this too is misleading. Whilst the Red Army made no further territorial gains after this date – indeed, *Gämse* resulted in the Soviet units being driven out of Lauban and the immediate environs – the fighting that erupted with the German counterattack must be seen as part of the same overall campaign. Nevertheless, Konev attempted to describe the operation as a success, though with some grudging praise for the ability of the Germans to coordinate their troops effectively even at this late stage of the war:

Let me summarise the results.

The Lower Silesian Operation lasted 17 days, from 8 to 24 February 1945. Not everything in it turned out as we had originally expected. The enemy, who suffered heavy defeats, managed to retain a foothold on the Oder line, put his defeated troops in order, brought up reserves, and managed to reorganise.

It would be wrong to belittle the degree of organisational skill shown by the Hitlerite command at this critical moment. But something else must also be kept in mind: hundreds of testimonies from prisoners confirmed the truly boundless cruelty and pure Fascism with which this organisation was conducted.

However, the collapse of the Third Reich was approaching inexorably. Despite the ever-increasing resistance of the Fascists and the fatigue of our troops, despite our incredibly overstretched lines of communication, despite the fact that during the entire operation there were only four days of flying weather and almost the entire burden of supporting the infantry fell on the artillery, which additionally still lacked ammunition – despite all this, the Front's troops broke the enemy's defences on the Oder with our right wing, overcame the intermediate defensive lines along the Bobr and Kweis Rivers, and reached the Neisse …

Compared to our gigantic leap from the Vistula to the Oder, the next leap – from the Oder to the Neisse – seems much more modest. But we must not forget two factors. Firstly, the second breakthrough was made by the same troops that had just marched from the Vistula to the Oder, without a single day of rest; secondly, during the 17 days of the Lower Silesian Operation, these troops, despite being at the limit of their physical strength, nevertheless moved between 100 and 150km [60 and 90 miles] closer to Berlin.

I am aware that there is an opinion that perhaps the Lower Silesian Operation should not have been carried out at all and it might have been more expedient to stop on the Oder, gather our forces, and then, breaking through the German defences, to cover the entire distance between 1st Ukrainian Front and Berlin in one fell swoop. But considering this, I in turn must ask: if we had not advanced forward from the Oder to the Neisse first at the cost of such tension and superhuman efforts, what would the last operation of the war, to reach Berlin, have looked like?

There is also an opinion that in February, we should have made a direct attack on Berlin. But the results of the Lower Silesian Operation completely refute this simplistic suggestion.[25]

The scale of the German success became the subject of huge differences of opinion. Soviet-era accounts rarely mentioned the battle at all. Where they did, they largely limited their accounts to mention that the weakened corps of Third Guards Tank Army fought off determined German attacks before defeating an attempt to lift the siege of Breslau. By contrast, German memoirs described highly unlikely numbers of destroyed Soviet tanks and assault guns. Hans von Luck claimed that his battlegroup accounted for 25 T-34s and that 17th Panzer Division destroyed a further 55 as they cleared the Red Army out of Lauban. This suggests that the elements of VII Guards Tank Corps that were engaged in and around Lauban lost at least 80 tanks. However, the daily reports submitted by the tank corps in the last week of February suggest that its strength at that moment was just 55 tanks in total. Even allowing for some reinforcements, this figure dates from before the bitter fighting in northern Lauban which cost the tank corps serious losses. The German figures for tank and assault gun kills on either flank of the battle are also improbably high. Collating the Soviet reports for the first eight days of March, the recorded losses of Third Guards Tank Army in the daily returns from its tank brigades come to a total of 84 tanks and 31 assault guns. Whilst this falls far short of the German estimate of a total of at least 250 tanks and assault guns, it still represents a considerable success, but even German accounts described the total haul of prisoners as disappointing, with fewer than 180 men captured. It is impossible to know whether this reflected, at least in part, the trend that Schörner had noted with approval, that German soldiers were now taking fewer prisoners than before.

The Germans recorded their losses as just ten tanks and assault guns, but this figure is as suspect as their estimates of Soviet vehicles destroyed. It was normal for German armoured units to describe only totally destroyed vehicles as losses; those that had been damaged and recovered were recorded elsewhere. If those damaged vehicles were later written off or abandoned, their numbers were not added to the recorded 'total losses'. Based on after-action reports from other battles, particularly when the Germans retained control of the battlefield at the end of the fighting and were therefore able to recover their damaged tanks and assault guns, it is likely that if only ten tanks and assault guns were totally destroyed, at least as many again would have been disabled in the fighting. Given the widespread shortages of spare parts in Germany at the time, only those with modest or minimal damage would have been returned to service.

In the immediate aftermath of the battle, there were many in the upper echelons of the German administration who were keen to make the most of this rare triumph. Amongst these was Goebbels, the propaganda minister, who visited the ruined town on 8 March with Schörner. Wilfred von Oven, a close acolyte of Goebbels, accompanied his master on the trip and some of his comments highlight the surreal world inhabited by the likes of Goebbels, and how – like politicians in most eras – they made highly selective use of what they were told:

There are fresh traces of fighting everywhere – and of the unspeakable atrocities committed by the Bolsheviks. It was particularly grim in the town's convent. All the nuns were raped, many were killed. Soldiers of all branches of the Wehrmacht gathered in the town square for a rousing speech by the minister. A 16-year-old Hitler Youth, in grey uniform, the recently awarded Iron Cross pinned to his tunic, shook the minister's hand. Schörner greeted him with enthusiasm. Afterwards, the minister drove to the front escorted by Schörner. He heard machine-gun and rifle fire, seeing the enemy with his own eyes for the first time. He spoke to officers and men. They were all still aglow after their recent triumph. They still felt greatly superior to the foe. They all agreed – the Russians ran just like in the good old days. The commander of the *Führer-Begleit* Division, General Mäder, said: 'Give me a thousand men, *Herr Reichsminister*, and I'll beat the whole Russian Army with my division!' When asked if he had sufficient weapons, he answered defiantly, 'Weapons? I don't lose any weapons if I have enough men!' The minister got not only the best impressions from these visits to the front, but also clear ideas. Front-line officers once more confirmed that it's soldiers, not weapons, that are needed in the front line. In the past we mocked Stalin for sending some of his soldiers unarmed into battle, but like so many of his measures this was wise. The soldier will find weapons for himself in battle, but weapons without soldiers are easily captured by the enemy. Another lesson is that it is wrong to allow battle-hardened veteran divisions to be bled white and to be crushed, and then to replace them, rather than replenishing the old formation ...

Schörner was full of confidence. If he had two [more] armies, he promised he could throw the Russians back to Warsaw with one blow. 'We must succeed,' said the minister when he returned to Berlin, 'in getting these two armies set up. I know Schörner always delivers his promises. What he's achieved with his limited forces is admirable. We must try to liberate the territory of the Reich, to stop the Bolshevik flood. That's the most important thing. Then everything will still turn out well.'[26]

Despite being involved in bitter fighting, first with the defenders of Lauban and then against the German forces attempting to retake the town, the soldiers of VII Guards Tank Corps had carried out multiple atrocities against the civilians who had not managed to flee in time. A report from Seventeenth Army gave a few examples from Bertelsdorf, on the edge of Lauban:

> The houses in Bertelsdorf suffered little from shelling. All destruction was carried out deliberately by the Soviets during their occupation. Almost all of the apartment furnishings were smashed, laundry, books, money etc. were torn and thrown around on the floors or out of windows.
>
> Of about 40 women who lived there, only one sick woman (with a severe facial rash) was not raped. All other women were raped on average 20–25 times in the most brutal and vile ways during the 14 days of occupation. In one case ... the woman was shot in the lower jaw by Soviet soldiers because she defended herself against rape. When the woman collapsed, the other residents of the house were forced into a basement so that they couldn't tend to the injured woman. After about four hours, the woman dragged herself to the basement and, since the Soviets had now left, received first aid from the residents. Two days later, when she was lying in bed with a makeshift bandage and running a high fever, three Soviet soldiers in their early 20s appeared and raped her one at a time in the most brutal manner at gunpoint.
>
> In a second case ... a 20-year-old woman and her two sisters-in-law were raped by a Soviet captain who, according to another Soviet who identified himself as a doctor, was seriously ill with syphilis. One sister-in-law, who is a nurse, saw the captain receive injections against syphilis.
>
> All the statements collectively give an identical picture of the most brutal treatment of women: The Soviets always appeared in their rooms drunk with their trousers open and dragged the women away to rape them in other houses or amongst the trees or, in one case, in the presence of the victim's parents ...
>
> The Soviets paid no attention to the remaining male population, almost all of whom were severely physically disabled. They were simply asked if they were former wounded soldiers and if they had fought in Russia, they were to be shot.[27]

Throughout the fighting around Lauban and in the weeks that followed, the battle for Breslau, the city whose resistance had hindered Konev's offensive into Lower Silesia, continued. In terms of food stockpiles, Breslau was in a good position to endure a prolonged siege; the city and the entire region had been used extensively to rehouse German civilians who had been made homeless by air raids on cities further to the west, and consequently large quantities of food were stockpiled in the region. In addition to warehouses full of sacks of flour, there were 32,000 sides of pork, 150,000 rabbits, 150 barrels of fat, and 5 million eggs.[28] When the Soviet ring closed around Breslau, part of the garrison – a battlegroup from 269th Infantry Division – took advantage of the relatively loose encirclement to break out to the west. The attack was aided by a group of ten German assault guns, which were brought to a halt by fire from anti-tank guns about ten miles (17km) to the west of Breslau and had to turn back together with the infantrymen accompanying them. However, the bulk of the division's remaining infantry managed to slip through the Soviet cordon.

Ahlfen, who was now the fortress commandant, issued a proclamation to the soldiers and civilians who remained in Breslau that was published in the city's newspaper, the *Schlesische Tageszeitung*:

> What matters is the Führer's order to defend the fortress of Breslau to the end. We will carry out the mission of this bastion of German culture on the Oder, which brave German warriors have defended and held for centuries with their blood and willingness to make the ultimate sacrifice …
>
> Warriors of Fortress Breslau! This is all there is! This is about our people, and our beautiful German homeland! We wish to defend both to our last breath. So to battle, in defiance of death and the devil! We will meet the Red invader wherever we can. Their skulls will run with blood in the ruins of our beloved city. We fight for a just cause. We believe in victory and God will stand by our resolute souls.[29]

There were over 150,000 Germans trapped in the city, of whom over half were civilians. The total number of combatants was probably fewer than 40,000, and they faced six rifle divisions of the Soviet Sixth Army, commanded by Lieutenant General Vladimir Alekseevich Gluzdovsky. He had about 50,000 soldiers, but the battle would not be decided purely by the numbers of combatants. Sixth Army had over 1,000 artillery pieces with adequate – if not plentiful – ammunition with which to hammer its way into the city. There had been an attempt to take Breslau with a sudden rush on 14 February when XXII Rifle Corps attempted to race through to the city centre from the southwest, but this made little headway. Three days later, Gluzdovsky began his first formal attempt to reduce the German defences. Several villages around the edge of the fortress perimeter were overrun, but as the battle moved into the urban area the casualties of both sides rose rapidly. Three days of hard fighting saw Sixth Army capture much of the southern part of Breslau and the leading units were just three miles from the city centre before being brought to a halt. The final act of this phase saw a battalion of Hitler Youth – the so-called *Kampfgruppe Hitlerjugend* – mount a determined counterattack that was the subject of a bombastic report in the *Völkischer Beobachter*, one of the leading Nazi newspapers. The truth was that the inexperienced but fervently motivated teenagers were slaughtered in the fighting.

Gluzdovsky paused to take stock. The next assault would be made by ten specially constituted assault battalions, each supported by several field guns and assault guns. The men were lavishly armed with submachine-guns – although these were less accurate than rifles, their greater rate of fire more than compensated for this in the short-range clashes in the city streets. There was a brutal artillery bombardment of Breslau early on 22 February, and then the assault battalions moved forward. The defenders had been reinforced by a few hundred paratroopers who had been flown into Breslau; in reality, these were largely Luftwaffe personnel who had been retrained as infantry and were far from the elite paratroopers that had featured in so many battles in the past. They lacked machine-guns and heavy weapons and Ahlfen was doubtful of their combat value, but *Gauleiter* Hanke insisted on their immediate deployment. Over several days, the Soviet groups battered their way closer to the city centre, but the fortress continued to hold.

Ahlfen had imposed a regime of iron discipline, sentencing officers and soldiers to death for deserting their posts, but his relationship with Hanke had deteriorated badly. Hanke was convinced that Ahlfen lacked the will to continue resisting with the required level of fanaticism, a view that was apparently shared by Schörner. The army group commander decided that a new fortress commandant was required. His choice was a surprise.

Generalleutnant Hermann Niehoff, the commander of 371st Infantry Division, had been stunned when Schörner visited the headquarters of the division at the beginning of March. Far from congratulating Niehoff and his men for having withdrawn from the disaster that had unfolded in central Poland, he raged that 371st Infantry Division was a disgrace and summoned the officers to appear before him; several were arrested and others dismissed on the spot. When Niehoff protested, he too was relieved of command. Less than a day later, Niehoff received a telephone call from Schörner, informing him that he had been appointed as the fortress commandant of Breslau in place of Ahlfen. At first glance, it seemed a strange decision given that Niehoff had just been dismissed in disgrace, but Schörner saw him as a man who could be pressured more easily than his predecessor. He concluded the telephone call with a threat: Niehoff had a wife and five children, and if he failed to defend Breslau resolutely and to the last man, his family would suffer the consequences.

Before he flew to Breslau, Niehoff dined with Schulz, commander of Seventeenth Army. Schulz informed him that Schörner had promised that the siege would be lifted in three or four days, but added that in his opinion, it would take at least two weeks to prepare such an operation. Niehoff's first two attempts to fly into Breslau were thwarted, one by Soviet anti-aircraft fire damaging an engine of his transport plane and the other due to icing on the control surfaces. Finally, he reached his new command during the evening of 5 March, having to take cover when Soviet soldiers on the airfield perimeter brought his plane under fire. He met Ahlfen, whom he knew well, and the two men had a depressing conversation. Although Ahlfen had been ordered to fly out of Breslau immediately, he agreed to stay in the city for a few days to help Niehoff familiarise himself with the overall situation. He added a warning about *Gauleiter* Hanke:

> Despite little combat experience and having spent only a short time in the field, Hanke believes he's the supreme commander of the fortress. The judgement of the *Gauleiter* counts for more than the judgement of the military commander.[30]

As February turned to March and Nehring's divisions commenced their limited counterattack around Lauban, Hanke reiterated his determination to hold out to the end in a speech that was reproduced in Breslau's newspapers. He also made clear to Niehoff that he expected the Wehrmacht officer to be subordinate to him. A few days later, when Schörner and Goebbels trumpeted the victorious conclusion to the Lauban battles, Hanke celebrated and it must have seemed likely that, despite the misgivings of Ahlfen and others, a relief operation might be mounted successfully. By the end of the second week of March, this hope had faded. *Gruppe Nehring* was redeployed closer to Breslau to make just such an attempt, but crises elsewhere intervened, requiring the precious panzer divisions to be dispatched to other theatres.

In the meantime, the brutal house-to-house fighting around the siege perimeter continued with city blocks reduced to heaps of rubble changing hands repeatedly. The airfield on the western side of Breslau at Gandau continued to be held, though it was within range of Soviet troops near to its western perimeter, and supplies were flown in regularly. On many occasions, planes attempted to drop supplies by parachute, particularly when Heinkel He-III bombers were used – they were unable to land at Gandau due to the limited length of the runway. Inevitably many of the canisters landed either in no-man's land or behind Soviet lines. Isaak Zalmanovich Rabinovich was a mortarman in Gluzdovsky's Sixth Army and he witnessed one such air drop:

> Once in the dark, Vasya Sopov and I came across a large metallic container dropped by parachute that had landed in the crater created by a large bomb. The company commander looked into the container and said, 'It's full of shells!' We opened the container fully and found it was full of German 81mm mortar bombs, painted red. We added propellant charges to each bomb and used them in our 82mm mortars.[31]

The planes that managed to land also evacuated some of the wounded, and over 5,000 were brought out of the city during the siege. Other casualties, civilian and military alike, were tended in improvised hospitals in cellars and the concrete bunkers that had been built originally as air defence centres and air raid shelters. Soviet shelling and air attacks continued every day and amidst so much destruction, many within the city adopted an increasingly nihilist outlook. Weapons were repaired in the still-functioning *Fahrzeug- und Motoren-Werke* ('Automobile and Engine Works', usually abbreviated to FAMO) factory in Breslau, and it was even possible to retrieve unexploded bombs dropped by Soviet aircraft; the explosives were then extracted using boiling water and re-used in improvised demolition charges. One of the largest improvised creations of FAMO was an armoured train that mounted four 88mm guns, a 37mm gun, and four 20mm guns with a few machine-guns. Despite being slow and cumbersome, the train intervened repeatedly in the battles around the airfield, accounting for several tanks.

Gradually, the fighting dropped in intensity as Gluzdovsky was forced once again to accept that Breslau wasn't going to be overrun quickly. The bombardment of the defences continued and to interdict flights into and out of the siege ring, increased numbers of Soviet anti-aircraft guns were deployed to the west of the airfield at Gandau. At first, the loss rate of transport aircraft had been acceptable, with about an eighth of those used being damaged or shot down, but this rose steadily in the second half of March. But the tenacious defence of the city drew the attention and approval of senior Nazi figures; many felt that Hitler's criticism of the Wehrmacht for 'prematurely' abandoning fortresses was being justified by the manner in which Breslau continued to hold firm. It was particularly noteworthy, they insisted, that *Gauleiter* Hanke had imposed his authority upon the Wehrmacht. But despite all the defiant proclamations issued by Hanke and Niehoff, the general mood in the besieged city was of fatalistic hopelessness. One soldier wrote to his wife in her home to the north of Berlin:

> We are all going under, no one will get out of here alive. The devil gets all those who began this game. We are the losers. Even an idiot knows that it's all over, but they still order us to continue dying.[32]

At the end of March, fighting flared up once more. There was a particularly heavy bombardment before dawn on 1 April by Soviet aircraft; operating from airfields no more than 15 miles (25km) from Breslau, the pilots barely had time to reach bombing altitude before they reached their target. The bombardment continued all through 1 April – Easter Sunday – and was resumed at slightly reduced intensity the following day. By the end of 2 April, much of Breslau was burning. Under cover of this savage bombardment, the Soviet ground forces made another attempt to overrun the city's defences. The main point of attack was in the west, around the vital airfield at Gandau. Briefly, the commitment of the last local reserves – two weak battalions of *Volkssturm* made up mainly of teenagers – managed to stiffen the defences, but Gandau was overrun late on 1 April. The following day, as the Red Army continued to make gains in the west, the northern perimeter also came under increasing pressure, but the Germans were puzzled by the failure of the Soviet troops to push forward in strength as they had attempted in the past. The reason would become clear to the defenders only after the war: attention had switched to the imminent battle that would take place for Berlin, and Gluzdovsky was working with limited resources.

But despite the constraints on his forces, Gluzdovsky continued to grind away at Breslau. Air raids continued every day, increasing in intensity again on 9–11 April. Rumours continued to circulate from time to time of an imminent relief of the city, but few believed them. A group of women protested outside Nazi Party offices demanding an end to the war and the safe return of their menfolk; many were arrested, and an unknown number were shot.[33] Slowly, the perimeter shrank. Elsewhere, the war rapidly approached its end, with the death of Hitler at the end of April and the fall of Berlin, but to the frustration of Gluzdovsky and his men the battle for Breslau raged on, giving rise to a grim joke in his army:

> Victorious Soviet soldiers are on their way from Berlin to Moscow to take part in a victory parade. Suddenly, they hear explosions and machine-gun fire.

'Is that a salute to welcome us?' asks one soldier.

'No,' replies his comrade, 'It's just Sixth Army. It's still busy trying to conquer Breslau!'[34]

Ground attacks on the city had almost ceased, but shelling and air attacks continued. On 1 May, a radio broadcast from Hamburg informed the garrison and the surviving civilians that Hitler was dead. Many hoped that this would trigger an immediate end to hostilities, but Schörner and Hanke – the latter had been declared head of the SS by Hitler in his will after the *Reichsführer-SS* was dismissed from his posts at the end of April – declared that the fighting would continue. Schörner promised Niehoff that a relief column would arrive imminently, but despite his earlier apparent commitment to the cause, the fortress commandant had had enough. On 4 May, he met senior clergymen who pleaded with him to order the garrison to surrender. Niehoff sent two officers under a white flag to commence negotiations, and was then confronted by Hanke who demanded that they should continue fighting. He threatened to arrest Niehoff, who coolly replied that if anyone was going to be arrested, it would he Hanke. The *Gauleiter* backed down and asked what he should do. Niehoff suggested suicide, but Hanke refused.

On 5 May, there was another brutal aerial bombardment of the shattered city. As the planes roared away, a Soviet delegation crossed the front line, accompanied by German soldiers who had surrendered at Stalingrad, and issued a final ultimatum. Unless Breslau surrendered immediately, there would be a fresh assault that would be continued until all the defenders were dead. With increasing reports of men in the front line surrendering to their Soviet opponents, Niehoff ordered a formal surrender. The long, bitter siege was over.

Hanke, who had demanded that the city be held at all costs to the last drop of blood and that fighting should continue even after the fall of Berlin, flew out of Breslau in a small liaison aircraft that took off from an improvised airstrip within the city. Despite coming under fire, the plane managed to reach Schweidnitz. From there, he travelled on to Prague where, dressed in the uniform of a private of the SS, he joined a group that attempted to reach Germany. There are numerous stories of what happened next, but the most probable account is that the group was captured by Czech partisans on 6 May and Hanke was taken prisoner, though nobody recognised him. On 8 May, he was part of a group of prisoners that attempted to escape by climbing onto a passing train. Their guards fired on them; Hanke was one of three men who were wounded. The guards then beat them to death, completely unaware that they had killed the last *Reichsführer-SS*. Niehoff, the man who was bullied and blackmailed by Hanke and Schörner, became a prisoner of war. He remained in captivity until 1955.

The death toll in the fighting in Breslau is open to dispute. Approximately 6,000 defenders were killed and perhaps 23,000 were wounded; 45,000 armed men – a mixture of regular military personnel, *Volkssturm*, and Hitler Youth – were taken prisoner.[35] Thousands of these prisoners died in captivity. The civilian death toll is where the greatest variation occurs, between a low estimate of 10,000 and a high estimate of 80,000. Red Army losses were about 7,200 killed and 24,400 wounded.

# CHAPTER 14

# CONCLUSION: DEFIANCE AND DESPAIR

At the beginning of 1945, with the outcome of the Ardennes offensive still apparently in doubt, there were many in Germany who still believed that the fortunes of war would turn in their favour. By the end of March, that number had dwindled to a tiny core of diehards. What Guderian had accurately described as a house of cards had collapsed in the face of a tremendous blow. The resultant catastrophic defeat of the Wehrmacht in Poland inflicted irreparable damage on the forces struggling to hold back the armies of the Allies. The end was now just a matter of time.

Casualties suffered by the two sides in the Soviet advance across Poland were heavy. When Stalin and Zhukov declared an end to the Vistula-Oder Operation on 2 February, the Red Army claimed that it had lost a little over 43,000 dead or missing and a further 150,000 wounded or sick, giving a total of about 193,000.[1] The two operations that followed – in Pomerania and Silesia – added a further 219,000 Soviet casualties and 8,700 Polish casualties, a grand total of about 420,000 killed, missing or wounded. German losses are difficult to calculate for several reasons. The Germans didn't necessarily classify their campaigns in the same manner as the Soviets; records were lost in the chaos of the collapse of the Third Reich; and large numbers of *Volkssturm* simply disappeared in the battles. Many were killed or captured, while others threw away whatever uniforms and weapons they had been given and attempted to return to their families. Nevertheless, the best estimates suggest that German losses were at least as great as those suffered by the Red Army.[2] The number of civilian casualties – Germans, Poles, and forced labourers from all parts of Europe – is impossible to calculate.

Although the totals of dead, wounded, missing, and prisoners suffered by the two sides were comparable, the impact was of course far greater on Germany than the

Soviet Union. The Red Army greatly outnumbered the Wehrmacht at the beginning of 1945; it therefore suffered a lower percentage of casualties than its opponent. Moreover, the resources of the Soviet Union were incomparably greater than those of the rapidly shrinking Reich. The crushing blows dealt to the German war machine in the summer of 1944 – in Normandy and northern France in the west, and in Belarus in the east – had been sufficient to doom Germany to eventual defeat. The further losses of the first three months of 1945 were proportionately greater.

Nor was the damage purely in terms of human losses, bad though those were. As Speer had warned, the loss of Silesian industrial resources rendered any prolonged resistance impossible. Hitler and Goebbels continued to talk of mobilising all Germans to fight fanatically for their homeland, but such concepts had far less meaning in the industrial era than in previous conflicts. Without tanks and guns, without ammunition and fuel, and just as importantly without the training to use these resources effectively, even the most optimistic mobilisation figures had no value. Fuel for tanks and trucks had been in short supply for the Wehrmacht from the very outset of the war and was now almost non-existent. The loss of the Silesian coalfields, after the similar loss of other vital mines in the Saar region and elsewhere, almost paralysed what remained of the German railway network. Speer and his staff worked miracles to improve efficiency of transportation, but even their most innovative solutions could not compensate for the further crippling of mobility and the loss of vital industrial production centres.

Militarily and industrially therefore, the Vistula-Oder offensive was a fatal defeat for Germany. But the campaign also had other far-reaching consequences. It left the Soviet Union in control of almost all of the territory that Stalin had wanted to occupy before the war came to an end, and thus paved the way for the creation of the power blocs that would dominate European and world history for decades to come. Almost as soon as the Red Army's ground troops moved on to the west from the Upper Silesian industrial area, experts began to dismantle factory equipment for shipment to the Soviet Union. A large proportion of the equipment would never be used. In some cases, German prisoners who provided much of the labour force for the work deliberately sabotaged machinery; on other occasions, essential parts of factory production lines were left behind or had been destroyed in the fighting, rendering the rest of the equipment almost useless; and entire trainloads of equipment were left to rust in railway sidings all across the Soviet Union. Sometimes, this was because nobody knew where it should be taken, or even what it was for. Much of it was simply forgotten and abandoned.

The German defeats in Poland, Silesia and Pomerania had a major impact on fighting elsewhere. To bring some semblance of order to the shattered Eastern

Front, many divisions were moved from other sectors – Hungary, Scandinavia, and the Western Front – as reinforcements. These transfers weakened those sectors and this contributed to the rapid collapse of German defences everywhere. The Red Army could claim with considerable justification to have facilitated the advance of its allies on other fronts, and Soviet historiography repeatedly stressed the importance of this. The Soviet-era accounts generally downplayed the value of the contributions of the Western Powers. But just as victory in the west would have been impossible without the hugely costly Soviet victories in the east, those victories would have been far harder to achieve – indeed, they may have been impossible – without significant German forces being tied down in the west, without the impact of American and British air raids on German industrial centres, and without the vast quantities of armaments and other supplies that were sent to the Soviet Union.

The dark side of the Nazi regime was widely known by 1945, and the Soviet advance to and beyond the Oder ripped away any remaining doubts. In many respects, Poland represented a model for how German rule of much of Europe would have unfolded following final victory for the Wehrmacht. Much of the remaining population had been reduced to little more than serfs, working for the occupiers with little or no payment and liable to be transported far from their homes with dubious prospects of ever returning. The large Jewish population of Poland had been almost exterminated, with about 90 per cent dying during the war.[3] Large numbers of ethnic Poles also died. In terms of percentage loss of life, Poland suffered more than any other country in the Second World War, losing over 20 per cent of its population. Only about 10 per cent of the approximately 6 million deaths were caused by fighting; the rest were either deliberately killed or died because of malnutrition or mistreatment. The western parts of the Soviet Union that fell under German control saw similar atrocities. These had already been uncovered by the Red Army over the preceding two years as the Wehrmacht was levered back to the western frontiers of the Soviet Union, and the drive across Poland in early 1945 by the armies of Zhukov and Konev laid bare the full horror of what Hitler had intended for the rest of Europe.

The atrocities that were uncovered by the Red Army – and were then loudly proclaimed to a shocked world – drew attention away from the crimes committed by the advancing Red Army. Almost inevitably, the misdeeds of the Germans were so great that an attitude of *Vae victis* – 'woe unto the defeated' – was widespread. Even when information about mass rapes and random killings became known in the west, it was largely ignored. Some believed that the Germans had brought such retribution upon themselves; others simply dismissed it as anti-Soviet exaggeration. When German accounts began to appear in the

1950s and 1960s, they highlighted the terrible ordeal of ordinary Germans, but often included phrases that were just as misleading as the blanket denials by Soviet writers. On the few occasions that German writers acknowledged that crimes had been committed by Germany in the occupied territories, they often added that the atrocities suffered by Germans were many times greater. This is simply untrue, but elements of this narrative persist.

The rapes, murders, and looting that took place in Silesia, Pomerania, Prussia and elsewhere were merely the beginning of the suffering of the civilian populations of these regions. The Yalta Conference had cemented earlier plans by the Allies to deprive Germany of much of its territory, and there was no intention of permitting Germans to remain in the areas that were to become parts of Poland and the Soviet Union. Such 'ethnic cleansing' was explicitly accepted by all Allied Powers even before the final details had been agreed. Churchill spoke to the House of Commons in December 1944, i.e. before the Yalta Conference, telling the British parliament that it was only by carrying out the expulsion of German civilians that a lasting peace could be secured.[4] Both before and after the end of the war, Churchill claimed that such population movements could be carried out with the minimum of hardship to German civilians, but this proved to be no more than a pious hope at best and a cynical misrepresentation at worst. The numbers involved were huge. Nearly 3 million Germans would be expelled from Prussia, many of them enduring several years of Soviet occupation, starvation, and forced labour before they were permitted to leave. A further 2.4 million were driven from Pomerania and the area to the east of the Oder estuary, and nearly 4.7 million were forced to leave Silesia. They left behind them their dead; tens of thousands had died as the Red Army stormed through German cities and towns, and many more perished in the months and years that followed. They departed from the ruins of their homes and of German culture east of the Oder. Centuries of settlement along the Baltic coast and in Silesia were at an end. Poles who were being expelled from the eastern parts of pre-war Poland – now to be absorbed by the Soviet Union – were settled in the newly gained lands to the west and north, and German names were rapidly erased. In many cases, Polish names for cities and towns already existed; in other cases, names were invented and imposed. The German towns of East Prussia that came under Soviet control were given new Russian names. In some cases, this was to honour senior Soviet figures – for example, the ancient German city of Königsberg became Kaliningrad, named after Mikhail Ivanovich Kalinin, a senior member of the Politburo, and Insterburg became Cherniakhovsk to commemorate General Ivan Danilovich Cherniakhovsky, commander of 3rd Belarusian Front who was killed in the closing weeks of the war. Other towns were renamed by the Russians who were settled there, recalling their hometowns elsewhere in the Soviet Union.

Many senior German commanders survived the war and wrote their self-exculpating memoirs, attempting to blame Germany's misfortunes on Hitler and his inner clique. The accounts of men like Manstein and Guderian concentrated on their military prowess and paid almost no attention to the terrible crimes being committed behind the front line – the few mentions of mass killings were always blamed on the SS or paramilitary police formations. There is ample evidence of the widespread involvement of every part of the German military machine in atrocities; it is inconceivable that Guderian's claim that he knew nothing about most war crimes is correct. He had a close relationship with Speer during his years as *Generalinspekteur der Panzertruppen* and while he was chief of the general staff, and given the tension between mobilising German men to replenish the depleted ranks of the Wehrmacht and the need to keep factories functioning, he must have had discussions with Speer about how manpower could be released. He must therefore have known about the use of slave labour in factories all across the Reich and the occupied territories. But like many of his contemporaries, he succeeded in compartmentalising his knowledge. Even during the closing months of the war, when retreating German units passed columns of concentration camp prisoners struggling along frozen roads during the 'Death Marches', almost no memoirs made any mention of this. Only the recollections of the march survivors reveal such encounters.

Few were innocent of choosing to look away. Dietrich von Saucken, one of the few commanders in this phase of the war to emerge with credit for his military performance, sent a signal to Berlin after he took command of the surviving German forces in the Vistula estuary about the remaining prisoners from the concentration camp at Stutthof, demanding that they be removed as he lacked the means to feed them. Many of these prisoners were marched into the waves of the Baltic Sea and machine-gunned by their guards; others were loaded into open barges and sent to the west, where they were caught up in the tragedy of the sinking of the liner *Cap Arkona* by British Typhoon aircraft with the resultant deaths of thousands of Jews who had been crammed into the ship. Just as Guderian's claims of ignorance are impossible to believe, it is almost inconceivable that Saucken was not informed of the shooting of concentration camp prisoners on the Baltic coast or their shipment in open barges across the bitterly cold sea. He took no action to intervene and appears to have regarded the logistic difficulty of looking after the prisoners as being solved.

Such behaviour gives a small glimpse into the various factors that led to Germans at every level, from the ordinary soldiers in the front line to the high command, to continue fighting. Some like Schörner clearly remained committed to the 'fanatical' struggle to impose Nazi rule upon the rest of Europe, but they were in a minority. Many senior officers shared the attitude articulated by Reinhardt, who was dismissed as commander of Army Group Centre before it was renamed Army Group North. In the midst of the catastrophe that was engulfing his forces in East Prussia in January, he wrote to his wife about a refugee column that he had seen after a Soviet air attack. He described the dead and wounded, the wrecked wagons and abandoned belongings, and explained why he continued the hopeless struggle:

> The machine of duty, willpower, and the sense of obligation to use our last strength work automatically within us. Only seldom do we ever think of the bigger picture of 'what now'.[5]

Kurt von Tippelskirch, who was chair of the standing court martial in Torgau that passed judgement on the officers who ordered the abandonment of Warsaw, would return to front-line command in the last phase of the war in April. Even at this late stage, when he and Heinrici, commander of Army Group Vistula, discussed the overall catastrophic situation, they agreed that the only means of preventing further widespread destruction and death was immediate capitulation. But whilst Hitler remained alive, any such act was impossible and in any case pointless, at least on the Eastern Front. Faced with the certainty of imprisonment in the Soviet Union and fully aware of the atrocities committed by Red Army soldiers, many soldiers would refuse to lay down their weapons and would continue to fight. This would result in Germany's enemies declaring that the terms of the capitulation had been ignored and the fighting would then continue.

Commanding the last German forces in northern Italy, Generaloberst Heinrich von Vietinghoff was in no doubt that by March 1945, the war was irreparably lost. In such circumstances, it was the duty of the highest authority – i.e. Hitler – to bring the war to an end. If he was unwilling to do so, every person who could exert any influence or control over events had to act – 'In this situation,' he wrote after the war, 'the duty of obedience reached its limits. Loyalty to the people and to the soldiers entrusted to [the commander] was the higher duty.'[6] For Vietinghoff, the main obstacle in taking such action was that he feared his men would refuse to lay down their arms unless it was part of a general surrender. The repression that followed the July Plot made it almost impossible to coordinate action with like-minded commanders or to take soundings on the mood of the troops. Even at the very moment that he negotiated a separate surrender – he contacted American and British representatives on 29 April and agreed terms of capitulation on 2 May – he was still concerned that significant parts of his command would refuse to obey. But whilst he was prepared to take that risk, it would have been unthinkable for any commander on the Eastern Front to take such measures.

It is difficult to assess with any accuracy just how many soldiers would have defied orders and fought on. By 1945, young recruits in the German forces would have few memories of anything other than Nazi rule, and the control exerted by the Party on all aspects of their upbringing conditioned them in ways that are hard to imagine from a modern western perspective. Unquestionably, there was widespread weariness of the war. Reports reaching Berlin described how soldiers who had left the front line demanded food and other goods from shops in German towns and cities, telling the protesting shopkeepers that the war was as good as over and that ration cards were now meaningless. However, others remained determined to fight against what they saw as the unacceptable threat of Soviet occupation. Even as late as April 1945, many soldiers shared the opinion of a man in 12th Panzer Division in Courland who wrote to his family:

The war is only lost if we surrender. Even if Germany should surrender, would that mean the war was over for us? No, the horror would only be beginning and we wouldn't even have the weapons to defend ourselves. If we have weapons and confidence in the justness of our cause, nothing is lost. I believe firmly there will be a decisive shift in our fortunes. Providence, which sent us the Führer, will not permit all our terrible sacrifices to have been in vain and will never abandon the entire world to the destructive terror of Bolshevism.[7]

Mail to and from the front line passed through the hands of censors and letters were written in awareness of this, complicating how accurately they portray opinions. A report from one censor's office at the end of March classified over 91 per cent of letters as being 'colourless', i.e. free of any political nuance; of the rest, those that were critical of the regime were slightly outnumbered by letters like the one quoted above. But Goebbels' propaganda had latched onto the term 'providence' to account for the Führer's survival in July 1944. Surely the same providence wouldn't abandon Germany now, in its greatest moment of need?

There were other factors that inhibited senior commanders from taking matters into their own hands. When General Otto Lasch, the commandant of 'fortress Königsberg' in East Prussia, defied Hitler's orders to fight to the bitter end and surrendered the city on 9 April, he was sentenced to death *in absentia*, but perhaps more importantly his wife and two daughters were placed under arrest. The families of senior officers could therefore be considered hostages of the regime. Other officers were aware of the atrocities in the east and in some cases knew that the Soviet Union intended to prosecute them for specific crimes; in such circumstances, surrender to the Soviet Union was inconceivable and many continued to cling to the hope that by holding back the Red Army in the east, they were buying time for larger parts of Germany to come under the control of the Western Allies. At the very top of the German state, the future partition of Germany into occupation zones was already known; but field commanders would not necessarily have been aware of this and continued to hope that they might spare thousands of German civilians from the ordeal of Soviet occupation as well as giving their men a greater chance of surrendering to the Western Allies.

Whilst soldiers and their commanders struggled with the conflicts of their wishes to bring the war to an end and their fear of Soviet occupation and the constant threat of arbitrary justice at the hands of field courts martial, the senior Nazi Party officials whose power had been greatly enhanced because of the July Plot remained fanatically determined, at least outwardly. The *Gauleiters*, accurately described by Ian Kershaw as 'diehards without a future', enforced draconian punishment of any civilians who showed what they regarded as defeatist tendencies; their subordinates generally obeyed such instructions inflexibly.[8] At the very top of the power structure, Hitler knew by the end of March that the end of the war was imminent, but for him there was no alternative but to continue. Whether Germany surrendered or was overwhelmed, his personal fate was that he would die in the near future and he wrapped himself in the mystique of seeking a glorious and heroic end that would inspire future generations. But some of those around him were wavering. Goebbels remained steadfastly loyal to his Führer's nihilistic vision – after the Western Allies crossed the Rhine, he too regarded the war as lost, but felt that embracing death and utter destruction was preferable to the ignominy of surrender. But others were attempting to find some means of negotiating an end to the conflict.

Himmler's attempts to contact the Western Allies via Swiss or Swedish intermediaries have already been described, and Speer was also encouraging everyone with any influence to take similar measures. Ribbentrop, the foreign minister, had far less power than in the glory days of the Third Reich, and at first limited himself to hoping that the Führer might experience a change of heart and agree to commence negotiations. But in March, as the Reich continued to disintegrate, he ordered Werner Dankwort, the German deputy ambassador in Stockholm, to fly home for discussions. He explained to Dankwort that Germany's new weapons would turn the tide, but it was important to buy sufficient time for their production and deployment. When he returned to Sweden, Dankwort was to take every step he could – even going as far as contacting Soviet diplomats – to persuade one or other of Germany's enemies to seek peace. But even at this stage, Ribbentrop lacked the courage to proceed without Hitler's explicit approval. When he spoke to the Führer by telephone, he was told that any such attempt was pointless. Dankwort's thoughts as he made the brief journey to the plane waiting to take him back to Sweden were mixed. He stared in horror at the devastated German capital, which had been hit repeatedly by bombing attacks since the beginning of the year, and reflected on the unreality of those at the very top of the German government. It was with considerable personal relief that he returned to the safety of a neutral country.[9]

Ernst Kaltenbrunner, head of the *RSHA*, was a brutal loyalist of the regime but nonetheless quietly contacted the Swiss Red Cross to explore the possibilities of a separate peace with the Western Powers, but his ambivalent behaviour is characteristic of many senior figures. At the same time, he denounced Obergruppenführer Karl Wolff, commander of SS forces in Italy, for attempting to negotiate capitulation with the Americans and British and actively tried to organise the so-called *Werwolf* resistance organisation to continue the fight even after the end of the war. At the very end, his pragmatism prevailed over his fanaticism and he fled from Berlin as the Red Army closed in.[10]

Curiously, there was a factor that provided motivation both for opponents of the regime and for its dwindling band of supporters to continue the fight: a fear of a repetition of the events of 1918. The collapse of the German government at the end of the First World War through civil unrest played a major role in the growth of the *Dolchstoss* ('stab-in-the-back') legend: the German Army was not defeated, many argued, but betrayed by the failure and opportunism of politicians. This legend was wholly false; the German forces in the west had passed the point of no return by the second half of 1918. In addition, the complete disintegration of their front line in the Balkans following the exit of Bulgaria from the war left an irreparable hole in the defences of the Central Powers, and the Austro-Hungarian Empire was accelerating towards dissolution. Moreover, as was the case in 1945, German industry was at the end of its resources and unable to continue producing arms and munitions in sufficient quantities for the war to continue. Nevertheless, the legend became an important factor in German politics in the decades after the war. As 1945 drew on and Germany's defeat was once more clearly just a matter of time, the regime's supporters clung to the view articulated by Hitler: there would be no betrayal of Germany's valiant soldiers by cowardly politicians in Germany. By contrast, those who were desperate for the war to be brought to an end were fearful that any attempt by them to bring this about might give rise to a new *Dolchstoss* legend. Many believed that Germany would have to suffer complete defeat and occupation to ensure that there was no resurgence of the mindset that had created the conditions for Hitler's rise to power. This view was shared by many of Germany's enemies.

Given the huge scale of German deaths, both civilian and military, in the last year of the war, it is worth considering what steps all parties might have taken to bring the conflict to an earlier end, and whether their actions prolonged the fighting and therefore contributed to the terrible death toll. In the case of Germany, the last realistic chance for an early end to the war disappeared on 20 July 1944 when Hitler survived the bomb blast in his headquarters in Rastenburg. The conspirators would not have been able to impose their preferred vision of peace upon the Allies, and would have struggled to secure control of Germany, but the resultant chaos would have made it almost impossible for German forces to put up prolonged resistance against the armies of the Allies. It is possible – even likely – that a new *Dolchstoss* legend would have arisen, with incalculable consequences for the post-war era, but the tightening of control of all aspects of German life after the failed coup attempt made it impossible for any coordinated attempt to oppose Hitler's will and to bring the war to an end. Individual commanders might have considered taking local action, for example by opening their lines to the armies of the Western Allies, but even if any such attempt had been made, it is likely that many of their subordinates would have refused to comply and would have fought on. There is nothing to suggest that any senior commander seriously considered such an act. German officers in British captivity discussed the matter amongst themselves in early 1945 and concluded unanimously that any such step would have been incompatible with military honour.[11] And of course, such a step would have once more fed a new *Dolchstoss* legend.

Were there any steps taken by the Allied Powers that prolonged the war, or were there any missed opportunities to bring it to an earlier end? In the summer of 1944, the Red Army launched its devastating Operation *Bagration*, which tore huge holes in the German front line and moved the fighting across Belarus into eastern Poland. Fighting in this part of the Soviet Union has historically been complicated by the existence of the Pripyat region, with its huge marshes and forests and comparatively few roads; *Bagration* deliberately took place to the north of this region. During Soviet planning for the summer offensive, there was consideration of an alternative attack to the south of the Pripyat region. This would aim to reach the middle Vistula and would then swing to the northwest, aiming to reach the Baltic coast somewhere in East Prussia. Such an offensive would have torn a gap between Army Groups Centre and North and the rest of the German forces, and the subsequent destruction of these two army groups would have left Germany unable to restore its front lines. But whilst the potential gains from such an operation were great, so too were the risks. Firstly, the Germans feared precisely such an attack. This actually contributed to the success of *Bagration*, as intelligence reports showed a great deal of confirmation bias and diverted several panzer divisions away from Belarus to the south in order to cover such a Soviet offensive. If the Red Army had attacked south of the Pripyat region, the Soviet policy of *Maskirovka* would undoubtedly have attempted to divert German attention away from this area, and it is impossible to assess how effective this would have been. But an offensive to the middle Vistula and on to the Baltic coast would have stretched Soviet logistic resources to the limit. As Soviet armies turned towards the northwest, they would have been faced with threats to both their flanks, and in such fast-moving encounter battles the Germans continued to demonstrate to the very end of the war that they retained a considerable advantage. It is therefore highly unlikely that the Red Army could have inflicted a war-winning blow on the Wehrmacht in 1944.

What of the Western Powers? Were there steps that they could have taken that brought the war to an earlier conclusion? Stalin had made repeated demands for much of the war for the British and Americans to bring forward their plans for an invasion of Western Europe, but despite Soviet suspicions that the Western Powers were content to allow Germany and the Soviet Union to bleed each other to death, there was no realistic possibility of an invasion prior to 1944. Nor could the military campaign that followed the successful capture of the Normandy bridgeheads have been conducted in a significantly different manner to bring about an earlier collapse of Germany. It had been Hitler's intention to hold back the Red Army while concentrating as much strength as possible in the west in anticipation of an invasion; he correctly identified the defeat of such an invasion as crucial if Germany was to avoid a two-front land war that it couldn't win. The result was bitter fighting in Normandy with daily casualty rates that were as bad as much of the fighting on the Western Front in the First World War. The Wehrmacht remained a formidable force and the two defeats inflicted on it in 1944 both in the east and west were essential precursors to Germany's final defeat; neither defeat could have been amplified sufficiently to bring about a complete collapse.

The July Plot took most US and British commanders and politicians by surprise. After a highly effective counter-intelligence operation earlier in the war in which German agents had masqueraded as anti-Hitler conspirators to lure British agents to a location where they could be captured, Churchill forbade any further contact with alleged opponents of the German regime. Despite this, there were reports that large parts of the German military hierarchy were disaffected and even making plans to try to kill Hitler, but Churchill remained adamant that there would be no British involvement. It is arguable that an opportunity was lost. At the very least, the costly British Operation *Goodwood* could have been timed to commence on the day of the assassination attempt, when German confusion was likely to be at its greatest.

In the years that followed the war, the policy announced in early 1943 after the Casablanca Conference – that the Allied Powers would pursue the war to the end and would accept only unconditional surrender – was blamed for leaving those in Germany who might have wished for a negotiated peace with little option but to continue fighting. In particular, the publication of what became known as the Morgenthau Plan was considered particularly damaging. Henry Morgenthau, the US Treasury Secretary, wrote a paper in 1944 that proposed how Germany was to be treated after the end of the war. His proposals outlined the complete demilitarisation of Germany and the dismantling of its armaments industry and considerable territorial changes. In the west, France would gain the Saar region, which had been under French control for a period after the First World War. East Prussia would be divided between Poland and the Soviet Union, and the former would also gain Upper Silesia. The rest of Germany would be divided into a South German State – roughly consisting of Bavaria, Württemburg, and Baden – and a North German State; the western parts of Germany would become an 'International Zone' that would be comprehensively de-industrialised. Although the plan was supported by many, including Roosevelt, others were strongly opposed, including many senior British figures.[12]

When the Morgenthau Plan was published, it was immediately exploited for propaganda purposes by Goebbels, who pointedly referred to it as a document drawn up by 'the Jew Morgenthau'.[13] There was also considerable opposition in the US press, and Roosevelt increasingly distanced himself from the plan. The extent to which the plan and the stance on unconditional surrender hardened the German will to continue the war is debatable. Clearly, the existence of such a radical proposal and its apparent support from at least parts of the US administration would have been greeted with widespread dismay across Germany. But it is worth noting that despite the insistence on unconditional surrender, many Germans – ranging from Stauffenberg and his fellow conspirators to Himmler, Ribbentrop and others – specifically intended to ignore any such demand. They interpreted the Casablanca Declaration – perhaps correctly – as stating that the Allied Powers would refuse to negotiate with the current regime.

Even as the fighting in Pomerania and along the Oder died down, both sides began to prepare in earnest for what everyone knew would be the last act of the drama: the Soviet assault on Berlin. Zhukov had been summoned back to Moscow on 7 March, and was told by Stalin to commence preparations for the

Berlin Operation. In his memoirs, he described how Stalin and other senior Soviet figures were still concerned about the possibility of Germany seeking a separate peace with the Western Powers, and that this added to the sense of urgency to deliver a killer blow. The damage inflicted on the Wehrmacht in the opening months of 1945 was immense. If the Eastern Front had been, in Guderian's words, a 'house of cards' at the beginning of the year, it was now little more than an array of names of divisions, corps and armies, reduced to shadows of their former strength. But despite this, Zhukov and Stalin both knew that in its final battle, the Wehrmacht would fight with all its remaining strength and determination.

From the perspective of the 21st century, the fanatical mindset of many Germans at this stage of the war isn't easy to understand. But they lived in a very different world, where their access to information was tightly controlled. Whether it was fanaticism or weary fatalism, there seemed no way out of the conflict for most Germans. Belief in Hitler and the Nazi Party was far from the delirious heights of earlier years, but despite the evidence on all sides, it remained strong in some parts of both civilian and military life. For the rest of Germany, there was a sense of hopelessness and of being trapped in a disaster that grew worse by the day and that would continue for a further few weeks. Hitler was still alive, and – one way or another – he remained an insurmountable obstacle to peace, even the peace of utter defeat.

# NOTES

## INTRODUCTION

1   *Kriegsende in Deutschland* (Ellert & Richter, Hamburg, 2005), p.55
2   M. Dönhoff, *Namen die Keiner Mehr Nennt* (Diederichs, Munich, 2004), p.21
3   J. Richter (ed.), *Die Tagebücher von Joseph Goebbels, Teil II Diktate 1941–1945* (Saur, Munich, 1993–96, 15 vols.), Vol. XIV, p.147
4   H. Schäufler, *Panzer an der Weichsel* (Motor Buch Verlag, Stuttgart, 1979), p.19–20
5   G. Koschorrek, *Vergiss die Zeit der Dornen Nicht* (Fleschig, Würzburg, 2005), p.435–36
6   Quoted in C. Merridale, *Ivan's War* (Faber & Faber, London, 2005), p.261
7   G. Baltuttis, *Auf Verlorenem Posten* (Rautenberg, Würzburg, 2006), p.13, 84–85
8   N. Zetterling, *Normandy 1944: German Military Organisation, Combat Power and Organizational Effectiveness* (Fedorowicz, Winnipeg, 2000), p.74; C. Wilmot, *The Struggle For Europe* (Wordworth, Ware, 2003), p.434

## CHAPTER 1: PREPARING FOR ARMAGEDDON: THE WEHRMACHT

1   T. Fontane, *Vor dem Sturm: Roman aus dem Winter 1812 auf 13* (Macmillan, New York, 1911), p.203
2   H. von Ahlfen, *Der Kampf um Schlesien* (Motor Buch Verlag, Stuttgart, 1998), p.25
3   R. Hinze, *19. Infanterie- und Panzer-Division: Divisionsgeschichte aus der Sicht eines Artilleristen* (self-published, 1994), p.719–20
4   H. Trevor-Roper, *Hitler's War Directives 1939–1945* (Sidgwick & Jackson, London, 1964), p.159–63
5   P. Buttar, *Germany Ascendant* (Osprey, Oxford, 2015), p.118–56
6   B. Shepherd, *Hitler's Soldiers: The German Army in the Third Reich* (Yale University Press, New Haven CT, 2016), p.470
7   R. Smelser, E. Davies, *The Myth of the Eastern Front: The Nazi-Soviet War in Popular American Culture* (Cambridge University Press, New York, 2008), p.107
8   S. von Lüttwitz, *LXXXV Corps 29 March to 7 May 45* (Historical Division US Army Europe, Karlsruhe, 1947), p.12–13
9   Quoted in Ahlfen, *Der Kampf*, p.29

10 M. Miller, 'Fritz Bracht', unpublished document

11 R. Evans *The Third Reich at War* (Penguin, Harmondsworth, 2010), p.675

12 *Oberschlesischer Zeitung* (Katowice, 22/10/1944), p.2

13 D. Yelton, *Hitler's Volkssturm: The Nazi Militia and the Fall of Germany 1944–1945* (University of Kansas Press, Lawrence KS, 2002), p.89–96

14 National Archives and Records Administration, College Park MD, *Befehl über die Aufstellung von Arbeitsabteilungen 23/5/1943* T-314 Film 688 Frame 1235

15 National Archives and Records Administration, College Park MD, *Kriegstagebuch der Quartiermeisterabteilung des LVI Korps 9/3/1944* T-314 Film 1438 Frame 914

16 J. Hürter, *A German General on the Eastern Front* (Pen & Sword, Barnsley, 2014), p.39–43

17 H. Pantenius, *Letzter Schlacht an der Ostfront* (Mittler, Bonn, 2002), p.54–55

18 *Bundesarchiv-Militärarchiv*, Freiburg, RH-10 Anlage 1 zu Fremde Heere Ost (I) 4012/44 gKdos 10/11/1944

19 H. Magenheimer, *Abwehrschlacht an der Weichsel: Vorbereitung, Ablauf, Erfahrungen* (Rombach, Freiburg im Breisgau, 1976), p.28

20 E. Kieser, *Danziger Bucht 1945* (Bechtle, Esslingen, 1978), p.12

21 Quoted in Ahlfen, *Der Kampf*, p.39

22 C. Messenger, *The Last Prussian: A Biography of Field Marshal Gerd von Rundstedt* (Pen & Sword, Barnsley, 2011), p.197

23 Kieser, *Danziger Bucht*, p.13

24 Ahlfen, *Der Kampf*, p.35

25 H. Guderian, *Erinnerungen eines Soldaten* (Vowinkel, Neckargemünd, 1960), p.352

26 J. Thorwald, *Es Begann an der Weichsel* (Steingrüben, Stuttgart, 1953), p.39

27 H. Hartmann, *Zwischen Nichts und Niemansland* (Machtwortverlag, Dessau, 2006), p.584–86

28 Ibid., p.588

29 Hinze, *19. Infanterie- und Panzer-Division*, p.725

## Chapter 2: The Red Army: 'Forward, forward at any cost!'

1 A. Vasilevsky, *A Lifelong Cause* (Progress, Moscow, 1981), p.488

2 S. Shtemenko, *The Soviet General Staff at War* (Progress, Moscow, 1970), p.384

3 Ibid., p.383

4 Vasilevsky, *A Lifelong Cause*, p.486

5 H. Salisbury, *The 900 Days: The Siege of Leningrad* (Da Capo, Cambridge MA, 2009), p.548

6 K. Rokossovsky, *A Soldier's Duty* (Lancer, New Delhi, 1992), p.85–86

7 P. Batov, *Von der Wolga zur Oder* (Deutscher Militärverlag, Berlin, 1965), p.311–13

8 G. Zhukov, *Vospomimaniya I Razmyshleniya* (Olma, Moscow, 2002, 2 volumes), Vol. II, p.237

9 Shtemenko, *The Soviet General Staff At War*, p.302

10   I. Konev, *Sorok Pyaty* (Voyenizdat, Moscow, 1970), p.5

11   Ibid., p.6–7

12   D. Lelyushenko, *Moskva-Stalingrad-Berlin-Praga* (Nauka, Moscow, 1987), p.288

13   Interview with A. Amanuti, available at https://iremember.ru/memoirs/tankisti/amatuni-ashot-apetovich/

14   Konev, *Sorok Pyaty*, p.7–8

15   Shtemenko, *The Soviet General Staff At War*, p.296

16   G. Zhukov, *Vospomimaniya I Razmyshleniy*, Vol. II, p.240

17   V. Chuikov, *Ot Stalingrada do Berlina* (Sovetskaya Rossiya, Moscow, 1985), p.516–17

18   V. Skorobogatov, *Berzarin* (Molodaya Gvardiya, Moscow, 2012), p.359–60

19   P. Buttar, *Meat Grinder: The Battles for the Rzhev Salient* (Osprey, Oxford, 2022), p.104–63

20   P. Belov, *Za Nami Moskva* (Voyenizdat, Moscow, 1963), p.182

21   Ibid., p.215

22   G. Blumentritt, 'Operations Against Rear Lines of Communications' in *Foreign Military Studies* (Historical Division, US Army Europe, 1947), B-684, p.6–7

23   M. Katukov, *Na Ostriye Glavnogo Udara* (Voyenizdat, Moscow, 1974), p.339

24   V. Antonov, *Put k Berlinu* (Nauka, Moscow, 1975), p.181

25   D. Glantz, *Soviet Military Deception in the Second World War* (Routledge, London, 1989), p.103

26   C. Duffy, *Red Storm on the Reich: The Soviet March on Germany, 1945* (Castle, New Jersey, 2002), p.32–33

27   D. Glantz, *Art of War Symposium 1986. From the Vistula to the Oder: Soviet Offensive Operations October 1944–March 1945* (Center for Land Warfare, US Army War College, Carlisle PA, 1986), p.507

28   Interview with N. Levin, available at https://iremember.ru/memoirs/saperi/levin-natan-markovich/

29   Ibid.

30   Interview with M. Grinstein, available at https://iremember.ru/memoirs/pekhotintsi/grinshteyn-mark-mikhaylovich/

31   Duffy, *Red Storm on the Reich*, p.33

32   Interview with M. Shinder, available at https://iremember.ru/memoirs/razvedchiki/shinder-mikhail-lvovich/

33   A. Babadzhanian, *Dorogi Pobedy* (Molodaya Gvardiya, Moscow, 1975), p.210–11

## CHAPTER 3: KONEV'S HAMMER BLOW: 12–13 JANUARY

1   Konev, *Sorok Pyaty*, p.12–13

2   For a discussion of the impact of the Ardennes offensive on Stalin's planning, see A. Beevor, *Ardennes 1944: Hitler's Last Gamble* (Viking, New York, 2015), p.331

3   See for example N. Bączyk, *Kielce 1945* (Widawnictwo Militaria, Warsaw, 2003), p.34–35

4   Hartmann, *Zwischen Nichts und Niemansland*, p.588
5   Ibid., p.589–90
6   Ibid., p.591
7   Duffy, *Red Storm on the Reich*, p.68
8   Interview with G. Melikov, available at https://iremember.ru/memoirs/pekhotintsi/melikov-georgiy-aleksandrovich/
9   Lelyushenko, *Moskva-Stalingrad-Berlin-Praga*, p.295
10  Ahlfen, *Der Kampf,* p.47
11  Glantz, *From the Vistula to the Oder*, p.617
12  A. Zhadov, *Chetyre Goda Voyny* (Voyenizdat, Moscow, 1978), p.268–69
13  D. Shein, *Tanki Vedet Rybalko. Boyevoy Put 3-y Gvardeskoy Tankovoy Armii* (Eksmo, Moscow, 2007), p.254–55
14  U. Saft, *Krieg im Osten* (Militärbuchverlag, Walsrode, 2002), p.108
15  W. Werthen, *Geschichte der 16. Panzer-Division – Weg und Schicksal* (Podzun, Bad Neuheim, 1958), p.268–69
16  Quoted in Ahlfen, *Der Kampf,* p.48
17  Glantz, *From the Vistula to the Oder*, p.613
18  Ibid., p.615
19  Konev, *Sorok Pyaty,* p.15
20  W. Rivers, 'The Repression of War Experience' in *Lancet* (Wakley, London, 1918), Vol. XCVI, p.513–33
21  Hartmann, *Zwischen Nichts und Niemansland*, p.593–94
22  Lelyushenko, *Moskva-Stalingrad-Berlin-Praga*, p.297
23  Konev, *Sorok Pyaty,* p.16
24  Shein, *Tanki Vedet Rybalko*, p.256
25  *Tsentralnyy Arkhiv Ministerstva Oborony Rossiyskoy Federatsii* (Moscow) RF, f.315, op.4440, d.567, L.17

## CHAPTER 4: ZHUKOV JOINS THE OFFENSIVE: 14–16 JANUARY

1   H. Grossmann, *Die Geschichte der Rheinissch-Westfälischen 6. Infanterie-Division 1939–1945* (Dörfler, Eggolsheim, 2005), p.238
2   Ibid., p.240–41
3   V. Antonov, *Put k Berlinu* (Nauka, Moscow, 1975), p.202
4   V. Chuikov, *Konets Tretyego Reykha* (Sovetskaya Rossiya, Moscow, 1973), p.106
5   O. von Knobelsdorff, *Geschichte der Niedersächsischen 19. Panzer-Division: Bis 31.10.1940 19. Infanterie-Division* (Podzun-Pallas, Friedberg, 1985), p.279
6   Grossmann, *Die Geschichte der Rheinissch-Westfälischen 6. Infanterie-Division*, p.248–49
7   Knobelsdorff, *Geschichte der Niedersächsischen 19. Panzer-Division*, p.280
8   Antonov, *Put k Berlinu*, p.209–10

9   Grossmann, *Die Geschichte der Rheinissch-Westfälischen 6. Infanterie-Division*, p.250–51

10  Interview with A. Vesterman, available at https://iremember.ru/memoirs/tankisti/vesterman-arkadiy-grigorevich/

11  Bączyk, *Kielce 1945*, p.48–49

12  Babadzhanian, *Dorogi Pobedy*, p.220

13  Chuikov, *Konets Tretyego Reykha*, p.107–08

14  A. Getman, *Tanki Idut na Berlin* (Nauka, Moscow, 1973), p.158

15  Antonov, *Put k Berlinu*, p.221–23

16  Interview with I. Uritskiy, available at https://iremember.ru/memoirs/tankisti/uritskiy-isaak-izrailevich/

17  Pantenius, *Letzter Schlacht an der Ostfront*, p.76

18  Ibid., p.77

19  W. Curilla, *Der Judenmord in Polen und die Deutsche Ordnungspolizei* (Ferdinand Schöningh, Paderborn, 2011), p.256

20  Interview with S. Tsvang, available at https://iremember.ru/memoirs/razvedchiki/tsvang-semen-ruvimovich

21  A. Gruber, *Das Infanterie-Regiment 213 (Grenadier-Regiment 70) 1939–1945* (Selbstverlag der Kameradschaft des Ehem. Infanterie-Regiments 213, Nuremburg, 1963), p.280–82

22  Pantenius, *Letzter Schlacht an der Ostfront*, p.88

23  Katukov, *Na Ostriye Glavnogo Udara*, p.348–49

24  *Institut für Zeitgeschichte* Munich, MS Zs 3095, p.6

25  E. Middeldorf, 'Die Abwehrschlacht am Weichselbrückenkopf Barabow' in *Wehrwissenschaftliche Rundschau* (Mittler, Darmstadt, 1968), p.72

# CHAPTER 5: WARSAW – KRAKÓW – ŁÓDŹ: 17–19 JANUARY

1   I. Loose, 'Kollektivgeschöpfe: die Berliner Juden im Getto Litzmannstadt 1941–1944' in *Einsicht: Bulletin der Fritz Bauer Institut* (Frankfurt am Main, 2009), Vol. 1, p.21–25

2   *Bundesarchiv-Militärarchiv* Freiburg, N 10/6 *Lüttwitz, Kampf der 9. Armee*, p.29

3   Antonov, *Put k Berlinu*, p.227

4   Getman, *Tanki Idut na Berlin*, p.216

5   Pantenius, *Letzter Schlacht an der Ostfront*, p.81–84

6   For a discussion of the various resistance groups, see K. Komorowski (ed.), *Armia Krajowa: Rozwój Organizacyjny* (Bellona, Warsaw, 1996), p.20–35

7   For a comprehensive account of the Warsaw Uprising, see N. Davies, *Rising '44: The Battle for Warsaw* (MacMillan, London, 2003)

8   A. Richie, *Warsaw 1944: Hitler, Himmler and the Warsaw Uprising* (Farrar, Strauss & Giroux, New York, 2013), p.242

9   Davies, *Rising '44*, p.279

10    K. Wituska, I. Tomaszewski, *Inside a Gestapo Prison: The Letters of Krystyna Wituska 1942–1944* (Wayne State University Press, Detroit MI, 2006), p.22

11    P. Friedrich, 'Kontaminerte Erinnerung: Vorn Einfluss der Kriegspropaganda auf das Gedenken an die Warschauer Aufstände von 1943 und 1944' in *Zeitschrift für Ostmitteleuropa-Forschung* (Herder, Marburg, 2008), Vol. 55/3, p.427; H. von Krannhals, *Der Warschauer Aufstand 1944* (Ars Una, Neuried, 2000), p.215

12    M. Berezowska, E. Borecka, J. Kazimierski, *Exodus Warszawy: Ludzie I Miasto po Powstaniu 1944* (Państwowy Instytut Wydawniczy, Warsaw, 1993, 2 vols.), Vol. 2, p.173–74

13    Z. Zaborski, *Tędy Przeszła Warszawa: Epilog Powstania Warszawskiego: Pruszków Durchgangslager 121: 6 VIII-10 X 1944* (Wydawnictwo Askon, Warsaw, 2018), p.55

14    I. Maliszewska, A. Iwaszkiewicz, A. Kubin, M. Jarmoszuk, *Wypędzeni z Warszawy 1944 – Losy Dzieci: Wystawa w Muzeum Historycznym m. st. Warszawy* (Wystawa w Muzeum Historycznym m. st. Warszawy, Warsaw, 2007), p.102–03

15    A. Tung, *Preserving the World's Great Cities: The Destruction and Renewal of the Historic Metropolios* (Clarkson Potter, New York, 2001), p.102–30

16    G. Semenov, *Nastupayet Udarnaya* (Voyenizdat, Moscow, 1986), p.193

17    B. James, *Moonless Night* (Pen & Sword, Barnsley, 2022), p.184–87

18    Ahlfen, *Der Kampf*, p.57

19    Saft, *Krieg im Osten*, p.114

20    Zhadov, *Chetyre Goda Voyny*, p.273

21    A. Polonsky, *The Jews in Poland and Russia* (Liverpool University Press, 2019, 3 vols.), Vol. 3, p.434

22    Babadzhanian, *Dorogi Pobedy*, p.228

23    P. Buttar, *Collision of Empires: The War on the Eastern Front in 1914* (Osprey, Oxford, 2014), p.356–87

24    M. Wardyńska, *Był rok 1939: operacja niemieckiej policji bezpieczeństwa w Polsce: Intelligenzaktion* (Instytut Pamięci Narodowej, Warszawa, 2009), p.203–05

25    L. Dobroszyki (ed.), *The Chronicle of the Łódź Ghetto, 1941–1944* (Yale University Press, New Haven CT, 1987), p.52

26    Ibid., p.lxi

27    A. Adelson, R. Lapides, *Lodz Ghetto: Inside a Community Under Siege* (Penguin, New York, 1991), p.440

28    Ibid., p.440–41

29    H. Spaeter, *History of the Panzerkorps Grossdeutschland* (Fedorowicz, Winnipeg, 2000, 3 vols.), Vol. 3, p.3–13

30    Ibid., p.175–80

31    Bączyk, *Kielce 1945*, p.56

32    Quoted in W. Paul, *Panzer-General Walther K. Nehring, Eine Biographie* (Motor Buch Verlag, Stuttgart, 2002), p.183

33    Konev, *Sorok Pyaty*, p.18–20

34    Chuikov, *Konets Tretyego Reykha*, p.546

35    Thorwald, *Es Begann an der Weichsel*, p.93

## CHAPTER 6: ROADS OF SUFFERING AND DEATH

1   W. Benz, B. Distel (eds.), *Der Ort des Terrors* (Beck, Munich, 2005–09, 9 vols.), Vol. 1, p.43–57

2   G. Paul (ed.), *Die Täter der Shoah: Fanatische Nationalsozialisten oder ganz Normale Deutsche?* (Wallstein, Göttingen, 2002), p.95–96

3   M. Allen, *The Business of Genocide: The SS, Slave Labor, and the Concentration Camps* (University of North Carolina Press, Chapel Hill NC, 2005), p.97–99

4   D. Czech, *Auschwitz Chronicle 1939–1945* (Henry Holt & Co, New York, 1990), p.261–62

5   R. Schnabel, *Macht ohne Moral: Eine Dokumentation über die SS* (Rödeberg, Frankfurt am Main, 1957), p.223

6   D. Blatman, *The Death Marches: The Final Phase of Nazi Genocide* (Belknapp, Cambridge MA, 2011), p.44

7   B. Smith, A. Peterson (eds.), *Heinrich Himmler Geheimreden 1933–1945, und andere Ansprachen* (Propyläen, Frankfurt am Main, 1974), p.203

8   J. Hoffman, *Das Kann Man Nicht Erzählen* (Konkret, Hamburg, 2008), p.82

9   International Military Tribunal Nuremburg, Himmler to senior SS officers, 21/6/44, PS-3683

10  International Military Tribunal Nuremburg, Bierkamp to Thiel, 21/7/44, O-053

11  Blatman, *The Death Marches*, p.58

12  Interview with G. Kornev, available at iremember.ru/memoirs/samokhodchiki/kornev-grigoriy-sergeevich/

13  Interview with P. Pudov, available at iremember.ru/memoirs/samokhodchiki/pudov-petr-dmitrievich/

14  P. Buttar, *Centuries Will Not Suffice: A History of the Lithuanian Holocaust* (Amberley, Stroud, 2023), p.267–68

15  Blatman, *The Death Marches*, p.63–64

16  Ibid., p.68

17  Ibid., p.69

18  A. Strzelecki, W. Brand, *The Evacuation, Liquidation and Liberation of Auschwitz* (Auschwitz-Birkenau State Museum, Oświęcim, 2008), p.38

19  *United States Holocaust Museum Memorial Archives*, Washington DC, Memoir of Katerina Feuer, RG-02.209, p.3

20  *Archives Nationales*, Paris, Testimony of Samuel Steinberg, 72 AJ 318-321

21  Blatman, *The Death Marches*, p.88

22  I. Sprenger, *Gross-Rosen: Ein Konzentrationslager in Schlesien* (Böhlau, Cologne, 1996), p.169–70

23  Quoted in Blatman, *The Death Marches*, p.97–98

24  Interview with P. Katsevman, available at iremember.ru/memoirs/letchiki-shturmovik/katsevman-petr-markovich/

25  Yad Vashem Archive, Jerusalem, Testimony of Yitshak Peri, 03/9952

26  F. Piper, 'Das Nebenlager Blechhammer' in *Hefte von Auschwitz* (Państwowe Muzeum, Oświęcim, 1971), no.12, p.37–39

27  W. Długoborski, F. Piper (eds.), *Auschwitz 1940–1945. Central Issues in the History of the Camp* (Auschwitz-Birkenau State Museum, Oświęcim, 2000, 5 vols.), Vol. V, p.230

28  Interview with L. Brandt, available at iremember.ru/memoirs/razvedchiki/brandt-leontiy-veniaminovich/

29  Interview with A. Limin, available at iremember.ru/memoirs/artilleristi/limin-aleksandr-leonidovich/

30  J. Steinhoff, P. Pechel, D. Showalter (eds.), *Voices from the Third Reich: An Oral History* (Da Capo, New York, 1994), p.420

31  Ibid., p.418

32  Quoted in Ahlfen, *Der Kampf*, p.72

33  Ibid., p.72–73

34  Yad Vashem Archive, Jerusalem, Testimony of Esther Harari, 03/9169

35  *Archiwum Pańsgwowego Muzeum Auschwitz-Birkenau*, Oświęcim, D-RF-3/RSHA/160, p.45–46

36  Quoted in Blatman, *The Death Marches*, p.87

37  R. Hargreaves, *Hitler's Final Fortress: Breslau 1945* (Pen & Sword, Barnsley, 2011), p.183

38  G. Knopp, *Die Grosse Flucht. Das Schicksal der Vertriebenen* (Edel, Hamburg, 2013), p.161–62

39  Hargreaves, *Hitler's Final Fortress*, p.185

40  R. Müller, N. Schönherr, T. Widera (eds.), *Die Zerstörung Dresdens: 13. bis 15. Februar 1945. Gutachten und Ergebnisse der Dresdener Historikerkommission zur Ermittlung der Opferzahlen* (V&R Unipress, Göttingen, 2010), p.48

## CHAPTER 7: DRACONIAN PUNISHMENT, FANATICAL DEFENCE

1  W. Widder, 'Auftragstaktik and Inner Führung: Trademark of German Leadership' in *Military Review* (US Army Press, Fort Leavenworth KS, 2002), Vol. 82/5, p.4

2  Quoted in G. Gunter, *Last Laurels: The German Defence of Upper Silesia January–May 1945* (Helion, Solihull, 2002), p.82

3  P. Hausser, *Soldaten wie Andere Auch* (Munin, Osnabrück, 1966), p.134

4  H. Eismann and F. Steinhardt, *Unter Himmlers Kommando 1945 – der Kampf von Heeresgruppe Weichsel an der Ostfront; die Persönlichen Erinnerungen von Oberst Hans-Georg Eismann, Ia von Heeresgruppe Weichsel* (Melchior, Wolfenbüttel, 2010), p.51

5  Ibid., p.55–56

6  M. Hastings, *Das Reich: The March of the 2nd SS Panzer Division Through France, June 1944* (BCA, London, 1981), p.36

7  Eismann and Steinhardt, *Unter Himmlers Kommando 1945*, p.65

8  Ibid., p.19

9  Ibid., p.61–63

10    This excerpt and the following account is from A. Clark, *Barbarossa: The Russian-German Conflict 1941–1945* (Macmillan, London, 1965), p.421–22

11    For Krüger's activities in the *Generalgouvernement*, see T. Pietrowski, *Poland's Holocaust: Ethnic Strife, Collaboration with Occupying Forces and Genocide in the Second Republic 1918–1947* (McFarland, Jefferson NC, 1998), p.23; M. Chodakiewicz, *Between Nazis and Soviets: Occupation Politics in Poland, 1939–1947* (Lexington, Lanham MD, 2004), p.92, 105, 118, 325; R. Hrabar, *Hitlerwoski Rabunek Dzieci Polskich: Uprowadzanie I Germanizowanie Dzieci Polskich w Latach 1939–1945* (Śląski Instytut Naukowy w Katowicach, Katowice, 1960), p.93

12    L. Thompson, 'Nazi Administrative Conflict. The Struggle for Executive Power in the General Government of Poland 1939–1943' (Dissertation, University of Wisconsin, 2000), p.320

13    J. Lifton, *The Nazi Doctors* (Basic Books, New York, 1986), p.159

14    E. Howell, *The Soviet Partisan Movement 1941–1944* (Verdun Press, Chicago, 2014), p.185

15    V. Hunt, *The Road of Slaughter: The Latvian 5th SS Division in Pomerania, January–March 1945* (Helion, Warwick, 2023), p.32

16    For details of the Torgau court martial, see Pantenius, *Letzter Schlacht an der Ostfront*, p.97–103

17    K. Dieckert, H. Grossmann, *Der Kampf um Ostpreussen* (Motor Buch Verlag, Stuttgart, 2002), p.116

18    R. Meindl, *Ostpreussens Gauleiter: Erich Koch – eine Politische Biographie* (Fibre, Osnabrück, 2007), p.443–44

19    E. Ziemke, *The US Army in the Occupation of Germany 1944–1946* (Center of Military History, US Army, Washington DC, 1990), p.232

20    A. Kunz, *Wehrmacht und Niederlage: Die Bewaffnete Macht in der Endphase der Nationalsozialistischen Herrschaft 1944 bis 1945* (Oldenbourg, Munich, 2007), p.113

## CHAPTER 8: POZNAŃ AND THE NORTHERN SECTOR

1    Chuikov, *Ot Stalingrada do Berlina*, p.449–450

2    Thorwald, *Es Begann an der Weichsel*, p.88

3    I. Kershaw, *Hitler, 1936–1945: Nemesis* (Norton, New York, 2001), p.759

4    J. Heller, G. Simpson (eds), *The Hidden Histories of War Crimes Trials* (Oxford University Press, Oxford, 2013), p.411–29

5    B. Kiekenap, *Der Stellvertreter aus Krähenwinkel: Biografische Notizen über Kurt Schmalz (1906–1964)* (Appelshans, Braunschweig, 2012), p.134–38

6    D. Schenk, *Hitlers Mann in Danzig: Gauleiter Forster und die NS-Verbrechen in Danzig-Westpreussen* (Dietz, Bonn, 2000), p.155

7    Wardzyńska, *Był rok 1939* p.102

8    M. Domarus, *Hitler, Reden und Proklamationen 1932–1945* (Süddeutscher Verlag, Munich, 1965, 2 vols.), Vol. 2, p.256

9    Katukov, *Na Ostriye Glavnogo Udara*, p.358

10 Saft, *Krieg im Osten*, p.150–51

11 Babadzhanian, *Dorogi Pobedy*, p.222

12 A. Speer, *Inside the Third Reich* (Weidenfeld & Nicolson, London, 1970), p.563

13 H. Berger, W. Girg, *In Hitlers Auftrag Hinter den Feindlichen Linien: Geheimeinsätze in der Uniform des Gegners. Ein Eichenlaubträger zwischen Skorzeny, CIA und BND* (Verlag für Wehrwissenschaften, Munich, 2014), p.62

14 Saft, *Krieg im Osten*, p.246–50

15 Katukov, *Na Ostriye Glavnogo Udara*, p.359

16 L. de Zeng, *Luftwaffe Airfields 1935–45 Poland* (Manuscript in preparation, 2014), p.38–40

17 I am grateful to Andrius Dirmeikis for providing me with copies of the relevant pages of the First Guards Tank Army war diary for January 1945

18 Chuikov, *Ot Stalingrada do Berlina*, p.451

19 Zhukov, *Vospomimaniya I Razmyshleniy*, Vol. II, p.242

20 Pantenius, *Letzter Schlacht an der Ostfront*, p.153–55

21 Chuikov, *Ot Stalingrada do Berlina*, p.452

22 A. Beck, *Bis Stalingrad 1941–1943* (Abt, Ulm, 1990), p.197

23 J. Ķīlītis, *Es Karā Aiziedams: Mani Raksturīgākie Piedzīvojumi Otrā Pasaules Karā* (self-published, Ottowa, 1956), p.182

24 Saft, *Krieg im Osten*, p.156–57

25 Ibid., p.176; Duffy, *Red Storm on the Reich*, p.150

26 Chuikov, *Ot Stalingrada do Berlina*, p.455

27 Hunt, *The Road of Slaughter*, p.107

28 P. Buttar, *Battleground Prussia: The Assault on Germany's Eastern Front 1944–1945* (Osprey, Oxford, 2010), p.186–88

## CHAPTER 9: THE WANDERING CAULDRON; KONEV TURNS SOUTH, 20–31 JANUARY

1 Saft, *Krieg im Osten*, p.116

2 Spaeter, *History of the Panzerkorps Grossdeutschland*, Vol. 3, p.185

3 Lelyushenko, *Moskva-Stalingrad-Berlin-Praga*, p.299

4 Ibid., p.300

5 Glantz, *From the Vistula to the Oder*, p.623–24

6 Spaeter, *History of the Panzerkorps Grossdeutschland*, Vol. 3, p.187

7 Konev, *Sorok Pyaty*, p.21

8 M. Miller and A. Schulz, *Gauleiter: The Regional Leaders of the Nazi Party and their Deputies* (R. James Bender, San Hose CA, 2012–21, 3 vols.), Vol. I, p.233, Vol. 3, p.556–63

9 Hargreaves, *Hitler's Final Fortress*, p.218

10 G. Reitor, *Vom Lager zum Lehrstuhl. Von Unten Nach Oben und Allem Daneben* (Reitor Libri, Gummersbach, 2001), p.48

11   U. Frodien, *Bleib Übrig: Eine Kriegsjugend in Deutschland* (DTV, Munich, 2004), p.118

12   K. Mammach, *Der Volkssturm: Das Letzte Aufgebot 1944–45* (Akademie Verlag, Berlin, 1981), p.68

13   Hargreaves, *Hitler's Final Fortress*, p.182

14   Frodien, *Bleib Übrig*, p.124

15   R. Becker, *Niederschlesien 1945: Die Flucht, die Besetzung* (Aufstieg, Munich, 1974), p.30

16   Ahlfen, *Der Kampf*, p.92

17   Speer, *Inside the Third Reich*, p.564

18   M. Bulsa and B. Szmatloch, *Sekrety Katowic* (Księży Młyn Dom Wydawniczy, Łódź, 2018), p.68–71

19   Konev, *Sorok Pyaty*, p.23

20   *Bundesarchiv-Militärarchiv* Freiburg, *Kriegstagebuch der Armeeoberkommando.17 26/1/45*, RH20-17

21   Ahlfen, *Der Kampf*, p.97

# Chapter 10: 1st Belarusian Front: The Advance to the Lower Oder

1   Zhukov, *Vospomimaniya I Razmyshleniy*, p.242

2   Katukov, *Na Ostriye Glavnogo Udara*, p.361

3   Eismann and Steinhardt, *Unter Himmlers Kommando 1945*, p.44

4   W. Lincoln, *Through Armageddon: The Russians in War and Revolution* (Oxford University Press, 1994), p.334–35

5   *New York Times*, 30/1/45

6   Quoted in F. Kohlase, *Als Küstrin in Trümmer Sank* (self-published, 1996), p.71

7   Speer, *Inside the Third Reich*, p.568

8   Quoted in H. Kissel, *Der Deutsche Volkssturm 1944/45. Eine Territoriale Miliz im Rahmen der Landesverteidigung* (Wehrwissenschaftliche Rundschau, Frankfurt-am-Main, 1962), p.165

9   Babadzhanian, *Dorogi Pobedy*, p.235

10   H. Höhne, 'Der Orden unter dem Totenkopf' in *Der Spiegel* (Hamburg, 1967), no.9, p.67

11   Eismann and Steinhardt, *Unter Himmlers Kommando 1945*, p.45

12   Katukov, *Na Ostriye Glavnogo Udara*, p.365–66

13   Quoted in Kohlase, *Als Küstrin in Trümmer Sank*, p.20–22

14   Ibid., p.26–27

15   F. Bokov, *Vesna Pobedy* (Mysl, Moscow, 1985), p.74

16   *TSAMO* Moscow, f.233, op.2307, d.194, p.111–13

17   Bokov, *Vesna Pobedy*, p.76–77

18   Kohlase, *Als Küstrin in Trümmer Sank*, p.89

19  F. Kohlase, *Brennendes Oderland. Miltärhistorische Fragmente der Ereigniss des Jahres 1945 aus dem Nordwestschlesicschen, Märkischen und Südpommerschen Oderland: Chronologie, Fakten, Schilderungen* (Verein für die Geschichte Küstrins e.V, Küstrin-Kietz, 2011, 4 vols), Vol. 4, p.73–74

20  Antonov, *Put k Berlinu*, p.233–34

21  Ibid., p.235

22  Chuikov, *Ot Stalingrada do Berlina*, p.581–82

23  T. Le Tissier, *The Siege of Küstrin, 1945: Gateway to Berlin* (Pen & Sword, Barnsley, 2009), p.85

24  Babadzhanian, *Dorogi Pobedy*, p.238

25  V. Chuikov, 'Na Berlin' in *Novaya i Noveyshaya Istoriya* (Rossiyskaya Akademiya Nauk I Institut Vseobshchey Istorii RAN, Moscow, 1965), No.2, p.7

26  V. Chuikov, 'Vislo-Oderskaya Operatsiya' in *Oktyabr* (Soyuz Pisateley RSFSR, Moscow, 1964), No.4, p.128–29

27  Zhukov, *Vospomimaniya I Razmyshleniy*, Vol. II, p.246; Chuikov, 'Na Berlin', p.6–7

28  Eismann and Steinhardt, *Unter Himmlers Kommando 1945*, p.49–50

# CHAPTER 11: 1ST UKRAINIAN FRONT: THE CONQUEST OF SILESIA

1   G. Gunter, *Last Laurels: The German Defence of Upper Silesia January–May 1945* (Helion, Solihull, 2002), p.125–26

2   Ahlfen, *Der Kampf*, p101–02

3   Ibid., p.103

4   Quoted in Ahlfen, *Der Kampf*, p.110

5   Quoted in ibid., p.112

6   Quoted in ibid., p.113

7   For an account of the failed attack by the *Grossdeutschland* Panzer Corps and Saucken's dismissal, see Spaeter, *History of the Panzerkorps Grossdeutschland*, Vol. 3, p.194–200

8   Quoted in H. Schäufler, *So Lebten und so Starben Sie: Das Buch vom Panzerregiment-35* (Kameradscaft ehemaliger Panzer-Regiment 35 e.V, Bamberg, 1983), p.229–30

9   G. Boldt, *Die Letzten Tage der Reichskanzlei* (Rowohlt, Hamburg, 1964), p.81

10  Konev, *Sorok Pyaty*, p.35

11  Lelyushenko, *Moskva-Stalingrad-Berlin-Praga*, p.302

12  Konev, *Sorok Pyaty*, p.36–37

13  W. Haupt, *Die 8. Panzer-Division im Zweiten Weltkrieg* (Pudzun, Friedberg, 1987), p.386–88

14  Quoted in Haupt, *Die 8. Panzer-Division im Zweiten Weltkrieg*, p.393

15  For a full account of the ensuing conference, see F. Harbutt, *Yalta 1945: Europe and America at the Crossroads* (Cambridge University Press, 2010)

16  S. Sebag Montefiore, *Stalin: The Court of the Red Tsar* (Weidenfeld & Nicholson, London, 2003), p.490

17  Ibid., p.494

18  Quoted in Haupt, *Die 8. Panzer-Division im Zweiten Weltkrieg*, p.393

19  Interview with I. Galitsky, available at https://iremember.ru/memoirs/partizani/galitskiy-iosif-bentsionovich/

20  Vesterman interview

21  Interview with D. Osinovsky, available at https://iremember.ru/memoirs/artilleristi/osinovskiy-dmitriy-filippovich/

22  J. Erickson, *The Road To Berlin* (Cassell Military Paperbacks, London, 2004), p.497

23  O. Wieviorka, *Normandy: From the Landings to the Liberation of Paris* (Belknap, Harvard University Press, Cambridge MA, 2010), p.329

24  M. Roberts, *What Soldiers Do: Sex and the American GI in World War II France* (University of Chicago Press, Chicago IL, 2013), p.210

25  S. Alexsijewitsch, *Der Krieg hat kein weibliches Gesicht* (Berliner Taschenbuch Verlag, Berlin, 2004), p.7

26  Interview with A. Bogachkin, available at https://iremember.ru/memoirs/artilleristi/bogachkin-anatoliy-ivanovich/

27  Interview with A. Vyatkin, available at https://iremember.ru/memoirs/letchiki-bombardirov/vyatkin-aleksandr-vasilevich/

28  Interview with A. Burimovich, available at https://iremember.ru/memoirs/artilleristi/burimovich-aleksey-grigorevich/

29  Interview with M. Grinstein, available at https://iremember.ru/memoirs/pekhotintsi/grinshteyn-mark-mikhaylovich/

30  Interview with S. Rozenberg, available at https://iremember.ru/memoirs/pekhotintsi/rozenberg-samuil-iosifovich/

31  Interview with B. Agaltsov, available at https://iremember.ru/memoirs/tankisti/agaltsov-boleslav-filippovich/

32  Vesterman interview

33  Ahlfen, *Der Kampf*, p.127–33

34  Konev, *Sorok Pyaty*, p.42

35  Hargreaves, *Hitler's Final Fortress*, p.249–50

36  Quoted in Haupt, *Die 8. Panzer-Division im Zweiten Weltkrieg*, p.394

37  Shein, *Tanki Vedet Rybalko*, p.277

38  Ahlfen, *Der Kampf*, p.152

39  O. von Natzmer, *Commitment of German Armor, 1943–1945* (US Army Historical Division, Karlsruhe, 1954), p.81

# CHAPTER 12: *SONNENWENDE* AND POMERANIA

1  Eismann and Steinhardt, *Unter Himmlers Kommando 1945*, p.50–52

2  See for example R. Hart, *Guderian: Panzer Pioneer or Myth Maker?* (Potomac Books, Washington DC, 2006), p.114–17; P. Batistelli, *Heinz Guderian: Leadership, Strategy, Conflict* (Osprey, Oxford, 2011), p.53–61

3   For a full discussion on this, see G. Gross, *The Myth and Reality of German Warfare: Operational Thinking from Moltke the Elder to Heusinger* (University Press of Kentucky, Lexington KY, 2016), p.189–258

4   Quoted in D. Bradley, *Walther Wenck: General der Panzertruppe* (Biblio, Osnabrück, 1981), p.330

5   Guderian, *Erinnerungen eines Soldaten*, p.374–77

6   E. Raus and S. Newton, *Panzer Operations. The Eastern Front Memoir of General Raus, 1941–1945* (Da Capo, Cambridge MA, 2003), p.319

7   Ibid., p.323

8   O. Carius, *Tigers in the Mud* (Stackpole, Mechanicsburg PA, 2003), p.196–99

9   I am grateful to Peter Caddick-Adams for describing this personal conversation that he had with Carius

10  R. Manvell and H. Fraenkel, *Heinrich Himmler: The Sinister Life of the Head of the SS and Gestapo* (Greenhill, London, 2007), p.230–33

11  T. Jentz, *Panzertruppen: The Complete Guide to the Creation and Combat Employment of Germany's Tank Force* (Schiffer, Atglen PA, 1996, 2 vols.), Vol. II, p.226–28

12  Bradley, *Walther Wenck*, p.331

13  Ibid., p.333–34; Guderian, *Erinnerungen eines Soldaten*, p.377–78

14  Raus and Newton, *Panzer Operations*, p.325

15  P. Oberhuber, quoted in Schäufler, *So Lebten und so Starben Sie*, p.251–52

16  R. Hufnagel, quoted in B. von Egloffstein, W. Hegen, and J. Huber, *Y-Rothenburg* (Self-published, 1994), p.149–50

17  Rokossovsky, *A Soldier's Duty*, p.294

18  Raus and Newton, *Panzer Operations*, p.326

19  Rokossovsky, *A Soldier's Duty*, p.295

20  Ibid., p.298–99

21  Ibid., p.300

22  Ibid., p.267

23  Semenov, *Nastupayet Udarnaya*, p.207

24  Katukov, *Na Ostriye Glavnogo Udara*, p.371

25  Raus and Newton, *Panzer Operations*, p.329–30

26  T. Gerritse, *Rauter: Himmlers Vuist in Nederland* (Boom, Amsterdam, 2018), p.467–71

27  Rokossovsky, *A Soldier's Duty*, p.305

28  Buttar, *Battleground Prussia*, p.275–76

29  Raus and Newton, *Panzer Operations*, p.330–33

30  Eismann and Steinhardt, *Unter Himmlers Kommando 1945*, p.60–61

31  Guderian, *Erinnerungen eines Soldaten*, p.381

32  H. Thrams, *Küstrin 1945: Tagebuch Einer Festung* (Landesmannschaft Berlin-Mark Brandenburg, Berlin, 1992), p.45

33  Kohlase, *Brennendes Oderland*, Vol. 3, p.44–45

34  Kohlase, *Als Küstrin in Trümmer Sank*, p.46

35  Guderian, *Erinnerungen eines Soldaten*, p.388–90

36 Batistelli, *Heinz Guderian*, p.54

37 P. Caddick-Adams, *1945: Victory in the West* (Hutchinson Heinemann, London, 2022), p.182–96

38 Le Tissier, *The Siege of Küstrin, 1945*, I, p.248

## Chapter 13: Lauban

1 A. Zwartsev, *3-ia Gvardeiskaia Tankovaia: Boevoi put 3-I Gvardeiskoi Tankovoi Armii* (Voenizdat, Moscow, 1982), p.277–78

2 Lelyushenko, *Moskva-Stalingrad-Berlin-Praga*, p.304

3 V. Zaitsev, *Gvardeyskaya Tankovaya* (Sredney-Ural, Sverdlovsk, 1989), p.123

4 Saft, *Krieg im Osten*, p.394–95

5 Zaitsev, *Gvardeyskaya Tankovaya*, p.124–26

6 Saft, *Krieg im Osten*, p.374–75

7 Grossmann, *Die Geschichte der Rheinissch-Westfälischen 6. Infanterie-Division*, p.258–61

8 G. Rottman, *Panzerfaust and Panzerschreck* (Osprey, Oxford, 2014), p.23–24

9 Interview with I. Stratievsky, available at https://iremember.ru/memoirs/pekhotintsi/stratievskiy-isay-borisovich/

10 Grossmann, *Die Geschichte der Rheinissch-Westfälischen 6. Infanterie-Division*, p.261

11 Ibid., p.269

12 Ibid., p.278

13 Shein, *Tanki Vedet Rybalko*, p.281

14 Haupt, *Die 8. Panzer-Division im Zweiten Weltkrieg*, p.397

15 Quoted in Paul, *Panzer-General Walther K. Nehring*, p.187

16 H. von Luck, *Panzer Commander: The Memoirs of Colonel Hans von Luck* (Cassell, London, 1989), p.249

17 R. Kaltenegger, *Generalfeldmarschall Ferdinand Schörner* (Flechsig, Würzburg, 2014), p.276

18 Tacitus, trans. A. Birley, *Agricola and Germania* (Oxford University Press, 2009), p.60

19 Grossmann, *Die Geschichte der Rheinissch-Westfälischen 6. Infanterie-Division*, p.278

20 M. Dörr, *Der Krieg Hat Uns Geprägt: Wie Kinder den Zweiten Weltkrieg Erlebten* (Campus Verlag, Frankfurt-am-Main, 2007), p.252

21 W. Nehring, 'Die Schlacht um Lauban' in *Deutsches Soldatenjahrbuch* (Schild-Verlag, Munich, 1970), p.56–58

22 Quoted in Haupt, *Die 8. Panzer-Division im Zweiten Weltkrieg*, p.286

23 I. Shkadov and A. Babakov, *Geroi Sovetskogo Soyuza: Kratkii Biograficheskii Slovar* (Voyenizdat, Moscow, 1987, 2 vols.), Vol. II, p.88

24 Konev, *Sorok Pyaty*, p.61–62

25 Ibid., p.62–63

26 W. von Oven, *Furioso: Mit Goebbels bis zum Ende* (Grabert, Tübingen, 1974), p.601–02

27    *BAMA* Freiburg, *Bericht für Fremde Heere Ost*, RH2/2685

28    Hargreaves, *Hitler's Final Fortress*, p.223

29    *Schlesische Tageszeitung* (Bergstadt Verlag Wilhelm Gottlieb Korn, Breslau), 18/2/45

30    Quoted in Hargreaves, *Hitler's Final Fortress*, p.289

31    Interview with I. Rabinovich, available at https://iremember.ru/memoirs/minometchiki/rabinovich-isaak-valentin-zalmanovich/

32    Quoted in Hargreaves, *Hitler's Final Fortress*, p.334

33    H. Gleiss, *Breslauer Apokalypse 1945: Dokumentarchronik vom Todeskampf und Untergang einer Deutschen Stadt und Festung am Ende des Zweiten Weltkrieges* (Natura et Patria Verlag, Wedel, 1986–97, 10 vols.), Vol. VIII, p.1188

34    R. Majewski and T. Sozanska, *Die Schlacht um Breslau Januar-Mai 1945* (Union, Berlin, 1979), p.115

35    A. Isaev, *Goroda-Kreposti Tretyego Reycha: Bitva za Festungi* (Yauza, Moscow, 2018), p.123

## CHAPTER 14: DEFIANCE AND DESPAIR

1    G. Krivosheeva (ed.), *Rossiya i SSSR Voynakh XX Veka: Poteri Vooruzhonnykh Sil* (Olma, Moscow, 2001), p.402

2    K. Bahm, *Berlin 1945: The Final Reckoning* (Motorbooks International, St Paul MN, 2001), p.51–52

3    H. Kochanski, *The Eagle Unbowed: Poland and the Poles in the Second World War* (Harvard University Press, Cambridge MA, 2012), p.119–24

4    G. MacDonogh, *After the Reich: From the Liberation of Vienna to the Berlin Airlift* (John Murray, London, 2007), p.163

5    Quoted in I. Kershaw, *The End: Germany 1944–45* (Penguin, Harmondsworth, 2011), p.197

6    *BAMA* Freiburg, *Nachlass Vietinghoff: 'Kriegsende in Italien'* N574/19, fos.44–45

7    *Württembergische Landesbibliothek* Stuttgart, *Sammlung Stertz, Unteroffizier Werner, F,* 1/4/45

8    Ibid., p.278

9    I. Fleischhauer, *Die Chance des Sonderfriedens: Deutsch-Sowjetische Geheimgespräche 1941–1945* (Siedler, Berlin, 1986), p.58–61, 268–75

10    C. Moorehead, *Dunant's Dream: War, Switzerland and the History of the Red Cross* (Carroll & Graf, New York, 1999), p.458–60; A. Read, *The Devil's Disciples: Hitler's Inner Circle* (Norton, New York, 2005), p.891–92

11    Kershaw, *The End*, p.376

12    For a comprehensive account of the Morgenthau Plan, see B. Greiner, *Die Morgenthau-Legende: Zur Geschichte eines Umstrittenen Planes* (Peter Lang, Lausanne, 1995)

13    M. Beschloss, *The Conquerors: Roosevelt, Truman and the Destruction of Hitler's Germany* (Simon & Schuster, New York, 2002), p.144

# BIBLIOGRAPHY

*Archives Nationales,* Paris
*Archiwum Pańsgwowego Muzeum Auschwitz-Birkenau,* Oświęcim
*Bundesarchiv-Militärarchiv,* Freiburg
*Institut für Zeitgeschichte,* Munich
*International Military Tribunal,* Nuremburg
*National Archives and Records Administration,* College Park MD
*Tsentralnyy Arkhiv Ministerstva Oborony Rossiyskoy Federatsii,* Moscow
*United States Holocaust Memorial Museum Archives,* Washington DC
*Württembergische Landesbibliothek,* Stuttgart
*Yad Vashem Archive,* Jerusalem
*Contemporary European History* (Cambridge University Press)
*Der Spiegel* (Hamburg)
*Deutsches Soldatenjahrbuch* (Schild-Verlag, Munich)
*Einsicht: Bulletin der Fritz Bauer Institut* (Frankfurt am Main)
*Foreign Military Studies* (Historical Division, US Army Europe)
*Hefte von Auschwitz* (Państwowe Muzeum, Oświęcim)
*Krasnaya Zvezda* (Ministry of Defence, Moscow)
*Lancet* (Wakley, London)
*New York Daily News* (New York)
*New York Times* (New York)
*Novaya i Noveyshaya Istoriya* (Rossiyskaya Akademiya Nauk I Institut Vseobshchey Istorii
    RAN, Moscow)
*Oberschlesischer Zeitung* (Katowice)
*Oktyabr* (Soyuz Pisateley RSFSR, Moscow)
*Schlesische Tageszeitung* (Bergstadt Verlag Wilhelm Gottlieb Korn, Breslau)
*Wehrwissenschaftliche Rundschau* (Mittler, Darmstadt)
*Zeitschrift für Ostmitteleuropa-Forschung* (Herder, Marburg)
www.iremember.ru

Adelson, A. and Lapides, R., *Lodz Ghetto: Inside a Community Under Siege* (Penguin, New York, 1991)

Ahlfen, H. von, *Der Kampf um Schlesien* (Motor Buch Verlag, Stuttgart, 1998)

Alexsijewitsch, S., *Der Krieg hat kein weibliches Gesicht* (Berliner Taschenbuch Verlag, Berlin, 2004)

Allen, M., *The Business of Genocide: The SS, Slave Labor, and the Concentration Camps* (University of North Carolina Press, Chapel Hill NC, 2005)

Antonov, V., *Put k Berlinu* (Nauka, Moscow, 1975)

Babadzhanian, A., *Dorogi Pobedy* (Molodaya Gvardiya, Moscow, 1975)

Bączyk, N., *Kielce 1945* (Widawnictwo Militaria, Warsaw, 2003)

Bahm, K., *Berlin 1945: The Final Reckoning* (Motorbooks International, St Paul MN, 2001)

Baltuttis, G., *Auf Verlorenem Posten* (Rautenberg, Würzburg, 2006)

Batistelli, P., *Heinz Guderian: Leadership, Strategy, Conflict* (Osprey, Oxford, 2011)

Batov, P., *Von der Wolga zur Oder* (Deutscher Militärverlag, Berlin, 1965)

Beck, A., *Bis Stalingrad 1941–1943* (Abt, Ulm, 1990)

Becker, R., *Niederschlesien 1945: Die Flucht, die Besetzung* (Aufstieg, Munich, 1974)

Beevor, A., *Ardennes 1944: Hitler's Last Gamble* (Viking, New York, 2015)

Belov, P., *Za Nami Moskva* (Voyenizdat, Moscow, 1963)

Benz, W. and Distel, B. (eds), *Der Ort des Terrors* (Beck, Munich 2005–2009, 9 vols.)

Berezowska, M., Borecka, E., and Kazimierski, J., *Exodus Warszawy: Ludzie I Miasto po Powstaniu 1944* (Państwowy Instytut Wydawniczy, Warsaw, 1993, 2 vols.)

Berger, H. and Girg, W., *In Hitlers Auftrag Hinter den Feindlichen Linien: Geheimeinsätze in der Uniform des Gegners. Ein Eichenlaubträger zwischen Skorzeny, CIA und BND* (Verlag für Wehrwissenschaften, Munich, 2014)

Beschloss, M., *The Conquerors: Roosevelt, Truman and the Destruction of Hitler's Germany* (Simon & Schuster, New York, 2002)

Blatman, D., *The Death Marches: The Final Phase of Nazi Genocide* (Belknapp, Cambridge MA, 2011)

Bokov, F., *Vesna Pobedy* (Mysl, Moscow, 1985)

Boldt, G., *Die Letzten Tage der Reichskanzlei* (Rowohlt, Hamburg, 1964)

Bradley, D., *Walther Wenck: General der Panzertruppe* (Biblio, Osnabrück, 1981)

Bulsa, M. and Szmatloch, B., *Sekrety Katowic* (Księży Młyn Dom Wydawniczy, Łódź, 2018)

Buttar, P., *Battleground Prussia: The Assault on Germany's Eastern Front 1944–1945* (Osprey, Oxford, 2010)

Buttar, P., *Collision of Empires: The War on the Eastern Front in 1914* (Osprey, Oxford, 2014)

Buttar, P., *Germany Ascendant* (Osprey, Oxford, 2015)

Buttar, P., *Meat Grinder: The Battles for the Rzhev Salient* (Osprey, Oxford, 2022)

Buttar, P., *Centuries Will Not Suffice: A History of the Lithuanian Holocaust* (Amberley, Stroud, 2023)

Caddick-Adams, P., *1945: Victory in the West* (Hutchinson Heinemann, London, 2022)

Carius, O., *Tigers in the Mud* (Stackpole, Mechanicsburg PA, 2003)

Chodakiewicz, M., *Between Nazis and Soviets: Occupation Politics in Poland, 1939–1947* (Lexington, Lanham MD, 2004)

Chuikov, V., *Konets Tretyego Reykha* (Sovetskaya Rossiya, Moscow, 1973)

Chuikov, V., *Ot Stalingrada do Berlina* (Sovetskaya Rossiya, Moscow, 1985)

Clark, A., *Barbarossa: The Russian-German Conflict 1941–1945* (Macmillan, London, 1965)

Curilla, W., *Der Judenmord in Polen und die Deutsche Ordnungspolizei* (Ferdinand Schöningh, Paderborn, 2011)

Czech, D., *Auschwitz Chronicle 1939–1945* (Henry Holt & Co, New York, 1990)

Davies, N., *Rising '44: The Battle for Warsaw* (Macmillan, London, 2003)

De Zeng, L., *Luftwaffe Airfields 1935–45 Poland* (Manuscript in preparation, 2014) [2024?]

Dieckert, K. and Grossmann, H., *Der Kampf um Ostpreussen* (Motor Buch Verlag, Stuttgart, 2002)

Długoborski, W. and Piper, F. (eds), *Auschwitz 1940–1945. Central Issues in the History of the Camp* (Auschwitz-Birkenau State Museum, Oświęcim, 2000, 5 vols.)

Dobroszyki, L. (ed.), *The Chronicle of the Łódź Ghetto, 1941–1944* (Yale University Press, New Haven CT, 1987)

Domarus, M., *Hitler, Reden und Proklamationen 1932–1945* (Süddeutscher Verlag, Munich, 1965, 2 vols.)

Dönhoff, M., *Namen die Keiner Mehr Nennt* (Diederichs, Munich, 2004)

Dörr, M., *Der Krieg Hat Uns Geprägt: Wie Kinder den Zweiten Weltkrieg Erlebten* (Campus Verlag, Frankfurt-am-Main, 2007)

Duffy, C., *Red Storm on the Reich: The Soviet March on Germany, 1945* (Castle, New Jersey, 2002)

Egloffstein, B. von, Hegen, W., and Huber, J., *Y-Rothenburg* (Self-published, 1994)

Eismann, H. and Steinhardt, F., *Unter Himmlers Kommando 1945 – der Kampf von Heeresgruppe Weichsel an der Ostfront; die Persönlichen Erinnerungen von Oberst Hans-Georg Wismann, Ia von Heeresgruppe Weichsel* (Melchior, Wolfenbüttel, 2010)

Erickson, J., *The Road To Berlin* (Cassell Military Paperbacks, London, 2004)

Evans, R., *The Third Reich at War* (Penguin, Harmondsworth, 2010)

Fleischhauer, I., *Die Chance des Sonderfriedens: Deutsch-Sowjetische Geheimgespräche 1941–1945* (Siedler, Berlin, 1986)

Fontane, T., *Vor dem Sturm: Roman aus dem Winter 1812 auf 13* (Macmillan, New York, 1911)

Frodien, U., *Bleib Übrig: Eine Kriegsjugend in Deutschland* (DTV, Munich, 2004)

Gerritse, T., *Rauter: Himmlers Vuist in Nederland* (Boom, Amsterdam, 2018)

Getman, A., *Tanki Idut na Berlin* (Nauka, Moscow, 1973)

Giordano, R., *Kriegsende in Deutschland* (Ellert & Richter, Hamburg, 2005)

Glantz, D., *Art of War Symposium 1986. From the Vistula to the Oder: Soviet Offensive Operations October 1944–March 1945* (Center for Land Warfare, US Army War College, Carlisle PA, 1986)

Glantz, D., *Soviet Military Deception in the Second World War* (Routledge, London, 1989)

Gleiss, H., *Breslauer Apokalypse 1945: Dokumentarchronik vom Todeskampf und Untergang einer Deutschen Stadt und Festung am Ende des Zweiten Weltkrieges* (Natura et Patria Verlag, Wedel, 1986–97, 10 vols.)

Greiner, B., *Die Morgenthau-Legende: Zur Geschichte eines Umstrittenen Planes* (Peter Lang, Lausanne, 1995)

Gross, G., *The Myth and Reality of German Warfare: Operational Thinking from Moltke the Elder to Heusinger* (University Press of Kentucky, Lexington KY, 2016)

Grossmann, H., *Die Geschichte der Rheinissch-Westfälischen 6. Infanterie-Division 1939–1945* (Dörfler, Eggolsheim, 2005)

Gruber, A., *Das Infanterie-Regiment 213 (Grenadier-Regiment 70) 1939–1945* (Selbstverlag der Kameradschaft des Ehem. Infanterie-Regiments 213, Nuremburg, 1963)

Guderian, H., *Erinnerungen eines Soldaten* (Vowinkel, Neckargemünd, 1960)

Gunter, G., *Last Laurels: The German Defence of Upper Silesia January–May 1945* (Helion, Solihull, 2002)

Harbutt, F., *Yalta 1945: Europe and America at the Crossroads* (Cambridge University Press, 2010)

Hargreaves, R., *Hitler's Final Fortress: Breslau 1945* (Pen & Sword, Barnsley, 2011)

Hart, R., *Guderian: Panzer Pioneer or Myth Maker?* (Potomac Books, Washington DC, 2006)

Hartmann, H., *Zwischen Nichts und Niemansland* (Machtwortverlag, Dessau, 2006)

Hastings, M., *Das Reich: The March of the 2nd SS Panzer Division Through France, June 1944* (BCA, London, 1981)

Haupt, W., *Die 8. Panzer-Division im Zweiten Weltkrieg* (Pudzun, Friedberg, 1987)

Hausser, P., *Soldaten wie Andere Auch* (Munin, Osnabrück, 1966)

Heller, J. and Simpson, G. (eds), *The Hidden Histories of War Crimes Trials* (Oxford University Press, Oxford, 2013)

Hinze, R., *19. Infanterie- und Panzer-Division: Divisionsgeschichte aus der Sicht eines Artilleristen* (self-published, 1994)

Hoffman, J., *Das Kann Man Nicht Erzählen* (Konkret, Hamburg, 2008)

Howell, E., *The Soviet Partisan Movement 1941–1944* (Verdun Press, Chicago IL, 2014)

Hrabar, R., *Hitlerwoski Rabunek Dzieci Polskich: Uprowadzanie I Germanizowanie Dzieci Polskich w Latach 1939–1945* (Śląski Instytut Naukowy w Katowicach, Katowice, 1960)

Hunt, V., *The Road of Slaughter: The Latvian 5th SS Division in Pomerania, January–March 1945* (Helion, Warwick, 2023)

Hürter, J. (ed.), *A German General on the Eastern Front* (Pen & Sword, Barnsley, 2014)

Isaev, A., *Goroda-Kreposti Tretyego Reycha: Bitva za Festungi* (Yauza, Moscow, 2018)

James, B., *Moonless Night* (Pen & Sword, Barnsley, 2022)

Jentz, T., *Panzertruppen: The Complete Guide to the Creation and Combat Employment of Germany's Tank Force* (Schiffer, Atglen PA, 1996, 2 vols.)

Kaltenegger, R., *Generalfeldmarschall Ferdinand Schörner* (Flechsig, Würzburg, 2014)

Katukov, M., *Na Ostriye Glavnogo Udara* (Voyenizdat, Moscow, 1974)

Kershaw, I., *Hitler, 1936–1945: Nemesis* (Norton, New York, 2001)

Kershaw, I., *The End: Germany 1944–45* (Penguin, Harmondsworth, 2011)

Kiekenap, B., *Der Stellvertreter aus Krähenwinkel: Biografische Notizen über Kurt Schmalz (1906–1964)* (Appelshans, Braunschweig, 2012)

Kieser, E., *Danziger Bucht 1945* (Bechtle, Esslingen, 1978)

Ķīlītis, J., *Es Karā Aiziedams: Mani Raksturīgākie Piedzīvojumi Otrā Pasaules Karā* (self-published, Ottowa, 1956)

Kissel, H., *Der Deutsche Volkssturm 1944/45. Eine Territoriale Miliz im Rahmen der Landesverteidigung* (Wehrwissenschaftliche Rundschau, Frankfurt-am-Main, 1962)

Knobelsdorff, O. von, *Geschichte der Niedersächsischen 19. Panzer-Division: Bis 31.10.1940 19. Infanterie-Division* (Podzun-Pallas, Friedberg, 1985)

Knopp, G., *Die Grosse Flucht. Das Schicksal der Vertriebenen* (Edel, Hamburg, 2013)

Kochanski, H., *The Eagle Unbowed: Poland and the Poles in the Second World War* (Harvard University Press, Cambridge MA, 2012)

Kohlase, F., *Als Küstrin in Trümmer Sank* (self-published, 1996)

Kohlase, F., *Brennendes Oderland. Militärhistorische Fragmente der Ereigniss des Jahres 1945 aus dem Nordwestschlesicschen, Märkischen und Südpommerschen Oderland: Chronologie, Fakten, Schilderungen* (Verein für die Geschichte Küstrins e.V, Küstrin-Kietz, 2011, 4 vols.)

Komorowski, K. (ed.), *Armia Krajowa: Rozwój Organizacyjny* (Bellona, Warsaw, 1996)

Konev, I., *Sorok Pyaty* (Voyenizdat, Moscow, 1970)

Koschorrek, G., *Vergiss die Zeit der Dornen Nicht* (Fleschig, Würzburg, 2005)

Krannhals, H. von, *Der Warschauer Aufstand 1944* (Ars Una, Neuried, 2000)

Krivosheeva, G. (ed.), *Rossiya i SSSR Voynakh XX Veka: Poteri Vooruzhonnykh Sil* (Olma, Moscow, 2001)

Lelyushenko, D., *Moskva-Stalingrad-Berlin-Praga* (Nauka, Moscow, 1987)

Le Tissier, T., *The Siege of Küstrin, 1945: Gateway to Berlin* (Pen & Sword, Barnsley, 2009)

Lifton, J., *The Nazi Doctors* (Basic Books, New York, 1986)

Lincoln, W., *Through Armageddon: The Russians in War and Revolution* (Oxford University Press, 1994)

Luck, H. von, *Panzer Commander: The Memoirs of Colonel Hans von Luck* (Cassell, London, 1989)

Lüttwitz, S. von, *LXXXV Corps 29 March to 7 May 45* (Historical Division US Army Europe, Karlsruhe, 1947)

MacDonogh, G., *After the Reich: From the Liberation of Vienna to the Berlin Airlift* (John Murray, London, 2007)

Magenheimer, H., *Abwehrschlacht an der Weichsel: Vorbereitung, Ablauf, Erfahrungen* (Rombach, Freiburg im Breisgau, 1976)

Majewski, R. and Sozanska, T., *Die Schlacht um Breslau Januar–Mai 1945* (Union, Berlin, 1979)

Maliszewska, I., Iwaszkiewicz, A., Kubin, A., and Jarmoszuk, M., *Wypędzeni z Warszawy 1944 – Losy Dzieci: Wystawa w Muzeum Historycznym m. st. Warszawy* (Wystawa w Muzeum Historycznym m. st. Warszawy, Warsaw, 2007)

Mammach, K., *Der Volkssturm: Das Letzte Aufgebot 1944–45* (Akademie Verlag, Berlin, 1981)

Manvell, R. and Fraenkel, H., *Heinrich Himmler: The Sinister Life of the Head of the SS and Gestapo* (Greenhill, London, 2007)

Martin, G., *The Holocaust: The Human Tragedy* (Rosetta, Munich, 2014)

Meindl, R., *Ostpreussens Gauleiter: Erich Koch – eine Politische Biographie* (Fibre, Osnabrück, 2007)

Merridale, C., *Ivan's War* (Faber & Faber, London, 2005)

Messenger, C., *The Last Prussian: A Biography of Field Marshal Gerd von Rundstedt* (Pen & Sword, Barnsley, 2011)

Miller, M., 'Fritz Bracht', unpublished document

Miller, M. and Schulz, A., *Gauleiter: The Regional Leaders of the Nazi Party and their Deputies* (R. James Bender, San Hose CA, 2012–21, 3 vols.)

Moorehead, C., *Dunant's Dream: War, Switzerland and the History of the Red Cross* (Carroll & Graf, New York, 1999)

Müller, R., Schönherr, N., and Widera, T. (eds), *Die Zerstörung Dresdens: 13. bis 15. Februar 1945. Gutachten und Ergebnisse der Dresdener Historikerkommission zur Ermittlung der Opferzahlen* (V&R Unipress, Göttingen, 2010)

Natzmer, O. von, *Commitment of German Armor, 1943–1945* (US Army Historical Division, Karlsruhe, 1954)

Oven, W. von, *Furioso: Mit Goebbels bis zum Ende* (Grabert, Tübingen, 1974)

Pantenius, H., *Letzter Schlacht an der Ostfront* (Mittler, Bonn, 2002)

Paul, G. (ed.), *Die Täter der Shoah: Fanatische Nationalsozialisten oder ganz Normale Deutsche?* (Wallstein, Göttingen, 2002)

Paul, W., *Panzer-General Walther K. Nehring, Eine Biographie* (Motor Buch Verlag, Stuttgart, 2002)

Pietrowski, T., *Poland's Holocaust: Ethnic Strife, Collaboration with Occupying Forces and Genocide in the Second Republic 1918–1947* (McFarland, Jefferson NC, 1998)

Polonsky, A., *The Jews in Poland and Russia* (Liverpool University Press, 2019, 3 vols.)

Raus, E. and Newton, S., *Panzer Operations. The Eastern Front Memoir of General Raus, 1941–1945* (Da Capo, Cambridge MA, 2003)

Read A., *The Devil's Disciples: Hitler's Inner Circle* (Norton, New York, 2005)

Reitor, G., *Vom Lager zum Lehrstuhl. Von Unten Nach Oben und Allem Daneben* (Reitor Libri, Gummersbach, 2001)

Richie, A., *Warsaw 1944: Hitler, Himmler and the Warsaw Uprising* (Farrar, Strauss & Giroux, New York, 2013)

Richter, J. (ed.), *Die Tagebücher von Joseph Goebbels, Teil II Diktate 1941–1945* (Saur, Munich, 1993–96, 15 vols.)

Roberts, M., *What Soldiers Do: Sex and the American GI in World War II France* (University of Chicago Press, Chicago IL, 2013)

Rokossovsky, K., *A Soldier's Duty* (Lancer, New Delhi, 1992)

Rottman, G., *Panzerfaust and Panzerschreck* (Osprey, Oxford, 2014)

Rudel, H-U., *Stuka Pilot* (Black House, London, 2013)

Saft, U., *Krieg im Osten* (Militärbuchverlag, Walsrode, 2002)

Salisbury, H., *The 900 Days: The Siege of Leningrad* (Da Capo, Cambridge MA, 2009)

Schäufler, H., *Panzer an der Weichsel* (Motor Buch Verlag, Stuttgart, 1979)

Schäufler, H., *So Lebten und so Starben Sie: Das Buch vom Panzerregiment-35* (Kameradscaft ehemaliger Panzer-Regiment 35 e.V, Bamberg, 1983)

Schenk, D., *Hitlers Mann in Danzig: Gauleiter Forster und die NS-Verbrechen in Danzig-Westpreussen* (Dietz, Bonn, 2000)

Schnabel, R., *Macht ohne Moral: Eine Dokumentation über die SS* (Rödeberg, Frankfurt am Main, 1957)

Schön, H., *Ostsee 45* (Motor Buch Verlag, Stuttgart, 1983)

Sebag Montefiore, S., *Stalin: The Court of the Red Tsar* (Weidenfeld & Nicholson, London, 2003)

Semenov, G., *Nastupayet Udarnaya* (Voyenizdat, Moscow, 1986)

Shein, D., *Tanki Vedet Rybalko. Boyevoy Put 3-y Gvardeskoy Tankovoy Armii* (Eksmo, Moscow, 2007)

Shepherd, B., *Hitler's Soldiers: The German Army in the Third Reich* (Yale University Press, New Haven CT, 2016)

Shkadov, I. and Babakov, A., *Geroi Sovetskogo Soyuza: Kratkii Biograficheskii Slovar* (Voyenizdat, Moscow, 1987, 2 vols.)

Shtemenko, S., *The Soviet General Staff at War* (Progress, Moscow, 1970)

Skorobogatov, V., *Berzarin* (Molodaya Gvardiya, Moscow, 2012)

Smelser, R. and Davies, E., *The Myth of the Eastern Front: The Nazi-Soviet War in Popular American Culture* (Cambridge University Press, New York, 2008)

Smith, B. and Peterson, A. (eds), *Heinrich Himmler Geheimreden 1933–1945, und andere Ansprachen* (Propyläen, Frankfurt am Main, 1974)

Spaeter, H., *History of the Panzerkorps Grossdeutschland* (Fedorowicz, Winnipeg, 2000, 3 vols.)

Speer, A., *Inside the Third Reich* (Weidenfeld & Nicolson, London, 1970)

Sprenger, I., *Gross-Rosen: Ein Konzentrationslager in Schlesien* (Böhlau, Cologne, 1996)

Steinhoff, J., Pechel, P., and Showalter, D. (eds), *Voices from the Third Reich: An Oral History* (Da Capo, New York, 1994)

Strzelecki, A., and Brand, W., *The Evacuation, Liquidation and Liberation of Auschwitz* (Auschwitz-Birkenau State Museum, Oświęcim, 2008)

Tacitus, trans. A. Birley, *Agricola and Germania* (Oxford University Press, 2009)

Thompson, L., *Nazi Administrative Conflict. The Struggle for Executive Power in the General Government of Poland 1939–1943* (Dissertation, University of Wisconsin, 2000)

Thorwald, J., *Es Begann an der Weichsel* (Steingrüben, Stuttgart, 1953)

Thrams, H., *Küstrin 1945: Tagebuch Einer Festung* (Landesmannschaft Berlin-Mark Brandenburg, Berlin, 1992)

Trevor-Roper, H., *Hitler's War Directives 1939–1945* (Sidgwick & Jackson, London, 1964)

Tung, A., *Preserving the World's Great Cities: The Destruction and Renewal of the Historic Metropolis* (Clarkson Potter, New York, 2001)

Vasilevsky, A., *A Lifelong Cause* (Progress, Moscow, 1981)

Wardyńska, M., *Był rok 1939: operacja niemieckiej policji bezpieczeństwa w Polsce: Intelligenzaktion* (Instytut Pamięci Narodowej, Warszawa, 2009)

Werthen, W., *Geschichte der 16. Panzer-Division – Weg und Schicksal* (Podzun, Bad Neuheim, 1958)

Wieviorka, O., *Normandy: From the Landings to the Liberation of Paris* (Belknap, Harvard University Press, Cambridge MA, 2010)

Wilmot, C., *The Struggle For Europe* (Wordworth, Ware, 2003)

Wituska, K. and Tomaszewski, I., *Inside a Gestapo Prison: The Letters of Krystyna Wituska 1942–1944* (Wayne State University Press, Detroit MI, 2006)

Wolff, G., *Kalendarium der Geschichte des KZ Sachsenhausen, Strafverfolgung* (Nationale Mahn- und Gedenkstätte Sachsenhausen, Oranienburg, 1987)

Yelton, D., *Hitler's Volkssturm: The Nazi Militia and the Fall of Germany 1944–1945* (University of Kansas Press, Lawrence KS, 2002)

Zaborski, Z., *Tędy Przeszła Warszawa: Epilog Powstania Warszawskiego: Pruszków Durchgangslager 121: 6 VIII-10 X 1944* (Wydawnictwo Askon, Warsaw, 2018)

Zaitsev, V., *Gvardeyskaya Tankovaya* (Sredney-Ural, Sverdlovsk, 1989)

Zetterling, N., *Normandy 1944: German Military Organisation, Combat Power and Organizational Effectiveness* (Fedorowicz, Winnipeg, 2000)

Zhadov, A., *Chetyre Goda Voyny* (Voyenizdat, Moscow, 1978)

Zhukov, G., *Vospomimaniya I Razmyshleniya* (Olma, Moscow, 2002, 2 volumes)

Ziemke, E., *The US Army in the Occupation of Germany 1944–1946* (Center of Military History, US Army, Washington DC, 1990)

Zwartsev, A., *3-ia Gvardeiskaia Tankovaia: Boevoi put 3-I Gvardeiskoi Tankovoi Armii* (Voenizdat, Moscow, 1982)

# INDEX

References to maps are in bold.